ETHNOGRAPHERS BEFORE MALINOWSKI

EASA Series

Published in Association with the European Association of Social Anthropologists (EASA)

Series Editors: Jelena Tošić, University of St. Gallen; Sabine Strasser, University of Bern; Annika Lems, Max Planck Institute for Social Anthropology, Halle

Social anthropology in Europe is growing, and the variety of work being done is expanding. This series is intended to present the best of the work produced by members of the EASA, both in monographs and in edited collections. The studies in this series describe societies, processes, and institutions around the world and are intended for both scholarly and student readership.

Recent volumes:

For a full volume listing, please see the series page on our website:
https://www.berghahnbooks.com/series/easa

ETHNOGRAPHERS BEFORE MALINOWSKI

Pioneers of Anthropological Fieldwork, 1870–1922

Edited by Frederico Delgado Rosa
and Han F. Vermeulen

berghahn
NEW YORK · OXFORD
www.berghahnbooks.com

First published in 2022 by

Berghahn Books

www.berghahnbooks.com

© 2022, 2024 Frederico Delgado Rosa and Han F. Vermeulen
First paperback edition published in 2024

Library of Congress Cataloging-in-Publication Data

A C.I.P. cataloging record is available from the Library of Congress
Library of Congress Cataloging in Publication Control Number: 2022016084

British Library Cataloguing in Publication Data

A catalogue record for this book is available from the British Library

ISBN 978-1-80073-531-6 hardback
ISBN 978-1-80539-148-7 paperback
ISBN 978-1-80539-566-9 epub
ISBN 978-1-80073-532-3 web pdf

https://doi.org/10.3167/9781800735316

Contents

Figures

Acknowledgments

The present volume is the result of over three years of dedicated efforts by the editors and a team of twelve scholars from ten countries in four continents to explore largely neglected aspects of the ethnographic archive and contribute to the history and theory of anthropology.

The editors wish to thank Adam Kuper, Regna Darnell, James Urry, Andrew Lyons, Ira Jacknis, Rosemary Lévy Zumwalt, Aleksandar Bošković, Paul Hockings, Guido Sprenger, Nicole Tonkovich, Bruce Grant, Sergei Alymov, Ira Bashkow, Fernanda Peixôto, Fermín del Pino, Marisa Karyl Franz, Peter Schröder, Akitoshi Shimizu, William Kelly, Chris Hann, Anna Sirina, Giordana Charuty, Dmitry Arzyutov, João Leal, Erik Petschelies, Auksuolė Čepaitienė, Roberto Malighetti, Marie-Claude Mahias, Thomas Beaufils, James McAllister, and Fabiana Dimpflmeier for their highly appreciated comments and suggestions. We owe a great debt of gratitude to Thomas Hylland Eriksen for his inspiring foreword.

Our special thanks go to Christine Laurière, co-convenor of the panel "Ethnographers before Malinowski [History of Anthropology Network]," which was virtually held in Lisbon, Portugal, at the EASA's 16th Biennial Conference on 21 July 2020. As panel co-convenor and discussant, respectively, the editors are grateful to the panel participants David Shankland, Herbert S. Lewis, Bryn Coldrick, Edward McDonald, João de Pina-Cabral, Anne F. Müller-Delouis, Ciarán Walsh, Christer Lindberg, and Sergei Kan, as well as to the attendees who contributed to the discussion, particularly Virginia Dominguez, Katja Geisenhainer, Maria Beatrice Di Brizio, and Diego Ballestero. We are indebted to all contributors to the present volume, two anonymous peer reviewers, as well as the EASA series editors, Jelena Tošić, Sabine Strasser, and Annika Lems. For institutional support the editors express their gratitude to the Centre for Research in Anthropology (CRIA) in Lisbon, Portugal, and the Max Planck Institute for Social Anthropology in Halle (Saale), Germany. Finally, our thanks go out to Marion Berghahn, Tom Bonnington, Elizabeth Martinez, Ben Parker-Jones, and their teams in Oxford and New York.

Foreword

Unearthing the Hidden Treasures of Early Ethnography

Thomas Hylland Eriksen

"A typical piece of intensive work is one in which the worker lives for a year or more among a community of perhaps four or five hundred people and studies every detail of their life and culture; in which he comes to know every member of the community personally; in which he is not content with generalized information, but studies every feature of life and custom in concrete detail and by means of the vernacular language."

This sounds like something Malinowski or one of his students might have said in the 1920s. In fact, the quotation precedes the "Malinowskian revolution" by about a decade and was written by a major immediate predecessor of Malinowski and the man responsible for sending Radcliffe-Brown to the Andaman Islands, namely W. H. R. Rivers (1864–1922). The quotation is from Rivers (1913: 7).

A major figure in early twentieth-century anthropology, Rivers, originally a medical doctor and a psychologist, was converted to ethnology as a member of the Cambridge Anthropological Expedition to the Torres Straits in 1898–99. Under the leadership of A. C. Haddon, a carefully selected half-dozen British scholars traveled to these islands between the northern tip of Queensland and New Guinea, where they worked collaboratively on a broad range of topics. In this group, Rivers would soon become the most influential contributor to anthropological theory and methodology. Notably, he introduced the genealogical method during his research on the Torres Straits islands, using kinship genealogies as a means to map social relations and social organization.

When the Royal Anthropological Institute decided, in 1907, to produce a new edition of the methodological handbook *Notes and Queries on Anthropology*, the committee charged with the task included most of the members of the Torres Straits Expedition of 1898–99. While previous editions had addressed itinerant travelers of various kinds, from missionaries to officers and colonial administrators, the committee—or a majority of it anyway (Urry 1973)—now felt it was time to address the professional ethnographer, he (or, occasionally, she) who went out into the field mainly in order to do research. Rivers's chapter on methodology is one of the longest, and arguably the most important, in the book. He describes the genealogical method in detail, notes the importance of corroborating one's findings with independent sources, and emphasizes the distinction between intensive fieldwork and survey work, describing the latter as superficial and often inadequate. Malinowski made good use of this methodological manual in his own training as an ethnographer but rarely refers to Rivers in his published writings.

There are good reasons for describing Rivers as "a lost ancestor" in the history of anthropology (Hart 2017), and he was written out of history rather unceremoniously, not least by Malinowski, who once told Brenda Seligman that he regarded Rivers as "the Rider Haggard of anthropology," while he himself intended to be its Joseph Conrad (Firth 1957: 6).

Yet, the moment we begin to ponder the forgotten legacy of Rivers, other lost ancestors come to mind, and there are many, as this book so splendidly demonstrates. For example, Rivers did not invent kinship studies. Decades earlier, the American L. H. Morgan, himself a skilled ethnographer, established a typology of kinship systems and a distinction between descriptive and classificatory kinship that remained influential through most of the twentieth century. As late as the 1980s, we still had to learn the difference between Omaha, Crow, and Hawaiian kinship terminologies as students in Oslo. As regards Rivers's alleged invention of the genealogical method, Gardner (2016) has shown that this method was used systematically by the Australian anthropologists Fison and Howitt in the 1870s and refined by their immediate successors Spencer and Gillen. Rivers did not relate to the achievements by his Australian colleagues, just as Malinowski failed to acknowledge Rivers's contributions to methodology.

"The age of armchair anthropologists," Rosa and Vermeulen point out in the conclusion to this book, "was also an age of ethnographers." Standard accounts of the history of anthropology often create a sharp break between evolutionist late Victorian anthropology and, in the United States, Boasian cultural relativism, and in the United Kingdom, functionalist microsociology. The "conjectural history" to which Rivers had fallen victim in his later years was treated disdainfully by some; critically but respectfully by his student Radcliffe-Brown. However, quite clearly there was continuity in ethnographic research and anthropological theorizing going back to the nineteenth century. It is true that people like Haddon and Rivers may rightly be seen as transitional figures creating a bridge between armchair anthropology and a slimmed-down, focused, systematic social anthropology, but everybody in the history of ideas can be seen as transitional: there have always been predecessors, and there were certainly numerous successors. There is no point zero where modern anthropology suddenly sprang, fully formed, from the ground.

This book identifies and describes a number of genealogies that have gone missing from official histories—partly owing to language issues, partly because of turf wars and the destructive effects of intellectual patricide, which is one of the least attractive aspects of modern academia. Elsdon Best, who spoke of Pacific islanders as argonauts decades before Malinowski, is saved from oblivion; Arnold van Gennep, known for his concept of *rites de passage* but not for his Algerian ethnography, is given his due, as is Edward Westermarck and the nonacademic explorer Henrique de Carvalho, among many others. Perhaps most tellingly, the most thoroughly forgotten of the pioneers of modern ethnography were often women such as the Australian Katie Langloh Parker and the American Alice C. Fletcher.

As the bibliography at the end of this book shows, the selection of authors and writings analyzed is far from comprehensive. A huge number of ethnographies were published between 1870 and 1922, many of them authoritative and reliable, and these accounts are in many ways more important to the development of anthropology than more famous but less grounded works such as Frazer's *The Golden Bough*. Thus, the actual immediate ancestors of Malinowski and his successors were not Tylor and Frazer but people like Best, Westermarck, Haddon, and Rivers.

What, then, is left of the so-called Malinowskian revolution? For one thing, Malinowski was a far better writer than his predecessors. (In this respect, his immodest comparison with Conrad has some merit.) His field methodology was also clearly formulated, systematically and succinctly laid out. His emphasis on participant observation also marked a departure from Westermarck and Rivers, although it remains an open question to what extent later ethnographers actually participated in everyday life. Doing so may be harder than it sounds. I have cut some sugar cane on steaming afternoons and gone fishing at five in the morning during fieldwork, but not regularly, and always as an inept and clumsy guest. It is worth mentioning that one of the most influential anthropologists of the last century, Marcel Mauss, remained an armchair anthropologist throughout his life, although he lectured extensively on field methodology. Malinowski's programmatic insistence on practice being prior to models had its merits, but also its limitations. It bears remembering in this respect that he never wrote his announced book about kinship among the Trobriand Islanders.

There was never a definitive break in the history of anthropology. Just as it would be futile to ask about the whereabouts of the first human being, searching for the first proper ethnographer can at best produce partial, tentative, and misleading answers. The authors of this book show why that is the case, but also that the past is far more exciting, colorful, and diverse than it looks from a distance, just as the societies explored by these pioneers of ethnography were more complex and in many ways more admirable than typically assumed in their own day and age.

Thomas Hylland Eriksen is professor of social anthropology at the University of Oslo. His research focuses on social and cultural implications of globalization. He has studied ethnic and nonethnic forms of identification and social organization in culturally complex plantation societies and published *Us and Them in Modern Societies* (1992), based on fieldwork in Trinidad and Mauritius, followed by *Ethnicity and Nationalism* (1993). He directed research programs on cultural complexity in Norway and more recently published on accelerated global change in *Overheating* (2016) and *Boomtown* (2018), the latter based on fieldwork in Australia. He published several textbooks, including *Small Places, Large Issues* (1995/2014), *A History of Anthropology* (with F. S. Nielsen, 2001/2012), and *What Is Anthropology?* (2004/2017). He is a member of the Norwegian Society of Science and Letters, an external scientific member of the Max Planck Society, and an honorary fellow of the Royal Anthropological Institute.

References

Firth, Raymond. 1957. "Introduction: Malinowski as Scientist and as Man." In *Man and Culture: An Evaluation of the Work of Bronislaw Malinowski*, edited by Raymond Firth, 1–14. London: Routledge & Kegan Paul.

Gardner, Helen. 2016. "The Genealogy of the Genealogical Method: Discoveries, Disseminations and the Historiography of British Anthropology." *Oceania* 86(3): 294–319.

Hart, Keith. 2017. "Rivers Is Our Forgotten Founding Father." The Memory Bank, retrieved 25 July 2021 from https://thememorybank.co.uk/2017/02/10/rivers-is-our-forgotten-founding-father/.

Rivers, W. H. R. 1913. "Report on Anthropological Research outside America." In *Reports upon the Present Condition and Future Needs of the Science of Anthropology*, edited by W. H. R. Rivers, A. E. Jenks, and S. G. Morley, 5–25. Washington, DC: The Carnegie Institution of Washington.

Urry, James. 1973. "*Notes and Queries on Anthropology* and the Development of Field Methods in British Anthropology, 1870–1920." In *Proceedings of the Royal Anthropological Institute of Great Britain and Ireland for 1972*, 45–57. London: Royal Anthropological Institute.

Introduction
Other Argonauts

Chapters in the History of
Pre-Malinowskian Ethnography

Frederico Delgado Rosa and Han F. Vermeulen

Predating Malinowski's *Argonauts of the Western Pacific* (1922) by fifteen years, New Zealand frontier man and salvage ethnographer Elsdon Best (1856–1931) made a comparison between a scriptless Oceanic people and the heroic navigators of ancient Greek mythology:

> And how came man to the land of the Maori and the *moa*? Whence came the Children of the Mist?
> *Tena!* Far away across the dark, wild waves of the Sea of Kiwa, away beyond the parts where the sky hangs down, there floats a primitive vessel upon the surging waters. It is a hewn canoe, of great length, and decked with many a strange device, such as were used by Polynesian Vikings in the days when the world was wide. ... How full of import is the progress of that primitive bark. ... For it is the old, old story of the Argonauts, of happening on a new world, of the conquest of the earth by man. (Best 1925: 2, 4, 5)

Considering that the manuscript of *Tuhoe: The Children of the Mist* (1925) was completed by 1907, it is clear that Best did not borrow the idea from Bronisław Malinowski (1884–1942). In fact, Best had already compared Māori to the Argonauts of Greek mythology as early as 1894, in the *New Zealand Mail*.[1] This coincidence is symbolic as it tells us something about the two men's respective destinies in the history of anthropology: undisputed fame in the case of Malinowski, significant oblivion in that of Best—except in New Zealand/Aotearoa and within the specialized field of Māori studies. To be sure, the words of one of Best's informants were famously quoted by Marcel Mauss (1872–1950) in *Essai sur le don*—better known as

The Gift: "I will now speak of the *hau* ..." (cited in Mauss 2016 [1925]: 70).[2] One would expect Elsdon Best's name to be an indispensable reference for any anthropologist, but the fact that a small parcel of his ethnography has become a part of the canon, witness the periodical *HAU: Journal of Ethnographic Theory*, does not mean that his immense work is known, let alone read. Unlike Malinowski's, his Argonauts are full of dust.

The present collection tries to recover other "Argonauts" or ethnographic accounts from the late nineteenth and early twentieth centuries. This provocative expression applies to forgotten or neglected monographies produced by ethnographers whose work, surpassed and overshadowed by that of later anthropologists, may both enlighten and question the dichotomy between canonic models of *writing culture* and "pre-Malinowskian" ones. At a time when anthropologists worldwide continually claim new fieldwork experiences and ethnographic results, from antipositivist to poststructural, from "gone native" to compassionate, a second chance should be given to older texts through a critical and creative combination of historicism and presentism. The disparate sensibilities of twenty-first-century practitioners reveal more than ever that once victorious criteria of professionalism are inadequate to assess the significance of previous ethnographic studies. Some deep-rooted assumptions are at stake, including the idea that intensive fieldwork in a single context by a single individual, with its corresponding output, the monograph, were twentieth-century inventions, and that nineteenth-century ethnographies were mere travelogues, expeditionary surveys or defective, fragmentary descriptions.

The present volume includes twelve case studies from a surprisingly large field. Shorter illustrations in this introduction and an appendix containing a selected bibliography of 365 ethnographic accounts, produced by 220 ethnographers, demonstrate how ethnography thrived during the fifty years between ca. 1870 and ca. 1922. The core idea underlying our project is that "pre-Malinowskian" ethnographies are a fundamental part of the history of anthropology, each ethnographic account containing several layers of meaning, style, and content that inspire open-ended readings and are projectable into the future.

"Four Ways" and World Anthropologies

The search for "the first true fieldworkers" (Eriksen and Nielsen 2001: 26–27) involves several hazards, even when there is a nuanced understanding of the complex historical processes underlying the development of ethnography as a scholarly field. One is the risk of Anglocentrism, viewing the history of the discipline mostly from an Anglo-American perspective. This is not to imply that historians of anthropology are unaware of this danger, but when scholars make it explicit that they are only addressing English-speaking countries, this does not necessarily prevent them and their readers from the temptation of generalizing from there, however subconsciously. Viewing British and North American anthropology as "major traditions" (Kuklick 2008) outshining less prominent ones worldwide affects the teaching of the history of the discipline. In the present volume, Anglophone monographs have been selected as case studies, but not to the exclusion of ethnographies from other settings conferring diachronic depth to lesser-known "minor traditions" brought to the fore by the world anthropologies paradigm.[3]

Anthropology has been portrayed as *One Discipline, Four Ways* in reference to the British, American, French, and German research traditions (Barth et al. 2005). But what about Brazilian, Italian, Chinese, Japanese, Indian, Nigerian, or Russian anthropologies, for example? The focus on four "major traditions" overshadows other important anthropological schools, in Europe and beyond. Even the history of German-speaking anthropology has fallen into oblivion and, due to two world wars, is no longer part of the anthropological canon (Eidson 2017: 49). Andre Gingrich refers to it as a "non-tradition of good anthropology" that has been "forgotten, repressed, and noticed only after tremendous time lags" (Gingrich 2005: 103; see Gingrich 2017). For example, the celebrity of Baldwin Spencer (1860–1929) and Francis Gillen (1855–1912) obfuscated the status of nonanglophone ethnographers, both in their own era and throughout the twentieth century, particularly of Carl Strehlow (1871–1922), their "rival" in the Arunta/Arrernte context.

In a 2019 special issue dedicated to "German-Speaking Anthropologists in Latin America, 1884–1945," editors Han F. Vermeulen, Cláudio Costa Pinheiro, and Peter Schröder identify a similar case of "amnesia" (p. 79) concerning the pivotal role of ethnographers from German-speaking countries working among Indigenous groups in Brazil and elsewhere, mainly in the period between 1880 and the end of World War I.[4] They speak of a "Great Age" represented by ethnographers such as Karl von den Steinen (1855–1929), Konrad Theodor Preuss (1869–1938), Theodor Koch-Grünberg (1872–1924), and Max Schmidt (1874–1950)—up to their last representative, Curt Nimuendajú (1883–1945). Despite several other efforts to unveil their ethnographic experiences, whether expeditionary or individual, and recent attempts to reassess their place in the history of anthropology as "forerunners of modern fieldwork," these figures still have a "restricted visibility" (Vermeulen et al. 2019: 72, 80).

In France, a good example of obliterated ethnography is Arnold Van Gennep's (1873–1957) monograph *En Algérie* (1914), which contains an important introductory section titled "Comment on enquête" (How to conduct field research): "I travelled through Algeria for five months: July–August 1911 and April–June 1912. That was too much, as now things that I thought were very simple are appearing to me with a distressing complexity. Or too little, because it would take years to untangle these complexities finally discerned" (Van Gennep 1914: 7–8). Christine Laurière highlights Van Gennep's constant "pleas for direct observation, for fieldwork, for the attention to detail" (Laurière 2021: 10). Known internationally for his classic study *Les rites de passage* (1909), Van Gennep distinguished "one single method, equally applicable in all countries and from morning to evening." Its cornerstones were empathy, respect, and conviviality: "It is only necessary to be introduced by individuals who have the confidence of the locals, to bend to the traditional rules of politeness, to lose track of time, to avoid any impatience, to avoid asking direct questions and to proceed by approximation" (Van Gennep 1912: 611; see also Van Gennep 1913).

When other European languages (not to mention non-European ones) are taken into account, the predicament of Anglocentrism becomes all the more obvious. At the same time, one should not lose sight of the extraordinary magnitude of the English-language ethnographic archive, namely, when the writings of amateur ethnographers are also considered. A prime example is *The Nuer of the Upper Nile Province* (1923), the first monograph on the celebrated Nuer, authored by army officer and colonial administrator Henry Cecil Jackson (1883–1962). First appearing in the *Sudan Notes and Records*, and subsequently published by El Hadara Printing Press in the Anglo-Egyptian Sudan, it is a rare book to this day and has never been properly analyzed by historians of anthropology. Both within and beyond the so-called major traditions, regionally focused studies on the history of anthropology often unveil long lists of ethnographers and ethnographies that require case-by-case considerations.[5] In *A Hundred Years of Anthropology*, T. K. Penniman faced this problem in lucid terms: "It is impossible to do more than mention the nature of evidence from the field without compiling an encyclopaedia" (1974 [1935]: 22).

The Anthropological Canon and the Drama of Selection

Historians of anthropology are well positioned to sense the drama of drastic selections, as when George W. Stocking Jr. (1928–2013) stated, in *After Tylor*, that he was "acutely conscious that much has been scanted or excluded" (1995: xvi). In *Victorian Anthropology* (1987), Stocking selected only three cases—George Grey (1812–98), Thomas Williams (1815–91), and Francis Galton (1822–1911)—to evoke the providers of data for the evolutionist founding fathers who were the actual subject of his book. In *After Tylor* (1995), the missionary ethnographers Lorimer Fison (1832–1907) and Robert Henry Codrington (1830–1922) stood for nineteenth-century fieldwork, along with Spencer and Gillen and Alfred C. Haddon (1855–1940). For the early twentieth century, Stocking highlighted the case of eight trained anthropologists, British or connected to British academia and more or less fallen into oblivion, who undertook "the intensive study of a limited area before the Great War" (1995: 117–19), namely, Gerald C. Wheeler (1872–1943), Rafael Karsten (1879–1956), Gunnar Landtman (1878–1940), John Layard (1891–1974), Maria Czaplicka (1886–1921), Barbara Freire-Marreco (1879–1967), Diamond Jenness (1886–1969), and Robert S. Rattray (1881–1938), while developing, in particular, the cases of Arthur M. Hocart (1883–1939) and Edward Westermarck (1862–1939). Three of these ethnographic anthropologists, Czaplicka, Rattray, and Westermarck, return in individual chapters of the present book (see Kubica, McFate, and Shankland, this volume).

In his seminal paper "The Ethnographer's Magic: Fieldwork in British Anthropology from Tylor to Malinowski" (1983), Stocking concluded:

> Something more than delayed or institutionally marginal careers . . . would seem to be involved in the lapsed remembrance of . . . other academic ethnographers of Malinowski's generation. Although some of them . . . are revealed in their field notes as extremely sensitive and reflective practical methodologists, their early monographs did not present them as self-conscious ethnographic innovators. (Stocking 1983: 31–32)

The recent tendency to recover forgotten or marginal figures, both within and beyond the four "major" traditions, is theorized in Richard Handler's *Excluded Ancestors* (2000). In its introduction, Handler reminds readers that "the same processes of inclusion and exclusion that affect the discipline of anthropology also affect [the] history of anthropology as a subfield." It would be impossible in any single volume to address "all the categorical omissions (not to mention individual forgotten ancestors) we might imagine" (Handler 2000: 8). The need for a more inclusive picture has been a guiding principle since the history of anthropology affirmed itself as a field during the 1960s and 1970s, with Stocking and Adam Kuper (b. 1941) taking the lead. Sometimes, attempts to account for lesser-known figures have been justified by the need to contextualize more prominent ones, but prominence, whether living or posthumous, is a relative condition (see Bieder 1986: xii; Stocking 1974). Meanwhile, other formulas respond to the same goal, such as "Neglected Pasts" (Kuklick 2008) or "Missing Ancestors and Missing Narratives," the title of a 2007 article in which Andrew Lyons addresses the problem in the following way: "We ask why some names, careers, and narratives are included in or excluded from histories of anthropology. These processes obviously influence our choices as to which books we shall read and which messages we shall heed. . . . A decision to omit someone from a historical survey may be overdetermined by many disciplinary and political traditions" (Lyons 2007: 148).

Have pre-Malinowskian ethnographers of the late nineteenth and the early twentieth centuries been excluded? The answer to this question depends on whether or not one considers the countless but scattered contributions to the reassessment of this or that particular case that may be found in biographies and monographic volumes, specialized journals and books within specific area studies or national traditions, online encyclopedias, and dictionaries. To name one example, Inuit studies specialists are fully aware of earlier ethnographies, such as the monumental descriptive volumes that were written in the 1870s, 1880s, and 1890s—mostly by natural scientists who, like Franz Boas (1858–1942), converted to anthropology (see Lewis, this volume). The title of the collective volume *Early Inuit Studies*, edited by Igor Krupnik in 2016, makes this historical sensibility explicit. The Danish administrator of South Greenland, Hinrich Rink (1819–93), is "widely recognized as one of the founding fathers of Eskimology" (Marquardt 2016: 35). Publishing extensively, both in Danish and in English, Rink's "best-known" work is the two-volume monograph *The Eskimo Tribes* (1887–91). To nonspecialists, however, he is a complete stranger.

A glimpse of the ethnographic archive's vastness has been made easier by the digital turn, and the present collection of essays aims at making pre-Malinowskian ethnography more visible. In view of the vast number of case studies that could have been considered for the present volume, our selection from the ethnographic archive is like the proverbial tip of the iceberg. In the process of reaching out to the international community of historians of anthropology, the editors of this volume were confronted with all kinds of warnings concerning this or that forgotten ethnographer whose omission from consideration would be unfair. "Do you include Bronisław Piłsudski in your volume? Hope you did!"[6]

Revisiting the "Revolution in Anthropology"

The history of anthropology in the nineteenth century is often equated with armchair anthropology because, as Thomas H. Eriksen and Finn S. Nielsen sustain, "the vast majority of anthropologists gathered their data through correspondence with colonial administrators, settlers, officers, missionaries, and other 'whites' living in exotic places" (2001: 24). This is only part of the story as the cases of two well-known founding fathers demonstrate. Lewis Henry Morgan (1818–81) was able to claim for himself the status of "witness" in the foreword to his ethnographic monograph on *The League of the Ho-dé-no-sau-nee, or Iroquois* thanks to his "frequent intercourse with the descendants of the Iroquois" (1851: x). The fact that this so-called armchair anthropologist was also a fieldworker is viewed as an exception—but the same applies to Edward B. Tylor's (1832–1917) Mexican experience and the resulting volume, *Anahuac: or, Mexico and the Mexicans, Ancient and Modern* (1861).[7] As to the ethnographic encounters and monographic accounts of amateur observers, they are often omitted under the pretext of their "uneven quality" (Eriksen and Nielsen 2001: 24), amalgamated as "mostly prejudiced and always inadequate" (Hogbin 1958: 18) and therefore undeserving of much attention or, at best, briefly and selectively enumerated. Disciplinary pasts may be subject to an unconscious myopia or to deliberate forms of exclusion in power-imbued narratives. There is a prevailing, even "conventional" tendency, as Efram Sera-Shriar puts it, "to depict the history of anthropology as fragmented into divergent methodological epochs" (2013: 3). Likewise, David Shankland notes that anthropology "sustains itself in its popular discourse by dividing its past into a number of stages each of which may be regarded as having been safely surpassed" (2019: 51). The typical narrative "goes something like this," he adds: "that anthropology contained a number of leading figures in the nineteenth century who proposed a form of evolutionism. These gave way to a 'revolution' in the 1920s headed by Malinowski, which created social anthropology and pioneered 'real' fieldwork" (ibid.).

According to Shankland, "Perhaps the archetypal work that sustains this understanding of the history, in its initial stages at least, of social anthropology is that by Adam Kuper" (ibid.: 52). Titled *Anthropology and Anthropologists: The British School 1922–1972*, Kuper's classic has gone through four editions (1973, 1983, 1996, 2015) and several reprints. His first chapter, titled "Malinowski," opens with powerful words: "Malinowski has a strong claim to being the founder of the profession of social anthropology in Britain, for he established its distinctive apprenticeship—intensive fieldwork in an exotic community" (1996 [1973]: 1). Kuper recalls the calls for professional ethnographic fieldwork by the generation preceding Malinowski. Despite the fact that "very little professional work involved more than a few days in any exotic area," forcing ethnographers "to rely upon interpreters, or évolué informants," Kuper added, "this represented a departure from the traditional system, whereby—as Marett described it—'The man in the study busily propounded questions which only the man in the field could answer, and in the light of the answers that poured in from the field the study as busily revised its questions.' It was now realized that the man in the field should be expert in the discipline, and that the European resident in the tropics was not generally a reliable informant. Some of these, particularly among the missionaries, had produced masterly ethnographies, but they were very much the exception; and even the best of them relied too heavily upon selected informants" (ibid.: 5–6).

While Kuper is right that Malinowski and A. R. Radcliffe-Brown (1881–1955) carried out intensive fieldwork and held important new chairs in anthropology at the London School of Economics (LSE) in 1927–38 and in social anthropology at the University of Oxford in 1937–46, respectively, his narrative does not accord enough attention to the so-called "exceptions" in the late nineteenth and early twentieth centuries, whether by professional or amateur ethnographers. His *Anthropology and Anthropologists* inadvertently influenced readers into formulating more simplified ways of dealing with the complexity of the discipline's archive. These are frequent in textbooks on the history of anthropology that cover several research traditions, as well as in guides to the theory and practice of ethnography (see, for example, Robben 2007: 30; Madden 2010: 27).

An earlier candidate for archetypal work on the epistemic shift brought about by Malinowski was Ian Jarvie, whose influential book *The Revolution in Anthropology* (1964) played a major role in consolidating a discontinuous perception of the history of the discipline, according to which there was "a shift of attention from speculative genetic theories of human society ... to intensive, thorough and accurate field-work" (Gellner 1964: v; see Shankland, this volume).[8] Jarvie did so by emphasizing Malinowski's coup de grâce to the era of armchair anthropology and by identifying James George Frazer (1854–1941) as the revolution's symbolical scapegoat. Ironically, this echoed the slain godly kings of *The Golden Bough* (1890): "The first battle-cry of the revolution is 'kill the chief-priest (or father) and his gang.' Translated this reads: 'overthrow the influence of these victorian intellectualist evolutionists' ... Bronislaw Malinowski plotted and directed the revolution. It was a genuine revolution, aiming to overthrow the establishment of Frazer and Tylor and their ideas; but mainly it was against Frazer" (Jarvie 1964: 43, 173; see also 1–2, 32–33). Jarvie's idea that Malinowskian ethnography overthrew Frazerian anthropology is unfair in that it practically ignores pre-Malinowskian ethnography. Indeed, the transition toward a new, field-centered anthropology appears more clear-cut, if not sudden and personal, when previous ethnographies are left out of the picture.[9]

In his enthusiasm, Jarvie turned Malinowski's critique of verandah ethnography into a metaphorical reference to the "verandah of western society," of the evolutionists or, for that matter, the diffusionists who refused to go into the field: "Into the quarrel between these two schools of thought stepped Malinowski. 'You both sit on the verandah spinning your theories and empty disputes,' he seems to have said. . . . 'Come down from the verandah of western society and look at men everywhere,' he says. . . . speculation on the verandah is not science, science is observation and description" (Jarvie 1964: 11, 13). In fact, Malinowski made quite explicit that he had in mind the actual "verandah of the missionary compound, government station, or planter's bungalow, where, armed with pencil and notebook and at times with a whisky and soda, he [the anthropologist] has been accustomed to collect statements from informants, write down stories, and fill out sheets of paper with savage texts" (Malinowski 1926: 122–23).[10] By disregarding the actual verandahs in the colonial settings where ethnography was done, Jarvie's abstract verandah of armchair anthropologists may be taken as a metaphor for something else: a deeply ingrained disregard for nineteenth-century and early twentieth-century ethnography, as if it were negligeable or irrelevant in the age of armchair anthropology.

Indeed, several ethnographers before Malinowski inhabited or were invited to the compounds, stations, and bungalows with verandahs where ethnographic encounters could happen. And this universe was certainly a target of his revolution, a crucial element if not the key to Malinowski's own charter myth. When Malinowski claimed to have "found out where lay the secret of effective field-work" and further asked, "What is then this ethnographer's magic . . .?" he answered that living "without other white men" was "the most elementary" of the "foundation stones of field work." In one swoop, previous ethnographies, written by colonial agents or visitors from the metropolis, were affected and seriously put into question by Malinowski's alleged finding of the ethnographer's magic. As white residents had "biassed and pre-judged opinions" in their "routine way of treating the natives" they could hardly be good company or good ethnographers themselves. Found "in the tone of the majority of white residents"—with "a few delightful exceptions"—such negative "features" were also identifiable "in the inferior amateur's writing," Malinowski stated (1922: 4, 5, 6), giving as illustration *Savage Life in New Guinea* (1902) by his former host on Kwato Island, missionary Charles William Abel (1862–1930), who portrayed the Indigenous people as "lawless" and only "governed by unchecked passions" (Abel 1902: 5; on Malinowski and missionaries, see Young 2004: 333).

In Malinowski's foreword to *Argonauts of the Western Pacific*, an opening statement made clear that the research "by men of academic training has proved beyond doubt and cavil that scientific, methodic inquiry can give us results far more abundant and of better quality than those of even the best amateur's work" (1922: xv; see also the conclusion in this volume).[11] Malinowski never gave any examples of such "modern scientific accounts," but it is unquestionable that he had in mind, at least, the production of his own mentors, the veterans of the celebrated Cambridge Anthropological Expedition to Torres Straits (1898–99), namely, Alfred Cort Haddon, William Halse Rivers Rivers (1864–1922), and Charles Seligman (1873–1940).

Academic versus Amateur Ethnography: A Fallacious Dichotomy

The myth of Malinowski as "self-proclaimed inventor of modern fieldwork" (Stocking 1995: 13) has long been shattered by historians of anthropology highlighting the decisive role of Rivers, Haddon, and Seligman during the expedition to the Torres Straits. There is a debate, however, on whether their expedition was fertile from the ethnographic and methodological point of view. The variety of survey methods within the expeditionary and multidisciplinary model compromises the idea that it pioneered ethnographic intensive fieldwork.

And even the famed genealogical method of Rivers (1900), dating back to the expedition, was "an instrument of survey research, useful to investigators spending only a brief time in the field" (Kuklick 1991: 140). In his introduction to *Argonauts of the Western Pacific*, Malinowski himself associated that method with the initial, sterile phase of his Melanesian experience, when he was still to discover "the ethnographer's magic." In spite of its "iconic status," the Cambridge Expedition's legacies are "diffuse" and difficult to grasp in any consensual manner (Herle and Rouse 1998: 21). Also, the notion that the expedition paved the way to the modern blending of ethnography and theory is counterbalanced by contrasting dimensions in the work of its members, from warnings against theory-infected records (ibid.: 19) to the carefree adoption of historical standpoints that were quite distant from the synchronic perspectives of their successors and most famous pupils, Radcliffe-Brown and Malinowski. In this, Rivers, Haddon, and Seligman are no different from the numerous pre-Malinowskian ethnographers who incorporated theoretical views in their writing, often addressing issues and approaches that were later relegated to the margins of canonic trends in social anthropology, such as cultural diffusion, the origins of particular institutions, or precolonial and colonial history.

To what extent did the Torres Straits experience make Haddon, Seligman, and Rivers realize the "limitations" of the expeditionary model and channel fieldwork in new directions? They produced independent monographs afterward, such as *The Todas* (1906) by Rivers and *The Veddas* (1911) by Charles Seligman and his wife Brenda Seligman (1883–1965). Nevertheless, survey techniques, intended to systematically and rapidly collect data from various groups inhabiting a relatively circumscribed but large region, were not discarded. Rivers himself resorted to alternative methods that were to be denigrated because of a long-lasting antidiffusionist bias. *The Todas* "was to remain Rivers' only attempt to produce an ethnography dealing with a single society," since his later "gang plank ethnography," James Urry writes, resulted in ethnographic accounts that were "fragmented in detail, lacking any sense of depth or internal coherence in their reporting" (Urry 1993: 50).[12] As Henrika Kuklick (1942–2013) put it in *The Savage Within*, "When anthropologists became fieldworkers, they did not necessarily become functionalists" (1991: 139; see Kuper 1996 [1973]: 8). So the idea of a unidirectional movement toward the modern monograph would be both misleading and teleological.

Moreover, Haddon and five of his Torres Straits colleagues were naturalists, trained in biological or biomedical disciplines, a circumstance that contributed to "a new sense of importance in the collection of data" (Urry 1993: 27; Urry 1984). The result of this "transfer of skills" — including the very word *fieldwork*, at the time spelled separately, as "field work" — may be disappointing. According to Urry, the influence of natural science and laboratory practice can be detected in their "dispassionate" reports, where facts are "pressed down, dried out or bottled in formalin" (Urry 1993: 7, 47). However determined these men were to professionalize fieldwork, they may be deemed "poorly qualified" under more humanistic criteria, namely for "lacking a background in languages, history or textual analysis"[13] (Herle and Rouse 1998: 7) — unlike the missionaries and government officials who were fluent in the vernacular languages and produced vernacular records that contrasted to Haddon's folktales in Pidgin English.

During the nineteenth century, several observers worked for scientific institutions and/or were academically trained in various fields of knowledge, other than anthropology, so there is no reason to make a difference between their diverse background and that of the British pioneers of professional fieldwork, Haddon, Rivers, and Seligman, who were never taught to be ethnographers or anthropologists anyway. Henrika Kuklick showed that the process of making British universities "hospitable to anthropology" was complex and gradual (1991: 31; see also 51–53); and if we combine this perception with avoiding Anglocentrism, the picture becomes more complex, considering that other European countries implemented university studies in anthropology or ethnology (among other designations) long before Britain.[14]

On top of this, there is the danger of reproducing a center-periphery model that systematically underscores the role played in the history of ethnography by metropolitan figures traveling from North to South, be they Haddon or Malinowski, to the detriment of colonial ethnographers whose lives were more entangled with indigenous reality. In a special issue of *Oceania*, edited by Helen Gardner and Robert Kenny in 2016, six historians of Australian anthropology challenged the notion that the shift from armchair anthropology to fieldwork was "autogenetic," that is, emanating from "those in the metropole" — a reference to Haddon and his teammates — "who realized that . . . anthropological research had to be hands-on and in place" (Gardner and Kenny 2016: 219). Highlighting the relevance of local ethnographic experiences predating the Torres Straits expedition (for example, the use of the genealogical method before Rivers), they deplore the fact that "standard historiography" has been "as heedless as the metropole itself" to the development of field practices in Oceania by no single "iconic figure" at no "clear moment." The fact that this was achieved in different ways by ethnographers with other primary tasks makes it difficult "to position colonial figures in the origins of the discipline." The recurrent impact of new data on evolutionary and other theoretical discussions in Europe may then be interpreted as a symptom of malaise: the insufficiently acknowledged import of the South in the emergence of the ethnographic sensibility and in bringing the armchair paradigm "to the limits of its viability." In sum, Gardner and Kenny claim that the history of anthropology "has been written upside down" (Gardner and Kenny 2016: 220, 223).[15]

If the line between trained and untrained observers is blurred, this is not just for reasons related to various academic pathways and institutional affiliations among nineteenth- and early twentieth-century ethnographers; it is also because, depending on various criteria, ethnographies produced by scientifically trained newcomers were not necessarily superior to amateur ethnographic texts.

Franz Boas and the Dawn of the Americanist Tradition

Franz Boas's ethnographic work, particularly along the Northwest Coast, has been the object of several in-depth studies (Codere 1966; Rohner 1969; Müller-Wille 1998; Müller-Wille and Gieseking 2011). Writing about his early explorations during the late 1880s, Rosemary Lévy Zumwalt (2019: 189) notes that Boas was "crafting innovative fieldwork techniques." Resorting to the correspondence between Boas and the veteran linguist Horatio Hale (1817–96), who was then monitoring his fieldwork on behalf of the British Association for the Advancement of Science, Zumwalt unveils the tension between both men, as Hale explicitly told Boas that he did not want him to make "a minute account of two or three tribes or languages" but "a general synopsis of the ethnology of the whole of British Columbia." Boas "disdained this approach" because it "must of necessity be very superficial" (Boas, quoted in Zumwalt 2019: 177). No wonder, then, that Boas kept complaining about the "senseless" instructions with which he had to conduct his ethnographic survey under Hale's orders (ibid.: 178).

The other side of the coin was Boas's tendency to overlook amateur ethnographies. It was with a grain of salt or as an exception to the rule that he acknowledged the work of this or that predecessor.[16] The main criterion in his consideration of previous ethnographies was their utility as more or less reliable raw materials for the analysis of precontact cultures, and his ethnolinguistic standards were high. "Excepting the old missionary grammars," he wrote as late as 1917, "there is very little systematic work, and we have no bodies of aboriginal texts" (p. 1). Other creative dimensions in the nineteenth-century ethnographic archive, whether literary, contextual, or theoretical, were basically neglected, and this also accounts for his severe scrutiny:

> There are very few students who have taken the time and who have considered it necessary to familiarize themselves sufficiently with native languages to understand directly what the people whom they study speak about, what they think and what they do. There are fewer still who have deemed it worth while to record the customs and beliefs and the traditions of the people in their own words, thus giving us the objective material which will stand the scrutiny of painstaking investigation. (Boas 1906: 642)

According to Regna Darnell (1999), the "Americanist tradition" encompasses both Boasian and pre-Boasian ethnographies. In their collective volume Theorizing the Americanist Tradition, Darnell and Lisa Valentine challenged the ingrained perception of it being a "merely descriptive" and "a-theoretical" anthropological paradigm (Valentine and Darnell 1999: 5, 12).[17] Boasian textualism has been criticized as a strategy that disembodied Indigenous interlocutors, presenting their oral literature "as if unmediated," and the same aversion befalls the historical precursors of that paradigm. "The idea of the text is little changed," wrote Michael Harkin against Boas, "from that of the brothers Grimm, who saw folktales as the texts that would reveal *der Geist* (the spirit) of the *Volk*" (Harkin 2001: 98), i.e., the Volksgeist. Indeed, the production of vernacular records, giving room to the Herderian concept of *Volksgeist*, had a significant part of its roots in late eighteenth- and early nineteenth-century Germany. We cannot restitute here the complex and diverse origins and developments of this broad tradition in the history of Western thought[18] — but no one will question that Boasian anthropology was one of its most flourishing branches. Historians of anthropology may choose to avoid overcritical readings of the pre-Boasian textualist tradition and search intellectual and spiritual idiosyncrasies reflected in the writings of Boas's predecessors in the United States, particularly the Bureau of American Ethnology's data collectors.

John Wesley Powell (1834–1902), the bureau's founding director, had an eye for amateur geniuses who could do the job, and his team included female ethnographers. In writing "Women in Early American Anthropology," a contribution to *Pioneers of American Anthropology* (1966), Nancy Oestreich Lurie (1924–2017) led the way in rediscovering Powell's female ethnographers, namely Erminnie Smith (1836–86), Alice Cunningham Fletcher (1838–1923), and Matilda Coxe Stevenson (1849–1915). From then on historiography followed its course, with biographies and other specialized studies on their legacies (see the conclusion in this volume). Some of these women were living legends at the end of her lives, but Lurie's verdict on their overall oblivion still resounds today as a bold appreciation of exclusion for reasons other than gender: "As it turned out, early women have been relegated to no more obscurity than have many of their male contemporaries who were also remarkable pioneer spirits" (Lurie 1966: 32).

Under auspices of the bureau, Regna Darnell writes, "participant-observation fieldwork was carried out, long before Malinowski, by Frank Hamilton Cushing, James Mooney, James Owen Dorsey, and Francis LaFlesche" (2001: 10). Indeed, Powell's team had several luminaries whose work was valued posthumously by twentieth-century anthropologists (see, for example, Lévi-Strauss 1958: 318) or brought to the fore by historians of the discipline. That is the case of the flamboyant Frank Hamilton Cushing (1857–1900) or the visionary ex-journalist James Mooney (1861–1921; see figure 0.1), whose status as excluded or included ancestors depends on the vantage point. Mooney's "The Ghost Dance Religion and the Sioux Outbreak of 1890" (1896) may be an inescapable reference for scholars working on this prophetic messianic movement or correlating similar phenomena from a sociological point of view. In comparison with the stronger memory of the Boasians, though, there is a feeling that Mooney remains "a forgotten man" (Nader 2002: 52). The perception of nineteenth-century anthropology would be very different if he was present instead of absent from handbooks informing each new generation of anthropologists. In fact, many ignore the fact that Mooney was "a political time bomb" (Nader 2002: 50, 52), actually a forerunner of colonial studies, on a collision course with the United States Indian policies. His ethnographic work was revolutionary for several reasons.

Thirty years before Malinowski boasted of discovering "the ethnographer's magic," Mooney put participant observation into practice in an incomparable way. Whether he spent the night at the Mennonite missionary's home or among the Cheyenne and Arapaho followers of the Ghost Dance is a minor question in the face of his first results

Figure 0.1. *James Mooney, undated. Courtesy of the Braun Research Library Collection, Autry Museum, Los Angeles; P. 36656.*

in Indian Territory. The myth of Malinowski's tent is meaningless in this context, as the tribal village gives way to the reservation. Not only did Mooney quickly understand that the traditionalist novelty, far from being a precolonial tradition, was related to oppression, he also participated in the dance, giving his hands to men and women for whom the new ritual embodied their faith in a better future. Produced in the postfrontier era, his collection of Ghost Dance songs transformed "salvage ethnography" into something new that should require the creation of a specific concept, since the sense of urgency and attention to vernacular detail were combined with a recognition of the colonial dimension of the cultural traits in question. "This is," according to Mooney, "the most pathetic of the Ghost Dance songs. It is sung to a plaintive tune, sometimes with tears rolling down the cheeks of the dancers as the words would bring up thoughts of *their present miserable and dependent condition*" (Mooney 1896: 977; our emphasis): "Father, have pity on me, I am crying for thirst, All is gone—I have nothing to eat."

Boas's harsh judgments on untrained ethnographers must be put into perspective since he considered, from the 1880s on and throughout his career, that they could positively contribute to anthropology. Ambiguity toward amateurs becomes more evident if we recall that the professional universe that Boas and his students wanted to consolidate for anthropology incorporated not only their Indigenous collaborators but also several amateur white ethnographers. Boas himself tried to "domesticate" them and influence their production and their ethnographic writings according to his methodological standards, but the outcome of this kind of rapprochement could be surprising (see Wickwire 2019).

The culturalists' "men on the spot" might have much in common with those of the *evolutionists*, including ambiguous forms of humility or "disobedience" toward their big-town mentors, culminating in daring, independent monographs such as *The Sun Dance and Other Ceremonies of the Oglala Division of the Teton Dakota* (1917) by James R. Walker (1849–1926), physician at the Pine Ridge Reservation from 1896 until 1914. The fact that the names and individual statements of Walker's informants were omitted in the published result—against the will of his supervisor, Clark Wissler (1870–1947)— arose the suspicion of Franz Boas, who asked Ella Cara Deloria (1889–1971) to confirm Walker's data onsite in 1937, but her own informants were "particularly incensed at the suggestion that the shamans might have held back from the people secret knowledge that they as shamans shared in common" (DeMallie and Jahner 1980: 44). The issue of authenticity was resolved by the discovery of the original manuscripts in the late 1950s and their publication in the 1980s by DeMallie and Jahner, who, while identifying some "antiquated" dimensions in Walker's monograph, risked the following statement: "That so much could have been lost in the twenty-four years since Walker left Pine Ridge is explainable only if some of the key parts of the information . . . were indeed secret. If this was really so, it places a truly enormous value on Walker's work—in fact, the value that he insisted it had" (ibid.: 45).

Postcolonial theorists and polemicists have made trenchant decon-
structions of white ethnographers' claims to be the vessels of a vanishing world, saved into print for posterity—mostly conceived of as
a Euro-American audience.

Beyond Postcolonial Anxieties

In their "Five Theses on Ethnography as Colonial Practice" (1994),[19]
Peter Pels and Oscar Salemink tried to demonstrate the ethnographic
nature of the colonial machine through the practice of late imperialism agents such as explorers, military officers, administrators, and
missionaries. Assuming a political continuity between such amateur
ethnographers and the later, professional ones, whose intellectual
and academic status forged the illusion of a lesser participation in
the system's violence, their accusatory historiography explicitly re-
jects the conventional genealogies of the discipline, focused on "the
great thinkers of anthropology, those whom we think revolutionized
its theories and methods, as the main carriers of the history of anthropology," and proposes to "consider the history of anthropology
from another angle," redirecting our attention to more or less obscure "colonial ethnographers" (1994: 1–4). The parallelism with the
present volume ends here. Following in the footsteps of historians of
anthropology who stressed, after Thomas Kuhn's *The Structure of
Scientific Revolutions* (1962), that paradigm shifts "are fuzzy, gradual,
and partial" (Hinsley 1981: 151), the editors and contributors of the
present volume admit connecting threads and continuities, more than
stereotyped ruptures, between nineteenth- and twentieth-century
ethnographies—except that colonial violence is not their criterion.

According to Pels and Salemink, the fact that various forms of
"proto-relativism," "proto-holism," and "proto-functionalism" may
be detected in the writings of colonial ethnographers is symptom-
atic if not proof that cultural relativism, holism, and functionalism
"are as much products of colonial practice as they are theoretical innovations of academic anthropology." In his countercritique of Pels
and Salemink, Herbert S. Lewis (2004, 2014) called attention to the
differences between professional anthropologists of the first half of
the twentieth century and imperial agents acting as ethnographers,
namely, from the point of view of colonial ethics. Focusing on the
example of the United States, Lewis adds:

> The doctrine of cultural relativism grew out of American anthropology
> and the ideas and teachings of Franz Boas, which were then adopted by

his students, and insofar as it had to do with colonialism it was a direct consequence of *opposition* to colonialism, cultural arrogance, and ethnocentrism! Johann Gottfried von Herder, and his predecessor Michel de Montaigne, were outraged by European overseas adventures and deeply troubled by ethnocentrism, and Franz Boas' genealogy includes these thinkers. (Lewis 2004: 253)

The present volume offers an alternative countercritique by admitting that the writings of amateur ethnographers can be imbricated, in varied and complex ways, in the Herderian as in other anthropological genealogies. What is of interest to us is the way in which ethnographic knowledge, in connection with observing and listening experiences that were never simply coinciding with colonial domination or ideology, is creatively transformed under text form. This perspective contrasts with a vast, critical literature that can hardly be listed here in any exhaustive way.[20]

If no idyllic portrait has been aimed at in the present volume, its contributors have tried to avoid the traps of radical postcolonial critique whenever it systematically puts "crime" and "horror" at the beginning of anthropology. This historiography of "hatred" (Lewis 2004: 247) or "self-aversion" (Singh and Guyer 2016: 199) is itself starting to be historically contextualized: "We need to question the motives of those who would burn the books" (Beals 2002: 225; Lewis 2014). New readings and positive ways of assessing the archive and its individual contributors are emerging. If our volume takes the decolonizing fever into account, it is by avoiding a triumphant gaze over anthropology's past and by joining other efforts in the same direction, as encapsulated, for instance, by Edvard Hviding and Cato Berg: "The factual contribution of our anthropological ancestors can now be appreciated in more generous ways than twenty years ago" (Hviding and Berg 2014: 30). Several titles speak for themselves, as representative of a recent tendency, following the postcolonial critique: "Acknowledging Ancestors" (Dureau 2014), "Voicing the Ancestors" (Handler 2016; Bashkow 2019), or "Exhuming the Ancestors" (Rosa 2019)—see also Karl-Heinz Kohl's "Plea for the Ethnographic Archive" (2014).

Salvage Ethnography as Indigenous Archive

Armchair anthropologist Marcel Mauss gave the following advice to ethnographers applying the "philological method." It was not enough to collect oral traditions: one should also "look for the magician who would supplement those formulas with the necessary comment." Preferably this work should be done "by an authoritative Indigenous expert," for "only the indigenous point of view matters." Mauss added that "the ideal option would be to transform those Indigenous individuals into authors, not just informants" (Mauss 1989 [1947]: 210, our translation), as happened with Omaha Francis La Flesche (1857–1932), and the part-Tuscorora John Napoleon Brinton Hewitt (1859–1937). In their decision to become ethnographers, and eventually ethnologists—hired as such by the Bureau of American Ethnology—La Flesche and Hewitt were influenced by foreign visitors. Hewitt started his career as a collaborator with Erminnie Smith, and, as developed by Joanna Cohan Scherer in the present volume, La Flesche was like an adopted son to Alice Fletcher, with whom he collaborated for over a quarter of a century. For these men, who had a European-American education and lived in a cross-cultural world, the publishing universe, even the white academy or the museum, was a matter of course.

In his introduction to a series of essays dedicated to the Boasians' fieldwork legacy from the point of view of the concerned Indigenous communities past and present, Ira Bashkow (2019) calls attention to the fact that salvage ethnography might be "co-constructed by the field researcher and the people researched" so that "it was not simply one-sided exploitation as one might imagine a colonial relationship." He added that "a humanistic idea of 'salvage' developed ... in the mid-twentieth century," according to which "the record might someday have value for a descendant community of the people studied" (Bashkow 2019: 218, 216).[21] The present volume aims to add more depth of space and time to this challenge, as there is room for discovering varied illustrations of indigenous participation in premodern ethnographic projects, well before the Boasian paradigm took off and far beyond North America. In several contexts where salvage ethnography took place, Native individuals were aware that books constituted a legacy to future generations, both of white and Indigenous peoples. Instead of being powerless or passively manipulated, informants and collaborators could be committed to preserving their knowledge in print and getting involved in salvage ethnography as a project that concerned their own lives and their communities.

To be sure, in some cases informants were not properly informed about the salvaging project they were taking part in. Baldwin Spencer and Francis Gillen published material, including photographs, on the most sacred items of the Arunta/Arrernte that should never be seen by women and noninitiated men. Analyzing the archive of the 1901–2 Spencer and Gillen expedition to the Northern Territory, Philip Batty (2018) unveils, however, the role of Aboriginal men, Erlikilyika and others, who not only were experts on the cross-cultural environment of that period but also acted as go-betweens in such a way that their dedication to the research goals influenced the shaping of the ethnographic field. Most meaningfully, Batty highlights the existence of an archive that involves Indigenous peoples, both in the past and the present (see Herle and Philp 2020). Therefore, it should not be reduced to mere Western imperial fantasies—and this is a powerful countercritique of the radical, postcolonial readings of Spencer and Gillen, in particular by Patrick Wolfe (1994), who equated ethnography with ethnocide.[22]

In their special issue of *Oceania*, "Before the Field," the editors Gardner and Kenny write: "The burial of colonial ethnographers beneath the practice of metropole grandees has meant that the Indigenous experts of the colonial ethnographers have been even more thoroughly hidden than their colonial collaborators and in need of a specific archaeology." Refusing to equate ethnography and colonialism in any simplistic or Manichaean manner, they "resist the efforts to bury Aboriginal agency and presence beneath this totalizing discourse" (Gardner and Kenny 2016: 222). Contemporary anthropologists estranged from the discipline's ethnographic archive should take the alert from this ongoing movement into serious account:

> The proof that these colonial records and texts are saturated with Indigenous knowledge can be found in their continued use by contemporary Aboriginal people, anthropologists, linguists, native title lawyers and historians who recognize the deep entanglement of Aboriginal peoples with those who wrote about them and the value of these documents for language, culture and the identification of boundaries. (ibid.: 222)

The value of early ethnographies can change according to present-day political realities, one important distinction being whether they relate to decolonized societies or to enduring settler colonial societies. These texts may be particularly relevant where First Nations further pursue their fight for acknowledgment in relation to current legislation on tribal boundaries and indigenous rights. Dichotomous views on the cosmopolitics of the ethnographic archive should, however, be avoided, considering the varied histories and historicities associated with political independence. Reassessments may also occur in decolonized societies where ethnographies pointing to the past are mined for culture and language for various reasons.

Exploring the intricacies of anthropological genealogy around figures claiming the title of pioneering ethnographers may be less significant for some readers than the here and now of the historical literature.
One may ask if the sole legitimate historiography of anthropology is
the one alert to contemporary political struggles echoing power relations in the colonial period. While we acknowledge the import of
this trend, we are also inclined to embrace diversity among historians
of anthropological and ethnological sciences.[23] Some of the contributors to this volume are entangled in present-day realities to the point
of combining their archival researches and fieldwork activities, while
others are more focused on disciplinary past per se and do not work
as anthropologists in the field, let alone as activists. In this sense, this
book echoes Regna Darnell's and Frederic W. Gleach's openness "to
all approaches," as "all of these debates and perspectives are part of
anthropology and thus of the histories of anthropology" — so they
reaffirm in each editorial of the *Histories of Anthropology Annual*
(2008: viii).

Structure and Aims of the Present Volume

Each contributor to the present volume was invited to give prominence to a particular ethnographic text and to select descriptive, vernacular, theoretical, methodological, historical, literary, or other significant
content from it. While keeping this selected textual content at the center
of the analysis, with purposely long indented extracts, contributors
were free to relate this content to other primary sources and to further,
sometimes external, questions, such as intersubjective experiences in
the field or colonial and sociopolitical contexts. The originality of
the present volume is thus related to a focus on ethnography as a
product, while the contributors never lose sight of ethnography as
a process. Thus, each chapter in this volume varies in creative ways
that flow from each contributor's scholarship within and beyond the
historiography of the anthropological sciences, with multiple dialog-
ing perspectives in their respective reading of the texts selected for
analysis. Ethnographic content related to specific aspects of the communities studied was, in several cases, a prime choice.

Part 1, "In Search of the Native's Point of View," is dedicated to
pre-Malinowskian versions of this Malinowskian theme par excellence. The selected case studies reveal that professional and amateur
ethnographers tried to apprehend the *Weltanschauung* of the people
studied, both their core values and the contextualized meaning of the

smallest cultural traits, resulting in some form of relativism and a critique of Western prejudice. By putting Malinowski's way of grasping "the native's point of view" into perspective, the ethnographic monographs under analysis open the horizons of disciplinary history.

In chapter 1, Herbert S. Lewis combines a thorough analysis of Franz Boas's first ethnographic monograph, *The Central Eskimo* (1888), with a selection of other texts produced during his one-year stay on Baffin Island in 1883–84. Lewis reveals Boas's fieldwork among the Inuit as an immersive, collaborative experience based on participant observation and an effort to increasingly grasp "the native's point of view." Quoting extensively from *The Central Eskimo*'s vivid accounts and detailed descriptions, Lewis questions the assumption that Boas "converted" from geography to anthropology and demonstrates how his intellectual and political background predisposed him to study and respect cultural difference in a fieldwork setting. Notwithstanding his faith in a revolution in ethnography, henceforth pursued by men of science to the detriment of amateurs, Boas believed in tutoring privileged collaborators in the field, a pattern he would continue to develop in the Northwest Coast but dating back to the period following his stay in Baffin Island.

In chapter 2, Barbara Chambers Dawson outlines how Katie Langloh Parker (1856–1940), a white settler in northern New South Wales for over twenty years, turned to the neighboring "Euahlayi" for companionship, learning their language and gaining their trust. This resulted in participant observation in ways that do not unfavorably compare with Malinowski, and Dawson quotes his formula—"to grasp the native's point of view"—in order to describe the core of Parker's ethnography. If her access to some of the knowledge of initiated men is "astonishing" (p. 94), Parker's intimate association with Indigenous women gave her unique access to the female native perspective, gaining insights into the agency of Aboriginal women that challenged the colonial stereotypes. According to Dawson, her book on *The Euahlayi Tribe* (1905) is a fundamental text in the history of anthropology by an unjustly excluded ancestor who, in her own words, "appreciated them [Aboriginal tribes] at their true value" (p. 108).

Chapter 3, by David Shankland, is dedicated to Edward Westermarck (1862–1939), professor of sociology at the LSE, close friend and supporter of Malinowski. Born in Finland into a Swedish-speaking family, Westermarck began ethnographic fieldwork in North Africa from 1898 on, with summer stays in Morocco for over two decades. His first ethnographic study, *Marriage Ceremonies in Mo-*

rocco, appeared in 1914. By analyzing a later two-volume monograph titled *Ritual and Belief in Morocco* (1926), Shankland sustains that Westermarck's ideas on the origins of ethical and moral behavior were applied to his ethnographic data in a relativist way. He believes that Westermarck's homosexuality was related to his understanding that "morals are rooted within different cultures' perceptions of behavior." Insisting on learning the vernacular, Westermarck concentrated on the meaning of folk Islamic religious concepts and "had no difficulty in assuming," Shankland concludes, "that the point of fieldwork was to give priority to the 'native's point of view.'" Shankland questions the motives why Westermarck was eventually excluded from the canon, being regarded as belonging to the nineteenth century.

Part 2, "The Indigenous Ethnographer's Magic," is dedicated to ethnographic accounts resulting from or unveiling particularly collaborative forms of ethnographic fieldwork. If the role of Indigenous informants and collaborators is transversal to the present volume, in part 2 they play the leading role of cultural experts, whether on an equal footing with the "white" ethnographers or assigning them a subordinate role as amanuensis or pupils.

In chapter 4, David Chidester proposes a vertiginous "deconstruction" of Anglican missionary Henry Callaway's (1917–1890) *The Religious System of the Amazulu* (1868–70), an ethnographic monograph that pioneered textual transliteration in two columns per page, namely in Zulu and English. While armchair anthropologists praised the authenticity of Callaway's raw ethnography for giving immediate access to the pristine beliefs of his Zulu informants, Chidester reveals that these men, including the monograph's chief authority, Mpengula Mbande (d. 1874), were figures from the margins, creatively struggling to adapt their traditional knowledge to Christian polemics and the disruptions of colonial encroachment. In conclusion, Chidester "reconstructs" Callaway's book, whose achievements are noteworthy from today's standards. The missionary recorded multiple voices to the detriment of his own and produced a text that voiced displaced and dispossessed individuals, "allowing the undercurrent of violence in the experience of his informants to surface in his monograph" (p. 180).

In chapter 5, Jeffrey Paparoa Holman explores the ten-year relationship between New Zealand ethnographer Elsdon Best and his foremost Māori collaborator Tutakangahau (ca. 1832–1907). Following a minute exegesis of *Waikare-moana* (1897), an ethnographic monograph under the guise of a tourist's guidebook, Paparoa Holman unveils the covenant taking place by the Waikaremoana lake in 1896, when Tutakangahau revealed that he was "an *ariki taniwha* [Lord of the Dragons]," willing to impart the esoteric lore of yore to Best. In reality, Tutakangahau was not the backward-gazing sage of romanticism but a modernizer who saw the opportunity to commission Best as his amanuensis and thus preserve traditional knowledge for future generations. Notwithstanding the asymmetric power relations that prevailed in colonial New Zealand, Best was in the subordinate position of a pupil, with Tutakangahau the expert. "What is enacted here," Paparoa Holman writes about the climax of their journey, "may legitimately be viewed as orality handing over its power to the written word" (p. 201).

In chapter 6, Joanna Cohan Scherer looks at the relationship between the Bureau of American Ethnology's ethnographer Alice Cunnigham Fletcher and her Omaha collaborator and protégé Francis La Flesche. Criticized in its time for classifying the collected material "according to canons of aboriginal rather than of scientific logic" (p. 219), their masterwork *The Omaha Tribe* (1911) resulted from a quarter of a century of joint and minute ethnographic fieldwork, as they both "lavished on details" (p. 229). A tribal member with privileged access to the lore of his people and pre-reservation cultural memories, La Flesche contributed to give the monograph "the true Omaha flavor" that Fletcher was searching for. Through the lens of archival correspondence and selected quotes from their book, Scherer brings *The Omaha Tribe* into our time as a monograph that was "a century ahead of other ethnographic publications," indeed "a prototype of collaborative research" (p. 239).

If all case studies in our volume are related to colonialism in one way or the other, the chapters in part 3, "Colonial Ethnography from Invasion to Empathy," offer a selection of ethnographic accounts whose colonial dimensions are particularly salient, albeit in contrasting ways. This section adds comparative depth to the volume by presenting one of the least "Malinowskian" among pre-Malinowskian ethnographies, under the form of invasive blitz ethnography. The section also discusses one of the most "Malinowskian" ethnographers, a surprising case of empathic "military anthropology" (McFate 2018). In between the two appears a missionary ethnography of the very type that Malinowski excoriated, resulting however from intimate observation of—and interference in—indigenous traditions. It can be taken as another counterexample of the volume's main narrative, reminding us of methodological and political diversity in late nineteenth- and early twentieth-century ethnographic practices.

In chapter 7, Ronald L. Grimes presents a troubling case study in the sense that John Gregory Bourke (1846–96) was an invasive ethnographer who captured indigenous sacred scenes during a short stay among the Hopi and against their will. Moreover, in *The Snake-Dance of the Moquis of Arizona* (1884) he constructed a category, "ophiolatry," that betrayed his culture-bound judgments. Grimes compares Bourke's ethnography with that produced by other nineteenth-century observers of Pueblo Indians, particularly Frank Hamilton Cushing, who in spite of his long stay and "gone native" attitude shares one important feature with Bourke: they were both dramatic performers of their own research. With due attention to current predicaments of Hopi studies by non-Indigenous scholars, Grimes explores the ritual dimension of *The Snake-Dance* as containing the clue to a more benevolent reading of Bourke's candid revulsion at the overwhelmingly olfactory sensations produced by the Snake Dance and the resulting vividness and sensuality of his writing.

In chapter 8, André Mary analyzes the case of *Chez les Fang, ou Quinze années de séjour au Congo français* (1912), written by the French missionary and ethnographer Henri Trilles (1866–1949). Combining monographic sections and missionary vignettes, *Chez les Fang* demonstrates the complexity of Catholic ethnography, from empirical soundness to literary fancy, from theoretical insights to ideological conundrums. On the one hand, Trilles practiced a manipulation of oral sources through his mytho-theological overinterpretation of native tales and legends. On the other, the narrative and dialogical style of *Chez les Fang*, the knowledge of and respect for Fang ritual specialists whenever he confronted them using their own codes and weapons, eventually reveal Trilles as a "genius of religious bricolage" (p. 283). Having fallen into oblivion, Trilles's work "affected Fang and Gabonese cultural life and history, which only adds to its complexity and makes its reassessment all the more challenging" (p. 300).

In chapter 9, Montgomery McFate unveils an ethnographic monograph, *Ashanti* (1923), published one year after Malinowski's *Argonauts of the Western Pacific* but resulting from fifteen years of intensive ethnographic fieldwork among the Ashanti in the British Gold Coast (now Ghana). A colonial officer eventually appointed government anthropologist in 1921, Robert Sutherland Rattray "was able to do what few anthropologists have done: stop what appeared to be an inevitable war between the Ashanti and the British" (p. 319). McFate describes Rattray's work as an unsettling combination of imperial anthropology and strenuous defense of Ashanti culture, portraying Rattray as an "extremely progressive, if not radical" (p. 327) figure in his own time, as well as a "proto-feminist" who understood the political import of women—particularly the Ashanti Queen Mothers—in a way that exposed both British colonial prejudice and the shortcomings of Indirect Rule. Regarded with suspicion by his peers, Rattray participated in the esoteric world of the Ashanti "as a believer," McFate sustains, while quoting inspirational passages from his monograph, such as: "I approached these old people . . . in the spirit of one who came to them as a seeker after truths" (p. 318).

Part 4, "Expeditionary Ethnography as Intensive Fieldwork," challenges the assumption that expeditionary, extensive surveys preceded stationary, intensive forms of ethnographic fieldwork, the first being associated with the nineteenth century and the latter with the twentieth. The selected case studies reveal how both models intertwined with each other, resulting in sound methodological reflections, participation on the move, and empathic descriptions.

In chapter 10, Frederico Delgado Rosa analyzes the 1890 ethnographic monograph of the Portuguese explorer Henrique de Carvalho (1843–1909), *Etnografia e história tradicional dos povos da Lunda*. As Carvalho joined the exiled Prince Samadiamb, whom the courtiers urged to return to the Lunda empire's capital, his expedition became like a traveling court if not the epicenter of local politics, with privileged conditions to pursue intensive ethnographic fieldwork. Carvalho stressed the importance of learning the native language and of experiencing "a close cohabitation and long-term work," to the point of affirming "the necessity of going native" (p. 343). According to Rosa, the difference between expeditionary and intensive fieldwork is brought into question by this case study, which unsettles the history of anthropology for other reasons as well, since the monograph's evolutionist and imperialist motives are related to relativistic and antiracist dimensions. Carvalho's reflections, Rosa sustains, "sound like a nineteenth-century version of Malinowski's charter myth" (p. 366).

In chapter 11, Grażyna Kubica reassesses the work of Maria Czaplicka as head of an anthropological expedition to Siberia at the outbreak of World War I. By attentively reading her travelogue *My Siberian Year* (1916), Kubica highlights the intensive tones of Czaplicka's expeditionary ethnography. If her experience was not stationary in comparison to that of her colleague and compatriot Malinowski, it was because she respectfully followed the nomadic rhythm of the people she studied, namely the Evenki (Tungus). Czaplicka's reciprocity, tactfulness, and humorous attitude gave way to engaging and reflexive portrayals of various native institutions and events, which can be considered "an early example of thick description" (p. 394). Following a feminist perspective, Kubica sustains that "*My Siberian Year* is no mere travelogue in the sense of continuing a nineteenth-century tradition, but a literary ethnographic text by a woman who had been trained in a male-dominated academic world to produce something quite different" (p. 394).

In chapter 12, Michael Kraus analyzes the ethnographic accounts of German ethnologists who participated in anthropological expeditions in the Amazon Basin during the late nineteenth and early twentieth centuries, particularly Karl von den Steinen, Konrad Theodor Preuss, Theodor Koch-Grünberg, Max Schmidt, and Fritz Krause (1881–1963). Their publications not only document indigenous cultures but also include methodological reflections on their increasingly intensive and stationary models of ethnographic fieldwork. The emphasis on learning the local languages, interacting with Indigenous people in their daily life, and trying to cover a complete annual cycle are some of the Malinowskian themes that this generation of German ethnographers anticipated. "It turns out," Kraus concludes, "that a significant number of the methodological principles discussed by Malinowski had already been debated and practiced by the ethnographers of the Amazon Basin and thus were far from being genuine innovations" (p. 429).

Conclusion: Ethnography, Ethnographers, and Empirical Anthropology

In *Before Boas: The Genesis of Ethnography and Ethnology in the German Enlightenment* (2015), Han F. Vermeulen concluded that before the eighteenth century ethnography existed only as "proto-ethnography" and demonstrated that "in a strict sense" ethnography and ethnology, including the coining of both terms in neo-Greek variants such as *ethnographia* (1767) and *ethnologia* (1783) or in German variants such as *Völkerkunde* (1771) or *Volks-Kunde* (1782), "were invented by eighteenth-century German-speaking historians," particularly Gerhard Friedrich Müller (1705–83), August Ludwig Schlözer (1735–1809), and Adam František Kollár (1718–83).[24] Having forged a terminological cluster and a corresponding new academic field from the 1730s to the 1780s, their program for a worldwide comparative description of peoples and nations was adopted by nineteenth-century scholars such as Gustav Klemm (1802–67), Theodor Waitz (1821–64), and Adolf Bastian (1826–1905), who form but one of the vertices in a triangle of intellectual diffusion from German-speaking countries to other European, American, and Asian centers of knowledge. While this intricate and thus far largely concealed genealogy concerns protagonist figures of the history of anthropology, from Edward Burnett Tylor to Franz Boas, it certainly implicates countless amateur ethnographers as well. Vermeulen states that "much of this process is unknown" (2015: 446, 449)—and perhaps it cannot be otherwise since the idea of ethnography was, by the mid-nineteenth century, on the loose, from Lithuania to Portugal, and beyond Europe, in a connected world in motion.

Thus, our volume deals with a period in which the term *ethnography* was fully established, meaning that it was self-evident and that its worldwide circulation no longer required justification or definition. In the late nineteenth and early twentieth centuries, the heydays of European colonialism, ethnography was a passion. Not only Boas and Cushing, or Bastian and von den Steinen, but scores of other scholars, travelers, and colonial agents tried their hand at describing peoples around the world (see the appendix to this volume). This means that it is virtually impossible to look for a unanimous, albeit tacit, understanding of the word *ethnography* in this period. As Urry noted, "The Greek suffix 'ology' or 'logy' means roughly 'the study of' with an emphasis on the scientific and the theoretical," whereas "the 'graphy' in ethnography indicates something denoted or described, connected in turn to the notion of something written or inscribed (graphe)" (Urry 2006: 28–29).

How did ethnography become limited to a specific fieldwork method of enquiry? It was mostly Malinowski and the graduate students of his seminar at the LSE who would equate the description of a people with participant observation. But there were others, notably in Britain. According to Meyer Fortes (1953: 16), the "first serious attempt" to carry out an "intensive study of a limited area" was made by Haddon's and Rivers's pupil, Radcliffe-Brown of Trinity College, among the Andaman islanders in 1906–8. The "full demonstration of its possibilities" appeared in 1922, when both Radcliffe-Brown's book on the *Andaman Islanders* and Malinowski's *Argonauts of the Western Pacific* were published (see the conclusion in this volume). "They introduced field-work of a kind that can only be carried out by trained investigators" (Fortes 1953: 17). Thanks to their efforts, the term "field work" or "field-work" became the modern-day equivalent of what previously had been generally known as "ethnography." Before 1900, *ethnography* referred to a descriptive and comparative study of a people, tribe or nation, a research program rather than a method of enquiry—even if it was evident for ethnographers before Malinowski that describing implied observing and comparing. Echoing the original uses of the word in the eighteenth century, ethnography might also apply—interchangeably with other concepts, particularly ethnology—to a broad research program that currently can be circumscribed as empirical anthropology.

Relevant ethnographies certainly existed before the affirmation of sociocultural evolutionism from the 1860s/1870s on. Many ethnographic sources perused by armchair anthropologists predated the Darwinian, archaeological, and geological revolutions. Therefore, it will not be a surprise if the present study involuntarily rejoins other histories of anthropology written for more distant periods (Palerm 2010 [1974]; Blanckaert 1996; Fabre and Privat 2010; Sera-Shriar 2013; Douglas 2014; Vermeulen 2015). For chronological coherence, however, our intent is to explore ethnographic texts produced from ca. 1870 on, i.e., *after Tylor*, in creative ways that bring them nearer to the twentieth century up to the year when *Argonauts of the Western Pacific* and *The Andaman Islanders* were published.

Mostly dedicated to selected monographs resulting from intensive, stationary fieldwork, this collection is attentive to other genres that had monographic hues or allowed for the inclusion of monographic sections. We do not see a shift from travelogues and expeditionary reports to monographs but a co-occurrence, both before and after Malinowski. Initiated in 1897—and therefore preceding the Cambridge Anthropological Expedition to Torres Straits—the equally famous Jesup North Pacific Expedition (1897–1902), collective and individual at the same time, expeditionary by name but intensive in practice, is evidence of this. It is a well-known fact that in spite of its ambition to unveil cultural-historical relations between Asia and North America thanks to a multisited network of North American and Russian ethnographers gathered around Franz Boas, "the Jesup Expedition did achieve a more restricted goal of producing a set of 'classical' ethnographic monographs" (Fitzhugh and Krupnik 2001: 9). Moreover, alternative pre-Malinowskian ethnographic genres existed, such as the ethnographic novel, the oral literature collection, and the indigenous autobiography, as well as blurred genres *avant la lettre*. The perspective underlying the present volume runs counter to an earlier historiographic attempt by Robert Thornton (1983) who insisted, possibly too much, on the characteristic features of the ethnographic monograph genre as it emerged in the nineteenth century.[25] Therefore, instead of identifying one coherent, "pioneering" genre, we aim at the identification of multifarious configurations within the monographic theme, as there were fluid boundaries between different genres that could have in common a monographic focus on a single group or various groups within a relatively circumscribed cultural region.

More than a paradigmatic shift, implying a consensus among anthropologists, what emerged with *Argonauts of the Western Pacific* was the notion of an ethnographic canon that manifested itself as a hegemonic trend within a diverse discipline. It relegated to its margins alternative ways of practicing it, such as expeditionary anthropology (Thomas and Harris 2018), with abundant but rather invisible illustrations in the twentieth century. The focus on participant observation has been productive and enriching but also reductive, ignoring the relevance of approaches such as comparative studies and ethnohistory.[26]

Therefore, it is time to render more visible the pre-Malinowskian side of the coin, by opening the ethnographic archive and bringing earlier ethnographies from the margins to the center of anthropology's history.

Frederico Delgado Rosa is lecturer at NOVA University, Lisbon (Portugal), and a researcher in the history of anthropology at CRIA: Centre for Research in Anthropology (Lisbon) and HERITAGES (Paris). He is the author, among other works, of *L'Âge d'or du totémisme* (CNRS Éditions, 2003); *Exploradores portugueses e reis africanos* (Portuguese explorers and African kings, A Esfera dos Livros, 2013, with Filipe Verde); and *Elsdon Best, l'ethnographe immémorial* (Les Carnets de Bérose, 2018). He is currently co-director, with Christine Laurière, of *BEROSE International Encyclopedia of the Histories of Anthropology* and co-convenor, with Fabiana Dimpflmeier, of the "History of Anthropology Network" within the European Association of Social Anthropologists (EASA).

Han F. Vermeulen is research associate at the Max Planck Institute for Social Anthropology in Halle (Saale), Germany, specializing in the history and theory of anthropology. He is editor or co-editor of a dozen books, including *Fieldwork and Footnotes: Studies in the History of European Anthropology* (1995); *Treasure Hunting? Collectors and Collections of Indonesian Artefacts* (2002); and *Tales from Academia: History of Anthropology in the Netherlands* (2002). His latest book, *Before Boas: The Genesis of Ethnography and Ethnology in the German Enlightenment* (University of Nebraska Press, 2015), was listed by the *Süddeutsche Zeitung* as one of the most important books of 2016, awarded the ICAS Book Prize 2017 by the International Convention of Asia Scholars, and published in a paperback edition in 2018. He is a founding member of the "History of Anthropology Network" (HOAN) within the European Association of Social Anthropologists (EASA).

Notes

1. Reprinted in the *Journal of the Polynesian Society* in 1901. As to the above quoted passage, it had appeared in an article published in the *Journal of the Polynesian Society* in 1913 (p. 153).
2. This quote was the transcription of a letter dated 23 November 1907, sent to Best by his Māori informant and collaborator Tamati Ranapiri (dates unknown; active 1872–1907).
3. The bibliography on world anthropologies is vast. See Ribeiro and Escobar (2006); Bošković (2008).
4. In the present volume, the words *Indigenous*, *Native*, and *Aboriginal* are capitalized when referring to Indigenous people or societies under settler colonialism and to individuals acting as experts of their own culture.
5. For Nigeria alone, see Jones 1974.
6. Email from Anna Sirina to the editors (30 September 2019). Reference is to Piłsudski's monograph *Materials for the Study of the Ainu Language and Folklore* (Cracow, 1912).
7. "Was Tylor really 'An Armchair Anthropologist?'" questions Maria Beatrice Di Brizio (2017) to challenge this perception (see also Sera-Shriar 2014). As to the nine research and acquisition "trips around the world" of Adolf Bastian, he "apparently spent less time in contact with the population than in the libraries of local scholars" (Fischer, Bolz, and Kamel 2007: 5). How much time Bastian actually spent with Asian, American, Oceanic, and African individuals or groups, and on what terms, deserves further attention in relation to his voluminous work (for Bastian's research expeditions, see Fischer, Bolz, and Kamel 2007; see also Penny 2021, who explains that Bastian contacted many Germans living abroad, as well as local experts on culture).
8. In fact, Jarvie criticizes the scientism underlying Malinowski's call to intensive fieldwork as a false religion comparable to cargo cults.
9. Jarvie made brief references to the forerunners of the "demand for direct observation," Alfred C. Haddon, W. H. R. Rivers, and Charles Seligman; strangely enough, he included Baldwin Spencer and Francis Gillen in this group. Jarvie also defined their demand as "the weapon" later used by Malinowski to fulfill the revolution (Jarvie 1964: 2).
10. This passage, which hardly lends itself to a confusion between the actual and the metaphorical verandah, was quoted by Jarvie as "the manifesto of the revolution" (1964: 2).

11. The same antiamateur bias can be detected in Malinowski's first Trobriand monograph, "Baloma: The Spirits of the Dead in the Trobriand
Islands" (1916). On its import, see Álvarez Roldán (1995).
12. Ten scholars have recently reassessed the ethnographic achievements
of the 1908 Percy Sladen Trust Expedition. The editors, Edvard Hviding and Cato Berg, recall that intensive ethnography and survey work
were considered as complementary. The division of subjects between the
three members of the expedition—Rivers, Hocart, and Wheeler—was
counterbalanced by the geographical partition they eventually made.
As a result, there were significant holistic dimensions in their writings.
Hviding and Berg conclude that Rivers and Hocart were "true pioneers
of fieldwork" who created "modern methodology on the spot," including participant observation. Even the "iconic tent" is not missing from
the comparison with Malinowski (Hviding and Berg 2014: 13, 23, 37).
13. With the exception of Sydney Herbert Ray (1858–1939).
14. Such as the Netherlands, one of the first countries to make ethnography
(*volkenkunde*) "a compulsory subject for those serving in the colonial
administration" in the 1830s and 1840s (Vermeulen 2015: 413). Germany, where museums became "the nuclei around which anthropology was established as an academic discipline," is another case in point.
"Very often," Karl-Heinz Kohl writes, "[museum directors and department curators] were accorded an honorary professorship at the nearby
university" (Kohl 2018: 2651).
15. This new understanding is also inscribed in the title of Helen Gardner
and Patrick McConvell's book on one of the most famous ethnographic
monographs of the nineteenth century, *Southern Anthropology: A History of Fison and Howitt's* Kamilaroi and Kurnai (2015)—thus highlighting its value beyond the theoretical influence of Lewis Henry Morgan.
16. A case in point, highlighted by Curtis Hinsley (1981), is the work of
the missionary ethnographer James Owen Dorsey (1848–95). Boas's appreciation of Dorsey's ethnographic work was ambiguous. On the one
hand, there was nothing "in the whole range of American anthropological literature" that might be compared to his publications on the Ponka
and the Omaha; on the other, they were also an instance—to be sure,
"the best"—of "how utterly inadequate the available collections are"
(Boas 1906: 643; see also Boas 1917: 1; Hinsley 1981: 174; Scherer, this
volume).
17. In the United States, the expression "Americanist tradition" had an explicitly linguistic sense during the 1960s (Regna Darnell, personal communication), while there are broader uses of the word *americanist* to
encompass anthropological traditions related to both North and South
American ethnographic contexts.
18. Jacob Grimm's (1785–1863) dramatic call to "fellow-labourers" who
could help him collect the remains of German "heathenism" is paradigmatic (Grimm 1882–83 [1835]: 1:12). The impact of his *Deutsche
Mythologie* (1835) on the history of European ethnography can hardly

be overestimated. "It is impossible to list them all," writes Hermann Bausinger about the collections inspired by Grimm's work (Bausinger 1993 [1971]: 44–45). If the romantic search for folk authenticity has been deconstructed as an ideological blend of emotions and science that justified disembodied collections (Bendix 1997: 48–49), these are, in reality, very diverse ethnographic products that also require case-by-case analysis. Illustrations and variants of this trend are detectable in various countries in transformed ways, with or without proper attention to the performative dimensions of orality.

19. The editor's introduction to a special issue of the journal *History and Anthropology*, followed by *Colonial Subjects: Essays on the Practical History of Anthropology* (Pels and Salemink 1999).

20. In association with other Africanist scholars, several African anthropologists warn against the risk of both denying colonialism and letting it "overdetermine intellectual debate" (Ntarangwi, Mills, and Babiker 2006: 12). Mwenda Ntarangwi, David Mills, and Mustafa Babiker propose to open an alternative dialogue with the past by foregrounding the early ethnographic work of African collaborators.

21. This benign understanding contrasts with more critical reassessments, namely by Margaret Bruchac (2018).

22. A similar warning may be found in Thomas (2011).

23. Including the right to avoid identifying oneself as a historian of anthropology.

24. In 1740, Gerhard Friedrich Müller coined the new research program "Völker-Beschreibung," a "description of peoples." The term *ethnographia* was used in Nördlingen, Swabia, as early as 1767, and *Ethnographie* in Göttingen, Hanover, in 1771–75. A first ethnographic journal titled *Allgemeines Archiv für Ethnographie und Linguistik* was published at Weimar in 1808 with the aim of examining the "physical, moral, and intellectual peculiarities of peoples, and their origins" (quoted in Vermeulen 2015: 344). With justice, Urry pointed out that some authors anachronistically applied the terms "ethnography" and "ethnographic" to earlier accounts and activities. These references to what was clearly proto-ethnography mostly come from outside anthropology, appearing in fields as varied as history, literary criticism, and cultural studies (Urry 2006).

25. Robert Thornton (1983) dealt with three monographs (presented as "the first" for Africa) by three missionaries: Callaway's *The Religious System of the Amazulu* (1868–70), Junod's "Les BaRonga" (1898), and Roscoe's *The Baganda* (1911). Thornton maintained that these authors deliberately sought to "emulate the monographs of the natural sciences" and distinguish their texts from other kinds of writing containing ethnographic data (such as travelogues and missionary diaries). Admitting that the content of the ethnographic monograph was "not radically new in appearance" and that other genres contributed to its development, Thornton chose to underscore its cohesive "format and rhetorical conventions" (Thornton 1983: 503, 507; see also Thornton 1981).

26. The relevance of comparative studies and ethnohistory has been shown by Adam Kuper (1982) and Marshall Sahlins (1985), for instance.

References

Abel, Charles William. 1902. *Savage Life in New Guinea: The Papuan in Many Moods*. London: London Missionary Society.

Barth, Fredrik, Andre Gingrich, Robert Parkin, and Sydel Silverman. 2005. *One Discipline, Four Ways: British, German, French, and American Anthropology*. The Halle Lectures, with a foreword by Chris Hann. Chicago: University of Chicago Press.

Bashkow, Ira. 2019. "Fieldwork Predecessors and Indigenous Communities in Native North America" (Introduction to dossier "Voicing the Ancestors"). In *Disruptive Voices and the Singularity of Histories*, edited by R. Darnell and F. W. Gleach, 211–229. Lincoln: Nebraska University Press (Histories of Anthropology Annual 13).

Batty, Philip. 2018. "Assembling the Ethnographic Field: The 1901–02 Expedition of Baldwin Spencer and Francis Gillen." In *Expeditionary Anthropology: Teamwork, Travel and the "Science of Man,"* edited by Martin Thomas and Amanda Harris, 37–63. New York: Berghahn Books.

Bausinger, Hermann. 1993 [1971]. *Volkskunde ou l'ethnologie allemande: De la recherche sur l'antiquité à l'analyse culturelle*. Paris: Éditions de la Maison des Sciences de l'Homme.

Beals, Alan R. 2002. "Anthropology Made New: Writing Against and Without Culture." *Reviews in Anthropology* 31: 213–29.

Bendix, Regina. 1997. *In Search of Authenticity: The Formation of Folklore Studies*. Madison: University of Wisconsin Press.

Best, Elsdon. 1901. "Te Whanga-Nui-A-Tara: Wellington In Pre-Pakeha Days." *Journal of the Polynesian Society* 10(3): 107–65. Reprinted from *New Zealand Mail*, 13 July 1894.

———. 1913. "Tuhoe, The Children of the Mist: I. A Lone Land and They Who Settled It." *Journal of the Polynesian Society* 22(87): 149–65.

———. 1925. *Tuhoe: The Children of the Mist*. 2 vols. New Plymouth: Thomas Avery & Sons.

Bieder, Robert E. 1986. *Science Encounters the Indian, 1820–1880: The Early Years of American Ethnology*. Norman: University of Oklahoma Press.

Blanckaert, Claude, ed. 1996. *Le Terrain des sciences humaines: Instructions et enquêtes (XVIIIᵉ–XXᵉ siècle)*. Paris/Montréal: L'Harmattan.

Boas, Franz. 1887. "Review of the Fourth Annual Report of the Bureau of Ethnology." *Science* 9(228): 597–98.

———. 1888. "The Central Eskimo." In *Sixth Annual Report of the Bureau of Ethnology to the Secretary of the Smithsonian Institution, 1884–1885*, 399–669. Washington, DC: Government Printing Office.

———. 1896. "The Limitations of the Comparative Method of Anthropology." *Science* 4(103) (new series): 901–8. Reprinted in Boas, Franz. 1940. *Race, Language and Culture,* 270–80. New York: Macmillan.

———. 1906. "Some Philological Aspects of Anthropological Research." *Science* 23(591) (new series): 641–45.

———. 1917. "Introductory." *International Journal of American Linguistics* 1(1): 1–8.

Bošković, Aleksandar, ed. 2008. *Other People's Anthropologies: Ethnographic Practice on the Margins.* New York: Berghahn Books.

Bourke, John Gregory. 1884. *The Snake-Dance of the Moquis of Arizona.* London: Sampson Low, Marston, Searle & Rivington.

Bruchac, Margaret. 2018. *Savage Kin: Indigenous Informants and American Anthropologists.* Tucson: University of Arizona Press.

Callaway, Henry. 1868–70. *The Religious System of the Amazulu.* 3 vols. Springvale, Natal: John A. Blair/Cape Town: J. C. Juta/London: Trübner.

Carvalho, Henrique Augusto Dias de. 1890. *Etnografia e história tradicional dos povos da Lunda.* Lisbon: Imprensa Nacional.

Czaplicka, Maria. 1916. *My Siberian Year.* London: Mills and Boon.

Codere, Helen, ed. 1966. *Kwakiutl Ethnography.* Chicago: University of Chicago Press.

Darnell, Regna. 1971. "The Professionalization of American Anthropology: A Case Study in the Sociology of Knowledge." *Social Science Information* 10(2): 83–103.

———. 1999. "Theorizing Americanist Anthropology: Continuities from the B.A.E. to the Boasians." In *Theorizing the Americanist Tradition,* edited by Lisa P. Valentine and Regna Darnell, 38–51. Toronto: University of Toronto Press.

———. 2001. *Invisible Genealogies: A History of Americanist Anthropology.* Lincoln: University of Nebraska Press.

Darnell, Regna, and Frederic W. Gleach. 2008. "Editors' Introduction." *Histories of Anthropology Annual* 4: vii–viii.

DeMallie, Raymond, and Elaine A. Jahner. 1980. "Physician and Anthropologist." In *Lakota Belief and Ritual,* edited by J. R. Walker, 3–45. Lincoln: University of Nebraska Press.

Di Brizio, Maria Beatrice. 2017. "Un anthropologue en chambre? Vie et œuvre d'Edward Burnett Tylor." In *BEROSE International Encyclopaedia of the Histories of Anthropology,* Paris.

Douglas, Bronwen. 2014. *Science, Voyagers, and Encounters in Oceania, 1511–1850.* New York: Palgrave MacMillan.

Dureau, Christine, 2014. "Acknowledging Ancestors: The Vexations of Representation." In *The Ethnographic Experiment: A.M. Hocart and W.H.R. Rivers in Island Melanesia, 1908,* edited by Edvard Hviding and Cato Berg, 44–70. New York: Berghahn Books.

Eidson, John R. 2017. "When a Great Scholarly Tradition Modernizes: German-Language Ethnology in the Long Twentieth Century." In *European*

Anthropologies, edited by Andrés Barrera-González, Monica Heintz, and Anna Horolets, 48–84. New York: Berghahn Books.

Eriksen, Thomas Hylland, and Finn Sivert Nielsen. 2001. *A History of Anthropology*. Sterling, VA: Pluto Press.

Fabre, Daniel, and Jean-Marie Privat, eds. 2010. *Savoirs romantiques: Une naissance de l'ethnologie*. Nancy: Presses Universitaires de Nancy.

Fischer, Manuela, Peter Bolz, and Susan Kamel. 2007. "Foreword." In *Adolf Bastian and his Universal Archive of Humanity: The Origins of German Anthropology*, edited by M. Fischer, P. Bolz, and S. Kamel, 1–8. New York: Georg Olms Verlag.

Fison, Lorimer, and Alfred William Howitt. 1880. *Kamilaroi and Kurnai: Group-Marriage and Relationship, and Marriage by Elopement*. Melbourne: George Robinson.

Fitzhugh, William W., and Igor Krupnik. 2001. "Introduction." In *Gateways: Exploring the Legacy of the Jesup North Pacific Expedition, 1897–1902*, edited by I. Krupnik and W. W. Fitzhugh, 1–16. Washington, DC: National Museum of Natural History.

Fletcher, Alice C., and Francis La Flesche. 1911. "The Omaha Tribe." In *Twenty-Seventh Annual Report to the Secretary of the Bureau of American Ethnology 1905-'06*, 17–672. Washington, DC: Smithsonian Institution; U.S. Government Printing Office.

Fortes, Meyer. 1953. *Social Anthropology at Cambridge since 1900*. An Inaugural Lecture by M. Fortes, William Wyse Professor of Social Anthropology in the University of Cambridge. Cambridge: Cambridge University Press, 1–30. Reprinted in Regna Darnell, ed. 1974. *Readings in the History of Anthropology*, 426–39. New York: Harper and Row.

Frazer, James George. 1890. *The Golden Bough: A Study in Comparative Religion*. London: Macmillan & Co.

Gardner, Helen, and Patrick McConvell. 2015. *Southern Anthropology: A History of Fison and Howitt's* Kamilaroi and Kurnai. Basingstoke: Palgrave Macmillan.

Gardner, Helen, and Robert Kenny. 2016. "Before the Field: Colonial Anthropology Reassessed." *Oceania* 86(3): 218–24.

Gellner, Ernst. 1964. "Foreword." In Ian C. Jarvie, *The Revolution in Anthropology*, v–viii. London: Routledge & Kegan Paul.

Gingrich, Andre. 2005. "The German-Speaking Countries: Ruptures, Schools, and Nontraditions; Reassessing the History of Sociocultural Anthropology in Germany." In *One Discipline, Four Ways: British, German, French and American Anthropology*, by F. Barth et al., 59–153. Chicago: University of Chicago Press.

———. 2017. "German-Language Anthropology Traditions around 1900: Their Methodological Relevance for Ethnographers in Australia and Beyond." In *German Ethnography in Australia*, edited by Nicolas Peterson and Anna Kenny, 29–53. Acton, ACT: Australian National University Press (Monographs in Anthropology Series).

Grimm, Jacob. 1882–83 [1835]. *Teutonic Mythology*. Translated from the 4th ed. with notes and appendix by James Steven Stallybrass. Vol. 1. London: G. George Bell and Sons.

Handler, Richard. 2000. "Boundaries and Transitions." In *Excluded Ancestors, Inventible Traditions: Essays toward a More Inclusive History of Anthropology*, edited by R. Handler, 3–10. Madison: University of Wisconsin Press.

Handler, Richard, ed. 2016. "Voicing the Ancestors: Readings in Memory of George Stocking." *Hau: Journal of Ethnographic Theory* 6(3): 367–86.

Harkin, Michael E. 2001. "(Dis)pleasures of the Text: Boasian Ethnology on the Central Northwest Coast." In *Gateways: Exploring the Legacy of the Jesup North Pacific Expedition, 1897–1902*, edited by I. Krupnik and W. W. Fitzhugh, 93–105. Washington, DC: National Museum of Natural History.

Herle, Anita, and Jude Philp, eds. 2020. *Recording Kastom: Alfred Haddon's Journals from the Torres Strait and New Guinea, 1888 and 1898*. Sydney: Sydney University Press.

Herle, Anita, and Sandra Rouse. 1998. "Introduction: Cambridge and the Torres Strait." In *Cambridge and the Torres Strait: Centenary Essays on the 1898 Anthropological Expedition*, edited by A. Herle and S. Rouse, 1–22. Cambridge: Cambridge University Press.

Hinsley, Curtis M. 1981. *Savages and Scientists: The Smithsonian Institution and the Development of American Anthropology 1846–1910*. Washington, DC: Smithsonian Institution Press.

Hogbin, Herbert Ian. 1958. *Social Change*. London: Watts.

Hviding, Edvard, and Cato Berg. 2014. "Introduction: The Ethnographic Experiment in Island Melanesia." In *The Ethnographic Experiment: A.M. Hocart and W.H.R. Rivers in Island Melanesia, 1908*, edited by E. Hviding and C. Berg, 1–43. New York: Berghahn Books.

Jackson, Henry Cecil. 1923. *The Nuer of the Upper Nile Province*. Karthoum: El Hadara Printing Press.

Jarvie, Ian C. 1964. *The Revolution in Anthropology*. Foreword by Ernest Gellner. London: Routledge & Kegan Paul.

Jones, Gwilym I. 1974. "Social Anthropology in Nigeria during the Colonial Period." *Africa: Journal of the International African Institute* 44(3): 280–89.

Junod, Henri-Alexandre. 1898. *Les Ba-Ronga: Étude ethnographique sur les indigènes de la baie de Delagoa*. Neuchâtel: Attinger Frères (*Bulletin de la Société de géographie de Nêuchatel* 10).

Kohl, Karl-Heinz. 2014. "The Future of Anthropology Lies in Its Own Past: A Plea for the Ethnographic Archive." *Social Research* 81(3): 555–70.

———. 2018. "Anthropology in Germany." In *The International Encyclopaedia of Anthropology*, edited by Hilary Callan, 5:2647–66. Hoboken, NJ: John Wiley & Sons.

Krupnik, Igor, ed. 2016. *Early Inuit Studies: Themes and Transitions, 1850s–1980s*. Washington, DC: Smithsonian Institution Press.

Kuhn, Thomas S. 1962. *The Structure of Scientific Revolutions*. Chicago: University of Chicago Press. 2nd enlarged ed. 1970.

Kuklick, Henrika. 1991. *The Savage Within: The Social History of British Anthropology, 1885–1945*. Cambridge: Cambridge University Press.

———, ed. 2008. *A New History of Anthropology*. Malden, MA: Blackwell Publishing.

Kuper, Adam. 1996 [1973]. *Anthropology and Anthropologists: The Modern British School*. 3rd rev. and enlarged ed. New York: Routledge.

———. 1982. *Wives for Cattle: Bridewealth and Marriage in Southern Africa*. London: Routledge and Kegan Paul.

Langloh Parker, Katie. 1905. *The Euahlayi Tribe: A Study of Aboriginal Life in Australia*. Introduction by Andrew Lang. London: Archibald Constable.

Laurière, Christine. 2021. "L'ethnographie pour raison de vivre: Un portrait d'Arnold Van Gennep." In *BEROSE International Encyclopaedia of the Histories of Anthropology*. Paris.

Lévi-Strauss, Claude. 1958. *Anthropologie structurale*. Paris: Plon.

Lewis, Herbert S. 2004. "Imagining Anthropology's History." *Reviews in Anthropology* 33: 243–61.

———. 2014. *In Defense of Anthropology: An Investigation of the Critique of Anthropology*. New Brunswick, NJ: Transaction Publishers.

Lurie, Nancy Oestreich. 1966. "Women in Early American Anthropology." In *Pioneers of American Anthropology: The Uses of Biography*, edited by June Helm, 31–81. Seattle: University of Washington Press.

Lyons, Andrew. 2007. "Missing Ancestors and Missing Narratives." In *Histories of Anthropology Annual* 3: 148–66.

Madden, Raymond. 2010. *Being Ethnographic: A Guide to the Theory and Practice of Ethnography*. Washington, DC: Sage.

Malinowski, Bronisław. 1916. "Baloma: The Spirits of the Dead in the Trobriand Islands." *Journal of the Royal Anthropological Institute* 46: 353–430.

———. 1922. *Argonauts of the Western Pacific: An Account of Native Enterprise and Adventure in the Archipelagoes of Melanesian New Guinea*. Preface by Sir James George Frazer. London: George Routledge & Sons.

———. 1926. *Myth in Primitive Psychology*. London: Kegan Paul & Co.

Marquardt, Ole. 2016. "Between Science and Politics: The Eskimology of Hinrich Johannes Rink." In *Early Inuit Studies: Themes and Transitions, 1850s–1980s*, edited by Igor Krupnik, 35–54. Washington, DC: Smithsonian Institution Scholarly Press.

Mauss, Marcel. 2016 [1925]. *The Gift. Expanded Edition* (selected, annotated, and translated by Jane I. Guyer). Chicago: HAU Books.

———. 1989 [1947]. *Manuel d'ethnographie*. With a preface and edited by Denise Paulme. Paris: Payot.

McFate, Montgomery. 2018. *Military Anthropology: Soldiers, Scholars and Subjects at the Margins of Empire*. New York: Oxford University Press.

Mooney, James. 1896. "The Ghost-Dance Religion and the Sioux Outbreak of 1890." In *Fourteenth Annual Report of the Bureau of Ethnology to the*

Secretary of the Smithsonian Institution 1892–93: Part 2, 641–1136. Washington, DC: Government Printing Office.

Morgan, Lewis Henry. 1851. *The League of the Ho-dé-no-sau-nee, or Iroquois*. Rochester, NY: Sage and Brother Publishers.

Müller-Wille, Ludger, ed. 1998. *Franz Boas among the Inuit of Baffin Island, 1883–1884: Journals and Letters*. Translated by William Barr. Toronto: University of Toronto Press.

Müller-Wille, Ludger, and Bernd Gieseking, eds. 2011. *Inuit and Whalers on Baffin Island through German Eyes: Wilhelm Weike's Artic Journal and Letters (1883–1884)*. Translated by William Barr. Montréal: Baraka Books.

Ntarangwi, Mwenda, David Mills and Mustaga Babiker. 2006. "Introduction: Histories of Training, Ethnographies of Practice." In *African Anthropologies: History, Critique and Practice*, edited by Mwenda Ntarangwi, David Mills, and Mustaga Babiker, 1–48. Dakar: Cosderia (in association with Zed Books, London and New York).

Nader, Laura. 2002. "Sleepwalking through the History of Anthropology: Anthropologists on Home Ground." In *Anthropology, History, and American Indians: Essays in Honor of William Curtis Sturtevant*, edited by William L. Merrill and Ives Goddard, 47–54. Washington, DC: Smithsonian Institution.

Palerm, Ángel. 2010 [1974]. *Historia de la etnología: Los precursores*. México: Centro de Investigaciones y Estudios Superiores en Antropología Social, Universidad Iberoamericana.

Pels, Peter, and Oscar Salemink. 1994. "Introduction: Five Theses on Ethnography as Colonial Practice." *History and Anthropology* 8(1–4): 1–34.

———, eds. 1999. *Colonial Subjects: Essays on the Practical History of Anthropology*. Ann Harbor: University of Michigan Press.

Penniman, Thomas Kenneth. 1974 [1935]. *A Hundred Years of Anthropology*. 3rd rev. ed. New York: William Morrow & Co.

Penny, H. Glenn. 2021. *In Humboldt's Shadow: A Tragic History of German Ethnology*. Princeton, NJ: Princeton University Press.

Piłsudski, Bronisław. 1912. *Materials for the Study of the Ainu Language and Folklore*. Edited by Jan Michał Rozwadowski. Cracow: Imperial Academy of Sciences.

Powell, John Wesley, ed. 1883. *Second Annual Report of the Bureau of Ethnology 1880–81*. Washington, DC: Government Printing Office.

Radcliffe-Brown, Alfred Reginald [Brown, A. R.]. 1922. *The Andaman Islanders: A Study in Social Anthropology*. Cambridge: Cambridge University Press. 2nd ed. 1933.

Rattray, Robert Sutherland. 1923. *Ashanti*. Oxford: Clarendon Press.

Ribeiro, Gustavo Lins, and Arturo Escobar, eds. 2006. *World Anthropologies: Disciplinary Transformations within Systems of Power*. Oxford: Berg.

Rink, Henry [Hinrich Johannes]. 1887–91. *The Eskimo Tribes: Their Distribution and Characteristics, Especially in Regard to Language; With a*

Comparative Vocabulary and a Sketch-Map. 2 vols. London: Williams and Norgate/Copenhagen: C. A. Reitzel.

Rivers, William H. R. 1900. "A Genealogical Method of Collecting Social and Vital Statistics." *Journal of the Royal Anthropological Institute* 30: 74–82.

———. 1906. *The Todas.* London: Macmillan and Co.

Robben, Antonius C. G. M. 2007. "Introduction." In *Ethnographic Fieldwork: An Anthropological Reader,* edited by A. Robben and J. A. Sluka, 51–55. Malden, MA: Blackwell Publishers.

Rohner, Ronald P., ed. 1969. *The Ethnography of Franz Boas: Letters and Diaries of Franz Boas Written on the Northwest Coast from 1886 to 1931.* Introduction by Ronald P. Rohner and Evelyn C. Rohner. Chicago: University of Chicago Press.

Rosa, Frederico Delgado. 2019. "Exhuming the Ancestors: A Reassessment of Fabian's Critique of Allochronism." *Critique of Anthropology* 9(4): 458–77.

Roscoe, John. 1911. *The Baganda: An Account of their Native Customs and Beliefs.* London: Macmillan and Co.

Sahlins, Marshall. 1985. *Islands of History.* Chicago: University of Chicago Press.

Seligman, Charles G., and Brenda Z. Seligman. 1911. *The Veddas.* Cambridge: Cambridge University Press.

Sera-Shriar, Efram. 2013. *The Making of British Anthropology, 1813–1871.* Brookfield: Pickering & Chatto.

———. 2014. "What Is Armchair Anthropology? Observational Practices in Nineteenth-Century British Human Sciences." *History of the Human Sciences* 27: 26–40.

Shankland, David. 2019. "Social Anthropology and its History." In "One Hundred and Fifty Years of the Zeitschrift für Ethnologie—a Look Back and Ahead," edited by Peter Finke, special issue, *Zeitschrift für Ethnologie* 144: 51–76. Berlin: Dietrich Reimer Verlag.

Singh, Bhrigupati, and Jane I. Guyer. 2016. "A Joyful History of Anthropology." *Hau: Journal of Ethnographic Theory* 6(2): 197–211.

Stocking, George W., Jr. 1974. "Some Problems in the Understanding of Nineteenth-Century Cultural Evolutionism." In *Readings in the History of Anthropology,* edited by Regna Darnell, 407–25. New York: Harper and Row.

———. 1983. "The Ethnographer's Magic: Fieldwork in British Anthropology from Tylor to Malinowski." In *The Ethnographer's Magic: And Other Essays in the History of Anthropology,* edited by G. W. Stocking Jr., 12–59. Madison: University of Wisconsin Press.

———. 1987. *Victorian Anthropology.* New York: The Free Press/London: Collier MacMillan Publishers.

———. 1995. *After Tylor: British Social Anthropology, 1888–1951.* Madison: University of Wisconsin Press.

Thomas, Martin. 2011. *The Many Worlds of R. H. Mathews: In Search of an Australian Anthropologist.* Crows Nest, NSW: Allen & Unwin.

Thomas, Martin, and Amanda Harris, eds. 2018. *Expeditionary Anthropology: Teamwork, Travel and the "Science of Man."* New York: Berghahn Books.

Thornton, Robert J. 1981. "Evolution, Salvation and History in the Rise of the Ethnographic Monograph in Southern Africa, 1860–1920." *Social Dynamics* 6(2): 14–23.

———. 1983. "Narrative Ethnography in Africa, 1850–1920: The Creation and Capture of an Appropriate Domain for Anthropology." *Man* 18(3) (new series): 502–20.

Trilles, Henri. 1912. *Chez les Fang, ou Quinze années de séjour au Congo français.* Lilles/Paris/Bruges: Société Saint-Augustin, Desclée, De Brouwer et Cie.

Tylor, Edward B. 1861. *Anahuac: Or Mexico and the Mexicans, Ancient and Modern.* London: Longman, Green, Longman, and Roberts.

Urry, James. 1984. "A History of Field Methods." In *Ethnographic Research: A Guide to General Conduct*, edited by Roy F. Ellen, foreword by Sir Raymond Firth, 35–61. London: Academic Press.

———. 1993. *Before Social Anthropology: Essays on the History of British Anthropology.* Chur: Harwood Academic Publishers.

———. 2006. "The Ethnographisation of Anglo-American Anthropology: Causes and Consequences." *Sites: A Journal of Social Anthropology and Cultural Studies* 3(2): 3–39.

Valentine, Lisa P., and Regna Darnell. 1999. "Introduction: Timely Conversations." In *Theorizing the Americanist Tradition*, edited by L. P. Valentine and R. Darnell, 3–18. Toronto: University of Toronto Press.

Van Gennep, Arnold. 1909. *Les rites de passage.* Paris: Émile Nourry.

———. 1912. *Religions, mœurs et légendes: Essais d'ethnographie et de linguistique.* Paris: Mercure de France.

———. 1913. "Quelques lacunes de l'ethnographie actuelle." *Scientia* 14: 404–11.

———. 1914. *En Algérie.* Paris: Mercure de France.

Vermeulen, Han F. 2015. *Before Boas: The Genesis of Ethnography and Ethnology in the German Enlightenment.* Lincoln: University of Nebraska Press.

Vermeulen, Han F., Cláudio Costa Pinheiro, and Peter Schröder. 2019. "Introduction: The German Tradition in Latin-American Anthropology." In "German-Speaking Anthropologists in Latin America, 1884–1945," special issue, *Revista de Antropologia* 62(1): 64–96.

Walker, James R. 1917. *The Sun Dance and Other Ceremonies of the Oglala Division of the Teton Dakota.* New York: American Museum of Natural History.

Westermarck, Edward. 1914. *Marriage Ceremonies in Morocco.* London: Macmillan.

———. 1926. *Ritual and Belief in Morocco.* 2 vols. London: Macmillan.

Wickwire, Wendy. 2019. *At the Bridge: James Teit and an Anthropology of Belonging*. Vancouver: University of British Columbia Press.

Wolfe, Patrick. 1994. "'White Man's Flour': Doctrines of Virgin Birth in Evolutionist Ethnogenetics and Australian State-Formation." *History and Anthropology* 8(1–4): 165–205.

Young, Michael W. 2004. *Malinowski: Odyssey of an Anthropologist, 1884–1920*. New Haven, CT: Yale University Press.

———. 2018. "Le Jason de l'anthropologie: Vie, œuvre et legs de Bronislaw Malinowski." In *BEROSE International Encyclopaedia of the Histories of Anthropology*, Paris.

Zumwalt, Rosemary Lévy. 2019. *Franz Boas: The Emergence of the Anthropologist*. Lincoln: University of Nebraska Press.

Part I

In Search of the Native's Point of View

1

"Adapt Fully to Their Customs"

Franz Boas as an Ethnographer among the Inuit of Baffinland (1883–84) and His Monograph *The Central Eskimo* (1888)

Herbert S. Lewis

Usually associated with the Kwakiutl or Kwakwaka'wakw of Vancouver Island, Franz Boas (1858–1942) was involved with this people from 1886 until his death and produced thousands of pages of text about their culture. Most of his field trips to the Northwest Coast were of relatively short duration, however, and his early work was largely a survey for the British Association for the Advancement of Science. Furthermore, he depended heavily on a local man, George Hunt (1854–1933), to collect much of the material he published. For all these reasons Boas's ethnography has often been criticized. Before meeting the Kwakiutl, however, Franz Boas lived for a year among the Eskimos of Baffin Island[1] and produced a very different ethnography.[2]

The Background

In July 1881, aged twenty-three, Franz Boas received his doctorate in physics from Kiel University "with *summa cum laude* on his thesis and *magna cum laude* on his doctoral examination" (Kluckhohn and Prufer 1959: 8). Almost two years later, in June 1883, he left Germany on the schooner *Germania* for a year of geographical research among the Inuit in the Arctic. This might have seemed like a radical change of topic and life's plan, but young Franz was remarkably well prepared for this work, and his research plans included ethnography.

Franz Boas was deeply involved with science and learning at least from the age of four, when he made his first herbarium and attended the Froebel kindergarten ("devoted to science") established by his mother in Minden, Westphalia. As his "Curriculum Vitae," produced at age nineteen, shows, he had interests in learning of every kind, including literature, music, and the arts. He mentions studying botany, physical geography, zoology, mineralogy, and astronomy by age eleven. In his teen years he added Goethe, Latin, Greek, French, geography, geology, physics, and mathematics. He also excelled in physical education and gymnastics, "acquiring indispensable skills and constitution for later in life when he would meet physical challenges such as travelling under Arctic conditions" (Müller-Wille 2014: 35).

His studies at the Universities of Heidelberg, Bonn, and Kiel included chemistry with Robert Bunsen (1811–99), physics with Rudolf Clausius (1822–88), and philosophy with the Kantian expert Benno Erdmann (1851–1921), as well as mathematics, geology, and marine biology (Kluckhohn and Prufer 1959: 7). He studied historical and cultural geography with Theobald Fischer (1846–1910), including a course on polar research (Cole 1999: 65). Late in life Boas wrote, "My university studies were a compromise. On account of my intense emotional interest in the phenomena of the world, I studied geography; on account of my intellectual interest, I studied mathematics and physics" (Boas 1938: 201).

Boas had hoped to do a dissertation in mathematics, but circumstances dictated a work in physics with minors in geography and philosophy (Müller-Wille 2014: 36). After a year of mandatory military service (1881–82), during which time he published seven papers on psychophysics, Franz Boas turned to geography and to his plan to do research on Baffin Island. This should not have been a surprise. By the age of ten Franz "dreamed of participating in a polar expedition," and when he was thirteen he wrote, "I would like to get to know new peoples and their customs and habits, including the already known Galla, Banda, Kaffer, and Hottentot peoples" (Boas, quoted in Zumwalt 2019: 95; Kluckhohn and Prufer 1959: 6).[3] He was born in 1858, one year before the death of Alexander von Humboldt (1769–1859). That German geographer, environmentalist, and explorer was one of the most famous men in Europe and the two Americas, and his magisterial work in five volumes, *Kosmos* (1845–62), had a major influence on Boas's thinking about science, as the latter demonstrated in his early paper "The Study of Geography" (1887b).

The 1880s were a rich time for European and American expeditions everywhere. Geography was a rapidly growing field in Germany, and as Ludger Müller-Wille notes, *Geographie* included *Ethnologie* or *Völkerkunde* as well (2014: 35). Karl Ritter (1779–1859), another founding figure of German geography, "had considered geography to be 'man-centered,' and had insisted that geographical provinces could not be defined absolutely but only relative to the perceptions of those people who lived in the area . . ." (Leaf 1979: 191). Theobald Fischer, Franz's teacher, friend, and loyal supporter, was influenced by Ritter.

In 1882 another geographer, Friedrich Ratzel (1844–1904), gained widespread prominence with the first volume of his work *Anthropogeographie*. Among his major concerns was the impact of environment on population distribution, migrations, and, more generally, societies. Boas was impressed by Ratzel, whom he had heard speak in Frankfurt about the importance of Polar research (Zumwalt 2019: 80). Boas planned to carry out physical exploration, mapping, and making meteorological, astronomical, and hydrological calculations, but "his real interest was the relationship between people and their natural environment through an investigation of . . . 'the dependence of contemporary migrating Eskimos upon the configuration and physical relationships of the land'" (Cole 1999: 65). He would study the ways in which Eskimos were able to adapt to the harsh Arctic environmental conditions. As he explained in a letter to his uncle, Dr. Abraham Jacobi (1830–1919), "I am studying the wandering of the Eskimo, their knowledge of the country they live in and of adjacent lands, in the hope to prove a close connection between the number of persons in a tribe, the distribution of food supplies and the nature of the country" (Boas, quoted in Zumwalt 2019: 73; cf. Stocking 1965: 53ff.).

Near the end of his life Boas gave another reason for his expedition. He wrote that "the writings of philosophers" had given him "a desire to understand the relation between the objective and the subjective worlds." Since he didn't have the opportunity to pursue this interest through psychological investigations, "by a peculiar compromise, presumably largely dictated by the desire to see the world, I decided to make a journey to the Arctic for the purpose of adding to our knowledge of unknown regions and of helping me to understand the reaction of the human mind to natural environment" (Boas 1938: 201–2). He gave a simpler reason to the German Polar Commission on 24 May 1883: "I intend to make a research trip to Cumberland Sound to study the conditions of the Eskimo and to explore the West Coast of Baffin Island" (Boas, quoted in Müller-Wille 1998: 41). Boas also thought that this trip would give him scientific credibility and that he would "be accepted among the geographers" (Zumwalt 2019:73–74).

Franz Boas had another form of preparation for ethnographic work, for studying the lives of peoples of a different "race" and culture from his own. He grew up in a German-Jewish family that took seriously the ideals of the Enlightenment. They thrilled to the notions of freedom and free thinking in the music of Beethoven, the works of Schiller, Lessing, and Goethe. They held to the ideals of the failed Revolutions of 1848, and he was brought up with faith in the liberal, even radical, values of democracy, equality, freedom of expression, individual rights, and the common humanity of all peoples. He was educated at a time when there was still a strong liberal tradition in Germany represented by Alexander von Humboldt (and his brother Wilhelm).[4] We know that Boas owned a set of the complete works of Humboldt's important predecessor, Johann Gottfried Herder (Kluckhohn and Prufer 1959: 10).[5] Herder and Humboldt were intellectual forerunners of the anticolonial, antislavery, and humanitarian tradition in German that was led in Boas's time in Germany by Rudolf Virchow (1821–1902) and Adolf Bastian (1826–1905).[6] A primary source of Boas's cultural and linguistic understanding came from the works of Heymann Steinthal (1823–99) and Moritz Lazarus (1824–1903), authors of the notion of *Völkerpsychologie*.[7]

Boas moved to Berlin in late September to prepare for his expedition. The year 1882–83 was designated the (First) International Polar Year, and Germany was one of the twelve nations participating in these coordinated scientific endeavors. Boas had entrée to the Gesellschaft für Erdkunde (Berlin Geographical Society) and was able to receive instruction in cartography, hydrology, meteorology, photography, astronomical observation, and terrestrial magnetism. He studied linguistics, Inuktitut, English, and Danish and read everything he could about Arctic exploration and Eskimos. He took the opportunity to get advice from the two major figures in the developing field of anthropology, Virchow and Bastian (Norman F. Boas 2004: 27). Virchow, one of Boas's role models, was Germany's leading figure in numerous scientific fields—cell biology, pathology, physical anthropology, archeology—as well as a leading liberal politician. Bastian was a rising figure in the development of German ethnography and the founder of the Königliches Museum für Völkerkunde (Royal Ethnological Museum) in Berlin. He would work with both of them on his return.

Boas had no official institutional backing or financing for his Arctic research, nor was he going as part of a team whose members had varied expertise and experience. He was the sole researcher, accompanied by his family's gardener and servant, Wilhelm Weike (1859–1917). Franz's father contributed funds for the undertaking, and the German Polar Commission aided him by lending and donating scientific instruments, expedition equipment, and supplies, to be collected from the polar station in Cumberland Sound. (These included a tent, a sled, two fur suits, equipment for hunting and fishing, "500 lb. of No.2 ship's biscuit and fine rye bread," and hefty amounts of butter, salt beef, mutton, beans, peas, barley, and above all, coffee. He also asked for ten bottles of lemon juice, presumably for the prevention of scurvy (Müller-Wille 1998: 41–42). The commission gave him free passage to Cumberland Sound on the schooner *Germania*, and he made an arrangement with Rudolf Mosse (1843–1920), the publisher of the *Berliner Tageblatt*, to write fifteen articles for that newspaper in return for 3,000 Reichsmarks, vouched for by his father in advance.

Boas decided to adopt the modus operandi of two American explorers, Charles Hall (1821–71) and Frederick Schwatka (1849–92). He would live like an Eskimo—eating what they ate, wearing what they wore, and traveling as they traveled, by dogsled and small boats (Müller-Wille 1998: 34). In an article for the *Berliner Tageblatt* about Hall's expeditions, published before he left on his own voyage, Boas wrote, "Since he believed ... that it was absolutely necessary to adopt an Eskimo life style, [Hall] dressed in seal's fur, slept with the Eskimos in their igloos, and participated in their joys as well as sadness. He soon made friends among the natives, who wished to help him in his task, and who familiarized him with the legends and the customs of their tribe" (Boas 1883a: 6).[8] He asked rhetorically in this early article,

> What happens when one is away [from the whaling station]? It [will be] impossible to take along provisions in the freezing North for many months because they would be far too heavy to be moved. There was no other recourse but to live as an Eskimo with the other Eskimos, to go hunting and fishing with them—in short, to adapt fully to their customs. But to be on the safe side we did take full provisions in order to have them in an emergency. (1883a: 10)

Boas and Weike left Hamburg with many other items and supplies, including "clothing, guns, ammunition, surveying instruments, sleds, a boat, tobacco, notebooks, writing instruments ..." and medicines

(Boas and Boas 2009: iii). They took "an array of plant presses, traps, implements to catch animals, glass vials for collecting, etc., and a small library" (Boas 1883a: 10). They also stocked pipes, needles, extra tobacco, ammunition, and handkerchiefs to be given as presents, payment, and barter. (Much of this equipment and supplies, as well as many artifacts, specimens, and photographs were lost or had to be abandoned during the difficult year.)

Boas left a detailed record of most of his days in Baffinland in notebooks and a "letter-diary" addressed to his beloved fiancée Marie Krackowizer (1861–1929) in New York—that she would not read until after his return from the Canadian Arctic. They tell of considerable hardships, including a diphtheria epidemic, the death of many sled dogs, frostbite, snow-blindness, and numerous misadventures due to bad weather, bad luck, and inexperience. The entries recall both "the times of hunger and worry and of bitter disappointment, and the hopeful, joyful times of creative and successful work" (1885b: 60). His professional ethnographic contributions are contained in his *Habilitation* thesis, *Baffin-Land: Geographische Ergebnisse* (1885a, in German), more than a dozen journal articles, and the important monograph *The Central Eskimo* (1888).

Ethnographic Research in the Arctic

Franz Boas and Wilhelm Weike left Hamburg on 22 June 1883, but their boat was held up for six weeks by ice. It wasn't until ten weeks later, the end of August, that they arrived at the Scottish whaling station in Kekerten Island in Cumberland Sound off Baffin Island. Boas had planned to take advantage of the late summer to begin geophysical exploration of a large portion of Baffin Island but arrived too late in the season, and even after their arrival they were beset by terrible weather. Forced to make the Scottish whaling station his home base for the next few months and engage in a series of more limited forays from there, his most ambitious plans had to be curtailed because of the weather and then the unavailability of dogs to pull the sleds.

According to Cole and Müller-Wille, "Boas did not shut himself up in Mutch's whaling station, a well-equipped compound with most of Cumberland Sound's Inuit population close by. Of his 364 days on the island, 209 were spent in tents (*tupik*) or igloos, usually in travel but often in outlying settlements. Even when based at Kekerten, he spent a full 30 percent of his nights away from the station or ships.

And at Kekerten, the 82 Inuit far outnumbered the two whites besides Boas and Weike" (Müller-Wille 1984: 54).

The two were Captain James Mutch, the long-time keeper of the Scottish whaling station, and a Dane named Rasmussen, the cooper of the American one. Mutch was welcoming, helpful, an important source of information and contacts, and a genial host. Boas maintained contact with him over the years, and Mutch would later contribute significant ethnographic observations and objects for publications and museum collections (see below).

Despite these setbacks, Boas, Weike, and their Inuit companions surveyed more than twenty-four hundred miles by boat and dogsled, carrying out cartographic, topographic, meteorological, astronomical, and other geophysical studies.[9] Baffin Island is the fifth largest island in the world, almost two and a half times as large as Great Britain, and Franz Boas is credited with accurately mapping about half of it. He also contributed knowledge about ice and currents (Kroeber 1943: 9).[10] His research was carried out several decades before missionaries or a Canadian government presence there, when its population was one thousand to eleven hundred souls, one-tenth of its current population (Boas 1964 [1888]: 18). Baffin Island was certainly not untouched by the outside world at that time; syphilis had been introduced there, along with guns, matches, and other goods acquired from the whalers, but the influence of Christianity or external authority had not been felt there yet.[11]

When Boas arrived on 28 August, the *Germania* was supposed to sail north to the German research station at K'ingwa to relieve the crew there, but the ship could go no further because of the ice. By 4 September, in this new and unfamiliar land, Boas volunteered to go with six Inuit men in a whale boat to tell the station personnel not to expect the ship as well as to pick up the supplies and gear for his own sojourn. "Though we had some very narrow escapes from being beset by the ice, and had to make a good number of roundabout journeys, as the passages were locked up, we succeeded in arriving at the station by September the 7th" (Boas 1884b: 249). This was immediate "total immersion" of the sort that would characterize most of his year among the Inuit. Fortunately, his companions spoke enough pidgin English that they could communicate, and he recruited the owner of the boat (Ssigna) to be his guide and companion for much of his stay (see figure 1.1).

Boas was on the move for his other scientific tasks as often as conditions permitted, but all the while he was accumulating material about Inuit life. "Every night I spent with the natives who told me

Figure 1.1. *One of the rare surviving photos taken by Boas on Baffin Island. Noon coffee break during boat trip in Cumberland Sound. Wilhelm Weike (left), with Nachojashi, Ssigna, and Ututiak. Photo by Franz Boas, 1883–84. Courtesy of the American Philosophical Society.*

about the configuration of the land, about their travels, etc. They re-lated the old stories handed over to them by their ancestors, sang the old songs after the old monotonous tunes, and I saw them playing the old games, with which they shorten the long, dark winter nights" (Boas 1884b: 253).

Placing special emphasis on their knowledge of the land, their names for places and geographical features, their migration routes, territories, and "tribal" affiliations, Boas took census data and looked at population distribution, settlement patterns, migratory move-ments, hunting practices, and the spatial use of resources. He spent a great deal of time working with key Inuit companions to have them transfer the maps in their head onto great sheets of paper. (Boas found these maps to be remarkably accurate according to his scientific cal-culations, and he reproduced several in his publications, always giv-ing credit to the mapmaker.) He interrogated the well-traveled Inuit he met about where and how they traveled at different seasons, the nature of the land and the waters they passed through, whom they met there, and how far they had traveled.

Afterwards, when I travelled all over the sound and visited all the settle-ments of the country, I saw quite a number of old men and women who remembered the old time thoroughly, when they were more numerous and no white men visited their land, when they hunted the whale and pursued the deer with bow and arrow only. By their help I filled up the lacunae of my knowledge and learned about the old wanderings of these tribes (Boas 1884b: 256).[12]

Boas collected as many Inuit place names as possible in order to track their routes, and when he produced his own maps and geographical descriptions, he only used Inuit names. "It is certainly more valuable scientifically to preserve the indigenous names than to write names of all meritorious or not so meritorious friends à la Ross and Hall on bays and foothills" (Boas, quoted in Müller-Wille 2014: 110). In the future he would urge his students to use the words and names of the cultures they were studying as an important general principal. As Rosemary Lévy Zumwalt writes, "Boas had identified as primary the native terms of classification. A worldview in anthropology would grow from this fertile point" (2019: 106).

Beyond his major concern with "demonstrating a certain relationship between the number of people in a tribe, the distribution of food . . . ," he was interested in the "mental life" of the Inuit, and so he collected material on their language, myths, songs, stories, and other oral traditions. Some was collected through formal interviews, but much he learned just by living with the people, especially during those long nights in their igloos and tupiks.

Franz Boas was a participant observer in the fullest sense, completely dependent on his Inuit companions. Although he set the agenda, knowing where he needed to go and what he needed to observe, he could only do it in their company and with their help. He was no "boss" sitting back while they worked. The diary indicates the extent to which he loaded and unloaded, hauled, scouted, hunted, cooked, chopped, steered, and, eventually, controlled the unruly dogs as he drove sleds. Admittedly, he wasn't the most skilled driver, and he got bored standing for hours over a blowhole waiting for a seal to come up for air to get speared in the snout, but he did it all.

I used to stay in the Eskimo villages and to survey the neighborhood. As soon as this work was finished, I proceeded to the next village, and thus worked my way all along the coast. In the villages I lived with the Eskimo in their snow-houses. Generally I proposed to a man who was well acquainted with the country to join me for a few days, and as I had better dogs and a better sledge than the Eskimo, my offer was gladly accepted. Such trips lasted generally about a fortnight, and during that time the man went sealing while I was surveying (1887a: 385–86).

He learned their seasonal variations and routines and became familiar with the material culture and its uses. While traveling he was usually in the company of just two or three Inuit men (as well as Wilhelm Weike), but they would often come to a settlement with families, women, children, and elders, and they would be welcomed into their tents and igloos. There Boas observed home and family life, singing, and storytelling. At the end, Boas and Weike spent a month on the coast of Davis Strait waiting for a whaling vessel to take them home accompanied by a group of Inuit families, eight tents full, planning to trade oil and skins with the whalers. This was a more relaxed time to learn life histories and songs and play and learn games with children and adults.

He wrote in his letter-diary, "As you see, my Marie, I am now truly just like an Eskimo; I live with them, hunt with them, and count myself among the men of Anarnitung. Moreover I scarcely eat any European foodstuffs any longer but am living entirely on seal meat and coffee" (15 February 1884; Müller-Wille 1998: 182).[13]

The Central Eskimo

Boas's major work on the Inuit, *The Central Eskimo*, was published in 1888 by the Bureau of Ethnology of the Smithsonian Institution.[14] The book opens with an impressive list of "Authorities Quoted"— almost entirely narratives and journals by Arctic explorers.[15] A wide-ranging geographic description of "Northeastern America," the habitat of the Inuit, is followed by a densely packed forty-page section titled "Distribution of the Tribes." This is prefaced by "General observation," in which Boas briefly lays out the fundamental facts of Inuit life. They are dependent for their lives on their ability to hunt and kill seals in winter and caribou in the warmer months. Above all they require seals for meat, blubber for heating and cooking, skins for summer clothing and for kayaks and umiaqs. Seal and other animal bones are used for frames for sleds, boats, and implements. They require reindeer above all for their thick hides for winter clothing, dwellings, and equipment. The people must migrate to follow their prey as the animals move and the conditions of weather, ice, water, and snow change.

Boas presents a detailed account of what he discovered about every Inuit group on Baffin Island. He lists group names, toponyms of their locations and migration routes, relationships among them, and distinctive features. He draws upon his own observations, many

hours of inquiry, and the accounts by earlier explorers like Hall and
Schwatka. He devotes several pages (20ff.) to a detailed account of
the annual movements of a single "settlement." To the nonspecialist
these accounts may seem excessive, but for the student of the Inuit in
those regions it is vital. The accounts are important for understanding the relationship between the environment and the people and
their knowledge of the land, and they are significant for their descendants in today's Nunavut.[16]

He discusses the drastic Inuit population losses and records a census of the settlements. He claims that the reduction in population is
due to disease, notably syphilis, and he contends that "the opinion
that the Eskimo are dying out on account of an insufficient supply of
food is erroneous" (Boas 1964 [1888]: 18). There are plenty of seals
and caribou but famine is caused when the environmental conditions
keep them from hunting, when ice floes don't form as they should,
or when dogs are not available to sniff out the seals' breathing holes
in winter.[17]

In a summary of the "Influence of Geographical Conditions Upon
the Distribution of Settlements," Boas wrote, "It is evident that they
are settled wherever extensive floes afford a good sealing ground
during the winter" (Boas 1964 [1888]: 52). And in summer, "After the
ice breaks up, the distribution of the deer regulates the location of the
summer settlements" (ibid.: 53). Presumably these are the (relatively)
simple answers to the anthropogeographical problem he set himself
before leaving home, but this did not satisfy the budding anthropologist. In 1887 he wrote to Major J. W. Powell (1834–1902), director
of the Bureau of Ethnology in Washington, "The longer I studied the
more I became convinced that the phenomena such as customs, traditions and migrations are far too complex in their origin, as to enable
us to study their psychological causes without a thorough knowledge
of their history. I concluded it necessary to see a people, among which
historical facts are of greater influence than the surroundings and selected for this purpose Northwest America" (in Stocking 1974: 60).[18]

After a short but wide-ranging section on "Trade and Intercourse
between the Tribes," the next ninety pages cover both the activities and the material culture involved in subsistence and existence:
hunting on land and sea and fishing; transportation by dogsleds and
boats; the construction of kayaks, umiaqs, tents, snow houses, and
all manner of "manufacturing." This includes the making of the vital
clothing and the work done preparing seal and caribou hides as well
as many "sundry implements" of stone, bone, wood, ivory, leather,
sinew, and metal.

There is a section on "adornment" of hair, bodies (tattoos), clothing, and the decoration of useful objects. At a superficial glance this section seems rather dry: many objects are discussed, accompanied by more than 150 drawings as in an old-fashioned museum. But it is a rich inventory of the material culture and the ingenuity and aesthetics of the Inuit.[19] These pages describe numerous innovations and inventions for maintaining life in their unforgiving land of snow, ice, water, and rocks. We also see the Inuit appetite and talent for artistry; they lavish time and effort to beautify their objects and their bodies. The accounts of the creation and use of these articles are often fascinating, demonstrating Inuit experience and skill.

Boas includes vivid accounts of the hunting of seals in winter (1964 [1888]: 67–77) and seals and walrus in summer (ibid.: 89–93), with a degree of realistic detail that might trouble modern readers (see figures 1.2 and 1.3).[20] He discusses travel by sled with a charming section on the peculiarities and temperament of the animals that pull them (ibid.: 121–30). He describes the process of building snow houses, quite complex structures when built for a whole winter, perhaps housing two or more families. He details the interior layouts with their sitting and sleeping ledges and arrangements for heating, cooking, light, dogs, and storage (ibid.: 131–38).

Here is the conclusion of a narrative of a "typical" winter's day in such a dwelling:

> While in times of plenty the home life is quite cheerful, the house presents a sad and gloomy appearance if stormy weather prevents the men from hunting. The stores are quickly consumed, one lamp after another is extinguished, and everybody sits motionless in the dark hut. Nevertheless the women and men do not stop humming their monotonous *amna aya* and their stoicism in enduring the pangs of hunger is really wonderful. At last, when starvation is menacing the sufferers, the most daring of the men resolves to try his luck. Though the storm may rage over the icy plain he sets out to go sealing. For hours he braves the cold and stands waiting and watching at the breathing hole until he hears the blowing of the seal and succeeds in killing it.[21]
>
> When those who have remained at home hear the sound of the returning sledge, they rush out of the houses to meet it. Quickly they help the bold hunter to get on shore. The sledge is unloaded, the seal dragged into the house, and every one joyfully awaits his share. The animal is cut up, every household receiving a piece of meat and blubber. The gloomy huts are again lighted up and the pots, which had been out of use for some days, are again hung up over the lamps. (ibid.: 166)

Figure 1.2. *According to the caption of the engraving in* The Central Eskimo, *this picture represents an "Eskimo awaiting return of seal to blowhole. (From a photograph.)" Courtesy of the American Philosophical Society.*

The ethnographer ends his account with a far less happy ending — when the hunter is unable to come home with food. But this scenario directly follows a much more pleasant section on "amusements" — games, gambling, exercise, jumping competitions, ball games, singing, storytelling, and cat's cradle — this last, an art they had perfected far beyond the Euro-American imagination. He continues with accounts of "Visiting" and "Social Customs in Summer" (ibid.: 166–

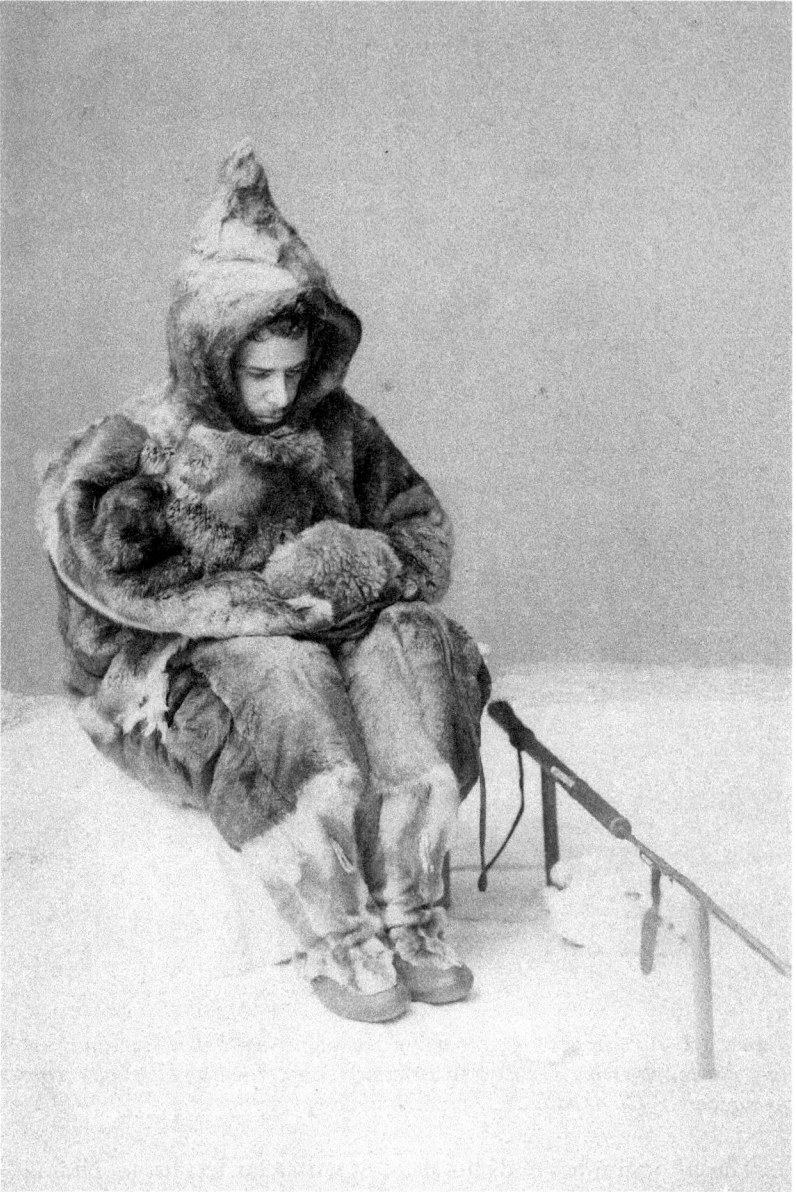

Figure 1.3. *Franz Boas dressed in Inuit winter clothing, posing to represent seal hunting at a breathing hole on the ice of Cumberland Sound. Photo taken by J. Hülsenbeck in a studio in Minden, Germany, in the fall of 1885. Courtesy of the American Philosophical Society.*

70). After reading in his diary of storms, dangers, hunger, and deaths, it is good to read of the people's imagination, artistry, and capacity for enjoyment.

Boas devotes only four pages to "Social Order and Laws." He begins with the statement that "the social order of the Eskimo is entirely founded on the family and on the ties of consanguinity and affinity between the individual families." This simple statement launched innumerable studies, commentaries, and disputes about the nature of "Eskimoan kinship"—a social system that is bilateral, without preference for either maternal or paternal side, and without larger kinship groups such as lineages or clans (see Stevenson 1997 for summary and sources).

Boas notes that residence after marriage is usually uxorilocal and mentions the gentle and loving treatment of children—but also infanticide—and the accepted practice of wife lending and exchanging. (He suggests that there can be a problem of jealousy with this arrangement regardless of ideology.) He writes of the importance of adoption and of unfortunate individuals—those without kin, crippled individuals, or those who have lost sleds and dogs—attaching themselves to more fortunate men and their families. "The position, however, is a voluntary one, and therefore these men are not less esteemed than the self dependent providers" (Boas 1964 [1888]: 173). One wonders, however.

There is a paragraph about the strictly limited "authority" of a *pimain*, "he who knows everything best," who has the prestige to suggest when and where to move settlements; but Boas stresses that families are independent and can decide for themselves. He writes of the distribution and sharing of major food animals, ownership, and murder, feuds, and vengeance. "There is no way of enforcing these unwritten laws and no punishment for transgressors except the blood vengeance" (ibid.: 174).

Many more pages are devoted to "Religious Ideas and the Angakunirn (Priesthood)" (ibid.: 175–201). He writes of phenomena he regards as central to Inuit culture, beginning with the origin myth of Sedna, a phenomenon that had already been the subject of one of his articles in the *Berliner Tageblatt*: "The old legends which mothers tell their frightened children during the long winter nights are all about her" (Boas 1884a: 38). Boas returned to the subject in *The Eskimo of Baffin Land and Hudson Bay* (1901–7), a two-part bulletin of the American Museum of Natural History from notes collected by Captain George Comer (1858–1937), Captain James Shepherd Mutch (1847–1931), and Reverend Edmund James Peck (1850–1924):

"This woman, the mother of the sea-mammals, may be considered as the principal deity of the Central Eskimo. She has supreme sway over the destinies of mankind, and almost all the observances of these tribes are for the purpose of retaining her good will or of propitiating her if she has been offended" (Boas 1907: 119). In the version told to Boas, whales and seals were born of Sedna's fingers, chopped off by her father as she clung to the sides of their boat—and then she sank. On the positive side, she is responsible for creating the animals without which the people could not live, but she is very vengeful and hates Inuit.[22]

After narrating and discussing the saga of Sedna, the author turns to "the *Tornait* and the *Angakut*" (sg. *Angakoq*). "A consideration of the religious ideas of the Eskimo shows that the *tornait*, the invisible rulers of every object, are the most remarkable beings next to Sedna. Everything has its *inua* (owner), which may become the genius of man who thus obtains the qualities of *angakunirn*" (Boas 1964 [1888]: 183). Three kinds of spirits protect the *angakoq*, those in the shape of men, bears, and certain stones. "These spirits enable the *angakut* to have intercourse with the others who are considered malevolent to mankind and though these three species are kind to their *angakut* they would hurt strangers who might happen to see them" (ibid.: 183).

Next comes an extended discussion of the operations of an *angakoq*. "The principal office of the *angakut* is to find out the reason of sickness and death or of any other misfortune visiting the natives" (ibid.: 184). Franz Boas had unhappy firsthand experience with this. An *angakoq* determined that he, Boas, was the cause of the illness that year and ordered his followers to shun him and not let him into their homes. Boas confronted this man, Napikang (aka Tyson), in front of all the men of the community, saying "all intercourse between us would cease until he invited me into his hut" (Boas, 23 January 1884, quoted in Cole 1983: 38). "In summer he will be travelling the same route as myself ... and I [told] him that he would never get anything from me until he had first invited me to come into his house" (Boas, quoted in Müller-Wille 1998: 172). "A few weeks later [the *angakoq*] came to [Kekerten] 'especially to reconcile me' with gifts of seal pelts and an offer of service. 'With this the incident closed and from then on nothing disturbed the friendly relations between the natives and me . . .'" (Boas, quoted in Cole 1983: 38–39). Boas and Napikang spent the last several months amicably enough.

Here are a few excerpts from a detailed description of the operations of an *angakoq*:

The Eskimo believes that he is obliged to answer the *angakoq*'s questions truthfully. The lamps being lowered, the *angakoq* strips off his outer jacket, pulls the hood over his head, and sits down in the back part of the hut facing the wall. He claps his hands, which are covered with mittens, and, shaking his whole body, utters sounds which one would hardly recognize as human.

Thus he invokes his *tornaq*, singing and shouting alternately, the listeners, who sit on the edge of the bed, joining the chorus and answering his questions. Then he asks the sick person: "Did you work when it was forbidden?" "Did you eat when you were not allowed to eat?" And if the poor fellow happens to remember any transgression of such laws, he cries: "Yes, I have worked." "Yes, I have eaten." And the *angakoq* rejoins "I thought so" and issues his commands as to the manner of atonement.

These are manifold. Exchange of wives between two men or adoption of a sick child by another family in order to save its life are frequently demanded. The inhabitants of a village are forbidden to wash themselves for a number of days, to scrape the ice from the windows, and to clean their urine pots before sunrise. Sometimes the *angakoq* commands that the clothing be thrown away or gives regulations for diet, particularly forbidding the eating of venison, working on deerskins, filing iron, &c. . . .

A great number of the performances of the *angakut* require much skill and expertness. Thus in invoking a *tornaq* or flying to a distant place they can imitate a distant voice by a sort of ventriloquism. In these performances they always have the lamps extinguished and hide themselves behind a screen hung up in the back part of the hut. The *tornaq*, being invoked, is heard approaching and shaking the hut. The *angakoq* believes that it is unroofed and flies with his spirit to their place of destination, to propitiate the wrath of a hostile *tornaq*, to visit the moon or Sedna's dismal abode. . . .

The performance of the *angakut*—in the Sedna feast . . . is quite astonishing. Some pierce their bodies with harpoons, evidently having bladders filled with blood fastened under their jackets beforehand, and bleed profusely as they enter the hut.

It is one of their favorite tricks to have their hands tied up and a thong fastened around their knees and neck. Then they begin invoking their *tornaq*, and all of a sudden the body lies motionless while the soul flies to any place which they wish to visit. After returning, the thongs are found untied, though they had been fastened by firm knots. The resemblance of this performance to the experiments of modern spiritualists is striking. (Boas 1964 [1888]: 184–86)[23]

Boas would meet with this sort of stagecraft and performance again among the Kwakiutl on Vancouver Island, and learn of very similar shamanistic practices from his colleagues who did important research among peoples of Siberia.

In his monograph, he added that "the angakut use a sacred language in their songs and incantations. A great number of words have a symbolic meaning, but others are old roots, which have been lost from common use in the lapse of time. These archaic words are very interesting from a linguistic point of view" (ibid.: 186).The narrative continues with a long list of taboos, "the numerous regulations referring to eating and working, many of which are connected with the Sedna tradition, and the observance of which is watched by the *angakut*" (ibid.: 187). These include not eating caribou and sea mammals at the same time, restrictions on women sewing clothes after a death, and limits on their activities during menstruation.

The next section, "Feasts, Religious and Secular" (ibid.: 192–207), begins with the "singing house" (*qaggi*), a large "snow dome" built for ceremonies and performances in winter. Major hunting successes, especially the killing of a whale, are celebrated there, and the most important occasions are associated with Sedna in the fall.

> When late in the fall storms rage over the land and release the sea from the icy fetters by which it is as yet but slightly bound, when the loosened floes are driven one against the other and break up with loud crashes, when the cakes of ice are piled in wild disorder one upon another, the Eskimo believes he hears the voices of spirits which inhabit the mischief laden air.
>
> The spirits of the dead, the *tupilaq*, knock wildly at the huts, which they cannot enter, and woe to the unhappy person whom they can lay hold of. He immediately sickens and a speedy death is regarded as sure to come. The wicked *qiqirn* pursues the dogs, which die with convulsions and cramps as soon as they see him. All the countless spirits of evil are aroused, striving to bring sickness and death, bad weather, and failure in hunting. The worst visitors are Sedna, mistress of the under world, and her father, to whose share the dead Inuit fall. While the other spirits fill the air and the water, she rises from under the ground.
>
> It is then a busy season for the wizards. In every hut we may hear them singing and praying; conjuring of the spirits is going on in every house. The lamps burn low. The wizard sits in a mystic gloom in the rear of the hut. He has thrown off his outer coat and drawn the hood of his inner garment over his head, while he mutters indescribable sounds, unnatural to a human voice. At last the guardian spirit responds to the invocation. The *angakoq* lies in a trance and when he comes to himself he promises in incoherent phrases the help of the good spirit against the *tupilaq* and informs the credulous, affrighted Inuit how they can escape from the dreaded ghosts. (ibid.: 195–96)

The *angakut* put on their magical shows, the men of the community run and jump and visit all the houses, and have a tug of war, with one side representing ptarmigans born in the winter and the other, ducks, children of the summer. After a ceremony in which each member of the community announces her or his name and where they were born, "now arises a cry of surprise and all eyes are turned toward a hut out of which stalk two gigantic [masked] figures." (There is a drawing by Boas of one of these frightening characters known as *qailertetang.*) All hell breaks loose, "screaming, running, jumping, spearing, and stabbing . . ." and a lot of hijinks, including an interesting custom. The *angakut* (in their disguises)

> solemnly lead the men to a suitable spot and set them in a row, and the women in another opposite them. They match the men and women in pairs and these pairs run, pursued by the *qailertetang*, to the hut of the woman, where they are for the following day and night man and wife. Having performed this duty, the *qailertetang* stride down to the shore and invoke the good north wind, which brings fair weather, while they warn off the unfavorable south wind. (ibid.: 197)

Following a discussion of "Birth, Sickness, and Death" (ibid.: 201–7), there are twenty-eight pages of narrative tales, a few of them illustrated with drawings by named Inuit artists. The book ends with a section called "Science and the Arts," which is a rare designation for a work on a so-called "primitive" people. The first part is about "geography and navigation." Boas writes of the Inuit's thorough knowledge of their country and reproduces several of their maps, crediting the mapmakers. The last section on poetry and music is illustrated with drawings by artists and Inuit carvings. He discusses the characteristics of the music and includes musical notations and words for nineteen songs, all but four of them from his own fieldwork.

In a story Boas wrote for his grandchildren, he told of Ututiak (aka Yankee),[24] one of his companions, who had drifted on an ice floe, alone, for eight days, and composed a song that "even made fun of his misfortune" as he faced death. "It's glorious on the ice; Here it is nice. Behold my lonesome path; all snow and slush and ice. This is nice. . . . Oh, when I reach the land—it will be nice! When will this roaming end? When will I be at home? Then it's nice." Boas continues, "This song has become a great favorite among the Eskimos, and they sing it everywhere in Cumberland Sound. So, you see our friend Ututiak is a poet as well as a composer among his people" (2007).

A year before the publication of *The Central Eskimo*, Boas published a paper called "Poetry and Music of Some North American Tribes" (Boas 1887c). He ends the article saying, "These few examples will show that the mind of the 'savage' is sensible to the beauties of poetry and music, and that it is only the superficial observer to whom he appears stupid and unfeeling." This was the era when evolutionist writers like Sir John Lubbock (1834–1913) contended that these people were not capable of appreciating beauty (e.g., Lubbock 1865: 323). From the beginning of his career as an anthropologist, Franz Boas attempted to change the image of "the primitive."

Franz Boas and the Human Angle in Baffin Island

Certain key passages from Franz Boas's letter-diary are well-known but bear repeating because they tell us so much about the man, his experience in the field, and the attitude he would take with him as he began his career in anthropology in America.[25]

Although his letters barely mention this problem, an early article in the *Berliner Tageblatt* begins with the revelation of his culture shock—or ethnocentrism—at his first sight of the people he was to live among for the next year. This twenty-five-year-old, "well-bred," middle-class German scientist, used to "good society" (his term, original in quotation marks) with its carefully groomed men and women, is taken aback. "Their long black hair, flat faces and watering eyes made a disturbing impression on me" (Boas 1883b: 25). Later he enters their summer tents (*tupiks*), made of smelly seal skins, full of smelly caribou skins and smelly stored meat, and according to his newspaper account, "I escaped as fast as I could" (ibid.). (In fact, in his notebook entry for 28 August 1883, he wrote, "We also visited many *tupiks*; they are not as dirty as I thought" [Boas, quoted in Müller-Wille 1998: 73]). In the next sentence he writes, "If somebody at the time had told me that before long I would live without disgust in similar circumstances, I would have vehemently rejected such a prediction. Yet it wasn't very long before conditions and daily routine made me share the beds of the natives that were made of piles of caribou skins" (Boas 1883b: 25).[26]

In the article he writes about cooking in the same kettle, welcoming the stored meat piled on the floor and the "friendly" oil lamp, and "How often did I appreciate my generous hostess who dried and cleaned my clothes!" (ibid.: 26). He gives a brief summary of the Inuit life through the seasons, and of his trips with them, ending thus: "In this way a year is fulfilled for these people who are easily satisfied under the most limited circumstances, whose hospitality and never-ending good nature I learned to appreciate and love during my stay with them" (ibid.: 28).[27]

It was far from an easy year. Here is one entry from his "letter" to Marie, referring to four deaths:

January 23, 1884—I just want to provide Ocheitu with provisions, because he may not go out for three days now [because of his wife's death]. . . . Isn't that really touching? I have noticed quite often here how calmly the Eskimos look death in the face, although they are unbelievably afraid of the dead . . . , and I have also seen such protestations of inner love between parents and children. I shall never forget coming into a small snow house in which a mother was sitting with her sick child which barely gave any sign of life, but still was voicing the most tender endearments to her child![28] And I'll always remember how Joe, who also is dead now, told me that thinking of his son, who had died the previous spring, made him so miserable.

These are "savages" whose lives are supposed to be worth nothing compared with a civilized European. I do not believe that we, if living under the same conditions, would be so willing to work or be so cheerful and happy! I have to say that as regards character, I am totally contented with the Eskimos . . . (Boas, quoted in Müller-Wille 1998: 173)

A month earlier he wrote to Marie from the same place, Anarnitung, a settlement off Cumberland Sound:

December 23, 1883—Now I am again sitting in Ocheitu's igloo celebrating a great feast with him. Today Ocheitu caught two seals and now every man in camp receives a piece. Isn't it a fine custom among these "savages" that they endure privations together, but all happily share in the eating and drinking communally when some game has been killed?

I often ask myself what advantages our "good society" possesses over the "savages" and the more I see of their customs, I find that we really have no grounds to look down on them contemptuously. Where among us is there such hospitality as here? Where are there people who carry out *any* task requested of them so willingly and without grumbling! We should not censure them for their conventions and superstitions, since we "highly educated" people are relatively much worse.

The fear of the old traditions and the old conventions is truly deeply implanted in humankind, and just as it controls life here, it obstructs all progress with us. I believe that in every person and every people . . . renouncing tradition in order to follow the trail of the truth involves a very severe struggle. But what am I struggling for? (ibid.: 159)

This passage from the field captures one of Franz Boas's central concerns. In 1938 he expanded on this subject: "The psychological origin of the implicit believe in the authority of tradition, which was so foreign to my mind and which had shocked me at an earlier time, became a problem that engaged my thoughts for many years. In fact, my whole outlook upon social life is determined by the question: how can we recognize the shackles that tradition has laid upon us? For when we recognize them, we are also able to break them" (Boas 1938: 202).

He continued his account:

> The Eskimos are now sitting alert, their mouths full, eating raw seal liver, and the blood stains on the other page will tell you how I was assisting them. I believe that if this trip has a significant impact on me as a thinking person, then it is the strengthening of my notion of the relativity of all *education* and the conviction of how the value of people lies in the guidance close to their heart [*Herzensbildung*], which I find or miss here, just as at home, and that thus all service which a person can render to humanity must depend on the furthering of *truth*, which may be sweet or bitter for humanity. Yes, whoever furthers it, whoever widely pursues the search for truth, may say that he has not lived in vain!
>
> But now back to the cold Eskimo country. Yesterday evening it gradually became quite comfortable in the igloo ... and I hoped I would sleep well, but I couldn't get warm in my sleeping bag which is not yet quite dry. (Boas, quoted in Müller-Wille 1998: 159)

Bildung was a key concept for the world into which Franz Boas was raised, that of the liberal "bourgeoisie" of nineteenth-century Germany, and especially for Jews. As historian George Mosse (grandson of Rudolf Mosse of the *Berliner Tageblatt*) explained, "The word *Bildung* combines the meaning carried by the English word 'education' with notions of character formation and moral education. Man must grow like a plant, as Herder put it, toward the unfolding of his personality until he becomes an harmonious, autonomous individual exemplifying both the continuing quest for knowledge and the moral imperative" (1985: 3). "The centrality of the ideal of Bildung in German-Jewish consciousness must be understood from the very beginning—it was basic to Jewish engagement with liberalism and socialism, fundamental to the search for a new Jewish identity after emancipation" (ibid.: 4). This describes Franz Boas (as George Mosse told me it would).

On 22 January 1884, Boas wrote:

> Will fortune favor me, so that very soon I may anticipate the fulfillment of our most longed-for wishes? It is *not* my wish to attain a German professorship, because I know that I am not dependent on my science and the teaching profession, to which I have little inclination. I would much rather live in America so that I can also work for the ideas in which I believe. But how? That I don't know. Well I can do nothing about it now

and must wait patiently to see how things turn out when I come back. And what I want, what I will live and die for, is equal rights for all, equal opportunities to [work] and strive for poor and rich! Don't you think that when one has done even a little towards this, this is more than the whole of science together? And that will certainly never be granted me in Germany. (Boas, quoted in Müller-Wille 1998: 171)

From these outpourings of thought and feeling to his absent and adored fiancée we learn of the impact of his intimate experience with the Inuit on his profound appreciation for "the relativity of education"—for which we can probably substitute "culture." And we see his conviction that his purpose in life is to search for the "truth" *and* to work for the same political causes that his mother, his mother's brother-in-law Abraham Jacobi, and his fiancee's father, Dr. Ernst Krackowizer (1821–75), worked for. As noted previously (Stocking 1965; Lewis 2008: 180), his experience in the field deepened the beliefs that he took with him to the Inuit. He was preadapted for the fieldwork and the career he chose.

Boas's Prescriptions for the Development of Ethnography

When Franz Boas met several whaling ships off the coast of Davis Strait in late August 1884, he chose the *Wolf* that took him to Newfoundland, whence he could get another ship bound for New York City. First, he wanted desperately to be reunited with Marie, and second, he hoped to connect with scientific circles in America to explore prospects for a career there. He was fortunate to have two prominent allies: his uncle, Abraham Jacobi, one of the most prominent physicians in the country, and Jacobi's best friend, the politically connected German American statesman and reformer, Carl Schurz (1829–1906).[29] Arctic exploration was an important topic in geographical circles in the United States as it was in Germany, and he stayed until March 1885, giving lectures (though embarrassed by his spoken English), publishing papers, and making important contacts. He met Otis T. Mason (1838–1908), curator of ethnology at the Smithsonian Institution, whose approach to museum display he would famously criticize two years later (Boas 1887d), and John Wesley Powell, director of the Bureau of Ethnology, who agreed to publish *The Central Eskimo*.

Among the numerous pieces he published while in New York was one in German in the *New Yorker Staats-Zeitung* of 18 February 1885, containing significant propositions about ethnographic research. He did not repeat them in *The Central Eskimo* or elsewhere in that form, but they are recognizable as basic to the field he was to develop and lead.[30]

He begins the discussion of his research by noting the drastic loss of population among the Inuit of Baffin Island due to diseases introduced by the foreign whalers: "death has played havoc among them, sparing no more than several hundreds of the many thousands . . ." and expressing his fear that "It won't be long before the Eskimo tribes will disappear. In time nothing but solitary graves, ruins of homesteads, and disintegrating tools will tell us something about the former inhabitants of this expansive land" (1885b: 58). Furthermore,

> It is not simply the threat of extinction . . . that demands immediate and thorough research in this field; it is also the rapid change in their old lifestyle which necessitates an immediate study of their customs and traditions. Otherwise one of the main tasks of ethnographers, i.e., the study of the lifestyle of primitive people in their unique development, will become too difficult or even impossible to carry out (1885b: 58).

The decrease in population affected their celebrations and migrations, and new needs and desires replaced old skills and old material culture. The gun replaced the bow and arrow, and the whaling boat supplemented the kayak. Trade links and travel for driftwood, iron, and pyrite for starting fires had broken down, replaced by traders around Hudson Bay. "It is, therefore, the solemn duty of the ethnographer to save what can be saved. Before it is entirely too late, he must collect the treasures hidden among the legends and oral histories of these tribes. He must familiarize himself with their customs and traditions" (1885b: 58). And later he writes, "Because of the seriousness of the situation, we are compelled not to hesitate another moment with our investigation of these Eskimos. We must make an all out effort. For this reason, in 1883 I decided to travel to Baffinland to undertake geographical and ethnological studies" (1885b: 59).

With postcolonial sensibilities, many anthropologists will cry, "Salvage! For Shame!" They will say that he should have had the prophetic wisdom to see that they would *not* die out, that they would survive with a heightened sense of their identity and heritage. This is not the place to explain and defend the ethos and theme of "salvage ethnography" (see Gruber 1970), but, supported by this notion and his desire to know other peoples, Boas left a record that is invaluable for their descendants today. As Ludger Müller-Wille writes, "Thus, to some degree, Boas's book . . . has become the encyclopedia of the Inuit in Cumberland sound and along the west shore of Davis Strait, for it illustrates how their ancestors lived and thought prior to the pervasive influence of Christian missions and Canadian government institutions. This is possible today only because Boas recorded this information in detail more than 115 years ago" (1998: 16). Neither ignominy nor apologies are called for.

A few pages later he turns to principles of ethnography.

> The young scholarly disciplines which have sprung up in our century suffer from one general shortcoming, namely: theory cannot keep pace with the overflow of incoming information. As in anthropology and in sociology we, in ethnography, only too often see true scholarship replaced by an eagerness to collect. We have hardly begun to classify collected facts according to scientific methods; we have not even clearly and firmly recognized the principles according to which basic research will have to be done. (Boas 1885b: 60–61)

After studying geography at university and spending a year in the Arctic, young Boas was now preaching to the inchoate field as an ethnographer. He continues:

> We recognize more and more that a scholar, who studies a primitive people, must not be content by simply studying the obvious customs and traditions of foreigners. He needs to become thoroughly familiar with the thinking and point of view of a people . . . before he can come to any reliable conclusions to be used by later theoreticians. . . .
>
> From this it follows that the collection of ethnographic material cannot be a task to be simply performed by any traveler. Such a task, as does any other kind of observation and any other kind of scholarly work, requires a thorough knowledge of the methods and of the goals of ethnography. . . .
>
> The researcher has to live entirely like a member of the tribe which is the object of his investigation. As long as a foreign people look upon a traveler as an intruder, or worse, as an enemy, the characteristics of its thought and of its emotional life will never be revealed to him. . . .
>
> Many of its customs will completely elude the researcher; others will remain incomprehensible. . . . The designation of so many primitive people as "savages" became popular and widespread only because travelers looked at the behavior of foreigners shortsightedly from the point of view of our European social institutions. They lacked a thorough knowledge of their languages, of their emotions, of their thinking, of their reli-

gious ideas, and of their traditions. Without this knowledge, the lifestyle of a primitive people, so far removed from our own thinking and our own way of life, may look absurd and unworthy of any kind of human society. Only because of such misunderstandings could the use of the term "savages" come about for tribes whose way of life is governed by strict religious rules, and whose rich imagination has created a plenitude of legends, songs, and inventions. (ibid.: 61)

After this Boas contrasts the "commonly accepted picture of the Eskimos" as dirty and dull, "hardly distinguishable from animals." But if we do our research correctly,

> with surprise, we will see that areas which almost constantly threaten the white man with death and destruction are successfully inhabited by these people. . . . These people, while fighting an inclement climate, wrest the necessities of life from the poorest natural habitat, and rise victoriously above their powerful enemy. Spirit and imagination are not impoverished; on the contrary, they unfold their wings with energy. Poetry and songs enhance life; music and dance shorten long winter nights, and the short summer brings joyful games. (ibid.)

Franz Boas continues with an upbeat picture of his experience among the Inuit of Baffin Island, emphasizing the pleasures he enjoyed with them—once the "first negative impressions" had been overcome. He speaks of the conversations that brought "a veritable treasure chest of knowledge" and adds: "But by simply listening one doesn't learn all about a people's thoughts and lifestyle. One needs to see and to observe most of their every day life and customs" (ibid.: 62). The article ends with these thoughts:

> I also became acquainted with the customs of the natives when we traveled together by sled; for days [we] had to depend on each other and had to hunt together. We shared hunger as well as good times. One needs to experience only a few weeks of this kind of life with the Eskimos to realize that they could not be considered "savages." It takes a much longer period of energetic work and rapt attention to every detail, even the most unimportant manifestation of life, to become better acquainted with their character and their customs and to understand their often strange manner. Every new observation brings material for reflection and helps to weave a web consisting of many other single observations until one day all of it will fall into place. Then, despite their strange ways of life, we will once again recognize the thinking and feeling human beings behind it all. They will be much closer to us in their characteristics than we could have seen after our first superficial impression. (ibid.: 63)

Conclusion

In "An Anthropologist's Credo," which Boas published in the journal *The Nation* of August 1938, he returned to his arctic experiences:

> A year of life spent as an Eskimo among Eskimos had a profound influence upon the development of my views, not immediately, but because it led me away from my former interests and toward the desire to understand what determines the behavior of human beings. The first result of my attempts to explain human behavior as a result of geographical environment was a thorough disappointment. The immediate influences are patent, and the results of this study were so shallow that they did not throw any light on the driving forces that mold behavior. (Boas 1938: 202)

George Stocking titled his well-known article "From Physics to Ethnology" (Stocking 1965), but this is a narrow reading of Franz Boas—both at the beginning and the end of his academic journey.[31] He did not begin as a physicist in a narrow sense, nor did he become only an ethnographer. We know of his interest in and knowledge of many sciences; by the time of his doctorate he was professionally competent in mathematics, physics, psychology, psychophysics, and geography: the last encompassing human geography or ethnology as well as physical geography. His sister Toni wrote, "After long years of infidelity my brother was reconquered by geography, the first love of his boyhood" (quoted in Cole 1999: 57). Furthermore: "My work on the Eskimos has given me more satisfaction than my trips," he wrote his parents (quoted in Müller-Wille 1998: 212).

The discipline that Boas finally turned to was not just ethnology but an integrated field that Americans called "anthropology." This scientist and scholar led the creation of a remarkably varied discipline—perhaps too varied to hold together for more than a century. With his own genius (it is not too strong a word) he made contributions to ethnography, ethnology, linguistics, biological anthropology, statistics, folklore, museology, and archeology. As part of this task of creation, the Baffin Island experience led to a new approach to anthropology in the United States. His family background as an "enlightened" German Jew, his training in German science, and his life among the Eskimos coalesced in Boas to produce the beginnings of a new way of thinking and doing research about peoples of the world—and not merely "primitive" peoples. He returned loudly proclaiming the proper way to learn about other peoples as well as the common humanity of all. He probably went into the field convinced of the latter, but his time with the Inuit showed him the importance of the former.

Within the decade after his return, Boas would make major contributions to the reorientation of ethnology, linguistics, physical anthropology, and museology. He drew on his wide and deep knowledge of science, history, ethnography, and the arts to influence the development of the distinctive "four field" anthropology in the United States.

Franz Boas ended one of his earliest articles writing:

> After all the many little adventures, and after a long and intimate intercourse with the Eskimo, it was with feelings of sorrow and regret that I parted from my Arctic friends. I had seen that they enjoyed life, and a hard life, as we do; that nature is also beautiful to them; that feelings of friendship also root in the Eskimo heart; that, although the character of their life is so rude as compared to civilized life, the Eskimo is a man as we are: that his feelings, his virtues, and his shortcomings are based in human nature, like ours. (1887a: 402)

These lines, written in English in an American journal, were not travelogue cliches for Boas. He was speaking to an incipient field of study whose amateur proponents were often under the spell of both racial determinism and evolutionary thought in which "the savage," "primitive man," was believed to be lacking such virtues as aesthetic enjoyment and friendship. From the moment of his immigration to the United States in July 1886 he started to demonstrate the falsity of those notions, as he would continue to do throughout his career. This was the message he brought home from his first venture as an ethnographer.[32]

Herbert S. Lewis, professor emeritus of anthropology, University of Wisconsin-Madison, has published extensively on the history of anthropology, particularly on Franz Boas and the Boasian school. His researches in political anthropology, ethnicity, and culture change are related to his fieldwork, conducted in Ethiopia, Israel, and the United States (Oneida). His vast work includes *A Galla Monarchy* (1965); *After the Eagles Landed: The Yemenites of Israel* (1989); *Oneida Lives: Long-Lost Voices of the Wisconsin Oneidas* (2005); and *In Defense of Anthropology: An Investigation of the Critique of Anthropology* (2014). Lewis is past president of the Association of Senior Anthropologists section of the American Anthropological Association.

Notes

1. Today Baffin Island is part of the vast Canadian territory of Nunavut. It was often called Baffinland in Boas's day. The two terms will be used interchangeably in the present chapter. The ethnonym "Eskimo," believed to be a name from the Montagnais language, has been replaced by the people's own term for "people," *Inuit*. In this chapter we use the older term in titles, quotations, and where appropriate in order to avoid anachronism.

2. There is a rich literature about Franz Boas and his year on Baffin Island. In addition to George Stocking, whose 1965 article can be called seminal, the late Douglas Cole and Boas's latest biographer, Rosemary Lévy Zumwalt, have contributed important work. Above all, Ludger Müller-Wille has been the most devoted contributor to tracing and publicizing Boas's experiences and scientific contributions in Baffinland. I thank Igor Krupnik for his careful reading of the manuscript and his useful suggestions. I am happy to acknowledge the support and friendship of Rosemary Lévy Zumwalt, Ludger Müller-Wille, and Nancy Parezo. Thomas Durkin of University of Wisconsin libraries was able to provide a high-resolution scan of the engraving of Franz Boas at the blowhole.

3. The names Galla, Kaffer, and Hottentot are no longer acceptable, but the Oromo of Ethiopia were still called "Galla" when I began my research with them in 1957, unaware of Boas's youthful interest in them.

4. See Walls (2009) on Alexander von Humboldt's liberal views and influence, and Bunzl (1996) regarding Boas and "the Humboldtian tradition."

5. Boas was a student at the time of a "neo-Kantian" movement of which Erdmann was a leader. Accounts of Boas's intellectual background usually allude to the influence of Kant, noting even that he wrote of reading Kant's work in an igloo one night! Boas's approach to matters of humanity and culture, however, was influenced much more by Herder, Kant's intellectual opponent, as Michael N. Forster points out (2010: 205–14).

6. Another important influence on Boas's skepticism about racial determination was Theodor Waitz (1821–64). Boas drew upon Waitz's *Anthropologie der Naturvölker* (1859–72) for his 1894 paper about race and incorporated much of that into *The Mind of Primitive Man* (1911). Waitz's position that "environment does not automatically stimulate a specific adaptation, which is itself a function of a people's culture" (Lowie 1937: 17), went back at least as far as Herder. (On Waitz, see Smith 1991: 46–51.)

7. As Kalmar (1987) and Bunzl (2003) point out, their conception of culture and of "Bildung" (see below) came from a similar place in German-Jewish Enlightenment ethos. Steinthal was also a teacher of Benno Erdmann.

8. Hall undertook three expeditions between 1860 and 1871 to find the remnants and records of the ill-fated Franklin expedition. He died sud-

denly aboard his ship off the coast of Greenland (apparently poisoned) on his final trip. Boas wrote, "Thus this man, remarkable in his loyalty toward his life's task, died. His enthusiasm for his favorite plans, his love for mankind and his self-sacrifice will hardly find their equal" (1883a: 8).

9. Wilhelm Weike was very helpful and uncomplaining, and Müller-Wille and Gieseking stress his contributions to tasks of travel and everyday life as well as to Boas's scientific collections and observations. Unfortunately, three of his toes were badly frostbitten, and he had to recuperate at the whaling station from early January until May, during which time Boas traveled without him. Müller-Wille points out that Weike would have lost his toes without the care of the Inuit and that he and Boas would not have survived without their concern and skill (personal communication).

10. According to Ludger Müller-Wille, Boas "made extensive observations of changing ice conditions and formations and their influence on mobility and resource utilization by both Inuit and whalers" and provided meteorological data that "are an important and extremely valuable source for the analysis of climatic change over the past one hundred thirty years" (2014: 132–33).

11. Reverend E. J. Peck established the first mission station in Cumberland Sound in 1896. He and Boas were in contact, and Peck contributed a number of tales and translated texts from Inuktitut that were included in the AMNH volumes of 1901 and 1907.

12. The clearest and most succinct account of his movements appears in this article.

13. Igor Krupnik, a specialist in Arctic anthropology, writes, "Many argued that the very pattern of scientific anthropological research among the Inuit originated with Boas's yearlong fieldwork on Baffin Island ..." (2016: 73). All the anthropologists who would follow Boas to the Arctic in subsequent years "emulated Boas's field paradigm based on active traveling on dogsled or in small boats with Native companions ..." (ibid.: 81).

14. A more accessible edition including a knowledgeable and laudatory introduction by Henry B. Collins, the dean of Arctic studies in America, was published in 1964. Two different versions of the original are available online, with different pagination. The 157 illustrations are more vivid online. Boas included an extensive account of Eskimo "Anthropogeographie" as one section of his *Habilitation* thesis, published in 1885 as *Baffin-Land*. The other sections of that work are a history of Arctic exploration, an account of his own journeys, and Baffin Island geography.

15. The one work of scholarship Boas cites is Hinrich Rink's *Tales and Traditions of the Eskimo* (1875). Boas would visit this Danish geologist, scholar, and administrator (1819–93) to consult on translations of Inuit tales and on linguistic matters. They coauthored an article in the *Journal*

of American Folklore (of which Boas was a recent cofounder). (See also Rink 1887–91.) According to Henry Collins, the other one of the "first scientific monographs on the Eskimo" was published by naval officer and Arctic explorer Gustav Frederik Holm (1849–1940) in Danish in 1888, the same year as Boas's work (in Boas 1964: v).

16. In 1984 Ludger Müller-Wille and Linna Weber Müller-Wille went to the people of Pangnirtung and showed them Boas's collection of 930 place names and the maps he and his companions had made. It was part of "a cooperative effort to react to and fulfill priorities set by local Inuit residents and organizations to preserve, maintain, and enhance Inuit cultural heritage for future generations" (Müller-Wille and Müller-Wille 2006: 217). They report that "despite all adversity, the results of Boas's cartographic and toponymic work ... are astounding and have withstood the rigor of later reviews by Inuit and others" (ibid.: 223). Marc G. Stevenson's *Inuit Whalers, and Cultural Persistence: Structure in Cumberland Sound and Central Inuit Social Organization* (1997) also makes considerable use of *The Central Eskimo*.

17. There once were many whales in Cumberland Sound, but only few remained by 1883, and the Inuit had largely given up the whale "fishery" and left it to the European and American whalers. According to Stevenson, however, whales are there again and hunted avidly, and the social division of labor and spoils is similar to that of Boas's time (Stevenson 1997: xviii–xx). Boas records seeing ruins of two large "ancient settlements" at Pangnirtung Fjord, abandoned at that time but today the largest settlement on Baffin Island. It is the site of the whale hunt that opens Stevenson's book.

18. To quote a contemporary version that corroborates Boas's findings in the 1880s, "It is absurd to think that the environment plays no role in shaping Inuit social organization. People 'gotta eat.' Nevertheless, the structure of productive social, political, and economic relationships— who hunts with whom, how the product of the hunt is distributed, who marries whom, etc.—and how these are given value and meaning is culturally determined, and not as preordained by environmental factors as many might suppose" (Stevenson 1996: xx).

19. These illustrations are beautifully reproduced in the original Bureau of Ethnology edition—less so in the 1964 reprint. Because Boas was not able to bring back most of his material culture collection, many of the illustrations are of items in the National Museum in Washington and the Museum für Völkerkunde in Berlin.

20. Franz Boas describes one practice as "... a most cruel way, by using the love of the dam for her pup to lure her to the surface of the hole." This section is accompanied by drawings produced from photographs of the stances of hunters. In fact, the "Eskimo" hunters are Boas and Wilhelm Weike, in appropriate dress, in a studio in Minden, their hometown. These impersonations were necessary because most of the photos Boas had taken on Baffin Island were lost.

21. Boas offered the readers of *Berliner Tageblatt*, 28 December 1883, another warm tribute to Inuit life and hospitality in a brief article translated as "With Your Host—Travel Sketch from the North" (Boas 1883d).
22. Boas inspired others, amateurs, to participate in the ethnographic project. Although the whaling captains Mutch and Comer preceded Boas in Cumberland sound, it was with his urging and support that they collected artifacts and recorded stories, rituals, and other cultural elements. As Kenn Harper claims, "Boas was, in fact, establishing a pattern that he would follow through much of his long career in anthropology, that of developing a research partnership with untutored men in the field" (2016: 89).
23. Houdini would appear about a decade later.
24. "Eskimo Story (Written for my Children)" was edited and published for the first time in 2007 by Franz Boas's grandson, Norman F. Boas.
25. Douglas Cole published a selection of these important letters (1983), and Ludger Müller-Wille's work (1998) contains translations of relevant materials from Boas's notebooks as well as almost the entire letter-diary. Boas urged Wilhelm Weike to keep a daily journal, and Weike's diary gives a complementary, sometimes more loquacious view of daily life (Müller-Wille and Gieseking 2011).
26. Carol C. Knötsch (1993: 11–14) discusses the newspaper article, demonstrating the way Boas purposely shows the reader his journey from initial shock and repulsion to appreciation.
27. In his letter to Marie on 22 January 1884 he wrote, "You can't imagine how one watches out for the ice foot [in front of a glacier] to appear on the horizon, the best sign that one is close to land, and how gladly one welcomes the comfortable igloo! One simply cannot express how comfortable and fine it seems as one crawls into this dirty, confined space, at the appearance of which I turned away full of horror the first time!" (Boas, quoted in Müller-Wille 1998: 170).
28. That child died in his hands—as would his own daughter Hedwig ten years later in a cold, crowded Chicago apartment (Cole 1999: 158–59).
29. For his 1884–85 stay in America, see Müller-Wille 2014: 83–88; for Jacobi and Schurz, see Lewis 2020.
30. Norman F. Boas and Doris W. Boas, Franz Boas's grandchildren, had their grandfather's newspaper articles translated and circulated privately as *Arctic Expedition 1883–1884: Translated German Newspaper Accounts of My Life with the Eskimos*. I am grateful to Rosemary Lévy Zumwalt for calling my attention to this translation and to Ludger Müller-Wille for sharing it with me. Müller-Wille 2014 contains a "List of People" (149–55) as well as a comprehensive annotated bibliography of Boas's publications from his Arctic work, in German and English, geographic as well as ethnographic.
31. Stocking (1965) dismisses Boas's students' contention that it was primarily his field experience that led to the Boasian conversion. He believed it was due to his work in Berlin with Bastian and Virchow in 1885–86. This is belied by the substance of Boas's writings immediately after his

return and the research projects he proposed to Bastian in late 1884. Above all, Boas's primary contacts in the United States in 1884 were Otis T. Mason of the National Museum and John Wesley Powell of the Bureau of Ethnology—where he wanted a job! (Zumwalt 2019: 133–34.)

32. Boas was so enthusiastic about fieldwork in the Arctic that he proposed a plan for four seasons of research, working his way westward from Labrador as far as Vancouver, studying and comparing all the Inuit and Indian groups along the way. "My chief idea . . . is that these tribes must be studied in relation to one another and that only someone who understands the East will be able thoroughly to understand the West" (letter to Bastian, 5 January 1886, in Stocking 1974: 87).

References

Boas, Franz. 1883a. "Polar Expedition of Charles Francis Hall." *Berliner Tageblatt*, 4 September. In Franz Boas, *Arctic Expedition 1883–1884: Translated German Newspaper Accounts of My Life with the Eskimos*, edited by Norman F. Boas and Doris W. Boas. Private edition, 2009.

———. 1883b. "The Eskimos of Cumberland Sound and Davis Strait." *Berliner Tageblatt*, 21 November. In Franz Boas, *Arctic Expedition 1883–1884: Translated German Newspaper Accounts of My Life with the Eskimos*, edited by Norman F. Boas and Doris W. Boas. Private edition, 2009.

———. 1883c. "To the Arctic Ocean! Travel Preparations and through the North Sea." *Berliner Tageblatt*, 4 August. In Franz Boas, *Arctic Expedition 1883–1884: Translated German Newspaper Accounts of My Life with the Eskimos*, edited by Norman F. Boas and Doris W. Boas. Private edition, 2009.

———. 1883d. "With Your Host—Travel Sketch from the North." *Berliner Tageblatt*, 28 December. In Franz Boas, *Arctic Expedition 1883–1884: Translated German Newspaper Accounts of My Life with the Eskimos*, edited by Norman F. Boas and Doris W. Boas. Private edition, 2009.

———. 1884a. "Sedna and the Religious Festival in Autumn." *Berliner Tageblatt*, 16 November. In Franz Boas, *Arctic Expedition 1883–1884: Translated German Newspaper Accounts of My Life with the Eskimos*, edited by Norman F. Boas and Doris W. Boas. Private edition, 2009.

———. 1884b. "A Journey in Cumberland Sound and on the West Shore of Davis Strait in 1883 and 1884." *Journal of the American Geographical Society of New York* 16: 242–72.

———. 1885a. *Baffin-Land: Geographische Ergebnisse einer in den Jahren 1883 und 1884 ausgeführten Forschungsreise*. Supplementary volume to/Ergänzungsheft no. 80 zu *Petermanns Mitteilungen*. Gotha: Justus Perthes. *Habilitation* thesis, University of Berlin.

———. 1885b. "Below the Polar Ice" [better: Below the Arctic Circle]. *New Yorker Staats-Zeitung*, 18 February. In Franz Boas, *Arctic Expedition 1883–1884: Translated German Newspaper Accounts of My Life with the*

Eskimos, edited by Norman F. Boas and Doris W. Boas. Private edition, 2009.

——. 1887a. "A Year among the Eskimo." *Journal of the American Geographical Society of New York* 19: 383–402.

——. 1887b. "The Study of Geography." *Science* 9 (210) (supplement, new series, 11 February): 137–41.

——. 1887c. "Poetry and Music of Some North American Tribes." *Science* 9: 383–85.

——. 1887d. "The Occurrence of Similar Inventions in Areas Widely Apart." *Science* 9: 485–86.

——. 1888. "The Central Eskimo." In *Sixth Annual Report of the Bureau of Ethnology Presented to the Secretary of the Smithsonian Institution 1884–'85*, 409–669. Washington, DC: Government Printing Office.

——. 1894. "Human Faculty as Determined by Race." *Proceedings of the American Association for the Advancement of Science* 43: 3–29.

——. 1901. *The Eskimo of Baffin Land and Hudson Bay: From Notes Collected by Capt. George Comer, Capt. James S. Mutch, and Rev. E. J. Peck*. Bulletin of the American Museum of Natural History 15, part 1. New York: AMNH.

——. 1907. *Second Report on the Eskimo of Baffin Land and Hudson Bay: From Notes Collected by Captain George Comer, Captain James S. Mutch, and Rev. E. J. Peck*. Bulletin of the American Museum of Natural History 15, part 2. New York: AMNH.

——. 1911. *The Mind of Primitive Man*. New York: Macmillan. 2nd ed. 1938.

——. 1938. "An Anthropologist's Credo." *The Nation*, 27 August.

——. 1964. *The Central Eskimo*. Introduction by Henry B. Collins. Lincoln: University of Nebraska Press.

——. 2007. "Eskimo Story (Written for my Children)." In *My Arctic Expedition 1883–1884*, edited by Norman F. Boas. Mystic, CT: Seaport Autographs Press.

——. 2009. *Arctic Expedition 1883–1884: Translated German Newspaper Accounts of My Life with the Eskimos*. Edited by Norman F. Boas and Doris W. Boas. Private edition.

Boas, Norman F. 2004. *Franz Boas 1858–1942: An Illustrated Biography*. Mystic, CT: Seaport Autographs Press.

Bunzl, Matti. 1996. "Franz Boas and the Humboldtian Tradition." In *Völksgeist as Method and Ethic: Essays on Boasian Ethnography and the German Anthropological Tradition*, edited by George W. Stocking Jr, 17–78. Madison: University of Wisconsin Press.

——. 2003. "*Völkerpsychologie* and German-Jewish Emancipation." In *Worldly Provincialism: German Anthropology in the Age of Empire*, edited by H. Glenn Penny and Matti Bunzl, 47–85. Ann Arbor: University of Michigan Press.

Cole, Douglas. 1983. "'The Value of a Person Lies in His *Herzensbildung*': Franz Boas' Baffin Island Letter-Diary, 1883–1884." In *Observers Ob-

served: Essays on Ethnographic Fieldwork, edited by George W. Stocking Jr, 13–52. Madison: University of Wisconsin Press.

———. 1999. *Franz Boas: The Early Years, 1858–1906*. Seattle: University of Washington Press.

Cole, Douglas, and Ludger Müller-Wille. 1984. "Franz Boas' Expedition to Baffin Island, 1883–1884." *Études/Inuit/Studies* 8(1): 37–63.

Forster, Michael N. 2010. *After Herder: Philosophy of Language in the German Tradition*. Oxford: Oxford University Press.

Gruber, Jacob W. 1970. "Ethnographic Salvage and the Shaping of Anthropology." *American Anthropologist* 72(6): 1289–99.

Harper, Kenn. 2016. "Collecting at a Distance: The Boas-Mutch-Comer Collaboration." In *Early Inuit Studies: Themes and Transitions, 1850s–1980s*, edited by Igor Krupnik, 89–110. Washington, DC: Smithsonian Institution Press.

Holm, Gustav F. 1914. *Ethnological Sketch of the Angmagsalik Eskimo*. Meddelelser om Greenland 39. Original in Danish 1888.

Humboldt, Alexander von. 1845–62. *Kosmos: Entwurf einer physischen Weltbeschreibung* [Cosmos: Outline of a physical description of the universe]. 5 vols. Stuttgart und Tübingen: J. G. Cotta'scher Verlag.

Kalmar, Ivan D. 1987. "The *Völkerpsychologie* of Lazarus and Steinthal and the Modern Concept of Culture." *Journal of the History of Ideas* 48(4): 671–90.

Kluckhohn, Clyde, and Olaf Prufer. 1959. "Influences during the Formative Years." In *The Anthropology of Franz Boas*, edited by Walter Goldschmidt, 4–28. Memoir 89, American Anthropological Association.

Knötsch, Carol C. 1993. "Franz Boas' Research Trip to Baffin Island 1882–1884." *Polar Geography* 17(1): 3–54.

Kroeber, Alfred L. 1943. "Franz Boas: 1858–1942." Memoir 61, American Anthropological Association.

Krupnik, Igor. 2016. "One Field Season and a 50-Year Career: Franz Boas and Early Eskimology." In *Early Inuit Studies: Themes and Transitions, 1850s–1980s*, edited by Igor Krupnik, 73–83. Washington, DC: Smithsonian Institution Press.

Leaf, Murray J. 1979. *Man, Mind, and Science: A History of Anthropology*. New York: Columbia University Press.

Lewis, Herbert S. 2008. "Franz Boas: Boon or Bane?" *Reviews in Anthropology* 37: 169–200.

———. 2020. "Who's Who in the Age of Boas: The Sponsors of Anthropological Papers Written in Honor of Franz Boas (1906)." In *BEROSE International Encyclopaedia of the Histories of Anthropology*, Paris.

Lowie, Robert H. 1937. *The History of Ethnological Theory*. New York: Rinehart and Co.

Lubbock, John. 1865. *Pre-historic Times, as Illustrated by Ancient Remains*. London: Williams and Norgate.

Mosse, George L. 1985. *German Jews Beyond Judaism*. Cincinnati: Hebrew Union College Press.

Müller-Wille, Ludger. 1984. "Two Papers by Franz Boas." *Ètudes/Inuit/Studies* 8(1): 117–20.

——, ed. 1998. *Franz Boas among the Inuit of Baffin Island, 1883–1884: Journals and Letters.* Translated by William Barr. Toronto: University of Toronto Press.

——. 2014. *The Franz Boas Enigma: Inuit, Arctic and Sciences.* Montreal: Baraka Books.

Müller-Wille, Ludger, and Bernd Gieseking. 2011. *Inuit and Whalers on Baffin Island through German Eyes: Wilhelm Weike's Arctic Journal and Letters (1883–84).* Translated by William Barr. Montreal: Baraka Books

Müller-Wille, Ludger, and Linna Weber Müller-Wille. 2006. "Inuit Geographical Knowledge One Hundred Years Apart." In *Critical Inuit Studies: An Anthology of Contemporary Arctic Ethnography*, edited by Pamela Stern and Lisa Stevenson, 217–29. Lincoln: University of Nebraska Press.

Peck, Edmund James. 2006. *Apostle to the Inuit: The Journals and Ethnographic Notes of Edmund James Peck, the Baffin Years, 1894–1905.* Edited by Frédéric Laugrand, Jarich Oosten, and François Trudel. Toronto: University of Toronto Press.

Ratzel, Friedrich. 1882–91. *Anthropo-Geographie.* 2 vols. Stuttgart: J. Engelhorn.

Rink, Henry [Hinrich Johannes]. 1875. *Tales and Traditions of the Eskimo — with a Sketch of Their Habits, Religion, Language, and Other Peculiarities.* London: William Blackwood & Sons.

——. 1887–91. *The Eskimo Tribes: Their Distribution and Characteristics, Especially in Regard to Language; With a Comparative Vocabulary and a Sketch-Map.* 2 vols. London: Williams and Norgate/Copenhagen: C. A. Reitzel.

Smith, Woodruff D. 1991. *Politics and the Sciences of Culture in Germany, 1840–1920.* Oxford: Oxford University Press.

Stevenson, Marc G. 1997. *Inuit Whalers and Persistence: Structure in Cumberland Sound and Central Inuit Social Organization.* Oxford: Oxford University Press.

Stocking, George W., Jr. 1965. "From Physics to Ethnology: Franz Boas' Arctic Expedition as a Problem in the Historiography of the Behavioral Sciences." *Journal of the History of the Behavioral Sciences* 1(1): 53–66.

——, ed. 1974. *The Shaping of American Anthropology 1883–1911: A Franz Boas Reader.* New York: Basic Books.

Waitz, Theodor. 1859–72. *Anthropologie der Naturvölker.* 6 vols. Leipzig: F. Fleischer.

Walls, Laura D. 2009. *The Passage to Cosmos: Alexander von Humboldt and the Shaping of America.* Chicago: University of Chicago Press.

Zumwalt, Rosemary Lévy. 2019. *Franz Boas: The Emergence of the Anthropologist.* Lincoln: University of Nebraska Press.

2

"A Sympathetic Chronicler of a Sympathetic People"

Katie Langloh Parker and
The Euahlayi Tribe (1905)

Barbara Chambers Dawson

The Euahlayi Tribe emerged from the cultural expertise of the Noongahburrah, who are acknowledged as co-contributors to its production. Readers are nevertheless notified that some words and descriptions are not culturally sensitive by today's standards. These terms reflect Katie Langloh Parker's use of words from the period in which she lived and are now considered inappropriate. The repetition of them is not intended to cause distress to readers, particularly Indigenous Australians. Aboriginal people are also advised that this chapter contains the names and images of deceased people. As a white Anglo-Australian woman, I underline my respect for the Yuwaalaraay people, past and present. For stylistic continuity, I will generally refer to the Yuwaalaraay as the Euahlayi or the Noongahburrah.

***

Katie Langloh Parker (1856–1940; see figure 2.1) recorded and documented a significant body of knowledge from the oral tradition of the Noongahburrah (Nhunggabarra) of the Narran River region—members of the larger Euahlayi (Yuwaalaraay) tribe—whose country stretched across forty-six hundred square miles in northern New South Wales. She was confident that her study of the "manners, customs, beliefs, and legends of the Aborigines of Australia"—whose full title is *The Euahlayi Tribe: A Study of Aboriginal Life in Australia*—was an important contribution to ethnographic enquiry (Parker 2018 [1905]: 17). By 1922, the study of human societies and their cultures was beginning to be recognized as the discipline of social anthropology.

Figure 2.1. *Katie Langloh Parker (Mrs. Stow). © National Library of Australia, Papers of Marcie Muir relating to Katie Langloh Parker (NLA MS 10182/3/19). This photograph appeared in* The Lone Hand *magazine (Sydney 1912).*

Parker's findings had joined, and been tested against, the work of contemporary Australian ethnographers. She was able to specifically locate and differentiate the Indigenous people, among whom she lived, from the 1904 anthropological work of Sir Alfred William Howitt (1830–1908), identifying them—neighbors of the people whom Howitt had termed the Wollaroi (Yualloroi) or Yualaroi—as the "Euahlayi" (Howitt 1996 [1904]). She revealed the depth of her acquired knowledge by explaining the pronunciation of "Euahlayi," with the accent falling on the second syllable. She had also learned the derivation and meaning of the word. The level of her recorded detail on Euahlayi beliefs about reincarnation, totems, and subtotems—and what was then termed "primitive monotheism"—enabled a comparison of Euahlayi knowledge with the beliefs of other Aboriginal people, such as the "Arunta" (Arrernte, Aranda) of Central Australia and those from the northern part of the State of Victoria, in southern Australia (Parker 2018 [1905]: 17–18). She stated that "the Euahlayi . . . present a mixture of ideas and usages which appears to be somewhat peculiar and deserving of closer study than it has received," adding that "Mr Howitt himself refers to the tribe very seldom" (Parker 2018 [1905]: 18). Her two previous publications—*Australian Legendary Tales* (1896) and *More Australian Legendary Tales* (1898)—were forerunners to her major ethnographic contribution.

In spite of his knowledge of Parker's work, which he quoted in his 1913 armchair monograph on *The Family among the Australian Aborigines: A Sociological Study*, it is unlikely that Bronisław Malinowski (1884–1942) had Parker's work in mind when he stated in 1922 that

> most . . . of the modern scientific accounts have opened up quite new and unexpected aspects of tribal life. They have given us, in clear outline, the picture of social institutions often surprisingly vast and complex; they have brought before us the vision of the native as he is, in his religious and magical beliefs and practices. They have allowed us to penetrate into his mind far more deeply than we have ever done before. (Malinowski 1972 [1922]: xv)

Although Malinowski's words serve to applaud the work of those schooled in scientific anthropological method or, as he calls it, the study of "comparative Ethnology," they equate closely with Parker's approach. Despite her acknowledged lack of formal theoretical training, she took her place in the evolving practice of the discipline.

Furthermore, with the cooperation of Indigenous women, she was granted access to women's societal contribution through the sharing of knowledge about their beliefs, customs, and practices—a field of study largely unexamined by male ethnographers.

Life in Outback Australia

Parker's opportunities for carrying out "fieldwork" were as close as the area outside her front door. In 1875, aged eighteen, she had married Langloh Parker, who in 1878 acquired a government lease for Bangate, a sheep and cattle station near Goodooga in far northern New South Wales, close to the Queensland border, 530 miles northwest of Sydney. The following year, Langloh and Katie moved there. They lived on the property for more than twenty years. As an established colonial pastoralist, Langloh Parker had built a reputation as a man of "high honour and great power."[1] Because her husband was popular and well-known, being much older than Katie Parker, she adopted her husband's first name "Langloh" for her publications, seemingly to give her books a notable profile.

The Parkers settled on the ancestral land of the Noongahburrah, forming a huge property typical of others "taken up" by Europeans in the remote outback regions of Australia. By 1887 it stretched across 215,408 acres (336 square miles), with more than 100,000 sheep and several thousand head of cattle (Muir 1982: 34–35). Bangate had a large, predominantly male workforce. Occasionally a white female cook or laundress might be employed on the station, but, as a lower-class worker, she was considered an unsuitable companion for the wife of the owner. A fall from a horse, soon after Parker's arrival at Bangate, precluded any further riding activities and prevented her from visiting neighboring females of her own class, who might live hundreds of miles away on distant properties. Childless, in a male-dominated and isolated environment, she turned to the Noongahburrah to compensate for loneliness, and for companionship. Intelligent and well read, she had been taught by parents with a high educational standard; her maternal grandmother could read the Old Testament in Hebrew and the New Testament in Greek. Her father, who had had a classical education, taught his children about Greek life and culture and also read to them aboriginal legends. Knowing about Greek and aboriginal mythology, she approached the Noongahburrah, curious to hear their traditional stories and eager to gain an intellectual outlet in her solitude.

Parker appears to have immediately felt comfortable among the Noongahburrah. Commentaries on her life refer to her former close proximity and friendly contact with Indigenous people. She was born on 1 May 1856 near Encounter Bay, South Australia, where her pastoralist father Henry Field farmed on the country of the Ramindjeri. In 1859 the Field family moved to Marra Station, ninety miles northeast of Wilcannia, on the Darling River, to Paakantyi country. She also had a family precedent to follow: her uncle, Simpson Newland, who was a partner with her father at Marra, wrote "humanitarian accounts of Aboriginal legends" and dealt "kindly and sensitively" with the Paakantyi, whose vocabulary he collected. In 1900 he wrote a novel, *Blood Tracks of the Bush*, in which he accurately depicted the murders of Aboriginal people by police and pastoralists (Jenkin 1988). Parker also invoked a memory of when, as a child of almost six years, she was saved from drowning in the Darling River by the family's Aboriginal nursemaid "Miola," who at the time was unable to save Parker's two sisters (Parker 2018 [1905]: 17). Miola subsequently joined the surviving Field children in the lessons provided by their mother.

Living among different groups of Aborigines from her young childhood, Parker understood that Australia was made up of many different Indigenous nations, living on their own separate country and with their own language and culture, their customary laws, beliefs, and stories. Over the many years that she lived alongside the Noongahburrah, she writes that she gained their trust, learned their language and associated dialects, and established close relationships. The Aboriginal women generously incorporated her into Noongahburrah society, giving her the aboriginal name "Innerah," which meant "a woman with a camp of her own" (ibid.: 100). She would join the women and girls when they went to swim in the Narran River, which wound through the property, or on their food-foraging trips and wrote that "they were on very good terms with me. They would exchange gifts with me: I might receive a carved weapon, and one of them [might receive] some tobacco. The giving was not on my side, by any means" (ibid.: 18; Dawson 2014: xx, 147–48).[2]

The Noongahburrah women cared for and protected the white woman on their land. When Katie Parker was left alone at the homestead during Langloh Parker's frequent trips to distant sheep stations or, with his workmen, to the far reaches of the property, perhaps thirty miles away, Bootha, a Noongahburrah female elder, would act as her spiritual protector, "smoking" the area around the house, as a

ceremonial protection to ward off evil spirits, until the menfolk returned. If Bootha had to temporarily leave the area and planned to
be absent for some time, she erected ceremonial poles in front of the
home to protect Parker from the visits of spirits of the dead until her
return. When the household almost ran out of flour, an Aboriginal
woman shared her own flour ration. Another woman walked sixteen
miles to ask for a cake of soap when she thought that Parker's supply
was low. One of the Aboriginal girls, whom Parker had trained to
work as domestic servants, would bring a blanket to sleep across the
threshold of her bedroom when she was alone (Parker 1899: 1482).
Bootha also shared her healing skills by diagnosing and, after conferring with spirits, curing a visiting white girl of illness caused by
mosquito bites.

Parker must be seen as complicit in colonization. She was the
daughter and wife of colonial landholders who had settled on huge
tracts of aboriginal territory at a time of pastoral expansion, and she
acted as mistress to young Aboriginal women who worked in menial
household jobs in a manipulative power imbalance—exploitative behavior deemed unacceptable today (Evans, Grimshaw, and Standish
2003: 15). It was through the friendly, accommodating, and kindly
attitude of the Noongahburrah that they accepted Parker, who grew
close to them and learned to know them as individuals.

Parker collected her data primarily through interactive conversations, by listening, and by observing the tribal rituals and ceremonies, with the same ethnographic methods as Malinowski's, cited
as "watching [the Trobriand Islanders] daily at work and at play,
conversing with them in their own tongue, and deriving all . . . information from the surest sources—personal observation and statements made to [the ethnographer] directly by the natives in their
own language" (Malinowski 1972 [1922]: vii–viii). Through these
means she was able to produce an account of Noongahburrah culture as she observed it, elements of which she could compare with
other ethnographic findings and relate to anthropological theories
of her time.

For her information, Parker was utterly dependent on Noongahburrah cultural experts, relying on five main "informants"; the chief
one was Peter Hippi to whom she dedicated her collection of *Australian Legendary Tales*. Through patient repetitions from the Noongahburrah, she learned some of the Euahlayi language and assiduously
transcribed their legends. At the end of *Australian Legendary Tales*,
she wrote down the story of Dinewan Boollarhnah Goomblegub-
bon in aboriginal language (Parker 1998 [1896]: 126–28), and in *Aus-*

tralian Legendary Tales, More Australian Legendary Tales, and *The Euahlayi Tribe,* she provided three different glossaries.

By her own assertion, Parker was scrupulous in reproducing the exact translation of Euahlayi knowledge, without any interpretation that might allow her own ideas or prejudices to intrude. She checked and rechecked the tales with various interpreters and recorded them exactly as they were told to her. While emphasizing that "the legends were told to me by the [Aborigines] themselves" (ibid.: xi), she explained that

> first I get an old, old Black to tell [the story] in his own language. . . . I get a younger one to tell it back to him in his language; he corrects what is wrong, then I get the other one to tell me in English. I write it down, read it, and tell it back again to the old fellow with the help of the medium, for though I have a fair grasp of their language, I would not, in a thing like this, trust to my knowledge entirely. (Muir 1982: 173)

And that

> we conversed in a kind of Lingua Franca. An informant, say Peter, would try to express himself in English, when he thought that I was not successful in following him in his own tongue. With Paddy, who had no English but a curse [swear word], I used two native women, one old, one younger, as interpreters, checking each other alternately. The younger natives themselves had lost the sense of some of the native words used by their elders, but the middle-aged interpreters were usually adequate. (Parker 2018 [1905]: 18)

Certainly, Parker stood fast in achieving what Malinowski would identify as the three-strata goal of ethnographic investigation: the study of "the organization of the tribe and the anatomy of its culture"; the *"imponderabilia of actual life"*; and the inclusion of "ethnographic statements, characteristic narratives, typical utterances, items of folk-lore and magical formulae"—the "documents of native mentality." Her modus operandi—even before Malinowski had formulated it as his own "final goal"—was, in his words, "to grasp the native's point of view, his relation to life, to realize *his* vision of *his* world" (Malinowski 1972 [1922]: 24–25).

As the daughter and granddaughter of a clever mother and a highly educated maternal grandmother, it seems natural that Parker went further in anthropological enquiry to include in her study the "vision" and the "world" of the women and the children as well as that of the men.

The All Father, Byamee,
and the Initiation of Young Males

During Parker's years on Bangate, the Noongahburrah were still able to maintain their connection to their land, where they continued to fulfill their sacred obligations and to respect their traditional laws through their ceremonial and social activities. Parker's informed knowledge on ritual observances and ethical teachings has contributed to the subject of "primitive monotheism"—the original belief in an All-Father "God" in precontact Indigenous societies—a topic that continues to engage anthropologists in historical debate.

Parker set down details of the Noongahburrah belief in Byamee (Baiame), meaning "big man" or "Great One"—known to the women as Boyjerh—a belief that she emphatically maintained had predated missionary contact. A mission at Brewarrina, one hundred miles to the southwest of Bangate, had opened in 1886, but the Noongahburrah—untouched by government coercion or missionary zeal—were able to remain on their land until the 1930s. An argument against a protective isolation from Christian influence could plead that distance was not an obstruction to aboriginal networking. But Parker's evidence for a belief in Byamee predating missionary input came from one of her informants, Yudtha Dulleebah, "said to have been already grey haired when [the European 'explorer'] Sir Thomas Mitchell discovered the Narran in 1846." The estimated date of the Aboriginal man's initiation (and his first knowledge of Byamee) was 1830. She adds that "[Byamee] was a worshipful being, revealed in the mysteries, long before missionaries came, as all my informants aver" (Parker 2018 [1905]: 20–21).[3] In *Australian Legendary Tales*, Byamee appeared as a *wirreenun* ("priest" or "doctor," "medicine man" or "wizard").

The Noongahburrah had met the clergyman, who visited Bangate to conduct Christian services, and sometimes attended a service out of curiosity. Parker also spoke with some young Indigenous women of an "overseeing providence, a King of All, to whom everything was possible" (Parker 1899: 1481). These transactions exposed the Noongahburrahs in the late nineteenth century to the idea of an omnipotent Christian God, that could have precipitated a changing version of belief in Byamee, which complied with changing times.

This is the argument adopted by Hilary Carey in her article "The Land of Byamee," in which she posits Parker's interpretation of Byamee within the Noongahburrahs' spiritual belief system that flourished during the "assimilation era." Carey argues that it developed as a reflection of the colonial impact of (often violent) dispossession and disease. Certainly, Parker's anthropological analysis incorporates the beliefs and fears—even "dread"—that the oldest *wirreenuns* instilled into the Euahlayi initiates at this time, regarding what they saw in their own sacred crystals or magical stones. They looked into the future and "foresaw" that the skin color of the Euahlayi "seemed to grow paler and paler, until only the white faces of the Wundah, or spirits of the dead, and white devils were seen, as if it should mean that some day no more blacks should be on this earth" (Carey 1998: 200–201, 205, 207; Parker 2018 [1905]: 88).

Parker's knowledge of Noongahburrah belief empowered her to oppose the views of her former intellectual hero, the English philosopher and sociologist Herbert Spencer (1820–1903). She expressed these views forthrightly to the Scottish folklorist and anthropologist Andrew Lang (1844–1912). Despite her geographical isolation, Parker had intellectual contact and connection to contemporary knowledge through books, journal subscriptions, and erudite visitors. Journals such as those of the Folklore Society of London—of which Lang was a member—and *Science of Man: Journal of the Royal Anthropological Society of Australasia*, edited by Dr. Alan Carroll (ca. 1823–1911), opened the way for her to correspond with a developing group of people (including Lang) who acknowledged that Australian Aboriginal people were worthy of serious study and respect. Another possible introduction to Lang may have occurred through his brother Dr. William Henry Lang (1859–1923), who was a medical doctor at Corowa, New South Wales, and who wrote of his love of horses in the *Pastoralists' Review*.

As James George Frazer (1854–1941) had godfathered, if not monitored, the ethnographic research of Sir Walter Baldwin Spencer (1860–1929) and Francis Gillen (1855–1912), Lang—among the fiercest critics of Frazer at the turn of the century—developed a special bond with Parker, who became a sort of protégée for him. Since the publication of *The Making of Religion* in 1898, Lang was the champion of primitive monotheism—and this partly explains his enthusiasm for her findings. When Lang and Parker started their exchange in the later 1890s, she was probably not aware that Herbert Spencer's repute in matters of primitive religion was dubious in the British anthropological milieu still dominated by Edward Tylor (1832–1917), who had accused Spencer of plagiarism. Lang wrote the introduction to *The Euahlayi Tribe* and reported the following:

Beginning as a disciple of Mr. Herbert Spencer in regards to the religious ideas of the Australians—according to that writer, mere dread of casual "spirits"—[Parker] was obliged to alter her attitude, in consequence of all that she learned at first hand. She also explains that her tribe are not "wild blacks," though, in the absence of missionary influences, they retain their ancient beliefs, at least the old people do; and, in a decadent form, preserve their tribal initiations, or Boorah. (Parker 2018 [1905]: 2)

Parker recognized and sympathized with the need of the Euahlayi to adapt and change their belief system during the disruptive period of assimilation with the European colonists. She represented the Euahlayi people's poignant assessment of a prophecy that, according to their view, emanated from Byamee himself, writing:

The reason of this must surely be that the tribes fell away from the Boorah rites, and in his wrath Byamee stirred from his crystal seat in Bullimah. He had said that as long as the blacks kept his sacred laws, so long should he stay in his crystal seat, and the blacks live on earth; but if they failed to keep up the Boorah rites as he had taught them, then he would move and their end would come, and only Wundah, or white devils, be in the country. (ibid.: 88)

Parker also made a significant contribution to anthropology through her descriptions and explanations of the long and complex preliminaries to the *Boorah* (the male initiation ceremony), and of the *Boorah* itself—details that touched on arcane Noongahburrah religious knowledge. The ceremony was defined as "a large gathering of [Aborigines], where the boys are initiated into the mysteries that make them young men" (Parker 1998 [1896]: 129). When a boy was about seven years old, his mother painted her son up "every day for about a week with red and white colourings." Thereafter, he was allowed to go to the "bachelors' camp" (*Weedegah Gahreemai*), where he went hunting with the men and boys and watched how fire was made in traditional times, before the currently used "wax matches" had become prevalent. Uninitiated boys were forbidden to practice this skill. Parker herself had witnessed this art many times, describing how the fire maker rubbed together two pieces of *Nummaybirah*—a soft, white wood—that, with the resulting sawdust and the addition of dry grass, soon caught alight. The precision of her watchful recording involved timing how long the process took from start to finish: the shortest span was three and a half minutes. But, she adds: "Sometimes it takes longer, but just under five minutes is the longest time I have ever seen it take" (Parker 2018 [1905]: 75–76).

She referenced the importance of the whirling boom of the bull-roarer, which informed the people that *Gurraymi*, the *Boorah* spirit (called by the women *"Gayandi"*), was near. Unseen, the *wirreenuns* swang their whirring *Gayandis*, filling the solitude of the Australian outback with an unworldly sound that inspired fear. She evocatively writes that "the function of the Gayandi is to inspire awe, and it fulfills it" (ibid.: 80). A ceremonial marching of the men and boys preceded a journey by the *Gooyeanawannah* (messengers), whose job was to disperse in various directions to summon neighboring tribes, from hundreds of miles around, to attend the *Boorah*. The *Dooloo-boorah* (message-stick) was handed to the first tribe, who took it to the neighboring tribe, and so on, until everyone had been contacted and invited. These different groups then brought along their boys to be initiated.

To prepare the sacred ground, the male Euahlayi elders cleared a large circle and built elaborate embankments; they carved the surrounding trees with the totems of the different tribes and painted them with mythical figures. In the *Bunbul* (smaller *Boorah* ring), wood was heaped together ready for the lighting of the sacred fire (*Yungawee*).

The Noongahburrah invited Parker and her husband to attend these preliminaries, allowing her to observe how the different men, boys, and women were ceremonially garbed and the order in which participants and onlookers entered the gathering place, and enabling her to hear the older women sing the *Boorah* songs. She wrote:

> The whole scene impressed us as picturesque—the painted figures of the men and boys, with the peculiarly native stealthy tread, threading their way through the grey Coolabah trees; the decorated women throwing their leafy missiles with accurate aim into the ranks of the boys, who did not dare to look at their assailants. A Boorah boy must give no evidence of curiosity; the *nil admirari* attitude then begun clings to a black man through life. The women of the tribe express voluble surprise, but a black man never except by the dilation of his eyes. (ibid.: 79)

Every night thereafter, a *corroboree* was held (see figure 2.2.). Parker recorded the mass organization and cooperation involved in accommodating such a huge gathering of people. Before each *corroboree*, the fully initiated of each tribe, as they arrived, helped prepare the inner sacred ground, while the younger men collected game and other foodstuffs. She described how the older men created huge earthen animals that represented their totems, which they plastered over with mud and painted in different colors and designs. Her commentary included details of intertribal wrestling matches and of the

Figure 2.2. *Noongahburrahs prepare for a* corroboree *at their camp on Bangate Station.* © *National Library of Australia, Papers of Marcie Muir relating to Katie Langloh Parker (NLA MS 10182/5/31).*

sporting and warfare games, such as sham fights, and the throwing of boomerangs and *boodthuls* (miniature war clubs) that tested the skills of the uninitiated boys.

Parker's portrayal of the *Boorah* was deep and extensive. It is astonishing how much she learned about these rites of passage, even if the arcane meanings behind the sacred objects and stories told to the boys were not revealed to her. She wrote that young women were banned from seeing the *Boorah* ceremonies, but, at specific times, the older women took part in dance and song. The mothers of the initiates were also present to remove the paint from the bodies of their sons on their return from the seven months' exclusion from the tribe. She did learn that, following the long period of initiation, the boys were prohibited from either speaking to or receiving food from a woman for twelve months, as if, as Parker observed, "they were monks of Byamee in training" (Parker 2018 [1905]: 90). Her descriptions speak of group cohesion, forged and emphasized by the corporate, symbolic skin painting and the wearing of decorative adornments, such as possum hair, kangaroo teeth, and feathers.

She was told that, during their time of exclusion from the tribe, the initiates endured physical trials and learned aspects of the sacred law and of magical objects. They were given small, white magical stones (*gubberah*), which Parker liked to compare with the "Baetyli" (sacred stones) of Greek antiquity. A period of starvation was followed by ongoing dietary restrictions. Her overview of this part of aboriginal lore was, "No wonder that the 'supernatural' was mixed up with their impressions of the Boorah: fasting nourishes hallucinations." She also noted that "the bush of Australia is a good background for superstition; there is such a non-natural air about its Nature, as if it has been sketched in roughly by a Beardsley-like artist" (ibid.: 86–87, 80).[4]

Parker was given access to some of the knowledge of initiated men, indicated by her copying down of "Byamee's song, which only the fully initiated may sing." An old Aboriginal man chanted the song to the Parkers "as the greatest thing he could do" (ibid.: 92). It was so ancient that its full meaning was said to be lost. She also reproduced an initiation chant that she had translated into English. Yudtha Dulleebah, "one of the oldest black men in the district," shared some of his experiences of initiation; for example, the strictness of behavior during the first stage was paramount: looking up or laughing was punished by death. Parker theorized on this inculcated veneration: "Only when the fear, the abasement, is gone does the true reverence come, which makes the most primitive creed a living religion" (ibid.: 84).

Adding to the descriptive elements of the ceremonial activities, Parker wrote about the ethical nature of Noongahburrah culture, as witnessed at the turn of the twentieth century. She learned that one of the qualities taught at initiation ceremonies was kindliness toward the old and sick—a strict command of Byamee. She also repeated the belief that, at a man's death, the "all-seeing spirit" reported on all breaches of his laws to Byamee, who judged that person accordingly. Three sins were "unforgiveable": unprovoked murder, lying to the elders of the tribe, and stealing a woman of the same hereditary totem—although there were extenuating factors that could absolve this last offense (ibid.: 91, 90). Parker does not give an opinion as to whether these were introduced Christianized elements, traditional beliefs, or a mixture of both.[5]

At the close of a *Boorah*, the oldest *wirreenun* said a prayer to Byamee, earnestly pleading for long life to the Euahlayi, because of their faithfulness to him, through the observance of the *Boorah* ceremony. Facing the east, he repeated his plea several times. Parker's exposition was that

> though we say that actually these people have but two attempts at prayers, one at the grave and one at the inner Boorah ring, I think perhaps we

are wrong. These two seem the only ones directly addressed to Byamee. But perhaps it is his indirect aid which is otherwise invoked. Daily set prayers seem to them a foolishness and an insult, rather than otherwise, to Byamee. He knows; why weary him by repetition, disturbing the rest he enjoys after his earth labours? But a prayer need not necessarily be addressed to the highest god. I think if we really understood and appreciated the mental attitude of the blacks, we should find more in their so-called incantations of the nature of invocations. When a man invokes aid on the eve of a battle, or in his hour of danger and need; when a woman croons over her baby an incantation to keep him honest and true, and that he shall be spared in danger, surely these croonings are of the nature of prayers born of the same elementary frame of mind as our more elaborate litany. I fancy inherent devotional impulses are common to all races irrespective of country or colour. (ibid.: 91–92)

Within the anthropological ideas of the day, Parker was recognized as a contributor to the ongoing High God or All Father debate. Following Andrew Lang's defense of her ethnography in Europe, other scholars took it seriously into account. For example, Émile Durkheim (1858–1917) asserted that, in the Australian context, the "ideas relative to the great tribal god are of indigenous origin" (Durkheim 1976 [1912]: 289). Acknowledging Howitt's work in particular, he included Parker in his discussion of the Baiame figure (ibid.: 285–89).[6] In 1917, the academic anthropologist E. O. James (1888–1972) also cited Parker's information on primitive monotheism in his discussion of both precontact belief and Christian influences (James 1917: 191–93). Parker's essential findings on Byamee joined and supported those of Howitt (Parker 2018 [1905]: 20, 21; Howitt 1996 [1904]: 488–508); her accounts of initiation ceremonies also contributed to the work done by Howitt and by Spencer and Gillen.

"Secret Women's Business"

In 1979, Diane Barwick, an Australian anthropologist and a pioneer in ethnohistory, and Diane Bell, a research scholar in prehistory and anthropology at the Australian National University, Canberra, suggested that "anthropologists have written little about the work and opinions and influence of women in Aboriginal society" (Barwick, Mace, and Stannage 1979: 179). They did, however, acknowledge four settler women whose writing about Aboriginal women contributed to the historical record: these were Daisy Bates (1863–1951) and

Olive Pink (1884–1975)—both of whom had close, long-term contact through welfare work with Aboriginal communities—and the first two Australian women who trained as anthropologists, Ursula McConnel (1888–1957) and Phyllis Kaberry (1910–77). Parker was not included in this list. Yet her close relationship with the Noongahburrah women, both young and old, resulted in a significant contribution to anthropology.

According to Julie Evans, Patricia Grimshaw and Ann Standish, Parker's writings "warrant serious attention" because of the evidence they offer of the lives of the Yuwaalaraay women, which is "not present in other literary sources and which exists for few Aboriginal women for this stage of the frontier." They argue that her ethnographic work was "unparalleled by any of her female counterparts" and further applaud her engagement with theory and the "anthropological debates of the day." Even the post–World War I Australian anthropologists, Pink and Kaberry, did not interact with Aborigines on the frontier in the same close way as Parker, but through the "artificially established avenue of anthropological fieldwork" (Evans, Grimshaw, and Standish 2003: 15, 16–17). These authors suggest that Parker's significance lies in her close observations of Euahlayi domestic and cultural life, as seen in the 1890s.

Parker's closeness to the Euahlayi women, and the trust they extended to her, is exemplified in her knowledge of what Aboriginal Australians now refer to as "secret women's business." Her chapter on "Birth—Betrothal—An Aboriginal Girl from Infancy to Womanhood" describes the legends surrounding the life events of an Aboriginal girl into adulthood. From firsthand knowledge, shared by the Aboriginal women and related to her in detail, she explains the complicated procedures (both spiritual and temporal) that accompany a girl at each significant stage of her life.

In reporting how "spirit-babies" are "usually despatched to Waddahgudjaelwon [a birth-presiding spirit] and sent by her to hang promiscuously on trees, until some woman passes under where they are, then they will seize a mother and be incarnated," Parker explained that "this resembles the Arunta belief, but with the Euahlayi the spirits are new freshly created beings, not reincarnations of ancestral souls, as among the Arunta" (Parker 2018 [1905]: 65). This relates Parker's ethnology to another major anthropological debate of the time (and during the twentieth century)—on supernatural or "virgin" birth—which predated but was particularly fueled by Spencer and Gillen's Arunta/Arrernte ethnology in their *The Native Tribes of Central Australia* (1899).

In other respects, Parker was able to open up new areas of enquiry: referencing the interposing spirits in myth and legend that result in the birth of a girl; noting the revulsion toward the birth of twins; describing the ceremonial activities and setting down the chants performed at the early milestones of a child's development. Knowledge of postbirth procedures indicates her presence at, or soon after, births: "The baby is bathed in cold water. Hot gum leaves are pressed on the bridge of its nose to ensure its flatness; the more bridgeless the nose the greater the beauty." The depth of detail about childrearing extended to indigenous methods of how to deal with sleepless babies, or with babies that cry too much—problems that plague mothers from all places and throughout time. Although not a mother herself, she recorded these "cures" with sympathy and understanding. One esoteric detail, revealed to her, was of the "muffled clicking sort of noise with her tongue rolled over against the roof of her mouth," performed by a baby's grandmother when a child clutched hold of something. The chant, accompanying this first reaching out to objects and people, contained the charm that encouraged the child to become a "free giver." Other applications of this tonal clicking accompanied the incantations sung over a baby about to crawl and in a ceremony performed by the mother on a four-year-old child, to promote a talent for strong swimming (Parker 2018 [1905]: 67–69). Parker presents each chant both "in language" and translated into English text.

The process of a girl's initiation involved a time of isolation and temporary dietary restrictions. Various marriage contracts, including baby betrothals *(Bahnmul)*—and the "great camp rows" that ensue when some girls struggle against marrying an old man—are set down and described. Details of a marriage ceremony involved flowers in the bride's hair and on her arms; her "bridal bouquet" was "a bunch of smoking Budtha leaves" (ibid.: 71–72).

Aspects of female experience included the belief in Euahlayi folklore that a common vaginal fungal infection was caused by a mother or her baby looking at the full moon. Only a female ethnographer in a long-term, confiding relationship with Indigenous women could be expected to elicit such privately held details. Phrases, such as "I have often heard," "I have often seen," "girls have told me," reveal the level of close association that the Noongahburrah women offered Parker.

Parker's accounts of activities associated with ceremonies sometimes adopt a light, even humorous tone, denoting not so much European patronization as perhaps reflecting a middle-aged woman's awareness of the foibles of humankind or an understanding of the manipulations of individual humans in the carrying out of a group's customary processes. Referring to the custom of spirit-women bringing presents to the women relations of the initiates a few days after the *Boorah*, she writes: "Then the old men—crafty old men—go out to where the 'bahing' [of the Kumbuy spirits] comes from, and bring in the gifts, which take the form of food, yams, honey, fruit principally" (ibid.: 73). Her reporting identifies the universal human trait of contrivance and adaptation and reflects her empathy with the Noongahburrah.

By her portrayals of Beemunny, one of Parker's chief informants, and of the authoritative powers of Bootha, Parker gives insights into the agency of Indigenous women. According to Patricia Grimshaw, "such personal interactions reveal something complex and important about intercultural exchanges between a pastoralist's wife and Aboriginal women" (Grimshaw 1995: 39). The example of Bootha, with her healing and magical powers, provides a strong indication that Aboriginal women gained power with age. As well as Bootha's reputed healing powers, she also had the power of rainmaking. Parker at least half believed in Bootha's magic, and she was influenced by Bootha and accorded her respect. When Bootha's prediction—that one of her sacred poles would fall to the earth when someone associated with the household died—came true at the exact time that the cook's mother died, Parker observed that "the camp were firm believers in Bootha's witch-stick after that" (Parker 2018 [1905]: 63).

Beemunny was another authoritative female elder. When she died, Parker wrote, perhaps patronizingly but mainly with empathy:

Poor old Beemunny! How the vanities of youth cling to one; how we are "all sisters under the skin."

She was ever so old, she was blind, her face was scarred with wrinkles, yet one of her beauties remained, and she absolutely joyed in its possession: it was her hair. Her hair was thick and fuzzy, when combed would stand nearly straight out, which is quite unusual with the native women's hair in that part. Beemunny one day asked one of the younger women if I had ever heard what a lot of lovers she had had in her youth, what fights there had been over her, and all because of her beautiful hair.

Poor old Beemunny! Something in my own woman nature went out to her in sympathy. She was old, she was ugly, her husband was dead, as were all men to her. . . . Having once learnt of her vanity, I never passed her without saying "Gubbah Tekkul!" "Beautiful hair!" at which she would beam and toss her head. (ibid.: 96)

Parker recorded the stories surrounding the death of Beemunny. During the days beforehand, the death spirits had been circling the camp in the movement of the air. A *boolee* (whirlwind) "watching to seize her fleeting spirit" sprang up. Her relatives guarded the old woman; and when the whirling eddy of air dissipated, Beemunny took her last breath. In this chapter of *The Euahlayi Tribe*, Parker's empathy for the people, whose grief she shared, evokes in her poetic expressions, not found in the more descriptive or analytical parts of her book. She refers to the impending death of Beemunny in poetic terms: "Round and round [the *boolee*] eddied. A dust-devil dancing a dance of death" (ibid.: 95–96). Whether these are her own words or a translation of Euahlayi dialect is unclear.

Granted permission to attend Beemunny's funeral as a mourner, Parker was accompanied by Bootha. Her presence at the graveside allowed her to be privy to the practices associated with death. She recorded the order of the procession to the gravesite, the birdsong from the sacred birds (through whom deceased women revisited the earth), the construction of the bark coffin, and the order in which different plants and the woman's belongings were placed in the grave. Mourning rituals included the smoking of the gravesite and of at-tendants, and wailing; Parker provided translations of the chants. As a confidante of the grieving group, she learned that part of the "etiquette" following the ritual "blood offering"—whereby a close relative drew blood by hitting her head with a sharp stone to prove her affection for the dead person—was the intervention of a friend to stop further injury.

Peter Hippi was in charge of the funerary rites, and he and Bootha shared with Parker the Noongahburrah beliefs of smoking and sweeping around the grave to cleanse and protect the site. She learned about the burial customs of other Indigenous groups, and Hippi de-scribed to her how the Noongahburrah practices had changed over time. Adding details about what she had seen or heard about these variations, she also offered both personal and acquired knowledge on the strict taboos of widows (ibid.: 97–105).

Another example that provides evidence of the agency of older Aboriginal women is in a story that Parker shares of an interaction between a European laundress on Bangate and an unnamed Noon-gahburrah female. The Indigenous woman had a hole through the septum of her nose, through which she often wore a bone (*mouyerh*). The laundress had pierced ears. The white woman said one day to the old Aboriginal woman:

"Why you have hole made in your nose and put that bone there? No good that. White women don't do that."

The black woman looked the laundress up and down, and finally anchored her eyes on the earrings.

"Why you make hole in your ears? No good that. Black gin no do that, pull 'em down your ears like dogs. Plenty good bone in your nose make you sing good. Sposin' cuggil—bad—smell you put bone longa nose no smell 'im. Plenty good make hole longa nose, no good make hole longa ears, make 'em hang down all same dogs." And off she went laughing, and pulling down the lobes of her ears, began to imitate the barking of a dog. (ibid.: 69)

Parker enjoyed "bush walks" with the women and girls. She acknowledged the depth of knowledge of young Aboriginal children, admitting that the walks "certainly . . . modified my conceit. I was always the dunce of the party—the smallest child knew more of woodcraft than I did, and had something to tell of everything." She added:

I had to hear the stingless little native bees before I could see them; and as to knowing which tree had honey in it, unless I saw the bees, that was quite beyond me, while a mere toddler would point triumphantly to a "sugar-bag" tree, recognising it as such by the wax on its fork, black before rain, yellowish afterwards. (ibid.: 122; cf. Dawson 2002)

Her long-term interaction with the Noongahburrah helped her to form ideas and proffer conclusions about their societal ethics. One emphatic reversal of a conventional notion was: "In books about blacks, you always read of the subjection of the women, but I have seen henpecked black husbands."

She theorized on Euahlayi life, expounding that

there are two codes of morals, one for men and one for women. Old Testament morality for men, New Testament for women. The black men keep the inner mysteries of the Boorah, or initiation ceremonies, from the knowledge of women, but so do Masons keep their secrets. (Parker 2018 [1905]: 73)

As to the Aboriginal women carrying most of the baggage on march, naturally so: the men want their hands free to hunt en route or to be in readiness for enemies in a strange country.

These stereotypes, handed down as derogatory elements of aboriginal culture, have in the past prejudiced white Australians against Indigenous men for their attitudes toward the women. With a paucity of other sources for understanding Aboriginal women's experiences, the European colonizers more often wrote negatively about Aboriginal people, and women suffered the worst vilification, typically por-

trayed as downtrodden slaves of their men (Evans, Grimshaw, and
Standish 2003: 18). Parker's broad knowledge of the Euahlayi provided evidence to refute these ideas. Her empathy enabled her to
equate their culture with aspects of Western society.

Although this valuable ethnographic information has reached
readers through the lens of a colonial woman's observation and understanding, it emanated from the generosity, particularly of the
Noongahburrah women, and because of Parker's close relationship
with them.

"Phratries, Totems, and Subtotems"

Parker's discussion of the complicated intratribal relationships extends
over a long chapter of *The Euahlayi Tribe*. Her work contributed to
the paramount anthropological debate on totemism and Australian
social organization. These social connections were still relevant and
practiced because, despite the push of colonization, the Noongahburrah continued to live in their tight-knit family groups, in coexistence
with the Parkers' pastoral endeavors. Enabled by the Noongahburrah,
who patiently informed and assisted her, Parker recorded in dense detail the plethora of names and meanings. This chapter bears witness to
her long-term engagement with her Indigenous informants, her acute
ear for recording their words, and her astute reasoning, the results of
which are produced in a clear, compartmentalized way.

According to Parker, the Euahlayi tribe was divided into four
"phratries," or "matrimonial classes"—derived through the maternal
line of descent—and further subdivided by their totems and subtotems. Parker explains the origins of these subdivisions and proceeds
to set out and decipher the complex marriage relationships. With due
reason, she refers to them as the "marriage law puzzles" (Parker 2018
[1905]: 37). Her contribution in recording these details is particularly
pertinent because she had learned that "in most Australian tribes the
meanings of the names of phratries are lost," and, in the case of the
neighboring Kamilaroi (the large Gamilaraay Indigenous group),
some phratries were of "unknown significance" (ibid.: 26). The no-
menclatures of the totem system ("the great Dhe") and its associated
intratribal relationships cover eight explanatory pages (ibid.: 30–37).

Parker's explication included idiosyncratic details, such as: "A
propos of names, a child is never called at night by the same name
as in the daytime, lest the 'devils' hear it and entice him away"; or
"Names are made for the newly born according to circumstances; a

girl born under a Dheal tree, for example, was called Dheala" (ibid.: 28). Connection to country was intrinsically maintained by the attribution of the place of birth in one of the baby's names (ibid.: 27; Evans, Grimshaw, and Standish 2003: 16).

Joining the network of contributors on debates about Aborigines, Parker corresponded with Howitt, particularly on marriage laws, referencing Howitt's findings on the Kamilaroi.[7] She also contributed information about the "yunbeai or animal familiar of the individual," observing that "the yunbeai has hitherto been scarcely remarked on among Australian tribes" and is perhaps "almost non-existent" in Australia, exceptions being—apart from the Euahlayi—the Wotjobaluk in Victoria, the Yaraikkanna (Yadhaykenu) of Cape York, and possibly groups from the western side of the Gulf of Carpentaria. Her humanistic taste for universal quotations, but surely also her awareness of the scholarly discussion on the subject of (allegedly totemic) guardian spirits—Frazer's "individual totems" (1887)—prompted her to include a reference to spiritual concepts from other continents. Her illustrations were anthropologically well-known at the time, namely the "Native American Manitu," the "Bush Soul" of West Africa, the "Nagual" belief in South America, and the "Nyarong" of Borneo (Parker 2018 [1905]: 41). The references to the Australian tribes are from an article by British anthropologist Northcote W. Thomas (1868–1936) (Thomas 1904). As Lang included non-Australian examples in his *The Secret of the Totem* (Lang 1905: 206), which was also published in 1905, there was probably an exchange between him and Parker on this matter.

Her respect for the Noongahburrah is particularly striking in this part of her ethnological study. She acknowledges Aboriginal expertise, disputing "savants [who] question the intellectual ability" (Parker 2018 [1905]: 26) of Indigenous Australians and declaring that

> [Aborigines] were early scientists in some of their ideas, being before Darwin in the evolution theory, only theirs was a kind of evolution aided by Byamee. I dare say, though, the missing link is somewhere in the legends. . . . One old man here was quite the Ibsen with his ghastly version of heredity. (ibid.: 39)

Anthropological Reputation: The Bumpy Road to Recognition

Julie Evans has called Parker's "reputation as a leader in the field of early ethnographic practice in Australia . . . far from clear-cut," despite her work continuing to attract critical attention for well over a century (Evans 2011: 18). Ambivalence toward the significance of her work was at play from her first editions. Because the publishing firm of David Nutt was interested in the popular trend of folklore or fairy tales, it published her first books within those genres, marketing them for children. Library catalogues continue to classify them as "For children," "Aboriginal folk-lore," or "Adventure stories." The addition to her *Legendary Tales* title of "Folk-lore of the Noongah-burrahs as told to the Piccaninnies" is thought to have been the publisher's initiative.

Having been identified as a female may have posed two problems to the growth of her reputation. The addition of the title "Mrs." to Parker's early publications exposed her identity as a woman at a time when men were beginning to assert their dominance in the developing science of anthropology. Citing Lynn Barber (Barber 1980: 125), Erica Izett notes that "women were not *expected* to achieve anything. Once their interest verged on real intellectual application it became 'fatiguing' and 'unhealthy'" (Izett 2014: 338). During the first half of the twentieth century, the bias of male researchers, talking mostly to Indigenous men, had failed to identify the cultural and religious depth of knowledge held by Aboriginal women (Barwick, Mace, and Stannage 1979: 179). Parker's contribution to the field was therefore largely excluded from the close network of Australia's emerging male anthropologists.

A contributing factor to her wavering reputation as an ethnographer may also have been due to a change in her name in 1905, the same year as the publication of *The Euahlayi Tribe*, when she became Mrs. Catherine Stow. Having been forced by drought and debt to leave Bangate in 1901, Langloh Parker died in 1903. In 1905 Katie married Percy Randolph Stow and left the outback to live an active but genteel life in the Adelaide suburb of Glenelg.

Another contributing factor, at least in Australia, may well have been white Australians' ignorance or indifference that relegated Parker's writing on Aboriginal people to one of unimportance. Dismissed as a "dying race" and viewed in derogatory terms, Indigenous Australians did not fit into the self-confident nationalism that was part of the newly federated (in 1901) Australia. When Parker mentioned to a friend that she proposed to write up the legends of the Noongahburrah, the response was: "But have the blacks any legends?" She adds that this showed that "people may live in a country, and yet know little of the aboriginal inhabitants" (Parker 1998 [1896]: ix).

Parker, however, continued to attract some recognition. Martin Thomas, the biographer of R. H. Mathews, her contemporary, writes that Mathews "read [*Australian Legendary Tales*] closely, and it probably influenced his decision to research and publish on this aspect of Aboriginal culture." In a footnote to a legend that Mathews published in the journal *Science of Man* (1898) as "The Hereafter," he expresses his "appreciation of the labours of Mrs. K. L. Parker" and states that she "deserves the thanks [for her collection and publication of these legends] of all who are interested in the folklore of the Australian aborigines." He affirmed that, "in its day, it was the most substantial book on Australian mythology" (Thomas 2007: 151, 131, 127; Mathews 1898: 143).

Like Parker, Mathews had "little or no formal training in anthropology" but was one of the "enthusiasts" who recorded aboriginal culture. Widely published, he had a distinguished career, and his *Australian Dictionary of Biography* entry acknowledges him as "anthropologist" (McBryde 1974). Catherine Stow's (Katie Langloh Parker) entry, from 1990, nominates her staidly merely as a "collector of Aboriginal legends" (Muir 1990).[8] Trivialized or discounted by most reviewers at the time of publication, *Australian Legendary Tales* had been extolled in the *Australasian Anthropological Journal* as "excellent work" and of "so admirable a quality that it is certain not only to attract considerable notice in England, and Australia at the present, but it is also likely to take a permanent place in the literature relating to the Australian blacks, which will be read by the future students who are studying the legends of the tribes."[9]

In his introduction to *The Euahlayi Tribe*, Lang happily acknowledged Parker, equating her work with those of Howitt, Spencer and Gillen, and Mathews. He recognized her credentials and contribution, writing that

> Mrs. Parker treats of a tribe which, hitherto, has hardly been mentioned by anthropologists, and she has had unexampled opportunities of study. It is hardly possible for a scientific male observer to be intimately familiar with the women and children of a savage tribe. Mrs. Parker, on the other hand, has had, as regards the women and children of the Euahlayi, [many] advantages. (Parker 2018 [1905]: 1)

Lang applauded Parker as a "close scientific observer" (ibid.) and contended that her work had shown that the Noongahburrahs' customary laws, ceremonials, and beliefs are "rich in variety" (ibid.: 3). He had read *The Euahlayi Tribe* in manuscript form, and his regard for her work is evident in the incorporation of her findings on the Euahlayi *yunbeai* and the Noongahburrahs' beliefs of reincarnation into his book *The Secret of the Totem* (Lang 1905: 19n3; 207n4).

Northcote W. Thomas also wrote favorably that

> both for the anthropologist who wants well-sifted and trustworthy mate-
> rial, and for the ordinary reader . . . this is a most useful book. In fact . . .
> it may . . . stand entirely alone. There is no other work on the Australians
> which gives anything like so good a general view: it is clear of superfluous
> technicalities, eminently readable, and written with so much sympathy
> that we cease to be surprised at the success of the writer in getting at such
> secret matters as male initiation ceremonies and beliefs about Byamee,
> all of which are strictly forbidden lore to the Euahlayi woman. (Thomas
> 1906a: 610)

His review in *Man* extols her book for offering details of "fundamental importance" and for its scope and depth of analysis on the "burning anthropological questions" (Thomas 1906b: 42–43).

The London *Athenaeum* similarly applauded *The Euahlayi Tribe*
as offering "first-hand evidence of the best kind" and found the
book—"full of material for discussion on [many] abstruse points"—
to be a "substantial contribution to our knowledge of the Australian
aborigines."[10]

Parker's standing in international terms is seen in a 1907 letter
from Robert Mathews to folklorist and anthropologist Edwin Sidney Hartland (1848–1927). Mathews explained a brutal review of
his own work by N. W. Thomas to the fact that it had been overlooked in favor of Baldwin Spencer, Alfred Howitt, and Katie
Langloh Parker. Here she takes her place alongside acknowledged
anthropologists of the time and supersedes Mathews in anthropological reputation. The following year, the German anthropologist
Moritz von Leonhardi (1856–1910) cited her findings in discussion
with Mathews (cit. in Thomas 2007: 246). Prior to his deprecation of
ethnographers who were not academically trained, Malinowski also
referred extensively to Parker in *The Family among the Australian
Aborigines* (1913), particularly in respect to Euahlayi marriage and
betrothal.

In Sydney, in 1912, *The Euahlayi Tribe* was assessed in the magazine *The Lone Hand* as part of a series of articles on prominent
Australian women. The author, Ann Cornstalk, wrote in somewhat
restrained terms that Parker brought to her task "affection and com-
prehension" and that she found in the people "poetic feeling, religious conception and a definite ethical code." She added that Parker's
"love of the aborigines and her sympathy with them goes deep";
she had "quick perceptive powers [and] a keen, though kindly, wit"
(Cornstalk 1912: xxxvi, xxxviii).

However, recognition of Parker's work, particularly in later years, was patchy. Robert Lowie (1883–1957) had referred to her "unimpeachable testimony" on the Euahlayi's "high-god" Byamee, in his dissertation on magic in primitive religions (Lowie 1925 [1924]: 145–46). Yet her contribution to anthropological knowledge in her intricate unpicking of the totem system could be overlooked in scholarly discussion. It is not to Frazer's credit that he ignored Parker's monograph—and the Euahlayi—in his quite exhaustive *summa totemica* (Rosa 2003: 231), the four-volumed *Totemism and Exogamy* (1910). When Durkheim argued his thesis on the evidence of totemism in Australia, he neglected Parker's chapter on "Relationships and Totems," restricting himself "in the main [to] the Arunta." In reporting on Durkheim's work, E. E. Evans-Pritchard (1902–73) also failed to reference Parker's contribution (Evans-Pritchard 1965: 66). Durkheim had nevertheless accepted and adopted her expression of the individual totem of the Euahlayi as "Yunbeai," paraphrasing her description of it as "the alter ego of the individual" (Parker 2018 [1905]: 39; Durkheim 1976 [1912]: 279).

Parker's reputation faded, although her *Australian Legendary Tales* was republished many times, including in 1897, 1953, 1955, 1966, 1969, 1973, 1998, and 2017. It had been produced for readers in Russia (1965), China (1986), Japan and Italy (1996), and India (2009). *More Australian Legendary Tales* (1898 and 1973) appeared in a combined "Legendary Tales" book in 1978 and in adapted selections by various authors in 1970, 1975, and 1993. Parker had continued to publish traditional stories: *My Best Boy and My Boy-in-Law and, Bobbity, a Bush Baby* (1901) and *The Walkabouts of Wur-Run-Nah* (1918). Her next collection, *Woggheeguy: Australian Aboriginal Legends*, did not appear until 1930.

This hiatus in her publishing career may have been a contributing factor to a loss of interest in her work. In 1965, Evans-Pritchard had also suggested that theories on religious beliefs and practices of primitive man were "as dead as mutton" for anthropologists and had ceased to occupy "men's minds" as they had in the late nineteenth and early twentieth centuries (Evans-Pritchard 1965: 100). Or the loss of interest in her work may have been due, from the 1960s onward, to the "slow awakening of historians' interest in Aborigines and ... anthropologists' tendency not to consider the historical dynamics of non-Western societies" (Rowse 2007).

Howitt, and Spencer and Gillen, however, have remained well-known names in anthropological history. A. R. Radcliffe-Brown (1881–1955), a "theoretician rather than a field worker" and described, along with Malinowski, as a founder of social anthropology, has maintained his reputation and was appointed foundation professor of anthropology at the University of Cape Town, South Africa, in 1921 (Hogbin 1988). Martin Thomas recently resurrected the work of R. H. Mathews (Thomas 2011).

As a woman in an increasingly male domain, Parker was self-deprecating. In 1930, on the publication of her Aboriginal tale collection *Woggheeguy*, she wrote:

> I need hardly explain that I had no scientific education, nor preparation for research, beyond desultory reading about primitive peoples and an intense interest in the genesis of races and their original mentality. Full of that interest I seized the time and opportunity of over twenty years' residence in juxtaposition to some of the finest aboriginal tribes in Australia to study them on the spot in an amateur way. And in all diffidence I think I may claim that I gained their confidence, for I appreciated them at their true value, nothing helping me better to understand them than their "Woggheeguy" [tales], in transcribing which I have always aimed at retaining their spirit. (Parker 1930: viii)

The following year, philosopher, sociologist, and anthropologist Lucien Lévy-Bruhl (1857–1939) was to include and acknowledge Parker's work in his *Primitives and the Supernatural* (Lévy-Bruhl 1936 [1931]).

After a long gap in interest, Marcie Muir's *My Bush Book: K. Langloh Parker's 1890s Story of Outback Station Life* (1982) catapulted Parker's writing into the consciousness of the Australian public. The author's husband, a bookseller and devoted "bookman," had purchased Parker's papers in 1940 and urged Marcie to write her biography. *My Bush Book* includes the release of Katie's own autobiographical work: "My Bush Book, Based on the notebooks of an old-time squatter's wife, 1879–1901, by K. Langloh Parker" (Parker, unpublished manuscript, in Muir 1982: 45–141).

In 1988 writer and historian Patricia Clarke helped to resurrect Parker's reputation as an early anthropologist, stating that she "wrote the first sympathetic and substantial account of Aboriginal legends and culture available to white Australians. At the time other writers were portraying Aborigines as barely human or as humorous characters of low intelligence. Where others observed without understanding, K. Langloh Parker listened to and recorded the legends of the Noongahburrah tribe whose language she learned while living in the far north of New South Wales" (Clarke 1988: 133).

In the last twenty years, scholarly research has revived Parker's reputation in academia. In 1998 Carey wrote that "Aboriginal legendary tales have been one of the most significant ways in which Aboriginality has been constructed in Australia" and that "Parker's importance as a source for popular notions of Aboriginality is difficult to overemphasize" (Carey 1998: 200, 201). Mary-Anne Gale refers to Parker's work as "seminal" and "prolific," adding that "one cannot undertake a study of the published Dreaming narratives of Australia's Indigenous peoples without paying considerable attention to the works and influences of Katie Langloh Parker" (Gale 2000: 75, 76). Serena Fredrick also acknowledged her contribution to ethnoastronomy through the legends she recorded from Noongahburrah knowledge, including those found in *The Euahlayi Tribe* chapter, "Something about Stars and Legends" (Fredrick 2008: 22).

Anthropologist Ian Keen's *Aboriginal Economy and Society* (2004) leaned strongly on Parker's work, particularly for his comparative analyses on indigenous belief and doctrines, social organization and mobility, the role of ancestral law, initiation ceremonies and power relations in social governance, and the economic factors in the control and organization of production (Keen 2004: 220–23; 112–14; 253–55; 283–85).

Nevertheless, there may yet be mountains to climb. In his 2014 *The Invention of God in Indigenous Societies*, James Cox cites Lang as a "chief player in discussions about the universal High God" and as "pivotal in advocating for the position that belief in a monotheistic Supreme Being is universal." This seems to imply that theory or Western ideology, more than ethnography, was responsible for the alleged invention. As Parker's significant contribution to the subject is overlooked (Cox 2014: 21), one may ask if the spotlight of late nineteenth- and early twentieth-century armchair anthropologists, such as Lang—replacing the ethnological results of fieldworkers such as Parker—is not being replicated in our century.

Conclusion

Parker was innovative in her quest to understand and value the importance of the legends and culture of Indigenous Australians and to present a "sympathetic and substantial account," available to white Australians. Her respect for the Euahlayi, at a time when the majority of European Australians disregarded Aboriginal people or viewed them with derision, has left a legacy that restores to Indigenous Australians their rightful strength and humanity. Her vital contributions to anthropological knowledge should place her in the annals of a discipline to which she deservedly belongs.

With her precise and idiosyncratic depictions of individuals, with their specific skills, she smashes stereotypical opinions about Indigenous Australians: not all Aborigines are good trackers or good hunters or expert boomerang throwers with exceptional eyesight. By portraying their intricate games and entertainments and their multiple riddles, often acted out in comic pantomime, she uncovers the depth of aboriginal intelligence and their cultural and artistic appreciation (Parker 2018 [1905]: 139). Her detailed exposition of *corroborees*— the chief form of entertainment—was that they were descriptive, narrative or ritualistic, and of great variety. Insight into the stage-craft through the devising of the "props" (theatrical property), particularly when the *corroboree* reconstructed a historical event, offers the reader a deeper level of analysis than could be achieved by mere reference to or a general description of a *corroboree* as a tribal dance. Parker posits that "the [Aborigines] are great patrons of art, and encourage native talent in the most praiseworthy way." Furthermore, elevating indigenous artistic expression to the "opera, ballet, and the rest" of Western entertainment, she calls those that create "new songs or corroborees" "poets and playwrights" (ibid.: 137, 136, 138).

An appreciation of the depth of Parker's recorded indigenous knowledge should not be assuaged by the style of her commentary. Often descriptive, with a smooth narrative flow, it enables the reader to visualize the vitality and beauty of the country and to situate the people within it. Her erudite allusions to classical and European literary figures, artists, or contemporary popular identities take her commentary to a deeper level of exposition and give the reader a rich source of comparison. The confidence with which she inserts into her narrative the occasional droll aside or a quirky mode of expression, when reporting a certain custom or belief, denotes her close understanding of the Euahlayi and reflects her empathy and understanding, not opprobrium. Lang summed up her representation and her attitude when he ended his introductory remarks to *The Euahlayi Tribe* with the following comment: "The Euahlayi are a sympathetic people, and have found a sympathetic chronicler" (ibid.: 16).

Parker brought detailed observations and perceptive understandings to the field of scientific ethnology. Her long-term access to her cultural experts surpassed some of her male contemporaries. Not confining her analyses to the Euahlayi alone, her incorporation of references to other Indigenous groups extends the scope and depth of her contributions. Eschewing the role of detached observer that later ethnography seemed to expect, she was able to work in partnership with the Indigenous women, through a close relationship and an apparent reciprocal trust, to record a unique source of female knowledge. Her interest and involvement in current anthropological thought, evidenced by her inclusion of the work of other researchers, set her firmly within the expanding discipline of anthropology.

As Antonella Riem Natale observed: "One needs to be aware of many differences and nuances in meaning when handling myths, words, ideas, concepts, stories belonging to a different culture." She added that, "on the other hand[,] it would be wrong to follow the idea that certain subjects can be treated, read, analysed only by those who 'belong' to that culture" (Riem Natale 2012: 113). Katie Langloh Parker embraced these issues with sensitivity and sympathy. Her ethnographic study, incorporating the culture, beliefs, and customary laws and practices of Australian Aborigines, has provided an invaluable source of saved indigenous knowledge that warrants due recognition and acknowledgment as crucial contributions to the history of anthropology.

Acknowledgments

I thank Helen Gardner and Amanda Lourie for information on A. W. Howitt's Papers; Rebecca Bateman, the National Library of Australia's Indigenous cultural reader; Kerry Willis, Helga Griffin, Martin Thomas, and Rosemary Jennings for insightful readings. And I extend my warm regards and thanks to Ted Fields Jr., Uallaroi/Yuwaalayaay Ngungaburra Elder, for permission to publish cultural images.

Barbara Chambers Dawson is a historian at the Australian National University, Canberra. She has written widely on Australian colonial history, specializing particularly in the relationships between Indigenous and settler women. Her publications in this field include *In the Eye of the Beholder: What Six Nineteenth-Century Women Tell Us about Indigenous Authority and Identity* (ANU Press, 2014); "Colonial Women in the *Australian Dictionary of Biography*" (2012); "Four Intrepid Scotswomen: Travellers to the Australian Colonies and their Representations of Aborigines," *History Scotland Journal*

9(4) (July/August 2009); and "Sisters under the Skin? Friendship: Crossing the Racial Gulf" in *Crossings* 7(3), Australian Studies Centre, University of Queensland (December 2002). For many years she was researcher and research editor for the *Australian Dictionary of Biography*, National Centre of Biography, Australian National University, Canberra.

Notes

1. *Morning Bulletin*, Rockhampton, Queensland, 24 August 1903, p. 5.
2. If Parker knew of the 1859 Hospital Creek massacre, in which about four hundred Aboriginal men, women, and children were shot not far from Bangate, she did not refer to it. The Noongahburrah would have been well aware of it, and their kind sympathy toward Parker, in that term of reference, outshone her own. The reasons given for the retributive attack are inconclusive.
3. In 2006 a Nhunggabarra man, Tex Skuthorpe, mooted that "Baayami" was never the Aboriginal equivalent of the Christian God, the idea having been "distorted by European 'interpretations'" (Sveiby and Skuthorpe 2006: 3).
4. Citing Aubrey Beardsley (1872–98), an Art Nouveau illustrator.
5. Parker equated "Numbardee, the first woman" in Noongahburrah legend, to the Judeo-Christian "Eve," but she did so through a biblical reference by the poet John Milton (1608–74); this attribution is probably no more than a linguistic device, similar to her other numerous literary associations (Parker 2018 [1905]: 97).
6. Durkheim added Parker's findings to those of Spencer and Gillen, Robert H. Mathews (1841–1918), Carl Strehlow (1871–1922), and Robert Brough Smyth (1830–89), who was the secretary of the Board for the Protection of Aborigines in 1860 and who wrote *The Aborigines of Victoria* (1876).
7. Papers of A. W. Howitt, MS 9356, box 1050 2(b), Australian Manuscripts Collection, State Library Victoria, referring to Howitt's "The Kamilaroi Marriage Law." *Science of Man*, 1902, The Royal Anthropological Society of Australasia, Sydney, vol. 5, no. 3, 46–47.
8. Parker had published two ethnographic articles in the *Australasian Anthropological Journal* containing information not covered in her book: "Gleanings of Black Folks' Medical Lore" (1897a) and "The Medicine and Witchcraft of the Blacks of Australia" (1898b).
9. *Australasian Anthropological Journal*, Anthropological Society of Australasia, Sydney, vol. 1, no. 5, 30 April 1897, 103.
10. *The Athenaeum: Journal of English and Foreign Literature, Science, the Fine Arts, Music and the Drama*, London, no. 4103, 16 June 1906, p. 735.

References

Archival Material

Papers of A. W. Howitt. Melbourne: Australian Manuscripts Collection, State Library Victoria, MS 9356, Box 1050 2(b).
Papers of Marcie Muir relating to Katie Langloh Parker, approximately 1838–2000. Canberra: National Library of Australia, MS 10182.

Published Sources

Barber, Lynn. 1980. *The Heyday of Natural History, 1820–1870*. London: Cape.
Barwick, Diane, Michael Mace, and Tom Stannage, eds. 1979. *Handbook for Aboriginal and Islander History*. Canberra: Aboriginal History.
Brough Smyth, Robert. 1876. *The Aborigines of Victoria*. Melbourne: J. Ferres.
Carey, Hilary M. 1998. "'The Land of Byamee': K. Langloh Parker, David Unaipon, and Popular Aboriginality in the Assimilation Era." *Journal of Religious History* 22(2): 200–18.
Clarke, Patricia. 1988. *Pen Portraits, Women Writers and Journalists in Nineteenth-Century Australia*. New York: Allen & Unwin.
Cornstalk, Ann. 1912. "Representative Women of Australasia." In *The Lone Hand: The National Australian Monthly Magazine* 12(68): xxxvi, xxxviii. Sydney: William Macleod for *The Bulletin*, 2 December.
Cox, James. 2014. *The Invention of God in Indigenous Societies*. London: Routledge.
Dawson, Barbara Chambers. 2002. "Sisters under the Skin? Friendship: Crossing the Racial Gulf." *Crossings* 7(3): 1–4. Australian Studies Centre, University of Queensland, December 2002. E-journal: http://pandora.nla.gov.au/tep/13231
———. 2012. "Colonial Women in the Australian Dictionary of Biography." *Australian Dictionary of Biography*, National Centre of Biography, Australian National University, 30 August. Retrieved 24 July 2019 from https://adb.anu.edu.au/essay/4/text26712.
———. 2014. *In the Eye of the Beholder: What Six Nineteenth-Century Women Tell Us about Indigenous Authority and Identity*. Canberra: ANU Press.
Durkheim, Émile. 1976 [1912]. *The Elementary Forms of the Religious Life*. 2nd ed. London: George Allen & Unwin.
Evans, Julie. 2011. "Katie Langloh Parker and the Beginnings of Ethnography in Australia." In *Founders, Firsts and Feminists: Women Leaders in Twentieth-Century Australia*, edited by Fiona Davis, Nell Musgrave, and Judith Smart, 13–26. Melbourne: University of Melbourne, eScholarship Research Centre.

Evans, Julie, Patricia Grimshaw, and Ann Standish. 2003. "Caring for Country: Yuwalaraay Women and Attachments to Land on an Australian Colonial Frontier." *Journal of Women's History* 14(4): 15–37. Bloomington: Indiana University Press.

Evans-Pritchard, Edward Evan. 1965. *Theories of Primitive Religion.* Oxford: Clarendon Press.

Frazer, James George. 1887. *Totemism.* Edinburgh: A. & C. Black.

——. 1910. *Totemism and Exogamy. A Treatise on Certain Early Forms of Superstition and Society.* 4 vols. London: Macmillan & Co.

Fredrick, Serena. 2008. "The Sky of Knowledge: A Study of the Ethnoastronomy of the Aboriginal People of Australia." MPhil thesis, Department of Archaeology and Ancient History, University of Leicester, UK.

Gale, Marie-Anne. 2000. "Poor Bugger Whitefella Got No Dreaming: The Representation and Appropriation of Published Dreaming Narratives with Special Reference to David Unaipon's Writings." PhD thesis, Linguistics and English, Faculty of Humanities and Social Sciences, Adelaide University.

Grimshaw, Patricia 1995. "Female Lives and the Tradition of Nation-Making." *Voices: The Quarterly Journal of the National Library of Australia* 5(3): 30–44.

Hogbin, Ian. 1988. "Radcliffe-Brown, Alfred Reginald (1881–1955)." *Australian Dictionary of Biography*, National Centre of Biography, Australian National University. Retrieved 10 September 2019 from http://adb .anu.edu.au/biography/radcliffe-brown-alfred-reginald-8146/text14233.

Howitt, Alfred William. 1902. "The Kamilaroi Marriage Law." *Science of Man and Journal of the Royal Anthropological Society of Australasia* 5(2): 46–47.

——. 1996 [1904]. *The Native Tribes of South-East Australia*, facsimile ed. Canberra: Aboriginal Studies Press for the Australian Institute of Aboriginal and Torres Strait Islander Studies (AIATSIS).

Izett, Erica Kaye. 2014. "Breaking New Ground: Early Australian Ethnology in Colonial Women's Writing." PhD thesis, Faculty of Architecture, Landscape and Visual Arts, University of Western Australia.

James, Edwin Oliver. 1917. *Primitive Ritual and Belief: An Anthropological Essay.* London: Methuen.

Jenkin, G. K. 1988. "Newland, Simpson (Sim) (1835–1925)." *Australian Dictionary of Biography*, National Centre of Biography, Australian National University. Retrieved 10 September 2019 from http://adb.anu.edu.au/ biography/newland-simpson-sim-7828/text13591.

Keen, Ian. 2004. *Aboriginal Economy and Society: Australia at the Threshold of Colonisation.* Melbourne: Oxford University Press.

Lang, Andrew. 1898. *The Making of Religion.* London: Longmans, Green, and Co.

——. 1905. *The Secret of the Totem.* London: Longmans, Green, and Co.

——. 2018 [1905]. "Introduction." In Katie Langloh Parker, *The Euahlayi Tribe: A Study of Aboriginal Life in Australia*, 1–16. London: Archibald Constable.

Lévy-Bruhl, Lucien. 1936 [1931]. *Primitives and the Supernatural.* London: George Allen & Unwin. (First edition: *Le Surnaturel et la nature dans la mentalité primitive.* Paris: PUF.)

Lowie, Robert Harry. 1925 [1924]. *Primitive Religion.* London: Routledge.

Malinowski, Bronisław. 1913. *The Family among the Australian Aborigines: A Sociological Study.* London: Hodder & Stroughton for the University of London Press.

———. 1972 [1922]. *Argonauts of the Western Pacific.* 8th impression. London: Routledge & Kegan Paul.

Mathews, Robert Hamilton. 1898. "Folklore of the Australian Blacks." *Science of Man and Australasian Anthropological Journal* 1(6): 142–43.

McBryde, Isabel. 1974. "Mathews, Robert Hamilton (1841–1918)." *Australian Dictionary of Biography*, National Centre of Biography, Australian National University. Retrieved 10 September 2019 from http://adb.anu.edu.au/biography/mathews-robert-hamilton-4169/text6693.

Muir, Marcie. 1982. *My Bush Book: K. Langloh Parker's 1890s Story of Outback Station Life, with Background and Biography.* Adelaide: Rigby.

———. 1990. "Stow, Catherine Eliza (Katie) (1856–1940)." *Australian Dictionary of Biography*, National Centre of Biography, Australian National University. Retrieved 24 July 2019 from http://adb.anu.edu.au/biography/stow-catherine-eliza-katie-8691/text15205.

Newland, Simpson. 1900. *Blood Tracks of the Bush.* London: Gay & Bird.

Parker, Katie Langloh. 1896. *Australian Legendary Tales: Folk-lore of the Noongahburrahs as Told to the Piccaninnies.* London: David Nutt/Melbourne: Melville, Mullen and Slade.

———. 1998 [1896]. *Australian Legendary Tales.* Middlesex: Senate, Tiger Books International.

———. 1897a. "The Folk-Lore of the Noongahburrahs." *Australasian Anthropological Journal* 1(5): 103–4.

———. 1897b. "Gleanings of Black Folks' Medical Lore." *Australasian Anthropological Journal* 1(6): 117–18.

———. 1898a. *More Australian Legendary Tales.* London: David Nutt/Melbourne: Melville, Mullen & Slade.

———. 1898b. "The Medicine and Witchcraft of the Blacks of Australia." *Science of Man and Australasian Anthropological Journal* [renamed title of *Australasian Anthropological Journal*] 1(1): 17–18.

———. 1899. "My Darkie Friends." *Sydney Mail*, 16 December, 1481–82.

———. 1901. *My Best Boy and My Boy-in-Law and, Bobbity, a Bush Baby.* Sydney: W. Dymock.

———. 1905. *The Euahlayi Tribe: A Study of Aboriginal Life in Australia.* London: Archibald Constable.

———. 1930. *Woggheeguy: Australian Aboriginal Legends.* Collected by Catherine Stow [Katie Langloh Parker]. Adelaide: F. W. Preece & Sons.

———. 1982. "My Bush Book, Based on the Notebooks of an Old-Time Squatter's Wife, 1879–1901." In M. Muir, *My Bush Book: K. Langloh Parker's 1890s Story of Outback Station Life, with Background and Biography Part Two*, 45–141. Adelaide: Rigby.

———. 2018 [1905]. *The Euahlayi Tribe: A Study of Aboriginal Life in Australia*. Indianapolis: Alpha Editions.

Riem Natale, Antonella. 2012. "The Pleiades and the Dreamtime: An Aboriginal Women's Story and Other Ancient World Traditions." *Coolabah*, no. 9, Observatori: Centre d'Estudis Australians, Australian Studies Centre, Universitate de Barcelona, 113–127.

Rosa, Frederico D. 2003. *L'Âge d'or du Totémisme: Histoire d'un Débat Anthropologique (1887–1929)*. Paris: CNRS Éditions, Maison des Sciences de l'Homme.

Rowse, Tim. 2007. "Barwick, Diane Elizabeth (1938–1986)." *Australian Dictionary of Biography*, National Centre of Biography, Australian National University. Retrieved 10 September 2019 from http://adb.anu.edu.au/biography/barwick-diane-elizabeth-76/text21837.

Spencer, Baldwin, and Francis James Gillen. 1938 [1899]. *The Native Tribes of Central Australia*. 2nd ed. London: Macmillan.

———. 1904. *The Northern Tribes of Central Australia*. London: Macmillan.

Spencer, Baldwin. 1914. *Native Tribes of the Northern Territory of Australia*. London: Macmillan.

Sveiby, Karl-Erik, and Tex Skuthorpe. 2006. *Treading Lightly: The Hidden Wisdom of the World's Oldest People*. Sydney: Allen & Unwin.

Thomas, Martin, ed. 2007. *Culture in Translation: The Anthropological Legacy of R. H. Mathews*. Canberra: ANU E Press and Aboriginal History Inc.

Thomas, Martin. 2011. *The Many Worlds of R. H. Mathews: In Search of an Australian Anthropologist*. Sydney: Allen & Unwin.

Thomas, Northcote Whitridge. 1904. "Further Remarks on Mr. Hill-Tout's Views on Totemism." *Man: A Monthly Record of Anthropological Science* 4(53): 82–85.

——— ["N.W.T."]. 1906a. "The Life of the Australian Blacks." *Nature: A Weekly Illustrated Journal of Science* 73(1904): 610–11.

——— ["N.W.T."]. 1906b. "The Euahlayi Tribe, a Study of Aboriginal Life in Australia." *Man* 27: 42–43.

3

Edward Westermarck, a Master Ethnographer, and His Monograph *Ritual and Belief in Morocco* (1926)

David Shankland

> Fieldwork so prolonged was never so wasted.
> —John Davis, *People of the Mediterranean: An Essay in Comparative Social Anthropology*, 1977

> No better field-work exists.
> —Bronisław Malinowski, "Anthropology of the Westernmost Orient," 1927

For a number of years, I have been considering Edward Alexander Westermarck (1862–1939) and his legacy. His brilliance is manifest in many ways: as a pioneer of modern kinship studies, as the founder of the anthropology of morality, as the teacher of Malinowski at the London School of Economics (LSE), and even as one of the first modern sociobiologists. Truly, then, a remarkable man. But the way I first came across him was through his ethnography, perhaps the part of his contribution that is most misunderstood today.

As I have elsewhere recounted (Shankland 2014), while an undergraduate in the 1980s I used the library of the Royal Anthropological Institute in London in order to write up the materials for my MA dissertation in social anthropology, for which I had conducted fieldwork in Morocco. I ordered from the stacks all the holdings on the ethnography of North Africa. Suddenly, I found myself looking with astonishment at Westermarck's *Marriage Ceremonies in Morocco* (1914). The detail it contained was unparalleled. I was immensely puzzled: I couldn't work out why this obviously very significant fieldworker had not played a greater role in our academic debates. My initial conclusion was that the idea that all ethnographic research that had preceded Malinowski was of poor quality evidently could not be true. I then turned my attention to Turkey, an area that was far away from Westermarck's. He remained in my mind, however, and it is with pleasure that I have in more recent times been able to turn back to him.

One of the great paradoxes of Westermarck is that, although he has been systematically overlooked in the way we understand the creation of modern anthropological thought, he did not suffer from lack of recognition in his own lifetime. He was widely published, reviewed, and cited; offered teaching positions; given senior posts; invited to lecture; and, through the award of the RAI's Rivers Medal (1926) and then its Huxley Medal (1937), acknowledged as having attained the peak of his profession. There are therefore at least two reasons to look at him and his ethnographic work again: to investigate why and when his writings were found unacceptable by the generation that followed him, and where, to our eyes today, in a more tolerant intellectual climate, we may find worth.

Career and Life

It may help initially to offer a recap of Edward Westermarck's career and his swift rise. Born in Finland into a native Swedish–speaking family in 1862, Westermarck was a conspicuously successful student. He used his time as a postgraduate at the University of Helsinki to develop the ideas that were later to be sketched out in more detail in *The History of Human Marriage* (1891), which by the fifth edition grew to become three thick volumes. By his own account (1929), Westermarck was drawn to studying overseas and, when looking to intensify his studies, deliberated as to whether to work with the British or the German traditions. Finding the work of James George Frazer (1854–1941) and Edward Burnett Tylor (1832–1917) more concrete, and attracted to the evolutionary theories of Charles Darwin (1809–82) and Alfred Russel Wallace (1823–1913), he obtained funds to come to London to study at the British Library where he continued his research.

The History of Human Marriage may be said to contain two main theses. The first is that when two persons are brought up in proximity with each other, they are disinclined to marry. This has been taken up by later generations of anthropologists, particularly evolutionary anthropologists, and continues to be debated. Though all of Westermarck's work is sensitive to the relation between human biology and culture, it is this theory for which he is sometimes known as the founder of sociobiology.

The second theory in *Human Marriage* is that there has never been a time when there has not been some form of human marriage, what we might call pair bonding today. One can see immediately the great force of this deceptively simple proposition. Once accepted, it means that anthropologists no longer needed to search for a transition whereby a hypothetical early promiscuity gave way to monogamy. It helps to crystalize modern comparative kinship studies because it becomes possible to look at the variations across human societies as to the way this bonding, now accepted as a constant, is achieved.

Westermark himself was fully aware of the significance this had for anthropology's theoretical relationship with the past, and throughout his life he spoke out strongly against the use of the kind of speculative quest for survivals for which there is no firm grounds. Sigmund Freud (1856–1939), for example, was dismissed by him in a further, late monograph, *Three Essays on Sex and Marriage* (1934), courteously but firmly:

> The facts that have been adduced in support of the supposed prehistoric events which Freud has attributed the inhibition of incest have thus in each case been found to be worthless as evidence. ... The role that the Oedipus complex plays in the psychology of the individual is in the first place to be decided by the neurologists; but the social facts underlying the supposition of its universality and the influence it is alleged to have exercised on the history of civilisation are matters that concern sociology. And objections raised by the latter cannot be ignored by those whose faith in Freud as a psycho-analyst has made them ready to swallow the unfounded sociological presumptions of his theory. (Westermarck 1934: 121–23)

The History of Human Marriage had the endorsement of Wallace, one of the founders of evolutionary theory, who writes most enthusiastically in the preface as to its great qualities, and the book was an immediate success. At the same time as he was deepening his acquaintance with London literary life, Westermarck quickly obtained a post at the University of Helsinki, eventually being made a full professor of moral philosophy there in 1906.

In London, Westermarck became friends with Martin White (1858–1928), a Scottish industrialist and member of Parliament, who was looking to expand his philanthropic work in the area of education. White founded two chairs in sociology at the LSE, and in 1907 Westermarck was appointed to the first of these, the other going to Leonard Hobhouse (1864–1929) (Husbands 2019). Westermarck had by now turned his hand to a more philosophical project, which resulted in *The Origin and Development of the Moral Ideas*, published in two volumes in 1906–8. In form, it emulates the typical major monograph of its time, in that it collates a massive amount of reading under specific and apparently disparate headings.

Seeing so many apparently diverse chapters, each with a plethora of detail, juxtaposed makes it difficult for a reader today to devise Westermarck's intent in putting the volumes together. However, in the long introductory passages of some two hundred pages, Westermarck did sketch out his underlying theory in detail, which is based on a form of interactionalism. Simply put, he regarded human interaction as being mediated through the collective norms of the cultures where a person lives and ethics as being shaped out of the negative or positive shared emotional reactions to which the collective interaction between them gives rise. From the causal point of view, his approach saw emotions as being primary, which when shared give rise to ethical judgments. For example, stealing gives rise to anger, which is then mediated through a collective ethical system that condemns theft and eventually is codified in religious or legal norms. Having sketched his approach, further detailed discussion follows, of homicide, slavery, property, truth, honor, altruism, suicide, diet, marriage, and celibacy, and how these are treated in different cultures.

To take a further example, this time from our own era: I have been struck as to how applicable Westermarck's ideas are to the 2020–21 pandemic; mask wearing was quickly turned into a moral issue, not simply a practical one. First, the epidemic struck. Then, in many parts of the world, lockdown was ordered and mask wearing declared compulsory, instituting a new collective rule. However, very soon, those persons, particularly public figures, who did not wear a mask were declared morally at fault, unable to appreciate the necessity of obeying the rules and often shamed or reprimanded. In this case, the shame is encouraged through the norms enacted by legislation, but it is explicitly sustained and evoked by emotions, the collectivized fear in the first place of the illness running out of control.

One of the most interesting aspects of Westermarck's thesis is the extent to which it relies on mutual empathy. It implies that only if individuals are highly sensitive to the mutual praise or approbation of their interlocutors will a moral code have any effect. Its roots, in this respect, lie in the Scottish Enlightenment and Adam Smith's (1723–90) *Theory of Moral Sentiments* (1759) (Stroup 1982b; Shankland 2018). Westermarck, however, is so far as I know entirely original in the way he has applied this to a mass of ethnographic material in a relativist way.

Westermarck was homosexual (Lyons and Lyons 2003). He himself never mentions this in his academic work, nor does he give homosexuality prominence in his discussions over any other human behavior. Nevertheless, I do think that it is at the root of his own searchings for the foundations of ethical and moral behavior. In his work he continually questions how collective expectations are coded in ethical expressions that serve to guide, or control, our conduct. The question he seems to be asking is, why should homosexual acts (or any other act for that matter) be regarded as unethical or immoral? His answer is in the emotive responses to which they give rise and the force they gain from their being judged within a collective ethical framework that permeates human interaction. It takes him to a form of relativism because it implies that there is no necessary essential universal moral code; rather, morals are rooted within differ-

Figure 3.1. *Westermarck in the field. Courtesy of Åbo Akademi University Library.*

ent cultures' perceptions of behavior and their complex, overlapping multiple responses to them.

Though expounded early on in his academic career, this philosophical position remained with Westermarck throughout his life. Realizing that the scissors and paste method provides a mass of ethnographic detail but can make an argument difficult to follow, he summed up his arguments in a monograph, *Ethical Relativity*, in 1932. He then expanded this analysis to a skeptical study of Christianity and its morals in his last monograph, *Christianity and Morals* (1939), written just before he died. Again, it is difficult not to see Westermarck's critical approach in this final monograph as being rooted in the way that he was unable to acknowledge his sexual orientation in his own milieu: nineteenth-century Sweden and early twentieth-century London. Indeed, in *Ethical Relativity* he not only commented on the way behavior is constrained but clearly believed that through understanding these constraints it is possible to overcome them (1932: 122). From this point of view, it would be possible to regard him as a kind of Henrik Ibsen (1828–1906) of the anthropological world, a seeker attempting to understand how constraints are embodied in our everyday lives and how they may be overcome.

Westermarck at the LSE

At the LSE, Westermarck had a reputation of being pleasant and affable (Montagu 1982). He ran a seminar on social institutions that was attended by Malinowski in 1910, and he very soon became his close friend and supporter. Much has been made of the apparently tempestuous way in which Malinowski created a new discipline. However, this image of an aggressive interloper does not fit in with at least this part of the record: on the contrary, the letters from the personnel files of Malinowski, Westermarck, and Charles Seligman (1873–1940) in the LSE show that both Westermarck and Seligman were strongly supportive of Malinowski. Indeed, Seligman even discretely paid for part of Malinowski's salary, something that is surely extremely unusual, and Westermarck joined forces with Seligman to support Malinowski to the LSE director as they were discussing his permanent appointment to the school (Shankland 2019).

Rifts did occur, it is true. Malinowski was openly hostile to hyperdiffusionist Grafton Elliot Smith (1871–1937), who was based at University College London (UCL). Seligman and Malinowski together asked William Beveridge (1879–1963), the director of the

LSE, not to go through with his idea to invite Radcliffe-Brown (1888–1951) to lecture while Malinowski was on leave. The conflict between Malinowski and Edward Evans-Pritchard (1902–73) is also well documented. On his side, Evans-Pritchard would make bitter, often caustic remarks. Malinowski appears to have reciprocated, even accusing him of appropriating his fieldwork (Morton 2007). Such rifts do not appear in the record, however, between Malinowski and Westermarck, or for that matter between Seligman and Westermarck. Their mutual warmth is borne out too in Michael Young's magisterial description of Malinowski's early life and arrival in London (2004).

Nevertheless, though happy in London, Westermarck clearly did not wish to separate from Finland completely. Inasmuch as he was politically engaged during his lifetime, it appears to be in the cause of Finland, its Swedish minority, and its intellectual life (Rantanen 2014). Early on in his career, he encouraged resistance against the Russian occupation of Finland (Shankland 2014: introduction). After he obtained his chair at Helsinki, he deepened his preoccupation with Finland by accepting an appointment as professor and rector of the University of Åbo, a Swedish-speaking university in the north of Sweden (Lagerspetz and Suolinna 2014).

A third significant commitment was his fieldwork. Early in his career Westermarck realized that fieldwork was necessary to become an anthropologist. Taking advantage of the very favorable terms of employment at Helsinki, he began research in North Africa already from 1898 onward. He continued these trips after he moved to the LSE, and even after his appointment at Åbo, meaning that he was very frequently in Morocco during the summer seasons, and eventually the Swedish consul in Tangier was able to let him take over his house there.

Westermarck seemed to have enjoyed his fieldwork and was fortunate to strike up a close friendship with a Berber man, Shereef 'Abd-es-Salam El-Baqqali, who helped him over many decades. Unusually for that time, however, Westermarck was extremely careful to acknowledge his great input, even eventually obtaining for him a major decoration from Finland.

> I have to thank my Moorish friend Shereef 'Abd-es-Salam El-Baqqali who has accompanied me on all my journeys in Morocco and given me invaluable assistance. I am happy to say that the president of the Republic of Finland has been pleased to confer on him knighthood of the order of "Finlands Vita Ros" as a reward for the services he has rendered me. (Westermarck 1926: vi)

He demonstrates his concern afresh in a private letter, this time to his parents early on during his fieldwork, written in 1899. Here, he is explaining to them that he has to break his stay in Morocco in order to support the cause of Finland, but he is concerned as to the safety of his assistant:

> Yesterday, I informed the Shereef of my decision. He received it with resignation and offered to send 1,000 men from his own tribe to help me. . . . He started to ponder how much money I was owing him and then announced that he wanted to use that to come to London with me. On considering the matter I found this suggestion quite satisfactory also from my point of view. I cannot be certain to find him still here when I come back. The fact that he had travelled with me without a single soldier, which was contrary to the pasha's orders, had made him most unpopular in the eyes of the latter. . . . I once received a telegram telling me that he was in danger of being put in jail. I telegraphed to the Russian ambassador who simply had the soldiers carted away who had been keeping an eye on his hiding place. . . . God only knows what would happen if he were left on his own. I have therefore decided to allow him to follow me to London. (translation by Mrs. Marjatta Bell; printed in full in Shankland 2014: 3–5)

These fieldwork trips often yielded very substantial articles in different journals, as well as his monograph on wedding ceremonies that so surprised me as a student, and a smaller but erudite work on proverbs and sayings with El-Baqqali, his assistant (*Wit and Wisdom in Morocco*, 1930). This extensive material is drawn together in a major, two-volume monograph titled *Ritual and Belief in Morocco*, which appeared in 1926, the year that Westermarck was awarded the RAI Rivers Medal.

The Reception of *Ritual and Belief in Morocco*

True to his teacher, Malinowski wrote a laudatory review of *Ritual and Belief in Morocco*, Westermarck's fieldwork magnum opus, in *Nature*:

> No better field-work exists . . . than that of Westermarck in Morocco. It was done with a greater expenditure of care and time than any other specialised anthropological research; it has brought to fruition Westermarck's comprehensive learning and special grasp of sociology; it revealed his exceptional linguistic talents and his ability to mix with people of other race and culture . . . (Malinowski 1927: 868)

The review continues along the same lines, with much fulsome praise, as well as remarking on various of its great strengths:

> The long chapter on the evil eye appeals no less to the antiquarian's imagination than to the interest of the sociologist. One of the oldest superstitions of the Mediterranean basin which still survives in the behaviour of civilised man, whether of Latin, Berber or Semitic race, is here described again with a fullness of detail and theoretical insight which defies comparison. A wealth of descriptive data, collected at first hand, is given, and then a comparative treatment of the problem, an analysis of the belief, and a number of interesting sidelights on its cultural influences. A description of the imprint of the evil eye upon decorative art, given with many interesting illustrations, will remain among the most illuminating contributions to comparative folk-lore. (ibid.)

Nevertheless, although Malinowski was so full of praise, is there perhaps also a sense that he was being a little dismissive? "Comparative folklore," "antiquarian's imagination" are very clearly nineteenth-century tropes, something that given Malinowski's great sensitivity to language he will hardly have inserted in the review unbeknowingly. Robert E. Park (1864–1944), in the *American Journal of Sociology*, was more explicit in his doubts, even if he, like Malinowski, was aware of the quality of the fieldwork:

> The author's method of procedure here, as elsewhere, has been to collect and classify his materials with respect to some more or less abstract category, with relatively little reference to temporal succession, geographical distribution, or relation to other traits of the prevailing cultural complex. The difficulty is that a classification which takes things out of their context inevitably tears apart things that belong together, and in doing so runs counter to the general principle that nothing human can be understood except in relation to the milieu in which it occurs. No one, I might add, has stated the principle better than Westermarck himself. On the other hand, what the author calls the "comparative method" does emphasize fundamental human traits, and by exhibiting the same motive in its varied cultural expressions does make intelligible and explicable what might otherwise appear unique and inexplicable. (Park 1927)

What might give rise to this uncertain response? *Ritual and Belief in Morocco* is a long work, as Westermarck was to favor when he wished to make a major statement. It is divided thematically into major chapters. Volume 1 covers *baraka* (which he translates as "holiness," and later writers often as "charisma"), its manifestations, and its sensitiveness; *jinn*, the ways of protecting oneself from them, and the origins of the belief in *jinns*; individual spirits; the evil eye; curses and oaths; and witchcraft. Volume 2 includes magic and dreams; rites whether associated with the religious, solar, or agricultural calendar; rites associated with the weather, with animals; childbirth; and death.

Though there is an astonishing wealth of detail, the ethnographic description is pitched most unusually at what we might call a middle level: Westermarck does not work at the level of abstraction that would make his work simply unacceptable—we do learn of the tribe and region from which he draws his remarks. Indeed, in the preface he identifies more than 140 places, tribes, or towns that he mentions specifically. But he does not link one cultural phenomenon with another, as was very quickly to become the hallmark of the British functionalist movement. In other words, where Malinowski would begin with magic, and then trace this in its interaction with technology, trade, sailing, myth, and kinship, each explained in a highly localized setting, Westermarck sticks resolutely to the subject at hand, whether it be saints, *baraka*, curses, magic, the evil eye, and so on, noting wherever he heard them discussed across the geographical extent of his trips throughout Morocco.

As he never—as Park remarked—explains the full, varied milieu in which these cultural phenomena are found, there is little relief for the reader, who is forced, like it or not, to follow the author inexorably through his exposition until the next chapter, when the process starts again. Though there are occasionally longer descriptions: the plethora of quotations are often limited to no more than a sentence or two. It is almost as if Westermarck, regarding the presentation style of Frazer's *The Golden Bough* (1890) as ideal, recreated it as a method of writing up fieldwork, transferring a method used to synthesize multiple written sources into the field. Indeed, this may be literally the case, as I strongly suspect that the way he worked was to compile card indexes of his different categories (e.g., *baraka*: animals with *baraka*, or food with *baraka*) from his notes or conversations that he could write up as sustained prose by stringing them together, just as Frazer did.

Be this as it may, his style has led to increasing bafflement by the generation that followed Malinowski, and then, as fieldwork—or rather highly concentrated community-based fieldwork—came to define the discipline, to Westermarck's effective banishment. The peak of his fame appears to coincide with the appearance of *Ritual and Belief in Morocco*, and already by the time of his Huxley lecture in 1936 he was aware of the way that the discipline was changing. By the time universities started up again in the postwar period of 1945–46, he was certainly no longer regarded as any kind of role model for younger scholars—indeed, quite the reverse. In his key work, *People of the Mediterranean*, which for a time achieved something like textbook status for undergraduates, John Davis (1938–2017) famously remarked that "fieldwork so prolonged was never so wasted" (1977: 1–2).

Today, almost one hundred years later and in a much more pluralistic intellectual environment, how might we reflect upon Westermarck's contribution? We can say immediately that those who specialize in Morocco have never been as dismissive as Davis, or at least not uniformly. There is clearly much to be used and learned from Westermarck's volumes (e.g., Herzfeld 1981), his writing is extremely accurate in detail, and he was emphatically not an armchair anthropologist. In fact, his 1926 monograph remains even today one of the most comprehensive works on what we might call vernacular Islamic religion.

Even leaving aside its undoubted great use as a reference point for subsequent anthropologists of the region, not least to check their understanding of a particular term or concept, there is I think a much more compelling reason to regard *Ritual and Belief* as a work of great importance for anthropology generally. There is a clear underlying message throughout Westermarck's text: his aim is to outline the way individuals in Morocco operate within a culture in which belief has a predominant role in guiding not just their relationship with God but also that with their fellow human beings: almost every conceivable interaction can be related to a supernatural impulse emanating from that interaction, whether it be sparked by malignity, danger, generosity, or chance transgression. This relates directly back to Westermarck's work on morality and ethics, in which he emphasized that morals are imbued within societal norms that function through the respective protagonists being able to empathize with each other, in either a positive or a negative way. In Westermarck's reading, culture and belief therefore become a constraining framework, one that is extremely difficult to escape if one is part of that society and wishes to function within it.

A further, perhaps obscure to our eyes today, contemporary review by Max Sylvius Handman in the *Southwestern Political and Social Science Quarterly* shows an understanding of this point:

> Having been led to the study of the Moroccans as a concrete instance in his general theory of the family, he now selects the same group for a concrete instance of his general theories concerning the origin and development of moral ideas. Ritual and belief are here studied not as quaint and curious lore, but as forms of social organization and methods of social control. The mechanism of spirits, the possession of the special gift, the

Figure 3.2. *Westermarck in midcareer. Courtesy of Åbo Akademi University Library.*

> Baraka, the prophylactic measures against the spirits, the function of the evil eye, the place of oaths, and the mechanism of witchcraft are studied as a consistent system of theory and practice which makes up the system of live and let live of this community. (Handman 1927: 310)

Appreciated as the detailed elucidation of a system of social control in which the religious, supernatural, linguistic, and symbolic elements of life interact with and reinforce each other, Westermarck's astonishing researches suddenly begin to make sense. We can also see much more clearly how they may have influenced other writers, most notably Evans-Pritchard. Much later, ironically, North Africa was once again to be the focus of an anthropological sociologist who came to influence a whole generation, one who also worked at a high level of generalization. Pierre Bourdieu's (1930–2002) development of the *habitus* clearly to my mind owes a great deal to Westermarck, whose work he certainly knew well.

Ritual and Belief in Morocco: Volume 1

Turning now to looking at these points in a little more detail, it is perhaps most helpful to examine the first volume of the set of two that makes up *Ritual and Belief in Morocco*. It opens with a discussion of *baraka*. The concept of *baraka* is not easy to translate. It approximates in some ways to the English word "holy," but it is wider than this. God—Allah—is all-powerful, capable of directly influencing the matters of those who live on earth. However, God's presence on earth may manifest itself, and become accessible, in different ways: it is this wider influence of God that is *baraka*. *Baraka* may diffuse through saints, the descendants of a saint, through anything they have touched; through their saliva, the earth where they are buried, or a horse they have mounted. *Baraka* may also be found in certain foodstuffs, such as wheat, or in certain trees or animals. It is found too in the Koran, and in texts drawn from the Koran. It may be found in auspicious names, in writing implements, in certain numbers, and also in the constellations. As *baraka* draws from and imparts God's strength, it enables a saint so blessed to transcend the everyday rules that govern our lives:

> A person who is possessed of *Baraka* in an extraordinary degree, a saint, is regarded quite as a supernatural being. He can see behind as well as ahead, he can see the whole world though it were expanded on the palm of his hand, he can see the seven heavens, the seven earths, and the seven seas. He knows what is happening in distant places, and foresees the future. He works miracles which fill the peoples with amazement. (Westermarck 1926: 148)

At the same time, through their proximity, a saint can be pleaded with to intercede with God in order to solve problems of any kind: health, procreation, sustenance, or success, whether a person is rich or poor. After death, a saint remains efficacious, and if successful a tomb may be built on their grave. Their extended family or relatives equally may become guardians of the tomb and act as host to pilgrims while accepting prestations in the name of the saint. If however, *baraka* is potentially a welcome panacea, there are multiple rules that have to be followed in order to gain access to it. Likewise, the wrath of the saint, if appropriate behavior is not followed, can be swift: it can result in death, paralysis, the loss of the use of a limb, or major misfortune. In other words, *baraka* is, as Westermarck puts it, sensitive (ibid.: chap. 3): it can be affected adversely by all sorts of different difficulties, not only through not behaving in the appropriate way near a saint or a saint's tomb. It can also be powerfully adverse should one attempt to steal or molest anyone within the vicinity of the saint's influence or that of his followers. Its purity can also be polluted if the correct behavior is not followed:

> *Baraka* is considered to be extremely sensitive to external influences and to be easily spoiled by them. . . . All sorts of bodily impurity are detrimental to *Baraka*. The ablution which is a necessary preparation for prayer is described by the Prophet as "the half of faith and the key of prayer." . . . Among the impurities of the body which may have an injurious effect on *Baraka* are also reckoned the breath and, in certain cases, blood. . . . *Baraka* may be spoiled by contact with the ground and its impurities. The prayer-place of a Muhammadan must be clean. . . . Neither the Koran, nor any other book containing the name of God, nor the writing-boards of schoolboys, must be placed on the ground . . . (ibid. 229–39)

The beneficial influence of the saint and *baraka* can be also affected by *jinn*, which Westermarck writes as *jnun*, who inhabit an alternative world. *Jnun* can appear as human beings (both men and women), exist in great profusion, live alongside human families, multiply, and be difficult to recognize.

> They have no fixed forms, but show themselves to man-kind in various shapes. They often look like men. Among the people at a market, for instance, there are many *jnun* disguised as human beings. There are also *jenn* scribes associating with human scribes and revisiting the Koran with them. . . . There are numerous instances of marriage or sexual intercourse between a man and a *jenniya* in the disguise of a woman. . . . Sometimes the *jnun* appear as monsters with the body of a man and the legs of a donkey. Very frequently they show themselves in the disguise of an animal . . . (ibid. 262–67)

Jnun can be warded off through different substances, especially iron, but also by bringing *baraka* to bear, for example, through recounting the words of the Koran. However, the possibility of their interceding into the lives of human beings is ever constant, all the more so as we may not be aware until much later that they have appeared in front of us or interacted with us in human guise.

Evil influences are made manifest not only through the *jnun* but also via the evil eye, the witting or unwitting propensity that human beings have to cause affliction or distress to other human beings by supernatural means. The evil eye is triggered by envy but also by greed, and its affects can be terribly severe, resulting in the death of children or ill fortune in life, illness, and disaster.

> Besides the *jnun* the evil eye is a very frequent cause of misfortune. It is said that "the evil eye owns two-thirds of the graveyard" or that "one half of man-kind dies from the evil eye." . . . So firmly is the evil eye believed in, that if some accident happens at a wedding or any other feast where a person reputed to have an evil eye is present, it is attributed to him and he may have to pay damages; and if such a person looks at another's animal and it shortly afterward dies, he is likewise held responsible for the loss . . . certain persons animals and objects are particularly liable to be hurt by the evil eye. This is the case with children—the younger they are the greater the danger,—with women in child-bed, brides and bridegrooms, horses, and greyhounds, milk, corn and vegetable gardens. . . . A person who is reputed to have an evil eye is generally shunned. (ibid. 414–23)

A person's life then and its attendant vicissitudes are beset on all sides through supernatural forces, whether emanating from God, beings of the other world, or other human beings, a struggle that appears almost Manichean, a constant tussle between good and evil, between purity and impurity. Nevertheless, Westermarck, it should be emphasized, is not depicting a culture where human beings are the passive butts of malevolent forces. On the contrary, there are many ways in which a beneficial outcome may be obtained: through being pious, avoiding transgressions, being generous. There are equally multiple ways that misfortune can strike. Misfortune is interpreted not only in the light of present dilemmas but also according to the past and the future: almost any action or happening can be explained in retrospect by invoking some rule or consequence that should have been predicted, whether deriving from a misbehavior, supernatural force, or another person. Likewise, many actions are prophylactic, in anticipation of another's ill will or envy in the future. Such anticipatory defense may take the form of a charm, device, crop, stone, prayer, or incantation and is particularly invoked at junctures that appear likely to be dangerous, such as marriage, death, entrance into a ruin, or proximity to ashes. Almost any action, then, can evoke a dense, complex cosmology that provokes and offers multiple possibilities and recourses.

In chapter 10, Westermarck draws together the threads of this argument in a most subtle way, through a description of *ar*, which he translated into English as a conditional curse, or oath. Running throughout this depiction is the idea that, given that individuals actively and continuously seek to ameliorate their position, one way open for them to do so is to invoke an oath or a curse, *ar*, by which the supplicant seeks to bind another person or agent to their will. The idea is introduced as follows:

> The assistance of saints is secured not only by humble supplications and offerings, but by means of a very different character; in numerous cases the petitioner puts pressure upon the saint by putting an *ar* on him. The word *ar* is used to denote an act which intrinsically implies the transference of a condition curse for the purpose of compelling somebody to grant a request; and *ar* is frequently cast on dead saints, as well as on living men and *jnun*. I shall, in a subsequent chapter, speak of various methods of putting *ar* upon saints such as the throwing of stones on a cairn connected with a saint, the tying of rags of clothing or hair to some object belonging to a *siyid* [saint], the knotting of palmetto leaves or white broom growing in the vicinity of a shrine or the killing of an animal. The *ar*-sacrifice is not meant as a gift but as a means of constraining the saint. . . . I have sometimes asked how it is that a saint, although invoked with *ar* does not always grant the request addressed to him. The answer has been that he no doubt does what he can, but he is not all-powerful, and God may refuse to listen to his prayer. (ibid. 188–89)

Ar is an appeal to another person for succor, not just an appeal but an attempt to bind them explicitly to a certain course of action, saying for example, "I place an *ar* on you for your help to relieve me of this stress, this bullying, this problem." It has a clear element of compulsion, such as the man who, in the most extreme example given by Westermarck, said that he would kill his daughter unless a powerful man helped him protect himself against another man who was threatening him. The person to whom the *ar* threat is made is supposed thereby to accede for fear of what may transpire should they not.

> The word *ar* literally means "shame" but in Morocco it is used to denote an act which intrinsically implies the transference of a conditional curse for the purpose of compelling somebody to grant a request. If a person

says to another "... Here is *ar* upon you" ... it implies that if the latter does not grant the request some misfortune will befall him on account of the conditional curse contained in the *ar*. A stronger expression is to represent the *ar* cast on a person as *ar* on God, the Prophet, or some saint with an implicit request to curse the person if he does not do what is asked of him. (ibid. 518)

Ritual and Belief in Morocco, then, is the specific ethnographic illustration of Westermarck's more abstract theoretical conception, which he outlined initially in *The Origin and Development of the Moral Ideas* and which he was to continue to explore and revisit until his death. In effect, we may say that the book is a study of individuals and the culture with which they interact: good is made manifest through saints, plants, the natural world, or material culture, but equally with negative aspects precipitating through envy; angering another person, especially a saint, through an inappropriate activity; or jealousy. Social control is largely assured through this immediate reciprocal impulse of positive reassurance or reprobation. Essential to Westermarck's conception of social control in this manner is the expectation of a positive or negative reaction as a result of human contact: it is this reciprocal anticipation that acts as the great inhibitor and controller of our actions.

By implication, most human beings are highly sensitive to such patterns of reinforcement, but not all. Indeed, Westermarck gives examples of where they are insensitive: he explains that there are individuals who appear to ignore the *ar* curses completely, in which case it is understood that the curse may not be effective. However, the general picture that Westermarck outlines appears to be operative for much of the time, that there is sufficient shared cosmology to bind the majority of individuals within its orbit.

From the point of view of anthropology more generally, another way of looking at this would be as follows: in the absence of physical coercion, how can human societies be kept in order? This question certainly attracted later British anthropologists to Morocco, notably Ernest Gellner (1925–95). However, Gellner's intellectual lineage was quite different and can be traced back to the Durkheimian-influenced, linked segmentary lineage theory that came to dominate British anthropology during the time of structural functionalism. Indeed, I recall discussing this very point with the late professor Paul Stirling (1920–98). Stirling explained to me that, at the time when he decided to take a doctorate in anthropology, Gellner was already a lecturer at the LSE in the Department of Philosophy. Gellner was initially supervised by Paul Stirling, who himself was a lecturer at the time in the LSE Anthropology Department. However, Stirling had trained at Oxford, with Evans-Pritchard as his supervisor (Shankland 1999). Stirling's doctorate in Anatolia had drawn very strongly on Radcliffe-Brown and the importance of social structure in village life. In tutorials, Stirling would stress to Gellner the great relevance of Evans-Pritchard's *The Nuer* (1940) to the ethnographic research he was conducting in Morocco. Eventually, Raymond Firth (1901–2002), finding Gellner's researches of great interest, asked to take over Gellner's supervision, but by that time Gellner was convinced, and the result is a model for social order among the Berbers, his *Saints of the Atlas* (1969), which relies on lineage theory for its explanatory power, an idea he was to expand further into *Muslim Society* (1981).

In contrast, we can see that the leading American anthropologist Clifford Geertz (1926–2006), who worked in Morocco, relies much more on culture as an explanatory concept and is much closer to Westermarck in spirit. Although Westermarck's and Geertz's style (1968) of course are very different, their solutions are in fact similar inasmuch as they both posit that it is within the ordered patterns of belief and the wider culture we all inhabit that the roots of social control must be found. Though Geertz's now famous summing up of his position in "Religion Considered as a Cultural System" (Geertz 1966) was written nearly thirty years after Westermarck's death, one cannot help thinking that Westermarck himself would have felt very sympathetic toward it, all the more so as it appeared in a series of volumes devoted to contrasting the British with the North American anthropological approaches of that time: "(1) a system of symbols which acts to (2) establish powerful, pervasive, and long-lasting moods and motivations in men by (3) formulating conceptions of a general order of existence and (4) clothing these conceptions with such an aura of factuality that (5) the moods and motivations seem uniquely realistic."

Compare this with Westermarck's definition of religion:

> By a religion is generally understood a system of beliefs and rules of behaviour which have reference to, or are considered to be prescribed by, one or several supernatural beings, who the believers call their god or gods—that is, supernatural beings who are the objects of a regular cult and between whom, and their worshippers, there are established and permanent relationships. (1926: 34)

It would be intriguing to look further at the extent to which Geertz may have found Westermarck's work stimulating when formulating his position. However that may be, it is clear that though a work of ethnography, *Ritual and Belief* is not social anthropology as it came to be understood; there is no exploration of kinship; there is no contextualized discussion of ritual and belief within a social structure; and there is no exploration of lineages or lineage theory. Nevertheless, we must grasp that this was a conscious choice by Westermarck, not the result of an unthinking replication of an earlier tradition: he felt that this form of presentation and analysis best suited the exposition of his ideas. Above all, Westermarck overtly did not wish to draw on Durkheimian theory and was careful indeed to distance himself from Émile Durkheim (1858–1917) and his opposition between the sacred and the profane: "There is not that impassable gulf between the holy and the profane which has been postulated by Durkheim" (Westermarck 1926: 147).

Instead, in his fieldwork monograph he was drawing upon the theoretical position that he himself had worked through in his *The Origin and Development of the Moral Ideas*, a wider cosmology influenced by, but not entirely congruent with, the formal religious framework of a society, one that leads individuals to act in a certain way through multiple collective sanctions, sanctions that become interpreted as justified responses to what was an ethically appropriate or inappropriate way to behave. The consequence being that all persons, whether men or women, become enmeshed in complex codes that are shifting, sometimes justified retrospectively, and can change depending on the way that circumstances unfold.

The Revolution in Anthropology

There are yet further ways that *Ritual and Belief in Morocco* takes Westermarck away from the anthropology that developed after him in Britain. In order to discuss this more specifically, we will need to appreciate that the influence of Malinowski at the LSE and the way that social anthropology came eventually to coalesce in Oxford under Radcliffe-Brown and Evans-Pritchard are rather different things; that is, we need to think of the creation of modern anthropology as occurring through a sequence of steps, not all in one bang as a revolution such as envisioned by Ian Jarvie (1964) (Shankland 2019).

At the LSE, as we have already seen, Westermarck himself contributed a great deal to anthropology's later formation; he inspired a modern framework with which to study kinship and was highly skeptical as to the worth of survivals. He insisted on the importance of fieldwork taking place in the vernacular and taught a course on social institutions to Malinowski. He espoused a form of relativism already in his early work on morals and, perhaps stemming from this, had no difficulty in assuming that the point of fieldwork was to give priority to the "native's point of view," something he did with consistency throughout his fieldwork exposition. Underlying his work too was an acceptance of the relations between the biological and social basis of behavior. Malinowski took all of this over into his own anthropology. He too learned the local, unwritten languages to a superb degree. He stayed an extended length of time in the field. By his own account, he regarded himself as a functionalist (Malinowski 1929); that is, he sought to discover how social institutions were based in and culturally responded to the biological reality that inevitably all human beings have to face, and his skepticism toward survivals was evident.

Nevertheless, there are important differences between Westermarck and Malinowski. One of the most important, or at least so it seems now, a century later, is that Westermarck made no effort to romanticize the discipline or the process of fieldwork. In his books, Westermarck preferred the matter-of-fact recitation of his nineteenth-century forebears, whereas Malinowski drew much more strongly on a literary trope that placed his work close to colorful travel literature. There is nothing in Westermarck at all that can be compared to the famous passages in the *Argonauts of the Western Pacific* (1922) or even in Firth's *We, The Tikopia* (1936), all of which enable these anthropologists' writings to be seen as heroic and adventurous, a trope that still resonates today (MacClancy 2013). Westermarck, by contrast, attracted no followers who would slash through the jungle and survive danger with him. His prose is as functional as he can make it, describing as evenly as he can the phenomenon he has been told, with studious references in brackets and extensive use of the vernacular terms. The below, for example, are the first lines (slightly simplified) of chapter 1 of *Ritual and Belief*:

> The Arabic word *Baraka* means "blessing." In Morroco it is used to denote a mysterious wonder-working force which is looked upon as a blessing from God, a "blessed virtue." It may be conveniently translated into English by the word "holiness." A person who possesses *Baraka* in an exceptional degree is called by a term corres-ponding to our "saint." The usual Arabic terms for a male saint, whether living or dead, are *siyid* (plur. *sadat*), *saleh* (plur. *salehin, salhin,* or *sullah*), *wali* (plural *auliya*), and *waliya llah* or *waliy allah*; and for a female saint *siyda* (plur. *siydat*), *saleha* (plur. *salehat*), and *waliya* (plur. *waliyat*). In Dukkala a frequent general name for a saint is *fqer* (plur. *foqra*). . . . (Westermarck 1926: vi)

The charisma of the lone explorer going to visit Argonauts in the Pacific, pitching his tent cheek by jowl with the local people, and writing about them with enthralling sympathy is an integral part of the myth that later was to make Malinowski, however wrongly, the creator of modern fieldwork-based anthropology and is thus entirely absent in Westermarck.

Even more disconcerting to later anthropologists, Westermarck's writing appears much less focused than Malinowski's, a characteristic that many of his followers then emulated so as to become the standard of all anthropological writings henceforth. As Gellner remarks in his *Anthropology and Politics*, "Westermarck, like Malinowski, was attracted by British empiricism, and much given to the practice of fieldwork; but he continued to be magpie-like in method and evolutionist in theory, and the fusion of empiricist philosophical background did not in his case, as it did in Malinowski's, engender the new functionalist style" (Gellner 1995: 235–36).

Can we defend Westermarck from this charge, or at least from its significance? I think that it is possible to do so. It is important to realize that there is no one way that anthropology has to be written; no *ur*-form, no Platonic essential conception that we are attempting to emulate and approach when we write our ethnography. It is certainly true that practical politics may come into play: any adoption of a new, sweeping fashion, even if it can never be fully imposed in practice, may lead to the effective exclusion of the old from popular acclaim.

Yet, any such change has potentially great intellectual costs, as well as benefits. To give a simple example, when a distinct social anthropology separated from archaeology in the 1930s, social anthropologists thereby distanced themselves from a close engagement with archaeology's theoretical and methodological developments in the application of stratigraphic recording and analysis, which became the greatest strength of British archaeology. This meant that social anthropologists rarely had the training, or the inclination, to conduct proper site recording, losing the possibility of a much better understanding of historical sequencing than they might have obtained (Shankland 2012).

Further again, social anthropology, almost as soon as it had formed into a distinct approach, became subject to a host of criticisms surrounding its use of history, conceptualization of science, lack of appreciation of gender roles, and mistaken objectivist or positivist worldviews (for a summary, see Kuper 2015 [1973]). In other words, the stream of work that later was recognized as becoming dominant in Britain under the rubric of social anthropology succeeded in convincing its followers that it was the *only* kind of anthropology that mattered. When they came to realize its faults, they equally assumed that all work from that period fell into the traps that they then identified as making it fallible.

Yet, with regard to Westermarck, none of these points is correct. We have seen already that *Ritual and Belief in Morocco* is a very substantial work of ethnography in its own right. More specifically, however, we need to realize that Westermarck was not looking, as social anthropologists typically came to do, for a closed society upon which to base his account. He did not see why his researches needed to be confined to a small community. He also did not for a moment seek to oversimplify the patterns that societies form. For this reason, he never fell into the trap, so often regarded as crucial, by later critics of anthropology of assuming that small communities are bounded entities. Instead, by concentrating on the individuals and their relations with the wider culture where they are found, Westermarck was able to trace the almost serendipitous way that different parts of a culture can become evoked at any one time—that the way that Moroccan individuals may regard themselves as being at fault can vary tremendously: it might be that they have not shown the right obeisance, that they have failed to remain pure, that they have failed to find the right protective amulet, that they have suffered from the evil eye, or from *jinn*, or from witchcraft, and so on. Their life is therefore, though constrained, at the same time fluid. Westermarck had no desire, and saw no need, to confine his exploration to a specific small locality or to invoke community or social structure as a means to explain an individual's place in society. We may say, then, that he did not fall into the trap that social anthropologists are said to have fallen into to, precisely because he saw already that it would be a mistake to focus too closely on one small community.

There is a further fascinating aspect of *Ritual and Belief in Morocco* that in parallel fashion avoids a later problem that was said to weaken social anthropology. Because Westermarck was not looking for structures and stuck firmly at the level of the individual, he privileges as much as possible both men and women in his account. Though, perhaps inevitably, most of his text is about men, there are nevertheless equally very many discussions on women and their roles, sufficient to make it clear that he was doing his best to bring in both. The below account, taken at random, is from the final chapter of volume 1, titled "Homeopathic Influences," describing the way a tent may be repaired:

Among the Ulad Buaziz the sewing takes pace in summer and is performed by the married women of the village. If the tent is made of four *flij* (sing. *felja*), or pieces of tent-cloth, only, the two new ones are inserted in the centre, side by side, whereas, if it is made of a larger number, an old one is sewn in between them. The women straighten the *flij* by beating them, and while doing so trill the *zgarit*. The mistress of the tent makes a quantity of *sersem*, by boiling chick-peas, durra, wheat, and beans with water and salt, and strews it over the *flij* at short intervals while the women are sewing them together; and the women and the children who are present pick it up and eat it as it falls down. When the sewing is finished, she brings three or four troughs containing *seksu* with *sersem* on top, and this is eaten by the women and children upon the ready-sewn tent . . . (Westermarck 1926: 592)

Likewise, Westermarck is careful to point out that both men and women may become saints and that the *jinn* may be both men and women, and though he occasionally uses the masculine pronoun to describe society more broadly, he is meticulous to denote wherever he can the way that gender may play a role in social life. The following is a further example, this time from the final chapter of the first volume of *Ritual and Belief in Morocco*, on "Witchcraft":

While the charm written by a scribe easily loses its efficacy before long, a woman's enchantment has generally a more enduring effect. Women can really do wonderful things by sorcery. . . . Mothers have recourse to *tqaf* [preventive magic] to preserve the virtue of their unmarried daughters. At Fez, the mother takes her daughter to a place where women are making silk ribbons and induces her to step seven times in the same direction over the threads which are twisted together. . . . The mother takes with her the ribbon, and preserves it till the day when she wants to remove the *tqaf*. She then separates the threats from each other and again makes the daughter step over them seven times. But while on the former occasion she stepped over them from the right of the woman who twisted them, she now does so in the opposite direction. (ibid. 571–74)

Thus, it is certainly true that Westermarck wrote more about men than women, but the famous strictures of Edwin Ardener (1927–87) in "Belief and the Problem of Women" (1975) simply would not have applied to Westermarck, who already included the women in his account, as explicitly as he could, and they were by no means occluded. We learn a very great deal about men's opinions on women; on relations and interaction between the sexes, and also about rituals or rites conducted by women alone. Indeed, the index entry on women takes almost one and a half columns.

There is yet a third great advantage in the way that Westermarck constructed his argument. Though he was extremely cautious concerning the use of survivals, he nevertheless felt that—however difficult—it was the task of the anthropologist to reflect broadly on the changing historical shifts within human cultures and to attempt to simplify them. This comes across strongly in his other major contributions, above all his early analysis of human marriage. It emerges in his North African work in various ways: in his speculations concerning the evil eye, and his readiness to consider a separation between Islam and the supposedly earlier folk beliefs of the Moroccan peoples, hence Malinowski's reference to antiquarianism. Of course, Westermarck was not wrong in this attempt, just unfashionable. The reluctance to engage with historical developments evinced in much anthropology simply meant that they pretended not to write about the past, not that history stopped, any more than diffusion stopped as a cultural phenomenon when Malinowski felt that he had worsted Elliot Smith.

Thus, although Westermarck disliked seeking after inherited characteristics where none could be found, he did not fall into the opposite approach of assuming that all aspects of culture must be explained in terms of a self-perpetuating, ahistorical system. On the contrary, Westermarck's approach assumed a process of continual change: by his account new forms of collective moral behavior could emerge at any time because they depended on the way emotional responses respond to changing events. Human beings are still profoundly embedded within society, but he seeks no underlying structure to explain or support their actions and no temporal inevitability to the way events may unfold. Thus, he certainly cannot be accused of either assuming a rarefied "ethnographic present" or ignoring social change, or confining it to a final chapter. His theoretical approach assumes that social change is an ever-present possibility, and he does his best to note such change where he feels that it may have taken place. Conjectural it might be, as he fully admits, but he is certainly not dogmatic about his suggestions, and his anthropological analysis makes no attempt to diminish the fluidity that he believes is an essential aspect of social life.

Conclusion

Westermarck was excluded from the canonical way that anthropology and the history of anthropology came to be visualized in the twentieth century, regarding him as belonging to the nineteenth. It is true that he was born in the nineteenth century and that he remained faithful, though not uncritically, to the memory of the thinkers who drew him to Britain, and to London in the first place; Frazer, and Tylor above all. It is also true that, philosophically, he remained close to Darwin and Wallace, the pioneer evolutionists who helped inspire his first book. But the work he produced was utterly original, and evolutionary explanations are markedly absent from his fieldwork description. Just as do the greatest thinkers, he first established his own theoretical position through exhaustive preparation, then he proceeded to spend decades in the field exploring ethnographic illustrations of his approach, learning at least two new languages in order to do so. That theoretical orientation, staunchly individualist, became difficult for those who came after him to understand as they embraced the structural functionalism later to be developed in Oxford. Out of favor in their eyes, he has therefore been ignored in accounts of the founding of anthropology at the LSE.

A slightly different way of asserting this conclusion would be to contrast two views of the history of the creation of social anthropology. The first of these is one that assumes that the genesis of social anthropology was at the LSE, forged in the crucible of the Malinowski seminar, whose attendees went on to take up positions across the country as new departments opened up. This is, for example, the impression that Kuper's *Anthropology and Anthropologists* gives, reiterated throughout its several editions to generations of undergraduates. That same approach feeds into much wider writing and analysis of the creation of modern anthropology, from Jarvie's *Revolution in Anthropology* onward. After many years of consideration, I now think it greatly erroneous.

In fact, Malinowski's chair was not in social anthropology; he himself preferred rather that it should be simply in anthropology (Shankland 2019). The LSE, perhaps following that lead, appears never to have a department of social anthropology. Social anthropology in Britain only became codified in recognizable form later, with Radcliffe-Brown's taking up the chair at Oxford, and specifically with his proposal for a reformulation of the Oxford diploma into distinct parts, the one social anthropology the other biological anthropology (Shankland 2019; see also Urry 1993b; Rivière 2007; Mills 2008). The social anthropology syllabus that Radcliffe-Brown came to outline after a series of exasperated exchanges with his colleagues indeed is prescient, recognizably similar to syllabuses of social anthropology as they came to be taught over the next fifty years in British universities. However, it marks a sharp break with Malinowski's attempted fusion of the biological, psychological, and social foundations of human behavior, which in any case his followers rejected almost immediately after his death (Gellner 1958).

Instead of what might be called the "big bang" theory, which the facts do not seem to support, a second view, to which I now adhere, and is perhaps closest to that formulated by Urry (1993a), I believe fits the historical record much better. It is that anthropology did not go through a revolution, even though its followers felt or hoped it had. Indeed, one of the reasons that Kuper's work, particularly in the early editions, is so powerful is that it is a concise and fluent writing out, a scripturalization of an oral tradition that imputes a single founder where in fact none exists. Modern anthropology actually gradually came into being through contributions by a number of different thinkers drawn from different institutions: Frazer, then Rivers and Haddon in Cambridge, who taught Radcliffe-Brown before he set off for his overseas peregrinations; Tylor, John Linton Myres (1869–1954), Robert R. Marett (1866–1943), and their diploma students at Oxford; and Seligman and Westermarck then Malinowski at the LSE.

These in turn, in their different ways, drew on a multitude of earlier thinkers, whether early fieldworkers, travelers, or philosophers of the Enlightenment, as Han F. Vermeulen exemplifies in his *Before Boas* (2015). When we realize this, we can see, for example why Evans-Pritchard (who certainly did not subscribe to the myth of Malinowski's being the founder of social anthropology), in the lectures later brought together by Andre Singer as his posthumous *History of Anthropological Thought* (1981), covers so much ground, taking in several centuries of earlier writers. Out of sympathy with his contemporary readers, these essays were roundly dismissed by reviewers (e.g., Stocking 1983). Social anthropology, instead of welcoming such ruminations from previous centuries, had found a much later founding figure to give strength to its message, providing it cohesion but foreshortening its historical vision.

We can now see too, why Westermarck sits so uneasily with this later codification of tradition. Nevertheless, when Westermarck's work is studied closely, the theoretical preoccupations that he developed in his fieldwork are surprisingly modern and much more sophisticated than his critics appreciate. He also was sympathetic and sensitive to women, both in his fieldwork and through encouraging women students, such as Hilma Grandqvist (Suolinna 2000).

However, from the point of view of his trajectory in the history of anthropology, he developed something that is very close to cultural anthropology as it took shape in North America under Clifford Geertz. He was preoccupied throughout his whole life with the achievement of social control of individuals, which he felt could be found not in an overarching, and perhaps rather abstract, social structure but rather in the interactions, mediated by culture infused by religion and ethics, that we inevitably find ourselves in when we wish to live and survive within the societies where we are found.

Nevertheless, it is possible, perhaps even desirable, that we disentangle as much as we can the different threads of his possible influence. Even though Westermarck is not regarded as a central figure in the creation of modern anthropology in Britain, we have seen the profound role that he had as Malinowski's teacher. Likewise, the Westermarck hypothesis concerning incest does regularly gain comment (Spain 1987; McCabe 1983). Equally, in Finland there has been systematic writing about him, often through the Transactions of the Westermarck Society (e.g., Heiskanen 1967). More recently, there has been a series of publications on his life and works from a new generation of Finnish researchers writing in both Finish and English (Lagerspetz, Suolinna, and Bruun 2014; Timosaari 2017; Lagerspetz et al. 2020), as well as monographs on specific aspects of his work, for example, Tuomivaara (2020) on the place of animals in Westermarck's thought and Pipatti (2020) on his moral theories.

Further, is his fieldwork really so bereft of those who have learned from it? The attention Evans-Pritchard's conflict with Malinowski has attracted is so great that it is easy to forget that Evans-Pritchard had at least three other teachers: Westermarck and Seligman in London, and his old tutor at Exeter College, Marett in Oxford, who rescued him after he was forced to leave the LSE by offering him first the possibility of giving lectures and then a research position (Shankland 2019; Shankland forthcoming).

Is it altogether fanciful to think that Evans-Pritchard has been influenced by Westermarck? Certainly, the way that Evans-Pritchard's *Witchcraft, Oracles and Magic* (1937) is presented, as a discussion of ritual and belief without feeling the need to draw in many other aspects of Azande life, parallels Westermarck's monographic presentation in *Ritual and Belief in Morocco. Nuer Religion* (1956), one of Evans-Pritchard's most confusing texts, with its refusal to construct an overarching narrative and its apparently contradictory expressions of beliefs in spirits, surely has echoes too of Westermarck's readiness simply to record without seeking to impose a constancy that he does not himself discern.

The same point could be made with regard to Bourdieu, in a slightly different way. Bourdieu was certainly very familiar with Westermarck's work and refers to him in his *Outline of a Theory of Practice* (1977). The level of abstraction that Bourdieu employs, and his conception of the habitus—that endless renegotiable cultural miasma in which we all have to struggle—appears to me strikingly familiar to Westermarck's understanding of the place of the individual in society.

Perhaps in the end there is no need to seek direct inheritors. Though anthropology, as all disciplines, likes to seek simple stages and demands hegemonies of thinking as each paradigm arrives, in reality this is only partially true. Social control over anthropological production—even if desired—is only ever partial, and only ever demanded in its purist state by some of those who claim to be part of a new or dominant school. There is surely room to study such great fieldworkers and thinkers as Westermarck without feeling that we have compromised our own *baraka*. Doing so enables us to realize that he elegantly avoided problems: rarefication of social structure, the overlooking of local assistance in the field, difficulty of coping with history and social change, overemphasis on small community studies, lack of understanding of the place of women that the later social anthropology has been frequently charged with.

Ultimately, then, our lack of subsequent appreciation of Westermarck and his varied contribution lies in the way that the social anthropologists who came to codify the discipline mistakenly regarded themselves as being part of a revolution that dismissed the work of those who came before. The resulting enthralling, exciting, but ultimately narrowing of their intellectual horizons meant that, just as we see in Davis's comment with which we began, not only did they no longer have the desire to read Westermarck's earlier writings, they no longer possessed the acuity to engage with them. Yet Westermarck was, at it were, part of the times: throughout the first half of the twentieth century his works were read, his pupils were many. We are fortunate that, in today's more pluralistic conception of the scholarly endeavor, we can at once begin to see these connections and explore Westermarck for what he was: an innovative, prolific, careful, and meticulous scholar and ethnographer, whose work is as relevant and stimulating today as it was when he wrote it a century ago. Today, with our more flexible approach, we can see that Westermarck can be read and deserves to be placed, indeed, at the heart of the anthropological problem that was faced by Bourdieu, Geertz, and Gellner in Morocco. To their great works—*Outline of a Theory of Practice*, *Islam Observed*, and *Saints of the Atlas*—when we turn to Morocco and the anthropological debates that have been inspired by ethnographers' engagement with its peoples, we should definitely add a fourth: *Ritual and Belief in Morocco*, treating it not as a historical curiosity but as a work whose theoretical approach and ethnographic findings remain entirely pertinent to our preoccupations today.

David Shankland is director of the Royal Anthropological Institute and honorary professor of anthropology at University College London. A social anthropologist by training, he has conducted many years of fieldwork in Turkey, especially among the Alevi community. As well as his field researches, he pursues a parallel interest in the history of anthropology, concentrating on the period in the late nineteenth and early twentieth centuries when modern disciplinary configurations emerged. He has published several books, including *The Alevis in Modern Turkey* (Routledge, 2003) and the edited ASA volume *Anthropology and Archaeology: Past, Present and Future* (Berg, 2012), and has made a special study of scholars such as F. W. Hasluck, J. L. Myres, R. R. Marett, and E. A. Westermarck.

References

Ardener, Edwin. 1975. "Belief and the Problem of Women." In *Perceiving Women*, edited by Shirley Ardener, 1–17. London: Dent.

Bourdieu, Pierre. 1977. *Outline of a Theory of Practice*. Cambridge: Cambridge University Press.

———. 1984. *Distinction: A Social Critique of the Judgement of Taste*. Translated by Richard Nice. London: Routledge & Kegan Paul.

Davis, John. 1977. *People of the Mediterranean: An Essay in Comparative Social Anthropology*. London: Routledge & Kegan Paul.

Evans-Pritchard, Edward Evan. 1937. *Witchcraft, Oracles and Magic among the Azande*. Oxford: Clarendon Press.

———. 1940. *The Nuer: A Description of the Modes of Livelihood and Political Institutions of a Nilotic People*. Oxford: Clarendon Press.

———. 1981. *A History of Anthropological Thought*. Edited by Andre Singer. London: Faber.

Firth, Raymond. 1936. *We, the Tikopia: A Sociological Study of Kinship in Primitive Polynesia*. Preface by B. Malinowski. London: George Allen and Unwin.

———, ed. 1957. *Man and Culture: An Evaluation of the Work of Malinowski*. London: Routledge & Kegan Paul.

Frazer, James George. 1890. *The Golden Bough: A Study in Comparative Religion*. London: Macmillan & Co.

Geertz, Clifford. 1966. "Religion as a Cultural System." In *Anthropological Approaches to the Study of Religion*, edited by Max Gluckman and Fred Eggan, 1–46. London: Tavistock Publications (ASA Monographs 3).

———. 1968. *Islam Observed: Religious Development in Morocco and Indonesia.* New Haven, CT: Yale University Press/Chicago, IL: University of Chicago Press.

Gellner, Ernest. 1958. Review of R. Firth, ed., *Man and Culture: An Evaluation of the Work of Bronislaw Malinowski. Universities Quarterly* 13(1): 86–92.

———. 1969. *Saints of the Atlas.* London: Weidenfeld and Nicholson.

———. 1981. *Muslim Society.* Cambridge: Cambridge University Press.

———. 1995. *Anthropology and Politics: Revolutions in the Sacred Grove.* Oxford: Blackwell.

Handman, Max Sylvius. 1927. Review of Edward Westermarck, *Ritual and Belief in Morocco. Southwestern Political and Social Science Quarterly* 8(3): 309–10.

Heiskanen, Veronica. 1967. *Social Structure, Family Patterns and Interpersonal Influence.* Helsinki: Academic Bookstore (Transactions of the Westermarck Society 14).

Herzfeld, Michael. 1981 "Meaning and Morality: A Semiotic Approach to the Evil Eye Accusations in a Greek Village." *American Ethnologist* 8(3): 560–74.

Husbands, Christopher. 2019. *Sociology at the London School of Economics and Political Science, 1904–2015: Sound and Fury.* London: Palgrave Macmillan.

Jarvie, Ian C. 1964. *The Revolution in Anthropology.* Foreword by Ernest Gellner. London: Routledge & Kegan Paul.

Kuper, Adam. 2015 [1973]. *Anthropology and Anthropologists: The Modern British School.* 4th ed. London: Routledge.

Lagerspetz, Olli, and Kirsti Suolinna. 2014. "Edward Westermarck at the Academy of Åbo, 1918–32." In *Westermarck*, edited by David Shankland, 28–66. Herefordshire: Sean Kingston Publishing (Royal Anthropological Institute Occasional Paper 44).

Lagerspetz, Olli, Kirsti Suolinna, and Niklas Bruun, eds. 2014. *Edward Westermarck: Intellectual Networks, Philosophy and Social Anthropology.* Commentationes scientiarum socialium 77. Helsinki: Finnish Society of Science and Letters.

Lagerspetz, Olli, Jan Antfolk, Ylva Gustafsson, Camilla Kronqvist, eds. 2020. *Evolution, Human Behaviour and Morality: The Legacy of Westermarck.* London: Taylor & Francis.

Lowie, Robert H. 1937. *The History of Ethnological Theory.* New York: Farrar and Rinehart.

Lyons, Andrew P., and Harriet D. Lyons. 2003. *Irregular Connections: A History of Anthropology and Sexuality.* Lincoln: University of Nebraska Press (Critical Studies in the History of Anthropology).

MacClancy, Jeremy. 2013. *Anthropology in the Public Arena: Historical to Contemporary Contexts in Britain.* Hoboken, NJ: John Wiley & Sons.

Malinowski, Bronisław. 1926 [1922]. *Argonauts of the Western Pacific.* London: George Routledge & Sons.

——. 1927. "Anthropology of the Westernmost Orient." Review of Edward Westermarck, *Ritual and Belief in Morocco. Nature* 120: 867–68.

——. 1929. *The Sexual Life of Savages in North-Western Melanesia: An Ethnographic Account of Courtship, Marriage, and Family Life among the Natives of the Trobriand Islands, British New Guinea.* London: George Routledge & Sons.

McCabe, Justine. 1983. "FBD Marriage: Further Support for the Westermarck Hypothesis of the Incest Taboo." *American Anthropologist* 85: 50–69.

Mills, David. 2008. *Difficult Folk? A Political History of Social Anthropology.* Oxford: Berghahn Books.

Montague, Ashley. 1982. "Edward Westermarck: Recollections of an Old Student in Young Age." In *Edward Westermarck: Essays on his Life and Works*, edited by Timothy Stroup, 63–73. Helsinki: Akateeminen Kirjakauppa.

Morton, Christopher. 2007. "Evans-Pritchard and Malinowski: The Roots of a Complex Relationship." *History of Anthropology Newsletter* 34(2): 10–14.

Park, Robert E. 1927. Review of Edward Westermarck, *Ritual and Belief in Morocco. American Journal of Sociology* 32(5): 833–36.

Pipatti, Otto. 2020. *Morality Made Visible: Edward Westermarck's Moral and Social Theory.* London: Routledge.

Rantanen, Pekka. 2014. "Edward Westermarck as a Finnish Patriot Abroad." In *Westermarck*, edited by David Shankland, 67–79. Herefordshire: Sean Kingston Publishing.

Rivière, Peter, ed. 2007. *A History of Oxford Anthropology.* Preface by Alan Macfarlane. Oxford: Berghahn Books.

Shankland, David. 1999. "An Interview with Professor Paul Stirling." *Turkish Studies Association Bulletin* 23(1): 1–23.

——, ed. 2012. *Archaeology and Anthropology: Past, Present and Future.* Association of Social Anthropology of the Commonwealth, ASA Monographs 48. Oxford: Berg.

——. 2014. "Introduction." In *Westermarck*, edited by David Shankland, 1–18. Herefordshire: Sean Kingston Publishing (Royal Anthropological Institute Occasional Paper 44, in association with the Anglo-Finnish Society).

——. 2018. "Westermarck, Moral Relativity and Ethical Behaviour." In *An Anthropology of the Enlightenment*, ASA Monographs in Social Anthropology, edited by Nigel Rapport and Huon Wardle, 69–80. London: Bloomsbury Academic.

——. 2019. "Social Anthropology and Its History." *Zeitschrift für Ethnologie* 144: 51–76.

——. Forthcoming. "Evans-Pritchard and Marett." In *Edward Evans-Pritchard*, edited by Andre Singer. Canon Pyon: Sean Kingston Publishing (Royal Anthropological Institute Occasional Paper).

Smith, Adam. 1759. *The Theory of Moral Sentiments.* London: A. Millar/ Edinburgh: A. Kincaid & J. Bell.

Spain, D. 1987. "The Westermarck-Freud Incest-Theory Debate: An Evaluation and Reformulation." *Current Anthropology* 28(5): 623–45.

Stocking, George W., Jr. 1983. Review of *A History of Anthropological Thought* by Edward Evans-Pritchard and Andre Singer. *Journal of Modern History* 55(1): 105–7.

Stroup, Timothy, ed. 1982a. *Edward Westermarck: Essays on his Life and Works*. Societas Philosophica Fennica, Acta philosophica Fennica 34. Helsinki: Akateeminen Kirjakauppa.

———. 1982b. *Westermarck's Ethics*. Åbo: Publications of the Research Institute of the Åbo Akademi Foundation.

———. 1984. "Edward Westermack: A Reappraisal." *Man* (n.s.) 19(4): 575–92.

Suolinna, Kirsti. 2000. "Hilma Granqvist: A Scholar of the Westermarck School in Its Decline." *Acta Sociologica* 43(4): 317–23.

Timosaari, Niina. 2017. *Edvard Westermarck — Totuuden etsijä* [Edward Westermarck: The seeker of truth]. Helsinki: Gaudeamus.

Tuomivaara, Salla. 2020. *Animals in the Sociologies of Westermarck and Durkheim*. London: Palgrave Macmillan.

Urry, James. 1993a. *Before Social Anthropology: Essays on the History of British Anthropology*. London: Harwood Academic Publishers.

———. 1993b. "Radcliffe-Brown's 'Pronunciamentos' on Anthropology and His Invention of British 'Social' Anthropology, 1913–1944." In Urry, *Before Social Anthropology*, 120–38.

Vermeulen, Han F. 2015. *Before Boas: The Genesis of Ethnography and Ethnology in the German Enlightenment*. Lincoln: University of Nebraska Press (Critical Studies in the History of Anthropology).

Westermarck, Edward. 1891 *The History of Human Marriage*. London: Macmillan and Co.

———. 1906–8. *The Origin and Development of the Moral Ideas*. 2 vols. London: Macmillan.

———. 1914. *Marriage Ceremonies in Morocco*. London: Macmillan.

———. 1926. *Ritual and Belief in Morocco*. 2 vols. London: Macmillan.

———. 1929. *Memories of My Life*. Translated by A. Barwell. London: George Allen and Unwin.

———. 1930. *Wit and Wisdom in Morocco: A Study of Native Proverbs by Edward Westermarck with the Assistance of Shereef 'Abd-es-Salam El-Baqqali*. London: George Routledge & Sons.

———. 1932. *Ethical Relativity*. London: Kegan Paul, Trench, Trubner.

———. 1934. *Three Essays on Sex and Marriage*. London: Macmillan and Co.

———. 1936. "Methods in Social Anthropology." Huxley Memorial Lecture. *Journal of the Royal Anthropological Institute* 66: 223–48. Reprinted in Shankland 2014: 178–207.

———. 1939. *Christianity and Morals*. London: Kegan Paul, Trench, Trubner & Co.

Wolf, Arthur P. 1995. *Sexual Attraction and Childhood Association: A Chinese Brief for Edward Westermarck*. Stanford, CA: Stanford University Press.

———. 2014. "Westermarck and the Westermarck Hypothesis." In *Westermarck*, edited by David Shankland, 96–103. Herefordshire: Sean Kingston Publishing (Royal Anthropological Institute Occasional Paper 44).

Young, Michael W. 2004. *Malinowski: Odyssey of an Anthropology, 1884–1920*. New Haven, CT: Yale University Press.

Part II

The Indigenous Ethnographer's Magic

4

Frontier Ethnography
and Colonial Theology

Mpengula Mbande and Marginal Informants in
Henry Callaway's *The Religious System
of the Amazulu* (1868–70)

David Chidester

In 1855 the Anglican bishop John Colenso (1814–83), the linguist
Wilhelm Bleek (1827–75), and the missionary Henry Callaway
(1817–1890) arrived in Natal, South Africa. All three embarked on
local Zulu research (J. W. Colenso 1855; Bleek 1952 [1857]). Eventually, Colenso shifted to critical biblical scholarship that resulted in
charges of heresy (Guy 1983); Bleek moved to Cape Town to advance
groundbreaking work on Khoisan language, culture, and religion
(Bank 2008); and Callaway became the leading nineteenth-century
authority in the world on Zulu religion. Based upon his collections
of oral tradition, Callaway's two major publications, *Nursery Tales,
Traditions, and Histories of the Zulus* (1868a) and *The Religious
System of the Amazulu* (1868–70), became the definitive statement
on Zulu religious beliefs and practices for European anthropology,
folklore, and comparative religion. European theorists, such as Edward B. Tylor (1832–1917), Friedrich Max Müller (1823–1900), John
Lubbock (1834–1913), Herbert Spencer (1820–1903), Andrew Lang
(1844–1912), and James George Frazer (1854–1941), depended heavily upon Callaway's texts not only to understand Zulu religion but
also for evidence in building their own general theories of the origin
and nature of religion (see Chidester 2014).

Tylor was impressed by the apparently unmediated access to savage religion afforded by Callaway's *The Religious System of the Amazulu*. Originally published in Springvale, Natal, in three installments

between 1868 and 1870 (Callaway 1868b; 1869; 1870a), a fourth section was added when the text was published as a whole (Callaway 1870b). This version was reprinted by the Folklore Society in London in 1884. A subsequent edition, with illustrations appropriated from previously published wood engravings by the Brothers Dalziel (Wood 1868–70), was published in 1913 (Callaway 1913). *The Religious System of the Amazulu* was composed in two columns, one in Zulu, one in English, comprising a bilingual transcription of Indigenous voices. Giving the sense of a work in progress, the final installment ended midsentence. In September 1871, Tylor tried to raise funds, by making an appeal through the *Colonial Church Chronicle*, to subsidize the completion and publication of Callaway's work, declaring that "no savage race has ever had its mental, moral, and religious condition displayed to the scientific student with anything approaching to the minute accuracy which characterizes" *The Religious System of the Amazulu* (Benham 1896: 247). In his major work, *Primitive Culture*, Tylor observed that Callaway's account represented "the best knowledge of the lower phases of religious belief" (Tylor 1871: 1:380). Reviewing an ethnography on the natives of South Africa (Fritsch 1872), Tylor criticized the author for "describing the Zulu religion without mention or apparently knowledge of the remarkable native documents collected by Dr. (now Bishop) Callaway, which throw such clear light not only on the religious ideas of these barbarians, but on the origin and development of religion among mankind at large" (Tylor 1874: 481). Intentionally ignoring the colonial context in which Callaway and his Zulu informants operated, Tylor harvested evidence for the cognitive origin of religion.

Henry Callaway belongs in the history of anthropology. He was one of the most important and frequently cited sources for data in the emergence of anthropology from the 1870s into the 1920s. He thought he was an anthropologist—serving as local secretary of the Anthropological Institute in Natal, presenting a paper to the Anthropological Institute (Callaway 1872), and corresponding with metropolitan theorists—even though his primary work was running a Christian mission. Callaway played a crucial role as a colonial middleman mediating between Indigenous informants and metropolitan theorists in the production of knowledge in anthropology. Although his major text might not look like the modern ethnographic monograph molded by Malinowski, *The Religious System of the Amazulu* is an ethnographic text, driven by theological interests but also informed by theory, that employs fieldwork methods of interviews, situated observation, and comparative generalizations that anticipate modern ethnographic practices. Clearly not a modern ethnographer, Henry Callaway nevertheless belongs in the lineage, or, better, the tributaries, of modern ethnography. As we will conclude, certain features of his work—its multivocality, intertextuality, and location in asymetrical power relations—resonate with our ethnographic present.

Henry Callaway's account of a Zulu religious system was entangled in the local conditions of the colonial frontier on at least four counts. First, Callaway framed his research agenda in terms of what he saw as the needs of the Christian mission. In this regard, he conducted his research on the Zulu "unknown God" in the context of a theological polemic against Bishop Colenso. On theological grounds, Callaway argued that Colenso's adoption of the God-name uNkulunkulu was inappropriate for a frontier mission that had to distinguish itself from a surrounding heathendom. Colenso had found two Zulu terms, *uNkulunkulu* and *umVelinqangi*, which he equated with Yahweh and Elohim of the Hebrew Bible, but he elevated uNkulunkulu as the God-name for the Christian mission. However, Callaway argued, the term *uNkulunkulu* was understood by the Zulu not as God but as the first ancestor (see Chidester 1996: 116–72; G. Colenso 2019; Gilmour 2006: 162–65; Weir 2005; Worger 2001).

Second, Callaway collected evidence for this conclusion primarily from informants who had sought refuge at his mission station in Springvale. Like the residents of other Christian missions, these informants were social outcasts or refugees from African communities (Etherington 1978: 68, 95, 102; 1987: 80). Furthermore, since they came from different regions that ranged from the remote northern Zulu territory to the eastern Cape, Callaway's informants had undergone different experiences of the expanding colonial frontier. As a result, instead of holding a single, coherent Zulu religious system, Callaway's informants asserted a spectrum of religious positions that can be correlated with varying degrees of colonial contact.

Third, Callaway operated in the midst of the colonial ethnogenesis of the Zulu. In nineteenth-century South Africa, Zulu identity was emergent, fluid, and contested. It was not anchored in a primordial ethnicity or a stable polity. Beginning with the military conquests by Shaka in the 1820s, the Zulu were a royal house, while tributary groupings of people, known collectively as *amantungwa*, were outsiders, often referred to by the Zulu with derogatory epithets, indicating their subordinate status from a Zulu perspective. Between the 1820s and the 1860s, this restricted notion of the Zulu persisted, although it came under pressure from the Boer Republic of Natalia established in 1838, which was usurped by the British as the Colony of

Natal in 1843. For these colonizers, every African in the region could be designated as Zulu by virtue of language, culture, and religion. Accordingly, considerable effort went into studying these features of Zulu life. Callaway embarked on his research in this colonial context of defining the Zulu (for a succinct summary of the political history, see Wright 2008).

Finally, the bulk of Callaway's authoritative account of Zulu religion in the *The Religious System of the Amazulu* was authored not by the missionary ethnographer but by the Zulu convert Mpengula Mbande [Umpengula Mbanda] (d. 1874). Although Callaway transcribed and edited the volume, providing footnotes and occasional commentary, the majority of the text appeared in the words of Mbande, reflecting, at many points, his own ambiguous position on the colonial frontier as a recent Christian convert. With one foot on either side of the frontier battle line that divided the colonial mission from African society, Mbande's ambivalent personal position defined the dominant perspective on Zulu religion that emerged in Henry Callaway's *Religious System of the Amazulu*.

Tylor's theory of religion, animism, was derived from the alleged primitive inability to distinguish between dreams and waking consciousness, among other psychological and empirical phenomena. When the primitive ancestors of humanity dreamed about deceased friends or relatives, they assumed that the dead were still alive in some spiritual form. Out of dreams, therefore, evolved "the doctrine of souls and other spiritual beings in general," a doctrine that was "rational" even if it was enveloped in "intense and inveterate ignorance" (Tylor 1871: 1:22–23). Certainly, Tylor found evidence of an active dream life among Callaway's Zulu. As many European reporters had observed, the Zulu often saw the shade or shadow of deceased ancestors in dreams (Tylor 1871: 1:430; citing Callaway 1870b: 91, 126). However, Callaway's volume included a detailed account about one Zulu man, an aspiring diviner, who had become so overwhelmed with visions of spirits that he had described his own body as "a house of dreams" (Callaway 1870b: 260). According to Tylor, all Zulu people, as "savage" contemporary representatives of "primitive" or original humankind, were subject to dream visions. A diviner, however, was a special case because "the man who is passing into the morbid condition of the professional seer, phantoms are continually coming to talk to him in his sleep, till he becomes as the expressive native phrase is, a 'house of dreams'" (Tylor 1871: 1:443).

Although Tylor appropriated him as an archetype of the "primitive," this particular Zulu man, who served Tylor as a savage representative of the original "house of dreams" from which religion originated, can be identified as James, a Christian convert for twelve years, who had recently left the mission with the initiatory sickness associated with becoming a diviner, torn between the promises of the Christian mission and the demands of indigenous tradition. While Mpengula Mbande went one way, becoming a catechist for the Christian mission, James struggled in the other direction, striving to keep an ancestral dream alive under increasingly difficult colonial conditions. In this case, therefore, the "house of dreams" was not

Figure 4.1. *Henry Callaway the year before embarking on his Anglican mission and ethnographic research in South Africa (from Benham 1896).*

a "primitive" but a colonial situation, the product of contemporary conflicts in southern Africa.

In order to distill a primitive religious mentality, Tylor had to erase all of the social, political, and military conditions under which his data was being collected. As a matter of method, he insisted on erasing the intercultural exchanges in which his ethnographic data was produced as "religious" data. In his use of evidence, Tylor was capable of entirely erasing the meaning and significance of data supplied by "experts" in colonial situations, such as Henry Callaway, who provided him with his classic case of animism in the account of the Zulu diviner who had become a "house of dreams." In the case of James, the "professional seer" who becomes a "house of dreams" because "phantoms are continually coming to talk to him in his sleep" (Tylor 1871: 1:443), Tylor substantially distorted Callaway's text. In Callaway's account, the phantoms were not coming merely to talk to the diviner. They were coming to kill him.

Callaway's uNkulunkulu

Born in 1817, Henry Callaway studied medicine in London between 1840 and 1844. He was admitted to the Royal College of Surgeons in 1842 and the Royal College of Physicians in 1853, and received his MD at Aberdeen in 1853. From the age of seventeen, Callaway had been a committed Quaker, even publishing a book, *Immediate Revelation*, on the "inner light" in 1841. In 1853, however, inspired by reading the work of Frederick Denison Maurice (1805–72), Callaway left the Society of Friends, gave up his medical practice, and offered his services to Colenso's mission to Natal (see figure 4.1). At Callaway's ordination at the cathedral church of Norwich on 13 August 1854, Colenso delivered a sermon that celebrated England's divine calling to surround the world with its colonial power so that "the lands, which our warriors have conquered, become the fair possessions of the Prince of Peace." Significantly, in the light of their subsequent controversies over the Zulu God-name, Colenso suggested at Callaway's ordination that this cooperation between colonial conquest and Christian mission was necessary "in order that God's name may be glorified" (J. W. Colenso 1854: 38–39). Having become a member of the Church of England in 1852, Callaway was made a deacon by Colenso, bishop of Natal, in 1854.

After arriving in Natal in 1855, Callaway spent his first three years in Pietermaritzburg. During that time he formulated his first ideas about Zulu religion. Callaway observed that the Zulu believed in spirits and the transmigration of souls into the bodies of animals, especially into a certain species of snake. Regarding any belief in a Supreme Being, however, he noted that the Zulu "also believe in a god; but I am not as yet quite clear as to what their precise notions are, or whether the belief is universal or even general among them." In 1858, wanting to pursue both his mission work and his research on Zulu religion far away from the corrupting influences of the colony, Callaway founded the Springvale mission station in southwestern Natal. There he began a more disciplined collection of oral evidence on the question of the Zulu "unknown God" (Callaway as quoted in Benham 1896: 53–54).

Even before establishing himself at Springvale, however, Callaway had arrived at the conclusion that Colenso was wrong about the term *uNkulunkulu*. In March 1856 he had proposed three theological objections to Colenso's introduction of uNkulunkulu into the Zulu prayer book. First, since uNkulunkulu was a proper name, it was unsuitable for representing a Christian concept of divinity as *Deus* or *Gott*. The Christian mission, Callaway suggested, might as well use the proper names Jupiter, Mercury, or Woden to represent divinity. The proper name uNkulunkulu was similarly inappropriate for the Christian mission. Second, Callaway referred to the Old Testament precedent in which the ancient Israelites had been forbidden to adopt the names of heathen gods. By introducing a heathen god-name into its worship, the mission risked violating biblical prohibitions against serving foreign gods. Third, recognizing that the Apostle Paul had used the Greek term *theos*, Callaway insisted that the crucial point was that Paul had used a generic term for divinity for Jehovah rather than using the name of any pagan Greek god. Repeating his point, Callaway insisted that since the God of the first-century Christian mission was not called by the name Zeus, the God of the nineteenth-century Zulu mission could not be called uNkulunkulu (Benham 1896: 55; Anon. 1855).

Did the Zulu have a generic term, like *theos*, for divinity? Callaway thought they did not. In conducting his research at Springvale, he replaced theological with ethnographical arguments against the use of uNkulunkulu in Christian worship. He questioned informants about their ideas of divinity. His ethnographic findings only confirmed his theological opposition to the use of the term uNkulunkulu for the Christian God. If it was bad to use a heathen god-name for the Christian God, Callaway found that it was even worse to adopt a name that actually did not refer to a god at all. As Callaway argued, the term uNkulunkulu was generally understood by the Zulu to refer not to a god but to the first ancestor. Since he was imagined as the progenitor of humanity, or of a particular tribe, uNkulunkulu could not be the "unknown God" of the Zulu.

As Callaway pursued his research during the 1860s, his argument about uNkulunkulu created some controversy among his colleagues. In 1862, for example, Callaway responded to a challenge from Wilhelm Bleek by insisting that he alone had penetrated the total system of Zulu religion. Instead of singling out one element of that system, uNkulunkulu, and then misinterpreting it as if it were a Zulu god, Callaway claimed to have captured the genuine spirit of the Zulu religious system. As he wrote to Bleek:

> It is not I who reject the tradition of the natives, my dear friend; it is you who reject all but one, and let aside nine-tenths of that by an arbitrary dictum. It is not I who do not enter into their spirit; it is you, who have failed to comprehend it, because you have interpreted not as they ever do or could, but by the light received from Christian Theology, and so have supposed the heathen to be that which you yourself believe; and which by a few ingenious twistings of their sayings, a few suppressions and a few additions, may be extracted from them.[1]

On the same day, Callaway wrote to Bishop Robert Gray (1809–72) in Cape Town, claiming not only that he had entered the Zulu religious system more deeply than any other European observer but that he had "entered far deeper, than the natives themselves could penetrate." Knowing Zulu religion better than the Zulu, Callaway was able to assert authoritatively that Zulu notions about uNkulunkulu had nothing to do with religious faith in a deity. Zulu regarded tales about uNkulunkulu as Europeans regarded fables, ghost stories, or idle gossip. Callaway insisted that the Zulu "have no religious convictions about [uNkulunkulu] whatever," because all of their "faith and religious convictions are devoted to . . . the Amatongo [ancestors]." Having developed a religious system based on ancestor worship, therefore, the Zulu had no "unknown God," as Colenso had insisted, that could be appropriated by the Christian mission.[2]

In the midst of prosecuting Colenso for heresy, Bishop Gray must have welcomed Callaway's implication that Colenso had been wrong not only about Christian faith but also about the character of Zulu religion. On two other issues, Colenso's principled tolerance of polygamy and his adoption of a comparative method in biblical criticism, Callaway also assumed an opposing position in the 1860s. Colenso tried to prevent Christian converts from entering into a second marriage, but he argued for tolerance in the case of converts who were already in polygamous marriages. In a sermon published in 1862, Callaway insisted that polygamy was in every instance a bar to membership in the Christian church. Regarding biblical criticism, Callaway published a sermon in 1866 that reduced its emerging comparative method to caricature. Callaway accused the "Higher Criticism" of destroying the unique sacred history of the Bible. According to Callaway, this comparative biblical criticism claimed that the ancient Israelites originally had "no national deity." In the beginning, they worshiped a stone. Gradually, the Israelites adopted religious beliefs from other nations, worshiping the gods of Egypt or Canaan. In developing their religious ideas, the ancient Israelites had taken their stories about the creation of the universe and the fall of humanity from the myths of Persia. In this comparative biblical criticism, Callaway complained, the nature of ancient Jewish religion was found not in the Bible but at Mecca, while the central Christian doctrine of the incarnation was derived from Hindu myths of Vishnu. These comparisons, Callaway asserted, had distorted both biblical revelation and the distinctive historical character of the religion of ancient Israel (Callaway 1862; 1866: 14).

While Callaway adamantly rejected the application of the comparative method to the Bible, which by then had a history of well over a hundred years, he nevertheless applied a similar method to the study of Zulu religion. Finding that the Zulu had "no national deity," Callaway proceeded to compare their beliefs and practices to the religions of the world. In asserting that the Zulu thought uNkulunkulu was the "first man," Callaway invoked the comparative example of the Hindu avatar Krishna, "the most ancient person." If the Zulu thought that uNkulunkulu broke off (*dabuka*) from the "source of being" (*Uhlanga*), then Callaway could cite a comparable instance from Hindu myth in which the original human being was "produced by a division (*ukudabuka*) of the substance of Brahma" (Callaway 1870b: 1–2, 43; with reference to Hardwick 1863: 1:242, 297, 305).

By drawing such comparisons, Callaway had no intention of suggesting that Zulu religion was historically derived from Hinduism. Rather, he invoked comparisons as precedents that lent support to his general reconstruction of the religious system of the Zulu. Comparisons were warrants that guaranteed the coherence and viability of the structure of that system. If it seemed unlikely that anyone, let alone the Zulu, could hold such a myth, Callaway's comparisons made it seem more likely. Comparison, in this sense, reinforced the credibility of the overall structure of Callaway's depiction of the

Zulu religious system. His reconstruction of a Zulu religious system was thereby made to appear more realistic by comparison with other religious systems.

While he compared the structures of religious systems, Callaway imagined the history of Zulu religion by resorting to the frontier theory of degeneration that had been such a prominent feature of missionary and settler theories of the indigenous religions of southern Africa. Where Bleek saw Zulu ancestor worship as a point of origin for a process of evolution, Callaway saw contemporary Zulu religion only as the end result of a "gradual deterioration of the religious opinions of the people." All that could be observed in the present was "the feeble representative of some old system."[3] The Zulu, Callaway assumed, had "degenerated from a much higher position intellectually and morally than they now hold" (Etherington 1987: 86). Echoing theories that had been popular on the eastern Cape frontier, Callaway argued that Zulu diviners were "probably the descendants of some old priesthood, and retaining all the evil influence and cruel tyranny of priestcraft over the minds of the people" (Benham 1896: 76).

These early reflections on Zulu religion provide important background to *The Religious System of the Amazulu*. In summary, Callaway formulated a three-stage history of Zulu religion. First, Callaway proposed, the Zulu must have originally believed in a Father in Heaven, a Heavenly Lord, or a Divine Creator. But that primitive belief had been obscured by ignorance and the "tyranny of priestcraft" that had supported the emergence of ancestor worship. Second, subject to their own ignorance and under the influence of devious priests, the Zulu had confused the Divine Creator with the first man. As a result, they had forgotten all about God. In their degenerate religious vocabulary, uNkulunkulu referred only to their first ancestor. Otherwise, they had no indigenous memory of God. Third, and finally, the Zulu were being reminded of their original belief in God by the advent of the Christian mission. If they were to remember God, however, they had to forget uNkulunkulu, their original ancestor.

On both structural and historical grounds, therefore, Callaway insisted that the mission could not adopt uNkulunkulu as the name of God without entangling Christianity in Zulu ancestor worship. Colenso remained unconvinced. As he wrote Bleek in 1868, "I am satisfied that Callaway is all wrong about Unkulunkulu. He has got a 'bee in his bonnet' on that subject, and runs wild after Unpengula [Mpengula Mbande] his catechist." According to Colenso, Callaway had been misled by his principal informant. After receiving a copy of

Callaway's *The Religious System of the Amazulu*, Colenso reviewed its findings with his own informants, including a son of the Zulu king Mpande, and was reassured that Callaway was "entirely wrong about uNkulunkulu . . . and in fact in all ideas on this particular subject."[4]

If his catechist was not the cause of Callaway's errors, Mpengula Mbande was at least the source of most of his primary data about Zulu religious beliefs and practices. In *The Religious System of the Amazulu*, a large portion of the first section on uNnkulunkulu was information either directly provided or indirectly collected by Mbande; the other three sections, on ancestors, divination, and magic, were almost entirely dictated and signed by Mbande. Callaway described Mbande simply as "an educated, intelligent, Christian native" (Callaway 1870b: 31). As such, Mbande became a hero of popular missionary literature (SPCK 1875: 29). However, Mpengula Mbande was also characterized by European commentators, such as Wilhem Schneider (1847–1909) in *Die Religion der afrikanischen Naturvölker*, as a "Zulu philosopher" (1891: 66). Mbande's depiction of Zulu thought and religion was taken as authentic. The Anglican missionary, Thomas B. Jenkinson,[5] active in Natal between 1873 and 1879 and author of *Amazulu: The Zulus, Their Past History, Manners, Customs and Language*, observed: "The account given by the late Native Deacon Umpengula of the state of the native mind on the subject of their ancestor worship and degraded state, is very good" (Jenkinson 1882: 28). As a Christian, a philosopher, and a comparative religionist, Mbande placed his distinctive mark on the formulation of a traditional Zulu religious system. Arguably, however, in working out his own ambivalent relationship with both the Christian mission and his African religious heritage, Mbande actually produced not an ethnographic account but a theological critique of traditional Zulu religion.

The Frontier Religious System of the amaZulu

Born into a "chiefly family" south of Natal in an area that would become known as Griqualand East, Mpengula Mbande found his way in the early 1850s to the mission station of Ludwig Döhne (1811–79) near Pietermaritzburg. A violent family conflict apparently forced Mbande to take refuge in the mission, since his move to Natal coincided with the outlawing of his brother for patricide. After Ludwig Döhne left Natal in 1857, Mbande and his wife Mary joined Callaway in his new mission station at Springvale. Prospering as a maize farmer, Mbande also assumed responsibilities as a catechist, Sunday school teacher, and, after 1871, deacon at Callaway's mission. Eventually, he was joined by two brothers, one who had been trained as a traditional healer, the other who developed the symptoms of the diviner's calling. As a sacred specialist in the new Christian religion, however, Mbande was able to exercise new sacred power not only as a priest but also in his sustained critique of the old Zulu religion that he conducted in collaboration with Henry Callaway.

The first section of *The Religious System of the Amazulu* contained conflicting testimony from a disparate collection of informants whose statements about uNkulunkulu reflected very different religious understandings. Evidence collected in this monograph, therefore, did not represent a single, coherent Zulu religious system. Rather, the voices in the text hinted at theological debates and arguments, as well as confusions and contradictions, that were situated on the colonial frontier. Although not systematized as such in Callaway's presentation, these reports can be organized in terms of a range of distinctive and, perhaps, representative religious positions.

1. *umVelinqangi is the Creator*: This assertion was attributed to Ufulatela Sitole,[6] who grew up on a Dutch mission station. Before the missionaries arrived, Sitole claimed, the Zulu knew of umVelinqangi as the divine creator who had brought forth human beings from a bed of reeds, but they did not know his name. Therefore, instead of worshiping the creator, they worshiped snakes. In giving this account, Sitole, displaying resentment against the Dutch, claimed that they refused to tell Africans about the creator because they said that black people were like dogs, lacking a spirit, and would therefore burn in hell (Callaway 1870b: 9–13).

2. *umVelinqangi is the Creator; uNkulunkulu refers to the first parents of humanity*: This solution to the relation between umVelinqangi and uNkulunkulu was proposed by Unsukozonke Memela. It was the only time in *The Religious System of the Amazulu* that any attempt was made to reconcile the two God-names identified by Colenso as equivalent to the Hebrew names for God, Elohim, and Jehovah (ibid.: 43–44).

3. *uNkulunkulu is the Creator*: The strongest, clearest statement of this position was provided by Mpengula Mbande, although he also suggested that this understanding of uNkulunkulu was a recent innovation. However, the identification of uNkulunkulu as creator was also made by Umfezi, a man living near

Springvale, who added that uNkulunkulu received no worship since the Zulu prayed to "their own people" (ibid.: 33–34). Another Springvale local, identified only as an old woman, was caught in a contradiction when one day she said that uNkulunkulu was above and the next day she said below. When Mbande went out to take her statement, she tried to resolve the confusion by declaring, "Truly uNkulunkulu is he who is in heaven." However, her understanding of uNkulunkulu's role as creator was only further confused when she followed this declaration by asserting, "And the white men, they are the lords who made all things" (ibid.: 52–55). Significantly, this confusion about the location of uNkulunkulu replicated Xhosa debates of the 1820s between the prophets Nxele and Ntsikana (Peires 1979). As an old Xhosa by the name of Ulangeni related those debates to Callaway and Mbande, Ntsikana had located God in the heavens, while Nxele had insisted that the God of the land dwelled underground (ibid.: 63–67). Therefore, a similar question about the ultimate location of sacred power was apparently raised around the Springvale mission station.

4. *uNkulunkulu is both Creator and the first parent of humanity*: This position was attributed to two anonymous strangers who happened to overhear Mbande and Callaway discussing uNkulunkulu. They provided an account of the original bed of reeds, the emergence of uNkulunkulu, and uNkulunkulu's generation of human beings (ibid.: 39).

5. *uNkulunkulu is the first ancestor of humanity*: In editing *The Religious System of the Amazulu*, Callaway gave precedence to this position, placing in the opening pages of the volume Uguaise Mdunga's report that uNkulunkulu was the first man and original parent of humanity (ibid.: 1–6). Significantly, Callaway identified this particular informant as "an Ilala." By the 1860s, European commentators generally assumed that the amaLala were a separate tribal group in Natal. In the 1820s, however, amaLala was a class designation, even a term of derision and abuse, referring to lower-class people who "sleep (*lala*) with their fingers up their anuses" (Webb and Wright 1976: 1:118). As an informant told the colonial administrator and amateur ethnographer James Stuart (1868–1942), conquering Zulu "called us *amaLala*, just as you Europeans call us *amakafula* ['Kaffirs'], for people that defeat others insult them" (Webb and Wright 1986: 4:14; see Hamilton and Wright 1990; Wright 2012).

These conquered and dispersed people were Callaway's main informants resident in and around Springvale. In *The Religious System of the Amazulu*, the interpretation of uNkulunkulu as the first ancestor of all humanity was expressed by "detribalized" amaLala. Uguaise Mdunga was corroborated on this point by the account provided by Unolala Zondi, who qualified his report, however, by saying that it was based on stories he remembered hearing when he was a child (Callaway 1870b: 35–36). The only other informant to take this position was an old man by the name of Ubebe, an amaNtanja whose people had been destroyed and scattered by Shaka. When questioned by Callaway and Mbande, Ubebe, who lived near a Roman Catholic mission station fifteen miles from Springvale, held that uNkulunkulu was the ancestor of all humanity. According to Ubebe, uNkulunkulu was nothing more than the first ancestor, but also nothing less, since other political groupings, unlike the shattered and dispersed amaLala and the amaNtanja, were claiming that the term *uNkulunkulu* referred specifically and exclusively to the first ancestor of their particular "tribal" lineage (ibid.: 56–60). As a variation on this position, a refugee from Zululand proposed that both the terms *uNkulunkulu* and *umVelinqangi* should be understood as the ancestor of all humanity (ibid.: 7–9). From these reports, it might be assumed that the interpretation of uNkulunkulu as the ancestor of all human beings depended upon informants who had suffered severe social dislocation. Torn from previous "tribal" allegiances, they identified uNkulunkulu as the original ancestor of all "tribes" in the world.

6. *uNkulunkulu refers to both the first man and to tribal ancestors*: One informant, Ungqeto Wakwatshange, seemed to recognize this tension between the universal and the particular in the significance of uNkulunkulu. He distinguished between the uNkulunkulu who emerged from the original bed of reeds and the uNkulunkulu who represented the generation of ancestors preceding his own great-great-grandfather (ibid.: 31–33). In these terms, all humanity had an uNkulunkulu; but each family also had its specific, genealogical uNkulunkulu.

7. *uNkulunkulu refers to only a "tribal" ancestor*: In terms of sheer number of informants, this position was most frequently represented in *The Religious System of the Amazulu*. Significantly, however, the informants who asserted that uNkulunkulu was only the first ancestor of their particular political grouping came from regions of the country that were farthest from the mission station and from the advance of colonial control.

An informant by the name of Ukoto, who was identified as an old Zulu of the Isilangeni, a tribe directly related to Shaka, reported that uNkulunkulu stood at the beginning of the genealogy of his own tribal ancestors (ibid.: 49). In agreement, a refugee from Zululand held that uNkulunkulu was the ancestor of the Zulu (ibid.: 83). However, this understanding of the term *uNkulunkulu* as original "tribal" ancestor was also claimed by informants from other political groupings. As Uludonga, identified as an Ngwane, put it, "All nations have their own Unkulunkulu" (ibid.: 51). Ushuguiwane Zimase reported that he knew of only the uNkulunkulu of his own tribe, not of all human beings (ibid.: 38). Likewise, a group of Bhaca informants held that uNkulunkulu was their first ancestor (ibid.: 86). Finally, four Dhlamini informants identified uNkulunkulu as only their "tribal" ancestor. When asked about uNkulunkulu, they related specific details of their own ancestral genealogy but claimed to know nothing about an uNkulunkulu of all humanity (ibid.: 97–99).

What Europeans called "tribes" were political alliances and allegiances, underwritten by ownership of cattle and access to territory, under the authority of a chief. While some of these political groupings remained viable during the 1860s, all were gradually disrupted by British and Dutch incursions and eventually absorbed into the Zulu kingdom that the British conquered in 1879 and organized into a system of indirect rule based on thirteen chiefdoms. If interpretations of uNkulunkulu as creator or ancestor of all humans depended upon reports from socially dislocated informants, the understanding of uNkulunkulu as genealogical ancestor was grounded in the political groups that remained viable on the colonial frontier. When that political independence was broken, it seems that they had two options: they could turn to an ancestor of all human beings or to the God of the mission.

This range of Zulu interpretations of uNkulunkulu was compressed in *The Religious System of the Amazulu*. However, it can be inflated and correlated with the dynamics of an advancing colonial frontier. While their indigenous political groupings remained functional, Zulu-speaking people could refer to uNkulunkulu as their own "tribal" ancestor. In Callaway's account, the remote Dhlamini maintained precisely such a localized understanding of uNkulunkulu as the progenitor of their own particular polity. Once their political independence was broken, however, Zulu-speaking people had to reinterpret their indigenous religious resources within the new colonial context. One option was to redefine uNkulunkulu as the original ancestor of all people. The amaLala, and other dislocated people, seem to have initiated such a universal reinterpretation of uNkulunkulu. However, under the same conditions of colonial disruption, and the rapidly expanding scope of socioeconomic relations and exchanges, Zulu-speaking people could reinterpret uNkulunkulu as a Supreme Being that overarched the entire world.

As the anthropologist Robin Horton (1971) proposed, the emergence of African Supreme Beings to prominence in the nineteenth century should be understood as a response to the conceptual dilemma posed by the increased scale of intercultural social relations. In that expanding social context, African spiritual resources could no longer be only local but had to encompass a broader range of cross-cultural contacts and conflicts. African "high gods" addressed that new situation. Accordingly, they increased in importance during the nineteenth century. They were reinterpreted to address a more global situation. Coincidentally, perhaps, Christian and Muslim "high gods" presented a similar solution to this new social situation by representing Supreme Beings that overarched the entire social world.

On a different frontier among Sotho-Tswana in the northern Cape, the missionary Robert Moffat (1795–1883) reported that an African ritual specialist, the *ngaka*, proposed a local compromise with the universal demands of the mission. According to Moffat, the *ngaka* suggested that his God dwelt in the north, while the God of the mission belonged in the Cape. As Moffat also reported, however, the argument was concluded as the Sotho-Tswana sacred specialist "looked rather stupid when I informed him that my God ruled over all the earth" (Northcott 1961: 77). The frontier, therefore, was an arena for such contests over local and global solutions to the meaning of sacred power.

As Callaway's collection demonstrates, the conflict between local and global interpretations of religion was not merely conducted between European missionaries and Africans. Clearly, Zulu-speaking people were engaged in ongoing internal debates about the meaning and significance of their indigenous religious vocabulary. They showed an interest in making subtle distinctions among different aspects of divinity. But they also adopted different, conflicting positions in a contemporary religious controversy. Instead of a single, coherent religious system, therefore, Callaway in fact recorded a religious argument among various Zulu-speaking people who had recently experienced, in different degrees, the disruptions of colonial conquest. As a Zulu translator, interpreter, and commentator in that argument, Mpengula Mbande assumed a prominent role in shaping the critical perspective on Zulu religion that appeared in *The Religious System of the Amazulu*. As a comparative religionist in his own right, Mbande advanced his own solution to the problem of the Zulu "unknown God."

Mbande's uNkulunkulu

While Callaway relied upon a three-stage theory of degeneration to make sense of the diversity of Zulu religious beliefs on the frontier, Mpengula Mbande developed his own theological rationale to derive religious significance out of the conflicts of the colonial situation. As a Christian theologian, Mbande held, agreeing on this point with Colenso, that uNkulunkulu should be identified with umVelinqangi. "For my part," Mbande observed, "I say they speak truly who say that Unkulunkulu is named Umvelinqangi" (Callaway 1870b: 16). According to Mbande, both terms referred to the "unknown God" of the Zulu. However, that god was not fully acknowledged before the Christian mission since, "as regards worship," Mbande noted, "they speak truly who say, he was not worshipped" (ibid.: 16–17). Echoing the biblical formula of Joshua 24, Mbande observed that no one ever said, "For my part I am of the house of uNkulunkulu" (ibid.: 18). Furthermore, Mbande revealed that uNkulunkulu had previously been understood by the Zulu as the first man, an understanding that bore no relation to the recent "account of uNkulunkulu we now see in books" (ibid.: 74). Nevertheless, he insisted, the Zulu knew about God before Europeans arrived to introduce the Christian mission. They knew about the Lord of Heaven because whenever the sky thundered, they used to say, "The king is playing" (ibid.: 20). As Mbande explained to Callaway, "This is why I say, that the Lord of whom we hear through you, we had already heard of before you came" (ibid.: 19). However, because they did not worship the Lord of Heaven, Mbande had to conclude that the Zulu knew something but not everything of the truth before the Christian mission. Although he affirmed a pre-Christian Zulu apprehension of religious truth, Mbande devoted most of his interpretation to a scathing critique of Zulu religious ideas.

According to Mbande, whatever black men said about religion "has no point; it is altogether blunt. For there is not one among black men, not even the chiefs themselves, who can so interpret such accounts as thus about Unkulunkulu as to bring out the truth" (ibid.: 22). Blacks suffered not only from ignorance but also from wickedness, greed, and drunkenness. Enveloped in this intellectual and moral darkness, they did not know the truth about uNkulunkulu. Nor did they know the truth about their own ancestors. "As regards the Amadhlozi," Mbande insisted, "we do not possess the truth. We worship men, who, when they too were departing from the world, did not wish to depart, but were very unwilling to depart, worrying us excessively, telling us to go and seek doctors for them, and that we wished them to die" (ibid.: 27). In Mbande's critique, the Zulu had been mistaken in worshiping their own ancestors. Instead, they should have worshiped the heavenly Lord that Mbande equated with the terms uNkulunkulu and umVelinqangi, as well as with the source of all life, *Uhlanga*, and with the *Itongo*, which depending upon context could refer to an individual ancestor or a collective term for the Great Spirit of all ancestors. Since these terms held different significance in the traditional religious vocabulary, Mbande's interpretation suggested that the Christian mission had taught the Zulu the genuine meaning of their own religion.

In one of his most important contributions to *The Religious System of the Amazulu*, Mpengula Mbande related the "account which black men give white men of their origin" (ibid.: 76). According to this creation myth, black men emerged first from the Uhlanga, the place of origin of all nations, coming out, however, with only a few things. They emerged with some cattle, corn, spears, and picks for digging the earth. Arrogantly, with their few possessions, the black men thought that they possessed all things. When the white men emerged, however, they came out with ox-drawn wagons bearing abundant goods and were able to traverse great distances. By displaying this new, unexpected use for cattle, the whites demonstrated a superior wisdom that had been drawn from the Uhlanga. In relation to the power and possessions of white men, black men recognized that they were defenseless. As Mbande explained:

> We saw that, in fact, we black men came out without a single thing; we came out naked; we left every thing behind, because we came out first. But as for the white men, we saw that they scraped out the last bit of wisdom; for there is every thing, which is too much for us, they know; they know all things which we do not know; we saw that we came out in a hurry; but they waited for all things, that they might not leave any behind. So in truth they came out with them. Therefore, we honour them,

saying, "It is they who came out possessed of all things from the great Spirit [Itongo]; it is they who came out possessed of all goodness; we came out possessed with the folly of utter ignorance." Now it is as if they were becoming our fathers, for they come to us possessed of all things. Now they tell us all things, which we too might have known had we waited; it is because we did not wait that we are now children in comparison with them. (ibid.: 78–79)

Therefore, Mpengula Mbande concluded, Europeans had not achieved victory over Africans by their superior force of arms. Rather, their wisdom and works had conquered. According to Mbande, European colonizers had been "victorious by sitting still" (ibid.: 79). They had not required military force. The knowledge, capabilities, and wealth that whites had drawn from the Uhlanga were sufficient to overpower the black people, who reflected among themselves, as Mbande reported, that "these men who can do such things, it is not proper that we should think of contending with them, as, if because their works conquer us, they would conquer us by weapons" (ibid.: 79–80). In this mythic account, therefore, Mbande recorded an indigenous religious rationale for submission to the colonial government and its Christian mission. Obviously, this myth was not some primordial Zulu cosmogony. It was a critical reflection on the contemporary Zulu colonial situation. In Mbande's account, this story was the relevant creation myth in the living religious system of the Zulu. Blacks had emerged too soon from uNkulunkulu with nothing, but "the white men came out from a great Itongo with what is perfect" (ibid.: 80). Another informant, a Zulu by the name of Usithlanu, placed a somewhat different interpretation on the same myth by telling Callaway that "you white men remained behind with *our* great Itongo" (ibid.: 94, my emphasis). In this subtle retelling of the myth, whites had acquired things that actually belonged to Africans because their wisdom, wealth, and weapons had been derived from the great creative spirit of the Zulu. In either case, the Zulu religious system revealed its most dynamic, creative character not in trying to recover a forgotten past but in these struggles to make sense out of the violent oppositions of a colonial present.

Mbande's Ancestors

In the Zulu conversations documented by Mpengula Mbande for *The Religious System of the Amazulu*, ancestors featured prominently

in relations of communication and exchange. Dreaming was crucial to transactions with ancestors, requiring principles of interpretation and practices of sacrificial offerings. In the interpretation of
dreams, according to Mbande, the Zulu had developed basic principles of correlation and contrast for discerning the meaning of dream
symbolism.

First, Zulu dream interpretation observed the correlation of summer with good dreams and winter with bad dreams. "People say, summer dreams are true," Mbande observed. By contrast, "winter causes
bad dreams" (ibid.: 238). Therefore, in this hermeneutics of dreams,
Zulu dream interpretation found a correlation—summer dreams are
true, winter dreams are false—which Mbande underscored by reporting that "it is said there is not much that is false in the dreams of summer. But when the winter comes the people begin to be afraid that the
winter will bring much rubbish, that is, false dreams." However, in
this Zulu hermeneutics of dreams, with its winter rubbish and summer revelations, Mbande introduced an element of indeterminacy by
cautioning about summer dreams that Zulu people "do not say they
are always true" (ibid.: 238–39). While the correlation was important
in establishing basic principles for interpretation, this indeterminacy
was even more important because it opened a space for creative and
critical reflection on the potential meaning of dreams.

Second, Zulu dream interpretation observed a principle of contrast, holding that dreaming "goes by contraries" (ibid.: 238; 240).
According to a number of Zulu informants recorded in *The Religious
System of the Amazulu*, dreaming of a wedding means that someone
will die, while dreaming of a funeral means that someone will get
married, or get well, or otherwise flourish. As Mbande related his
own experience, he recalled, "I have dreamt of a wedding dance, and
the man died; again, I have dreamt of the death of a sick man, but he
got well" (ibid.: 237).

In Britain, imperial theorists of religion were intrigued by this
principle of contrast. Referring to these Zulu reports, Edward B.
Tylor noted that "this works out, by the same crooked logic that
guided our ancestors, the axiom that 'dreams go by contraries'" (Tylor 1871: 1:110; citing Callaway 1870b: 241). Similarly, Andrew Lang
took these reports to indicate that "Dr. Callaway illustrates this for
the Zulus," proving that "savages, indeed, oddly enough, have hit on
our theory, 'dreams go by contraries'" (Lang 1898: 114). However,
the conversations collected in *The Religious System of the Amazulu*
about this hermeneutical principle, "dreams go by contraries," reveal
profound struggles with indeterminacy. Like the correlation of good

summer dreams and bad winter dreams, the principle "dreams go by contraries" was true but not always. As Mbande acknowledged, "I have not yet come to a certain conclusion that this is true; for some dream of death, and death occurs; and sometimes of health, and the person lives" (ibid.: 238). His friend, Uguaise Mdunga, accepted the principle that dreams go by contraries, but then recounted that he had just dreamed of a wedding and a funeral. According to the principle of contraries, "your dream of a funeral lamentation is good; the dream of a wedding is bad" (ibid.: 242). But what if you dream of both?

As these Zulu deliberations about the hermeneutics of dreams indicate, dreams could be correlated with the seasons, but not always, and dreams could go by contraries, but not always. And sometimes, as Uguaise observed, "sleep has filled my mind with mere senseless images" (ibid.: 246). This indeterminacy in the interpretation of dreams was related to the uncertainty and instability of daily life under colonial conditions. Dreams were not merely "texts" to be interpreted. They were calls to action. They demanded a practical response, whether through exchanges with ancestral spirits or through asserting ancestral claims on a territory.

In the first instance, as Uguaise Mdunga observed, dreams often required a sacrificial offering for an ancestor, calling the dreamer to action. "You will see also by night, you will dream; the Itongo [ancestor] will tell you what it wishes," he observed. "It will also tell you the bullock it would have killed" (ibid.: 6). This exchange between the living and the "living dead," the ancestors, was a central feature of Zulu religious practice. Dreams were a medium of communication; but they were also a call to action, with detailed attention to the specific ancestral spirit, sacrificial offering, and, of course, the dreaming human being who must be brought into relationship with the deceased ancestor in this exchange.

In the second instance, dreams often required actions to assert or reassert claims on territory, as when dreaming of the dead (or, according to one report, even not dreaming of the dead) required the living to perform certain ritual actions so the dead might be "brought back from the open country to his home" (ibid.: 142). In such ancestral dreams, practical steps had to be taken to reestablish the territorial integrity of domestic space shared by the living and the dead.

Under colonial conditions, the meaning of dreams might have become increasingly uncertain. But the energetics of dreams was radically disrupted. As Africans were deprived of the means of exchange and access to territory, dream life was dramatically altered. Increasingly, according to reports collected in *The Religious System of the Amazulu*, Africans turned to ritual techniques for blocking dreams because they were unable to fulfill the practical obligations to their ancestors that were conveyed by dreaming. Techniques for blocking dreams included using a black medicinal herb, performing symbolic actions to throw the dream behind (without looking back), and enacting rituals to remove the dream from the home and secure it in a remote place (ibid.: 160–61). Conversion to Christianity could also be a technique for blocking ancestral dreams.

In the ritual energetics of exchange, Africans deprived of cattle could not fulfill the requirements of sacrifice. Recounting a recent dream, Uguaise Mdunga noted, "I have seen my brother." His deceased elder brother, appearing in a dream, called for a sacrificial offering, which placed a solemn and sacred obligation on Uguaise to respond. But Uguaise had no cattle. Addressing the spirit of his brother, he cried, "I have no bullock; do you see any in the cattle-pen?" (ibid.: 146–47). Unable to achieve the necessary exchange, Uguaise could only feel the anger of his brother. "I dreamed that he was beating me," he reported, noting that in further dreams this spirit kept "coming for the purpose of killing me" (ibid.: 157). The result of this blocked exchange, he felt, would only be suffering, illness, and death.

A few decades earlier, European Christian missionaries had complained that they could not gain converts among the Zulu because the people were too wealthy in cattle (Poland, Hammond-Tooke, and Voigt 2003). Now, ironically, when people had less cattle, ancestors were increasingly appearing in dreams to demand sacrifice. As a result, people dreamed, but they did not talk about their dreams. As Mbande observed, "Although they have dreamed and in the morning awoke in pain, [they] do not like to talk about it themselves; for among black men slaughtering cattle has become much more common than formerly, on the ground that the Idhlozi [ancestor] has demanded them" (Callaway 1870b: 172). Under colonial conditions of dispossession, dreams of ancestors calling for cattle apparently increased, but the living, unable to fulfill this exchange, no longer were able to talk about what they had seen in their dreams. Increasingly, Africans sought ritual means to block their dreams, as Callaway himself observed, "lest the frequent sacrifices demanded should impoverish them" (ibid.: 190n50).

Under colonial conditions, Africans tried to block their dreams, but their dreams were also blocked by colonial conditions. In addition to calling for sacrificial exchange, dreams also called upon people to keep their ancestors in the home or bring them back to the home.

However, for people displaced from their homes, this aspect of the energetics of dreams became very difficult. As Mbande recounted, his own family, which had been displaced by colonial warfare, struggled with their ancestral dreams of home. Forced to flee to another country, they employed the traditional ritual means of transporting ancestors under the sign of snakes. As a symbolic trace of the ancestor, the snake communicated through dreams, as Mbande noted, "Perhaps the snake follows; perhaps it refuses, giving reasons why it does not wish to go to that place, speaking to the eldest son in a dream; or it may be to an old man of the village; or the old queen" (ibid.: 212).

In the case of Mbande's family, however, their ancestral dreams were blocked by the colonial incursions of the Dutch and the British. As they were "flying from the Dutch," the head of the family, Umyeka, dreamed that their paternal ancestor was demanding that they reclaim their home as "it was said to him in a dream, 'Why do you forsake your father?'" But they could not return home, "fearing their feud with the Dutch." Blocked from returning to their ancestral territory, they dreamed of relocating their ancestor. As Mbande recalled, "Our father whilst asleep dreamt the chief was talking with him, [saying] it would be well for you to make a bridge for me, that I may cross on it and come home; for I am cold, and the water makes me colder still" (ibid.: 206–7). With considerable ritual effort, they built a bridge for their ancestor to relocate to a new home. But this dream of a new home was also shattered, as Mbande recounted, because they were soon driven out at the order of the British colonial administrator, Secretary of Native Affairs Theophilus Shepstone (1817–93). As a result, Mbande reported, "We were scattered and went to other places" (ibid.: 209). The energetics of dreams, therefore, was radically disrupted by such colonial conditions of dispossession and displacement.

In *The Religious System of the Amazulu*, a convert at Callaway's mission station, who is identified only as James, features prominently as a dreamer. After living for over ten years at the Christian mission, James left to pursue his own dreams. Showing all of the symptoms of being called by the ancestors to be a diviner, suffering an illness, which, Mbande notes, "is not intelligible among Christians" (ibid.: 185), James went off to live alone, subject to dreams, his body becoming a "house of dreams" (ibid.: 260). When Mbande and his fellow Christian convert Paul went to see him, James related that his initiatory sickness had caused him to leave the mission, noting that "this disease has separated me from you," but he also observed that his dreams had given him new access to the entire world because "there is not a single place in the whole country which I do not know; I go over it all by night in my sleep; there is not a single place the exact situation of which I do not know" (ibid.: 187–88). In this new freedom, however, his dreams were still blocked. In his dreams, he was told where to find medicinal plants, but he did not find them; he dreamed of antelope telling him where to find an aloe tree, but it was not there. He dreamed of ancestors calling for meat, but he could not provide the cattle. The Word of God and the bell of the church, Mbande advised, would drive away all of these dreams. But James seems to have found these ancestral dreams already blocked. Nevertheless, he continued to dream. As he told Mbande and Paul, "On the night before you came I saw you coming to me, but you were white men" (ibid.: 192). Going by contraries, perhaps, this dream nevertheless suggested that James now perceived these African Christian converts as aliens.

Every night, in dreams, James saw wild animals, dangerous snakes, and rushing rivers. "All these things come near to me to kill me," he said. On the day of his meeting with his Christian friends, James reported that the previous night he had been attacked by men. As James explained, "I dreamt many men were killing me; I escaped I know not how. And on waking one part of my body felt different from other parts; it was no longer alike all over." As a result, James found, "My body is muddled today" (ibid.: 260). The Zulu term for "muddled"—*Dungeka, Ukudunga*—was a metaphor derived from stirring up mud in water. Although it could be applied to a state of mind, signifying confusion, it could also be applied to the disturbance of a household by a house-muddler (*Idungandhlu*) or the disturbance of a village by a village-muddler (*Idungamuzi*) (Doke and Vilakazi 1958: 175). All of these meanings, certainly, were at play in the dreams of a Zulu man who experienced his body, his home, his family, and his sense of community stirred up and under attack by forces threatening to kill him.

Mbande reminded James of an old dream, which James had related to Mbande when they were both Christians, in which James crossed a river in a boat of faith and was saved from being killed by wild dogs. In African indigenous religion, the river was a powerful liminal zone in between the sacred space of home, which was built up through ritual relations with ancestors, and the wild, dangerous zones of the bush or forest that contained alien spirits. Mediating between home space and wild space, the river represented both ancestral protection and spiritual danger, a place of potential for both life and death (Chidester 1992: 3–6; 2012: 27–28). As James learned during his initiatory sickness, the dreams of a diviner were filled with rushing rivers. Mbande, as a Christian, interpreted these dream rivers as a test of faith. The dreamer, according to Mbande, must cross these rivers in the boat of Christian faith. Remembering this old dream, in which he had been saved by the boat of faith, James had now arrived at a new interpretation. Yes, James said, "the boat is my faith, which has now sunk into the water. And the dogs which I saw are now devouring me." If he could not be saved by Christian faith, Mbande demanded, "Who will save you?" No one, James replied: "I am now dead altogether" (Callaway 1870b: 188–89).

Under colonial conditions, all of the Zulu dreams we have considered bear traces of a changing world, a colonial world in which indigenous people were undergoing dispossession, displacement, and despair. As a result, in the hermeneutics and energetics of dreams, the principles of dream interpretation became increasingly indeterminate, and the ways of practically engaging with the demands of dreams by entering into ancestral exchange or affirming ancestral territory became increasingly impossible. These were realities of the colonial situation revealed through dreams in *The Religious System of the Amazulu*.

Afterlives

Henry Callaway and Mpengula Mbande had extraordinary afterlives in the anthropology of religion. As we have seen, Edward B. Tylor relied upon their data to develop his dream theory of the origins of religion, although Callaway's *The Religious System of the Amazulu* also provided Tylor with evidence of several aspects of primitive animism, the belief in spiritual beings. For example, in analyzing the theology of sneezing, "best shown among the Zulus," Tylor cited the "native statements" provided by Henry Callaway. Accounts were abundant of Zulu people invoking their ancestors whenever they sneezed. "Sneezing reminds a man that he should name the *Itongo* (ancestral spirit) of his people without delay," as one of Callaway's informants reported, "because it is the *Itongo* which causes him to sneeze, that he may perceive by sneezing that the *Itongo* is with him." In this case, the *Itongo* was evidence of a prominent feature of primitive animism, the "savage doctrine of pervading and invading spirits," demonstrating the earliest form of religion when sneezing was still in its "theological stage" (Tylor 1871: 1:88–89). Whether dreaming or sneezing, Callaway's Zulu were Tylor's best evidence for his definition of religion as animism and for illustrating animistic phenomena such as the cult of the ancestors ("manes-worship") and metempsychosis. In Tylor's hands, this colonial and missionary material was not only transformed into prehistoric evidence but also fragmented and dispersed throughout the different chapters of *Primitive Culture*, and therefore the idea of a system that Callaway had in spite of everything tried to imprint on Zulu's religious ideas and practices was lost.

Friedrich Max Müller, often identified as the founder of the academic study of religion, also relied on Henry Callaway. In his preface to the first volume of the Sacred Books of the East, *The Upanishads*, the first footnote was to Callaway's *The Religious System of the Amazulu*, referencing uNkulunkulu, first ancestor, as primordial evidence that religion originated in a sense of the infinite (Max Müller 1879: xiii). Max Müller also depended upon Henry Callaway to argue for the universality of religion, especially since the Zulu had been accused by earlier accounts as lacking any religion. In the case of the Zulu, he observed: "Thus we find among a people who were said to be without any religious life, without any idea of a Divine power, that some of the most essential elements of religion are fully developed" (Max Müller 1873: 185). During the 1890s, Max Müller got caught up in a scam perpetrated by the Catholic missionary Alfred T. Bryant (1865–1953), who pretended in print to be a Zulu by the name of uNemo contradicting Callaway, so Max Müller could only complain, "If we can no longer quote Callaway on Zulus . . . whom shall we quote?" (Max Müller 1897: 1:204–5). This controversy demonstrated the foundational role of Callaway and Mbande in the study of religion and the instability of that foundation (see Chidester 2014: 227–31).

Shifting to early twentieth-century anthropology, Mpengula Mbande appeared in the work of the anthropologist Paul Radin (1883–1959), *Primitive Man as Philosopher* (1927). Fighting against the denigration of indigenous people as unthinking, Radin got caught in the frontier conflicts of nineteenth-century South Africa. Identifying Mbande as a philosopher, Radin cited Mbande's colonial positionality as if it were philosophical skepticism. As a Christian convert, catechist, and eventually deacon, Mbande had observed that what black men say about uNkulunkulu "has no point; it is altogether blunt. For there is not one among black men, not even the chiefs themselves, who can so interpret such accounts as those about Unkulunkulu to bring about the truth" (Radin 1927: 380; see 379–84). Over six pages

in the culmination of his argument that primitive peoples could produce primitive philosophers, Radin quoted Mbande's Christian in-
vective against Zulu ancestral religion. As an exemplar of primitive
man as philosopher, Mbande was certainly a strange choice, since he
had been enlisted in a Christian campaign against primitive religion.
Despite Radin's good intentions, any invocation of primitive religion
was entangled in the mediations—imperial, colonial, and indigenous—that produced and circulated knowledge about religion.

Henry Callaway's *The Religious System of the Amazulu* must be valued not only by recalling how the text was used as raw material by metropolitan theorists but also by recognizing what the text accomplished.
In conclusion, we should consider four major accomplishments.

First, Callaway recorded multiple voices, variously situated in colonial frontier zones, which can be disaggregated and recalibrated to
reveal the specific contours of a history of relations, contexts, and
exchanges. As we have seen, the range of understandings of uNkulunkulu, which can be correlated with the advance of colonialism,
clearly demonstrates the rich potential of Callaway's text. But the
fact that he diligently collected all of these voices, despite his theological position or theoretical interest, is an accomplishment of transparency that makes *The Religious System of the Amazulu* a signal
achievement of intertextuality.

Second, the voices Callaway recorded were not only multiple
but also embedded in the asymmetrical power relations of advancing colonialism. The prominence of displaced and dispossessed informants, often identified as amaLala, shows Callaway's attention,
however it might have been determined by the refugees attracted to
his mission, to the broader assemblages of power in which his data
was collected. Colonial power relations, as we have seen, formed the
material subtext of *The Religious System of the Amazulu*, but only
because Callaway allowed that messy and often brutal reality to reg-
ister throughout his text.

Third, Callaway anticipated questions about the authorship of any
ethnographic monograph that can be triangulated among a nominal
author, mediating conditions of production, and Indigenous informants, who in *The Religious System of the Amazulu* were a diverse
range of people encountering colonialism and were facilitated by
Mpengula Mbande and orchestrated by Henry Callaway to come together in the pages of a single published book. As a result, this text
is a landmark example of the multiple authorship of an ethnographic
monograph before Malinowski entrenched the model for asserting
sole and exclusive authorship.

Fourth, Callaway's *The Religious System of the Amazulu* records the violence permeating his research field. Despite the interest of metropolitan theorists in erasing all of the social, political, and economic conditions in which their data was collected, Callaway provided evidence from his informants that they were displaced and dispossessed by colonial interventions. The meaning of uNkulunkulu shifted according to exposure to colonial warfare, the relations with ancestors were altered by colonial violence, and the Zulu diviner, who encountered spirits in dreams, found that they were coming not to speak to him but to kill him. Allowing the undercurrent of violence in the experience of his informants to surface in his monograph was a crucial accomplishment of Henry Callaway's *The Religious System of the Amazulu*.

Henry Callaway's greatest achievement was to let all the seams show in stitching together an ethnographic monograph of ambiguous authorship, multiple voices, intertextuality, and transparency in revealing the means of its own production in the asymmetrical power relations of colonialism. *The Religious System of the Amazulu* is a text worthy of revisiting not merely as a precursor of the modern ethnographic monograph, not merely as a relic of the past, but also as an index to the ethnographic challenges of the present.

Acknowledgments

In this chapter, material has been adapted from David Chidester, *Savage Systems: Colonialism and Comparative Religion in Southern Africa*, 152–67, © 1996 by the Rector and Visitors of the University of Virginia, reprinted by permission of the University of Virginia Press; and David Chidester, "Dreaming in the Contact Zone: Zulu Dreams, Visions, and Religion in Nineteenth-Century South Africa," *Journal of the American Academy of Religion* 76(1): 27–53, 2008, with permission of Oxford University Press.

David Chidester is emeritus professor of religious studies and senior research scholar at the University of Cape Town in South Africa. He is the author or editor of over twenty books on North American studies, South African studies, and comparative religion, including *Savage Systems: Colonialism and Comparative Religion in Southern Africa* (University of Virginia Press, 1996); *Christianity: A Global History* (Penguin; HarperCollins, 2000); *Empire of Religion: Imperialism and Comparative Religion* (University of Chicago Press, 2014);

and *Religion: Material Dynamics* (University of California Press, 2018). He has twice received the American Academy of Religion's Award for Excellence in Religious Studies.

Notes

1. "Callaway to Bleek, July 8, 1862," Manuscript Collection, 9.10.c.6, South African Library, Cape Town.
2. "Callaway to Bishop Gray, July 8, 1862," Manuscript Collection, 9.10.c.6, South African Library, Cape Town.
3. "Callaway to Bleek, July 8, 1862," Manuscript Collection, 9.10.c.6, South African Library, Cape Town.
4. "Colenso to Bleek, September 20, 1868," Special Collections, BC151, A111, University of Cape Town Library.
5. Dates unknown.
6. Unless stated otherwise, all dates of birth and death of Callaway's informants are unknown.

References

Anon. 1855. "Bishop Colenso and his Kafir Words for the Deity." *African Christian Watchman* 2: 273–380.

Bank, Andrew. 2008. *Bushmen in a Victorian World: The Remarkable Story of the Bleek-Lloyd Collection of Bushman Folklore*. Cape Town: Double Storey.

Benham, Marian S. 1896. *Henry Callaway M.D., D.D., First Bishop of Kaffraria: His Life History and Work; A Memoir*. London: Macmillan.

Bleek, W. H. I. 1952 [1857]. *Zulu Legends*. Edited by J. A. Engelbrecht. Pretoria: Van Schaik; orig. ed. 1857.

Callaway, Henry. 1862. *Polygamy, a Bar to Admission into the Christian Church*. Durban: John O. Brown.

———. 1866. *The Last Word of Modern Thought: Two Sermons Preached at St. Peter's Cathedral and at St. Andrew's Church, Pietermaritzburg Natal, December 1865*. Springvale, South Africa: J. Blair/Pietermaritzburg, South Africa: Davis.

———. 1868a. *Nursery Tales, Traditions, and Histories of the Zulus in Their Own Words*. Springvale, Natal: J.A. Blair/London: Trübner.

———. 1868b. *The Religious System of the Amazulu: Part I. Unkulunkulu; or, The Tradition of Creation as Existing among the Amazulu and Other Tribes of South Africa, in Their Own Words, with a Translation in English, and Notes*. Springvale, Natal: John A. Blair/Cape Town: J. C. Juta/London: Trübner.

———. 1869. *The Religious System of the Amazulu: Part II. Amatonga; or, Ancestor Worship as Existing among the Amazulu and Other Tribes of South Africa, in Their Own Words, with a Translation in English, and Notes.* Springvale, Natal: John A. Blair/Cape Town: J. C. Juta/London: Trübner.

———. 1870a. *The Religious System of the Amazulu: Part III. Izinyanga Zokubula; or, Divination, as Existing among the Amazulu and Other Tribes of South Africa, in Their Own Words, with a Translation in English, and Notes.* Springvale, Natal: John A. Blair/Cape Town: J. C. Juta/London: Trübner.

———. 1870b. *The Religious System of the Amazulu.* Springvale, Natal: John A. Blair/Cape Town: J. C. Juta/London: Trübner; reprinted London: Folklore Society, 1884.

———. 1872. "On Divination and Analogous Phenomena among the Natives of Natal." *Proceedings of the Anthropological Institute* 1: 163–83.

———. 1913. *The Religious System of the Amazulu.* Edited by Willibald Wanger. Illustrations by Brothers Dalziel. Mariannhill, South Africa: Mariannhill Mission Press; reprinted Cape Town: Struik, 1970.

Chidester, David. 1992. *Religions of South Africa.* London: Routledge.

———. 1996. *Savage Systems: Colonialism and Comparative Religion in Southern Africa.* Charlottesville: University Press of Virginia.

———. 2012. *Wild Religion: Tracking the Sacred in South Africa.* Berkeley: University of California Press.

———. 2014. *Empire of Religion: Imperialism and Comparative Religion.* Chicago: University of Chicago Press.

Colenso, Gwilym. 2019. "uNkulunkulu: Bishop John William Colenso and the Contested Zulu God-Name in Nineteenth-Century Natal." In *Translating Wor(l)ds: Christianity across Cultural Boundaries*, edited by Sabine Dedenbach-Salazar Saenz, 97–126. Baden-Baden: Academia Verlag.

Colenso, John William. 1854. *The Good Tidings of Great Joy, Which Shall Be to All People: A Sermon Preached in the Cathedral Church of Norwich, on Sunday, August 13, 1854, on the Occasion of Ordaining Henry Callaway, M.D. as a Missionary among the Heathen in the Diocese of Natal.* London: Bell.

———. 1855. *Ten Weeks in Natal: A Journal of a First Tour of Visitation among the Colonists and Zulu Kafirs of Natal.* Cambridge: Macmillan.

Doke, Clement M., and Benedict W. Vilakazi. 1958. *Zulu-English Dictionary.* 2nd ed. Johannesburg: Witwatersrand University Press.

Etherington, Norman. 1978. *Preachers, Peasants, and Politics in Southeast Africa, 1835–1880: African Christian Communities in Natal, Pondoland, and Zululand.* London: Royal Historical Society.

———. 1987. "Missionary Doctors and African Healers in Mid-Victorian South Africa." *South African Historical Journal* 19: 77–91.

Fritsch, Gustav. 1872. *Die Eingeborenen Süd-Afrikas,ethnographisch und anatomisch beschrieben.* Breslau: Hirt.

Gilmour, Rachael. 2006. *Grammars of Colonialism: Representing Languages in Colonial South Africa.* New York: Palgrave Macmillan.

Guy, Jeff. 1983. *The Heretic: A Study of the Life of John William Colenso, 1814–1883.* Johannesburg: Ravan Press.

Hamilton, Carolyn, and John Wright. 1990. "The Making of the *Amalala*: Ethnicity, Ideology and Relations of Subordination in a Precolonial Context." *South African Historical Journal* 22: 3–23

Hardwick, Charles. 1863. *Christ and Other Masters: An Historical Inquiry into Some of the Chief Parallelisms and Contrasts between Christianity and the Religious Systems of the Ancient World.* 2nd ed. London: Macmillan.

Horton, Robin. 1971. "African Conversion." *Africa: Journal of the International African Institute* 41(2): 85–108.

Jenkinson, Thomas B. 1882. *Amazulu: The Zulus, Their Past, History, Manners, Customs, and Language.* London: W. H. Allen & Co.

Lang, Andrew. 1898. *The Making of Religion.* London: Longmans, Green and Co.

Max Müller, Friedrich. 1873. *Introduction to the Science of Religion: Four Lectures Delivered at the Royal Institution with Two Essays on False Analogies, and the Philosophy of Mythology.* London: Longmans, Green.

———. 1879. "Preface to the Sacred Books of the East." In *The Upanishads, Volume 1*, ix–xxxviii. Edited and translated by Friedrich Max Müller. Oxford: Oxford University Press.

———. 1897. *Contributions to the Science of Mythology.* 2 vols. London: Longmans, Green.

Northcott, Cecil. 1961. *Robert Moffat: Pioneer in Africa, 1817–1870.* London: Lutterworth Press.

Peires, J. B. 1979. "Nxele, Ntsikana, and the Origins of the Xhosa Religious Reaction." *Journal of African History* 20(1): 51–61.

Poland, Marguerite, David Hammond-Tooke, and Leigh Voigt. 2003. *The Abundant Herds: A Celebration of the Nguni Cattle of the Zulu People.* Vlaeberg, South Africa: Fernwood Press.

Radin, Paul. 1927. *Primitive Man as Philosopher.* New York: D. Appleton.

Schneider, Wilhelm. 1891. *Die Religion der afrikanischen Naturvölker.* Münster: Aschendorff.

SPCK. 1875. *May, the Little Bush Girl.* London: Society for Promoting Christian Knowledge.

Tylor, Edward B. 1871. *Primitive Culture.* 2 vols. London: John Murray.

———. 1874. "Fritsch's 'South African Races.'" *Nature* 9(234): 479–82.

Webb, Colin, and John B. Wright. 1976. *The James Stuart Archive of Recorded Oral Evidence Relating to the History of the Zulu and Neighbouring Peoples.* Vol. 1. Pietermaritzburg, South Africa: University of Natal Press.

———. 1986. *The James Stuart Archive of Recorded Oral Evidence Relating to the History of the Zulu and Neighbouring Peoples.* Vol. 4. Pietermaritzburg, South Africa: University of Natal Press.

Weir, Jennifer. 2005. "Whose Unkulunkulu?" *Africa* 75(2): 203–9.

Worger, William H. 2001. "Parsing God: Conversations about the Meaning of Words and Metaphors in Nineteenth-Century Southern Africa." *Journal of African History* 42(3): 417–47.

Wood, John George. 1868–70. *The Uncivilized Races; or, Natural History of Man, Being a Complete Account of the Manners and Customs, and the Physical, Social and Religious Condition and Characteristics of the Uncivilized Races of Men throughout the Entire World.* 2 vols. London: George Routledge.

Wright, John. 2008. "Reflections on the Politics of Being 'Zulu.'" In *Zulu Identities: Being Zulu, Past and Present*, edited by Benedict Carton, John Laband, and Jabulani Sithole, 35–43. Scottsville, South Africa: University of KwaZulu–Natal Press.

Wright, John. 2012. "A. T. Bryant and the 'Lala.'" *Journal of Southern African Studies* 38(2): 355–68.

5

At the Feet of the Lord of the Dragons

Tutakangahau, Elsdon Best, and *Waikare-moana:*
The Sea of the Rippling Waters (1897)

Jeffrey Paparoa Holman

Since 2002, when I began working on the influence of the New Zealand ethnographer Elsdon Best (1856–1931) on the writing about
Māori origins, history, and culture, I have been struck by how pervasive his presence is in the literature and public discourse in Aotearoa/
New Zealand as well as in private opinions expressed to me along
the way. On my first visit in 2004 to the tribal area of Ngāi Tūhoe,
the iwi (people),[1] among whose ancestors Best had lived, worked,
and done his collecting and note-taking between 1895 and 1910, gave
me at least three versions of Te Peehi (Best's Māori name). The first
was from my host, Materoa Nikora (1935–2019), a Ruātoki kuia (female elder), who told me of childhood raids on the fruit trees of his
long-abandoned homestead, "te ngahere a Peehi" (Best's forest). She
had his magnum opus, *Tuhoe—Children of the Mist* (1925 [1897]) on
her bookshelf and a child's memory of this mysterious Pākehā (European) who had written down their stories.

Materoa introduced me to my next informant, local leader Tamati Kruger (b. 1955), now chair of a Tūhoe tribal body and a claims
negotiator with the Crown over treaty settlement issues. She made
this appointment in some haste: the arrangements she had initially
made for me to meet some kaumātua (elders) of the tribe had fallen
through, as the remote area where they lived had been overtaken by
massive flooding that prevented access. Mr. Kruger gave me a short
interview and short shrift: Best was a tahae (thief) who had sat in the
Native Land Courts and listened to claims but had no real knowledge
of Tūhoetanga (Tūhoe lifeways). Materoa Nikora then introduced

me to a well-known tohunga (healer, wise man), Hohepa Kereopa, who is widely respected for his writings on Tūhoe lore, especially medicinal plants. Kereopa kindly received me in the premises of the Presbyterian Centre in Whakatāne (the main town) and asked me to wait while he consulted the library (Presbyterian missionaries had a long and respected association with the tribe, especially with the prophet Rua Kenana [1868?–1937] and his remote community at Maungapōhatu).

When Mr. Kereopa returned, he told me something of his history and training but revealed that his researches in the archive had not yielded any fruit; however, he knew that "Te Peehi (Best) had a Māori wife." This was news to me, as I knew that in 1903, while involved in his work, Best had married Adelaide Wylie, a local Pākehā schoolteacher. He told me that, while still a child, he had overheard this information from a very elderly tohunga (expert) who was living up at Maungapōhatu while Best was doing his research there in the early 1900s.

It has never been possible to verify this claim. This record of meetings over an initial week spent among Tūhoe is indicative of how entwined Elsdon Best as a Pākehā ethnographer had become in tribal memory; many subsequent examples could be cited as my research progressed, focusing on the archival written material from the time Best spent in the area, his writing afterward as he rose to prominence during his tenure as "museum ethnologist" in the Dominion Museum from 1910 until his death in 1931 lauded as that of the country's foremost expert on matters Māori. The focus of my research also moved to include the writings of his informants in the same period and earlier, especially that of the Tamakaimona chief, Tutakangahau (1832?–1907), his principal source (see figure 5.1).

Best, controversial at times in his day and in the Māori renaissance of the 1970s, remains so today. A recent Twitter storm has broken out among younger Māori, who attack him for his "racist" ethnography, write of their anger at his presence in the archive, and speak in one case of the pain it causes them to read this Pākehā writing about their tūpuna (ancestors). All of this underlines once more that Best is, through his writings, very much alive in the culture of Aotearoa/New Zealand; so too, I would assert, are Tutakangahau and his fellow Tūhoe, as well as other Māori tribal informants. It is this side of the archive that these objectors miss: Best's informants were neither victims nor passive actors but willing participants in their own ethnographic creations. A final example: some years ago, in the 1980s, a local member of Parliament (MP), a Pākehā woman distantly related

Figure 5.1. *Portrait of Urewera chief, Tutakangahau, wearing a kākahu (Māori cloak), in 1898. Photographer, and location, unidentified. © Alexander Turnbull Library, Wellington, New Zealand (PAColl-7273-04).*

to Best, was examining roses growing wild on the roadside in the Urewera Range near Te Whaiti, a place where Best and his wife had actually lived and planted the blooms. An elderly Tūhoe man from a house nearby approached and asked her what she was doing; she explained she was the electorate MP and a relative of Te Peehi (Elsdon Best). He walked back to his house and reappeared, in tears, carrying copies of the ethnographer's books, the stories of his people. Ethnography is made by, for, and about flesh-and-blood human beings; this was as true in Best's day as it is in ours. We are as flawed now, in our own peculiar ways, as were the dead who left these works behind them.

Te Ao Hurihuri: The Changing World of Ngāi Tūhoe, 1840–90

Some context is necessary here: the situation in the Urewera (the principal Tūhoe tribal area) prior to Best's arrival and the tribe's relationship to the settler government; biographical information about the informant and the ethnographer; the origins of the Polynesian Society and its mission to study the Indigenous peoples of Oceania; why they commissioned Best to go to the Urewera; and a brief background to the book itself, *Waikare-moana, The Sea of the Rippling Waters: The Lake; The Land; The Legends, with a Tramp through Tuhoe Land*. The geographical area in which this encounter took place is a predominantly mountainous region in the northwest of Aotearoa/New Zealand's North Island (called Te Ika a Maui). It is generally agreed that Polynesian double-hulled canoe voyages from the Pacific enabled the ancestors of today's Māori to reach these southern islands between 1250 and 1300.[2] The majority resident tribe of the area in question—Ngāi Tūhoe—take their name from Tūhoe-Pōtiki, a grandson of Toroa, captain of the Mataatua canoe, in one of the major migrations from the north. According to Rangi McGarvey, a Tūhoe elder, earlier inhabitants such as Ngā Pōtiki, Te Tini a Toi, and Te Hapū-oneone have, over time, "through conquest and intermarriage," made up the composition of the tribe as it exists today.[3]

Such areas—settled and disputed, fought for and cultivated over the next five to six hundred years—were those in which a unique Tūhoe character developed: the hardy mountain dweller who, living in a demanding physical environment, had a reputation as a fierce fighter, as a famous proverb defines them to this day: "Tūhoe moumou kai, moumou taonga, moumou tangata ki te Pō" (Tūhoe wasteful of food, wasters of treasures, wasters of men to Death). It would be the fact of their physical isolation and this inhospitable environment that left much of their territory out of the hands of the incoming settlers and the colonial troops who fought the midcentury wars (1860–70), at least until the very last decade of the nineteenth century. It was their relative isolation that also left their language and lifeways available—in an imaginary pristinity—to Elsdon Best in his search for those he would come to term as "the mythopoetic Māori." This was a concept he had derived from his study of the nineteenth-century German linguist and scholar Friedrich Max Müller (1823–1900) and his theories of a mythological, or mythopoetic, stage in human intellectual development (Max Müller 1881).[4]

Tutakangahau, chief of Tamakaimona and Best's principal source, was born into a Tūhoe world, living a largely traditional hunter-gatherer lifestyle in a remote area of a forbidding mountain fastness. The Tamakaimoana hapū (clan) of the tribe were distant from the lowland-dwelling and coastal members of their people, yet they were not untouched by early missionary activity—and literacy—in their domain. Tutakangahau was present when the missionary William Colenso (1811–99) arrived at his home marae (village) in 1844, where the Pākehā evangelist recorded the presence of a small group of catechists reading Bible portions translated into Māori. The Word had beaten the bearer of the good news; Māori converts from the north had already brought the printed word into Tutakangahau's world (Bagnall and Petersen 1948: 173). Along with print technology had come the power of firearms; the tribal wars of the 1840s that decimated Māori populations once guns were introduced eventually reached the Urewera, where historic intertribal conflict was ongoing. The wars between the settler government and Māori tribes from Taranaki to Waikato in the 1860s to the 1870s soon entangled Tūhoe and therefore the men who would become Best's sources. Millennial prophetic movements arose in this period, whose leaders, disillusioned with land-hungry European duplicity, deployed biblical texts of betrayal and deliverance—prophets, priests, and kings—as a syncretic indigenous theology where the oppressed Hebrew tribes of the Old Testament offered a template for Māori in their struggle against Pākehā pharaohs and their legions.

This formative period of Māori history and thought shaped Tutakangahau's thinking. In the late 1860s, he is recorded as fighting alongside the Ringatū prophet and warrior, Te Kooti Arikirangi (1832–91), an alliance that was to prove damaging to his tribe in the end. This brought other Māori tribes, such as Ngāti Porou, fighting alongside the settler troops, into Tutakangahau's domain as conquerors and occupiers. Tūhoe were repaid for their support of Māori brethren with raupatu—the confiscation of millions of acres of tribal lands—and client status. In the twenty years that followed, up until his meeting with Elsdon Best in 1895, Tutakanghau, appears in the literature (newspapers, government reports, letters) among several other leaders as a mediator, supplicant, and diplomat, doing all in his power to adapt to change and preserve what was left of chiefly authority, their rangatiratanga (Holman 2010).

We can summarize the shaping forces of Tutakangahau's later life as the practice of syncretic Māori religion, a struggle to effect the return of confiscated lands, and mana motuhake (local autonomy) for Tūhoe and their tribal relatives. He emerges as both a religious and a civic leader who had come to believe that the settlers could not be defeated by force of arms. He had accepted that the prophecy—"Mā te ture anō te ture e āki" (only the law can prevail against the law)—of his co-religionist Te Kooti Arikirangi signaled the end of warfare and an appeal to the rule of law (Binney 1995: 490). With other Māori leaders of his era, faced with engagement or retreat, he found his available choices limited by military weakness yet susceptible at the same time to the material benefits of European culture. It was this experience of *engagement* that made him so accessible to Best when the ethnographer arrived in his territory. By 1895, Tutakanghau was a modernizer who had once lived traditionally but was now fully present to modernity as played out in late colonial New Zealand.

There *were* no "old-time Māori" by the 1870s, let alone by 1895 when Best came looking—none were left untouched by the arrival of the Pākehā. The Tamakaimoana chief was able to pass on what he knew of the old world because of his place in the new dispensation, attached as he was by this time to Pākehā power and culture. It was here that the role of literacy most counted: he wrote letters to newspapers and officials, disseminated his views and opinions in Māori and Pākehā publications, and read parliamentary debates on land and law, all of which indicates the *present* mode of Tutakangahau's cultural life. He had become a literate and forward-looking political figure who was anything but the backward-gazing sage of European romanticism with a "barbaric" psychology shaped and fixed by oral modes of transmission. Alongside Best, he would become the co-author of a new literature of the Māori world. His later years of involvement with Best and the ethnographer's project of recovery and preservation also coincided with the period of his final political role. As a commissioner in the Urewera Native District Reserve (1896), Tutakangahau would experience final bitter disillusionment with Pākehā power in the last decade of his transformed and transformative life (see Holman 2010: 104–24).

Elsdon Best, the man who would become Tutakangahau's amanuensis (see figure 5.2), was born in June 1856 at his parents' settler farm block at Tawa Flat north of Wellington; this area of the North

Figure 5.2. *Elsdon Best. Undated. © Alexander Turnbull Library, Wellington, New Zealand. Craig, Elsdon Walter Grant (1917–80): Photographs (PAColl-8066-09-28).*

Island had already seen tensions between the colonial government and Māori, and by his fifth birthday, the Land Wars had begun in Taranaki. His farming father was enrolled in the local militia, and as the young Elsdon grew in his teenage years, wars continued through the 1860s, until the last shots were fired in 1872 in the pursuit of Te Kooti Rikirangi, Tutakangahau's leader and co-religionist. From the ages of six to sixteen, he lived in a country where war—or rumors of war—was an ever-present part of life (Craig 1964: 11–21).

At the same time, he was living alongside, playing with, and fishing with Māori children in the area, hearing the language spoken all around him. This free-ranging childhood did not equip him for city life; however, in 1866, his parents sold the farm and moved into urban Wellington, where they sent the teenage boy to school. He had gone from a world of Māori traders around the bustling village of Tinipia (a transliteration of "ginger beer") on Paremata Harbour into the confines of schoolrooms and into studying for the Junior Civil Servant exam, which he passed in 1873.

The seventeen-year-old only held a civil service post for one year, 1874, before he fled the top-hatted and striped-trousered misery of being an office boy, for his brother-in-law's Poverty Bay cattle farm to the northeast. Thus he returned to his earlier life and—vital to his later development—the sites of the East Coast wars where Tutakangahau, the man who would become his Tūhoe teacher, had fought. While the Tūhoe elder's intellectual maturity had been shaped by opposing forces of Māori tradition and biblical literacy, Best's mind maps were forged by the very opposite: emerging evolutionary theory and a scientific model of the universe. If any two individuals might be seen to embody the history and conflict of powerful ideas and influences on the New Zealand colonial frontier, it is difficult to find a pair more seemingly opposed than Best and Tutakangahau (Holman 2010: 44). As a ten-year-old boy, Best devoured *Vestiges of the Natural History of Creation* (1844) by Robert Chambers (1802–71), which shaped his views on evolutionary theories and hierarchical models of human development. He continued his autodidactic studies as he worked on the farm, and he gained fluency in the language first acquired as a child around Tawa and Paremata during his explorations of recent battle sites and conversations with local Māori.

Over the next three years, he continued farming; in 1877 he began a new venture as a logging contractor. Its failure led to his joining the Armed Constabulary, which took him north to Taranaki. This gave rise to further explorations of local archaeological sites—allowing him to further sharpen his Māori language skills with the local people—and resulted in a fateful meeting with two local Pākehā authorities on matters Māori: Stephenson Percy Smith (1840–1922) and Edward Tregear (1846–1931). These two influential Māoriphiles shared Best's fascination for Māori history and supplied him with many books. The relationship would bear fruit in 1892, when Best would become a founding member of the Polynesian Society, "the first ethnological society in the Southern Hemisphere" (Sorrenson 1979: 75–76). Over the period of his service in the Armed Constabulary—which included the sack of the peaceful settlement at Parihaka in November 1881 and the imprisonment of the pacifist prophets Te Whiti-o-Rongomai (1830–1907) and Tohu Kakahi (1828–1907)— Best continued his studies in the existing literature. He made a point of violent disagreements with such missionary ethnographers as the Rev. Richard Taylor (1805–73), a copy of whose 1870 [1855] study, *Te Ika a Maui, or New Zealand and Its Inhabitants*, he possessed and extensively annotated with comments fiery and dismissive: "And this man Taylor an M.A.!" (Taylor 1870).[5] He mocked the cleric for asserting on page 66 of the work that "puerile myths" common to other religious traditions could not "invalidate the scriptural account of man's creation." Best's comprehensive marginalia (sighted by the present author in the ethnographer's original copy) give a fascinating picture of his mental universe and foreshadow a coming embrace of the Darwinian intellectual revolution in the later nineteenth century as well as his own eventual emergence as a secular intellectual. He would also manifest a yearning for the esoteric and the exotic origins of Māori precontact culture, both material and spiritual.

Discharged from the Armed Constabulary, he returned to Poverty Bay and to farming; the deaths of two of his sisters and the move of his brother-in-law and wife Isabel to Argentina persuaded the disconsolate Best to begin learning Spanish in order to follow them. After a peripatetic sojourn in the United States (1883–86), where he moved from job to job, and later working his passage home, he returned to sawmilling in New Zealand. After a time he again moved back to Wellington and reconnected with Edward Tregear and other Māoriphiles, who together would create a core of autodidactic ethnographers, giving Best the opportunity to write and publish the first of his ethnographic studies—"The Races of the Philippines"—in their new journal. It seems that his passion for self-improvement had borne fruit in his ability to read early Spanish ethnographers—no mean feat for a man with, supposedly, no higher education (Best 1892).

It may later appear that Best never considered himself an anthropologist. In *The Maori* (Best 1924: 1:xi), he prefaces his remarks as being "the jottings of a bush collector." In the introduction that follows, however, he opens this major two-volume study with a reference to "*later* anthropological works" (my emphasis). An untrained fieldworker by academic disciplinary standards, he may be referring to the growing ranks of trained professionals:

> The science of anthropology is one that has made great strides within the past thirty years and increasing numbers of people continue to take up the study of man. This has naturally led to a demand for works describing the customs, arts and institutions of savage and barbaric man. Data on these subjects, if collected by responsible persons, are always welcomed by ethnographers. This quickening interest in the subject has led to the collection of much additional matter pertaining to races and tribes concerning whom many works had already been published. A marked feature in many of the later anthropological works is the attention given to detail, combined with a more methodical and scientific manner of compilation. (Best 1924: 1:xiii)

Both in 1924 and when *Waikare-moana* was published almost thirty years earlier, he certainly conceived of himself as a member of that tribe: the anthropologists, ethnographers included. On the very first page of *Waikare-moana*, referring to himself, he writes of the "sensation of vivid interest . . . felt by the ethnologist" (Best 1975 [1897]: 9). It is important to recognize that Best was a master of self-deprecation, yet he was subject to outbursts of rage when he felt his anthropology was being stolen or demeaned by others. In this regard, it is worth mentioning his clash with the Dominion Museum director Augustus Hamilton (1853–1913), an ethnologist (and biologist) who claimed coauthorship of Best's first bulletin, *The Stone Implements of the Maori* (Dominion Museum Bulletin no. 4, 1912). Best never forgave him, even pursuing his quarry beyond the grave (see Holman 2010: 220–22). It is important to take his "bush collector" remark with a grain of salt, as it perhaps reveals the gnawing inferiority complex of an autodidact with no university qualifications in a class-ridden colonial society. In my view, Best clearly saw himself as an anthropologist.

While this background might seem an unlikely training ground in terms of modern anthropological studies, Best's unusual curriculum vitae fitted him perfectly for the task ahead: there were no universities in New Zealand offering to teach him anthropological theory (he had not matriculated and was therefore ineligible for tertiary study), so he taught himself; he was confident from childhood in his relationships with Māori, so he learned the language as he went; he was involved in hard physical labor in the bush, in dangerous environments, so he was physically hardy and able to move through the dense forests and cross treacherous rivers; and he was ambitious to prove himself in his chosen passion. For all his lack of formal educational achievements and his own low estimation of his abilities, his elders in the Polynesian Society saw in Best their opportunity to rescue and preserve the treasures of an imagined dying culture—what Best would come to term "the kura huna," the hidden knowledge (Holman 2010: 94). All that was needed was the opportunity to get him into the field, which came in 1895 as the settler government pursued its policy of roading troublesome areas to bring the benefits of civilization to isolated Māori communities—all the while implementing what amounted to a Pax Romana, building roads that gave military access to any regions that might need pacification. Not all Tūhoe welcomed the Rotorua-Waikaremoana-Wairoa project that aimed to connect the central North Island with the East Coast and open up the Urewera for further development—principally, forestry and mining. Tutakangahau, it seems, was amenable, and he would later become one of a number of local leaders who gained mail contracts in their areas of influence.[6]

It was for this project that Elsdon Best left Wellington for Galatea in April 1895 in order to take up his new role as quartermaster on the Waikaremoana section of the road and to oversee the provisioning of the works and the payment of wages. His real purpose, however, was to do what his employer—the head of the Lands and Survey Department and fellow Māoriphile, Percy Smith—with the support of all other members of the Polynesian Society, had dispatched him there to achieve. Best was to find and record the hidden treasures of Māori knowledge—the aforementioned kura huna—before it disappeared forever with the death of its last bearers, such as Tutakangahau. Best's real job was to locate such experts, the oldest and wisest men of Tūhoe, gain their confidence, and persuade them to commit to paper and preservation the secrets of a mythopoetic culture that was vanishing like the Urewera mists in the heat of the rising sun. It was this Arthurian quest that would produce the book that became *Waikare-moana, The Sea of the Rippling Waters*.

According to Best's biographer and grand-nephew Elsdon Craig (1917–80), when Tūhoe discovered Best was a Māori speaker, "they flocked to see him."[7] Tutakangahau was one of those, and early in 1896 Best wrote to Percy Smith that "Tutaka Ngahau, a leading man of the Tamakaimoana and Ngai-Tawhaki hapus . . . [is] willing to accompany an exploring party in search of a route for the Road."[8] By

April of the same year, Tutakangahau wrote to Percy Smith himself, about a journey to Waikaremoana, "Kua ki mai a pehi kia haere au hai hoa mona" (Best has asked me to go as his companion). He continues, "Ko au hoki he ruanuku i roto i a Tuhoe, a kua whakae au hai hoa mona" (I am the wise man among Tuhoe, I have agreed to be his companion).[9] He also asks for payment for his services. What this remarkable exchange signifies is the depth of the intellectual and cultural revolution that has taken place in the sixty years since the elder's birth in the mid-1830s. The two worlds that gave birth to both men have converged, and at the heart of the meeting is literacy; it will be the power of the written word that Tutakangahau will appeal to when he gets Best to himself, in August 1896, as the journey to the great lake Waikaremoana takes place. In the very next year, Best will publish an account of the journey. Events were moving at a remarkable pace, which indicates a ripeness and an urgency on both sides to get these histories, these ideas, on the written record (see figure 5.3).

This photograph taken by Best (probably at a roadman's camp near Te Whaiti) also tells a story. In the image, which appears on page twelve of the book, we see Tukua-i-te-rangi, Tutakangahau's son,

Figure 5.3. *Tūhoe group, with Tutakangahau, his son Tukuaiterangi, his daughter-in-law Te Kura, and Te Kokau.* © *Alexander Turnbull Library, Wellington, New Zealand. Craig, Elsdon Walter Grant, 1917–80: Photographs (PA1-o-1240-12-1).*

holding a dog, a relaxed, domestic note. This group photograph—complete with a tent (Best's) and a bowler hat on the far right (also Best's)—is important in the way it shows the culture of the moment, the mixture of native and European dress styles. Te Kokau, the man on Tutakangahau's right, is wearing a European jacket and blanket kilt but no shoes; Tutakangahau is also kilted with a blanket and a korowai (traditional cloak); Tukua-i-te-rangi is in complete European dress, with shoes, trousers, braces, and bowler hat, holding a puppy; and his wife is attired in European clothing. Here is a telling image of transitional culture in 1896, at the moment Best and his informant are meeting and establishing what will become a seminal relationship in the history of New Zealand anthropology: a European enquirer and a Māori elder and expert. If these are the visible externals at this moment in time, what exactly is occurring here, what is happening within this group of people that draws them into Best's orbit and he into theirs?

Waikare-moana: The Book

The book under consideration here would hardly have appeared to Victorian readers in late colonial New Zealand as being an ethnographic study of the Tūhoe people. The preface declares that "the following account has been printed by direction of the Hon. John McKenzie, Minister of Lands, with a view of furnishing information to tourists as to the various scenes of beauty on the lake: and at the same time an attempt has been made to invest the different places with a human interest by preserving the old Maori history relating thereto" (Best 1925 [1897]: 6–7). This sounds like every pro forma tourist guidebook ever written, clichéd and bland, with the underlying preservationist instinct betraying a definite sense that Tūhoe were no longer in control of their homeland. However, within what was ostensibly a travel book, published by a government agency, overseen by Percy Smith as surveyor general, is Best's announcement to the ethnological culture in his day and age of both his presence and his mission.

The book Best writes is cloaked in the guise of a travelogue, but in reality it is his first essay in a local ethnography, opening on the very first page with a whiff of romanticism mixed with realpolitik. Along with his desire to "look upon the unwrought wilderness" where "primitive man" has waged war with nature, he is quick to note that "neolithic man"—who blazed trails through forests "he could not

conquer"—has opened up routes "by which the incoming pioneers of
the Age of Steel shall pass along, to leave behind them peace in place
of war, thriving hamlets for stockaded pas, fields of waving grain for
jungle and forest" (ibid.: 9). In reality, this is a lapse into propaganda
that obscures the history and the present political reality faced by
those very people upon whose hospitality Best's research and writing
depended. There is no indication that it was war on Tūhoe by the
settler government and its Māori allies that had displaced them. That
war was waged not with nature but with another culture, and it was
genocidal in application and effects.[10] Only through an early twentieth-century revival of Māori political life and a consequent cultural
rebirth after the World War I—where the influenza pandemic struck
Māori communities far harder than the settler population—would
their expected demise and extinction fail to materialize. It was this
expectation that was part of the pressure on Best to record what was
seen to be passing away forever—the knowledge of precontact Māori
cultural practices and beliefs.[11]

Best was keen to get on the road, overcome as he was with the
anticipation "felt by the ethnologist, botanist, and lover of primitive
folk-lore when entering on a new field for research. For the glamour
of the wilderness in upon him and the *kura huna*—the 'concealed
treasure' (of knowledge)—loometh large in the Land of Tuhoe"
(ibid). The Arthurian quest of the Victorian romantic is hard to ignore
in this declaration, yet behind the language is a serious intent. Best is
determined to record whatever he can from the accounts of such elders as Tutakangahau. He is correct in assuming that most of what
Tūhoe have been taught and have experienced, in the century now
ending, is for the settler cultureboth unknown and of great value. For
the man who will become his principal informant, the same is true for
his people and for their descendants; the profound cultural changes
overtaking Māori society have made it imperative also for him to engage in a preservationist project, with entirely different motives. Best
presents Tutakangahau to his readers as the journey begins, authenti-
cating his account with a vivid portrait.

> A word here as to the Kaumatua, for me thinks he is the leading charac-
> ter of this sketch. An old man, probably sixty-five years of age, yet both
> strong and active, a leading chief of the Tuhoe tribe. . . . A warrior of the
> olden time, his face deeply scored by the chisel of the tattoer, possess-
> ing, moreover, a large-minded contempt for the habiliments of the white
> man. Here is a man who has faced death in many a fierce struggle, and
> [had] led his hill-bred clan in many a gallant charge. And yet withal a

quiet-mannered and courteous companion, ever ready to allay strife among his tribesmen, or to assist the stranger within his gates, be that stranger Pakeha or Maori. Such is the Kaumatua. (ibid.: 11)

Here is Best's kaitakawaenga (mediator), his necessary guide through the world in which he will begin a life's work: his ethnographic studies of Te Iwi Māori, New Zealand's Indigenous people.

Traveling onward, we read Best's depiction of the journey, where "conversation supplies the place of literature" (ibid.: 17). The stories are located, centered on place; at Te Umu-roa, Best hears the story of Moetere and Houhiri who died in the snows of Huiarau while hunting kiwi to obtain the bird's precious feathers, which are used for the korowai (cloaks) of high-ranking persons. Best relates the account as it was told to him by Tutakangahau—"Even so, O Pakeha! did Moetere and her lover perish on the great mountain ... [and] you shall look upon the stream, which yet bears the name of Moetere, and camp amid the snows of Huia-rau" (ibid.: 19). Best comments: "Such is the story of Moetere, as related by her descendants in the *wharepuni* (meeting house) at Te Umuroa. But it is past midnight, and we must follow the example of the Kaumatua, and sleep that we may acquire strength" (ibid.: 20). The placement of this early episode is significant for a number of reasons: it sets the method of dialogic explanations, the voice of Best (as author) foregrounding Tutakangahau as teacher (the Kaumātua) and himself as student (the Pākehā). It also dramatizes Māori storytelling techniques and methods of locating whakapapa (descent lines) and history (territorial rights), both of which establish Māori storytellers as those to whom the place belongs. Best proceeds in this manner throughout, connecting stories the old man tells him with the geography of the area, alerting the reader to the links between conquest, place, ritual, whakapapa, and the ensuing kōrero (conversations, stories) that link these lines of descent to the land. Tutakangahau is physically dramatizing these kōrero in a quintessentially Māori way, by taking Best to the places that are stories *in themselves*, forever peopled by men and women and by spirits, the living and the dead.

The ethnographer is not averse to a little lexicography and giving the derivation of place names. Kapiti—where the traveling party pauses to "sling the billy" (brew tea)—comes from a tale of snaring ducks (*kawai parera*), which signifies the way the birds were caught. It is also the place in the text where Best first uses direct quotes to show that this is Tutakangahau speaking. "The Kaumatua seats himself by the fire and relates the origin of this place name:—'In olden times, certain men of Ngati-Ruapani went to Lake Waikare-iti to snare the wily *parera* [ducks]'" (ibid.: 22). The reader is also given a number of descriptions of native flora, their names, and their uses by Tūhoe—remembering that at the outset, the writer has styled himself as both an ethnologist and a botanist. Some flora are used in perfumes, "the oil of the titoki berries was scented with the gum of the tarata and the kopuru," in which the skin of the swamp hen (pūkeko, *Porphyrio melatonus*) was immersed (ibid.: 23). Formed into a ball and suspended from the neck, this love charm here attracts an early example of Best's deep antipathy toward the influence of Christianity on Māori society: "But when the missionaries of the Pakeha came they condemned this practise as savouring of the Evil One, and calculated to lead the Tuhoe soul to perdition" (ibid.).

As he proceeds, moving always toward the goal of the journey—the private audience with Tutakangahau, which is the centerpiece of this work—Best demonstrates his ability to combine careful botanical descriptions, a sincere appreciation of the attractions of the myriad fern species, with a social scientist's appreciation of the human uses of these plants. On the one hand, he can write, "The heart of the Pakeha goes forth in love for these youngest and fairest children of Tane, the god of forests"; on the other, he describes the limitations of the inferior flaxes in the Urewera ranges and how Tūhoe had to make use of the common mauku fern. This he illustrates by citing the local proverb, "*Rua-tahuna kakahu mauku*—Rua-tahuna of the mauku garments" (ibid.: 24).

But this is no botanical expedition: the real reason Tutakangahau invites Best to share this journey to the sacred mountain of Panekiri and the great lake Waikaremoana is to commission the Pākehā as his amanuensis, a scribe to gather all that the koroua (elder) wishes to record and preserve for future generations. Having long since become literate in Māori, Tutakangahau is deeply aware of the erosion of the authority of oral transmission and the growing power of the written word.

As the account progresses, Best makes it clear that this is a valedictory moment for Tutakangahau, as the elder "trudges on barefooted, with a serene indifference, through the ice-cold snow, dislodging heavy masses of the same from the sturdy bushes as he pushes his way through the thicket" (ibid.: 26). They stand on the crest of Hui-arau, emerging from the bush country to see below them "the grand panorama of the lower country . . . the voiceless forest, the rugged crags, the shimmering waters—silent, imposing and grand" (ibid.: 28). Tutakangahau stands alone on the cliff's brow and chants "a long

wailing lament for his old comrades who have passed on to the Re-
inga (place of departed spirits) . . . for his ancestors who dwelt and
fought here in the long ago" (ibid.). Tutakangahau calls to the land
itself and to the hunga mate (the dead) whose bones still lie "beneath
dark waters, in the burial caves of old." The smoke of their campfires
no longer rises, he cries, "and I alone of your generation am left . . .
of the fighting men of old," though his strength to avenge them has
left him. As his lament ends, he cries out that he may never return
to climb "this great *ika whenua* (backbone) to greet you. *E noho ra!*
(farewell)" (ibid.: 29). This powerful event early in the relationship of
the two men has the literary effect of dramatizing Best's role as the
witness while establishing the voice of Tutakangahau as emblematic
of a passing generation and a vanishing world, a somber valediction.

The old man is well aware that he is passing through one world
into another, and he deliberately grants the Pākehā an audience at a
private and historic moment. What is enacted here may legitimately
be viewed as orality handing over its power to the written word; this
will become even more apparent a few pages later when Best, alone
with Tutakangahau at Maahu on Wairau—the young carriers sent
away to replenish the supplies—writes of what the kaumātua expects
of him. Best concludes his description of the old man's lament: "As
the old patriarch of the 'People of the Mist' finished the tangi for the
dead of his tribe [he] grabbed his staff and strode forward without
a word. As silently the carriers take up their burdens and move on
after the Kaumatua" (ibid.). What follows over the next twenty pages
combines a more conventional journalistic account with further botanical examples, explanations of place names and their significance,
and, with Best donning his ethnographer's hat, explanations of customs such as the placing of a newborn's umbilical cord (iho) as a tohu
whenua, a sign to preserve the influence of future generations "over
the lands adjacent" (ibid.: 33).

Traveling east, through "the famous Strait of Manaia," they enter
a branch of the lake, Wairau Moana, leaving behind the main body,
"Waikare-whanaunga-kore (Waikare, the relationless)"—a warning
about the unpredictable and dangerous nature of this major body
of deep water: 54 square kilometers, 600 meters above sea level, and
over 250 meters at its deepest point. Crossing the lake, they will
make landfall after drifting "back into the remote past . . . [when] the
ao marama (or world of light and being) is far behind us" (ibid.: 41).
This is a journey through time as much as space. They land their canoe at Waiopaoa and pitch their tents. Having completed their preparations and rested, the bearers now leave Best and Tutakangahau to

their mission: "The boat has gone away in the care of the 'children' [of the Mist, i.e., Tūhoe]; gone to One-poto, the parts trodden by the white man, and the Kaumatua and the Pakeha are left in the realm of Maahu (a powerful ancestor), the lonest spot in lone Wairau" (ibid.: 48). Best has set the scene for an encounter somewhere between the magical, the metaphysical, and the ethnographic—but most of all, he is about to relate how, where, and from whom he derives his authority to record for this world, the secrets of another.

From the viewpoint of contemporary anthropology, Best's weakness would primarily be his romanticism (though his writing can be hugely entertaining, and the picture of the lake and surrounding bush-clad hills is highly evocative). It is difficult for the reader, however, to discover quite when and where the old man is speaking and where the writer is commenting, but there are a number of cues and clues. While this is not modern anthropology, there are certainly some clear indications, such as what Tutakangahau says to Best when he opens his storehouse of knowledge and why he is telling these histories and legends. "It is well," Tutakangahau begins, "that I should tell you the legend of the 'Sea of Rippling Waters,' for that is why I followed you [here] ... it is not an idle journey, but one in which there is much to be learned and much to be seen" (ibid.). Best should not be alarmed, Tutakangahau tells him, "at the monsters which inhabit this 'Sea of Waikare,' for I am an *ariki taniwha* [Lord of the Dragons]. I am descended from Rua-mano, and Nga-rangi-hangu, and Te Tahi-o-te-rangi, who were *taniwha* ancestors of mine" (ibid.: 48–49).[12] In proclaiming himself a descendant of—and equal to— supernatural beings, Tutakangahau moves his disclosures into another realm, one of magic and danger, and great spiritual power. Best is safe with him—"no *taniwha* will molest me," Tutakangahau adds. He now instructs his pupil: the ethnographer must be "strenuous in retaining what I will impart," because the Pākehā, while under his protection, has not partaken of traditional ceremonies that bind oral knowledge from expert to pupil (ibid.: 49).

This will be a new form of cross-cultural teaching, a necessary exchange, as Tutakangahau laments that his children "have little love for the gallant stories of old." Te Ao Mārama (the world of light, a poetic coinage for the literate modernity of Europe), has severed the link with a past that preserved its reality through oral traditions. "I will tell them to you," he declares, "and one other and no more, that you may preserve the traditions of my people and record their ancient customs, that they may be retained in the world of light" (ibid.). Preserve, record, retain: it is difficult to interpret this historic moment as anything other than a paradigm shift—undergone long before in the world of Best's English forebears—where we see the power of memory in the culture of orality delivered to the world of the book, the written word. What this inevitable declaration signifies is the end of tradition, lived prior, as known and practiced by the old man's Tūhoe forebears. He bows to the pressures of modernity, inducting Best and his pen into the whare takiura (a school of esoteric teaching, often undertaken at night). Tutakangahau seems acutely aware that if he does not take this step, much of what he and others know will die with them. What was their alternative? Māori with a level of literacy, bilingualism—and the access to the power and privilege to record and publish such material—were those such as the members of Parliament, James Carroll (1857–1926) and Apirana Ngata (1874–1950), who were fully engaged elsewhere in the struggle to ensure the survival of their people. Formerly, there were traditional prohibitions on who was taught such knowledge and who retained and transmitted it. Relying now on publication for the transmission and retention of sacred knowledge and traditions meant opening all things to the light; to this day, some Māori dispute that this was the case, arguing without necessarily offering proof that the real esoterica was withheld from Best.

Yet Best's arrival in the Urewera must have seemed greatly providential to someone like Tutakangahau, who wasted no time in making himself known to the Māori-speaking Pākehā quartermaster on the Waikaremoana roading project. He had come to realize that his son's generation belonged to a new age and could not be trained as he himself had been, in the world that existed before the encroachments of the Europeans, whose appearance had led to disastrous wars—and defeat for his people. He now instructs Best as if he were a pupil: "Do you plainly write them [customs and traditions] in your *paipera* [Bible, record book], that all who love such things may understand" (ibid.). This is a moment of great poignancy; the kaumātua is clearly distressed about the loss of interest in the ancient stories he knows so well, at the broken circle of Māori thought, ripped open like a cobweb by invaders from the white world (Perham 1988: 173–74).[13] More than this: he is placing his faith in a man he has known, at most, for fourteen months (Best arrived at Galatea in April 1895, and this journey was undertaken in August of the following year). He looks ahead to an uncertain future: "I would even hope that my children may yet return to the *kura* (knowledge, valuable possession) of Tuhoe and of Potiki and be proud of the achievements of their ancestors. *Tena!*" (Best 1925 [1897]: 49).

Following this is a thirty-page account of "the ancient people of Waikaremoana," their legends and their wars, with accompanying whakapapa (descent lines, genealogies), karakia (prayers), laments, and a more recent history of Ngāti Ruapani and Tūhoe, traditional enemies (ibid. 49–83). This consists of direct recordings of what Tutakangahau declares to Best, interspersed with commentaries by the Pākehā. At one moment, we read Best, at another, the Kaumātua—there is no certainty about exactly what the old man said (due to a lack of recording technology) or of the way Best edited or shaped his notes into the book we have before us. Nevertheless, this was the opening up of the kura huna (hidden knowledge), beyond the boundaries of the Urewera to a degree that it was not available to the world before—and it would almost certainly not have survived Tutakangahau's passing on.

The book continues, after Best has set the scene, with a three-page account by the elder of the ancient peoples of Waikaremoana, stories concerning god-men such as Maahu and Haere. "We do not know the history of that old, old race, but merely retain a few legends concerning them and their doings. But it was far back in the ages of darkness when Maahu and his people lived in this land, for he and others were *atua* (gods) themselves, and held strange powers," Best records Tutakangahau, beginning what will be a long night of storytelling (ibid.: 49). After assuring the ethnographer that he is an ariki taniwha, a Lord of the Dragons, Tutakangahau links himself immediately to these ancestors, as possessing supernatural origins. Here is the portal between the new world and the old, a world where "Maahu must have lived many generations ago, for did he not engage in combat with Haere, the rainbow god, and each destroyed the other by supernatural powers?" (ibid.: 50). The story and the genealogies that accompany the telling open to Best and his readers a window on indigenous explanations of origins and authority—explanations that are now challenged by the European presence and their scientific conceptions of human progress. Best then links these traditions, localized here among Tūhoe but carried "from older lands across the ocean in times long passed away," indicating the northern Polynesian origins of this account. He is anxious to point out that this Maahu, the powerful ancestor who caused the formation of the great lake beside which they are seated in their camp, has now been identified to him—the Pākehā—by Tutakangahau, the Kaumātua. This is important in that Tutakangahau's imprimatur on Best's reinscribing of these stories is the conferral of authenticity on the ethnographic project. Maahu's work in forming the lake is enlarged upon in "the more

generally-received version of that most ancient and wondrous legend," that of Maahu's son, Hau-Mapuhuia, and his place in the formation of Waikaremoana—which follows over the next four pages
(ibid.: 55–58).

Best is once again asserting a measure of authority, showing that
he knows there are other versions of the story he is being told. His
description of why the lake has certain geographical features—as
recounted by Tutakangahau in terms of legendary explanations—is
a clear indication of the cross-cultural nature of the exchange. The
father drowned the son for insolence and disobedience, and in the
son's struggle to escape, "he reached the *komore* (end), where the
waters rush forth" and became fixed there where he lies to this day
(ibid.: 56). Tutakangahau sings a lament of Maahu for his dead son,
which speaks of "water gushing forth at Te Whangaromanga,/ Where
Hau-mapuhia rumbles down below."[14]

Best reappears in the text to elaborate on the legend, describing it
in Eurocentric terms as follows:

> A strange legend and an ancient, viewed from the standpoint of an unlet-
> tered people possessing no knowledge of graphic art, and relying entirely
> upon oral tradition. It originated probably in the widespread and univer-
> sal desire implanted in the human mind to assign a cause and origin to all
> material objects and manifestations of Nature. (ibid.: 58)

As if this were not a rich enough interpolation for analysis, the aster-
isk sends the reader to a footnote, ascribed to the "EDITOR." In the
absence of any other indication, it makes sense to credit this observation to the commissioner of Best's text, Stephenson Percy Smith,
his boss and the author of the book's preface: "There is little doubt
that the lake was formed by a vast land-slip, now covered with forest,
which fell from the slopes of the mountains on the east of the outlet,
and filled up what was formerly a valley. Probably this took place
before the advent of the Maori; but he is quite equal to understanding
the cause, and with his love of the marvellous, to inventing a supernatural reason for it" (ibid.: 58).

It is difficult—reading this and Best's observations—not to have
some sensation of patronage, of adults speaking of children, or alien
visitors from another planet explaining the inhabitants of earth to
their own satisfaction. It is hardly surprising that many Māori today
are angered by such comments, but there is no avoiding the fact that
in the times Tutakangahau and other senior Tūhoe leaders lived, there
was little alternative to engagement with such Māoriphiles in order
to get Māori histories and mythologies onto paper and into the new

world of print for preservation. Engagement was a compromise, in full realization of the assymetrical power relationships that prevailed at the time. Conquest and colonization allowed the ethnographers access; print and preservation gave the Indigenous authors their foothold on the future. What Tutakangahau said to Best in commissioning him can hardly be interpreted any other way. He used his power and prestige to access the channels that would ensure erasure could not be complete. The evidence before us here—and in many other publications Best completed using the material supplied by such elders—proves that Tutakangahau was far-sighted, a true matakite (a seer).

What follows over the next ten pages are three legends recounted by Tutakangahau: that of the Tauira, the aboriginal people of Waikaremoana; that of Rua and Tangaroa, ancestors of the ancient Ngā Potiki tribe; and an extensive account of Ruakapana, a great bird that carries an important ancestor, Pourangahua, back from his journey to Hawaiki (the traditional origin site of Māori mythology). What these stories provide—beyond their rich detail of intertribal storytelling and relationships—are further opportunities for Best to display his own learning in the area of Polynesian traditions, citing also other writers such as the Rev. Richard Taylor's *Te Ika a Maui* and explaining to the reader the significance of the whare-potae, the house of mourning referred to by the Tūhoe elder in his aforementioned accounts (ibid.: 69–70). Here is the relationship that empowers the work: Tutakangahau speaks; then, Best glosses and elaborates, beginning a shared ethnographic project that over the next ten years will record as much of Tūhoe history, myth, beliefs, and lifeways as the two men are able to collect and preserve in their historic collaboration.

The final section of the work divides into interwoven themes: histories of ancient battles with traditional Tūhoe enemies (Ngāti Ruapani, Ngāti Kahungunu), interspersed with descriptions of flora and fauna, and other meditations as the journey winds down (73–83, 83–102), concluding with an account of more recent battles during the 1870s in an appendix (103–6).

Rejoined by the youthful paddlers, we hear Tutakangahau commence his tangi, a farewell lamentation. As they pass Pa Pouaru and Te Waiwai, he declares that the weapons of the Pākehā now mean that war parties hardly need leave home to fight each other, "for a bullet will travel a hundred miles—or is it a hundred yards?" (ibid.: 92). It is a graphic acknowledgment of the speed of change and his awareness of what has overcome his world. Rather than emphasizing the elder's sense of the present, however, Best is at pains to construct Tutakangahau as a man living in the past, *a man of the past*—a living example of the mythopoetic Māori whose authentic being he seeks to capture and embalm in the museum of progress.

Best writes this story in his persona as curator, a recorder of the psychology of "the old time Māori." All that he goes on to do later will be influenced by these assumptions: that a preexistent level of spiritual development is laid open to be harvested in the very being of such men. This does not invalidate the parallel account he will also preserve, of Māori material culture in his own day and age, and of its origins; rather, his quest to discover an authentic Māori being derived from a romantic cast of mind, the seeker of an anthropological Holy Grail that had to be captured alive before it was lost in the onward march of an urban civilization he secretly despised (Holman 2010: 286–89).[15] In its own strange fashion, Best's affection for this man—and many other Māori elders he befriended—marks him as a man out of time, at odds with that same progress he appears to laud. His final imaging of Tutakangahau at journey's end suggests as much:

> There is no holding him now; for the old fighter is once again started on the beloved subject of the men of yore—their deeds, evil and otherwise, in the world of light—and tale after tale comes of wars and sieges and priestly craft, as the *Kaumātua* drifts back over the stormy sea of his adventurous life, and greets again his old companions of the war-path, and again takes his place at the camp fires whose ashes have been cold for half a century. (Best 1975 [1897]: 94–95)

It is difficult not to feel that Best is in some measure speaking of himself, as the outsider he will increasingly become in the years ahead (see Holman 2006). While the story here recorded in print is designed for and intended to be read by a Pākehā audience, Best uses Māori orature and pedagogy as both method and material. This is a far cry from armchair anthropology; it is a seminal moment in the development of a local ethnography that attempts to foreground the character of an indigenous culture in the midst of colonial swamping, military defeat, and the rapid loss of land and authority. Best is, of course, a partaker of that colonizing culture, hardly a disinterested observer. There are a number of asides throughout the book where he reminds his settler readers that another world—one of their making—impinges on that of Tutakangahau and his own: "Yet the Steel Age is here and the stone *toki* (axe) is replaced by the products of Sheffield and Pittsburgh" (Best 1975 [1897]: 21). On the one hand, he is writing a tourist's guidebook for his employer; on the other, more significant side, he is making the most of an opportunity to get his years of autodidactic ethnographic readings into print. The book weaves together three contrasting visions of nature from one individual, Elsdon Best: the sublime nature beloved of the Romantics; the allegedly *supernatural* nature of Māori, peopled by gods and dragons; and the blind nature of deterministic social evolutionism. Yet it also gives to the outside world an entry of sorts into late nineteenth-century Tūhoe society, the opening chapter in a writing life whose prolific output would continue until Best's death in 1931. He makes the most of the opportunity presented to him and leaves the reader with a unique view of the world inhabited by his informant, Tutakangahau, and his people. These writings have since been contested and even discounted by some Tūhoe tribal members; yet, had they never been recorded at the time, Tūhoe would surely have been left the poorer.[16]

This reading of Tutakangahau's presence in the literature is of a leader constantly engaged with life—with modernity; and while he may have related to Best in a way that the ethnographer encouraged, Tutakangahau had his own lived reality beyond Best's construction of the vanishing primitive, "the old time Māori." His engagement with Best is forward, future focused rather than backward looking. In passing on the rich trove of material he gave to the ethnographer, he was engaged in an act of cultural transference between equals. This was not the surrender of esoteric knowledge to an envoy from a superior stage of social development—which is the logical outcome of Best's views, absorbed from his readings and the climate of the times; rather, Tutakangahau's life was one of action and power, no matter how Best records him in his final years, losing his memory and embracing "the cult of the 'New Messiah,' Rua Kenana of Maungapōhatu" (Best, letter to Percy Smith, 2 January 1908).[17]

Elsdon Best in his age and long after was regarded as New Zealand's foremost authority on Māori history, their origins, language, and culture. There were some private challenges in the 1920s to his expertise and authority, exemplified through personal correspondence between leading Māori intellectuals Te Rangi Hiroa (Sir Peter Buck) (1877–1951) and Tā Apirana Ngata, both of whom were significant cultural and political leaders (Holman 2010: 261–62). In the same historic moment, others such as Raymond Firth (1901–2002), the New Zealand–born anthropologist and London-based former student of Malinowski, were lauding Best's "unrivalled research" (Firth 1929: xx). Today, his work also lives on beyond New Zealand, mostly thanks to Marcel Mauss's *Essai sur le don* (The Gift, 1969 [1923–24]), and here in his natal land through the magisterial Williams' *Dictionary of the Māori Language* (1844–1971), to which he was a significant contributor through his interviews of Māori respondents and his hard-won prowess in their native tongue (Holman 2010: 154–57). Elsdon Best was a pioneering fieldworker, hastening the end of armchair anthropology; his interviews and notes from activity undertaken in the challenging and inhospitable mountain region inhabited by Ngāi Tūhoe, and later his extensive publications, became the foundational library of New Zealand anthropological writings. Although rightly and often contested since the Māori Renaissance of the 1970s and in the years that have followed, they remain foundational, and most are still in print. Behind these works stand the figures of those leaders he would call his "academy," principal among them Tutakangahau of Maungapōhatu, who did not live to see his commissioning of Te Peehi (Best) fulfilled, as he hoped, in the generations of his people to come.

Conclusion

Literacy was and is a primary agent in the creation of what we have now figured as *modernity*; modernity in turn empowers and extends literacy. Spoken language was over time subject to scribal recording; the written word, which later became the printed word with the arrival of the printing press, was transmitted as mass media; latterly, the emergence of digital texts and online transmission has birthed a virtual world of instant information. Ethnographers of preliterate oral cultures were recording a rapid transition to modernity by capturing the spoken word in text; at the same time, they were helping to supplant and destroy the very thing they were intent on preserving—indigenous realities. As they recorded histories, systems of knowing, and ways of being, they were not just translating language and ideas, they were effectively translating ways of *being human*. Oral cultures were never completely overcome, but they could no longer be as they were once the printed word had marched in and captured the narratives. Some ethnographers—such as Best—were working in fields where literacy was already well embedded in formerly preliterate oral cultures. Tutakangahau was never that chimera—an "old time Māori"—but a man of his time, bilingual, bicultural, literate in his native tongue.

As it was then, so it is today; change runs in parallel lines, mingling currents and actualities impossible to disentangle. Digital nativity is overtaking, while not yet completely destroying, a deeply embedded print culture in a process of generational change, the outcomes of which are not clear. This is not postmodernity—modernity was never supplanted by a mere idea, or philosophical speculation; it was always too deeply embedded in the material world for that. Instead, we have today what may be termed *über-modernity*, the logical outcome of technologies that place print and publishing back in the hands of each tribal member. Since the arrival of Twitter and other information sharing technologies, we are now enabled to send our smoke signals and drumbeats to unseen followers with each and every tweet. From Hebrew scribes to the Diamond Sutra of the Tang Dynasty, from Gutenberg to Einstein to Greta Thunberg and Barack Obama, the word made flesh still dwells among us, awaiting tomorrow, always restless, on the move and leaving a trail. Tutakangahau and Elsdon Best in their time were voyagers on these seas of change, navigating with the skills they possessed in order to create lasting meanings for a future they could not imagine but knew was coming.

Jeffrey Paparoa Holman was born in London in 1947 and came to New Zealand in 1950. He is a Pākehā writer of history, memoir, and poetry, a specialist in Māori studies, and the author of *Best of Both Worlds: The Story of Elsdon Best and Tutakangahau* (Penguin, 2010). His 2013 memoir, *The Lost Pilot*, involved travel to Japan in 2011 to meet the families of kamikaze pilots who had died attacking his father's aircraft carrier HMS *Illustrious* in 1945. His most recent works are *Dylan Junkie* (Mākaro Press, 2017), a collection of poems to Bob Dylan, and a memoir, *Now When It Rains* (Steele Roberts, Aotearoa, 2018). He was the 2012 New Zealand Writer in the International Writers Program at the University of Iowa; in 2016, he was the invited New Zealand poet to the Festival Internacional de Poesia de Granada, Nicaragua. He has recently retired as a senior adjunct fellow at the University of Canterbury's School of Humanities and Creative Arts, where he served from 2010 to 2019.

Notes

1. With regard to Māori words in the text, since the 1970s it has ceased to be the practice in Aotearoa/New Zealand academic writing (and writing in general) to italicize lexical items from one of the country's three official languages: Te Reo Māori, English, and Sign. It is now considered inappropriate to treat Māori as a foreign language. Where quotes of original material contain italicized Māori words—as in Best's usage here in *Waikare-moana*—the italics are retained. Where a Māori word is used, a translation is given in parentheses, e.g., iwi (tribe, people).
2. https://nzhistory.govt.nz/culture/encounters/polynesian-voyaging.

3. https://teara.govt.nz/en/ngai-tuhoe/print.
4. Best also possessed a copy of Max Müller's *Anthropological Religion* (1892), which he had personally annotated (see Craig 1964: 239). The nineteenth-century genealogy of the scientific use of terms borrowed from the Greek μυθοποίησις (mythopoeia, mythopoiesis, mythopoetry, mythopoetics) goes back at least to the Victorian Hellenist George Grote (1794–1871) and in particular to his colossal *History of Greece* (1846–56). Their etymological meaning—creating stories about the gods—does not exhaust their connotations, which vary according to the authors and the currents of thought. It is clear that for Best, the term *mythopoetic*, which he used quite often, allowed him to insist, like Friedrich Max Müller, on the different dimensions of the mythological phenomenon, the poetic dimension, and, in particular, a primitive developmental stage in human psychology (Rosa 2018: 78n2).
5. Best's personal copy of Taylor's *Te Ika a Maui* (1870) was extensively annotated by Best, in this case on page 66. The book was sighted by the present author in 2009, when a descendant of one of Best's sisters auctioned many of his works. This copy was purchased by a rare books dealer in Auckland, who allowed me to view it. See Holman (2010: 84–85), where images of Best's remarks are reproduced.
6. A mail contract was a government contract to deliver letters, a postal service that was a form of income to tribal leaders.
7. Elsdon Craig, Notes for *Man of the Mist*, MS-Papers-7888-024, Craig Papers, Alexander Turnbull Library (Wellington), 77.
8. *Repro. 1801*, LS-1, 21734/64, Archives New Zealand/Te Rua Mahara o te Kāwanatanga, Wellington. Letter from Best to Percy Smith, Surveyor General, Wellington, from Te Whāiti, 20 February 1896.
9. LS-1, 21734, Archives New Zealand/Te Rua Mahara o te Kāwanatanga, Wellington. Letter from Tutakangahau to Percy Smith, Surveyor-General, Wellington. Te Whāiti, 10 April 1896: a Tūhoe "wise man" who will go as a guide with Best ("Pehi") to Waikaremoana.
10. On the issue of Māori views on the outcome of the wars of the 1860s onward, see http://nzetc.victoria.ac.nz/tm/scholarly/tei-KawRena-t1-g1-t1.html. This page contains *parts of an exchange of letters* between a Māori leader in the 1860s and a regional superintendent about the outbreak of what would become the New Zealand Wars. Renata Tamaki-Hikurangi (1808?–88) was from 1860 on well placed to describe what this meant for Māori (he took part in the fighting) and was not shy in pointing out its genocidal implications. He writes that the governor had sent to England for soldiers "to exterminate these tribes of ours" ("a tae atu ki Ingarangi hei whakangaro i ena iwi o matou"). What happened in the next ten years was only to prove him right. The original text of this exchange of letters contains a powerful portrayal of New Zealand colonial history at the very beginning of the war on Māori. In 1860 Renata quotes a speech by the senior Waikato chief Pōtatau Te Wherowhero on what these wars implied. Te Wherowhero declared to the governor

that Māori, under Christian evangelism, have given up their old gods, including Uenuku, "the man-eater" (i.e., a cannibal god). But "now the Governor, the supporter (*kaupapa*) of Jehovah, has stepped forward and carried off Uenuku, the cannibal of Taranaki, as his god *for the destruction of man*" (my emphasis). Meaning, the governor (and the settlers) are abandoning their Christian God (Jehovah) and adopting our god (Uenuku), that is, they are going to devour Māori. A prescient Te Wherowhero recognized genocide when he saw it coming. (NB: The actual quote from Pōtatau Te Wherowhero is not in the link above but appears in the original exchange of letters in the *New Zealand Spectator*, Wellington, 7 November 1860.)

11. See also Head (2001), "The Pursuit of Modernity in Māori Society."
12. Ibid. 48–49. A taniwha is a fabulous monster, residing principally in deep waters; a powerful spiritual being.
13. For more on this point, see Holman, *Best of Both Worlds* (2010: 247–48), where the British colonial historian Margery Perham (1895–1982), during a visit to New Zealand in 1929, is quoted on her meeting with the elder Best and cites his view that the Māori circle of life and ideas had been torn apart by the arrival of European thought, by the "gun, money and Christianity" (Perham 1988: 173–74).
14. The same site of the lake's outlet can be visited today, but sadly the diversion of the Waikaretaheke River for a hydroelectricity scheme has covered the area in a landslide, and those physical features that led Māori to ascribe a human form therein— "head downhill" and legs extended up the hillside, "hair floating and waving in the foaming waters"—are now gone (Holman 2010: 57).
15. For a discussion of Best's eugenicist leanings, see Holman (2010: 286–89).
16. This is certainly true of some critics in the postwar generation of Tūhoe and other Māori tribal scholars, but most certainly not by all, nor by the parents and grandparents of these "baby boomers" active since 1945.
17. Letter to S. Percy Smith, Ruatoki, 2 January 1908. See Craig, Elsdon, Notes for a Biography of Elsdon Best (267), MS-Papers—7888-024, Alexander Turnbull Library, Wellington, New Zealand. This disparaging comment refers to the religious community Iharaira (Israelites) founded deep in the Urewera by the prophet Rua Kenana, upon his syncretic teachings—on Tutakangahau's home ground. The atheist in Best despised what he saw as the inauthenticity of this last Tūhoe prophet and objected to his power over his followers.

References

Bagnall, A. G., and G. C. Petersen. 1948. *William Colenso, Printer, Missionary, Botanist, Explorer, Politician: His Life and Journeys*. Wellington: Reed.

Best, Elsdon. 1975 [1897]. *Waikare-moana: The Sea of the Rippling Waters.* Wellington: A.R. Shearer, Government Printer [1st ed., Wellington: Government Printer, 1897].

——. 1892. "The Races of the Philippines/Prehistoric Civilisations of the Philippines," pts. 1–2. *Journal of the Polynesian Society* 1 (Wellington: The Polynesian Society): 7–19, 118–125, 195–201.

——. 1912. *The Stone Implements of the Maori.* Dominion Museum Bulletin no. 4. Wellington: Government Printer.

——. 1924. *The Maori.* 2 vols. Wellington: Harry H. Tombs.

——. 1925 [1897]. *Tuhoe—The Children of the Mist: A Sketch of the Origin, History, Myths, and Beliefs of the Tuhoe Tribe of the Maori of New Zealand; with Some Account of Other Early Tribes of the Bay of Plenty District.* 2 vols. New Plymouth: Thomas Avery & Sons.

Binney, Judith. 1995. *Redemption Songs: A Life of Te Kooti Arikirangi Te Turuki.* Auckland: Bridget Williams Books.

Chambers, Robert [anon.]. 1844. *Vestiges of the Natural History of Creation.* London: John Churchill.

Craig, Elsdon. 1964. *The Man of the Mist.* Wellington: Reed.

Firth, Raymond. 1929. *The Primitive Economics of the New Zealand Maori.* London: Routledge.

Grote, George. 1846–56. *A History of Greece: From the Earliest Period to the Close of the Generation Contemporary with Alexander the Great.* 12 vols. London: John Murray.

Head, Lyndsay. 2001. "The Pursuit of Modernity in Māori Society—The Conceptual Bases of Citizenship in the Early Colonial Period." In *Histories of Power and Loss: Uses of the Past—A New Zealand Commentary,* edited by Andrew Sharp and Paul McHugh. Wellington: Bridget Williams Books.

Holman, Jeffrey Paparoa. 2006. "Elsdon Best: Elegist in Search of a Poetic." *Ka mate ka ora: A New Zealand Journal of Poetry and Poetics.* The New Zealand Electronic Poetry Centre, no. 2, July. Retrieved 25 November 2020 from http://www.nzepc.auckland.ac.nz/kmko/02/ka_mate02_holman.asp.

——. 2010. *Best of Both Worlds: The Story of Elsdon Best and Tutakangahau.* Auckland: Penguin Books.

Mauss, Marcel. 1969 [1923–24]. *The Gift* [Essai sur le don]. Translated by Ian Cunnison. London: Cohen & West.

Max Müller, Friedrich. 1881. *Selected Essays on Language, Mythology and Religion.* Vol. 1. London: Longman, Green & Co.

——. 1892. *Anthropological Religion: The Gifford Lectures.* Vol. 3. London: Longman.

Perham, Margery. 1988. *Pacific Prelude.* London: Peter Owen.

Rosa, Frederico Delgado. 2018. *Elsdon Best, l'ethnographe immemorial: Sauvetage et transformation de la mythopoétique maorie.* Preface by Herbert S. Lewis. Paris: BEROSE International Encyclopaedia of the Histories of Anthropology (Les Carnets de Bérose 9).

Sorrenson, M. P. K. 1979. *Maori Origins and Migrations*. Auckland: Auckland University Press/Oxford University Press.

Taylor, Rev. Richard. 1870 [1855]. *Te Ika a Maui, or New Zealand and Its Inhabitants*. 2nd ed. London: William McIntosh/H. Ireson Jones/ Wanganui.

6

Partnership with a Native American Family

Alice C. Fletcher, Francis La Flesche, and *The Omaha Tribe* (1911)

Joanna Cohan Scherer

In 1911 Alice Cunningham Fletcher (1838–1923) published with Francis (Frank) La Flesche (1857–1932) *The Omaha Tribe*, a monograph on the Omaha, a Siouan group. It appeared in the Smithsonian Institution's *27th Annual Report of the Bureau of American Ethnology*.[1] The monograph describes the pre-reservation culture of this tribe during the first half of the nineteenth century, making a record of Omaha customs that the authors believed were largely disappearing. It was initially based on Fletcher's (see figure 6.1) own studies beginning in 1881.[2] Later, it was viewed by her as a collaborative effort with La Flesche. In order to evaluate the extent of this unusual partnership, this chapter looks at the relationship of Fletcher and La Flesche through the lens of archival correspondence and via selected quotes from the personal reflections of La Flesche found in *The Omaha Tribe*. In Fletcher's signed foreword to the book, she states:

> The following account of the Omaha tribe embodies the results of personal studies made while living among the people and revised from information gained through more or less constant intercourse throughout the last twenty-nine years. . . . The following presentation of the customs, ceremonies, and beliefs of the Omaha is a joint work. For more than twenty-five years the writer has had as collaborator Mr. Francis La Flesche. . . . Having had awakened in his mind the desire to preserve in written form the history of his people as it was known to them, their music, the poetry of their rituals, and the meaning of their social and religious ceremonies, Mr. La Flesche early in his career determined to perfect himself in English and to gather the rapidly vanishing lore of the tribe, in order to carry out his cherished purpose. (Fletcher in Fletcher and La Flesche 1911: 29–30)

Figure 6.1. *Alice C. Fletcher, seated left, with Native and non-Native women at a Presbyterian mission on the Omaha Reservation, Walthill, Nebraska. Photographed by an unknown photographer, 1883–84. © Smithsonian Institution, NAA, B.A.E. collection (gn-04473 enhanced and cropped).*

Although the collaborative authorship is clear on the title page, it would appear that Francis La Flesche long considered this work to be the product of Alice Fletcher. In his obituary of Fletcher, La Flesche credits *The Omaha Tribe* as one of the three "most important papers" she wrote (La Flesche 1923: 115).[3] He does not acknowledge himself as co-author, but a plural formula—"the writers"—is used throughout *The Omaha Tribe*. It will be shown that La Flesche's voice distinctively appears in it.

Alice Fletcher first met Francis La Flesche when he was chaperoning his sister Susette La Flesche (1854–1902), also known as Bright Eyes (see figure 6.2), in 1879 during a speaking tour of the eastern

Figure 6.2. *Francis La Flesche and his sister, Susette La Flesche. Photographed by an unknown photographer, ca. 1879, probably during the La Flesches' eastern tour. © Smithsonian Institution, NAA, B.A.E. collection (NAA INV 0689800 enhanced).*

United States. The La Flesches were accompanying their Ponca uncle Standing Bear (ca. 1829–1908) and Thomas Henry Tibbles (1840–
1928) to aid the cause of the Ponca, who had been forcibly removed
from their reservation in Nebraska to Indian Territory in 1877.[4] One
of the lecture stops was Boston where Fletcher and the La Flesche siblings met. A friendship sparked, and in the summer of 1881 Fletcher
began to plan her first trip west with Susette and Susette's new husband Tibbles. In the fall of 1881 they arrived at the La Flesche family
home (Fletcher 2013 [1923]: 233–36), and she began her Omaha research with the help of Francis and his family. Their partnership (as
close as mother and son) lasted the rest of their lives—Fletcher died
in 1923 and La Flesche in 1932—creating significant contributions to
the written scholarship of the Omaha.

The Omaha Tribe's Reception

The Omaha Tribe has 640 pages, including an index, a list of original
owners of allotments on the Omaha Reservation, and an accompanying title map. It includes 192 illustrations (65 plates and 132 figures).
The contents describe: location and linguistic relations with related
tribes including the Ponca, Osage, Kansa, and Quapaw (Fletcher and
La Flesche 1911: 33–69); data regarding the environment including
village sites, fauna and flora (ibid.: 70–114); rites pertaining to the
individual (ibid.: 115–33); tribal organization and government (ibid.:
134–216); the quest for food, including hunting, agriculture, and fishing (ibid.: 261–312); social life, including kinship terms, women's and
men's roles, and clothing (ibid.: 313–70); music (ibid.: 371–401); warfare (ibid.: 402–58); societies both sacred and social (ibid.: 459–581);
disease and death (ibid.: 582–94); religion and ethics (ibid.: 595–604);
and language (ibid.: 605–7). An appendix includes information on the
history of Omaha and white interrelations, detailing early trader and
missionary contacts, treaties with the United States, and reservation
creation, and also features a section on Francis's father, the Omaha
leader Joseph La Flesche (1822–1889),[5] the 1881 appeal for land patents, and the tribe's status in 1910 as a result of land allotment, "not
all of which has been happy" (ibid.: 640).[6]

The scholarly reception of this work was mixed. In the thirty
years between Fletcher's first fieldwork and the publication of *The
Omaha Tribe*, anthropology had developed rapidly, shifting its base
from museums to an academic curriculum within universities. In the
United States, under the influence of Franz Boas (1858–1942) Fletch-

er's research was being relegated to anthropology's past. It was the ideas of Boas, spread by the growing number of his students, which came to dominate American anthropology. Lacking professional training and associated with the social evolutionary perspective of the nineteenth century, Fletcher appeared to younger anthropologists as an anachronism.

The authors of *The Omaha Tribe* were first and foremost criticized for ignoring both historical accounts and the earlier ethnographic studies of James Owen Dorsey (1848–95). Dorsey, an Episcopal missionary to the Poncas and a linguist, had been sent to the Omaha Reservation in 1878 by John Wesley Powell, founding director of the Smithsonian Institution's Bureau of [American] Ethnology. Dorsey carried out ethnographic and linguistic work on the Omaha Reservation from 1878 until his death in 1895.[7]

Writing in *Science*, the prestigious publication of the American Association for the Advancement of Science, Robert H. Lowie (1883–1957), an assistant curator of anthropology at the American Museum of Natural History in New York and one of Boas's students, wrote a scathing review of Fletcher's and La Flesche's book. He noted that the authors had not accomplished their stated task of giving a definitive study of Omaha ethnology principally because they had not cited research done by "their great predecessor" J. O. Dorsey, who worked among the Omaha in 1878–80. Lowie wrote:

> The most obvious thing about this monograph is the authors' well-nigh complete neglect of the work of their predecessors. It is their avowed purpose (p. 30) to borrow nothing from other observers and to present "only original material gathered directly from native people." Apart from any considerations of historical justice, this principle is unjustifiable from the standpoint of the student ... as a field report it will ... be found wanting in several respects. In the first place, the tremendous wealth of concrete material is classified according to canons of aboriginal rather than of scientific logic. ... Secondly, there are large fields of ethnological interest that the authors either do not touch at all or treat in a very unsatisfactory manner. Foremost among these is mythology and folklore ... another very remarkable deficiency appears in the discussion of material culture and art. (Lowie 1913: 910–12)

Responding to this review, La Flesche explained that Lowie had misinterpreted the objective of the authors by not giving the whole reason for their approach as presented in the original foreword by Fletcher. La Flesche then quoted from that foreword:

When these studies were begun nothing had been published on the Omaha tribe except short accounts by passing travelers or comments made by government officials . . . In the account here offered nothing has been borrowed from other observers, only original material gathered directly from the native people has been used and the writer has striven to make, so far as possible, the Omaha his own interpreter. (La Flesche 1913: 982, quoting Fletcher 1911: 30)

La Flesche went on to state that it was his (and Fletcher's) goal:

to present the results of independent and original investigations on the Omaha . . . [and] avoid criticism of other writers. The final adoption of this plan was due in a large degree to the regard which the authors felt for the late Rev. J. O. Dorsey. They honored his personal character and his conscientious efforts, and preferred silence to the unwelcome task of pointing out the numerous errors throughout his work when he was no longer living to rectify them. (La Flesche 1913: 983)

La Flesche continued regarding Dorsey:

Regrettably his imperfect knowledge of the language, as can readily be seen in his Omaha texts, accounts for misconceptions that now appear in his writings. . . . The misconceptions of Mr. Dorsey, cited by the reviewer, they corrected in the interest of truth, but without caring to detract from the credit due to the deserving author. Their competency to do so comes from the long and careful study of the tribal institutions and the beliefs on which they were founded, made in conjunction with practically all those men of the tribe who by position and ability were qualified to explain and to interpret tribal life and thought and also to point out the differences between teachings that were to be taken literally and those which were symbolic in form and character. (ibid.: 983)

Finally, La Flesche further justified their divergent views from Dorsey's by stating: "One of the authors is not only himself an Omaha and well versed in his native language, but is [also] equipped with a knowledge of English, so that niceties of the meaning and of the usage of words are made clear" (ibid.: 983).

Another critical review by Herbert J. Spinden (1879–1967), a student of Frederic Ward Putnam,[8] written in a new journal published by the American Anthropological Association, was less scathing but hardly complimentary. He wrote:

This book, the result of long research and exceptional collaboration is very rich in material. . . . As a rule, interpretations of the inner life and thoughts of the Indian in European terms are labored and unconvincing.

... The authors, however, brought to their task unusual qualifications of information and sympathy: Miss Fletcher has spent a large part of her life among the Omaha, while her collaborator has an inborn interest in the subject. (Spinden 1912: 186)

Spinden went on to say:

But while there is much to praise ... [*The Omaha Tribe*] has certain limitations ... One may be permitted to question the wisdom of attempting a thorough report on any subject of scientific interest while disregarding completely the work already done by other investigators in the same field ... the pioneer efforts of J. O. Dorsey have been of the greatest value to anthropologists ... the Indian as his own interpreter is not an unbiased witness. ... Anthropology has gone beyond the descriptive stage and with the greater mass of material at its disposal has become analytical and comparative. This book we have just considered is a worthy monument to an older order. (ibid.: 186–89)

Reviews of the book in Britain and France, where social evolution was still the dominant perspective (even within the otherwise innovative Durkheimian school), were generally positive. Ever attentive to North American ethnography, Marcel Mauss (1872–1950) wrote a review in *L'Année sociologique*, considering it a work of significant scholarship and much better than the "fragmentary" and "superficial" analysis of J. O. Dorsey (Mauss 1912; see Mark 1988: 339). Then Émile Durkheim (1858–1917)—who had recently completed his important book on Australian totemism, *Les formes élémentaires de la vie religieuse* (*The Elementary Forms of the Religious Life*, 1912)—published a second review in *L'Année sociologique* giving high praise to Fletcher and La Flesche. Alfred C. Haddon (1885–1940) also extolled *The Omaha Tribe* in the British journal *Nature* (1912). In May 1913 Fletcher wrote Frederick Webb Hodge (1864–1956), ethnologist-in-charge of the Bureau of American Ethnology: "Many thanks for your kindness in letting me see ... the very pleasant notice of *The Omaha Tribe* written by Dr. Haddon. ... Evidently Dr. Haddon has read the book & not merely 'looked at the pictures,' and I am grateful to him."[9]

The Fletcher/Dorsey Rivalry

Fletcher's disagreements with Dorsey were long-standing and are important in understanding the reasons why she did not cite his work in *The Omaha Tribe.* The following will give some of the essence of this schism. In a letter to Putnam from September 1882, Fletcher noted, "Have not written Mr. Dorsey yet."[10] On 29 December 1884 she wrote to Putnam:

> As to the Articles I will try [and] get the names & sketch of the social organization ready. I would like to get that to you soon, because I think Mr. Dorsey's work will soon be out, & I find he has been misled. He has organized the gens or rather the subdivisions too closely, giving a man as at the head of a subdivision & then mentioning those who acknowledge his authority & as he wrote from hearsay of Indians who did not understand what he was driving at they have given him the man's sons' names as those acknowledging authority. He has made other mistakes. While it would not be best to call attention by name, would it be well to speak of this mistake having been made, making the statement general rather than particular?[11]

In January 1886 Fletcher wrote Putnam:

> My Omaha work moves but moves slowly. Mr. Dorsey's is out. I am surprised to see how mine will vary from his. He is quite off in many places. His illustrations are some of them wrong. He is all off on the pipes. When he saw them in my room he said that he was wrong. He is off on the painting of the men, and as to customs he is often far from the fact. When my account is out I wonder what will be thought of the difference. It will make needful a statement of my living with the people and finally confiding to them the fact of my writing an account & of being corrected in my notes by the people. Mr. Dorsey has made mistakes thro[ugh] his lack of familiarity with the language. I could point to places where he has mistaken words and so changed the whole thing. I don't mean to in any way criticize Mr. D.'s paper, but simply make my statement. F. [Francis] is quite annoyed at some things.[12]

Fletcher's rivalry with Dorsey was also evident in that they frequently used the same consultants to gather information. In February 1889 Fletcher wrote to Putnam:

> Wahapa is here. He is an Omaha working with Mr. Dorsey. I use him on evenings. I am at work on my *ms.*, which I hope to lay before you one of these days. There is much to present. . . . I am a little embarrassed for the lack of time to work over the old records. . . . [Francis] is working quite faithfully and I can assure you that there are many inducements much held out to him to give what he has elsewhere.[13]

Examples of such early "inducements" can be seen in letters from Fletcher to Putnam. In 1884 Fletcher remarked about La Flesche: "I did not get a chance to tell you that they are after Frank [Francis] in Washington. Mr. D[orsey] tried to get a promise that F[rank] would work with the Bureau [of Ethnology], but I can hold him and he is valuable."[14] In 1885 Fletcher wrote: "Francis has saved a week or 10 days of his time to go to Cambridge & complete among other things the ethnological photographs. ... You can't fancy how many plans are on foot to get him away from me & turn his work off from the [Peabody] Museum. He is to be a member of the Anthropological Society & he is also offered other things. He holds so far. This is all between us."[15]

Her competition with Dorsey led to years of anxiety for Fletcher.[16] It must also have strained the relationship between Dorsey and La Flesche. As early as June 1886, La Flesche was finding that he did not agree with Dorsey's phonetic spelling for Omaha.[17] La Flesche had in the early 1880s helped Dorsey gather Omaha data, and, in fact, Dorsey had taught the La Flesche children, including Francis, how to write Omaha. Dorsey often praised Francis's quick learning. He thought enough of his scholarship that he recruited him to join the American Association for the Advancement of Science in the summer of 1884 and to give a paper in its anthropology section at the September meeting in Philadelphia. The suggestion surprised Fletcher, but she and Francis did give a joint paper on the sacred pipes that was very well received. In a letter to Putnam, Fletcher explained that

> I mean to write on the Sacred Pipes, exhibit them, but Mr. Dorsey was here the other eve. and suggested ... that Frank ... give a paper. Frank wants to write on these pipes & all things considered it is not best for me to object. Altho. I feel sure he cannot go as deeply into the matter as it ought to be done from lack of objective knowledge & general culture. Still I will help him, & have no doubt a valuable contribution will be given by him. Surely no one will dare dispute an Indian's statements of his Sacred Articles of his own Tribe. In many ways I am glad he is going to take it up altho. it had seemed to me well that the article should be joint & so cover all the ground open at present.[18]

The pipes themselves were given to Fletcher and La Flesche in May 1884 and for a while were on the wall in Fletcher's home. They were later donated to the Peabody Museum, as were many other ethnographic items.[19]

The strained relationship between Dorsey and La Flesche did not improve. When Dorsey sent him some queries in 1894, La Flesche refused to answer them. He wrote to Dorsey:

I have looked over the questions you submitted to me, and after thinking over them I decline to answer them in the way they are put. . . . I think that too much of the private affairs of many of the Omahas has already been published in the Bureau of Ethnology reports without their consent and I do not wish to add more, or have it done with my assistance. . . . Some things you have published about me which I did not wish published but you took the liberty to do it.[20]

The conflicts plagued Fletcher even after Dorsey's death in 1895. For example, in April 1896, in response to questions she had sent to Rosalie La Flesche Farley (1861–1900), Francis's half-sister, Fletcher received the following reply:

We asked mother the questions and her answers I send numbered according to [the] questions [these have not survived with the letter]. She said whoever got the information in regard to the Omahas believing they came from animals and addressed the dying in the words, "You came hither from the animals and you are going back hither," must have got it from Betsey Dick. She laughed at the idea, said father had told Mr. Dorsey to be careful from whom he got his information.[21]

Fletcher's and La Flesche's disagreements with Dorsey's ethnographic data reflect a fundamental difference in their approaches. Dorsey felt compelled to report differences of opinion among his informants (whose name he always gave), treating their varying and often contradictory statements as integral parts of his ethnographic reports. In his juxtaposition of diverging versions, however, he allowed himself to suggest that this or that account was "doubtful" (Dorsey 1884: 221) and often reached decisions that reinforced his own anthropological authority. Fletcher and La Flesche, by contrast, sought to present a seamless and definitive ethnographic account in which differences of opinion among individual Omahas were silently resolved. This is why most accounts are presented in an anonymous way or resorting to formulas such as "Tradition says . . . ," "Some of the old men said . . . ," etc. (Fletcher and La Flesche 1911: 72–73). Unlike Dorsey's, their joint ethnographic expertise is thus practically indistinct from that of "the old Omaha men, who are the authority for the interpretations of tribal rites and customs contained in this memoir . . ." (ibid.: 211). Working year after year with Francis, Fletcher attempted to leave no loose ends and to present a portrayal of the Omaha as seen through the lens of one family, the La Flesches.

The Writing of *The Omaha Tribe*

Fletcher studied the Omaha tribe with La Flesche throughout the 1880s. From her first fieldwork in 1881 on, she was welcomed into the La Flesche family and was especially drawn to Joseph La Flesche (her own father had died before she was two years old) and he to her. After his first meeting with Alice Fletcher, Joseph La Flesche told Francis: "Your sister [Susette La Flesche Tibbles] has gone up to the Sioux with a white woman. . . . Your sister's friend is a remarkable woman; in thought and expression she is more like a man than a woman."[22] Francis absorbed the significance of his father's words—a potentially useful ally had come into their life.

Thus it is not surprising that, at the insistence of Joseph La Flesche, Fletcher began to work on securing Omaha traditional lands. Fletcher lobbied prominent Washington legislators and was successful in helping get an Omaha land ownership bill passed in 1882. In the Spring of 1883 she was appointed to allot these Omaha lands.[23]

In 1883 Fletcher began planning a comprehensive publication on the Omaha. She wrote to Putnam on January 20:

> I mean to get the music of the various dances from Frank, and write out all I can that is available. The following is the plan of the 12 articles. I have tried to have the discussion of the festivals as the Hunt & Pole Ceremony to come in the appropriate months.
>
> Omaha Life
> 1 Migrations, camp circle (with maps & sketches).
> 2 Home life—gens life—naming of children, etc.
> 3 Games of boys & girls. Stories told them/Piercing ears etc.
> 4 Ceremony of putting the blue mark on the girls.
> 5 Pipe Dance—with music.
> 6 The Hunt.
> 7 Ceremonies of the pole with music.
> 8 Religious societies & rites.
> 9 War path & warlike customs etc.
> 10 The Societies among the men & music.
> 11 Courtship, marriage, death & burial customs.
> 12 The struggle toward civilization.
> All will be illustrated—
> I propose to copyright these articles & later collect them in a book form with more elaboration. The series ought to be valuable—for much will be entirely new.[24]

This earliest evidence of her intent to write a book shows that she was already relying on Francis to do a detailed gathering of data. In

February, Fletcher wrote to Putnam, "Frank is rendering very valuable assistance."[25] When something happened to La Flesche, the work stalled. In May 1883, in writing to Putnam about her almost completed article on the Pipe Dance (Fletcher 1884), she mused "Frank has gone over & over it & been very patient. It is all here but two ritual songs. These I could not get for Frank's mother died a week ago & he will not even hum a song."[26]

In July 1886 Fletcher wrote to Putnam again about the importance of La Flesche's research:

> Francis goes with me to the Omahas, he is charged with gathering some ethnological materials. He is going to try & get the sacred pole & pack ... it may cost him a beef for a feast. If he has to do it can't the animal be paid for out of the fund you hold for my work? It will cost $25 to $30. If he gets the pole you will then have all the sacred articles of the Omahas. F[rancis] is working on the music ... This all goes into the complete setting forth of one tribe. When the Omaha book is out & you have all the articles, you will show forth one thing thoroughly.[27]

Then, in September 1888, Fletcher wrote emotionally to Putnam:

> Francis when here last month secured the sacred pole from the *Hunga* gens. This is a great prize. . . . We have it at Mrs. Farley's (his sister) in Bancroft and it is proposed, although this is a secret for it is by no means certain it can be brought about, to have next summer the full ceremonies so that F[rancis] & I can photograph them, and take down all the songs and all the details ... now for the great grief and disaster. Francis' Father lies dead. He died Monday. . . . How this sore calamity will effect our work I can't tell. . . . I was with the family staying up the last nights & I go back to attend the funeral. I was very much attached to Joseph La Flesche. . . . Civilization & science have lost a friend in Joseph La Flesche.[28]

In 1888, after the death of his father, La Flesche advised Putnam:

> No doubt Miss Fletcher has written you how I secured the sacred pole ... and why we did not send it to the Museum and kept it out there. The question of securing the full ritual and songs of that sacred article has become a serious and a puzzling one since the death of my father shortly after the passage of that relic out of the tribe ... it will be hard to make them believe that my father's death was in no way the result of the taking away of the pole. . . But still there may be some way of getting a few of the songs, at least. Of these we have two.[29]

Because Fletcher needed to find paid work that allowed her to support herself, she could not always choose to do the research and

writing she wanted. She expressed distress that her government contracts kept her from the Omaha publication, but she couldn't afford
to turn down the monetary support. In 1887 she was asked by President Grover Cleveland (1837–1908) to allot land to the Winnebago.[30]
Then in 1889, while working on the Nez Perce allotment, she wrote
to Putnam:

> I never have had to bear a keener disappointment [than the one] that
> has come to me this summer. I refer to my unfinished ms. over which I
> worked every moment I had the opportunity and thought to do so. You
> may not have received my letters telling you how I was hurried away
> here, and not given a day's grace even. I had to obey, or lose my position.
> . . . So instead of having a fortnight or so which would have put my *ms.* in
> training so I could have completed that part which was to be published.
> Away from Francis, I was obliged to pack it up, and cross the continent a
> saddened woman.[31]

In 1890 a fellowship initiated by Mary Thaw (1843–1929), a private
philanthropist, through the Peabody Museum at Harvard University,
finally allowed Fletcher to concentrate on the Omaha manuscript.[32]
In January 1890 she had written to Putnam:

> The book is progressing. I have the first chapter finished which gives[:]
> Location; Present Status; Table of population; The Omaha word for
> Tribe; the name Omaha; Tribal Organization; the *Hoo'thuga*, or tribal
> Circle; the divisions of Gentes of the tribe; Description of Gentes &
> sub-gentes (each gens & its sub-gentes given with its function, taboo,
> symbols, & decoration, etc.) an appendix giving gens of Ponca etc. The
> names in use among the Omahas, arranged alphabetically, occurring
> within gens & sub-gens, characters & sex. This much is almost done.
> I have examined [illegible] the tradition of migration, geographic rela-
> tions to other tribes, enemies & allies, historic [illegible] and mention by
> early writers, map containing names of [illegible] location. . . . Then too
> I want to add something about the pipes of peace and fellowship . . . &
> to introduce the [illegible] music & open the way for the other songs I
> have already.[33]

While Fletcher was working on the Omaha book she was at the
same time writing articles on the Omaha that were published in more
popular venues such as *Science* (1885), *Journal of American Folk-Lore*
(1888), and *Century* (1895), to name a few. She knew there was a conflict between popular writing and scientific papers, and she would
solicit Putnam's advice frequently as to how to use her materials. In
March 1890 she wrote to Putnam:

As for the *Century* if Mr. Gilder will carry out your [publication] plan it will be a good thing all round. . . . Of course I shall be grateful to earn a little money for one must pay butcher & baker, but I think my chief feeling is that it will be well for the Museum and for the much misunderstood Redman.

I have thought & sent you a sketch of 9 papers. . . . I don't think I can use chapters in our book for there must be detail in the book which would not interest the general reader. The papers can be compiled from the book material but they should be less minute in description. If I am correct in my judgement the book is for scientific study as a means by which to compare the Omaha with other tribes . . . while the articles are to present in popular form the pictures of Indian life now fast dying out . . . I want to use my material just as you deem best. I hold myself subject to your direction.[34]

Then again in August 1891 Fletcher wrote to Putnam:

Dear Prof. Putnam, believe me I will bring all I can, but I must finish [the Nez Perce allotment assignment]. . . . I have been working too hard & worrying over the Century Articles, but I'll send another before long & get them all done one of these days. I was troubled lest you were not pleased with what I had done. You do not say anything & I accept silence as approval. . . . I think the Omaha work will be good. I know now that the music is fully correct. . . . And indeed I am not troubled any more about Mr. Dorsey's getting things into print first. He has his point of view and I mine & it does not hurt either of us, but helps science.[35]

Throughout her career Fletcher sought and heeded Putnam's advice.

As Francis La Flesche's research on the Omaha became more involved and detailed, he began to assert himself regarding credit for his work. In April 1893 Fletcher wrote to Putnam:

I find that Francis has a great deal of feeling concerning the recognition of his share in the work involved in this monograph ["A Study of Omaha Indian Music," Fletcher (1893)]. He wants his name to appear on the title page—so as to read, "aided by Francis La Flesche." He has spent several hundred dollars, and given much time and labor, moreover he first had the idea of writing out the music. . . . I shall be glad to have his name added as I have put it in the page & hope you will be willing.[36]

It appears as if Fletcher felt the need to justify and appeal to Putnam regarding the importance of La Flesche's contributions and that he should be receiving more recognition and possibly even a professional museum appointment at the Peabody Museum (Mark 1988: 264).[37] In 1896 she wrote to Putnam:

Francis' uncle left me last night to return to the [Ponca] Reservation, having been with me about ten days. . . . I have taken over eighty songs belonging to various rituals and societies. I have also taken on the graphophone the "Counting of Honors." . . . Francis has worked night and day, and will have to work night and day for some time to come, with me. It would have been absolutely impossible for anyone to have gained this material without him. His uncle's regard for him has opened many a secret. Francis said jokingly that he thought he was doing enough for the Museum to win him a place among its workers.[38]

On 23 August 1897 Fletcher returned to the Omaha Reservation with La Flesche and stayed until 9 September. This was her first visit in seven years, and she stayed with members of the La Flesche family. She reported to Putnam: "Francis and I took between seventy and eighty photographs & a large number of graphophone records. We secured some valuable material & paved the way for securing a ritual in a year or so."[39]

Fletcher and La Flesche's ethnographic inquiries seemed endless, and while they enriched their work it also delayed the book. For example, Fletcher's response to a query from F. W. Hodge of the B.A.E. about Omaha war bonnets is indicative of the care she and La Flesche lavished on details. She wrote to Hodge in November 1902:

As to the War-bonnet. There was quite a ceremony attending the making of it and the arrangement of the feathers. The account of this regalia forms one of the chapters in my work on the Omaha Tribe not yet completed & published. I intend to give a joint paper with Mr. La Flesche on this subject at the meetings of section H [anthropology section of the American Association for the Advancement of Science] this winter . . . The subject is too complex to answer in a few words, I regret to say.[40]

As time went on Fletcher included La Flesche even more actively in her research. She wrote to Hodge in August 1905: "Mr. La Flesche is back from the Omahas and from his letters I judge he has made a very rich gleaning. This will help in completing the record we shall put in shape as soon as I get home."[41]

In 1906 an unanticipated chain of events once again derailed the Omaha publication. That year La Flesche, now fifty years old, met and married Rosa Bourassa (born ca. 1871), a mixed-blood Chippewa who had studied at Carlisle. At first Fletcher had high hopes for the marriage and wrote to Charles F. Lummis (1859–1928)[42] that Rosa was "a charming young lady who will be a daughter to me. They will live here."[43] But the marriage quickly dissolved, and the couple divorced in the fall of 1907. Bourassa publicized their private affairs, including innuendo about La Flesche's relationship with Fletcher. In response to the pressure of scandalous gossip and anticipating the legal proceedings surrounding the divorce, Fletcher in April 1907 went through her files of correspondence and papers, destroying everything except what related to her professional work.[44] Then she left for an extended trip to Europe.

In September 1907 William H. Holmes (1846–1933), chief of the Bureau of American Ethnology, wrote La Flesche: "A year or more ago I talked with Miss Fletcher regarding your work on the Omaha and she informed me that it was practically ready for publication and that she would be glad to have it published by the Bureau . . . if this paper is now ready, it could be introduced into our next Annual Report."[45] La Flesche responded:

> I would rather have you discuss the matter with her as she can tell you better than I can what shape the work is in. I do not think that as a whole the work could be put in readiness for publication for some time but there are parts of it that deal with the religious ceremonials and secret societies that can be put in shape for printing in a short time and they can fill a volume.[46]

When Fletcher returned to Washington in the fall of 1907, she and La Flesche resumed their work on the manuscript. In October she wrote to Putnam:

> Just before I reached home Francis had a letter from Mr. Holmes suggesting that I furnish the Omaha material for the next Bureau [of American Ethnology] Report. . . . I have already been at work & Francis will take his leave & work with me . . . the book will be a complete record of the tribe & the work done. It is quite a task to formulate the mass of material that we have & Francis & I are at work on the plan. He will do [a] considerable part of the book. He will have to write it for I want it to have the true Omaha flavor and not be diluted thro[ugh] me.[47]

Rather than follow the usual ethnographic models, they chose to structure the work from an Omaha point of view. By excluding any material recorded by others, they produced a work that presented Omaha culture from the perspective of the La Flesche family. At the time, this was a unique approach. As a tribal member who had privileged access to the lore of his people, La Flesche surely felt he had the freedom to decide what a definitive account of the Omahas would or would not include. Fletcher wrote Francis in February 1911: "You and I will do our utmost to extract from the language the thought and the belief of the people and try to show the world that the Omaha did think. . . . I am glad you like the Omaha book. I've done my best in my share of it and I think it will help in the way we want it to help the race & all mankind."[48]

There were negotiations with the Bureau of American Ethnology whether the Omaha manuscript would be long enough to fill a whole annual report. At the end of August 1908 Holmes wrote Fletcher:

> It appears that your paper will fall short of making a volume of the desired thickness, and I have therefore asked Doctor [Jesse W.] Fewkes [1850–1930] to at once prepare his report on recent work at the Spruce-tree House in Mesa Verde Park. . . . Although I would much rather have the volume of the report limited to the work of one person or to a particular subject, I think that the association of the Omaha with the cliff dwellings will not be objectionable.[49]

Fletcher insisted that the work be printed by itself:

> I think it will be a mistake to add any outside matter to the book. The purpose of the work has been to make as complete a record of the Omaha tribe as possible. To add an outside subject will make the index to the volume complex and take from the usefulness of the book.
>
> As the *ms.* represents over 25 years of research & study and the expenditure upon it of hundreds of dollars drawn from my own pocket I feel justified in expressing to you my serious objection to any plan except that of publishing the material in a volume by itself.[50]

Holmes conceded, but the Bureau requested the addition of an appendix summarizing relations between the Omahas and the government.[51] It took the authors a number of months to pull together this material, but then the book was completed. Hodge sent Francis La Flesche a copy of the *The Omaha Tribe* with this note in November 1911: "I am sending you one of the first copies of the *Twenty-seventh Annual Report.* We are congratulating ourselves on its final appearance after its long and annoying delay . . . wishing you continued success, believe me . . ."[52]

Francis La Flesche may have begun his career in anthropology as Fletcher's clerk, interpreter, and consultant, but in the end he was recognized as an ethnologist in the Bureau of American Ethnology in his own right. Their extraordinary partnership extended past the publication of *The Omaha Tribe*. La Flesche continued to live in Fletcher's home, and she devoted much effort to furthering his anthropological work, placing his career ahead of her own.[53]

In 1919 she revised her 1891 will that stated in part:

> Second, I give and bequeath all my household furniture and personal
> effects including my jewelry to the said FRANCIS LA FLESCHE
> ... I have for many years regarded and treated the said FRANCIS LA
> FLESCHE as an adopted son and have for him the affection of a mother.
> I have not, however, formally and legally adopted him as a son for rea-
> sons which are well know to him and to me.[54]

Fletcher's will also arranged for the establishment of a fellowship at
the Archaeological Institute of America, part of Santa Fe's School of
American Research after La Flesche's death. In the summer of 1922
La Flesche accompanied Fletcher on her last trip to Santa Fe and to
the Omaha Reservation. "At both places she was highly honored."[55]
In February 1923 Alice Fletcher suffered a stroke and died on 6
April. In 1926 Francis La Flesche, too, suffered a stroke. He retired
from the Bureau of American Ethnology on 26 December 1929 and
returned to live with his brother, Carey La Flesche (1872–1952), on
the reservation in July 1930. He died there on 5 September 1932.

Francis La Flesche's Reflections

The Omaha Tribe is rich in ethnographic content. It is impossible to
convey this richness in this short chapter. Instead, this section will
share quotes from the monograph in the voice of Francis La Flesche.
He spoke authoritatively because he was the son of a former chief
and knew the various ritual leaders who were custodians of Omaha
knowledge, including the last keeper of the Sacred Pole, the relic that
was the symbol that bound the tribe. The correspondence previously cited demonstrates that important Omaha artifacts had been,
through the effort of the La Flesche family, donated to the Peabody
Museum for their safekeeping. This section includes personal recollections about the Sacred Pole by La Flesche, who clearly stands out
in it not only as a privileged witness but also as a participant. His
autobiographical account is presented as "the boy memory of these
ancient ceremonies of the Sacred Pole, now forever gone, by one of
the present writers, the only living witness who is able to picture in
English those far-away scenes" (Fletcher and La Flesche 1911: 245).
Francis recounts:

> One bright summer afternoon the Omahas were traveling along the val-
> ley of one of the streams of western Kansas on their annual buffalo hunt.

... There was an old man walking in a space in the midst of this moving host. ... the solitary old man [carried] a dark object that looked like a black pole. From one end hung a thing resembling a scalp with long hair. ... with measured steps he kept apace with the cavalcade. ... Five horses broke into a swift gallop through the open space, and the gray and the black, one after the other, ran against the old man, nearly knocking him over. (ibid.)

Accompanied by a friend, who told Francis's father what had happened, Joseph La Flesche responded:

"Now, boys, you must go to the Sacred Tent. Take both horses with you, the gray and the black, and this piece of scarlet cloth; when you reach the entrance you must say, 'Venerable man!' we have, without any intention of disrespect, touched you and we have come to ask to be cleansed from the wrong that we have done."
We [Francis and his friend] did as we were instructed and appeared before the Sacred Tent in which was kept the "Venerable Man," as the Sacred Pole was called and repeated our prayer. The old man who had been so rudely jostled by our horses came out in response to our entreaty. He took from me the scarlet cloth, said a few words of thanks, and reentered the tent; soon he returned carrying in his hand a wooden bowl filled with warm water ... sprinkled us and the horses with the water. ... This act washed away the anger of the "Venerable Man," which we had brought down upon ourselves. (ibid.)

A few weeks later, Francis was summoned to the Holy Tent to present buffalo meat as an offering. There he saw a pole standing aslant in the middle of the tent and "recognized this pole as the one that was carried by the old man whom my horses ran against only a few weeks before" (ibid.: 246). When all offerings had taken place "the priests began to sing the songs pertaining to this peculiar ceremony. I was now very much interested and watched every movement of the men who officiated" (ibid.).

Years passed, and with them passed many of the brave men who told the tale of their battles before the Sacred Pole. So also passed the buffalo, the game upon which the life of this and other tribes depended. During these years I was placed in school, where I learned to speak the English language and to read and write. ... The Omaha had given up the chase and were putting all their energies into agriculture. They had abandoned their villages and were scattered over their reservation upon separate farms, knowing that their former mode of living was a thing of the past and that henceforth their livelihood must come from the tilling of the soil. (ibid.: 247)

La Flesche then introduced Alice Fletcher:

> While driving over the reservation one day we came to a small frame
> house. . . . There stood in the back yard an Indian tent, carefully pitched,
> and the ground around it scrupulously clean. My companion [Fletcher]
> asked, "What is that?" "It is the Holy Tent of the Omahas," I replied.
> "What is inside of it?" "The Sacred Pole," I answered. "I want to see it."
> "You can not enter the Tent unless you get permission from the Keeper."
> The Keeper was not at home, but his wife kindly conducted us to the
> entrance of the Tent, and we entered. There in the place of honor stood
> my friend, the "Venerable Man," leaning aslant as I saw him years before
> when I carried to him the large offering of choice meat. He had served a
> great purpose; although lacking the power of speech, or any of the fac-
> ulties with which man is gifted, he had kept closely cemented the Seven
> Chiefs and the gentes of the tribe for hundreds of years. He was the ob-
> ject of reverence of young and old. . . . He now stood before us, aban-
> doned by all save his last Keeper, who was now bowed with age. The
> Keeper seemed even to be a part of him, bearing the name "Smoked Yel-
> low," a name referring both to the age and to the accumulation of smoke
> upon the Pole. Silently we stood gazing upon him, we three, the white
> woman in the middle. Almost in a whisper, and with a sigh, the Keeper's
> wife said, "I am the only one now who takes care of him. . . . Many were
> the offerings once brought to him, but now he is left all alone. The end
> has come!" (ibid.: 248)

A few years later Francis returned to the house of Smoked Yellow:

> As my visit was drawing to a close, . . . I suddenly swooped down upon
> the old chief with the audacious question: "Why don't you send the
> 'Venerable Man' to some eastern city where he could dwell in a great
> brick house instead of a ragged tent?" A smile crept over the face of the
> chieftain as he softly whistled a tune and tapped the ground with his pipe
> stick before he replied, while I sat breathlessly awaiting the answer, for I
> greatly desired the preservation of this ancient and unique relic. . . . He
> gave me his answer: "My son, I have thought about this myself but no
> one whom I could trust has hitherto approached me upon this subject. I
> shall think about it, and will give you a definite answer when I see you
> again." (ibid.)

When Francis visited Smoked Yellow again, he was entrusted with
the Pole and related objects. "This was the first time that it was purposely touched by anyone outside of its hereditary Keepers. It had
always been regarded with superstitious awe and anyone touching
even its Tent must at once be cleansed by the priest. . . . Thus it was
that the Sacred Pole of the Omaha found its way into the Peabody

Museum in 1888" (ibid.: 249). Fletcher and La Flesche acknowledged that many discussions took place about salvaging not only the Sacred Pole and related objects but also the Sacred Legend that explained their history. Francis related:

> The disposition to be made of these sacred objects, which for generations had been essential in the tribal ceremonies and expressive of the authority of the chiefs, was a serious problem for the leading men of the tribe . . . it was finally decided that they should be buried with their keepers.
>
> For many years the writers had been engaged in a serious study of the tribe and it seemed a grave misfortune that these venerable objects should be buried and the full story of the tribe be forever lost. . . . The importance of securing the objects became more and more apparent, and influences were brought to bear on the chiefs and their keepers to prevent the carrying out of the plan for burial . . . for which great credit must be given to the late Inshta'maza (Joseph La Flesche, f 49). . . .
>
> When the Pole was finally in safe keeping it seemed very important to secure its legend, which was known only to a chief of the Hon'ga. The fear inspired by the Pole was such that it seemed as though it would be impossible to gain this information, but the desired result was finally brought about, and one summer day in September, 1888. . . . Smoked Yellow . . . figure 50, came to the house of Joseph La Flesche to tell the legend of his people treasured with the Sacred Pole (Fletcher and La Flesche 1911: 221–23).

Alice Fletcher was an active agent in the effort to save the sacred items and collect associated history about them. So it is not surprising that she is one of "the four actors" in the drama of finally acquiring the legend that went with the Sacred Pole. The other participants were Joseph La Flesche (former principal chief), Smoked Yellow (keeper), and of course Francis, who recounted:

> It was a memorable day. The harvest was ended, and tall sheafs of wheat cast their shadows over the stubble fields that were once covered with buffalo grass. The past was irrevocably gone. The old man had consented to speak but not without misgivings until his former principal chief said that he would "cheerfully accept for himself any penalty that might follow the revealing of these sacred traditions," an act formerly held to be a profanation and punishable by the supernatural. While the old chief talked he continually tapped the floor with a little stick he held in his hand, marking with it the rhythm peculiar to the drumming of a man who is invoking the unseen powers during the performance of certain rites. His eyes were cast down, his speech was deliberate, and his voice low, as if speaking to himself alone. The scene in that little room where sat the four actors in this human drama was solemn. . . . The fear inspired

by the Pole was strengthened in its passing away, for by a singular coincidence the touch of fatal disease fell upon Joseph La Flesche almost at
the close of this interview, which lasted three days, and in a fortnight he
lay dead in the very room in which had been revealed the Sacred Legend
connected with the Pole. (ibid.: 224)

Echoing the letter to Putnam, December 1888, La Flesche writes
about his father's death shortly after the Sacred Pole and its legend
had been transmitted. In the 1911 publication, the fact that Joseph La
Flesche's death was felt by many Omaha to be related to the power
of the Sacred Pole can be read as a continuation of the traditional
pre-reservation culture rather than its end. Fletcher and La Flesche
had good intentions, but as noted in Francis La Flesche's reflection
above, the passing of the Sacred Pole out of the tribe had the opposite effect to what they thought would happen. Despite the massive
loss of tribal land through allotments and attempts to assimilate the
Omaha into mainstream American culture, the Omaha did not lose
their tribal identity. In fact, a revival of cultural traditions in the 1980s
culminated in the repatriation of the Sacred Pole from the Peabody
Museum. It was displayed at the Omaha powwow of 14 August 1989
and gave the people back their collective tribal symbol.

The Omaha Tribe Reevaluated

In a history of the Bureau of American Ethnology written by Neil
Judd in the 1960s, he remarked that *The Omaha Tribe* was "one of
the most sought-after studies ever published by the B.A.E." (Judd
1967: 52). As a result it is not surprising that it was reprinted in both
1970 and 1992. In his elegant (really poetic) preface to the 1992 edition, Robin Ridington stated that "*The Omaha Tribe* ... is the single most important and comprehensive study ever written about a
Native American tribe. If I had to choose one book to rescue from a
pyre of burning ethnographies, it would probably be this one" (1992:
1).[56] He went on to say:

Anthropology has now come full circle. We can appreciate the language
and interpretation of nineteenth-century writers like Fletcher and La
Flesche. We have become aware that anthropological representation requires more than the repetition of ethnographic facts. We know that we
construct the information we place upon the page in collaboration with
the people who inform us. We recognize that ethnographic description is
inherently interpretive. We realize that the ultimate ethnographic instru-

ment is human, not mechanical. True objectivity requires understanding and interpretation.... *The Omaha Tribe* is remarkable because it resulted from the collaboration of a Native and non-Native ethnographer.... The book is remarkable for the wealth of songs, prayers, and ceremonies it documents. It is remarkable for a sometimes overwhelming abundance of ethnographic details about clan names, place names, emblematic clan hair cuts given to children, vision quests, social organization, government and history. As a balance to this detail, the book is remarkable for passages that are clear, beautiful, and philosophically interpretative. (Ridington 1992: 5)

Ninety years after the publication of *The Omaha Tribe*, the authors of a chapter on Omaha ethnography in the encyclopedic *Handbook of North American Indians* described the original 1911 work as a "comprehensive historical and ethnographic study that is an idealized account of traditional culture" (Liberty, Wood, and Irwin 2001: 415). In that chapter, summarizing the scholarly research on the Omaha written in the twentieth century, *The Omaha Tribe* was cited about forty-eight times.[57] Despite the fact that much of Fletcher's work is associated with nineteenth-century social evolutionary theory, the truth is that her ethnography has much in common with that of the Boasians. Regna Darnell highlights the continuities within the Americanist tradition, namely between the untrained ethnographers of the Bureau of American Ethnology and those academically trained by Boas himself (1999). In their reconstructions of cultural history, not all Boasians resorted to historical accounts as defended by Lowie (1913) in his critique of *The Omaha Tribe*. Lowie, who has been described as a "marginal Boasian" (Kan 2019), actually disregarded fundamental aspects of the monograph, namely that it is language-centered, that it presents "culture as it appears to the Indian himself," and that Fletcher's and La Flesche's approach is clearly historical. They made use of native oral traditions and customs in order to reconstruct not a static condition but a dynamic and complex past, made up of migrations, cultural diffusion, and cultural change.

Fletcher's aim in much of her fieldwork was to capture and publish, in both popular format and scholarly detailed articles, aspects of Omaha life that she feared were fast dying out. She was always encouraging Omaha dancing and singing in the performance of traditional ceremonies, as Nancy Lurie, a pioneer in the reassessment of Fletcher's ethnography, correctly pointed out (1966: 52). La Flesche's determination to write down the many details, both sacred and mundane, of Omaha society, leads one to believe that he too felt the imperative of capturing a way of life that might not survive. In his autobiographical sections published in *The Omaha Tribe*, La Flesche's views on the subject are clear as he describes the pains it took to record the songs of the Sacred Pole ceremony when the elder singer was reluctant. The argument that eventually persuaded the elder was this, in La Flesche's own words:

> Grandfather, last summer . . . I asked you to teach me the songs of the Sacred Pole. You replied that you knew the songs, but could not sing them for me, because they belonged to the other side of the house and were not yours to give. . . . I respected your purpose to keep inviolate your obligations to maintain the respective rights and offices of the two houses that were so closely allied in the preservation of order among our people . . . believing that you would soon see that the object for which that Sacred Tree and its accompanying rites were instituted had vanished, never to return. Our people no longer flock to these sacred houses as in times past. . . . I have been . . . among the members of the opposite side of the house . . . to find some one who knew the songs of the Sacred Pole, so that I might preserve them before they were utterly lost; but to my inquiries the invariable answer was, "I do not know them" . . . Therefore I have made bold to come to you again. (Fletcher and La Flesche 1911: 249)

The elder then replied:

> My eldest son, all the words that you have just spoken are true. . . . The men with whom I have associated in the keeping and teaching of the two sacred houses have turned into spirits and have departed. . . . No one can now with reason take offense at my giving you the songs of the Sacred Pole. . . . Make ready, and I shall once more sing the songs of my fathers." (ibid.: 249–51).

La Flesche described his own reaction:

> It took but a few moments to adjust the graphophone to record the songs for which I had waited so long. As I listened to the old priest his voice seemed as full and resonant as when I heard him years ago, in the days when the singing of these very songs in the Holy Tent meant so much to each gens and to every man, woman, and child in the tribe. Now, the old man sang with his eyes closed and watching him was like watching the last embers of the religious rites of a vanishing people. (ibid.: 251)

By viewing Omaha culture through the language and lens of the people themselves, Fletcher and La Flesche emphasized what was important to the Omaha and showed how the Omaha's worldview was very different from the worldview of Western cultures. They made explicit reference to this in passages like the following, on the subject of *Wakon'da*, the most important spiritual concept of the Omaha:

> It is difficult to formulate the native idea expressed in this word. The European mind demands a kind of intellectual crystallization of conceptions, which is not essential to the Omaha, and which when attempted is apt to modify the original meaning. Wakon'da stands for the mysterious life power permeating all natural forms and forces and all phases of man's conscious life. The idea of Wakon'da is therefore fundamental to the Omaha in his relations to nature, including man and all other living forms. (Fletcher and La Flesche 1911: 597)

It is quite evident that, by prioritizing the subjects's view, the 1911 publication *The Omaha Tribe* was a century ahead of other ethnographic publications. The fact that one of the two anthropologists involved was a Native of that culture made this approach possible.

In hindsight, the partnership between Alice C. Fletcher and Francis La Flesche worked in a unique and highly productive way. Fletcher provided academic contacts and the perseverance of a scholar. La Flesche provided an insider's view of a Native American culture and a scholar's determination to document it. Together they made an impressive team that created one of the greatest ethnographies of the period. *The Omaha Tribe*, highly criticized when published for its "aboriginal" presentation as well as for its nineteenth-century descriptive organization, is today seen as an irreplaceable foundation for Omaha ethnography. It stands as a prototype of collaborative research, very much used in the twenty-first century.

Acknowledgments

Many thanks to Nicole Tonkovich, friend and colleague, for sharing transcriptions of Fletcher's correspondence from the Nez Perce allotment period, and to Ruth Selig, a Smithsonian colleague, for her assistance in proofreading the manuscript. This chapter is based on years of collaborative research with Raymond J. DeMallie, chancellors' professor emeritus, Indiana University, and director emeritus, American Indian Studies Research Institute, Indiana University. DeMallie died on 25 April 2021.

Joanna Cohan Scherer is emeritus anthropologist in the Department of Anthropology, Smithsonian Institution, Washington (USA). She is an authority on photographs of Native Americans and was a key researcher for the *Handbook of North American Indians*, a twenty-volume encyclopedia on the history and culture of all Indigenous peoples of North America. Fifteen volumes of the *Handbook* were published between 1978–2008 by the Smithsonian, and another volume, an introduction, is currently being edited by Igor Krupnik (of the Department of Anthropology), for which Scherer is contributing chapters on the history of the *Handbook* series. She has written a number of books, including *A Danish Photographer of Idaho Indians: Benedicte Wrensted*, which won the Idaho Book Award of the Year in 2006 as well as two other national awards. Her last book was *Life among the Indians: First Fieldwork among the Sioux and Omaha by Alice C. Fletcher*, edited with an introduction by Scherer and Raymond J. DeMallie (University of Nebraska Press, 2013).

Notes

1. The Bureau of Ethnology was established in 1879 by the U.S. Congress within the Smithsonian Institution. Its first director, John Wesley Powell (1834–1902), who was also director of the Geological and Geographical Survey of the Territories, had lobbied for its creation in order to have an organization devoted to anthropology. In 1897 its name was changed to the Bureau of American Ethnology (B.A.E.). For the history of the B.A.E., see Hinsley (1994).
2. Fletcher's earliest fieldwork is detailed in her autobiographical memoir *Life among the Indians: First Fieldwork among the Sioux and Omaha* (2013). The best overall biography of Alice C. Fletcher is Mark (1988), and a biography of Francis La Flesche by Mark (1982) is also excellent.
3. The two other "most important" works of Fletcher in La Flesche's opinion were: "The Hako: A Pawnee Ceremony," with James R. Murie (1904); and *Indian Story and Song from North America* (1900).
4. The Ponca fled back north in January 1879, and after extensive litigation were allowed to remain in Nebraska.
5. For a biography of Joseph La Flesche and his accomplished family, see Green (1969).
6. For a discussion of the resulting aftermath of allotment among the Omaha, see Scherer and DeMallie 2013: 55–59.
7. Like Fletcher, J. O. Dorsey was closely allied with the La Flesche family and, in fact, taught Joseph La Flesche's children how to write Omaha. Dorsey's study of *Omaha Sociology* was published in 1884.
8. Frederic Ward Putnam (1839–1915) was one of the first museum anthropologists in the United States. He became curator of the Peabody Museum of American Archaeology and Ethnology at Harvard University, Cambridge, Massachusetts, in 1875 and remained in that position until

1909. A professor of American archaeology and ethnology at Harvard from 1886–1909, he was also Fletcher's mentor.

9. Fletcher to Hodge, 1 May 1913, Southwest Museum of the American Indian, Fletcher-Hodge, B.A.E., 1910–13, Manuscript Collection., 7.EIC.1.64.

10. Fletcher to Putnam, 30 September 1882, Peabody Museum records, box 4, folder 1882 C-G.

11. Fletcher to Putnam, 29 December 1884, Peabody Museum records, box 5, folder 1884 C-F. For information on Omaha social organization and gens, see Fletcher and La Flesche 1911: 134–96.

12. Fletcher to Putnam, 17 January 1886, Peabody Museum records, box 7, folder 1886 A-I. For information on the painting of the Omaha men, see Fletcher and La Flesche 1911: 349–50.

13. Fletcher to Putnam, 4 February 1889, Peabody Museum records, box 9. Copy from Nicole Tonkovich.

14. Fletcher to Putnam, 11 September, Thursday [1884], Peabody Museum records, box 5, folder 1884 C-F.

15. Fletcher to Putnam, 11 December 1885, Peabody Museum records, box 5 folder 1885 F-J.

16. Recovering from a prolonged illness, Fletcher to Putnam, June 1886: "There is one thing that troubles me, I wanted you to have the Omaha volume, but as I work on it and look over Mr. Dorsey's work we vary so much in some things, that I think I shall submit mine to some of the leading Indians, one of us is wrong. F. [Francis] says Mr. D. is. I don't know. I want to make mine complete" (Fletcher to Putnam, 27 June 1886, Peabody Museum records, box 7, folder 1886 A-I). And again, in May 1890 to Putnam: "Dorsey is pushing on and I want to get my work out before he takes the wind from my sails, but I do not fear it much [as] we are on very different standpoints & he has not got inside very far as yet. I think I had better try the phonograph, don't you? The songs to be published must be in the form I have them" (Fletcher to Putnam, 17 May 1890, Ft. Lapwai [Idaho]. Peabody Museum Directors records, Putnam, [unaccessioned], box 2, folder 1).

17. "I want Francis to give his paper on tanning skins, and also one on newly formed words in the Omaha language, both are good, and the Ass[ociation = American Association for the Advancement of Science] will like them. He bids me [to] tell you he is having a fight with Mr. Dorsey on Omaha phonetic spelling" (Fletcher to Putnam, 27 June 1886, postscript to letter, Peabody Museum records, box 7, folder 1886 A-I).

18. Fletcher to Putnam, 28 July 1884, Peabody Museum records, box 5, folder 1884 C-F.

19. The objects, used in the Omaha sacred pipe ceremony, included two gourd rattles, bladder tobacco pouch, wildcat skin, and two pipes made of ash. According to the Peabody Museum accession records, these items were collected by La Flesche in 1883 (an apparent error in the early record, for surely this was in 1884) and donated to the museum. On 18

September 1990, these objects were returned to the Omahas, except for the wildcat skin, which is still in the Peabody Museum. For detailed information on the Omaha sacred pipes, including music and songs, see Fletcher and La Flesche 1911: 376–400.

20. La Flesche to Dorsey, 8 June 1894, NAA, J. Owen Dorsey General Correspondence, ms. 4800, box 65. La Flesche may have been referring to Dorsey's publication of information about Joseph La Flesche's lineage and the validity of his status as chief. See Barnes 1984: 18–25.

21. Rosalie La Flesche Farley to Fletcher, 19 April 1896, NAA, Fletcher & La Flesche Collection, ms. 4558, box 1, Incoming Correspondence, folder 1896–98. In fact, as Fletcher must have been aware, the ritual exhortation that Rosalie La Flesche ridiculed came not from Betsey Dick (dates unknown) but from Lewis Morris, also known as Two Crows (1826–94), a respected elder whose portrait Fletcher and La Flesche included in *The Omaha Tribe* (1911: 210). Dorsey included the ritual in English as part of the account of the *Hunga* clan in his *Omaha Sociology* (1884: 233) and considered it significant enough to publish in the original Omaha, with translation, in his *A Study of Siouan Cults* (1894: 421). For information about the Omaha view of the relationship between humans and animals, see Fletcher and La Flesche 1911: 599–601. Fletcher was close to all of La Flesche's siblings (Green 1969), and they often sent greetings to her in letters to La Flesche. For example, in 1895 in a postscript to a letter to Francis, Rosalie wrote, "My love to dear Miss Fletcher, the older I grow the more I love her" (Rosalie La Flesche Farley to Francis La Flesche, 30 December 1895, Nebraska State Historical Society, La Flesche Family Papers).

22. Francis La Flesche, "Alice C. Fletcher's Scientific Work," drafted 1923, NAA ms. 4558, box 15. Using Fletcher's journals, La Flesche wrote about the first month of her fieldwork. This manuscript was used as the foreword to Fletcher's *Life among the Indians*, published posthumously (La Flesche 2013: 83–95).

23. In a letter to the commissioner of Indian affairs, Thomas Jefferson Morgan (1839–1902), on 6 October 1890, Fletcher summarized her efforts: "In 1881 while pursuing my scientific studies ... I found every household shadowed by the fear of ... removal to Indian Terr[itory]. ... Every thoughtful Omaha desired to own his land individually by patent. ... To this end I ... [sent] a short petition to Congress [December 1881] urging that the tribe be given titles to their lands ... Receiving no reply ... I went to Washington in the Spring of 1882, at my own expense to state their case. ... The result was the passage of the Act of Aug. 7, 1882, giving the Omaha their land in severalty. ... In the Spring of 1883 I was appointed to allot the Omaha lands ... and Mr. Francis La Flesche was detailed as my interpreter and clerk" (National Archives and Records Administration, RG 75: 31703. Copy from Nicole Tonkovich).

24. Fletcher to Putnam, 20 January 1883, Peabody Museum records, box 5, folder 1883 D–F.

25. Fletcher to Putnam, 1 February 1883, Peabody Museum records, box 5, folder 1883 D-F.

26. Fletcher to Putnam, 1 May 1883, Peabody Museum records, box 5, folder 1883 D-F. Fletcher (1884: 308) published on the pipe ceremony, and in the first footnote in this publication she notes: "To Mr. Frank La Flesche I desire to acknowledge my indebtedness for most valuable assistance in the preparation of this article."

27. Fletcher to Putnam, 27 July 1886, Peabody Museum records, box 7.

28. Fletcher to Putnam, 26 September 1888, Peabody Museum records, box 8, 1888 A-Z. Copy from Nicole Tonkovich. The sacred tree from which the pole came was a symbol of life and tribal unity. For an ethnographic account of the pole used by the Omaha, including origins, ceremony, ritual songs, and dances associated with it, see Fletcher and La Flesche 1911: 217–60.

29. La Flesche to Putnam, 3 December 1888, Peabody Museum records.

30. "I was telephoned to [*sic*] the Indian Commissioner [John D.C. Atkins (1825–1908)], and told that I had been designated by the President to allot the lands to the Winnebago Indians under the Severalty Act . . . I accepted. The pay is excellent, just the same as the men. . . . My going out will help my Omaha work. I shall take all my ms. along and do my best to make it worthy of your acceptance" (Fletcher to Putnam, 14 January 1887, Peabody Museum records, box 7).

31. Fletcher to Putnam, 20 September 1889, Peabody Museum records, box 9, folder F. Copy from Nicole Tonkovich.

32. "On my way west, Mrs. Wm. Thaw of Pittsburgh telegraphed me to stop & see her. . . . I will give you $1200 per annum & more if it is needed . . . devote yourself to your work. . . . I propose to put my work in good shape among the Nez Perce & ask for a leave of absence without pay from August 1890 to April 1891 then I will resume my work & complete allotment. That will give me 7 months for writing & Omaha work. I will spend September with Francis in the field" (Fletcher to Putnam, 1 April 1890, Peabody Museum Directors records, Putnam, [unaccessioned], box 2, folder 1).

33. Fletcher to Putnam, 20 January 1890, Harvard University Archives, Putnam papers, box 6. Copy from Nicole Tonkovich.

34. Fletcher to Putnam, 6 March 1890, Harvard University Archives, Peabody Museum, Putnam Papers, box 6. Copy from Nicole Tonkovich.

35. Fletcher to Putnam, 6 August 1891, Peabody Museum records, box 11. Copy from Nicole Tonkovich.

36. Fletcher to Putnam, 13 April 1893, Peabody Museum records, box 13, 1893 D-G.

37. There is no evidence that a professional appointment at the Peabody Museum ever was initiated. La Flesche did succeed in gaining professional status in his appointment as an Ethnologist at the B.A.E. in 1910 (Mark 1988: 325).

38. Fletcher to Putnam, 22 January 1896, Harvard University Archives,

Putnam Papers, box 9, folder F 1891–1900. A Graphophone is a device that records sounds on wax cylinders. Fletcher was among the first anthropologists to use a Graphophone, purchasing it in 1894 (Scherer and DeMallie 2013: 60, 71). For information on the gathering of honors by Omaha and Ponca warriors, see Fletcher and La Flesche 1911: 434–46.

39. Fletcher to Putnam, 29 September 1897, Peabody Museum records, box 17, 1897 D-G.

40. Fletcher to Hodge, 8 November 1902, Southwest Museum of the American Indian, Fletcher-Hodge at Smithsonian 1902–1905, Manuscript Collection, 7.SI.142. The war bonnet is discussed in Fletcher and La Flesche (1911: 446–48).

41. Fletcher to Hodge, 5 August 1905, Southwest Museum of the American Indian, Fletcher-Hodge at Bureau of Ethnology 1902–05, Manuscript Collection, 7.B.A.E.1.70.

42. Charles Fletcher Lummis was a California journalist who became heavily involved in the American committee of the Archaeological Institute of America, founded in 1879. Fletcher was an early member; a close friendship with Lummis resulted (Marks 1988: 298–304). Their correspondence dates from February 1900 to January 1922.

43. Fletcher to Lummis, 26 February 1906, Southwest Museum of the American Indian. Lummis Manuscript Collection, 1879–1928, Ms. 1.1.1456, Correspondence 1900–06.

44. Fletcher's 1907 personal diary April 4–19, NAA, Alice C. Fletcher and Francis La Flesche Collection, ms. 4558, box 12A.

45. Holmes to La Flesche, 17 September 1907, NAA, Records of the B.A.E., Letters Received 1907, box 121.

46. La Flesche to Holmes, 20 September 1907, NAA, Records of the B.A.E., Letters Received 1907, box 121. For information on Omaha secret societies including music and songs, see Fletcher and La Flesche 1911: 486–575; for a description of religious ceremonials pertaining to the individual, see Fletcher and La Flesche 1911: 115–33.

47. Fletcher to Putnam, 10 October 1907, Harvard University Archives, Putnam papers, box 15.

48. Fletcher to La Flesche, 13 February 1911, NAA, Fletcher & La Flesche Collection, ms. 4558, Correspondence on Specific Subjects, 1881–1925, box 5.

49. Holmes to Fletcher, 31 August 1908, NAA/B.A.E., Letters Received 1908, box 124.

50. Fletcher to Holmes, 2 September 1908, NAA/B.A.E., Letters Received 1908, box 124.

51. Fletcher wrote to Lummis: "My book on 'The Omaha Tribe' is done, but Mr. Hodge wants me to add an appendix to give data as to the relations of the Omaha to Gov't etc. That will take a little more time." Fletcher to Lummis, 22 January 1909, Southwest Museum of the American Indian, Lummis Collection, Correspondence, Ms. 1.1.1456B.

52. Hodge to La Flesche, 1 November 1911, NAA, Records of the B.A.E., Letters Received 1909–49, box 188.
53. Fletcher transcribed the Osage ritual texts and songs La Flesche had recorded and organized his research materials. La Flesche published five volumes on the Osage (three are listed in the bibliography) and an Osage dictionary. Unlike the overall treatment of the Omahas given in their 1911 publication, the Osage works were detailed accounts of religion, ritual, political structure, clans, and mythology.
54. The revised will was dated 18 September 1919. In a deposition made on 2 July 1925, La Flesche stated that a formal adoption did not take place because, as the son of a former chief of the Omaha tribe, he did not want to change his name. The deposition also stated that he and Fletcher had lived together as mother and son since 1884, some seven years before 3 April 1891, when Fletcher made the first written testament of her intention to consider La Flesche as her son and make provision for him in her will. NAA, Fletcher–La Flesche Collection, ms. 4558, box 13, Biography and memorabilia folder: Will and Estate 1919–25. See also Smith 2001: 597–98.
55. Letter from Francis La Flesche to his niece, Marguerite Conn (1890–1954) in La Flesche family papers, Nebraska Historical Society, Lincoln, quoted in Marks 1988: 346.
56. Introduction to reprint of *The Omaha Tribe*.
57. For the record, James Owen Dorsey's Omaha publications are cited about thirty-three times in the *Handbook of North American Indians'* Omaha article.

References

Manuscript Collections

Harvard University, Pusey Library, Harvard University Archives, Cambridge, Massachusetts.
    Peabody Museum of Archaeology and Ethnology records, correspondence 1851–1968, ms. no. UAV 677.38.
    Frederic Ward Putnam papers, 1851–1916, general correspondence, ms. no. HUG 1717.2.1.
National Archives and Records Administration, Washington, DC.
    Records of the Bureau of Indian Affairs, RG 75.
Nebraska State Historical Society, Lincoln, Nebraska.
    La Flesche Family Papers.
Smithsonian Institution, Washington, DC, National Anthropological Archives (NAA).
    Records of the Bureau of American Ethnology (B.A.E.), Correspondence Files.
        James Owen Dorsey Collection, ms. no. 4800.
        Alice C. Fletcher & Francis La Flesche Collection, ms. no. 4558.

Southwest Museum of the American Indian, Los Angeles.
  Charles Fletcher Lummis Manuscript Collection, 1879–1928.
  Frederick Webb Hodge Manuscript Collection.

Published Sources

Barnes, R. H. 1984. *Two Crows Denies It: A History of Controversy in Omaha Sociology*. Lincoln: University of Nebraska Press.

Darnell, Regna, 1999. "Theorizing Americanist Anthropology: Continuities from the B.A.E. to the Boasians." In *Theorizing the Americanist Tradition*, edited by Lisa P. Valentine and Regna Darnell, 38–51. Toronto: University of Toronto Press.

Dorsey, James Owen. 1884. "Omaha Sociology." In *3rd Annual Report of the Bureau of [American] Ethnology to the Secretary of the Smithsonian Institution 1881–'82*, 205–370 [vol. index, 595–606]. Washington, DC: Smithsonian Institution; U.S. Government Printing Office. Repr. New York: Johnson Reprint Company, 1970.

——. 1894. "A Study of Siouan Cults." In *11th Annual Report of the Bureau of [American] Ethnology to the Secretary of the Smithsonian Institution 1889–'90*, 351–544 [vol. index, 545–53]. Washington, DC: Smithsonian Institution; U.S. Government Printing Office.

Durkheim, Émile. *1912. Les Formes élémentaires de la vie religieuse*. Paris: Presses Universitaires de France. English translation by Karen Fields, *The Elementary Forms of the Religious Life*. New York: Free Press, 1995.

——. 1913. Review of "The Omaha Tribe." *L'Année sociologique* 13: 366–71.

Fletcher, Alice C. 1884. "The 'Wawan,' or Pipe Dance of the Omahas." *Peabody Museum Annual Report 16–17* 3(3–4): 308–33.

——. 1885. "An Evening in Camp among the Omahas." *Science* 6(139): 88–90.

——. 1888. "Glimpses of Child Life among the Omaha Tribe of Indians." *Journal of American Folk-Lore* 1(2): 115–23.

——. 1893. "A Study of Omaha Indian Music." Aided by Francis La Flesche and John C. Fillmore. Archaeological and Ethnological Papers, *Peabody Museum of Archaeology and Ethnology* 1 (1893): 237–87.

——. 1895. "Hunting Customs of the Omaha: Personal Studies of Indian Life." *Century: A Popular Quarterly* 50(5): 691–702.

——. 1900. *Indian Story and Song from North America*. Boston: Small, Maynard & Company. Repr. New York: AMS Press, 1970, and Lincoln: University of Nebraska Press, 1995.

——. 1911. "Foreword" in "The Omaha Tribe." In *27th Annual Report of the Bureau of American Ethnology to the Secretary of the Smithsonian Institution 1905–'06*, 29–31. Washington, DC: Smithsonian Institution; U.S. Government Printing Office. Repr. New York: Johnson Reprint Company, 1970; and Lincoln: University of Nebraska Press, 1992.

———. 2013 [1923]. *Life among the Indians: First Fieldwork among the Sioux and Omahas.* Edited with an introduction by Joanna C. Scherer and Raymond J. DeMallie. Lincoln: University of Nebraska Press.

Fletcher, Alice C., and Francis La Flesche. 1911. "The Omaha Tribe." In *27th Annual Report of the Bureau of American Ethnology to the Secretary of the Smithsonian Institution 1905–'06,* 17–672 [vol. index, 655–72]. Washington, DC: Smithsonian Institution; U.S. Government Printing Office. Repr. New York: Johnson Reprint Company, 1970; and Lincoln: University of Nebraska Press, 1992.

Fletcher, Alice C., and James R. Murie. 1904. "The Hako: A Pawnee Ceremony." In *22nd Annual Report of the Bureau of American Ethnology to the Secretary of the Smithsonian Institution 1900–'01,* 1–368 [vol. index, 369–72]. Washington, DC: Smithsonian Institution: U.S. Government Printing Office. Repr. Lincoln: University of Nebraska Press, 1996.

Green, Norma Kidd. 1969. *Iron Eye's Family: The Children of Joseph La Flesche.* Lincoln, NE: Johnson Publishing Company.

Haddon, Alfred C. 1912. "The Significance of Life to the Omaha." *Nature* 90 (24 October): 234.

Hinsley, Curtis M. 1994. *The Smithsonian and the American Indian: Making a Moral Anthropology in Victorian America.* Washington, DC: Smithsonian Institution Press.

Judd, Neil M. 1967. *The Bureau of American Ethnology: A Partial History.* Norman: University of Oklahoma Press.

Kan, Sergei. 2019. "Mainstream or Marginal Boasian? An Intellectual Biography of Robert H. Lowie." In *BEROSE International Encyclopaedia of the Histories of Anthropology,* Paris.

La Flesche, Francis. 1913. [Reply to review of] "The Omaha Tribe." *Science* 37: 982–83.

———. 1921. "The Osage Tribe: Rite of the Chiefs; Sayings of the Ancient Men." In *36th Annual Report of the Bureau of American Ethnology to the Secretary of the Smithsonian Institution 1914–1915,* 37–640. Washington, DC: Smithsonian Institution; U.S. Government Printing Office. Repr. New York: Johnson Reprint Company, 1970.

———. 1923. [Obituary of] "Alice C. Fletcher." *Science* 58 (July–December): 115.

———. 1925. "The Osage Tribe: Rite of Vigil." In *39th Annual Report of the Bureau of American Ethnology to the Secretary of the Smithsonian Institution 1917–1918,* 31–630. Washington, DC: Smithsonian Institution; U.S. Government Printing Office.

———. 1928. "The Osage Tribe: Two Versions of the Child-Naming Rite." In *43rd Annual Report of the Bureau of American Ethnology to the Secretary of the Smithsonian Institution 1925–1926,* 23–164. Washington, DC: Smithsonian Institution; U.S. Government Printing Office.

———. 1932. "A Dictionary of the Osage Language." *Bureau of American Ethology Bulletin* 109. Washington, DC: Smithsonian Institution; U.S.

Government Printing Office. Repr. St. Clair Shores, MI: Scholarly Press, 1986; and Brighton, MI: Native American Publishers, 1990.

———. 2013. "Foreword." In Alice C. Fletcher, *Life Among the Indians: First Fieldwork among the Sioux and Omahas*. Edited with an introduction by Joanna C. Scherer and Raymond J. DeMallie. Lincoln: University of Nebraska Press.

Liberty, Margot P., W. Raymond Wood, and Lee Irwin. 2001. "Omaha." In *Handbook of North American Indians*. Vol. 13: *Plains*, edited by Raymond J. DeMallie, 399–415. Washington, D.C: Smithsonian Institution.

Lowie, Robert. 1913. Review of "The Omaha Tribe." *Science* 37 (new series): 910–15.

Lurie, Nancy Oestreich. 1966. "Women in Early American Anthropology." In *Pioneers of American Anthropology: The Uses of Biography*, edited by June Helm, 31–81. Seattle: University of Washington Press.

Mark, Joan. 1982. "Francis La Flesche: The American Indian as Anthropologist." *Isis* 73(4): 497–510.

———. 1988. *A Stranger in Her Native Land: Alice Fletcher and the American Indians*. Lincoln: University of Nebraska Press.

Mauss, Marcel. 1912. Review of "The Omaha Tribe." *L'Année sociologique* 12: 104–11.

Ridington, Robin. 1992. "Introduction." In Alice C. Fletcher and Francis La Flesche, *The Omaha Tribe*, 1–8. Lincoln: University of Nebraska Press.

Scherer, Joanna C., and Raymond J. DeMallie. 2013. "Introduction." In Alice C. Fletcher, *Life Among the Indians: First Field Work among the Sioux and Omahas*. Lincoln: University of Nebraska Press.

Smith, Sherry L. 2001. "Francis LaFlesche and the World of Letters." *American Indian Quarterly* 25(4): 579–603.

Spinden, Herbert J. 1912. Review of "The Omaha Tribe." *Current Anthropological Literature* 1(3): 186–89. Lancaster, PA: American Anthropological Association and American Folk-Lore Society.

Tonkovich, Nicole. 2012. *The Allotment Plot: Alice C. Fletcher, E. Jane Gay, and Nez Perce Survivance*. Lincoln: University of Nebraska Press.

Part III

Colonial Ethnography from Invasion to Empathy

7

Stepping into a Pit of Snakes

John Gregory Bourke and *The Snake-Dance of the Moquis of Arizona* (1884)

Ronald L. Grimes

John Gregory Bourke (1846–96), a United States Cavalry officer, survived the American Civil War at age sixteen and weathered two fierce Indian wars with the Lakotas (1866–68, 1876–77) and Apaches (1849–86).[1] He was regarded by soldiers and Indigenous people alike as dogged, courageous, fair, and literary minded. His Apache friends called him "Captain Cactus" or "Paper Medicine Man." When Apaches wanted something, Bourke, ever the scholar, traded favors for religious knowledge. He wrote, "I did not care much what topic he [an Apache] selected; it might be myths, clan laws, war customs, medicine—anything he pleased, but it had to be something, and it had to be accurate" (Bourke 1984 [1884]: 124) (see figure 7.1).

In 1881 Bourke, a seasoned soldier and military ethnologist, used Santa Fe, New Mexico, as the base for a seven-month (April–November) ethnographic scouting mission. He visited twenty-two villages (Pueblo, Zuni, Navajo, Hopi). Despite vast language and cultural differences, he assumed their commonalities out-

Figure 7.1. *Only known photograph of Captain John Gregory Bourke in civilian dress, ca. 1893. © Nebraska History Museum (RG2955 Bourke, John Gregory, 1846–1896).*

weighed their differences: "Certain it is that every symbol seen here this day has been seen at other times among the Zunis, Moquis [Hopis], and Jemez people, with whose heathenism they are linked, and if heathenish in those Pueblos, they can scarcely be Christian in Santo Domingo" (Bourke 1984 [1884]: 44). Bourke used these assumed similarities to challenge the orthodoxy of Christianity at Santo Domingo Pueblo.

Here is the Victorian-style title of this first ethnographic account of the Snake Dance: *The Snake-Dance of the Moquis of Arizona: being a narrative of a journey from Santa Fé, New Mexico, to the villages of the Moqui Indians of Arizona, with a description of the manners and customs of this peculiar people, and especially of the revolting religious rite, the Snake-Dance; to which is added a brief dissertation upon serpent-worship in general with an account of the Tablet Dance of the Pueblo of Santo Domingo, New Mexico.*

Foreshadowing Hopi

The first third of *The Snake-Dance of the Moquis of Arizona* is a travelogue. The next third is Bourke's description of the Snake Dance at Walpi. The final third of the book is theory, comparison, and speculation. Bourke characterizes the volume as "a work intended for popular perusal," presenting "incidents which may serve to entertain and amuse, if they do not instruct" (Bourke 1984 [1884]: x, xix). He tells readers that he resisted the temptation to write "a pretentious volume of travel" (ibid.: 57). Instead, we have a 364-page tome containing 31 plates of sketches, drawings, and diagrams.[2] Bourke claims he was "the first white man to carefully note this strange heathen rite" (ibid.: 1) and declares his book to be "a truthful description of religious rites" (ibid.: xix).

Since I am a religious studies scholar whose field is ritual studies, I focus here on Bourke's perception and interpretation of that "revolting religious rite." Bourke's compulsive diary keeping and candid accounts allow scholars to peer into his methods, theories, and assumptions for studying ritual.[3] His writing is transparent, enabling contemporary readers to see what the study of ritual looked like during the Second Conquest, the one carried out by the English rather than the Spanish.

The Hopis live in northeastern Arizona on high desert mesas. No site in North America has been continuously inhabited for a longer time. The Hopis sustain one of the most enduring ritual traditions in

North America. Compared with many other First Nation ceremonies, which were obliterated, radically modified, or subsumed into Christianity, Hopi rituals remained largely intact in the late nineteenth century.

Early in the narrative a foreshadowing event occurs at Santo Domingo Pueblo (now called Kewa), south of Santa Fe. Bourke writes:

> It was evident that whatever *secret* ceremonies were connected with the festival had been held at dead of the previous night. . . . As it might be a good thing to obtain a correct description of the little that was transpiring within the Estufas [*estufa* is the Spanish word for kiva, an underground ritual chamber], Moran [Bourke's sketch artist] and I laid our heads together, and concluded that an attempt should be made to penetrate the larger edifice.
>
> Our note-books were gripped tightly in one hand, and our sharpened pencils in the other, the theory of our advance being that, with boldness and celerity, we might gain an entrance and jot down a few memoranda of value before the preoccupied savages could discover and expel us.
>
> My pulse beat high as we reached the roof and passed the sacred standard floating from the top of the ladder. Everything looked propitious, and I had gotten down four rungs of the ladder, within two of the bottom, when a yell was raised, repeated from point to point in warning tones, and from every conceivable spot—from out of the earth as it seemed to me—Indians fairly boiled.
>
> The Estufa itself buzzed like a hive of bees. Before I could count ten I was seized from above by the neck and shoulders, and from below by the legs and feet, and lifted or thrown out of the Estufa, the Indians yelling at the tops of their voices, "Que no entres, amigo, mañana Bueno"—"You mustn't enter, friend—to-morrow (will be) good (or proper for that)." They reiterated: "To-morrow, to-morrow; you can come in to-morrow; it isn't good now."
>
> There was no disguising the fact; I was "fired out . . ."
>
> I laughed very heartily at my discomfiture, and the Indians, seeing that I was taking the affair good-naturedly, became very much appeased, and joined in my hilarity. (Bourke 1984 [1884]: 21–23)

Bourke was a military man so, despite his ejection, he returned with reconnaissance: notes about a fire ready for lighting, glimpses of pipes, corn fodder, old farming tools ready for use as ritual objects. But Santo Domingo literally and figuratively left a bad taste in Bourke's mouth: "While at Santo Domingo we breathed so much that was offensive and even putrid, probably dead meat and other effete matter accumulated on account of the feast, that until this morning we were certain we could taste the foulness each time we opened our mouths" (ibid.: 66).

Entering Hopi

Frank Hamilton Cushing (1857–1900), an ethnologist working among the Zunis in New Mexico (160 miles southeast of the Hopi reservation in Arizona), urged Hopis to admit Bourke to the Snake Dance, claiming that Bourke was coming to write everything down for "the Great Father" (Washington personified). In fact, Bourke's visit had no official government status, and the kivas were not open to most Hopis, much less to American soldiers. Bourke anticipated resistance since he had already been removed from a sacred site at Santo Domingo Pueblo. So he and his men staged an improvised ceremonial entry, the tawdry Anglo equivalent of Hispanic rites of reduction.[4] Bourke's men paid him exaggerated homage as if he were a revered personage on a mission of great consequence.[5] Consequently, when Bourke arrived at Walpi on First Mesa, the Hopis responded with a ceremonial display of courtesy.

When Bourke and some of his men invaded the kivas, the Hopis protested, but Bourke feigned ignorance, pretending not to understand. Hoping to distract them, he aggressively shook their hands, pump-handling them like a whistle-stop politician. He pushed past those who obstructed him, climbed down the ladder, and entered the underground ritual chamber where he remained for four hours. Bourke tells his adventure-hungry readers what he encountered:

> The stench had now become positively loathsome; the pungent effluvia emanating from the reptiles, and now probably more completely diffused throughout the Estufa by handling and carrying them about, were added to somewhat by the rotten smell of the paint, compounded, as we remember, of fermented corn in the milk, mixed with saliva! I felt sick to death, and great drops of perspiration were rolling down forehead and cheeks, but I had come to stay, and was resolved that nothing should drive me away. (Bourke 1984 [1884]: 150)

These words came from a man who had sweated only half as much in the face of Geronimo (1829–1909) and his greatly feared Apache warriors. Bourke's description was more than a confession of fear. It was also the report of a sensory assault. The underground portion of the ritual, enacted in close, dark quarters, required the handling and herding of rattlesnakes with eagle feathers. The visual, auditory, tactile, kinesthetic, and olfactory power of the scene terrified the soldier-observer. But, as Bourke tells the story, he drew on his military discipline and did not abandon his post, although his compatriots evacuated theirs.[6]

The Snake-Dance of the Moquis of Arizona is a description of parts of the ceremony propped up by two bookends: a travel narrative and a theory. This volume is considered a classic of early American ethnology and a rare work of observation, even though neither John Bourke nor his sketch artist, Peter Moran (1841–1941), could keep up with the pace of the actions. The Snake Dance was a nine-day ceremony. The first eight days were enacted secretly in kivas. On the final day, dancers appeared with snakes for less than an hour. By the end Bourke was exhausted even though he had witnessed only a small portion of the ceremony. He had no idea what the costumes, objects, and spaces meant, nor did he know what would happen next. He was keenly aware that the complexity of the event far exceeded his language abilities as well as his capacity to observe and document. Consequently, his arrogance in breaching the secrecy of the kiva was softened a bit by his humility regarding his ethnographic account of the ritual. Bourke carried away what tourists and photographers would soon be carrying away: scenes. Whereas his scenes were mainly verbal, those of tourists would be photographic. But Bourke also carried away memories of sensory experiences. In the end, I believe these experiences covertly determined the tenor of the theory, eventually undermining it.

Bourke describes the aboveground public scene. He estimates that a thousand spectators were there:

> Fill every nook and cranny of this mass of buildings with a congregation of Moqui women, maids and matrons, dressed in their graceful garb of dark-blue cloth with lemon stitching; tie up the young girls' hair in big Chinese puffs at the sides; throw in a liberal allowance of children, naked and half-naked; give colour and tone by using blankets of scarlet and blue and black, girdles of red and green, and necklaces of silver and coral, abalone, and *chalchihuitl* [turquoise]. For variety's sake add a half-dozen tall, lithe, square-shouldered Navajos, and as many keen, dyspeptic-looking Americans, one of these a lady; localise the scene by the introduction of ladders, earthenware chimneys, piles of cedar-fuel and sheep manure, scores of mangy pups, and other scores of old squaws carrying on their backs little babies or great ollas [clay pots] of water, and with a hazy atmosphere and a partially-clouded sky as accessories, you have a faithful picture of the square in the Pueblo of Hualpi, Arizona, as it appeared on this eventful 12th day of August 1881. (Bourke 1984 [1884]: 156; see figure 7.2)

In Bourke's written portrait his visualist preferences dominate. The description reads like a picture postcard.[7]

Figure 7.2. *The Snake Dance of the Moquis by Alexander Francis Harmer (1856–1925), 1881. From Bourke 1884, Plate II.*

Hopis say they sing and dance not for themselves alone but also for the planet. Despite this planetary aim, Hopi ritual knowledge is not public. To give away kiva and Snake Clan secrets would be to court disaster, even death. Then, as now, Hopis say their lives depend on the enactment of the Snake Dance. Without rain, which their deadly ancestors the serpents bring, the Hopis would die. They dance in order to be Hopi, in order to be human.

Bourke was unable to make friends with the Pueblos and Hopis in the way he had with the Lakotas and Apaches, even though he had fought the Lakotas and Apaches and only observed and intruded upon the Hopis. To his credit, Bourke recorded a discussion with Nanahe, a frank Hopi, who told him the truth to his face:

> I saw you in the Estufa at the dance; you had no business there; when you first came down we wished to put you out. No other man, American or Mexican, has ever seen that dance, as you have. We saw you writing down everything as you sat in the Estufa, and we knew that you had all that man could learn from his eyes. We did not like to have you down there . . . , but we knew that you had come there under orders . . . , so we concluded to let you stay. . . . One of our strictest rules is never to shake hands with a stranger while this business is going on, but you shook hands with nearly all of us, and you shook them very hard. . . . You being a foreigner, and ignorant of our language, can do us no harm. . . . A secret

order is for the benefit of the whole world, that it may call the whole world its children, and that the whole world may call it father, and not for the exclusive benefit of the few men who belong to it. . . . If they [the secrets] became known to the whole world, they would cease to be secrets, and the order would be destroyed, and its benefit to the world would pass away. (Bourke 1984 [1884]: 150)

In this stinging critique of Bourke's imperialism and visualist ethnocentrism, Nanahe both compliments and criticizes him in a succinct sentence: "We knew that you had all that man could learn from his eyes." Bourke's sensory revulsion was pronounced: "These people stink atrociously; their garments and skins emit the foulest of smells . . ." (ibid.: 296). He complains about decay and abandoned houses; he notices "grotesque wooden idols, painted in gaudy colours . . ." (ibid.: 306).

Bourke left Walpi to visit other Hopi villages, where he traded for goods, carried on short conversations, and noted what ethnographers often note: clans, crops, clothing, children, animals, gender distinctions, material culture (pots, tools, weapons, ruins), trails, spaces and places, stacks of stones.

Bourke was told not to return. He returned anyway, this time with Navaho bodyguards. His reasoning was stereotypical: "Moquis are vacillating, deceitful, good-natured, industrious and filthy, miserly. Navajoes [sic] are generous, bold, arrogant, good-humored, true to their word" (Porter 1986: 111).

With Bourke's intrusiveness challenged and his capacity to understand the Snake Dance confounded, he left plagued by insomnia, exhaustion, and the weather. He descended from the Hopi mesas to visit nearby *Mo-mo-nees* (Hopi for Mormons), who, like Mennonites, were busy trying to convert Hopis into Christians. Although Bourke turned something of an ethnographic gaze upon the Mormons, mostly he was relieved at being away from the kivas and rattlesnakes. He attended worship and was impressed by the power and folk-qualities of the sermon. He took note of Mormon "energy, patience and industry" and remarked upon all the "nice boys" in their "astounding uniformity" (Bourke 1984 [1884]: 356, 358). Although a little strange, Mormons were insufficiently "other" to hold his attention for long.

Bourke's conclusions were shaped partly by ethnography, partly by reading. Some of his comparisons were driven by the desire to show that American ways of life were superior to those of the Hopi. Occasionally he inverts the hierarchy, suggesting the superiority of

Hopi ways of life. On the basis of his reading, he compared what he has witnessed among the Hopis with what he could learn from books about rituals in Greece, Guinea, Scandinavia, and Polynesia. Out of his several comparisons, he constructed a theoretical category, "ophiolatry," the idolatrous worship of serpents. This classificatory act was his most fundamental theoretical move. He prepared his readers for this conclusion with three chapters (18–20) consisting almost exclusively of quotations from "approved authorities" about snakes (ibid.: 196–225).

For Bourke, who dared to step down into a snake-filled kiva, this stepping back to write, lecture, and theorize was also a stepping up. His book earned considerable cultural and academic capital.[8] In 1896 he was elected president of the American Folklore Society. His ethnographic foray and publications presaged a tourist flood. A few years after the publication of *The Snake-Dance of the Moquis of Arizona*, other anthropologists arrived at the mesas. In the wake of scientific and popular publications by Bourke and other social scientists, a sea of gawking tourists swamped the Hopis.

The Santa Fe Railroad issued a tourist's guide for the Snake Dance and began using Snake Dance images on posters to attract ticket-buying tourists. The Hopi Snake Dance became one of the most photographed, painted, and written-about indigenous rituals in the Americas (see also Forrest 1961 [1906]; Voth 1973 [1905]). In 1904 Edward Sheriff Curtis (1868–1952) began visiting and photographing Hopi rituals, resulting in the pictures of volume 12 of *The North American Indian* (Curtis 1997 [1907–30].). The aggressions and abuses of photographers led the Hopis to sequester the ritual from public view. Even as late as 1984, Emory Sekaquaptewa (1928–2007), a Hopi anthropologist, complained about white people who simulate Hopi performances, acting as if Hopi rituals were in the public domain.[9]

In 1895, the year before Bourke's death, he was patronized by Buffalo Bill's Wild West show. Along with defeated Indians, some of whom Bourke had fought and written about, he and other aging soldiers were put on display. Only in his late forties, he was already being cast as an old war horse. Ironically, when he died at forty-nine, this lifelong student of indigenous ritual was buried without ceremony in Arlington National Cemetery.[10]

Because John Bourke was an American soldier who lived in the nineteenth century, it is easy to debunk his theory of ritual and religion. Nonsoldiering academics cannot help noticing how culture bound he was. When he confesses his antipathy toward snakes, referring to them as "mankind's first enemy" rather than as promising but dangerous relatives, we can feel him shiver (Bourke 1984 [1884]: 141). We shiver at his shiver, because casting snakes as enemies rather than as ancestors twists his theorizing into a Christian judgment on serpents and those who supposedly worship them. Whereas Bourke's seeing the rituals as drama or as art *may have been* constructive, his sensory response to snakes eventuates in their becoming symbols of evil. So his theory is really a judgmental, Victorian Christian theology: "Phallic and obscene worship . . . has a deep root in all the towns of the sedentary Indians, especially those of the Zunis and Moquis, and it may briefly be said that no part of the world has more to present that is repugnant and disgusting to the sentiments and judgment of people brought up in the schools of a Christian civilization" (ibid.: 260).

Bourke, Fewkes, Stevenson

It is instructive to compare Bourke's *The Snake-Dance of the Moquis of Arizona* with works of his contemporaries who were doing ethnography in the Southwest: Jesse Walter Fewkes's *Tusayan* [Moquis, Hopis] *Snake Ceremonies* (1894–98) and Matilda Coxe Stevenson's *The Zuñi Indians* (1901–2). Bourke spent a week (11–18 August 1881) among the Hopis and observed the Snake Dance on 12 August. By contrast, Jesse Fewkes's research among the Hopis was not a scouting mission; it lasted six years (1891–97).

Bourke appears very much in front of the scenes he narrates, while Fewkes (1850–1930) and Stevenson (1849–1915) stand in the shadows, farther behind the surface of their writings. Bourke creates characters. Fewkes and Stevenson rarely do. Fewkes employs a narrative style but uses first person only to claim authority: "I witnessed," "I know," or "I am told."

Matilda Coxe Stevenson did not visit Zuni to make friends or do exciting things. She was there to gather information, so her rhetoric is descriptive and distanced. She avoids both narrative and first person, choosing circumlocutions: "It was the writer's privilege. . ." She does not tell readers what happened to *her* but what Zunis *do*—in the ethnographic present, as if she expects them to keep on doing it.

Like Bourke, Fewkes provided scenes, but Fewkes's scenes were less dramatic, weighed down with objects and locations. The objects were described and enumerated. The actions were described and oriented: east-west, left-right. The actions were often dated and timed: on the third day, at 2 o'clock. . . . Fewkes lets readers know the Snake Dance was not a ritual; it was a *phase*, a *part*, of a ritual. He did confess, however, that he had not witnessed any of the secret rites (Fewkes 1986 [1894–98]: 287). Fewkes's *Tusayan Snake Ceremonies* was comparative. He examined variants of the Snake Dance at other Hopi villages. His comparisons were ethnographic and local, not like Bourke's: global, ancient, speculative, and text based. Armed with more data and details than with drama and literary flourishes, Fewkes concluded that the Snake Dance was not about idolizing snakes but about ancestor veneration and rainmaking (Fewkes 1986 [1894–98]: 307). Only a few years after the publication of *Snake-Dance*, Bourke's theory of Hopi ophiolatry crashed, whereas Fewkes's view of their main purpose is still widely accepted today.

Ritual in Frank Hamilton Cushing's *My Adventures in Zuni*

Since Bourke writes with literary flair, a more apt comparison is with Frank Hamilton Cushing (1857–1900), who opened the way for John Bourke to enter Hopi territory. Like Bourke, Cushing intruded upon rituals, observed them, described them, and authorized sketches of them. When Cushing first arrived at Zuni, he horrified Matilda Coxe Stevenson by moving into the village instead of remaining in the camp outside. He thrust himself into Governor Paliwahtiwa's home, believing he could understand a people and their rituals only to the extent that he could penetrate their inner sanctum and identify his life with theirs. He told his superiors at the Smithsonian Institution in Washington that he was being initiated into the Bow Priesthood to have access to information that would otherwise be closed to him. He used the Zunis, but they also put him to political use. Holding a Bow Priesthood position obligated him to enter into the fray with Zuni enemies, Navahos, and the U.S. government.

Cushing organized *My Adventures in Zuni* (1883) on a ritual model. The book condenses into a year what probably took two years. The narrative begins in the summer of 1879 with his "call" in the Smithsonian tower and ends with a funeral in the summer of the following year. He seems to have woven together two cycles: a seasonal-ritual pattern that follows the Zuni year, and a birth-to-death cycle running from his "birth" into Zuni society to the death of an adopted Zuni relative—a scene in which Cushing plays the role of favorite son.[11]

The literary device of weaving his individual life into the collective ritual life of Zuni emphasizes their harmony and deemphasizes their dissonance. The story he tells is not about the clash of cultures but their convergence; *My Adventures in Zuni* is the tale of Cushing's enculturation as a Zuni. The structure of the book prevents readers from dwelling on the incompatibilities of nineteenth-century Zuni and Victorian-American cultures. He employs stories and rites as devices to ensure such synchrony precisely because it does not exist naturally.

One of the striking features of *My Adventures in Zuni* is the number of rituals it incorporates. At the very least there are eight in eighty-eight pages of text. There could be as many as sixteen, depending on whether you count greeting gestures (such as breathing on the hands) and preliminary rites (such as smoking) as rituals in their own right, and depending on what is considered a rite per se or a phase of a rite.

Cushing not only took rites as primary objects of ethnography, standing outside them, he also underwent them, a strategy very different from Bourke's. In one sense Cushing won his struggle to have access to Zuni rites; they gave up trying to prevent his intrusion.[12] In another, however, they won by co-opting him. He lurched from ritual violation into ritual initiation, then became a ritual publicist. Rites sometimes served both Cushing and the Zunis as means of publicity and pedagogy.

Cushing and a small group of Zunis made two trips back East. Accompanied by media people, they visited women's clubs, Harvard University, the Smithsonian Institution, the president of the country. Cushing staged media events and gave ritual demonstrations, workshops, and performances based on his personally appropriated ritual knowledge. For Cushing this was a way of publicizing his work, raising money, and educating the readers of his ethnographic and popular writings.

For Zunis the trip was a pilgrimage to the waters from whence the sun rises; they hoped to secure sacred sand from the beaches. They also wanted to see "Washington," which had so much interest in and power over them. The Zunis pressured Cushing to take them to Washington by insisting that his initiation into the priesthood could proceed only if he did so. For him the trip was also the first phase of a rite of passage into a secret society. No sooner had the Zunis secured their sand than they turned to Cushing and began their rituals on the beaches of Boston harbor. All of this happened with media spectating on the event.

Cushing's archaeological research (as distinct from his ethnographic research) was, you might say, "divinatory." He had an uncanny way of discovering long-buried objects and figuring out how such objects were used.[13] He used the phrase "manual concepts" to describe his ritualizing technique; he believed human hands have a wisdom of their own. He felt one could learn about an object by making one like it. Left to work meditatively with a material or found-object, his hands could discern its purpose. The hands, like the brain, could recognize concepts worked out in physical materials. Cushing thought ethnologists should not merely observe or interview but also work alongside the people who descended from those who produced such objects.

As with the Zuni so with Cushing: storytelling was a ritualized activity. Not only did Cushing observe and study Zuni storytelling but he also told stories, not only *about* Zunis but *as* a Zuni. From the point of view of later anthropology, his rhetoric was too literary, too free, too embellished: an ethnographer should transcribe, not invent.

What the Zunis probably did not understand—and what Cushing could never forget—were his ceremonial obligations to the reading-consuming public and the ever-collecting Smithsonian Institution. According to the canons of American coup counting, an ethnographer was obliged to collect objects and tell secrets that Indigenous people preferred to keep to themselves.

What does all this tell us about the Zunis and Cushing? Probably no one has put it more succinctly or provocatively than Andrew Peynetsa (1904–76), a Zuni. When Dennis Tedlock (1939–2016) asked about Cushing's initiation into the Priesthood of the Bow, Peynetsa said, "Once they made a white man into a Priest of the Bow, he was out there with the other Bow Priests—he had black stripes on his white body. The others said their prayers from their hearts, but he read his from a piece of paper" (Tedlock 1983: 329).

Bourke and Cushing

Bourke and Cushing were "paper medicine men" but in different ways (Porter 1986). Bourke observed rituals firsthand and turned them into paper when he got home. Unlike Cushing, he stayed only a short time, did not learn the language, and did not dress like, or self-identify as, a Hopi. He did not participate in indigenous rituals or live among the people he studied. He did not use paper as a prompt in Hopi rituals. He used notes on paper as a mnemonic device for writing.

Both ethnographers took copious notes and sketched or brought sketch artists. Bourke mobilizes his readers' senses with metaphor. Watching his sketch artist, Bourke writes, "As long as he could manage to endure the noisome hole, his pencil flew over the paper, obtaining material which will one day be serviceable in placing upon canvas the scenes of this wonderful drama" (Bourke 1984 [1884]: 141). Bourke wraps the ritual scene in artistic and dramatistic metaphors. He sees the Snake Dance *as if* it were visual art or drama. Insofar as he is able to capture the ritual's sensuousness, he is a better writer than many scholars who write about ritual today. We would do well to imitate the sensuality of his writing but probably not its sensorium organization,[14] because it tends to render *multi*sensory activity into *mono*sensory, visualist or verbal scenes, although his revulsion at the overwhelming olfactory dimensions of the Hopi Snake Dance threatens to upend these scenes.

Cushing's research, like that of Fewkes, was long-term. Bourke's book on the snake ritual was preliminary, the outcome of a scouting mission; he does not claim otherwise. *The Snake-Dance of the Moquis of Arizona* is neither a fully developed ethnography nor a full-blown theory. The book is a mixed-genre patchwork rather than a systematically applied theory governed by a scientific method. In my judgment, Bourke's conclusions were determined less by his theory than by his worldview—the taken-for-granted values and the sensory prejudices of Victorian America. Then, as today, scholars' *implied* theories may differ from their *declared* theories.

Although both men were courageous and showed more respect for Native people than many of their contemporaries, both theatricalized dishonestly and invaded sacred precincts without proper invitation. By today's standards, their fieldwork ethics were imperialistic and disrespectful. Scholars of ritual traverse the distance from home to field, from circumference to center and back (Grimes 2011). Fieldwork often requires both movements. Sometimes the distance is geographical, sometimes not. Ethnographic researchers' stances are dynamic, shuttling across the circle of ritual enactment. This moving in and out is both bodily and conceptual, generating perspective by the constant shifting of observation angles and vectors of participation.

Method is how one negotiates the distance between center and periphery. Method requires bodily, therefore sensory, action. Since Bourke stepped into Hopi liturgy in order to know, rather than to be or become, from a Hopi point of view, he didn't "get it." His not getting it eventually motivated Hopis to sequester the ritual, but not getting it was also the irritant that drove Bourke to theorize about the ritual.

From a Hopi perspective, the Snake Dance was, and is, a sacred rite, a liturgy, with practical and political consequences. From Bourke's viewpoint, the ritual was a verbal-visual illustration of a theoretical category, ophiolatry. From the point of view of the tourists who soon followed, it was a spectacle. From my point of view, Bourke's account of his encounter with the Hopi Snake Dance is an illustration of a research performance, a dynamic loop that knots together a religious ritual with the sensory data of field research, the methods of ethnography, and the tenets of a budding theory.

It would be unfair to stress Bourke's theoretical conclusions since he and his ethnographer colleagues were known more for descriptions than for theories. In the late nineteenth century, American ethnological reputations were made mainly on the basis of descriptions, often embedded in journey narratives. Even though Bourke felt obliged by scholarly convention to tilt his data in the direction of theory, narratives gave his book popular appeal.

Studying Hopi Ritual Today

To write about the Hopi Snake Dance today is to step into a pit of snakes. If you imagine snakes as your enemy, flee. If you imagine snakes as ancestors, pause, take a deep breath, and listen. With historical hindsight, which, as we all know, is perfect, there are plenty of negative lessons to learn by reading John Bourke's *The Snake-Dance of the Moquis of Arizona*: how *not* to act; what *not* to do; how *not* to theorize. Thanks to Lieutenant-become-Captain Bourke and other ethnographic ancestors, ritual studies scholars and ethnographers will not likely witness, much less study, the Hopi Snake Dance. There are a few exceptions. In the late 1970s Peter Whitely reported witnessing a Snake Dance (Whitely 1998: 20–21). Later he regarded that first experience as cultural tourism or quasi-ethnography, but it became part of his inspiration to return in 1980 to do serious ethnography.

Lomayumtewa Ishii, a contemporary Hopi, insists that white ethnographies are cultural fictions, "a contrived rendition of anglophone recursive ideations about each of the authors' own intellectual and academic authority." Consequently, Ishii says, "aesthetic freedom becomes the guise for the justification of intellectual genocide" (Ishii 2002: 33–35). Ishii's criticism of Bourke in particular was that he used an imperialistic model, the adventure story, a genre designed to keep readers on the edge and reinforce their own authority (ibid.: 34–35). In adventure stories, says Ishii, Hopis are cast as exotic but disgusting others. The ritual scenes in which they appear are repulsive yet inviting. Worse still, adventure stories begin and end in "civilization," white civilization.

I have not observed the Snake Dance or any other Hopi ritual. I am writing on the basis of paper—books and articles written by white men in the late nineteenth century. I am writing about their publications and perspectives, not the ritual itself. I am also reading contemporary Hopi academics. I try to "listen" to their voices, "hear" their writing. Readers in a similar situation might begin by watching and listening to Leigh Kuwanwisiwma, director emeritus of the Hopi Cultural Preservation Office (Kuwanwisiwma 2014; 2018b). In the virtual land of video perhaps viewers can see the semblance of Leigh's face, hear the hint of a voice, sense a tone.

Even in recent research, where Hopis are cast as participants rather than as subjects, they are seldom authors, so it is crucial to seek out Hopis as live or virtual speakers, sole or joint authors.[15] At the invitation of Hopis, cooperation can happen, albeit rarely. Well-known are the collaborations of Leigh Kuwanwisiwma and Peter Whiteley.[16] Kuwanwisiwma writes:

> Previously, my life had been focused on my village of Paaqavi, but through Whiteley's research I was exposed to the whole history of Third Mesa—including the history of Orayvi, its famous split in 1906, and the subsequent establishment of the villages of Kiqötsmovi, Paaqavi, and Hotvela. My eyes were suddenly opened by the many interviews of older Hopi people, which I helped conduct and interpret. Together Whiteley and I captured a lot of information. Whiteley proposed to publish a book on Paaqavi history and the Board of Governors agreed. This work—published in 1988 as *Bacavi: Journey to Reed Springs*—further motivated me to pursue the position [first director of the Hopi CPO] with the tribe. (Kuwanwisiwma, Ferguson, and Colwell 2018: 4)

Much of the current published discussion about Hopi ritual is precipitated by the repatriation of human remains and ceremonial objects.[17] At one point in its history the catalog for Chicago's Field Museum listed over eleven thousand Hopi items (Robbins and Kuwanwisiwma 2017: 63). Leigh Kuwanwisiwma, collaborating with Helen Robbins, reports that the Hopis and the Field Museum have been consulting for thirty years about repatriating the museum's collections, although the connection began earlier, in 1897, when the museum sent a representative to Hopi to buy materials from Henry R. Voth, a Mennonite missionary living at Oraibi.

Kuwanwisiiwma and Robbins make the telling point that legalized procedures of the American government, as prescribed by the Native American Graves Protection and Repatriation Act (National Park Service 1990) coupled with the museums' procedures and protocols, are themselves highly ritualized:

> Although museums' specific policies and procedures vary, the ritualized process a federally recognized tribe must adhere to is exemplified by the following steps at the Field Museum. The tribe must submit a letter on letterhead; demonstrate that the person/group who has written the letter has been authorized by the tribe; address the questions of affiliation, that is, make the argument that the requested items are affiliated to the tribe, especially in cases where provenance is not clear-cut; request each item by museum catalog number; identify the legal category under which the items is being requested (i.e., unassociated funerary object, sacred object, object of cultural patrimony); and "present evidence which, if standing alone before the introduction of evidence to the contrary, would support a finding that the Federal agency or museum did not have the right of possession." (Robbins and Kuwanwisiwma 2017: 66)

Ritualized bureaucracy, designed to remedy, often inhibits the process of repatriation. Although the aim of the Protection and Repatriation Act may be to empower, Hopis "come on their knees" to museums (ibid.: 68).

Theories and Methods, Post-Bourke

With the benefit of historical hindsight, reading *The Snake-Dance of the Moquis of Arizona* offers a long list of prohibitions, but there are positive lessons too: learn about visitor etiquette—ceremonially required rituals of respect (Hopi Cultural Preservation Office 2019); reflect on your own postures and performances, stories, and descriptions, since they underwrite theories and methods.

Journeys and narratives about these journeys continue to shape ethnographic research on ritual, but the tendency in twenty-first-century scholarship is to shrink, omit, or publish separately autobiographical travel narratives, leaving ritual descriptions to serve as grist in the mill of theory. Whereas many nineteenth-century descriptions of rituals were narrative driven, twenty-first-century ones are expected to be theory driven. The *intention* of making this shift is to render research publicly accountable and scientifically respectable, but the *effect* is also to disembody research, severing it not only from the researcher and the researched but also from the research narrative (which one typically hears over a beer) and the research performance (which one hears on ceremonially framed academic occasions).

The outcome of much current theorizing about both religion and ritual is often to disembody, desensualize, and hypervisualize them (see, e.g., Wiebe 2018). As Nanahe noted, outside observers may learn what can be learned using only their eyes, but the noses, feet, and tongues are probably as ignorant as they were in Bourke's day. Because scholars' theories and methods sometimes require of us performances that are inept if not imperial, because our theories and methods often do not require of us kinesthetic, tactile, gustatory, and olfactory attentiveness, we have much information about, but little sense for, the Snake Dance and other indigenous rituals.

By comparing and contrasting Hopi ritual practices with ethnographic and ritual studies practices, my intention is not to set up a binary opposition. It is to distinguish and relate ritualizing and researching by examining the arc that leads from the former to the latter and back again. Research is not only analytical; it is also narrative and performative. "Research is ceremony," argues Shawn Wilson, a First Nations scholar (Wilson 2008).

By transposing ritual into data, scholars exercise ceremonial power by stepping back, then up into positions of academic authority. The rituals of researching, teaching, and publishing constitute the academic ceremony that goes on after the indigenous liturgy ends. Theorists of ritual, like snake-handling Hopis, engage in a dangerously elevated activity, so it is only proper that we who write about ritual receive instruction (and maybe a few whiplashes) from practitioners. We should learn not only *about* Hopis but *from* Hopis and *with* Hopis. What Hopis do with their own worst fears and greatest hopes is to sequester or mask them, rendering them sacred. Then in public they set loose ritual clowns, who both police and mock liturgical activity. The play of power is eventually downplayed.

The Koyemsi, or mudhead clowns, are sometimes depicted as dolls riding Palölökong, the feathered water serpent who slithers out of a jar, becoming erect in the process. He rises up precipitously toward the sky. Such serpent-ancestors are as essential as rain, but they are also as dangerous as the devil. The Hopi scenario requires that sacred clowns, like scholars, ride high. However, it also requires that they be thrown off into the dirt. So be assured: like others who aspire to think theoretically and write methodologically about ritual, our landing spot is predetermined.

Besides embracing the ground, another way to humanize research is to embody and contextualize it. In this respect a theory is no different from a ritual. Theories and methods, like rituals, should be understood in their several contexts: bodily, social, historical, religious, cultural, ecological. Because scholarly bodies are embedded in landscapes, eras, and communities, we comprehend methods and theories best if we understand their relation to the lives and times of those who create, consume, and misuse them. If we can make sense of these relations, theories and methods will no longer seem superior to rituals; they will be just two different kinds of enactment.[18]

Methods are tools of intervention aimed not only at ensuring objectivity and fairness but also at insulating researchers from danger and disorientation. However much research is governed by data gathered into notes, it is also driven by a desire to escape alive and tell the story, erect a theory, or otherwise generate academic capital. Management-by-method is an attempt to control an object of perception experienced as unmanageable by stepping back and then taking up a tool that renders the ritually dangerous event into a visual or verbal scene or a theory that is more predictable and less threatening.

The labor of research, like that of ritual making, arises from and generates its own conceptual space.[19] Method-operationalized theory is an act performed, and it transpires in a setting or on a set. However much the magic of words makes it appear that theories dwell either nowhere or everywhere, they, in fact, arise and decline somewhere. Theorizing is place and time specific. Since scholars sometimes write histories of theories, we are more accustomed to recognizing a theory's time-boundedness than its space-boundedness. It may be true that theorizing enables perspective, but the theorizing eye is not really panoptic; it is neither universal nor divine. As Apaches say, "Wisdom sits in places" (Basso 1996), so it would be wise to follow methods and formulate theories as if the place where we do so matters.[20]

Like ritualizing, thinking theoretically and acting methodically are bodily acts. Although performing them requires stepping back or returning home, these places are nevertheless places; they are not everywhere or nowhere. However godlike this disappearing act may appear from the perspective of local people in the fields where we study, we who come and go to conduct research are merely human. Hopis and other Indigenous people have known this for a very long time, but we non-Indigenous immigrants sometimes forget.

I regret that John Gregory Bourke is unceremoniously in his grave. He deserves better. His *Snake-Dance of the Moquis of Arizona* is a rare book, a collector's item that no one needs to collect since the book is a freebie, downloadable as a PDF from Archive.org (Bourke 1884). We readers will someday join John as ground partners, and our books will undergo the same fate as his. We who write for a living should honor Bourke ceremoniously with a sacrifice. Since libraries no longer want scholars' paper-filled libraries after they retire from writing and making intellectual capital, stack Bourke's book on top of ours, ready for the funeral pyre, and lift a toast: "Here's to you John—a drink of cool, clear water, for which Hopis pray."

Ronald L. Grimes is professor emeritus of religion and culture at Wilfrid Laurier University, Waterloo (Canada), where he taught courses on religion and the performing arts, field research in the study of religion, and ritual studies. Exploring the intersections of religious practice and performance, Grimes has written profusely in the realm of ritual studies, most recently publishing a monograph titled *The Craft of Ritual Studies* (Oxford University Press, 2014). Other publications include *Fictive Ritual* (Ritual Studies International, 2013); *Rite Out of Place: Ritual, Media, and Conflict* (Oxford University Press, 2011); and *Deeply into the Bone: Re-inventing Rites of Passage* (University of California Press, 2002). He is coeditor of the Oxford Ritual Studies Series and director of Ritual Studies International.

Notes

1. This chapter revises and combines parts of previously published works: Grimes 1994; 2006; 2014a. Joseph Porter (1986) has written a good biography of John Bourke.
2. The drawings were by Sargent A. F. Harmer, not Peter Moran, the sketch artist who accompanied Bourke. The original Moran sketches are missing.
3. Volume 5 of his diary (Bourke 2003a [1872–76]) parallels the account in *The Snake-Dance of the Moquis of Arizona*.
4. The best account of these ceremonies of reduction is by Patricia Seed (1995).
5. Accompanying Bourke were, at a minimum: the ambulance driver (unnamed) and Peter Moran. At a maximum his party included: the driver, Thomas Keam, Peter Moran, Mr. Sinclair (a Fort Defiance clerk, no first name given), two soldiers (Gordon and Smallwood, no first names

given), Alexander Stevens, Webber (no first name), Barney Williams, Lorenzo Hubbel, Whitney (no first name).

6. Later he was promoted to captain.
7. Figure 2, a large-scale foldout in some editions, was made later by A. F. Harmer for the *Snake Dance*. Emory Sekaquaptewa, a Hopi anthropologist, who wrote the foreword for a recent edition of *Snake-Dance*, is critical of Bourke's intrusion and of some details in the illustration, but Sekaquaptewa also calls this a "picture-perfect formation of the snake dancers" (Bourke 1984 [1884]: xvi).
8. Bourke grew disillusioned with the military, becoming an active critic of governmental Indian policy and in trouble with Washington bureaucrats. He later wrote other important works such as *Scatalogic Rituals of All Nations* (Bourke 2003b [1891]) about the religious character and ritualistic use of urine and human feces. He also wrote treatments of Mexican nativity plays, delivered public lectures, served on panels, and in 1893 played a role in the World's Columbian Exposition, which hosted the World's Parliament of Religions.
9. Sekaquaptewa is complaining specifically about the "Smoki Tribe," a pseudo-Indian group from Prescott, Arizona, that began performing in 1931. The performances stopped in 1990.
10. Frank Cushing thought Bourke was "killing himself with too many hours a day at the Congressional Library," wearing himself out by trying to turn fifteen years of journal writing into publications (cited in Turcheneske 1979: 333). Bourke's doctor told him that nature was calling a halt, but soldiers do not obey orders from nature.
11. This suggestion is made by Joan Mark (Mark 1967: 455–56) and followed by Jesse Green in his introduction (in Cushing 1979: 38)
12. Jesse Green (in Cushing 1979: 33n39) examined photographs in the Anthropological Archives at the Smithsonian and says most of the illustrations for the published *Adventures* were based on photographs taken by Jack Hillers, the B.A.E. expedition's photographer. They were probably executed by Willard Leroy Metcalf, who also illustrated popular articles on Cushing written by Sylvester Baxter, a Boston journalist.
13. However, in two scandalous affairs he was accused, although officially exonerated, of forging artifacts.
14. A person's or culture's way of organizing, selecting, and attending to sensory data, often tuning in some kinds and tuning out others. The term is from Walter Ong (Ong 1977).
15. Some examples: Gilbert 2013; Kuwanwisiwma 2018a; Sheridan et al. 2015.
16. The fullest, most critical account of Hopis and ethnographers was written by Peter Whitely (1998).
17. A good discussion of repatriation and other culturally contentious issues is *Who Owns Native Culture?* (Brown 2003).
18. Terry Eagleton articulates a similar view: "If theory means a reasonably systematic reflection on our guiding assumptions, it remains as indis-

pensable as ever. But we are living now in the aftermath of what one might call high theory" (Eagleton 2003: 2).
19. For more on sensorium organization, see Grimes (2010: 53, 94).
20. Spatializing theory helps counteract the danger that words assume a "godlike agency in western culture" (Stafford 1998: 5).

References

Basso, Keith. 1996. *Wisdom Sits in Places: Landscape and Language among the Western Apache*. Albuquerque: University of New Mexico.

Bourke, John Gregory. 1884. "The Snake-Dance of the Moquis of Arizona." Retrieved 22 November 2019 from https://archive.org/details/snakedancemoqui00bourgoog/page/n5.

———. 1984 [1884]. *The Snake-Dance of the Moquis of Arizona*. Tucson: University of Arizona Press.

———. 2003a [1872–76]. The Diaries of John Gregory Bourke: November 20, 1872, to July 28, 1876. *The Diaries of John Gregory Bourke*. Denton: University of North Texas.

———. 2003b [1891]. *Scatalogic Rites of All Nations*. Whitefish, MT: Kessinger Publishing Company.

Brown, Michael F. 2003. *Who Owns Native Culture?* Cambridge, MA: Harvard University Press.

Curtis, Edward Sheriff. 1997 [1907–30]. *The North American Indian: The Complete Portfolio*. London: Taschen.

Cushing, Frank Hamilton. 1970 [1883]. *My Adventures in Zuñi*. Palo Alto, CA: American West.

———. 1979. *Zuñi: Selected Writings of Frank Hamilton Cushing*. Edited with an introduction by Jesse Green. Lincoln: University of Nebraska Press.

Eagleton, Terry. 2003. *After Theory*. London: Penguin/Allen Lane.

Fewkes, Jesse Walter. 1986 [1894–98]. *Hopi Snake Ceremonies*. Albuquerque, NM: Avanyu.

Forrest, Earle R. 1961 [1906]. *The Snake Dance of the Hopi Indians*. New York: Tower.

Gilbert, Matthew Sakiestewa. 2013. "Foreword." In *Don C. Talayesva, Sun Chief: An Autobiography of a Hopi Indian*, ix–xv. New Haven, CT: Yale University Press.

Grimes, Ronald L. 1994. "Ritual and Autobiography in Frank Hamilton Cushing's *My Adventures in Zuni*." In *Other Selves: Biography and Autobiography in Cross-Cultural Context*, edited by Phyllis Granoff and Koichi Shinohara, 207–21. Oakville, Canada: Mosaic.

———. 2006. "Reimagining Ritual Theory: John Bourke among the Hopis." Retrieved 4 August 2019 from https://repository.ubn.ru.nl/handle/2066/27447.

———. 2010. *Ritual Criticism: Case Studies in Its Practice, Essays on Its Theory*. Waterloo, Canada: Ritual Studies International.

———. 2011. "Field and Home in Ritual Studies." Retrieved 21 November 2019 from http://vimeo.com/ronaldlgrimes/field-home-ritual-studies.

———. 2014a. *The Craft of Ritual Studies*. Oxford/New York: Oxford University Press.

———. 2014b. "The Craft of Ritual Studies." Film retrieved 1 January 2014 from https://vimeo.com/album/2450305.

Hopi Cultural Preservation Office. 2019. "Visitor Etiquette." Retrieved 4 December 2019 from http://www8.nau.edu/hcpo-p/visitorInfo.html.

Ishii, Lomayumtewa C. 2002. "Hopi Culture and a Matter of Representation." *Indigenous Nations Studies Journal* 3(2): 33–52.

Kuwanwisiwma, Leigh J. 2014. "Going Home 11: Native Community and Agency Perspectives." Retrieved 4 November 2019 from https://www.youtube.com/watch?v=YXEOhiQxqO0.

———. 2018a. "The Collaborative Road: A Personal History of the Hopi Cultural Preservation Office." In *Footprints of Hopi History: Hopihiniwtiput Kukveni'at*, edited by Leigh J. Kuwanwisiwma, T. J. Ferguson, and Chip Colwell, 3–15. Tucson: University of Arizona Press.

———. 2018b. "Corn as Teacher." Retrieved 17 November 2019 from https://www.pbssocal.org/programs/native-america/leigh-kuwanwisiwma-corn-teacher-lx4fyr/.

Kuwanwisiwma, Leigh J., T. J. Ferguson, and Chip Colwell, eds. 2018. *Footprints of Hopi History: Hopihiniwtiput Kukveni'at*. Tucson: University of Arizona Press.

Mark, Joan. 1967. "Frank Hamilton Cushing and an American Science of Anthropology." *Perspectives in American history* 10: 449–86.

National Park Service. 1990. "Native American Graves Protection and Repatriation Act." Retrieved 6 December 2019 from https://www.nps.gov/subjects/nagpra/index.htm.

Ong, Walter J. 1977. *The Presence of the Word*. Minneapolis: University of Minnesota Press.

Porter, Joseph C. 1986. *Paper Medicine Man: John Gregory Bourke and His American West*. Norman: University of Oklahoma Press.

Robbins, Helen A., and Leigh J. Kuwanwisiwma. 2017. "Hopi Renewal and (Ritualized) Performance under American Law." *Museum Worlds: Advances in Research* 5: 60–73.

Seed, Patricia. 1995. *Ceremonies of Possession in Europe's Conquest of the New World, 1492–1640*. Cambridge: Cambridge University Press.

Sheridan, Thomas E., et al., eds. 2015. *Moquis and Kastiilam*. Tucson: University of Arizona Press.

Stafford, Barbara Maria. 1998. *Good Looking: Essays on the Virtue of Images*. Cambridge, MA: MIT Press.

Tedlock, Dennis. 1983. *The Spoken Word and the Work of Interpretation*. Philadelphia: University of Pennsylvania Press.

Turcheneske, John A., Jr. 1979. "John Bourke: Troubled Scientist." *Journal of Arizona History* 20(3): 323–44.

Voth, H. R. 1973 [1905]. *The Traditions of the Hopi*. Millwood, NY: Krause Reprint.

Whitely, Peter. 1998. *Rethinking Hopi Ethnography*. Washington, DC: Smithsonian Institution Press.

Wiebe, Donald. 2018. *The Science of Religion: A Defence*. Leiden: Brill.

Wilson, Shawn. 2008. *Research Is Ceremony: Indigenous Research Methods*. Halifax, Canada: Fernwood.

8

Totemic Relics and Ancestral Fetishes

Henri Trilles's *Chez les Fang*, or Fifteen Years in the French Congo (1912)

André Mary

Chez les Fang, ou Quinze années de séjour au Congo français (Among the Fang, or fifteen years in the French Congo, 1912), by the French missionary and ethnographer Henri Trilles, belongs, according to the preface he wrote himself, to a kind of travel narrative about Fang villages and rivers in which he greatly invested. In 1910 *Au Gabon: Dans les rivières de Monda* (In Gabon: Across the rivers of Monda) appeared. In his later work, *Fleurs noires et âmes blanches* (Black flowers and white souls, undated, ca. 1914), Trilles cultivated stories of sorcerers and anthropophagi largely for his French readership (he apologized to his readers for telling them that he had lived among the anthropophagi for fifteen years), but he also gave a great deal of space to his catechists, the healed baptized and Christian martyrs. This lively and edifying genre of the hero of faith who adventures into the villages, conquering the souls of the black people, always includes a dedication to the missionary's beloved mother, but it is not to be confused with the "letters to parents" genre, like those of his colleague Prosper Augouard (1852–1921) in his *28 années au Congo* (28 years in the Congo, 1905).

In a later book, *Milles lieux dans l'inconnu, en pleine forêt équatoriale chez les Fang anthropophages* (A thousand miles into the unknown, in the heart of the rainforest among the anthropophagous Fang), published in 1931, Trilles related his participation in the so-called Lesieur expedition of 1900 with Father Joseph Tanguy (1872–1941). Wounded and seriously ill, he engaged in an extraordinary adventure of one year, at the end of which, in the absence of news home, he and his companion were considered missing. Recruited for their language skills by the Société d'exploration coloniale, the two missionaries had been placed under the authority of Henri Lesieur,[1] whose mandate was to establish territory contracts with the Fang chiefs and to carry out a topographical survey of the disputed French-Spanish border on the Ntem from Bata to the village of Nkina. Trilles wrote a true step-by-step diary along the forest trails and the course of rivers, with geographical descriptions and well-documented botanical and ornithological observations of the forest's resources.

Henri-Louis-Marie-Paul Trilles (1866–1949) (see figure 8.1) was a Roman Catholic priest who worked as a missionary in the French Congo, now Gabon. Born in Clermont-Ferrand, where his father was stationed as a soldier, Trilles had gone to school in Cherbourg and been trained at the small seminary of Sées in Normandy. Having opted for the missionary apostolate among the Fathers of the Holy Spirit, or Spiritans, he left for Africa in 1893 and returned to France in 1907.

Chez les Fang, more than other travel writings, was inspired by the spirit of the monograph and the scholarly study of the Fang, the social and family life of this ethnic group, and especially its "religious life." The book is a narrative synthesis, often a comparative one, nourished by Trilles's experience of Fang culture and his readings since his return to France in 1907. The chapters open with thematic windows—the legend of migration, language, kinship, beliefs and rituals, "Fang theology"—that bear witness to ethnological and linguistic erudition, acquired through the observation in situ of ritual sequences of the Bieri and Ngil cults, as well as through the study of tales and legends collected from old village chiefs. But Father Trilles's "signature" is his lyrical and patriotic outbursts on the national "totemic god" of the Fang people and the testimonies of his fight against the *féticheurs*, agents of the devil.

Chez les Fang and Its Companion, *Le totémisme chez les Fân*

1912 was in fact the year of publication of two clearly distinct works by Henri Trilles: *Le Totémisme chez les Fân* (Totemism among the Fang) and *Chez les Fang*. Published by the Anthropos Library in its series of monographs, the first book is a well-documented "theological sum" of nearly six hundred pages, commissioned by Monseigneur

Figure 8.1. *Henri Trilles, undated. From* Chez les Fang, ou Quinze années de séjour au Congo français, 1912 *(author's collection).*

Alexandre Le Roy (1854–1938)—the Bishop Le Roy, who wrote the preface—and by Father Wilhelm Schmidt (1868–1954), director of the Pontifical Lateran Museum in Rome. An encyclopedic synthesis of scholarly readings of the totemic phenomenon, it partly takes up the issues and debates that the journal *Anthropos* had echoed since its founding in 1905 with two major goals: (1) to show that totemism exists in equatorial Africa and particularly among the Fang in an "integral" form; and (2) to draw on the Catholic ethnography of the beliefs and practices of fetishism as well as totemism in order to invalidate any scholarly reading that sought to account for the superior religion of the Christian faith deriving from the inferior forms of religion. In a way, this was the application of the program set out by Monseigneur Le Roy in *La Religion des primitifs* (The religion of primitive peoples, 1910) in response to the challenge of the theses of the Durkheimian sociologists at the Sorbonne (Mary 2015).

After his arrival in Gabon, Trilles had become acquainted with the "country of the blacks" from Lambaréné, on the Ogooué River, a true crossroad of tribes: Galoa, Mpongwe, Vili, Seke, and Fang. As Trilles summed it up in his preface to *Chez les Fang*:

> Then, when I was acclimatized by these few months of my stay and was familiar with the various idioms spoken in our colony, in a word, when I was sufficiently "black," I began this long series of diverse explorations among the Fang, which were to last fifteen years, the most beautiful of my life as a man. And it was in the course of these journeys that I came to know this interesting race of the Fang, "the race of the Future, the race of Men," said the great explorer Savorgnan de Brazza; I learned to know it; I also learned to love it, by living its life, by sitting at the fires of their villages, by collecting their traditions, by accompanying them in fishing, hunting, and war, by becoming one of them, so to speak. (Trilles 1912b: 7–8)[2]

After returning to France, Trilles wrote that the manuscript on totemism expected by *Anthropos*, to which he was a regular contributor, was ready by 1908 (Trilles 1912a: 9). But at this point a serious setback intervened: the publication of the work of Le Roy on *La Religion des primitifs* (1910), with theses on totemism and fetishism that would be the subject of a serious dispute between Trilles and his superior (see below), all in view of the announced publication of the work of Émile Durkheim (1858–1917) on *Les Formes élémentaires de la vie religieuse* (*The Elementary Forms of Religious Life*, 1912). The words of Trilles in his introduction to *Le Totémisme chez les Fân* are not lacking in irony: "At several points, we may find ourselves in contradiction with the eminent author [Le Roy]. We will frankly admit that hovering higher, he must have seen truer. We have persisted, however, not out of a vain overstatement or attachment to our own ideas, but to allow for further research that will bring out the truth more clearly" (1912a: 10). Trilles's critique of the "great writer" Le

Roy, the "pioneer" of studies on the *Négrilles*[3] (Le Roy 1905) whom Trilles had accompanied in the field, was to be more frank twenty years later, when he returned to the question of totemism among Pygmies at the invitation of Wilhelm Schmidt (Trilles 1932). Yet, in his essay on totemism, Trilles had already denounced the idea of a "Pygmy tribal totem," which he saw as a confusion between totemic and sacred animals (Trilles 1912a: 146).

The parallel edition of *Chez les Fang* in 1912, with a preface in which "the author introduces himself and says what he wants to do," appears in this context as a "double" or reverse discourse. It values the personal missionary experience of the native (the black) in his own language and the "intimate" knowledge of "*nos Fang*" (our Fang), in contrast to the experience Le Roy claimed about his "initiation" to totemism with Chief Foumba on the heights of Kilimanjaro in 1892: "Then after a white goat's throat was slit, Foumba's arm and mine were gored and blood was spilled, the victim's liver, divided into six pieces, was rubbed with the blood, and we gave them each other to eat. ... Foumba's blood was now mine, mine was his, and we were 'brothers' ..." (Le Roy 1910: 119). Le Roy acknowledged that this was not quite totemism, and Trilles continued to ironicize about those passing visitors who did not speak the language and called themselves "initiates." In his great work on *Les Pygmées de la forêt équatoriale* (Pygmies of the rainforest, 1932), Trilles returned to the "blood covenant"—the paradigm of totemism according to Le Roy—only to subtly scoff at it: "In his Kilimandjaro book, Mgr Le Roy humorously echoed a very colorful account by Father Baur, recounting how on the East Coast he became blood brothers with one of the little kinglets there" (Trilles 1932: 499).

However, there was an obvious gap between the conclusion of the essay on totemism—"totemism exists in Africa, I have found it among the Fang," it is even "integral totemism" (Trilles 1912a: 38)—and the missionary and ethnographic testimonies of Trilles (and his colleagues), which gave little place, if any, to the celebrated "totemism" that agitated the scholarly world. The most common category of missionary discourse in the field was that of fetishism, with its fetishes, its *féticheurs*,[4] and fetish cults.[5] The occasional reference to the "tribal fetish" of the crocodile and its Nguranengurane legend, or to individual acts of "nagualism" (Trilles 1912b: 232)—a category taken up by Trilles under the authority of Robert Hamill Nassau (1835–1921), corresponding to the incarnation of the soul of a living human being in an animal (in this case a leopard)—should not be taken as confirmation of the presence of totemism. The issue Trilles was asked to address in his essay on totemism by Le Roy—and Schmidt—was the respective place of totemism and fetishism, but it has to be borne in mind that their overlapping, interlocking, or intertwining meanings were self-evident to Trilles as far as the empirical evidence of worship was concerned.

Let us recall that the tension and hesitation over these terms, *totem* or *fetish*, if not over the phenomena themselves, somewhat divided the Durkheimian circle at the time (Mary 2012). Upon reading *The Native Tribes of Central Australia* (1899) by Baldwin Spencer (1860–1929) and Francis Gillen (1855–1912), Durkheim wrote in a letter to Marcel Mauss (1872–1950): "The connections between the totem and things other than the totemic species are obvious. There is a fetishism, indistinct from common fetishism, whose totemic origin and character are indisputable" (Durkheim 1998: 224). Mauss, on his part, did not hesitate to consider it necessary, in view of the data on Bantu Africa, to "replace the concept of fetish with that of mana for the whole of Africa" (Mauss 1968 [1907]: 20). Semantics apart, it must be stressed that Trilles's common reference to a world of hidden forces embodied in fetishes or totems is quite close to the Melanesian category of mana that inspired the concept of sacredness of the Durkheimians.

It must be said that Reverend Robert Hamill Nassau (1835–1921), recognized by Trilles as an undeniable ethnographic authority, with forty years of presence (1861–1906) in Equatorial Africa (despite his affiliation with the Presbyterian "ministers of error"), hardly mentioned totemism in *Fetichism in West Africa: Forty Year's Observation of Natives*, and denied the importance of a totemic cult among Bantu peoples (Nassau 1904: 191). On the other hand, similar to Mary Kingsley (1862–1900), Nassau, to the dismay of the Durkheimians at the Sorbonne,[6] retained the all-encompassing category of fetishism[7] by a significant mixing of the French and English spellings of the term, originally derived from the Portuguese *feitiço*:

> The charms that are most common are material, the fetich—so common, indeed, that by the universality of their use, and the prominence given to them everywhere, in houses and on the person, they almost monopolize the religious thought of the Bantu Negro, subordinating other acknowledged points of his theology, dominating his almost entire religious interest, and giving the departmental word "fetich" such overwhelming regard that it has furnished the name distinctive of the native African religious system, viz., fetichism. (Nassau 1904: 80)

The Legendary Fang and the Invention of the God Nzame

The settling of the Mission Sainte Marie (Libreville) in the coastal country of the Mongwe (then called the Gabonese) allowed Trilles to encounter the first Fang villages—like that of Ayeng—a few days away from the mission by boat or canoe, before embarking on "tours" through the interior of the country. The Fang, this "beautiful race" of warriors and conquerors, was at the gates of the colony, its identity built "at the frontier" in the encounter with the first explorers, Pierre Savorgnan de Brazza (1852–1905), Paul Du Chaillu (1831–1903), and Victor de Compiègne (1846–77). The first "informants" of Trilles, to whom he paid tribute in his accounts by means of photographs, were the former pupils, the "recruited" apprentices and faithful catechists of the mission who guided him to their fathers and introduced him to the guardians of the oral tradition, the elders who "know."

Trilles's relationship with Fang men, the almost "white" black men that some geographers associated with the Ethiopian branch, was profoundly ambivalent:

> As the in-depth study of his language—and especially of the genius of his language—irrefutably demonstrates today, the Fang undeniably belongs to the Bantu race,[8] a race so powerful that it throws its prolific branches over nearly half of the African continent, from Sudan to the Cape.
>
> But the Fang is also the least Bantu of all Bantu. Cast in the limelight at one of their extremities, the Fang are true warriors of the Marches opposing the progress of Islamism with an impenetrable block, and one of the intermediate links that connect the races of the Nile and Libya to the Chamitic races, properly speaking. Also, their manners and customs partake of the one and the other. They may be hunters, but also shepherds; black, but also red and sometimes blond; ferocious, and often of easy and pleasant welcome. (Trilles 1912b: 14)

The young Spiritan missionary invested himself in the Fang language with the publication of a lexicon, a grammar, a method of learning, and especially a Fang catechism (1897) in continuity with the work begun by his predecessor Monseigneur Louis Martrou (1876–1925). He became known from 1898 on through a series of articles, first titled "Chez les Fang" in *Les Missions catholiques* (1898), then in the geographical societies of Lille and Neuchâtel (1906–7), until his return to France. *Les Missions catholiques: Bulletin hebdomadaire de l'œuvre de la propagation de la foi* (Catholic missions: Weekly bulletin of the work of spreading the faith) published a regular column titled "À la suite" (follow-up) from January to December

1898, with specific headings, the first being "Chez les Fangs: Leurs mœurs, leur langue, leur religion" (Among the Fang: Their manners, their language, their religion). It continued like this: "Ce qu'ils sont, où ils vont et d'où ils viennent" (What they are, where they are going, and whence they come). Everything had a place there: sections on "race" (81), "traditions" (92), "language" (101, 116, and 128), "events: medical and missionary" (136), "theological quarrels" (166), "mass and baptism" (188), "some legends" (199), "in the village" (212), "unexpected baptism" (226), etc. But in the pagination of *Les Missions catholiques*, selected pieces concerning the life of the Fang intermingle with sections on the Kanak or the Tonkinese in the same "universal" Catholic world. The beginning of the séries has a particularly edifying note on page 6: "Mgr Le Roy, the eminent Superior General of the Fathers of the Holy Spirit only passed through Gabon; however, he left there the imprint every superior man leaves on the works and the men he directed. So our readers will easily recognize in Father Trilles, in the charming, alert, moving, interesting story we publish, a disciple of the master. There is no doubt that our dear associates will have the same impression as we do."

Thus, the publication of the 1912 work, *Chez les Fang, ou Quinze années de séjour au Congo français*, was a continuation and resumption of these fifteen years of "serial" publications, often reproducing the articles in their first version. First of all, Trilles takes up the study of Fang tales and legends as a tool for learning the language "as it is spoken," along with their corresponding encyclopedia, from bestiaries to parables, which aided the elaboration of Fang lexicons and catechisms. Linguistically and ethnographically, the collection of the great narratives of the legendary Fang migration is marked by the ambiguous notion of a "Chamitic," if not Nilotic, people from the "Northeast" and Upper Nile, by Trilles's own version of Egyptology, with its tables of parallels between Fang and Egyptian, matching the legendary genealogy of the Fang old men. For him, it was a question of making the link between "the natural people" and its legendary heroes. But what particularly motivated his research was the saga of the origin of the first ancestors: Nzame, Mebeghe, Nkwa, and Nyingone, the matrix of a pantheon of ancestor gods—or a "Fang theology" of the divine trinity, in the words of Trilles. The Fang genealogy of ancestral figures has a derivative relation to the biblical or Adamic genealogy, which was eventually supposed to embody the universality of the original unity of humankind according to the "dogma" of original monotheism. But, according to Trilles, who never doubted that the Fang had a religion, this same religion was also the locus of all perversions and degradations, in the image of the original incest of their mythology.

It must be emphasized, however, that the stories collected by Trilles and their "context of enunciation,"[9] like the legends of the Fang migration, are perfectly situated (the village of Ayeng of Monda, but also other places of evocation, with variants as far away as Cameroon) and related to narrators to whom he paid tribute (such as the old chief Nkoro). The same goes for the legend of Ngurangurane, the "son of the crocodile, the first chief of the Fang" (Trilles 1912b: chap. 7, 83ff.), told for the first time on the river Ebe by a native Christian named Henri (ibid.: 211). The subsequent publication of these stories, taken out of their ritual context,[10] ignores the fact, first, that these stories were sung during evening gatherings by the players of Mvet (the name of the harp and the epic of the Fang), with Trilles giving us musical versions of them; and second, that these songs also provide material for the *mebara*, the genealogical accounts of the initiatory society of Bieri, and even go so far as to list the names of the fetishes mobilized or conjured up. This legendary thread of tribal memory would nourish the dramatization of the ritual sequences of the Fang initiatory society Bwiti during the 1930s–50s. The legend of the crocodile that was sacrificed by the chiefs of the Ngan society, a variant of the Ngil initiatory society described by Trilles (see below), makes delicate reference to "the image, roughly reproduced in clay, lying in a corner of the forest" (ibid.: 211), with the white clay casts found in the "house of the Ngil" of which Günter Tessmann (1884–1969) provided us with some very beautiful and strange photos as part of the initiation to the So.[11]

It will come as no surprise that the living accounts of ritual sequences imparted by Trilles and included in *Chez les Fang* are often intermingled with exchanges with informants and based on in vivo descriptions extrapolated from the personal comments and memories of the initiates. The mytho-theological overinterpretation of the tales and legends of the ancients were to be perfectly assimilated by the learned young seminarians who forged the Fang tradition. It differs from Nassau's more "sociological" reading of the tales he collected in the same period (1878–90) and the same regions along the Ogooué River: the stories of the bloodthirsty leopard who seizes the "meat of others" and of the slow but cunning tortoise tell above all of the tensions in a clan society in the midst of a crisis in parental relations, as this society was confronted with the fratricidal disparities engendered by the riches of white people (Cinnamon 2006a: 39–40). Trilles did not ignore the moral lessons, including the evangelical, that can be drawn from this confrontation between the great hoarders of wealth and the small ones with no other weapons than cunning; he ignored even less the justification of the inequalities conveyed by these myths of tribal origin, in the guise of role-playing between whites and blacks under the amused gaze of Nzame. The competition between legendary "totems" can also be translated in terms of an unresolved conflict between the emerging associations: the famous "leopard men" and the Ngil cults called in to engage in witch hunting.[12]

The missionary work of bricolage of the heroes of the Fang traditions, which led to the invention of the god Nzame in the second half of the nineteenth century and to the promotion of an ancestor-god of the tribal genealogy or a legendary village chief to the status of Supreme Being or God "in person," owes much to Trilles's transcriptions. Jean-Émile Mbot portrayed Trilles as the inventor of the Fang god and denounced his misinterpretation as a "missionary manipulation" (Mbot 1975: 112; 2002: 8). But over time we can see in Trilles's translation of God's name a kind of working misunderstanding, associating the process of incomprehension of the other with the real genius of religious bricolage. After all, Nzame's village affairs, the jealousies of his wives, and the betrayals of his beloved sons are images of the intrigues of the kingdom of God and the legend of Adam and Eve, not to mention the "forbidden fruit" and the original incest.

The welding between Adamic mythology and the genealogy of Fang ancestors had been at work in missionary practice since at least the middle of the nineteenth century. Trilles was not surprised to find at the heart of the legend of Bingo, the presumed son of Nzame and Mboya, a passing woman who, while human, was quite a match for a divine hero. This echoed the dogma of the Divine Trinity; and the original monotheism thus wove its spider's web between the Semitic and Nilotic traditions (Trilles 1912b: 142–43). Moreover, Trilles recounts how he presented himself upon his arrival in the villages by reciting the family genealogies he had learned thus far, adding to them, as in the *mebara*, the names of the ancestral couple, Nzame and Nyingone (Trilles 1912a: 5; see above). But, as we know, living history has the ability to transform these manipulations, misunderstandings, and misinterpretations of the original legends and names of the ancestral gods into intercultural productions and authentic traditions—through a "collaborative" ethnology or "inculturation" anticipated by the missionary and his catechists. For all Fang in Gabon today, Christian or not, Nzame and Nyingone Mebeghe are indeed their Adam and Eve, as they have learned in catechism or songs since childhood. Thus, as a good "son of the Fathers," Mbot, a former seminarian and professor of ethnology at the Université Omar Bongo in Libreville, can today consider the "manipulation" of Trilles as a contribution to the memory heritage of the Fang, and the missionary as a "precursor apostle of interculturality" (Mbot 2002: 5).

The Initiation Complex: Fetishes and Totems

Descriptions of the major rituals among the Fang and their initiatory societies (Bieri, Bwiti, Melan, Ombwiri) and especially of the anti-witchcraft cult of the Ngil, occupy a central place in *Chez les Fang*. The book features an ethnographic section of more than twenty pages (174–97) about this cult and its offshoots or counterparts such as the Ngan, the Akhung, or the Evodu, a myriad of ritual societies that offer various opportunities for combination or accumulation adapted to the lineages, alliances, and circumstances within the initiates' life cycle. Trilles made a major contribution to this subject "among the Fang," with no equivalent at the time other than Tessman's account of the Yaunde of South Cameroon.[13] Pierre Alexandre (1922–94), a specialist on the Pahouin,[14] was astonished by the absence of the great interclan initiatory ritual of the So in the rites listed by Trilles, but as he himself acknowledged, the initiatory cycle of the So gradually became segmented and diluted in its expansion south of the N'tem (Alexandre and Binet 1958: 97). Tessmann (1991 [1913]: 266) had insisted on the multiple variants of the So he observed in southern Cameroon: the Bokung-elong, the Ndong-ba, and the Shok with its zoomorphic clay figurines. Sequences of the fragmented So reappear in the Ngil, the Bieri or the Bwiti,[15] and the complex intertwining of the rituals of the Fang initiation system, encouraged by the overlapping of totemism and fetishism, was well rendered by Trilles.

The initiation complex was structured around three poles: (1) the zoomorphic entities, their dwellings (outside the village), and their representation in the form of a mask or a clay animal sculpture (elephant, gorilla, crocodile, snake), which could be described as "totemic"; (2) the "coarse" statues of carved wood and the bark boxes that keep the "fetish" skulls of the ancestors in the chiefs' hut; and (3) the *biang*, fetishes or medicines provided by the *féticheur* (*nganga*), with the sorcerer's power in the background, embodied by the "universal" category of the Fang world, the *evu*, the devouring evil that some individuals possess in their womb as told in the original myths. From Nassau to Tessmann and including Trilles, the consensus on the omnipresence of the category of the *evu* (or *evus, evur*, depending on the clan regions of the Fang) is obvious.

Trilles had an acute sense of nuance and, in a manner reminiscent of Evans-Pritchard (1902–73), denounced the confusion between the *sorcier*, the agent suspected of wrongdoing, and the *féticheur*, with a recognized social status as diviner or healer, without ignoring their complicity:

> These two words are almost always used interchangeably: *sorcier* and *féticheur*. Nothing could be more inappropriate. The *féticheur* is the man of public worship, of ritual, with rank and legal place in the tribe. He plays a religious role accepted by all. The *sorcier*, on the contrary, is the man of secret, extra-legal worship. He is the man of the night, the hated man par excellence. The *féticheur* is honored; on the contrary every *sorcier*, accused of a crime, must drink the poison of trial. Convicted, he is burned without remission. (Trilles 1912b: 9n1)

The distinction in principle between totemic worship and "manes-worship," formulated in *Le Totémisme chez les Fân* (1912a: 371ff.), is marked by the difference between *esayôn* (clan) and *mvamayôn* (totemic group) and at the same time by a very close relation between the two, an interweaving and overlapping that results in each being the part and the whole of the other: "Just as totemism, therefore, is part of fetishism and constitutes one of its aspects, but nevertheless is profoundly different from it, so the totem forms one of the aspects of the fetish, mingles and merges with it, but nevertheless remains profoundly distinct from it by its cult and the object of that cult" (Trilles 1912a: 635).[16] Trilles was not yet familiar with the concept of "participation" that Lucien Lévy-Bruhl (1857–1939) would develop to account for this "primitive" logic.

The narrative and dialogical style of *Chez les Fang* allows us to restore the pragmatic and contextual dimensions of the categories that we tend to "fetishize" too much:

> But first of all, what does this word, *fetish*, which so often drops from our pen, mean?
> For many, the fetish is a gri-gri, an amulet, a thing of some kind, animal tail, animal remains, nail clippings, fragments of skin or antelope horn that the black man hangs in his hut, wears on his chest, attributing virtue or real power to it. And indeed, let us take, for example, an explorer or a colonial officer facing a black man:
> "What are you wearing on your side, your neck, your belt?" he will ask him, pointing to his fetish.
> And the black man replies at once:

"It's the *biang*, the consecrated medicine that will keep me safe from bullets, from accidents, that will make me rich!"

"But do you believe in it? Do you really believe in it?"

"Oh! Certainly, my *biang* is infallible!"

And the white man mocks the black, mocks the simplicity of this naive man who attributes an imaginary power to some object, which he himself believes has no force or virtue. And he leaves, disdainful, without suspecting that he is the naïve one!

Is it really to this object, this horn, this bell, the nail clippings or bone debris, that the black man attributes virtue? This is where the white man is strangely mistaken! For the black man this fetish is a "sign," a token, a material object reminding us of an idea. It is the counterpart of "our medals," it is the memory of the propitiatory offering made to his god and of which this fetish contains the remains; and that is why he attributes to it a real, and often proven, value.

It is for him so much a "sign" and only a "sign"—a sacramental one, if you like—that at the moment of danger, of action, our black man will seize his fetish, and say to him: "Evalega, remember." And who should remember? The inanimate object? No, the Spirit instead, to whom he went to offer some bloody sacrifice in the dark forest, and of whom he keeps a material remembrance in his "fetish."

Remember, Spirit protector, that I offered you a sacrifice! But when his expectation has been deceived several times, he will scornfully throw away his fetish and care no more about it: "the fetish is bad." This does not mean that the Spirit has lost his power, but simply that he has not accepted the sacrifice. Some are astonished that the black man, disappointed many times over, should nevertheless continue to have faith in his fetish. How surprisingly naive! Was the fetish bad? This is because the sacrifice was worthless, and the Spirit did not listen to it, or because the intermediary, the *sorcier*, was impotent, malevolent, I know not what! It is therefore necessary to begin again and the faith of the black man in the fetish remains intact. (Trilles 1912b: 198–99)

As Trilles repeated, the Fang do not believe that they are the children of the Crocodile; if one can say so, they do not "fetishize" the fetish: whether fetish or totem, their faith in the power of the thing stems from the spirit of the sacrificial covenant. In the didactic presentation of his essay on Fang totemism, his concern about highlighting differences goes hand in hand with pedagogical illustrations of the complexity of the total object (to use Mauss's term).

Fetishism does not merely consist of worshipping the material object that is influenced by the spirit: one must also attach to it everything that constitutes witchcraft or magic, mantic or medicine as usually practiced in savage countries, as well as the initiations, the secret societies, and finally the various beliefs and ceremonies that make this caricature of a religion a very complicated whole. Take, for example, a spirit or a genius, that of thunder, the sea or the winds: it has, naturally, its name, its gender (it can be male, female, or both), its history, and its legends; it has its material fetish: a statuette, a plant, an animal, a special stone, a particular shell or a horn filled with various products, each of which has its own meaning; it has its symbol: a bracelet, a ring, a necklace, a tattoo or a mark that its followers wear as a sign of consecration or of rallying; it has a special color dedicated to it, red, green, white, etc.; it has its own *féticheur*, the only one authorized to compose and consecrate its fetish, to offer it the prescribed sacrifices, to gather the faithful around it, to conjure it up and, if necessary, to expel it; it has its brotherhood or secret society, its feasts that distinguish it from others, its particular dances, the offerings or sacrifices it accepts and the oracles, spells or services within its competence.

With regard to a genius, this is part of fetishism. But at the same time, as it happens, this genius may be the totem of a clan, or a secret society, and by this very fact this already so complex whole reproduces itself a second time, finds itself doubled: for example, it will have its color as genius, and it will have another one as a totem. (Trilles 1912b: 198–99)

This inclusion of the part in the whole and the whole in the part was reflected at the ritual level by the fact that "totemic ceremonies are the prelude to or continuation of the ceremonies relating to the cult of the ancestors" (Trilles 1912a: 374), the same ritual sequence and the same sacred objects being repeated from one "system" to the other (by changing colors). Trilles insisted on the fact that the skulls smeared with the blood of sacrifices that the initiates had to identify as they were taken out of the bark boxes by reciting their genealogy (*mebara*) were associated with the pieces of bones or the ashes of animals preserved in the horns of antelopes (Trilles 1912b: 378, and 632). The consecration of the link between the *nsek Bieri*, the bark box in which the marked skulls were kept, and the antelope horn that kept the burnt "remains" of the sacrifice (*evalega*), explains why Trilles spoke indifferently of "totemic relics" or "ancestral fetishes," thus underlining the hybridization of cults beyond their difference.

The *catechism* of the primacy of the individual, which was dear to Wilhelm Schmidt's modern ethnology, was placed at the forefront of chapter 1 of *Chez les Fang*; and the concern for the elective and intimate relation of the individual with his patron totem was at the heart of Trilles's encounters, concerned as he was about the nature of the pact between the individual, the group, and the totem. Nevertheless, the personal link of identification with the "real totem" (such as the pet snake in the chief's hut) was subordinated to a "totemic right" of which the chief of the tribe (or the "chief of the race"), and his proxy, the male head of the family (*esa*), was the sole guardian in the name of the covenant, renewed by bloodshed, with the totemic animal and its "sons." Thus, the interlocking of the totemic affiliation in the cult of the ancestors was obvious to Trilles and the place given to the Bieri, the "national" fetish, and its totem was at the core of all antiwitchcraft cults, as illustrated by the Ngil and its *féticheurs*.

"Whitening" Bieri or Reverse Fetishism

Fang oral tradition always makes reference to a god from above (*Nzame e yo*) and a god from below (*Nzame e si*). And while the distant Mebeghe, or the Nzame of folktales fleeing men after the original sin, could be identified with the heavenly god of the Christians, the Nzame from below is always there—in this case Bieri, the ancestor god, somewhere between a devil and a good god, the only recourse for men in misfortune and need. The moment of bravery in *Chez les Fang* is the encounter with this "devil" called Bieri (also Biéri, or Byeri), whom the missionary—so he said—had the privilege of visiting in his hut in the village (apart from the initiation rites):

> Above this box [the bark box containing the skulls] is often placed a crude and hideous statue, carved from a shapeless black wood trunk with an axe. This, strictly speaking, is Bieri, the national god, the universally dreaded fetish of the uninitiated. The statue is a representation of the invisible god of evil, the one to be reconciled with, to whom from time to time, especially during the full moon, the victims of sacrifice are offered in a remote corner of the dark forest.
> Bieri is the strong god, the powerful one, the Teutates of the tribe, the Odin of our fierce warriors. As the old men tell you, this divinity was recently introduced, in relation to the Ye-Ngol and prevailing everywhere over the ancient leopard, the hieratic crocodile. Once universally adored, the latter is now relegated to the background with the ideas of yesteryear, as a fallen god who is barely remembered in some nocturnal party by a few old men, a remnant of a past that will fade away, slowly forgotten. . . . Bieri is the national god of the Fang! (Trilles 1912b: 246–47)

The attitude toward that fetish god, a phantom of former totems, revived by the recent cults of the Ye-Ngol and promoted to national god, is totally ambivalent, a mixture of fascination, confrontation, and denigration if not self-pitying over the "remains." It is easy to see how Trilles's Catholic patriotism can also be found in this Fang fetishist patriotism nourished by the blood of sacrifices and the land of ancestors, which Fang scholars relay to each other.

To speak of an "officiant" of the Bieri cult who would expose the relics and the box is implausible and hides the artificiality of the assemblage, whereas the Sango ethnic reference (southern Gabon) suggests that the image is unrelated to the Fang.

The missionary fetishism of the manufactured postcard, exposing "fetish remnants," open bark boxes and skulls brought out in the open, fetishes of all kinds spread around (see figure 8.3), has nothing to do with photographs of authentic initiatory life. Instead, it is part of an apologetic strategy that had been widespread in the "Congolese" regions since the 1880s.[17] The photo (see figure 8.2) accompanying the presentation of Bieri in *Chez les Fang* (246) is, however, even less authentic. In fact, it is unique and, if one may say so, "signed," because unlike the known original photo (see figure 8.3), which was also used elsewhere (notably by Augouard), here the white "smearing" of the body of the "fetishist" gives him the appearance of an "altar boy" in his cassock. The initial article in the series of *Les Missions Catholiques* only includes the drawing of a statue of Bieri placed on a box containing human skulls (1898: 436), but no photos or postcards. Therefore, this is not a simple operation of substitution from one im-

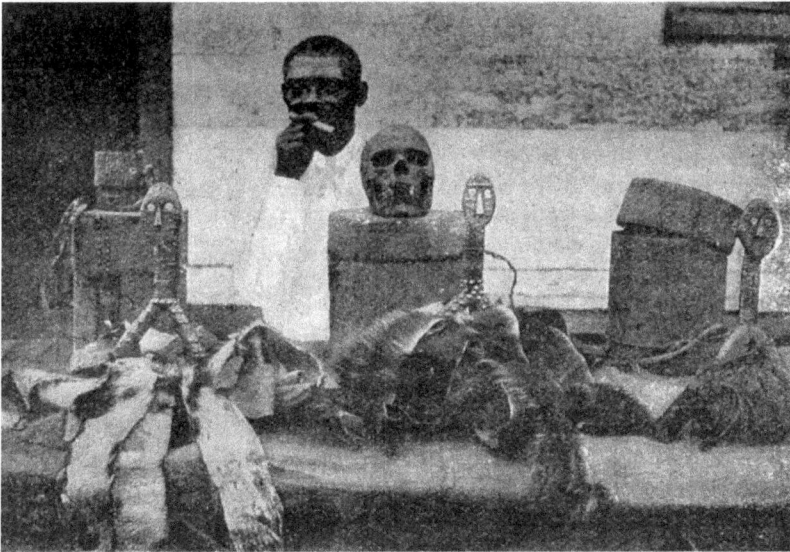

Figure 8.2. *"Whitened" postcard, reprinted by Henry Trilles in* Chez les Fang, *1912, p. 246 (author's collection).*

Figure 8.3. *"Officiant of the Sango cult of the ancestors," Father Augouard collection, no date. From Perrois 1979 (author's collection).*

age to another, in this case the use of fetish objects and bark boxes of Sangho origin, from southern Gabon, in order to illustrate a Fang initiation context. This is a bleaching operation involving a "gross" (and sacrilegious) falsification: a very significant symbolic gesture of inversion and perversion of the traditional whitening by *foem* (white clay) used by the initiated actors, transfigured as ancestors in the ceremonies of the Bwiti or the Ombwiri. Trilles, it should be noted, practiced photography in the field but mostly made drawings from it that were meant to be naturalistic and faithful. He knew what he was showing and continued his fight against the "devil's fetishes" and his confrontation with the fetishists, using their codes and their own weapons.

The White *Sorcier*'s Challenge to the *Féticheur*

The most dramatic passages in *Chez les Fang*, in fact, are those in which Trilles defied the *féticheurs*. Taking place in the village square, in front of the missionary's audience (both Christian and pagan), this was a theatrical confrontation between the "white sorcerer," who gambled his prestige in the trial, and the "satanic" *féticheur*, who was doomed to lose face, as can be seen in the following excerpt titled "An eventful interview":

Around Ngil's master.

A child, a page of some sort, appears first. This figure is not masked, but wears a special loincloth, made of bark and thread, which covers him entirely. He carries a bell in his hand and goes around the whole village shouting: "Close the doors, close the windows, turn off your lights, shut up, Ngil is coming, here is the Ngil."

The child then returns to the outskirts of the village, and walks a few steps before the Ngil. Behind him is a man with a masked face, carrying a bundle of long poisoned arrows, wooden sticks sharpened at their ends and impregnated with the juice of onai,[18] a strychnine-based poison with staggering effects, now well known in Europe. Then finally, behind him, with arrows in one hand, and a skull blackened and covered with poison in the other, at the end of a short stick, appears the famous Ngil. On this occasion, against his usual habit, he is not masked, but on his head wears a crown of blue and red feathers, and he is dressed in a sort of garment woven with the thread of the banana tree. A minute goes by, and there we are in each other's presence.

From as far as he sees me, probably amazed by my audacity, he summons me with that strange voice which makes the natives unable to recognize the human voice, and orders me to withdraw immediately.

I stay still, of course, staring straight at him, not moving at all. He takes a few steps, repeats his order to me; but I move no further.

Suddenly then, he throws his arm backwards, brandishes one of his assegais and throws it at me with all his strength: vigorously thrown, it whistles in my ears and is driven into the ground about twenty steps behind me. Lamenting that he missed me, he screams with fury, brandishes a second assegai and throws it again at me; I see it coming at me, and it stops in the folds of my clothes. But already he has taken a third one: at the same time, I coldly raise my revolver: one of my children, who anxiously contemplates the scene through the crack of a neighboring hut, cries out: "Father, don't kill him! We would all be dead." A moment of inattention, the assegai is already gone, but I turn it away with the cylinder of my revolver, right on time. In my turn, with my weapon held high, I walk to the sorcerer, who does not move back a step.

And as I came upon him: "Ngil," I said, "why did you want to kill me? Three times you have missed me; now it is my turn."

"Kill me," answers the Ngil, "your life is my life, your death is my death."

"Ngil," I replied, "go on your way at once. Besides, you have no right to touch me, I know you, I know your laws, go and pass."

"Why do you despise me?"

"I don't despise you, but you see, you can't scare me. I'm much stronger than you. Go and let me go."

Then Ngil came very close to me, an angry look on his face, rolling his bloody and deranged eyes: "Since you know me," he said, "I am going to ask you some questions. We'll find out if you're one of us."

"So be it. Interrogate me."

And he shakes over my head the human skull that he carries, he makes the poisonous ashes, the famous *Nshou* or Ngil's poison, fall on my shoulders and on my head: "Who am I, what is my name, what is my duty?"

"You are Ngil, and it is said that you discover guilty women, thieves and murderers: I have known you for many years, but I have not yet seen your power put to the test. I would like to see it." (Trilles 1912b: 175)

The sense of intrigue, the self-control of the strong man, the respect of his adversary, but also the knowledge of the other, of his genealogical identity (who is your father?), as well as the knowledge of substances and weapons, are the main ingredients of this captivating tale. With the crucifix on his heart and revolver in hand, as lucid and cunning as his adversary, the soldier of Christ unscrupulously uses as many tricks and traps in this fight against the satanic agents of the Ngil as necessary. Yet in another scene, by the magic of the pole suspended in the air through the use of supernatural power (ibid.: 212), Trilles knew how to make room in his account for doubt and questioning about the sincerity of the *féticheur*: "Are the féticheurs convinced"? (ibid.: 217).[19] Do they believe in the power of their fetishes? The missionary from Normandy, familiar with the healers and spell casters of the Bocage countryside, displayed a certain level of pagan complicity as well as peasant common sense in his fight against Satan.

Between the "Root of the World" and the "Race of the Future"

It is significant that the essay on totemism concludes with a final reference to the ritual of brotherhood through blood (Trilles 1912a: 626ff.), the key to "*totémisation*" according to Father Le Roy (1910: 119ff.), and that *Chez les Fang* (Trilles 1912b: 276ff.) has as its epilogue the funeral of the great chief Nzogo of Ayeng, initiator of the young missionary. This entails the preparation of his skull smeared with oil from padauk wood (evoking sacrificial blood) by his son, who recalls the personal history and deeds of his father before he joins the other skulls of the clan in the Bieri box. The "Christic" paradigm of exchange by blood and the sacrificial pact applies to the community of the living and the dead.[20]

In *Chez les Fang*, in all "good faith," so to speak, and without any hesitation, Trilles practiced the manipulation of oral sources, falsified iconographic collections, and wrote fictional literature on human sacrifices and the anthropophagy of his "dear Fang." The conclusion is obvious: in spite of his positivist professions of faith, his lessons in language skills against administrators such as Victor Largeau and even against his own superior, Le Roy, Trilles was a bricoleur of genealogies and mythologies. He participated in the consecration of the Nzame ancestor as God the Creator and in the election of his "dear Fang" as a beautiful "Nubian" race, a tribe lost in the forest, who by the grace of missionary heroes, and for its own survival, became the eldest daughter of the Equatorial Church.[21] Let us recall the unabashed confession of this "innocent deception" by the "diligent" missionary ethnographer:

> So when I arrived in an unknown village, after the customary greetings, I hastened to ask the chief for his *mebara* [the recitation of the list of ancestors, in the absence of distinctive tattoos] because a reincarnated spirit [a white man] obviously had the right to interrogate a mere mortal first. As I already knew a great number of genealogies, as soon as I had heard his first generations, and especially knowing his tribe, I quickly entered his cycle. When, in my turn, I had to recite my *mebara*, he would invariably find that, to his astonishment, and by an innocent deception, not only did we find ourselves to have the same ancestors, but I was always of a family more closely related than he was to the primitive strain! Even when I arrived at this primal stem, I went even higher than my interlocutor in the list of ancestors, thanks to the patriarchal genealogies of the Bible; and so, very slowly, relying on both my memory and my notes, we arrived at Adam, son of God, where it was necessary to stop! (Trilles 1912a: 5)

"Mé ne Mone Nzame, I am the son of Nzame," said the white-bearded Christian missionary to old Ndoume (Trilles 1912b: 145). After all, Ethiopian converts did not act differently by letting the tribes of Israel hear that their god was the god of their fathers, Abraham, Jacob, etc.

Trilles, on the other hand, was surprisingly discreet about the presence of the Baka in *Chez les Fang*, even though this group of Pygmies often welcomed him in their camp during his forest tours. It was indeed Trilles who had accompanied Monseigneur Leroy to the camps of southern Gabon, with the Ajon-go of the Fernan Vaz lagoon, "pure mixed" Négrilles (like the famous Mba Solé, dancer and informant for Le Roy). Trilles also encountered Aka Pygmies (an Egyptian name, according to him) in Fang country when he traveled with Father Tanguy to northern Gabon. It was, however, in a simple note that he explained: "The word *Baka*,[22] in the Fang language, designates the Pygmies of Africa, the famous Dwarves about whom so much has been said. Today subjugated and reduced to half-slavery, the Pygmies of central Africa have indeed long fought against the Fang, invaders of their forests" (Trilles 1912b: 98). It appears that this reminder of the Fang's "master slaver" role is not to the credit of this "race of the future."

Nevertheless, these people of the forest, providers of meat for their Fang masters, incarnate the original man, above all in the ethnology of the missionary milieu revolving around the journal *Anthropos* (Wilhelm Schmidt's *Urmensch*). The whole demonstration was based on the key idea that one can find survivors of pure primitive humanity in these "little men": "the root of the world," the "elders of the earth." Now the Pygmy, by a miracle, as Le Roy had maintained since 1904, ignores both fetishism and totemism, black magic and witchcraft, and prays to a supreme deity, who takes the divine names—Anyambie and Nzame respectively—of his Nkomi neighbors or the Fang. The Pygmy thanks the supreme deity for its blessings with offerings and libations, without even spilling the slightest sacrificial blood—which is not self-evident, even for a good Catholic. "Our Négrilles" of the equatorial forest are thus promoted as "exceptional" witnesses of the primitive divine revelation and, by an astonishing reversal, it is the Fang, the "race of the future," their masters, who were supposed to introduce their degraded morals and corruption into this innocent world before the Fall. Again, missionary apologetics are paradoxically in tune with local indigenous traditions: the long-standing master-slave or patron-client relationships that existed between the Bantu black men and the Négrilles never prevented the former from combining contempt and fascination toward the latter. Without mentioning the stories of the Pygmies themselves, all Fang origin myths of the Bwiti cult agree that everything originally came from the Pygmies, those little men of the forest who also transmitted all their secrets to black men (in regard to religion and art), first and foremost the "secret of life and death" revealed through the transmission of *iboga*, the sacred hallucinogenic plant at the foundation of the Melan and Bwiti cults.

It was not until twenty years later, with the publication of his other great work, *Les Pygmées de la forêt équatoriale* (The Pygmies of the Equatorial Forest, 1932) that Trilles, having returned to his native Normandy, did full justice to these little black men, children of God. Once again, he was in agreement with Schmidt, but this time in clear contradiction to Le Roy, who unfavorably compared Pygmy spirituality to that of the Fang. For Le Roy, the problem with the Bantu was that, in spite of their feelings for Mebeghe, they considered this supreme and distant God to be indifferent to men, so that he could in no way be a reliable interlocutor and least of all be solicited by prayer and offerings. To illustrate this attitude, Le Roy even took pleasure in quoting an excerpt from a tale collected by Trilles in the Fang context: "God is God, Man is Man. Each in his own house. Each in his own home." This cosmic compartmentalization could also be found in the response to the missionary offers: white men's ways vs. black men's ways. According to Le Roy, the consequence of this "theological" posture was that for everything that concerns their daily affairs and interests, the Bantu blacks relied on the cult of more or less impersonal fetishes, ancestors, or geniuses. Everything that "ethnologists" had classified under the terms *naturalism, fetishism, animism, polytheism,* or even *totemism* was not without empirical relevance, but the process that led to fetishizing objects, personifying natural beings (sun, moon), or deifying human beings was for the Catholic ethnographer the consequence of a loss of sense of the divine and of the pure idea of God.

The convictions put forward on the "theology of the Négrilles" by Le Roy in 1905 were based on extremely tenuous testimonies. Thus, the God of the Baka had the same name as the Nzame of their Fang masters; the Nzambi of the A-jongo of the Fernan Vaz lagoon was clearly, according to their own statement, the Anyambie of their neighbors, the Nkomi. The individual testimony about the reward of the good and the punishment of the wicked after death (the good souls being buried underground and the wicked being thrown by God into the fire above) among the A-jongo—described by Le Roy as "populations of half-breed Négrilles who claim to have preserved their primitive traditions"—was reported without the slightest discernment (as Mauss himself would be surprised to find out (1968 [1913]: 507). At the same time, the testimony of a certain Mba Solé, of the Baka group, about the condemnation of the wicked in Totolane was clearly interpreted as subject to the influence of the Fang (Totolane is indeed translated as "hell" or "purgatory" in Fang catechisms). Thus, Trilles, in 1932, returning to sources and informants he had met with Le Roy, drove home the point by declaring about this alleged "Pygmy of pure race living among the Fang," so dear to his superior, that "the traditions and accounts he provides do not in any way emerge from the Négrille background, they are clearly and uniquely Bantu" (Trilles 1932: 71).

Worship, the great annual feast of the first fruits, the offering of the Kola nuts—so well told by Le Roy, according to Trilles—was for him "the testimony of the high religiosity of the Négrilles, a thousand-year-old witness to the sacrifice offered by man in the first

eras of the world, a touching testimony of the humble children of the
earth, to the Father in heaven" (ibid.: 92). In reality, Trilles added,
this corresponds to very classical offering rites practiced during the
harvest of honey or *nkula* nuts in the forest (the indigenous walnut
tree), a "feast of the first fruits" which, as everywhere, included the
obligation to reserve their share first for the gods or the ancestors
(ibid.: 94–95). To top it all, Trilles—acknowledging that he himself never attended this *nkula*-picking ceremony in the forest (even
though he had all the details confirmed)—pointed out that the description of this great seasonal festival, presented by Monseigneur Le
Roy as a "procession," was in fact a second- or even thirdhand account. It was transmitted to Trilles by Father André Raponda Walker
(1871–1968), the first Gabonese priest and ethnographer of Mpongwe origin, then a student at the seminary, and subsequently taken
up by Le Roy (Trilles 1932: 98–99). However, the refrain has nothing
Négrille about it since it was in Mpongwe, and the lyricism of its
translation into French directly echoed the hymns of the Catholic
processions during the harvest festival: "Forward, forward to gather
the Lord's gift."

In short, Trilles expressed severe criticism of surveys not carried
out in the indigenous language. Siding with Father Schmidt, he provided stronger ethnographic support to the thesis of the original
piety of the Pygmies, for in this "spiritual" battle the argument in-
validating opponents on both sides, and especially Monseigneur Le
Roy, was the use of interpreters, considered to be contributing to a
secondhand ethnography.[23]

But Trilles was also a good pupil in terms of reproducing or creating fantasies about the piety of the little men of the forest—as in
using iconographic devices that dressed indigenous rites in Christian
garb. Over time, however, the Christian mask could be turned against
the face itself and eventually left its mark on it, contributing to an in-
depth recasting of African ethnic identities, in spite of Trilles's intentions. The encounter between colonial Catholicism and Fang culture,
of which Trilles, among others, was one of the actors, was similar
in this sense to that described by John Peel in *Religious Encounter
and the Making of the Yoruba* (Peel 2000): in the affirmation of their
ethnolinguistic identity but also in their historical awareness of being
God's chosen people, the Yoruba became Yoruba in the same movement by which the first literate individuals (catechists or interpreters)
converted to Christianity and recognized in the biblical fabric of the
Hebrew people their own history.

From Blacklisting to Oblivion

Henry Trilles's masterpiece, *Chez les Fang*, has been practically ignored by contemporary anthropologists of the Fang, from Georges Balandier (1920–2016) to James W. Fernandez (1930–), including Pierre Alexandre and Philippe Laburthe-Tolra (1929–2016). His monograph has fallen into oblivion between his 1905 collection of Fang proverbs, legends, and tales and his 1912 essay on Fang totemism. It has entered the realm of forgotten or erased works. However, the reactions of his own congregation suggest a more general "blacklisting" of Father Trilles from 1912 on, in relation to the ethnological questions raised by his work, even its peculiar style and genre.

In their 1958 summary of "the group known as Pahouin," Pierre Alexandre and Jacques Binet (1916–2009) quoted Father Trilles's magnum opus on Fang totemism, acknowledging that "fine and exact observations are mixed with sometimes hazardous conclusions and unexpected gaps" (1958: 146). Even if to them Trilles remained "the great authority on the Fang," they gave priority to the "more exact" information in the encyclopedia of their fellow administrator Largeau (1901). Phillippe Laburthe-Tolra, an ethnographer of the Beti of South Cameroon who was also familiar with the Fathers of the Holy Spirit Missions and who translated selected extracts of Tessmann's work, kept the latter's comments on the state of research about the Southern Pahouin in the late 1890s. In Tessmann's introduction to *Die Pangwe*, Trilles was referred to as "by far the most fruitful but also the most boring author," not to mention the countless "exaggerations" which had no other excuse than the deceptions of his "mission pupils"[24] (Tessmann 1991 [1913]: 171; see Tessmann 1913: 1:xvi–xvii). In fact, Tessmann mainly cited the entries on "Chez les Fang" published by *Les Missions Catholiques* for the origin myths of the Fang and the worship of the Ngil that he himself had observed among the Yaunde of Cameroon.

Nevertheless, Trilles's commitment to the enterprise of the *Anthropos* journal was unfailing, and his name was in good company in the international circle of totemism specialists during the "Das Problem des Totemismus" symposium of 1913, alongside Van Gennep who, however, was not very happy with this editorial cohabitation with Catholic ethnologists (Mary 2018: 71). Despite this, Trilles was never considered a credible anthropologist, let alone a great but little-known ethnographer. In the same generation of missionary ethnographers or in the same lands, his fate was not comparable to that of Robert Nassau or even Martin Gusinde (1886–1969) who also worked on the Pygmies with Paul Schebesta (1887–1967) and under the direction of Wilhelm Schmidt. To anthropologists, Trilles has always been "the little soldier" of Le Roy, of Schmidt, of Catholic ethnology, as his great treatise on the Pygmies (1932) would confirm.

The paradox is that it was clearly this 1932 publication—obviously commissioned and supported by Schmidt, director of the Pontifical Lateran Museum, who expected Trilles's manuscript to be a complement to Father Schebesta's work on the Pygmies of the Ituri forest (1931)—that practically led to the "blacklisting" of Trilles within his own congregation. In fact, it is significant that Father Maurice Briault (1874–1953), in his 1929 summary work *Polythéisme et fétichisme*, prefaced by Monseigneur Le Roy, never cited the work of Father Trilles, which was absent from the bibliography. In *Sur les pistes de l'A.E.F.* (On the tracks of French Equatorial Africa, 1948: 67), the same Briault mentioned the "circle of specialists" on Pygmies consulted by Le Roy in 1905, of which, according to Briault, Trilles was not a member, while quoting the "anonymous author of a work from 1930 [*sic*]," which can be none other than Trilles's 1932 book. His thesis about the existence of an "idiom peculiar to the little men of the forest," which would be close to the Nilotic or Ethiopian languages and similar to the pristine language of an original humanity, was, Briault argued, totally invalidated by Reverend Charles Sacleux (1856–1943). This is a startling critique when one realizes that the same Trilles would be persistently solicited after his retirement by Father Smith, who eventually signed the introduction to his tome of nearly six hundred pages on the subject!

A curious contrast exists between the scientific recognition of Trilles's work by the eminent scholar of the Lateran Museum after more than twenty years of collaboration, placing him in a rank of honor among Pygmy specialists next to Schebesta (Trilles 1932: xiv), and his blacklisting by the "eminent writers" of his own congregation, Le Roy and Briault. This leads to a few questions being raised. Basically, in view of the mixed nature of the Bantu encampments, Trilles was the first to put into perspective the quest for the pure Pygmy, the hypothesis of an "original" language, and the evidence of authentic religious piety. But it was above all his persistent impertinence with regard to the 1905 "picturesque book" of his superior—whose references were declared obsolete, while the author's pretensions regarding field experience and mastery of the Bantu languages were deemed "exaggerated"—that was punished by Father Briault, the private secretary to Bishop Le Roy. The same applies, and even more so, to Trilles's revelations "between the lines" about the writing secrets of the Spiritan "tribe."[25]

Upon his return from Africa in 1908, Father Briault was promoted to the rank of private secretary to the superior general of the congregation, Monseigneur Le Roy, and beginning in 1913 he reigned over the Annals of the Fathers of the Holy Spirit for more than thirty years. John Cinnamon (2006b: 415) quotes from Briault's "Notes sur le Père Trilles: Cas du Père Trilles et de son ouvrage sur les Pygmées" (Notes on Father Trilles: The case of Father Trilles and his work on the Pygmies), which take up the entire dispute of the "Trilles affair," his fabrications and exaggerations, and his scientific discredit. Thanks to a revealing note by Joseph Bouchaud,[26] published in 1954 and dedicated to Briault's biography, we can fully appreciate the crossed destinies of these "enemy brothers," Trilles and Briault, two "Normans," one the son of a soldier, the other of a farmer. They both had an impulsive temperament and unbridled imagination, according to their superiors' reports, and left for Africa to live among the "anthropophagous savages" in the same period of missionary settlements at the beginning of the twentieth century, and in the same regions of the Pahouin. Both had passed through Fribourg, Switzerland, for their scholarly training, including geography and ethnology, and both aspired to be recognized as "writers," as model fathers, and they were undoubtedly so, in view of the academic and literary tributes they received. But in the end they were caught up in the mesh of the busy court and the "boisterous spirit" of Bishop Le Roy, who, in the words attributed by Bouchaud to Briault, "let his friends down easily in order to please his enemies."[27]

Considering Father Wilhelm Schmidt's systematic search for ethnographic illustrations of primitive monotheism and the complicity of his "little soldier" Henri Trilles, who was always ready to serve when he was called upon, it is impossible to consider the latter as a martyr of science joining the common destiny of missionary ethnographers—like Father Francis Aupiais (1877–1945) and many others—who were recognized by the scientific community and academia but at the same time disowned and sanctioned by their congregation. Instead, Trilles reveals himself to be the "patriotic" victim of the contradictions of the scientificity of a Catholic ethnology caught between its concern for methodological seriousness and empirical proof, and its apologetic intentions at the service of "universal" religion (Mary 2010). Both through his commitment to the "Propagation of the Faith" and his scholarly works, first as a "good disciple" of his superior and fellow traveler Bishop Le Roy and then following his promotion to the auxiliary of the great scholar Wilhelm Schmidt, Father Henry Trilles revealed himself "in all good faith" as an exemplary "critical" and "polemical" personality.

After the World War II, Trilles returned to the subject with *L'âme du Pygmée d'Afrique* (The soul of the African Pygmy, 1945), taking up the essence of his observations on the religious life of the Négrilles of the equatorial forest. Always well informed about recent publications by specialists on a matter that was close to his heart, he was delighted by the flattering reception the learned world of ethnologists gave to his work and the prize awarded him by the Académie française. He particularly underlined the convergences with firsthand observations of that "conscientious" scholar, Reverend Paul Schebesta (whose conclusions were by then accessible to the French-speaking public; see Schebesta 1931), even if there were significant differences between the Bayaga (or Akka) of South Cameroon and the Bambuti of Ituri. In that concert of great scholars "with a missionary soul" who brought the Pygmies into history, Trilles reiterated his homage to the two beautiful and learned books, *La Religion des Primitifs* and *Les Pygmées*, by the "eminent author" Monseigneur Le Roy.

In sum, *Chez les Fang* is not an isolated work but a link in a chain that goes from the articles published in *Les Missions catholiques*, via the essay on totemism, and ends at *Les Pygmées de la forêt équatoriale*, if not *L'âme du Pygmée d'Afrique*. As a combination of blurred genres, from monographic sections to missionary vignettes within a regionally if not ethnically circumscribed traveling context, *Chez les Fang* may be a strange ethnography for twenty-first-century readers; but it is also a good illustration of the multiple layers in a single book within a pre-Malinowskian frame. For better or for worse, caught between theoretical insights and ideological conundrums, empirical soundness and literary fancy, Trilles's ethnography affected Fang and Gabonese cultural life and history, which only adds to its complexity and makes its reassessment all the more challenging.

André Mary is emeritus director of research at the CNRS and a member of the Institut Interdisciplinaire d'Anthropologie du Contemporain, EHESS, Paris. His work focuses on the logics of syncretism within prophetic forms of African religiosity and the bricolage of African versions of Christianity. He also devotes himself to the history of anthropology and the contribution of missionary ethnography to the anthropology of African religion. He has published *Le bricolage africain des héros chrétiens* (2000), *Visionnaires et prophètes* *de l'Afrique contemporaine* (2009), and *Les anthropologues et la religion* (2010).

Notes

1. On the numerous expeditions, whether ministerial or private, linked to the disputed Franco-Spanish border of Gabon, see Mangongo-Nzambi (1969).
2. "Puis, acclimaté par ces quelques mois de séjour, familiarisé avec les divers idiomes qui se parlent dans notre colonie, devenu en un mot, suffisamment « Noir », je commençai chez les Fang cette longue série d'explorations diverses qui devaient se prolonger pendant quinze années, les plus belles de ma vie d'homme. Et c'est au cours de ces voyages que j'appris à connaître cette race si intéressante des Fang, 'la race de l'Avenir, la race des Hommes', disait le grand explorateur Savorgnan de Brazza; j'appris à la connaître; j'appris aussi à l'aimer, en vivant de sa vie, en m'asseyant aux feux de leurs villages, en recueillant leurs traditions, en les accompagnant à la pêche, à la chasse, à la guerre, en devenant pour ainsi dire l'un d'entre eux" (Trilles 1912b : 7–8).
3. In the colonial period, the French word *Négrilles* (literally "small negroes"), was used to designate Pygmy peoples.
4. Translating the French term, *féticheur*, of Portuguese origin, into the English categories and terms used by Evans-Pritchard, namely, witch or sorcerer, would be incorrect. Therefore, I will keep *féticheur* throughout.
5. In the preface to *Chez les Fang*, a "book on fetishism" was evoked as a possible alternative monograph to Trilles's own travel narrative (1912b: 9).
6. See the review of Nassau by R.H. (Robert Hertz) in *L'Année sociologique*, IX, 1904–1905: 191–194.
7. Father Maurice Briault (1874–1953), a missionary writer who arrived in Gabon in 1898, a few years later than Trilles, and who was to be editor of the Annals of the Fathers of the Holy Spirit, also used the term *fetishism* for primitive religions in his synthesis on "fetishist religions" (1929).
8. Note by Trilles: "The Bantu race is so named, because all tribes belonging to it and descending from the same stock designate "a man" by *tu* or *N-tu*, in the plural: *Ba-ntu*, men. This word varies according to the languages of the various tribes, but is always related to the same root. The Fang call "a man" *mur*, in the plural *Bur* – it is the same root. Generally speaking, *Ba* always indicates the plural: *I-vili*, a Vili individual, and *Bavili*, several Vili people." [In the original: "I-vili, un Ivili, Bavili, des Bavilis."]
9. See, for instance, the work of Jean-Émile Mbot (1975).
10. See Henri Trilles, *Contes et légendes fang du Gabon* (1905), republished in 2002 by Henry Tourneux from "Proverbes, légendes et contes fang," originally published in *Bulletin de la Société neuchâteloise de Géogra-*

phie 16, 59–295. The transcription of these narratives does not include Trilles's introductions and comments, nor the photos.

11. Tessmann 1991 [1913].
12. For the link between the characters in the Leopard and Turtle tales, and the ritual associations, see Mbot 1974: 669.
13. Tessmann (1991 [1913]: 268) found in it "the most sympathetic of the forms of worship," which is not without a degree of misunderstanding considering the particularly cruel ordeals imposed on initiates or supposed sorcerers. For an updated ethnographic version of the Ngi or Ngil, see Laburthe-Tolra 1985, chap. 12, which emphasizes the complementary and competing links between the Melan, the cult of the ancestors, and the anti-witchcraft Ngi among the Beti.
14. *Pahouin* is the name of a larger group in which the Fang are the dominant ethnic group, but "pahouin" has a colonial connotation attached to it, and is considered to be rather pejorative (nevertheless, it was taken up again by the translator of Tessmann's work – *Die Pangwe* – from German to French). The name *Fang*, which Trilles used as equivalent to *Pahouin*, is considered to be the more correct ethnological term (see Trilles 1912b: 18; Alexandre and Binet 1958).
15. I have witnessed, in my own work on the Bwiti of the Fang, this segmentation of initiatory societies and the accumulation of initiations, which is still a current issue (Mary 1999).
16. "De même donc que le totémisme rentre dans le fétichisme et en constitue un des aspects, mais s'en différencie toutefois profondément, de même le totem forme un des aspects du fétiche, se mêle et se confond avec lui, mais en reste toutefois profondément distinct par son culte et par l'objet de ce culte" (Trilles 1912a : 635).
17. As illustrated by another photo representing an old "chief" of Vili origin, a *fiot* (the Fang name for the ethnic groups of southern Gabon). A photo by the Bishop Le Roy on the divinatory consultation of antelope horns among the Kikuyu of Kenya (Le Roy 1910: 249), which had been renamed by Le Roy himself as "The remission of sins" (*sic*), was again reprinted by Trilles in *Chez les Fang* in order to illustrate the practices of the Ngil (Trilles 1912b: 176). This is a case of good editorial use of the available iconographic stock.
18. Footnote by Trilles: "*Strychnos Onai* [*sic*], of the *Apocynaceae* family. The black men extract its juice by incision from the roots and the mother stem. This juice is mixed with the sap of a ficus which gives it the necessary binder. A paste of crushed ants exposed to the sun is added. The resulting product is carefully stored away from light and humidity. It is most often used either for war or for hunting monkeys and birds. In the latter cases, the arrow thrown silently hits the animal, which falls to the ground after a few seconds without frightening its companions, who are thus struck one after the other" (Trilles 1912b: 175, note 1).
19. Le Roy (1910: 285) had already raised the same question, to which he supplied the following answer: "I believe so. And curiously enough,

they are 'convinced' even though they know, without a doubt, that one of their operations is pure phantasmagoria . . . In other words, there are results, and that is why sorcerers believe in their art . . . ."

20. This "blood covenant" can be found in the Christian reading that Father Aupiais and his disciple Paul Hazoumé retained from the Vodun initiation in Dahomey (Hazoumé, *Le Pacte de Sang*, 1937).

21. In Trilles's imaginary, this was comparable to the idea of France being the "eldest daughter of the Church."

22. In the original, "Békü."

23. It must be admitted, however, that the thesis of a language pertaining to the Pygmies, which went hand in hand with the idea of their pristine spirituality, had against it the paradox of a mixed situation: The interaction of the Pygmies with neighboring groups necessarily involved their use of neighboring languages, Eshira, Punu, and especially the language of the Fang. Trilles, caught in his own trap, got away with it by arguing the existence of an original language that, adapted by the Pygmies, was a mixture of Fang and partial elements of archaic languages close to those of the Nilotic or "Egyptian" peoples: a kind of cultural Pidgin. As a good native from Normandy, Trilles pointed out the problem both lucidly and humorously: "Let us say that very often, through his scientific training, the missionary manages to decompose, to understand these archaic words that the Pygmy no longer understands. Doesn't the same thing happen in our Norman countryside? A brave woman, mother of a large family, told me one day that she had a 'pourchignée de gnats', that is to say a large family. . . She would have been incapable of explaining whence these words come. And yet they do come directly from the Latin: progenies gnatorum!" (Trilles 1945: 15). The "miracle" allowing us to overcome the communication problem with an ancestral and pure people without being caught in the web of their borrowed words can also be found in the testimonies of those other ethnographers of the "Divine Word," Martin Gusinde and Paul Schebesta, following their encounter with the Pygmies of Ituri. After reading their writings, Trilles declared in 1934 that he agreed with them. Given the impossibility of accessing the "truth" of divine language, Trilles, as a good Catholic, pushed his own thesis to its limits and was supported all the same by Schmidt. Trilles's thesis is interesting in that it formulates the methodological and theological problem behind the ethnographic challenge of proving God's existence through the Pygmies (Mary 2010). Incidentally, it provided a basis for the critique of "second-hand" ethnography by his "fathers" and brothers of the Holy Spirit.

24. In the French translation, "petits pensionnaires de la mission"; in the original, "seiner Missionszöglinge."

25. See Joseph Bouchaud, untitled, in *Bulletin de la province de France*, no. 66, January 1954, 193 ff.

26. Dates unknown.

27. Ibid., unnumbered note.

References

Alexandre, Pierre and Jacques Binet 1958. *Le Groupe dit Pahouin (Fang-Boulou-Beti)*. Paris: Presses Universitaire de France.

Augouard, Prosper. 1905. *28 années au Congo: lettres de Mgr Augouard*. 2 vols. Poitiers: Société française d'imprimerie et de librairie.

Briault, Maurice. 1929. *Polythéisme et fétichisme*. Preface by Mgr Le Roy. Paris: Librairie Bloud & Gay.

———. 1930. *Sous le zéro équatorial. Etudes et scènes africaines*. Preface by Mgr Le Roy. Paris: Librairie Bloud & Gay.

———. 1948. *Sur les pistes de l'A.E.F.* Paris: Editions Asaltia.

Cinnamon, John M. 2006a. "Robert Hamil Nassau: Missionary Ethnography and the Colonial Encounter in Gabon: "Le Fait Missionnaire, Missionnaries and Ethnography." *Social Sciences and Missions* 19 (December): 37–64.

———. 2006b. "Missionary Expertise, Social Science, and the Uses of Ethnographic Knowledge in Colonial Gabon." *History in Africa* 33: 413–432.

Durkheim, Émile. 1912. *Les Formes élémentaires de la vie religieuse*. Paris: Felix Alcan.

———. 1998. *Lettres à Marcel Mauss*. Paris: Presses universitaires de France.

Hazoumé, Paul. 1937. *Le Pacte de Sang*. Paris: Institut d'Ethnologie.

Laburthe-Tolra, Philippe. 1985. *Initiations et sociétés secrètes au Cameroun. Essai sur la religion beti*. Paris: Karthala.

Laburthe-Tolra, Philippe and Christiane Falgayrettes-Leveau. 1991. *Fang*. Paris: Musée Dapper.

Largeau, Victor. 1901. *Encyclopédie pahouine, Congo français. Éléments de grammaire et dictionnaire Français-Pahouin*. Paris: Ernest Leroux.

Le Roy, Alexandre. 1905. *Les Pygmées. Négrilles d'Afrique et Négritos de l'Asie*. Tours: Maison Alfred Mame et fils.

———. 1910. *La Religion des primitifs*. Paris: Bauchesne.

Mangongo-Nzambi André. 1969. "La délimitation des frontières du Gabon (1885–1911)." *Cahiers d'études africaines* 9(33): 5–53.

Mary, André. 1999 *Le défi du syncrétisme. Le travail symbolique de la Religion d'Eboga (Gabon)*. Paris: Editions EHESS.

———. 2010. "La preuve de Dieu par les Pygmées." *Cahiers d'études africaines* 198–199: 881–890.

———. 2012 "Retour aux choses sacrées: emblèmes, empreintes et fétiches." *Archives de Sciences Sociales des Religions* 159: 203–223.

———. 2015. "Science de l'Homme ou 'Science de Dieu'? Révélation primitive et formes élémentaires du religieux." In Christine Laurière (ed.), *1913. La recomposition de la science de l'Homme*. Paris: BEROSE International Encyclopaedia of the Histories of Anthropology (Les Carnets de Bérose n° 7), 196–222.

———. 2018. "Le totémisme vrai et vivant de Van Gennep." In Daniel Fabre and Christine Laurière (eds.), *Arnold Van Gennep, du folklore à l'ethnographie*. Paris: Éditions du CTHS, 71–95.

Mauss, Marcel. 1968. *Œuvres*. Tome 1: *Les fonctions sociales du sacré*. Paris: Éditions de Minuit.

Mbot, Jean-Émile. 1974. "La tortue et le léopard chez les Fang du Gabon." *Cahiers d'Etudes Africaines* 56: 651–670.

———. 1975. *Ebughi bifia, "démonter les expressions."* Énonciation et situations sociales chez les Fang du Gabon. Paris: Institut d'ethnologie, Museum national d'histoire naturelle, Mémoires 13.

———. 2002. "Préface." In Henri Trilles, *Contes et légendes fang du Gabon* (edited by Henry Tourneux). Paris: Éditions Karthala, 5–11.

Nassau, Robert Hammil. 1904. *Fetichism in West Africa: Forty Year's Observation of Natives Customs and Superstitions*. London: Duckworth & Co.

Peel, John David Yeadon. 2000. *Religious Encounter and the Making of the Yoruba*. Bloomington, IN: Indiana University Press.

Perrois, Louis. 1979. *Arts du Gabon*. Paris: ORSTOM (Arts d'Afrique Noire series, n°240).

Raponda-Walker, André and Roger Sillans. 1962. *Rites et Croyances des peuples du Gabon*. Paris: Présence Africaine.

Schebesta, Paul. 1931. *Les Conceptions religieuses des Pygmées de l'Ituri* [translated from the German by Jean Leyder and Ed. De Jonghe] Bruxelles: Goemaere.

Schmidt, Wilhelm. 1910. *Die Stellung der Pygmäen Völker in der Entwicklungsgeschicte des Menschen*. Stuttgart: Strecker.

Spencer, Baldwin and Francis Gillen. 1899. *The Native Tribes of Central Australia*. London: MacMillan and Co.

Tessmann, Günther. 1913. *Die Pangwe. Völkerkundliche Monographie eines westafrikanischen Negerstammes* (Ergebnisse der Lübecker Pangwe-Expedition 1907–1909 und früherer Forschungen 1904–1907). 2 vols. Berlin: Ernst Wasmuth.

Tessmann, Günther. 1991 [1913]. "Les Pahouins." In P. Laburthe-Tolra and C. Falgueyrettes-Leveau, *Fang*. Paris: Musée Dapper, 166–313 [translated extracts from G. Tessmann, 1913].

Trilles, Henri. 1897. *Catéchisme Fang*. Tours: L. Dubois.

———. 1898. "Chez les Fang, leurs mœurs, leur langue, leur religion." *Les Missions catholiques*, January-December: 6 ff.

———. 1905. "Proverbes, légendes et contes fang." *Bulletin de la Société Neuchâteloise de Géographie* 16: 59–295. Republished by Henry Tourneux in 2002.

———. 1906. "Un peuple du Congo français, Les Fang, croyance et religions (Première grande conférence)." *Bulletin de la Société de Géographie de Lille*, December: 368 ff.

———. 1907. "Un peuple du Congo français, Les Fang, croyance et religions (2ème conférence, compte rendu)." *Bulletin de la Société de Géographie de Lille*, February: 7–9.

———. 1910. *Au Gabon. Dans les rivières de Monda*. Lilles/Paris/Bruges: Société Saint-Augustin, Desclée, De Brouwer et Cie.

———. 1912a. *Le totémisme chez les Fân* (Preface by Mgr Alexandre Le Roy). Münster: Bibliothek Anthropos.

———. 1912b. *Chez les Fang, ou Quinze années de séjour au Congo français.* Lilles/Paris/Bruges: Société Saint-Augustin, Desclée, De Brouwer et Cie.

———. No date (ca. 1914). *Fleurs noires et âmes blanches.* Lilles/Paris/Bruges: Société Saint-Augustin, Desclée, de Brouwer et Cie.

———. 1931 *Milles lieues dans l'inconnu, en pleine forêt équatoriale chez les Fang anthropophages. Vingt illustrations d'après les croquis de l'auteur.* Paris/Bruges: Desclée, De Brouwer et Cie.

———. 1932 *Les Pygmées de la forêt équatoriale* (Preface by Henri Pinard de la Boullaye; Introduction by Wilhelm Schmidt). Paris: Librairie Bloud et Gay.

———. 2002 [1905]. *Contes et légendes fang du Gabon* (edited by Henry Tourneux; Preface by Jean-Émile Mbot). Paris: Éditions Karthala.

9

"The Stream Crosses the Path"

Robert Sutherland Rattray and *Ashanti* (1923)

Montgomery McFate

> The stream crosses the path,
> The path crosses the stream;
> Which of them is the elder?
> Did we not cut a path to go and meet this stream?
> The stream had its origin long, long ago,
> It had its origin in the Creator.
> —Ashanti traditional drum poetry,
> in R. S. Rattray, *Ashanti*, 1923

In 1907, when Robert Sutherland Rattray (1881–1938) first arrived in the Gold Coast (now known as Ghana), the series of brutal wars between the British and the Ashanti had ended only a few years earlier.[1] The territory was still not completely "pacified, and there was a lively business in gun-running across the Volta [River]" (Machin 1998: 23).[2] Among the British colonial officers in Africa, the Gold Coast was known as the "White Man's Grave," both because of the variety of dangerous tropical diseases and the ferocity of indigenous tribal groups. Although his first impression when he disembarked in Accra was that it was very hot and dreary, Rattray spent the next twenty-three years of his life in the Gold Coast, primarily among the Ashanti.

Rattray remains noteworthy as an anthropologist in part because of his long-term participant observation among the Ashanti. Participant observation is generally assumed to be a research paradigm inspired by Malinowski's exhortation to get "off of the verandah" and is associated with later generations of anthropologists. Early colonial anthropologists (such as Rattray) are assumed to have conducted their research while sitting comfortably in their armchairs. Yet, Rattray conducted his anthropological research in the field with the Ashanti, immersed in their world. Because of this deep connection to the Ashanti, Rattray came to be known by Africans and Europeans alike as *oboroni okomfo*, which means "white witch doctor" (ibid.: 90).

Rattray was appointed as the first and only head of the newly created Gold Coast Anthropological Department in 1921, after a variety of government appointments in the colony. When he accepted the position, he decided that he would not merely collect the materials and observations produced by others in a "Central Office or Clearing House" but would instead "begin work by himself, making a detailed investigation into the beliefs and customs of this people" (Rattray 1923: 6–7). In his view, "in Ashanti really valuable anthropological information is possessed by comparatively few of its inhabitants. Those who have accurate knowledge are the older men and women who have few dealings with the foreigner, live secluded lives in remote villages, and are ignorant of or indifferent to the social and religious changes brought about by the European" (ibid.: 7). Moreover, these individuals were unlikely to trust anyone who could not converse with them in their native language, "usually becom[ing] reticent and suspicious." Rattray, however, spoke fluent Ashanti and was able to "converse directly with them" (ibid.).

Accordingly, in his new official capacity Rattray set out on an extended research trip across the territory in 1921. He was accompanied by a local guide named Kakari,[3] "an old Ashanti aristocrat" who left his village to assist Rattray in his wanderings (ibid.: 15). Instead of sitting on "the verandah," Rattray immersed himself in the lives of the "ancients" in the hinterlands, producing "minute and exact studies with accurate detailed accounts of social and religious beliefs, rites, and customs" (Rattray 1923: 8) (see figure 9.2). During his first five months as a government anthropologist, Rattray produced six papers that were submitted to his colonial superiors but otherwise unpublished: the "Ashanti Family System," "Queen Mothers," "the Golden Stool," "Gold Weights," "*Ntoro* Exogamous Divisions," and "Neolithic Implements" (see Machin 1998: 82). These papers became the basis of his book *Ashanti*, which was published in 1923.

As a text, *Ashanti* is simultaneously flowery and dry, passionate and scientific, and does not accommodate the casual reader. Partly as a result of the haphazard method of the book's organization and

partly due to the style of early ethnographies, *Ashanti* does not describe Ashanti society as a system in which the parts function to
maintain the equilibrium of the whole, as found in later functionalist
writings. Nor does the book attempt to articulate a unified picture
of Ashanti culture and society organized along a single overarching,
unifying theme as do many of the classical ethnographies, whether
the ritual cycles of the Iatamul as recounted by Gregory Bateson
in *Naven* (1936) or the oscillating social structure described in Edmund Leach's *Political System of Highland Burma* (1954). Rather,
each chapter presents a richly detailed, scientifically objective view
of various aspects of Ashanti society. Each chapter stands alone and
has limited thematic intersection with other chapters, even if Rattray
does note that "there is hardly an art, a rite, a custom, or belief that is
not bound up or connected in some way with some separate art, rite,
custom, or belief" (Rattray 1923: 22). Only in later writings—such
as *Ashanti Law and Constitution* (1929)—did Rattray fully explore
and articulate the scope, complexity, and significance of the tapestry
of Ashanti social life as an integrated whole. And only in the essays
written shortly before his accidental death in a hang gliding accident
in 1938 did Rattray fully articulate his keen observations regarding
the unintended consequences of British colonial policy, which was
inadvertently destroying the very social institution (democracy) that
it purported to create.

Despite the limitations of its prose and the unpolished structure
of the manuscript, *Ashanti* nevertheless ought to find a place in the
anthropological canon because it establishes the ethnographic foundation upon which Rattray's later works rest, and also because it articulates a surprisingly harsh view of the British colonial enterprise.
The book contains three significant features that are unusual for its
time and place, which are the subject of this chapter. First, in *Ashanti*
Rattray describes his efforts conducting what later became known
as participant observation, an anthropological research method most
commonly associated with those scholars who came after Bronisław
Malinowski (1884–1942). Second, *Ashanti* recounts the resolution of
a potentially violent political dispute between the Ashanti and the
British government, which provides an early example of anthropology being applied to ameliorate and resolve conflict. Third, *Ashanti*
describes the matriarchal kinship system of the Ashanti and the political power of the Queen Mothers. Rattray believed that the political
force of women had been overlooked by the British and that it was at
the core of Ashanti law and kinship. One might thus view Rattray as
a proto-feminist.

Rattray and Colonial Anthropology

Like all scholars, Rattray was a product of a particular political moment; in this case, that moment was the British consolidation of indirect rule in their colonial possessions in Africa during the first decades of the twentieth century. Historians and anthropologists have written tomes regarding indirect rule and its complexities, a review of which is beyond the scope of this chapter (see, for example, Perham 1935; Asad 1973; Mair 1975; Kirkby and Coleborne 2001). For the purposes of this chapter, the most important feature of indirect rule was the use local institutions of power to facilitate control over the population (see Lugard 1922). Instead of imposing a foreign tax system, for example, the British would (in theory) utilize the indigenous means of collecting taxes. If the British intended to use local institutions in order to avoid the imposition of their own forms of law and government on the local society, they obviously required some knowledge of these indigenous institutions. At a minimum, British colonial officials required an understanding of the local system of government, the distribution of power, and the legal process for each and every society they annexed. In short, indirect rule created a new imperative for knowledge about African traditional political, social, and legal systems. Thus, it has been said that "the need for anthropologists arose from the introduction of Indirect Rule as a form of government" (Lackner 1973: 147). For the most part, however, the knowledge imperative of indirect rule was not fulfilled by professional anthropologists but by "the old hand, the man on the spot" whose knowledge was a "working knowledge of the surfaces of African societies" that was "incomplete and provisional" (Ranger 1976: 119). British colonial officials—which Henrika Kuklick described as "amateur civil service anthropologists" (1978: 104)—frequently relied on informal, personal knowledge to accomplish their mission.

The unsystematic studies produced by civil servants dabbling in anthropology were swiftly recognized as inadequate by figures such as Major Fitz Herbert Ruxton, formerly lieutenant governor of the Southern Provinces in Nigeria (1925–29), who wrote in 1930: "Very many District Officers have a considerable knowledge of native law and custom, gained by personal observation and through their intimate knowledge of the proceedings in the native courts, but this individual knowledge gained through experience is no basis on which to rest a judicial system or to develop native administration" (Ruxton 1930: 2–3). Beginning in the early 1900s, there was a "tide of public policy and learned opinion" that was impatient "with European ig-

norance of 'colonial' peoples" (Laue 1976: 35). Sir Richard Temple
(1850–1931) advocated in 1904 for the creation of a School of Applied
Anthropology at Cambridge University to train consular and administrative officers (Temple 1914: 80) and repeatedly stressed the need
for colonial officials "to know the culture of the people one is dealing
with" (ibid.: 2). Thus, in 1908 Sir Reginald Wingate asked Oxford
and Cambridge to provide anthropological training for the new civil
service of the Anglo-Egyptian Sudan (Temple 1914: 29; Myers 1929:
47; Feuchtwang 1973: 82), which was the first instance in which a
British colonial administration formally recognized the importance
of anthropological knowledge for its officials (Foster 1969: 186–87).

In addition to providing anthropological training to the civil
service, the British government began to appoint professional anthropologists to the colonies to conduct systematic research on indigenous people. For example, the British Colonial Office appointed
Northcote W. Thomas (1868–1936) to the position of government
anthropologist in Nigeria in 1909 with the objective of averting an
impending crisis among the Ibo- and Edo-speaking peoples whose
authochthonous social structure proved a barrier to indirect rule
(ibid.: 187). The relations between these government anthropologists
and British civil servants were often fraught with misunderstanding,
conflicting objectives, and frequent suspicion. Northcote Thomas,
for example, was seen by British administrators as eccentric and difficult to work with. According to a colonial office administrator, he
was "a recognised maniac in many ways. He wore sandals, even in
this country, lived on vegetables, and was generally a rum [strange]
person" (as quoted in Lackner 1973: 135).

In 1921, Rattray was appointed special commissioner and head of
the Anthropological Department, which was a rather grand title for
the job of government anthropologist (Machin 1998: 65). The chief
commissioner of Ashanti, Sir Charles Harper (1876–1950), had requested Rattray by name. "I want an expert," he wrote, "to collect
and report upon all manner of customs, fetish, stool, marriage, burial,
family, games, etc. etc. and to codify native law and custom with regard to land, timber, hunting, fishing, travelling. Such work would be
of scientific value and of incalculable importance from an administrative point of view."[4]

Rattray's path to becoming a government anthropologist among
the Ashanti was a strange and winding one. Rattray, an impish, red-
haired child with enormous ears, was by nature rebellious and adventurous. While still a teenager, he volunteered against his family's
wishes as a scout during the Boer War (1899–1902).[5] After the war, he

signed on to work for the African Lakes Corporation in what is now Malawi (see figure 9.1.), herding cattle and selling dry goods (Machin 1998: 4, 10, 12). Despite the fact that Rattray was most probably dyslexic, he had a remarkable facility for spoken languages and began collecting local folklore, stories, and songs in order to learn the Chinyanja language (a member of the Bantu language family). These collected materials were published as *Some Folk-Lore Stories and Songs in Chinyanja, with English Translation and Notes* (1907), "a dry, meticulous little book" (ibid.: 21).

While recovering back in Britain from a dangerous fever, Rattray's family tried to convince him to apply for the Indian Civil Service. Rattray, however, said India was *too civilized* for him. Instead, he joined the Gold Coast Customs Service, a remote outpost of the empire associated in the minds of the British public with a series of wars against the Ashanti. James George Frazer (1854–1941), the author of *The Golden Bough* (1890), wrote Rattray a letter complimenting his book *Chinyanja Folk-Lore* (*sic*) as "valuable" and suggesting research areas and offering help in publishing further research (Machin 1998: 22). Now that the British government was paying an incentive of forty pounds for passing language proficiency exams, Rattray began learning Hausa by collecting traditional stories. This became the basis of *Hausa Folk-Lore*, published in 1913 (ibid.: 26).

Figure 9.1. *Robert S. Rattray in Malawi, 1905. Courtesy of Nicole Rattray.*

In 1909 Rattray matriculated to Exeter College, Oxford, as part of a scheme to educate colonial servants in the new field of anthropology. "From his first days in Oxford he developed an ambivalent attitude towards the academic world: he liked to impress it and he liked to be thought of as a scholar, but at heart he despised any learning which could not be immediately related to 'real life'" (ibid.: 27). As a means to promotion in the Colonial Service, Rattray also joined Gray's Inn and started on the chain of law exams. (Almost ten years later, Rattray was finally called to the bar in 1918 [ibid.: 28].)

Rattray returned to the Gold Coast from Oxford in 1912, triumphant with his own academic success. His new job as assistant district commissioner involved supervising the provision of labor for building a new, paved road, inspecting the police, and observing legal procedures in native courts. (During this tour in 1912, Rattray produced a small *Mole-English Vocabulary, with Notes on the Grammar and Syntax* [1918], which was the first book on the language. Unfortunately, he did not receive any incentive pay for the Mole language exam, because no one was qualified to examine him.) Probably as a result of his close contact with the Ashanti people, Rattray's interest shifted from language to culture, and he began work on a book titled *Ashanti Proverbs: Primitive Ethics of a Savage People* (1916), "a not altogether satisfactory bundle of anthropological and linguistic notes" (ibid.: 37–38, 40).

When World War I was declared, Rattray obtained a commission in the British army as a captain in the intelligence corps (ibid.: 45). He fought against the Germans in Togoland during World War I, being mentioned in dispatches (Laue 1976: 34). Though he rose steadily through the British colonial ranks, he was not particularly well suited to administration. Fluent in Hausa, Twi, and a variety of other West African languages, Rattray was known to the Ashanti as *amoako* (red pepper) because of his feisty personality and red hair (ibid.). He was strongly opinionated, believing that the government should embrace the "values and structures authentic to the West African peoples" (Robertson 1975: 54) and resented government interference in scientific research. He observed that "the success of work of this especially difficult scientific nature lies—at least in my experience—on its freedom as far as possible from the fetters and trammels of Departmental interference" (Rattray 1929: xii). Probably what most irked his colleagues in the colonial administration was his empathy and identification with the people of West Africa: "Rattray was certainly an oddity among colonial officers of his time, displaying now and then a not altogether respectable tendency to 'go native'" (Robertson 1975: 54).

Though he had hoped for further promotion in the regular civil service, Rattray's highest and final posting was as a government anthropologist in 1921. This position "compartmentalized" his activities and prevented any potential embarrassment to the government (ibid.).[6] In the view of his superiors, Rattray had "an artistic temperament" and was "completely unsuited for administrative work."[7] Accepting that he would never become governor of the Gold Coast—his early ambition—Rattray spent time living in "remote villages" (Rattray 1923: 7), producing "minute and exact studies with accurate detailed accounts of social and religious beliefs, rites, and customs" (Rattray 1923: 8).

Participant Observation:
From Drum Language to Ta Kora

Unlike the ethnological theorists content in their armchairs, Rattray invested a tremendous amount of time and attention to understanding the material and spiritual world of his local informants and conducted detailed examinations of their culture and society through a research method that we would now term "participant observation." This approach was not always seen as valuable or appropriate by Rattray's contemporaries. As late as 1933, a British colonial official sniped at Rattray for conducting actual ethnographic field research on the ground among the Ashante. "Captain Rattray ... chose to work by himself rather than to correlate, verify and edit the accumulated knowledge of previous writers, and the records of present-day observers in the field" (Vivian 1933: 29, cited in Machin 1998: 197–98). In the eyes of colonial officials, it was appropriate and valuable to spend time correlating, verifying, and editing secondhand sources. Indeed, many colonial officials conducted amateur anthropological research in the evenings as a hobby. Rattray's type of firsthand, in situ research was seen by his colleagues as an unnecessary waste of valuable government time and resources. Despite the official preference for correlation and organization of secondhand sources, in the end it was Rattray's field research that stood the test of time and ultimately resulted in *Ashanti*.

Two examples of Rattray's approach to participant observation found in *Ashanti* are his investigation of drum language and his observation of the rituals associated with the supreme god of the Ashanti, Ta Koro.

For many years the British had known that a variety of West African societies communicated over great distances using "talking drums," but they erroneously assumed that the mode of transmission was something similar to Morse code. Rattray first corrected this misperception in *Ashanti Proverbs* (1916: 133–38). Then, in *Ashanti*, he further developed the subject, establishing as the basic principle that "among the Ashanti the drum is not used as a means of signaling in the sense that we would infer, that is, by rapping out words by means of a prearranged code, but (to the native mind) is used to sound or speak the actual words. ... Tympanophony, or drum-talking, is an attempt to imitate by means of two drums (a 'male' and a 'female') set in different keys the exact sound or words of the human voice" (1923: 243).

Despite this breakthrough in understanding drum language, Rattray had failed to show how two drums of different notes could possibly be made to reproduce "actual spoken words" (ibid.). From the moment he was appointed as government anthropologist, Rattray planned to investigate this question and to record the talking drums. He immediately requested funds to purchase a "cinematograph" and sound recording equipment, "which at that time still consisted of a His Master's Voice horn attached to a machine which scratched lines on copper cylinders" (Machin 1998: 65).

Once in the field, Rattray "prevailed upon some of the experts to give me lessons in drumming." While drumming instruction might not appear to contemporary readers as unusual or significant, the drums were considered sacred by the Ashanti. The Ashanti believed that drumming summoned different types of spirits that then physically entered the drums. "The drums, thus, for a time, become the abode of the spirits of forest trees and of the 'mighty elephant.' The deities of Earth and Sky are called upon in like manner" (Rattray 1923: 265). Rattray was the first Westerner permitted to handle the sacred drums and learn how to play them, which shows the degree to which the Ashanti trusted him with their esoteric knowledge and spiritual practices.

With the help of Christaller's *Grammar* (1875),[8] Rattray developed a phonetic analysis of the drum language, showing how the features of speech—tone, accent, gesture, pauses, and duration—were transmitted by drums. "In Ashanti, every syllable, in every word, has assigned to it a more or less arbitrary tone or musical pitch. These tones do not depend upon the will or caprice of the speaker, and are not employed for emotional, oratorical, or grammatical purposes" (Rattray 1923: 245). Drum language, as Rattray concluded, depended equally on the tonal and holophrastic nature of the Ashanti language.

After mastering Ashanti drum language, Rattray asked an Ashanti chief, Osai Bonsu, *omanhene* (chief) of the political division of Mampon, permission to have the old court drummer, Osai Kojo, set up his drums in Rattray's bungalow and perform the long drum-history of Mampon. As the old court drummer played, Rattray recorded the performance. He then transcribed the sounds of the drum into drum language, transposed it into Ashanti, and then translated it into English. The drum history recorded and transcribed in Ashanti by Rattray relates the history, in chronological order, of one of the most important Ashanti political divisions. "It may not be generally recognized that such a history has a deeply sacred significance," wrote Rattray. "The names of dead kings are not to be spoken lightly, and the recounting of such a history comes with no small sadness to the listener" (Rattray 1923: 264). Again, Rattray was one of the few Westerners (perhaps the only one) permitted to hear the sacred history of a political unit of the Ashanti.

Drum language was not the only esoteric knowledge that the Ashanti shared with Rattray. During his years of living and working among the Ashanti, Rattray witnessed and participated in many ceremonies and feasts held for their pantheon of divine beings. The Ashanti believed in a supreme being called Nyame, "who dwells somewhat aloof in His firmament, down to those to whom He delegates some of His powers, as His vice-regents on Earth" (ibid.: 86). In addition to this Supreme Being, the Ashanti believed in a variety of nonhuman spirits (*abosom*), including those who inhabited lakes and streams, those who took the form of ancestors, and those who inhabited various inanimate objects (*suman*).

"These beliefs," observed Rattray, "have for centuries been described as 'fetishism' or 'fetish worship,' but the religious conceptions of the Twi-speaking peoples of the Gold Coast and Ashanti have, in my opinion, been grievously misrepresented" (ibid.). Indeed, the prevailing attitude of many Europeans (including members of the British colonial administration) was that the Africans were, in the words of an old slave trader,

> stupid and unenlightened hordes; immersed in the most gross and impenetrable gloom of barbarism, dark in mind as in body, prodigiously populous, impatient of all control, unteachably lazy, ferocious as their own congenial tigers, nor in any respect superior to these rapacious beasts in

intellectual advancement but distinguished only by a rude and imperfect organ of speech, which is abusively employed in the utterance of dissonant and inarticulate jargon.[9]

Rattray's ongoing research agenda was to counter such biased, erroneous stereotypes in the minds of the administration through empirical research. In 1916 he wrote in the introduction to *Ashanti Proverbs* that the isolated, forest-dwelling Ashanti not only had a highly developed system of government but also practiced a monotheistic religion. "These few words the present writer has felt in duty bound to say, lest the reader, astonished at the words of wisdom which are now to follow, refuse to credit that a 'savage' or 'primitive' people could possibly have possessed the rude philosophers, theologians, moralists, naturalists, and even, it will be seen, philologists, which many of these proverbs prove them to have had among them" (1916: 11). Once the complexity and beauty of Ashanti customs and religion were recognized, Rattray believed, it would be impossible to dismiss them—as Noel Machin puts it in his biographical monograph on Rattray—as mere "heathens bowing down to sticks and stones" (Machin 1998: 102).

Figure 9.2. *Robert S. Rattray, 1906, location unknown (probably Upper Volta). Courtesy of Nicole Rattray.*

Ten years later and now in his official capacity of government anthropologist, Rattray began to systematically record the complexity of Ashanti cosmology. He was able to demonstrate, contrary to the prevailing view, that the Ashanti supreme God Nyame had not been introduced into Ashanti mythology by Christian missionaries but had always been a central feature of it.[10] "The conception, in the Ashanti mind, of a Supreme Being has nothing whatever to do with missionary influence, nor is it to be ascribed to contact with Christians or even, I believe, with Mohammedans." In Rattray's view, the concept of a Supreme Being could certainly be the product of people "who live face to face with nature, perhaps unclothed, sleeping under the stars, seeing great rivers dry up and yet again become rushing torrents, seeing the lightning from the heavens rending great trees and killing men and beasts ..." (Rattray 1923: 140). Belief in a Supreme Being, according to Rattray, was not the prerogative of Western civilization: "I can see no reason ... why the idea of a one great God, who is the Firmament, upon Whom ultimately all life depends, should not have been the conception of a people living under the conditions of the Ashanti of old" (ibid.: 141).

Unlike many of his anthropological contemporaries, Rattray participated in the world of the Ashanti not just as an observer but also as a believer:

> I approached these old people and this difficult subject (their religious beliefs) in the spirit of one who came to them as a seeker after truths, the key to which I told them they alone possessed, which not all the learning nor all the books of the white man could ever give me. I made it clear to them that I asked access to their religious rites such as are herein described for this reason. I attended their ceremonies with all the reverence and respect I could well accord to something which I felt to have been already very old, before the religion of my country had yet been born as a new thought yet not so entirely new, but that even its roots stretched back and were fed from that same stream which still flows in Ashanti today. (ibid.: 11)

Rattray's reverence for Ashanti religious beliefs and his respect for its antiquity enabled him to gain access to esoteric elements of Ashanti society normally closed to outsiders. In May 1922, for example, he set out to visit the temple of the greatest of the Ashanti gods upon earth, Ta Kora. On the evening he arrived, he sat in the moonlit courtyard with the chief of the town and the high priest of Ta Kora, Kori Duro, "a perfectly charming old gentlemen with a benign and intellectual face." Rattray explained that the object of his visit was to ask permission for the creation of a new shrine that he could bring back to England (ibid.: 175). The high priest explained that the request would be placed before the god the following day. That night around midnight a tornado split a tree from top to bottom.

> As I was standing in my pajamas examining it, one of the villagers came up and, after looking at it, said that God's axe (*Nyame akuma*) had, after splitting the tree, passed underground to the river where no doubt it would someday be found. I was told later that the fact that no house was struck and no one was killed was taken as a favorable omen. Had I been killed, I am afraid the cause of anthropology in these parts would have received a set-back from which it would have hardly recovered. (ibid.: 176)

The next day Rattray was allowed into the sacred temple of Ta Kora where a ceremony took place. The high priest went into religious convulsions as the spirit of the god entered his body. Speaking through the voice of the high priest, the god Ta Kora spoke directly to Rattray: "The man who loves me comes to me, and when he goes away I shall stand behind him and accompany him on a good path that he may go his way. And this one who has come, grant him permission to go to my rock should he wish to go. Let him go and behold the place where I reside" (ibid.: 181). The following day Rattray was allowed to visit the source of the Tano River and the sacred caves that housed the god Ta Kora. He was the first Westerner to be so honored. "I feel that I do not need to make any excuses," he wrote, "for having taken part in what old Bosman [a Dutch Protestant merchant] undoubtedly would have called 'Heathen and Idolatrous rites' in order to elucidate the origin of religious beliefs" (Rattray 1923: 11).[11]

Conflict Avoidance and the Golden Stool

As a result of Rattray's deep knowledge of Ashanti religious, legal, and political life, he was able to do what few anthropologists have done: stop what appeared to be an inevitable war between the Ashanti and the British. To provide some context, it is worth noting that over the course of one hundred years, the Ashanti and the British had gone to war five times, for reasons such as control of coastal territory, defense of alliances, territorial incursions, or refusal to abide by treaties (Edgerton 2010). Beginning in 1806, British economic penetration of West Africa in the form of the African Company of Merchants resulted in conflict with the Ashanti Empire. Between 1823 and 1831, in what is now known as the First Anglo-Ashanti War, the British initiated a war against the Ashanti nominally to stop the Ashanti slave trade but also to defend coastal territory belonging to the Fante, with whom they were allied. This war ended with a British withdrawal and thirty years of peace. The Second Anglo-Ashanti War (1863–64) erupted when the Ashanti made incursions into British territory in pursuit of a fugitive and ended in a stalemate after both sides were decimated by sickness. The Third Anglo-Ashanti War (1873–74) was initiated by the Ashanti, who wanted to protect their coastal access after the British purchased the Dutch Gold Coast from the Netherlands, including territory that was claimed by the Ashanti. The Treaty of Fomena, which ended the war in July 1874, mandated that the Ashanti pay reparations, give up territorial claims, terminate various alliances, withdraw troops from the coast, keep trade routes open, and end human sacrifice. The Fourth Anglo-Ashanti War (1895–96) was initiated by the British after the Ashanti refused to become a British protectorate. The Ashanti were defeated, and their king was exiled to the Seychelles (Edgerton 2010). Although the monarchy did not survive British indirect rule, many of the social structures (such as the institution of the Queen Mother and political divisions) remained in place. In 1900, six years before Rattray arrived in the Gold Coast, the British and the Ashanti went to war over the Golden Stool, the most sacred ritual object of the Ashanti. This conflict is known as the War of the Golden Stool (1900).

The Golden Stool was first created during the reign of King Osai Tutu, the fourth known king of the Ashanti who ruled from 1700 to 1730. As a physical object, the Golden Stool was constructed of wood with three supports, partially covered with gold, and decorated with bells. As a spiritual object, the Ashanti believed that the Golden Stool contained the *sunsum* (soul or spirit) of the Ashanti nation and embodied "their power, their health, their bravery, their welfare" (Rattray 1923: 289). If this stool was taken or destroyed, then "just as a man sickens and dies whose *sunsum* during life has been injured, so would the Ashanti nation sicken and lose its vitality and power" (ibid.: 90). Historians have subsequently claimed that the Golden Stool was not just an "object of sacred veneration"—it was also "a political weapon." Possession of the Golden Stool conferred political legitimacy on the individual who controlled it and "helped deliver into the outstretched hand the reins of power and government" (McCaskie 1983: 198, 199).

Because of the Golden Stool's political and religious power, not even the king of the Ashanti was permitted to sit upon it. That sacred prohibition did not deter the governor of the Gold Coast, Sir Frederick Hodgson (1851–1925), from demanding to sit on the Golden Stool. "Where is the Golden Stool? Why am I not sitting on the Golden Stool at this moment?" (as quoted in Rattray 1923: 292).[12] Lacking the requisite knowledge about Ashanti culture and religion, this "stupendous and costly blunder" by the British unnecessarily provoked the War of the Golden Stool (Laue 1976: 36). Led by the Queen Mother Yaa Asantewaa (1840–1921), in 1900 Ashanti forces attacked and besieged the British fort of Coomassie (now spelled Kumasi), resulting in the death of the governor and several thousand Africans. In 1900, four years after the British finally defeated the Ashanti, the remaining members of the royal court were exiled to the Seychelles, and the Ashanti territory finally came under the control of the British Crown. Clearly annoyed with the British colonial administration's blundering, Rattray writes, "I am sure if the Government of that day had ever known what is here very briefly described it would never have asked for the stool 'to sit upon,' and possibly it would not have asked for it at all, and there would have been no siege of Coomassie in 1900" (Rattray 1923: 292).

Although they lost the war, the Ashanti still possessed the Golden Stool. After the war, the Ashanti buried the Golden Stool in the bush between two great brass pans. In 1921, laborers building a road uncovered it, and thieves removed the golden ornaments that adorned the stool. The British locked the thieves up in prison, saving them from being killed by an irate mob. A few hours later, the whole of Ashanti "was in a state of national mourning and tribulation, far greater than the loss of any king" (ibid.: 9). Rumors were flying that the British had seized the stool. British officials, in turn, were concerned that another bloody uprising was imminent.

Rattray was not in Coomassie when the thieves were arrested and detained by the British, but he rushed back from the town of Bekwai where he was conducting fieldwork on Queen Mothers. He immediately began conducting interviews with informants, including his venerable friend Kakari whose genealogy had earlier provided the model for the Ashanti kinship system (Machin 1998: 77). Working as quickly as possible because of the explosive political situation, Rattray produced a confidential memorandum on the history of the Golden Stool with recommendations about how the British administration ought to approach the issue.

Over the past hundred years, both historians and anthropologists have written about Rattray's role in preventing yet another bloody Anglo-Ashanti war (Smith 1926; Myatt 1966; Laue 1976; McCaskie 1983). While these secondary sources are valuable, the book *Ashanti* contains the actual confidential memorandum Rattray wrote for the British administration a few days after the events had occurred. The memorandum captures the atmosphere in the Gold Coast at the time extremely well. In the memorandum, Rattray began by noting a lack of information on the topic of the Golden Stool. He himself had "avoided any questions, direct or indirect, concerning this subject, not wishing to offend the susceptibilities of the Ashanti" (Rattray 1923: 287). He noted that neither the archives of the British government nor the classical texts dealing with this part of Africa contained information about the Golden Stool. Yet, "a knowledge of the facts now recorded would possibly have prevented at least one Ashanti war, had its bearing on local feeling and Ashanti politics been fully grasped . . ." (ibid.: 288).

Rattray then described the origins and significance of the Golden Stool to the Ashanti people, concluding "that we have the key to this delicate situation." He offered three recommendations to the British government. The first and most important was that the British should not take possession of the Golden Stool—even to keep it safe. British possession of the Golden Stool might have deadly consequences:

> I do not think we . . . fully grasp the results which I believe might follow were we ever to take it from this people. I believe it will be found to be the case that all the obedience, the respect, and great loyalty we have been given by the Ashanti is given through and by reason of the Golden Stool. I believe that, so far from benefiting, had we ever taken this stool—which would have been little more than a "trophy" to us—that its power would have then worked against us. I go further and say that if it be true that this symbol of Ashanti nationality has now been lost or destroyed, that the results will soon be felt by us in a way we can hardly grasp. (ibid.: 293)

Rattray's second major recommendation was that justice ought to be left in the hands of the Ashanti chiefs. The third was that although a sentence of death was demanded under Ashanti law for the theft and defilement of the Golden Stool, the British should plea for mitigation of the punishment. This plea should only be made after the Ashanti chiefs had reached their final adjudication. The chief commissioner of Ashanti, Sir Charles Harper, accepted Rattray's recommendations and let the trial of the thieves proceed under the jurisdiction of the Ashanti chiefs. Rattray attended the trial, during which three thousand Ashanti spectators watched in almost complete silence as the chiefs and elders heard evidence. On the fourth day of the trial, the suspects (whose ethnicity was not specified in the text) were found guilty and sentenced to either death, life imprisonment, or a "drink fetish" (a type of ordeal by oath). Following the adjudication of the sentences, Harper commuted the sentences to lesser forms of punishment as Rattray had suggested.

Rattray's role was officially recognized in the 1921 *Annual Report for Ashanti*, which he did not abstain from quoting in the preface to *Ashanti*: "Captain Rattray's researches have already proved of practical value, for it is due to his investigations that much that is new in the history of the 'Golden Stool' has come to light, and with such knowledge Government has seen its way to deal in a sympathetic spirit with the disturbing event of its desecration" (as quoted in Rattray 1923: 9–10).

A few months after the trial, one of the chiefs of the Ashanti, Chief Totoe, invited Rattray to visit the shrine of the Golden Stool and told him to bring two sheep for sacrifice. As Rattray later recalled in his article "The Golden Stool of Ashanti," published in 1935 in *The Illustrated London News* in 1934, when they arrived at the shrine,

> we were in a room, lighted only through the open doorway, which contained as its almost sole article of furniture, a round table ... covered with a piece of red carpet, with some faded design upon it. On top of this table were arranged three bells, all different sizes. ... All were so thickly covered with congealed blood that it was quite impossible to see of what metal they were made. ... Behind the regalia now described lay a small bundle tied up in cloth, or large handkerchief. This had, I think, once been white. On the fabric was a design of dark-coloured butterflies. The cloth was stained with blood. This little bundle—for all the world like some navvy's dinner tied up in a kerchief—contained the Golden Stool. Later it was reverently opened, and the contents were seen to consist of a piece of wood, about 3 in. by 5 in., stained quite black with blood. This, I was told, was a corner of the base of the Stool. Besides this, the largest piece, were several smaller fragments and a few handfuls of what was almost wood-dust. This was all that remained of the almost mythical Golden Stool, which, of course, was originally a wooden stool heavily ornamented with gold plates. (Rattray 1935: 334)

Rattray was the first European to actually see the Golden Stool, and he kept his visit a secret for ten years. "I do not think I am betraying a secret I have thought fit to keep for ten years," he wrote in his 1935 article; "the old greybeard is now dead who, because he believed I had the Ashanti cause at heart, revealed to me, a solitary individual, what armies had tried in vain to discover" (Rattray 1935: 334). He described the honor of seeing the Golden Stool as "the proudest day of my life" (Rattray 1935: 334). Rattray's deep satisfaction at viewing the most sacred object of the Ashanti was (perhaps) confirmation to him of his special relationship with the Ashanti. With mutual trust and cooperation, the Ashanti shared their esoteric knowledge with Rattray, and he in turn acted as transcriber and guardian of their cultural knowledge.

Queen Mothers

The third significant feature of *Ashanti* is the description of the matriarchal kinship system of the Ashanti and the political power of the Queen Mothers, which was quite unusual for the time. Contrary to the views of other British colonial officers in West Africa, who rarely considered the role and position of women, *Ashanti* treats them as a central political feature of Ashanti society.

Rattray began the chapter on "Matrilineal Descent in Ashanti" in a rather conventional way, noting that descent was matrilineal and matripotestal, meaning that clan descent was traced through the female. He then went on to clarify how matrilineal descent effects the status of women among the Ashanti: "The most obvious results of a social organization framed on such lines is to raise immediately the status of women in the community." Among the Ashanti, women had significant legal rights, including custody of children, the right to inherit and alienate property, and "when she dies, no male even of her own clan may be her heir until all her female blood (clan) relations are extinct" (Rattray 1923: 78, 79).

This dry and technical discussion of matrilineal descent and its social consequences quickly shifted to an exegesis on the political power of Queen Mothers in Ashanti society and British failures to understand their authority. "There is indeed one fact," Rattray wrote, "that I believe to have militated against [the Queen Mothers] being known as widely as the circumstances would appear to warrant, the very small number of Europeans who have ever known or made friends with the old Ashanti mothers" (ibid.: 81). Rattray did not advance a hypothesis as to why the British failed to grasp the extensive authority of the Queen Mothers, but certainly part of the reason was structural sexism in Britain at the beginning of the century. In Britain during the 1910s and 1920s, women had no parliamentary vote, educational opportunities were scarce, and upperclass women were expected to be good wives and mothers. Despite the fact that the titular head of the British government was Queen Victoria, women in Great Britain had very limited political power. For British administrators to recognize the extraordinary power of women among the Ashanti would have caused some cognitive dissonance with contemporary British gender roles, and thus it was preferable to simply ignore it.

Rattray's objective in this chapter, if one follows his argument carefully, was to point out the consequences of this failure to recognize the Queen Mothers and advance a number of suggestions for alterations to British administrative policy in the Gold Coast. He began by explaining that the Queen Mother (*Ohema*) was the senior female of the ruling clan. She was not necessarily the biological mother of the king but often his sister. Indeed, among the Ashanti, her political position was recognized as superior to the king. But for women's physical "inferiority" and the prohibition against women going to war during their menstrual cycle, argued Rattray, "Ashanti women under a matrilineal system, would, I believe, eclipse any male in importance. A king's son can never be the king, but the poorest woman of the royal blood is the potential mother of a king" (ibid.: 82). In addition to the transmission of royal blood, Queen Mothers played a significant political role, including determining the royal succession, advising the ruler, choosing his senior wife, receiving petitions, presiding over certain legal cases, and going to war if they were postmenopausal, which is when the taboos concerning contact with menstruating women would be moot (ibid.: 82–84).

Historically, the Ashanti Queen Mothers were not just the "power behind the throne," they actually wielded more power than the king himself. Successive generations of Europeans had simply missed this essential fact, giving all their attention to the chiefs (Machin 1998: 83). "To-day [*sic*] the Queen Mothers are unrecognized by us," wrote Rattray.

> Some of us may have been in the habit of going out of our way to speak to the old lady, feeling rather than knowing she was a power to be reckoned with. Official recognition she has none. I have myself been surprised at the results of my investigations. . . . I have asked the old men and women why I did not know all this—I had spent very many years in Ashanti. The answer is always the same: "The white man never asked us this; you have dealings with and recognize only the men; we supposed the European considered women of no account, and we know you do not recognize them as we have always done." In other words, the Ashanti have simply accepted the fact that our system seemed to take no official cognizance of women as a power in the family and in the State, and therefore did not question our methods. (Rattray 1923: 84)

In effect, Rattray was pointing out that the Ashanti understood the British approach to government and administration much better than the British understood the Ashanti approach to government and administration. Because they had been ignored and their power demeaned, the Queen Mothers resented the British presence and resisted British governance. "How could their influence have been used otherwise but against us when these shrewd old women saw the whole weight of our power apparently used against them, breaking up their former pride of place in society and the state?" (ibid.).

Rattray then shifted from a critique of British administrative shortfalls to advocating a policy shift. "I feel convinced that, without the expenditure of public funds, we could by some official recognition of the Queen Mothers do more for the moral welfare of the Ashanti race than by the expenditure of many thousands of pounds . . ." (ibid.: 85). In Rattray's view, political recognition of the Queen Mothers would empower them to use their considerable influence to combat infant mortality, improve hygiene, limit tetanus, and forestall "the slow collapse of the former rigid moral standards" (ibid.).

Failure to recognize the Queen Mothers, Rattray argued, was unintentionally achieving the opposite result from official British policy. "If . . . we really wish to break up the clan system, then we are doing the right thing by ignoring the position of these women, for they are the keystone of the whole structure" (ibid.). In fact, the British objective in indirect rule was to retain and even strengthen the clan system. Thus, one can detect that Rattray's ironic tone in this passage in *Ashanti* conceals a deeper anger at the bumbling British administration that inadvertently destroyed what it intended to protect. In later articles and books such as *Ashanti Law and Constitution* (1929) and *The Tribes of the Ashanti Hinterland* (1932), Rattray returned to the theme of British colonial ineptitude. For example, he argued that encouraging Christian missionaries to convert the Ashanti effectively eroded the foundation of traditional religion upon which the Ashanti political and legal system was based: "We are encouraging on the one hand an institution [law] which draws its inspiration and vitality from the indigenous religious beliefs, while on the other we are systematically destroying the very foundation [religion] upon which stands the structure that we are striving to perpetuate" (Rattray 1928: 103). In short, Rattray's many years of living among the Ashanti had enabled him to see the interlocking structures of the political, legal, kinship, and religious systems. And his intimate knowledge of these systems made him understand how British ignorance was destroying the very structures they were trying to uphold.

Conclusion

Sadly, Rattray's work is now seldom being read in anthropology programs. Only scholars who specialize in Ghana are likely to have read
his books, and they often dismiss Rattray as a "romantic" with a limited grasp of historical facts (McCaskie 1983: 191) who contributed
to the "reification of 'tradition'" (Robertson 1975: 55). Despite these
dismissals, his *Ashanti* monograph illuminates many current issues of
interest to the discipline, including the early use of participant observation, complex relations between anthropologists and governments,
the use of cultural knowledge in a conflict environment, and feminist
approaches to power. In addition to these mundane topics, Rattray's
book also evokes the illicit spectre of anthropologists who "go native" during fieldwork and potentially compromise their objectivity.
Rattray not only valued African spirituality as an expression of the
diversity of human cosmologies, but actually adopted the religious
beliefs of the Ashanti as his own.

Unfortunately, current scholarship on Rattray is plagued by the
tendency to evaluate him according to current-day politics (Robertson 1975; McCaskie 1983) without considering the overall political
and social context in which he lived and worked. Considered from
the perspective of his own era, Rattray's views of the Ashanti and
British colonial policy in the Gold Coast were extremely progressive,
if not absolutely radical.

In the political discourse of the 1920s, there were two main schools
of thought regarding the "progress" of West Africans (the Ashanti
among them). On the one hand, scholars and officials believed that
African society and culture was fundamentally maladapted to the
modern world and that Western civilization ought to be imported
as a substitute. As Margery Perham (1895–1982) noted, "The attitude of the nineteenth-century humanitarian to native culture arose
from his absolute confidence in his own civilization as a substitute"
(Perham 1934: 325). Rattray found untenable and objectionable the
notion that Western norms, religion, and social organization could
be substituted for Ashanti culture. As he wrote in an article on "Anthropology and Christian Missions," published in 1928:

> The older school would relegate all that curious spiritual past which it
> has been my endeavour to set forth, if not to the African's own kitchen
> middens (*suminaso*), at least to the shelves and glass cases which have be-
> come accepted as the mausolea of dead or dying cultures, where—if I

may draw another analogy which my Ashanti friends will understand—
the souls of the peoples whom our civilization has robbed of these heritages, now seek a lonely and unhonoured refuge. This school, working by
what seems to me a standard of purely material and economic prosperity,
argues that because the African's beliefs appear to have served him but indifferently well in the past as stepping-stones to real progress, his culture
has been tried and found wanting. For these beliefs this school would
therefore substitute European civilization and thought. There is much, of
course, to be said for the supporters of such logic and of methods which
are frank and clear cut; they would prefer a tabula rasa on which to start
afresh; they are free from sentimentalism; and are purely materialistic.
(Rattray 1928: 100)

On the other hand, there were scholars and administrators who believed that African social institutions and cultural patterns had value
in and of themselves, and therefore ought to be preserved. Instead
of relegating traditional African culture to the "mausolea of dead or
dying cultures," the goal, Rattray wrote,

should be, not to become pseudo-European, but to aim at progress for
their race based upon what is best in their own institutions, religion, their
manners and customs. I have told them that they will become better and
finer men and women by remaining true Ashanti and retaining a certain
pride in their past, and that their greatest hope lies in their future, if they
will follow and build upon lines with which the national sunsum or soul
have been familiar since first they were a people. (Rattray 1921: 12)

In Rattray's view, indirect rule should promote "the retention of all
that is best in the African's own past culture" (Rattray 1928: 101).

As an advocate for preservation of Ashanti culture, Rattray was
determined to counter the biased, erroneous stereotypes in the minds
of the administration through empirical research. Once the complexity and the beauty of Ashanti customs and religion was recognized,
Rattray believed, it would be impossible to dismiss them as mere
primitive people whose culture had no value. To that end, *Ashanti*
can be understood as a text intended as proof for the British colonial administration that indigenous African societies were unique,
complex, and worthy of preserving. In *Ashanti*, Rattray provided his
observations neither on the basis of a theory of social evolution (an
approach that was still commonly accepted among contemporaneous
scholars) nor on the basis of haphazard subjective observations (as
was often the case among missionaries and colonial officers) but on
the foundation of 348 pages of empirical observations drawn from
twenty years of ethnographic fieldwork among the Ashanti.

Rattray employed the accepted rhetorical conventions, the incontrovertible belief in the scientific method, and convictions of moral rectitude of the British colonial administrator to challenge their assumptions about the Ashanti and undermine their logic about indirect rule. The objective, scientific approach Rattray adopted in *Ashanti* intentionally trapped contemporary British readers in a dungeon built of their own logic. Because the conclusions that follow from the empirical data cannot be easily dismissed or contravened, Rattray might convince his British colonial audience to shift their policy positions. For example, through his meticulous description of the matriarchal kinship system of the Ashanti, Rattray was able to conclusively establish the political power of the Queen Mothers and make an argument about how the British administration ought to approach governance among the Ashanti. Similarly, by including the confidential memorandum that Rattray produced for the colonial government in Ashanti, Rattray offered actual evidence of the importance of cultural knowledge in administering the colonies. But perhaps the most significant contribution Rattray made to ethnography (at a time when most anthropologists were sitting on the veranda, smoking pipes, and debating racial phrenology) was his demonstration of the efficacy of an objective, scientific approach to obtaining this type of knowledge.

Montgomery McFate is a professor at the US Naval War College in Newport, Rhode Island (USA). Formerly, she was senior social scientist for the US Army's Human Terrain System. She has held positions at RAND, the Institute for Defense Analyses, and the US Navy's Office of Naval Research, where she was awarded a Distinguished Public Service Award by the secretary of the navy. She has served on the Army Science Board and the Defense Science Board and was an instructor at the Johns Hopkins School of Advanced International Studies. She is the editor of *Social Science Goes to War* (Oxford University Press, 2015) and the author of *Military Anthropology* (Oxford University Press, 2018).

Notes

1. The Ashanti are also referred to as the Asante. Since this is a transliteration, either spelling is acceptable. Rattray used "Ashanti," and so that is the spelling employed here.
2. Noel Machin became interested in African art, Akan culture, and R. S. Rattray while working in Ghana. Machin began to collect material for a full-length biography of Rattray in the early 1970s. Very little of Rat-

tray's correspondence survived a fire in his family home, so Machin solicited the help of Rattray's friends, colleagues, and relatives to reconstruct his life from original documents and personal memories. Before his book on Rattray was finished, Machin died in 1986. His friends at the Centre for Social Anthropology and Computing at the University of Kent at Canterbury edited Machin's book on Rattray and published it posthumously as a monograph in 1998. Outside of very limited archival material at the Pitt-Rivers Museum, Machin's biography is the most comprehensive and reliable source on Rattray's life.

3. Dates unknown. All other dates unknown if unmentioned.
4. C. H. Harper, Memoranda, Correspondence and Diaries 1904–35, Rhodes House MSS Brit. Emp.; cf. Machin 1998: 65.
5. Rattray fought in five engagements, during both the conventional and guerilla phases of the war.
6. Rather than promoting him further, the governor of the Gold Coast, Sir Frederick Gordon Guggisberg (1869–1930), on the initiative of Sir Charles Harper (1876–1950), the civil commissioner of Ashanti, created a position for Rattray in 1921.
7. Foreign Office file on Rattray, as quoted by Machin 1998: 15–16; 125.
8. German missionary Johann Gottlieb Christaller (1827–95) was a self-trained philologist and ethnolinguist. Apart from his 1875 Asante grammar, which had an exceedingly long title (see references), he also published dictionaries and vernacular translations of the Bible.
9. Anon.: Slavery No Oppression, 19C pamphlet, as quoted by Machin 1998: 100–101.
10. Furthermore, the statues and bags of hair that Western colonialists had interpreted as mere fetishism were, according to Rattray, sacred objects that possessed magical efficacy derived from their relationship to the Ashanti gods (Rattray 1923: 141n; see also Machin 1998: 103).
11. Very likely a reference to Dutch merchant Willem Bosman (1672–1703), whose 1704 work *Nauwkeurige beschrijving van de Guinese Goud-Tand- en Slavekust* was published in London (Ballantyne and Co.) in 1907 as *A New and Accurate Description of the Coast of Guinea Divided into the Gold, the Slave, and the Ivory Coasts.* Rattray probably read this edition.
12. Sir Frederick Hodgson's wife claimed that this was an error of translation and that he never said these words.

References

Asad, Talal, ed. 1973. *Anthropology and the Colonial Encounter.* Atlantic Highlands, NJ: Humanities Press/London: Ithaca Press.
Bateson, Gregory. 1936. *Naven: A Survey of the Problems Suggested by a Composite Picture of the Culture of a New Guinea Tribe Drawn from Three Points of View.* Cambridge: Cambridge University Press.

Bosman, Willem. 1907. *A New and Accurate Description of the Coast of Guinea Divided into the Gold, the Slave, and the Ivory Coasts.* London: Ballantyne and Co. [1704]

Christaller, Johann Gottlieb. 1875. *A Grammar of the Asante and Fante Language Called the Tshi (Chwee, Twi): Based on the Akuapem Dialect with Reference to the Other (Akan and Fante) Dialects.* Basel: Basel Evangelical Missionary Society.

British Colonial Office. 1921. *Annual Report for Ashanti.* London: His Majesty's Stationery Office (printed in the Gold Coast).

Foster, George M. 1969. *Applied Anthropology.* Boston: Little, Brown, and Company.

Frazer, James George. 1890. *The Golden Bough: A Study in Comparative Religion.* 2 vols. London: MacMillan and Co.

Kirkby, Diane Elizabeth, and Catharine Coleborne. 2001. *Law, History, Colonialism: The Reach Of Empire.* Manchester: Manchester University Press.

Edgerton, Robert B. 2010. *Fall of the Asante Empire: The Hundred-Year War for Africa's Gold Coast.* New York: The Free Press.

Feuchtwang, Stephan. 1973. "The Discipline and Its Sponsors." In *Anthropology and the Colonial Encounter*, edited by Talal Asad, 71–100. London: Ithaca Press.

Kuklick, Henrika. 1978. "The Sins of the Fathers: British Anthropology and African Colonial Administration." *Research in Sociology of Knowledge, Sciences and Art* 1: 93–119.

Lackner, Helen. 1973. "Colonial Administration and Social Anthropology: Eastern Nigeria 1920–1940." In *Anthropology and the Colonial Encounter*, edited by Talal Asad, 123–52. Atlantic Highlands, NJ: Humanities Press.

Laue, Theodore H. von. 1976. "Anthropology and Power: R. S. Rattray among the Ashanti." *African Affairs* 75(298): 33–54.

Leach, Edmund R. 1954. *Political System of Highland Burma: A Study of Kachin Social Structure.* London: G. Bell & Sons. Repr. 1964; London: The Athlone Press, 1970.

Lugard, Lord Frederick. 1922. *The Dual Mandate in British Tropical Africa.* Edinburgh: W. Blackwood & Sons.

Machin, Noel. 1998. *Government Anthropologist: A Life of R.S. Rattray.* Canterbury: University of Kent (Centre for Social Anthropology and Computing).

McCaskie, Thomas C. 1983. "R.S. Rattray and the Construction of Asante History: An Appraisal." *History in Africa* 10: 187–206.

Mair, Lucy. 1975. "Anthropology and Colonial Policy." *African Affairs* 74(295): 191–219.

Myatt, Frederick. 1966. *The Golden Stool: An Account of the Ashanti War of 1900.* London: William Kimber.

Myers, John L. 1929. "Presidential Address: The Science of Man in the Service of the State." *Journal of the Royal Anthropological Institute of Great Britain and Ireland* 59: 19–52.

Perham, Margery. 1934. "A Re-statement of Indirect Rule." *Africa: Journal of the International African Institute* 7(3): 321–34.

———. 1935. "Some Problems of Indirect Rule in Africa." *Journal of the Royal African Society* 34, no. 135: 1–23.

Ranger, Terence Osborn. 1976. "From Humanism to the Science of Man: Colonialism in Africa and the Understanding of Alien Societies." *Transactions of the Royal Historical Society* 26: 115–41.

Rattray, Robert Sutherland. 1907. *Some Folk-Lore Stories and Songs in Chinyanja, with English Translation and Notes.* London: Christian Knowledge Society.

———. 1913. *Hausa Folk-Lore.* Oxford: Clarendon Press.

———. 1918. *Mole-English Vocabulary, with Notes on the Grammar and Syntax.* Oxford: Clarendon Press.

———. 1916. *Ashanti Proverbs: Primitive Ethics of a Savage People.* Oxford: Clarendon Press.

———. 1923. *Ashanti.* Oxford: Clarendon Press. Repr. *Ashanti.* New York: Negro Universities Press, 1969.

———. 1927. *Religion and Art in Ashanti.* London: Clarendon Press.

———. 1928. "Anthropology and Christian Missions: Their Mutual Bearing on the Problems of Colonial Administration." *Africa: Journal of the International African Institute* 1(1): 98–106.

———. 1929. *Ashanti Law and Constitution.* Oxford: Oxford University Press.

———. 1931. "The Tribes of the Ashanti Hinterland: Some Results of a Two-Years Anthropological Survey of the Northern Territories of the Gold Coast." *Journal of the Royal African Society* 30(118): 40–57.

———. 1932. *The Tribes of the Ashanti Hinterland.* 2 vols. With a chapter by Diedrich Westermann (1875–1938). Oxford: Clarendon Press. Repr. 1969.

———. 1934. "Present Tendencies of African Colonial Government." *Journal of the Royal African Society* 33 (130): 22–36.

———. 1934. *The Leopard Priestess: A Novel.* London: Thornton Butterworth.

———. 1935. "The Golden Stool of Ashanti." *Illustrated London News*, 2 March, 333–35.

Robertson, A. F. 1975. "Anthropology and Government in Ghana." *African Affairs* 74, no. 294: 51–59.

Ruxton, Fitz H. 1930. "An Anthropological No-Man's-Land." *Africa: Journal of the International African Institute* 3(1): 1–12.

Smith, Edwin Williams. 1926. *Golden Stool: Some Aspects of the Conflict of Cultures in Modern Africa.* London: Edinburgh House Press.

Temple, Sir Richard Carnac. 1914. *Anthropology as a Practical Science.* London: G. Bell.

Vivian, C. 1933. "Anthropology in the Gold Coast: Discoveries of Known Facts." *West African Review*, February, 29.

Part IV

Expeditionary Ethnography as Intensive Fieldwork

10

From Savages to Friends

Henrique de Carvalho and His *Etnografia e História Tradicional dos Povos da Lunda* (1890)

Frederico Delgado Rosa

One would expect to read the following lines in a travelogue, as they recount a recurrent scene of delusional illness and risk of death in many accounts by European explorers in nineteenth-century Central Africa. However, these words by the Portuguese officer Henrique de Carvalho (1843–1909),[1] who lived in the country of Lunda between December 1884 and October 1887, can be found in a detailed monograph on the Lunda (or Aruwund) and other peoples (*povos*) who were historically subjects of or related to the Lunda "empire"[2]:

> During a serious illness in which I lost all consciousness, when I no longer had even the most insignificant resources for the purchase of food and in the locality there was only cassava, corn and tomatoes, I was treated by them with the closest of interest and the most remarkable affection. . . . They took so great care, subjected me to such baths, and performed so many adorations to their idols that I returned to myself after about eight days, so they told me. Then I found myself surrounded, not by savages, but by dedicated friends who manifested their joy and felt truly happy to have saved my life. (Carvalho 1890a: 45)

One of the reasons for this sudden mix of genres is that Carvalho wanted his readers to know that his decision to gather the ethnographic and historical material scattered in his diaries in a separate volume was taken at that precise moment, while convalescing "among pillows, unable to move, swollen and beset with pain" (ibid.: 47). This was no minor undertaking, as his daily writing habits had never been interrupted in the preceding two and a half years. The only exception is that one week of unconsciousness, between 3 and 11 April 1887, created a void in the journal that was immediately preceded and followed by short entries such as: "Bad day, bad night, wild fever. Lips, nose and mouth, all bursting. No doctor, no resources. I'm at God's mercy. . . . My head's not quiet, I've been hallucinating a lot."[3] As Carvalho feared being "near the end of [his] existence," he worked hard and fast. In the next two months, he produced four ethnographic notebooks, full of erasures, with dense paragraphs in small handwriting, and dispatched them to Lisbon "at the first opportunity" (ibid.: 384). They are the prototype for Carvalho's monograph, *Etnografia e História Tradicional dos Povos da Lunda*, written in Portuguese (1890a).[4]

Considered "a privileged witness" (Vellut 1972: 67) by scholars working on this historical region of what is now Angola and the Democratic Republic of Congo, stretching from the river Kwango to beyond the Luapula, the colossal dimensions of Carvalho's work, its denseness, and the fact that he wrote in Portuguese are against him. All this makes his work illegible to many, which is the reason why it is practically ignored by nonspecialists, historians of anthropology and anthropologists outside the lusophone (Portuguese-speaking) world. In four massive volumes, his travelogue was adapted from the eight handwritten volumes that composed Carvalho's journal. Titled *Descrição da Viagem à Mussumba do Muatiânvua* (1890b), this is a minute account of his journey to the capital, or *Musumb*, of the great Lunda or Ruwund "sovereign": the *Mwant Yaav*.[5] In any case, the monograph that he conceived while convalescing in Africa encapsulates Carvalho's legacy as a pre-Malinowskian ethnographer whose imperialist ideals and evolutionist views did not prevent him from reaching the humanity of the people he learned to live with, from savages to friends.

The main primary sources to be considered are: (1) Carvalho's journal in eight handwritten volumes (1884–88), preserved at the Overseas Historical Archive in Lisbon; (2) his four ethnographic notebooks, handwritten in Africa in 1887, preserved at the same archive in Lisbon; (3) Carvalho's ethnographic monograph, *Etnografia e História Tradicional dos Povos da Lunda* (1890a); and (4) his travelogue, *Descrição da Viagem à Mussumba do Muatiânvua* (1890b), published in four volumes.[6]

Born in Lisbon into a liberal family of intellectual tradition, Carvalho (see figure 10.2) attended the Colégio Militar (a military boarding school), the Escola do Exército (army academy), and a civil engineering course. He joined the army as an infantry officer in 1863 and entered on a career that took him to the Portuguese colonies of Macao (1867–73), São Tomé and Príncipe (1873–76), Mozambique (1877–78), and Angola (1878–82)—each time employed in public works—which explains his role in planning an expedition to the Lunda empire.

The "Portuguese Expedition to the Mwant Yaav" (1884–88) was conceived by him—in association with two former colleagues from the Colégio Militar, namely Luciano Cordeiro (1844–1900), president of the Geographical Society of Lisbon, and Manuel Pinheiro Chagas (1842–95), minister of the navy and of overseas affairs)—as both a political and a scientific enterprise. On the one hand, Carvalho's mission, as entrusted to him by the Portuguese government, was a diplomatic one. Its aim was to sign political treaties with the *Mwant Yaav* and related rulers in the name of the Portuguese crown in order to renew old connections and make them official. (These connections between the Portuguese colony of Angola—particularly its slave and ivory traders—and Central African independent "kingdoms" dated from the sixteenth and seventeenth centuries.) The resulting treaties should allow the establishment of a Portuguese "civilizing mission" directed "by a permanent political resident."[7] The expedition was neither military nor commercial, but it was intended to pave the way to postslavery trade with the Lunda.

On the other hand, his mission had scientific purposes: the practical knowledge of the white and mestizo *sertanejos* (frontiersmen) of Angola and their Luso-African employees should give way to scientific studies in cartography, botany, ethnography, and so on. The expedition was carried out under the aegis of the Geographical Society of Lisbon, which had promoted other scientific explorations in Africa and was, in Carvalho's eyes, "the perpetuator of our glories"—a reference to the Portuguese *descobertas* (maritime discoveries) in Africa, Asia, Oceania, and the Americas during the fifteenth and sixteenth centuries.[8] In fact, the scientific and political dimensions of Carvalho's ethnography were deeply intertwined, not least because of their common idealistic dimension. As historian Richard J. Hammond (1966) states in a classic work about *Portugal and Africa 1815–1910*, by the end of the nineteenth century no other colonial power was so strongly motivated by the chimera of a splendorous past, which the book's subtitle summarizes well: *A Study in Uneconomic Imperialism*.[9] Carvalho's expedition coincided with the Berlin Conference of 1884–85, during which Portugal—a severely impoverished country since the independence of Brazil, its most important colony, in 1822—claimed historical rights to the territories between Angola and Mozambique. This was against British pretensions to link the Cape to Cairo and German and Belgian interests in the country of the Lunda. Indeed, German explorations in the area, undertaken in 1878 and 1881, were one of the catalysts for dispatching the "Portuguese Expedition to the Mwant Yaav," which was also designed to counterbalance them.

Most of Carvalho's volumes are profusely illustrated with engravings made in Lisbon from photographs taken during the expedition. The original photo album, with handwritten captions describing each portrait, scene, or landscape, is a fundamental part of Carvalho's work since it contains biographical notes and comments on each character, from the most aristocratic figures of Lunda society to the humblest members of the expedition, such as porters.[10] In the travelogue, practically all engraved portraits appear with names underneath, while in the ethnographic monograph these are mostly used to illustrate ethnic and social types. There are exceptions, however, particularly in passages of *Etnografia e História Tradicional dos Povos da Lunda* (1890a) where the two genres are again mixed. Labeled portraits also helped Carvalho express his gratitude to those who stood by him under the most adverse circumstances—and who made the book possible by saving his life. "I care not," he wrote, "about the color of their skin, their origins, their place of birth, their humble position, their social status or where they come from! I know they are men of feelings" (Carvalho 1890b: 4:12; see 1890a: 217, 680, 688). Naturally, the profound human bond between Carvalho and his African interlocutors, whether they came from Lunda or from Portuguese Angola, is particularly perceptible in his diaries and the resulting travelogue. Empathy, however, is an unsuspected undertone of his ethnographic monograph as well.

"To Feel Like the Indigenous People," or "The Necessity of Going Native"

Notwithstanding the thematic coherence of some chapters in *Etnografia e História Tradicional dos Povos da Lunda*, several of them have disconcerting overlaps, and two out of ten—both titled "Most Remarkable Ways and Customs"—are quite chaotic.[11] This is probably due to the difficulties Carvalho had in managing the bulk of his own manuscripts during and after his convalescence. As he wrote in chapter 8: "I shall proceed by presenting my observations as I registered them on the spot . . . , although the order I follow is not strictly scientific" (Carvalho 1890a: 443). The monograph's interest does not lie in its structure but in its content, and this applies not only to historically relevant ethnographic data but also to Carvalho's views on a number of broader issues that remain anthropologically relevant. To start with, his position against racism and prejudice runs through the entire volume.[12] Notwithstanding Carvalho's imperialistic fervor—which he deemed compatible with a humane attitude—the monograph may be read as a critique of colonial violence by virtue of passages like this:

> We [Europeans], without understanding them [Africans], without studying them if only to do them justice, penetrate the places where they live and expect immediately to be understood, imitated and served, as if it were easy to impose other customs and another religion on the most intimate life of a people. . . . We ignore the environment around us . . . and, having only ourselves as our model, believe that we have transported civilized Europe into Africa. . . . We take the realities that present themselves to be savagery, treat the black with contempt and then come to the sad and erroneous conclusion . . . that the people of Africa are dull-witted and that, consequently, it is only possible to subject them to our customs by force; or that nothing can be done with them since they are resistant to any teaching. (ibid.: 45–46)

Focusing on his experience among the people of Lunda, Carvalho put cultural institutions and social occurrences that could be distorted by a rushed or biased gaze into perspective. He warned his readers against the way in which many travelers described a particular people as savage "on the basis of isolated facts," leading them to portray them "in the ugliest colors" (ibid.: 443, 8). For example, the explorer John Hanning Speke (1827–64) wrote that in Africa he found "a mad contempt for life itself." And "with this warning," Carvalho commented, "I would have said so myself if I were to judge by appearances" (ibid.: 724). In reality, he explained, homicides and even injuries were "extremely rare" (ibid.: 437). In three years he had only learned of two murders, and therefore "it seems to me that the unfavorable lessons that have been inferred from isolated cases at great intervals of time are very far from the truth, especially when we compare them with what happens among civilized peoples" (ibid.: 684)—possibly a reference to the dueling culture in nineteenth-century Europe. Homicides for political reasons were a different thing, to be sure (see below). As to the right of the Lunda potentate to take the lives of his subjects, it was met with resistance, Carvalho noted, if abusively exercised. Once again, the comparison was not necessarily favorable to "civilized nations," even if Portugal was the first European country to abolish the death penalty for civil crimes in 1867. Tormented by the dilemma of opposing it in Africa, he wrote in his journal: "How unjust we are!!! In one day we want the Lunda regenerated in terms of what still has to be regenerated (after so many centuries) among the most advanced in civilization, the great European nations!"[13]

Carvalho's approach reveals an openness to African society that, in spite of his firm belief in progress, inspired a critique of some aspects of European "civilization"—thus renewing, probably without him knowing it, the tradition of Montaigne, Rousseau, and others. His comparisons about issues as delicate as homicide, theft, lying, hygiene, and so on point toward a relativist frame of mind. For example, on the question of African seminudity, which several observers found outrageous, he wrote:

> If we look at women's clothing, subject to fashion as it is among us, we find more reason to condemn it as contrary to decorum and good customs than the simple rag or leaves with which blacks cover the genitalia. . . . we try to give a woman artificial and tempting forms so that she pleases the society in which she lives, and these artifices cannot be to the credit of modesty and honesty. (ibid.: 679)

Carvalho professed and recommended "the cult of truth," which demanded that its followers "strip themselves of all prejudice, of all vanities of race, religion and intellectual culture" (ibid.: 9). He did not realize that he was himself judgmental on several occasions, while resorting to unquestioned evolutionary ideas—that reflected diffuse more than precise theoretical influences. On the subject of "superstition," he wrote: "In fact, nor can we boast that we have no superstitions; . . . I believe some of our own are much worse, and do not provide much proof in favor of our sophistication" (ibid.: 431).

Among the most sensitive subjects on which he spoke in relativistic terms was slavery. On the one hand, he considered it a calamity that the sale of human beings was still a reality in Africa. On the other, he maintained that the daily existence of slaves in African societies such as Lunda was not as violent as trafficking to Brazil—overtly in the past, illegally in the present: "The less keen observer would see among them not the slave, but the servant who actually sits at the boss's table, wears his clothes, hunts with his guns and like him has a say in tribal affairs" (ibid.: 439). Against negative generalizations, Carvalho resorted to abundant examples of the "good character" of Lunda people, their generosity, their charitable habits as well as their outbursts of gratefulness. As to the feeling "we would call love," he insisted that "the word also exists in Lunda" (ibid.: 489) and that its use was not restricted to the mutual affection between spouses. His overall "good impression" was reinforced by the fact that, as he himself experienced, they did not abandon their sick—"and their dedication to me can serve as an example" (ibid.: 463).

This positive depiction is inseparable from the ethnographic sensibility Carvalho developed during his long sojourn in the region. This is reflected in passages of *Etnografia e História Tradicional dos Povos da Lunda* that make explicit reference to the methodological need for empathic immersion in native society. One should ask, of course, how this was possible if Carvalho led an expedition that was supposed to keep moving toward its preestablished destination, the *Musumb*.[14] Before answering this question, allow me to respond to a few other remarkable passages in his monograph.

Aware that descriptions about Central Africa lacked "homogeneity" in terms of research methods, with a prevailing tendency to what he called the "subjective method" (ibid.: 56)—that is, an inextricable mixture of ethnographic data and biased opinions—Carvalho affirmed that studying "uncivilized" peoples was harder than studying "civilized" ones. It demanded "persistent observation" and "a particular way of registering things in great detail" (ibid.: 443). Most of all, it required linguistic skills:

> Linguistics is the main research tool with which anyone trying to solve the main problems of the ethnography of a people must equip themselves. For this reason, in order to be understood in my attempts, I immediately endeavored to study the dialects of the tribes with which I wanted to establish relations. (ibid.: xxi–xxii)

Hundreds of references to his daily lessons and exercises pervade Carvalho's journals. Thanks to his learning the Lunda or Uruwund language, there was a gradual loss of importance in having interpreters, even if their presence could never be fully dispensed with. In any case, direct relations between Carvalho and his many African interlocutors were reinforced. His emphasis on the need to learn native languages is reflected in some of his reading choices, particularly *La Linguistique* (1877) by Abel Hovelacque (1843–96); but he clearly had a predisposition to language-centered ethnography. This was related not only to his long overseas experience but also, most probably, to his personality.[15] There can be no doubt that the opening pages of Carvalho's monograph also reflect his transformative experience in Lunda:

The greater the difference between our civilization and that of the people we wish to study, the more necessary it becomes for us to speak and understand their language or dialect, *to live the life of that people or that tribe* and to think in the closest of terms, using the same references and the same allusions. These should bring to our brains the images and sensations of local objects according to the same psychic emotions and comparisons that these objects provoke in the minds of that people. Only then can we feel these emotions or understand them as they feel them, as they conceive them. . . . But to feel like the indigenous people themselves is to transform oneself psychologically; and whoever leaves an environment such as ours cannot immediately transform his mentality, shut down, so to speak, his whole physical, moral and intellectual life and keep it mute, forgotten for a certain period, and have the indispensable courage and resignation to take place among those with whom he intends to live for some time. (Carvalho 1890a: xxii: my emphasis)

The need for a long sojourn is a leitmotif of *Etnografia e História Tradicional dos Povos da Lunda*; it actually precedes the book, as Carvalho wrote about it while convalescing in Lunda. This is the opening paragraph of his handwritten notebook titled "Notes on the Ways and Customs of the Peoples of Central Africa and More Particularly the Lunda": "One has to live among these people for a certain period of time, months and even years, in order to be able to talk about their ways and customs with full knowledge, as well as their traditional history, their politics, their manner of living."[16] He resumed this idea by using a Portuguese verb—*permanecer*—that combines the existentialist dimensions of remaining within space-and-time dimensions of staying. Otherwise it was impossible to know any people, he felt: "And how is one to know any people without remaining among them, by studying their habits and customs, their language (not yet written), and the products they obtain from the soil or from their industry?" (ibid.: 4). Despite, or precisely because of, the many occasions he had to feel exasperation and to express that to his African interlocutors, he insistently preached "resignation, prudence and the utmost self-sacrifice" as requirements to achieve an "authorized experience" (ibid.: 7)—that is, an ethnographic experience. "If there is any study that demands the greatest peace of mind and the greatest impartiality of opinion," he added, "it is without question that of the African tribes with which one manages to be in contact. Without such a relaxed study, ethnography will not be able to progress nor to establish itself on a secure footing" (ibid.: 8).

Unfortunately, it is impossible to ascertain with any precision how and when Carvalho became acquainted with the concept of ethnography, which he used in the title of his monograph but abstained from defining. His studies and military career did not have many points of contact with ethnological sciences, as in Portugal there was no special kind of training for officers working in the colonies. Diffuse influences are likely, all the more so because the peripheral condition of Portugal, whose bourgeoisie was both francophile and anglophile, propitiated eclectic options. Spencerism and French *anthropologie*, Tylorian evolutionism, and the comparative mythology of Friedrich Max Müller (1823–1900) could be combined in unexpected ways, along with references to minor works by lesser-known international figures. A scientific event having great impact on Portuguese society was the 9th International Congress of Anthropology and Prehistorical Archaeology, which took place in Lisbon in 1880 following important archaeological findings in Portugal.

Indeed, the anthropological scene of a peripheral country can be complex in comparison with more cosmopolitan ones. The fact that Carvalho lived in the colonies for many years accentuates the blurry nature of his theoretical background. His references are often incomplete or vague, for example when he writes, "According to some ethnologists . . ." (ibid.: 54) without specifying their names or their works. After his return from Lunda, Carvalho considered presenting a paper on the Ruwund language at the 10th International Congress of Orientalists, planned to take place in Lisbon in 1892 under the patronage of the king of Portugal—which, however, was canceled following a political dispute between European Orientalists.

In any case, Carvalho's ethnography should be regarded as a process. It followed a clearly distinguishable path from the dissipation of cultural misunderstandings to a participation in local ways, to the point of saying: "Day after day, I recognized the necessity of going native."[17] This implied, again, "maximum resignation" so as to accept the local rhythms and to act accordingly (ibid.: 406). Already before "slow ethnography" had become an epistemological and political manifesto against neoliberal academia in the early twenty-first century, the Portuguese historian Maria Emília Madeira Santos used the word *slow* to describe Carvalho's fieldwork, adding that he was the first to practice it this way (Santos 1998: 493). Problematic as identifying pioneers in this regard may be, Carvalho's case surely makes a contribution to questioning the history of anthropology, as he carried out both participant observation and observant participation:

It was the Lunda people—with whom I had a relationship for three years—who attracted my attention the most; and I managed to be introduced to their customs, their dialects and their intimate life, entering their huts not as a stranger, or as an honored guest, but as a friendly and trustworthy person. I even ended up taking my place at their meals and learning about their domestic life. I was constantly called for, constantly sought to help resolve their disputes. I was asked for advice on delicate matters. If at the beginning they mistrusted me, they understood that I was a just man and presented their cases to me so that I could plead them before the potentates. (Carvalho 1890a: 43–44)

Carvalho's deep involvement in local politics deserves special attention, but for the moment let us focus on his persistent critique of the European "explorer-traveler" who did not have time to "dwell on the particularities of the regions he travelled through" and who could do no more than "appreciate the people with what he could observe during a short stopover" (ibid.: 46). In fact, the best they could attain in terms of communication with Central Africans — grasping Portuguese as a lingua franca in the hinterland of Angola — was below his own minimum: "In the course of an ephemeral journey — and what is more, surrounded by interpreters with only a limited knowledge of just one of the modern languages, Portuguese — one cannot learn it sufficiently to understand the interpreters and therefore the people one is visiting" (ibid.: xx). This was also an understanding of the linguistic limitations African brokers might have:

> Without learning the languages, only via the speech of the interpreter who transmits no more than a summary of what he has been able to perceive . . . one cannot grasp what there is of feelings in the expression of the native individual who intends to communicate with those who observe him. And, in most cases, the lessons that are drawn from the interpretation contradict the thought of the individual who speaks. (ibid.: 723)

These shortcomings resulted in problematic and "always boring" (ibid.: 6) dialogues that made the European traveler lose his patience and ultimately resort to violent gestures. Carvalho's readings before and after his fieldwork varied but, more or less haphazardly, included a significant corpus of foreign travelogues. The ones produced by two German explorers who had been to Lunda in previous years and who had visited the *Musumb* deserve special mention: Paul Pogge (1838–84), who had traveled to Lunda in 1878 and published *Im Reich des Muata Jamwo* (1880), and Max Buchner (1846–1921), who had traveled to Lunda in 1881 and wrote "Das Reich des Mwata Yamvo und seine Nachbarländer" (1883; also 1879–81, 1882; see Heintze 2007). After perusing the "colorful" literature produced by European explorers, Carvalho asked: "What do they tell us? Very little" (1890a: 384). What he missed in Pogge's and Buchner's reports, which are full of cultural misunderstandings, was a deeper description of Lunda ways and values, only possible by learning the language during a long sojourn, combined with a more empathic and less unprejudiced attitude.

"So-Called Savages Have Culture": Culturalism in an Evolutionist Framework

> The peoples whose civilization is coarse and whom we call savages also have *their* culture.[18] It reveals itself through language, its mirror, with a subtlety of meanings and nuances sometimes so diverse and almost always so characteristic of their intellectual development and moral level that it *can only be grasped after a close cohabitation and long-term work.* (ibid.: v; my emphasis)

The history of the anthropological concept of culture is a matter of debate. George W. Stocking Jr.'s reading of the pioneering definition of "culture or civilization" by Edward Tylor (1832–1917) in *Primitive Culture* (1871: 1) has been influential. In his 1966 seminal article on "Franz Boas and the Culture Concept in Historical Perspective," Stocking makes a distinction between Tylor's "singular and hierarchical" nomenclature, applied to "cumulative human creativity" (Stocking 1966: 868–69; see also Stocking 1963), and the plural, particularistic usage of the culture concept of modern anthropologists by Franz Boas and his students. To be sure, Tylor "recognized the existence of custom and tradition," but "culture was definitely not their synonym." Stocking suggested that "the argument from Tylor can be generalized" (1966: 870). One might look for previous occurrences of the word in the German tradition of Bastian, Humboldt, and Herder—Boas's cradle—but only, Stocking proceeds, to find the notorious distinction between peoples with and without culture: *Natur-* and *Kulturvölker*. This reading has been questioned by James Urry (1998) and Ivan Kalmar (1987). "Most anthropologists accept Stocking's assessment," Kalmar writes. "Boas may have been the first to use the word 'culture' in the plural, *in English*. But not in German. In Germany, *Kultur* was used in the plural (*Kulturen*) as early as the 1880s" (Kalmar 1987: 670, 682; see also Vermeulen 2015: 434; Bunzl 1996; and Kroeber 1949).[19] Henrique de Carvalho's usage of the word *culture* also represents a challenge to Stocking's distinction. Indeed, it is a symptom of a more complex picture, all the more so because Carvalho does not mention where he took the word from.

While he, at other moments, spoke of peoples "without culture" (or "uncivilized"), this is necessarily because the word had two different meanings for him: culture or civilization as strictly applied to a literate society, deemed to be spiritually and materially sophisticated, and culture as the specific traits of any people, deemed backward or progressive. When he wrote that so-called savages had "*their* culture," the plurality behind this phrasing is implied. Carvalho's understanding of *usos e costumes* (manners and customs) was thus summarized by the word *culture* in this rare but interesting passage. Only the collection of "ethnological documents" (*documentos etnológicos*) made it possible to appreciate "the differences that characterize each tribe" (Carvalho 1890a: 4). He enumerated "weapons, instruments, tools, artifacts, clothing, ornaments, food, . . . drinks, . . . buildings, agriculture, administration and government, funeral ceremonies, births, hunting, dances, the trade system, superstitions, migrations, fights, wars, family life, skills," or, in a nutshell, "everything that can best characterize a people" (ibid.: 16). In spite of the monograph's focus on the Lunda, eight other ethnic groups or "tribes," particularly the Cokwe, also featured, with constant comparisons between them.[20] He also highlighted variations "within a single tribe [*na mesma tribo*]" (ibid.: 728).

But, more importantly, Carvalho's notion of culture dialogued with folk perceptions of it, particularly African perceptions. Albeit dispersed through his work, parts of Carvalho's ethnography belong to the category *corpus inscriptionum*, with oral traditions, such as songs and proverbs, fixed in the original language with a Portuguese translation. One of the most curious passages of his monograph is the transliteration of conventional messages transmitted by the biggest drum in the region. And Carvalho himself used this instrument of communication too.

Etnografia e História Tradicional dos Povos da Lunda has undeniably "culturalist" (albeit pre-Boasian) tones, owing to Carvalho's insistence on regional studies—"the most important to carry out" (ibid.: 46)[21]—the search for an indigenous description of objects and gestures, and an explanation of their meaning, or his perception that the phenomena of diffusion between neighboring peoples did not mean that the shared traits had the same significance: "From one tribe to another, there are differences which have become characteristic, which have, so to speak, a special imprint, and the observer must notice them, because what could often be taken for a loan, is not quite the case" (ibid.: 383). Carvalho's review of the relevant literature made him aware of the level of detail of his own ethnography and the gaps it filled for the Lunda region: "Comparing these works of mine with the investigations of many foreign travelers, explorers and missionaries who have been more closely involved in these matters, I have come to the conviction that they are all superficially and incompletely studied" (ibid.: xxiii).

In his warning against the risks of anachronism in appreciating nineteenth-century uses of the word *culture*, Stocking calls attention to how evolutionary status was "frequently argued in racial terms" (Stocking 1966: 870). Initially, Carvalho wanted to take the "biological conditions" (Carvalho 1890a: 12) of the peoples of Lunda into account, as he believed that all kinds of factors, including climate, could explain their "backwardness." In spite of his comments on bodily aspects of the people of Lunda—"light-colored," with heads "as beautiful as at any meeting of Europeans" (ibid.: 172)—he actually gave up doing a study in (physical) anthropology. Various reasons made him abandon this plan. Carvalho mistrusted the reliability of skulls and skeletons, if only because the complex "intertribal" history of Central Africa, and especially of Lunda, made their provenance dubious. He was aware that craniology (which had its representatives in Portugal) was fashionable; but he refused to plunder graves, a shameful activity that, on top of it, could jeopardize his reputation in Lunda. The same applies to anthropometry.

Without specifying his readings on the matter, Carvalho makes reference in chapter 1, titled "Origin of the Lunda Peoples," to "well-known" (ibid.: 56) monogenist and polygenist theses on the origins of African "races," but he criticizes the defective materials on which divergent theories were based. In chapter 2, titled "Tu or Antu Dialects," he focuses instead on the three scholars who had identified and characterized the Bantu language group, namely Wilhelm Bleek (1827–75), Friedrich Müller (1834–98),[22] and Johannes Theophilus Hahn (1842–1905). Sustaining that *tu* or *antu* should be used to the detriment of the word *bantu*, his main message was that more detailed regional studies would be necessary before broader conclusions could be reached—all the more so because both Bleek and Müller, influenced by Darwin's proselyte Ernst Haeckel (1834–1919), considered that language allowed answers to evolutionary questions framed in racial terms (Gregorio 2002). In addition, he criticized those scholars for ignoring important "tribes" under the "great and famous states of the central region" (Carvalho 1890a: 121).[23]

It was difficult to ascertain if the Lunda had been through a Stone Age; Carvalho believed they already knew iron before migrating from the north. There is a "diffusionist" dimension to his evolution-ism. But in fact, to dwell on the unknown origins of a people would be "rash," in his understanding, so his monograph makes an inflection after this kind of "palaeo-ethnological" speculation and resolutely moves on to "ethnography" (ibid.: 3, 33, 13). It is this emphasis that makes his work relevant today.

Origins and Political Organization
of Lunda Sacred Kingship

In addition to *etnografia*, the title of Carvalho's book contains two other terms—*história tradicional*—that reveal his historical sensibility, which functions like a driving force behind the monograph as a whole. Indeed, his ethnography included historical data going back three or four centuries, or so he believed. As there were no physical remains or written records of the past, oral traditions on the history of the Lunda "empire" should be duly collated, alongside the linguistic work. These might not be as "rigorous" as desired, but it was certain that "they elucidate greatly" (ibid.: 47).

For Carvalho, it was self-evident that Lunda was a "state" (*estado*) and, more than that, an "empire" (*império*). His political vocabulary also included the words "kingship" (*realeza*), "sovereign" (*soberano*) and "government" (*governo*). But his favorite term—abundantly used in all his writings, both handwritten and published—was *potentado*, from the Latin *potestas* (power). The less commonly used English word *potentate*, applied to a powerholder, does not have the same impact as the Portuguese *potentado*, which designates a powerful ruler but implies the political unit in question as well, with a sense of geographical vastness.[24] The *Mwant Yaav* was a *potentado*, but other rulers subjected to him were also called *potentados* by Carvalho in order to reinforce the imperial status of the Lunda top ruler. There are two dimensions to Carvalho's terminology. On the one hand, it was visibly inherited from an older Portuguese tradition that applied the references of European monarchy to African contexts. On several occasions, Carvalho presents the *Mwant Yaav*'s Lunda as the "once famous great empire," "the famous empire of other centuries," the "long ago renowned empire of central Africa" (1890b: 3:124; 4:206, 239). On the other hand, his ethnographic—and historical—research contributed to reinforce his conceptualization of the Lunda political organization as a state and a pluriethnic empire with a Lunda or Ruwund ruling class.[25]

According to accounts collected by Carvalho, the "state" of Lunda resulted from the friendship (*lunda* or *runda*) between chiefs who had gathered around the heiress of one of them, Princess Ruwej.[26] At the expense of her brothers—particularly Kinguri[27]—who had been removed from succession for misbehavior toward their father, she won the title of *Nswaan Murund*,[28] lady of the country, henceforth called Lunda. She was to put a bracelet made from human veins, *rukan*, a symbol of sovereignty, on the arm of her future husband. On the banks of the Nkalaany River, she fell in love with a foreign hunter, Cibind Yirung,[29] a prince from the declining Luba "state," who eventually was invested with the following powers by the *rukan*: "to gather all small states into a single one under the dominion of his future son, who was to expand it [the dominion] by making vassals and conquering peoples . . . ; to have sorcerers, criminals and those who disobeyed him killed; to dispose of the life and possessions of all subjects in favor of his son's greatness and well-being, as they were slaves of his mother, the lady of the lands" (Carvalho 1890a: 72). When Cibind Yirung's first son was born, he was given the title of *Mwant Yaav*, the lord of all riches.

A split led to the abandonment of the capital by the dissatisfied gathered around Kinguri, who set out for new territories, taking a similar conception of sovereignty with them and thus founding new *potentados*, particularly Imbangala and Cokwe,[30] whose historical connection with the Lunda or Aruwund was constantly emphasized by Carvalho.

The history of the Lunda state was Carvalho's obsession from the beginning. Even before entering the country of Lunda, he was already making inquiries on this subject. Among the many interlocutors with whom Carvalho discussed it, the first was the black Angolan Lourenço Bezerra,[31] an old man who was almost blind, with cataracts covering his eyes and who had lived in the *Musumb* during the 1860s and 1870s. He was the elder brother of the main interpreter of the expedition, António Bezerra—who further strengthened the Portuguese aspect of his surname by adding "de Lisboa" (of Lisbon) "so that everyone would know," he said, "that his great-grandfather came from the kingdom" (Carvalho 1890b: 1:145).[32] Early interviews on the origins of the "state" of Lunda took place while Carvalho was in the small town of Malanje, in Angola, making his final preparations. "[Lourenço] Bezerra was unsatisfied with today's explanations," wrote Carvalho on 24 August 1884, "so he will write me . . . on this subject from the information he has at home. Let us see if I can do something about it before going to Lunda."[33] These written historical accounts have not been found in the archive. Due to illness, António Bezerra joined the expedition only later but "confirmed the information old Bezerra had given me in Malanje about the foundation of the state of the Ant Yaav."[34] Later Carvalho collated versions heard from several Lunda/Ruwund, Cokwe, and Imbangala informants,[35] but one might say this variety of sources reinforces his claim to historical reconstruction, considering that the original *lenda* (legend) (Carvalho 1890a: 112) was shared by and concerned all three groups.

Understanding that the foundational mytho-history of the Lunda empire was inextricably linked to its political organization in the present, Carvalho was a pioneer in the identification of perpetual kinship and positional succession, as twentieth-century Africanists designated these institutions. Irrespective of age and exact genealogical relation, they established artificial kinship ties between aristocratic representatives of alleged eponymous figures. By the same token, they were incumbents of specific political titles and functions. This is one of the reasons why narratives connecting the past and the present were often staged during the many royal audiences Carvalho attended: "The Mwant Yaav and in general all potentados of these peoples occupy their time by telling ancient stories under any pretext, and they always find one" (ibid.: 421).

The highest royal state dignitaries were two female figures: the *Rukonkish*[36] and the *Nswaan Murund*.[37] According to Carvalho, both embodied the same historical character in the present: Ruwej, the mother of the first Mwant Yaav. The *Nswaan Murund* represented Ruwej before her son inherited the state. In accordance with this role, she was the guardian of a vault containing the *rukan* bracelets. Although he never had the chance to attend the investiture ceremony around the *rukan*, Carvalho reported on it in detail as it was described to him. The *Rukonkish*, in the version fixed by him, represented Ruwej after the death of her husband and the investiture of her son. The title meant "she who takes care," as she had to look after the *Mwant Yaav* and his children.[38]

The titles Carvalho chose for most chapters are inaccurate. The scope of chapter 4, "Tu Peoples' Dwellings," for instance, is much deeper than this formula suggests. While focusing on the *Musumb* of the *Mwant Yaav*, it goes well beyond the mere architectural or urban dimensions of the capital of the empire. Instead, this is only a pretext for explaining Lunda political organization, its imperial rites and court etiquette, the interdictions surrounding the *potentado*, and the connections between the present and the mytho-historical foundations of the kingship institutions.[39] According to Carvalho, the *Musumb* had the shape of a turtle drawn on the ground, although following an orthogonal layout (see figure 10.1). As it was about two to three miles long from head to tail, this matrix was not visible as a whole to the naked eye, not least because there were plebeian clusters around it. Carvalho describes in detail how the *Musumb* had strictly stipulated places for the different titles of nobility, including the subordinate *potentados* of the Lunda "empire," who could also have specific functions in its *governo* (government) beyond local representation. He identified and described over fifty noble ranks related to the royal family, with their respective manor houses of perishable materials. Even when the noblemen spent seasons in their own domains, they kept a representative close to the *Mwant Yaav*.

The actual residence and seraglio of the ruler stood out in height among the others, not exactly at the center of the capital but facing the center, where there was a large open space corresponding to the turtle's belly and where the great and most solemn audiences attended by the entire court took place. If the *Mwant Yaav* wanted to talk to a more select group, he would not leave the courtyard of his residence. The different categories of staff also occupied their own premises, and the degree of detail in their duties echoed the complexity of the *Musumb* ways. According to Carvalho's detailed description, the function of some officials consisted only in guarding very specific objects, including several power insignia such as the tail used to brush away flies.

There are, however, two sides of the coin in Carvalho's ethnography: on one side, we have the account of the sacred kingship institutions and of its mytho-historical foundations, symbolically reflected in the *Musumb* turtle drawing; on the other side, we find Carvalho's depiction of the late nineteenth-century political turmoil. In fact, the state of Lunda was undergoing a severe crisis at the time, probably its most serious since the establishment of the kingdom and empire. This was both due to external pressures, related to European prohibitions on the slave trade, to ivory shortage and Cokwe encroachments, and to internal factors related to palace maneuvers and despotic rulers. This side of the coin, to which we now turn, is complicated by the fact that, from August 1885 on, the Portuguese expedition and especially its leader were deeply involved in local politics, as Carvalho decided to travel with a leading figure he had met on the way. This was the exiled old prince Samadiamb (see figures 10.2 and 10.3),[40] whom important noblemen had urgently called to the *Musumb* in order to occupy his legitimate place as *Mwant Yaav*. Since the expedition lent security and prestige to that cause, and several dignitaries gradually joined it, Carvalho had the opportunity to not only witness but also experience the intricacies of a traveling court of an empire in decline.

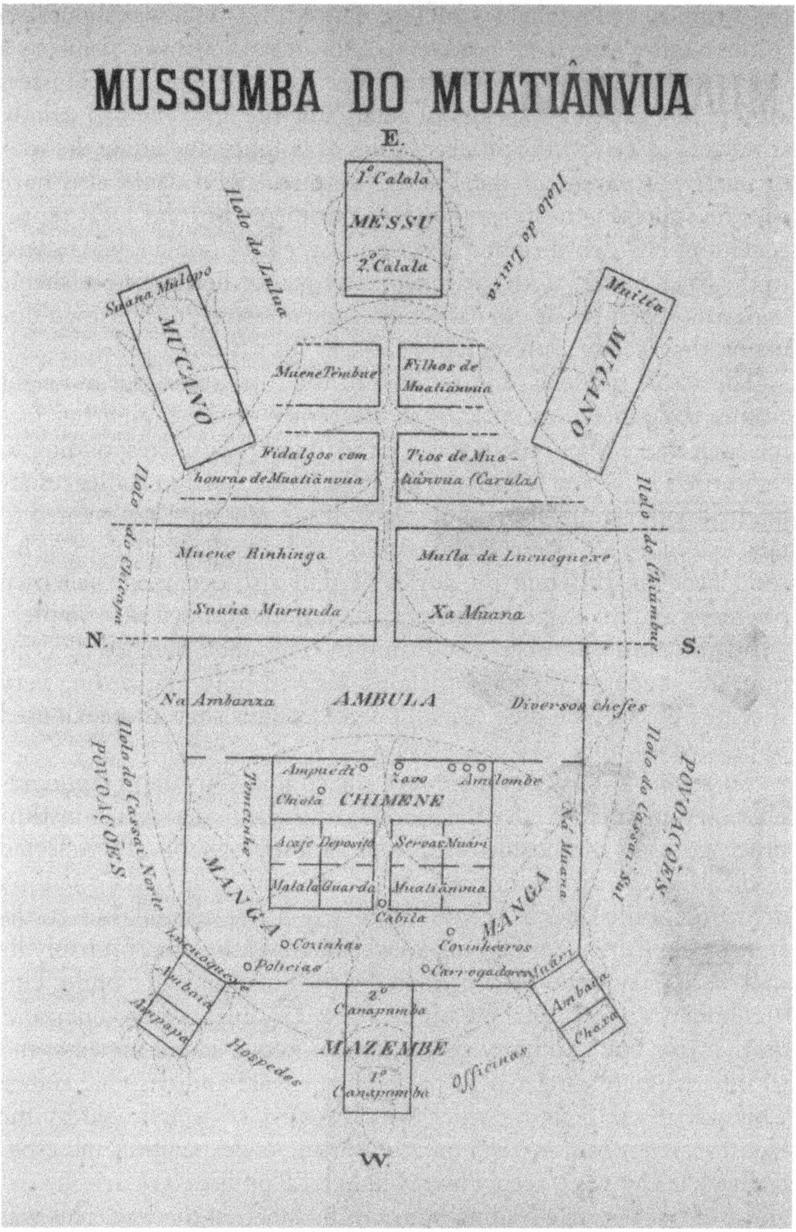

MUSSUMBA DO MUATIÂNVUA

E.

Figure 10.1. *The* Musumb *of the* Mwant Yaav. *From Henrique de Carvalho,* Etnografia e história tradicional dos povos da Lunda, *1890. Courtesy of Sociedade de Geografia de Lisboa.*

Figure 10.2. *Henrique de Carvalho and Samadiamb in Lunda, undated, ca. 1884–87. Photo by Manuel Sertório de Aguiar. From H. de Carvalho and M. Sertório de Aguiar (phot.), "Álbum da Expedição ao Muatiânvua," 1890. © Sociedade de Geografia de Lisboa.*

Mwene Puto: An Ethnography of Colonial Contact

The way in which Carvalho meddled in Lunda political life is inseparable from the fact that he was a representative of *Mwene Puto*, the
century-old vernacular designation of the king of Portugal (sometimes confounded with the governor-general of Angola). This was a
well-known but almost mythical entity, perceived as a very powerful
slave consumer (see Miller 1988). In Carvalho's travelogue (as in the
original journal), the expression *Mwene Puto* appears constantly; it
was a subject of discussion with African interlocutors, and it designated Carvalho himself as his sovereign's "ambassador."[41] The dense
political web in which he became involved is less explicit in the ethnographic monograph, but Portuguese[42] cultural influence is a recurrent subject in several of its chapters.

The descriptions of Lunda royal mysteries and prophecies involving *Mwene Puto* count among the most dramatic passages of
Carvalho's monograph. Even the foundational myth of the Lunda
empire saw its historicity reinforced by the fact that Ruwej's brother,
Kinguri, received lands and a flag from the hands of the governor-
general of Angola, Dom Manuel, whom he had helped in wars that are
inscribed in the Portuguese colonial records: "It is difficult to ascertain dates among the natives because of the irregular way they divide
time. . . . In this case, however, there are traditional sources on which
all are unanimous" (Carvalho 1890a: 78). While in Lunda, Carvalho
guessed that Kinguri's interaction with the Portuguese[43] took place in
the early eighteenth century. In December 1885 Carvalho wrote in his
journal: "I estimate this refers to the beginning of the last century. We
will see in our archives if I can find out anything else."[44] In Lisbon, he
was indeed able to correct his estimate in the following way:

> With such references, Kinguri's men may have entered Luanda at the time
> of Dom Manuel Pereira Forjaz, from 1606 to 1609, or that of Dom Man-
> uel Pereira Coutinho, from 1630 to 1635. . . . In any case, it can be said
> that the state of the Mwant Yaav was organized shortly before and that it
> was established at the end of the sixteenth century. (ibid.: 78)

Although one of Carvalho's goals consisted of replacing on paper the
strictly mental maps of Africans, Luso-Africans and Portuguese *sertanejos* (frontiersmen) by scientific ones, he considered himself to be
less an explorer than a diplomat with responsibility for concluding
political treaties with the *Mwant Yaav* and other *potentados* who had
long known about Mwene Puto.[45] "Que não corra como novo, o que
para nós é antigo" (Let what for us is old not pass as new; ibid.: 727).

This sentence encapsulates Carvalho's vision. Against what he (and Portuguese cultivated society in general) perceived to be a European conspiracy consisting of ignoring or denigrating Portuguese achievements after the "glorious Age of Discovery," he also highlighted the written output of the four-century-old Portuguese experience in Africa, whether sixteenth- and seventeenth-century Jesuit grammars of native languages, an eighteenth-century map with the empire of the *Mwant Yaav* on it, or surviving records by frontiersmen who had been at the *Musumb* during the nineteenth century. Carvalho carried with him the most important one all the time: the journal kept by *sertanejo* and former envoy of the *Mwene Puto*, Joaquim Rodrigues Graça, whom the Portuguese government in Angola had commissioned to convince the *Mwant Yaav* to stop selling slaves. Rodrigues Graça, who lived in the *Musumb* in 1846–47, described it in splendorous terms that ignited Carvalho's imagination: "The traveler feels as if he has been transported to a civilized country, on account of the police he finds, the cleanliness of perfectly straight streets and the spacious squares" (Graça 1890 [1867]: 452).

In chapter 4 of *Etnografia e História Tradicional dos Povos da Lunda*, Carvalho quoted these passages in full and mentioned an Angolan "colony" that had settled near the *Musumb* "after Rodrigues Graça" (Carvalho 1890a: 258). Its leader, known as Lufuma at the Lunda court, was none other than Lourenço Bezerra, whom Carvalho had encountered and interviewed in Malanje about Lunda history (see above). They were *ambaquistas*, a Portuguese word derived from the once flourishing slave trading post of Ambaca, where the missionary actions of the Jesuits had produced a class of literate Africans who, after the expulsion of this religious order in 1759,[46] continued to be renowned (and coveted by independent African potentates) for their scriptural skills and craftsmanship. From a linguistic point of view, Carvalho could not help saying that *ambaquistas* had altered the Portuguese language by mixing words and expressions from Kimbundu, while sometimes keeping a rather precious ancien régime style; from a religious point of view, he only saw a veneer of Christianity in them. Yet it was indisputable to him that they perpetuated European customs, participated in representations of Portugal and *Mwene Puto*, and, above all, promoted them. More than that, he considered that Bezerra and his community had accomplished a "civilizing work" (ibid.: 261).

After many perils that made him order the withdrawal of his subordinate officers in November 1886, Carvalho finally arrived at the *Musumb* in January 1887. He was greeted with patriotic outcry by

Figure 10.3. *Audience of Samabiamb, Lunda, 17 April 1886. Photo by Henrique de Carvalho. © Sociedade de Geografia de Lisboa.*

the Angolan colony, whose new leader was the cousin of the Bezerra brothers, Manuel Correia da Rocha.[47] This "impeccably dressed" black gentleman (Carvalho 1890b: 4:208) told Carvalho that the German explorers had (unsuccessfully) tried to undermine the reputation of the *Mwene Puto* before the *Mwant Yaav*'s court by portraying him as one of the poorest and least powerful kings in Europe. Paul Pogge and Max Buchner had hidden the presence of this Europeanized community in the Lunda capital as much as they could, as that would have put their alleged discovery of a virgin continent into question (Heintze 2011: 100–101). In contrast with most explorers who glorified themselves by peddling this kind of cliché, Carvalho deliberately contradicted it. The Central Africa he described, crossed by trade caravans whose drivers were familiar with the local geography and populations, was made up of monarchical courts exchanging letters in *ambaquista* Portuguese and knowledgeable about European products, to the point of incorporating some of them, beyond recognition, in their own traditions. To be sure, this dimension of Carvalho's work is inseparable from his nationalism, his idealistic cult of the *Pátria*, the Fatherland that "had not taken its eyes off his son . . . when he had been devoured by fever and despair."[48] The fact remains that the descriptive nature of chapters 5 and 6, dedicated to "Indigenous Industry" and "Clothing, Personal Adornments, and Musical Instruments," overrides his tendency to equate borrowing with progress. Alongside the detailed presentation of local handicraft, both in words and through engravings (from drawings he himself had made in Lunda and some photographs),[49] there was room for reference to the uses of china, rifles, earrings, beads, parasols, and needles, not to mention a love for fabrics, which were the main currency to pay for African products and services. The number of foreign products also included American plant species, from tobacco to manioc.

In Carvalho's Lunda, letters and other documents were called *mukanda*. Since the alphabet was far from unknown, the daily hours he spent writing were perceived by his hosts as an undeniable sign of knowledge, if not of learned activities. "He doesn't just walk around," it was said of him; "at night he reads and writes books to get to know the country well" (Carvalho 1890b: 2:298–99). Indigenous perceptions of writing facilitated positive reactions to his ethnographic work:

> The passion and tenacity with which we conducted our research was what struck them most. For example, when in a village, in front of or next to a straw hut, we saw a figure roughly carved with a knife to imitate a man, or a plant arranged with great care, we were never content to know its name. . . . In order to interpret the whole thing properly, we pursued a series of investigations. . . . They were very appreciative of such a request for information and it aroused their curiosity, as they wanted to know what, in comparison, existed in the lands of the Mwene Puto. (Carvalho 1890a: 435–36)

In this passage, Carvalho makes reference to religious practices and conceptions, but he was less successful in studying them. Regarding witchcraft, and particularly the persecution of the accused, his ethnocentric prejudices were counterbalanced, curiously enough, by his evolutionist relativism, according to which Europeans should remember their own past in order to refrain from critique of African beliefs. In the following chapters on "Remarkable Customs," however, he paid attention to *Zambi*, a word the interpreters translated as "God" but that was also applied to crucifixes. To those who would doubt the presence of monotheistic notions in Central Africa, Carvalho anticipated the following reply:

> It can be said, and it is true, that the religious principles I differentiated from fetishism are still poorly defined and are partly due to the influence of Christianity which, since the early days of the Portuguese conquest, had been introduced in the hinterland of Angola and spread throughout the central region. This only proves that the transition was well accepted and perfectly matches the mental state of these peoples. (ibid.: 723)

"The Succession of the Ant Yaav"

The Mwant Yaav never dies. He is always the same.
— Words attributed to the Lunda monarch Yaav Nowej,
eighteenth century (in ibid.: 540)

The "progressive capacities" of the Lunda peoples, of which the adoption of European products and ideas was a barometer, are a dominant theme in Carvalho's monograph. But its highlight is chapter 8, the longest (comprising 144 pages), dedicated to the "Succession of the Ant Yaav."[50] The political history of Lunda kingship had always been his main interest, nay, his obsession, in accordance with his own monarchist worldview and the expedition's goals. The fact remains that this was an appropriate option to the ethnographic context in question, in which dynastic events were clearly a major theme of orally transmitted narratives. The bulk of the chapter was written in Africa during Carvalho's convalescence, based on a selection and collation of hundreds of passages from his journal.[51] An entire notebook was filled under the heading: "Historical notes or collection of notes for the History of the Ant Yaav[52] from 1820 until this date, April 28, 1887. Collection obtained from the best informants and from what I have witnessed as head of this Expedition, Henrique Augusto Dias de Carvalho, Major of the Army of Portugal."[53] Behind this formula was a plethora of sources. While the expedition's goals make it hard to distinguish between political interlocutors and ethnographic informants, he nonetheless made explicit reference to these.

Whether in the journal, historical notebook, or printed chapter, Carvalho sometimes resorted to general formulae, such as: "So say the narrators . . . an informant told me . . . according to informants" (Carvalho 1890a: 539, 548, 554). Some of them showed a greater personal attention or taste for historical narratives, so he also highlighted the special input of this or that figure, whose name might also appear underneath a portrait.[54] Notwithstanding the interpreters' salary, Carvalho always refused to pay his informants. "I had to put him out today," he wrote about an individual whom he had invited to talk about Lunda history but who had asked him, "with an imbecile face, how much I would pay him for it."[55] None other than Prince Samadiamb (figure 3) stands out among his Lunda informants, followed by a former high dignitary called Kalaw,[56] who "was a great connoisseur and had a deep knowledge of the tradition of all these peoples." This man, Carvalho added, "had a blessed memory, he used every occasion for narrations, and it is thanks to him that I obtained many clarifications about the past." When other Lunda elders were asked about old events, they began by saying "as the old man Kalaw said …" in order to show how good the source of their knowledge had been (ibid.: 575). Cokwe and Imbangala informants were, again, important. Here is an example: "This information was given to me by the old Cokwe Mona Kiesa[57] … with whom I lived for almost two months, and who provided me with many data about Cokwe and Lunda from the past. He was an old man of about seventy, and held in great regard among these people … As a hunter, he had lived in the Musumb of Mwant Yaav Nawej"[58] (ibid.: 557). Then, of course, the *ambaquistas*—the Bezerra brothers and Manuel Correia da Rocha, among others—contributed a great deal of information about events they had witnessed or that had been confided to them by the Lunda royal family.[59]

The final version of the chapter, prepared in Lisbon after his return, included more material from his journals concerning older periods of the empire—actually since the reign of the first Mwant Yaav: Ruwej's and Cibind Yirung's son. As he states in the opening paragraph: "The notes I have been able to collect from oral tradition about the succession of Lunda's potentates from the death of Yirung[60] until my return from the Musumb in 1887 … sum up what I was able to ascertain on the subject" (ibid.: 523). Carvalho was aware of the probable gaps in the record, but then again (to the dismay of skeptical scholars who insist on the strictly contemporary, political uses of the past in Central African contexts to the detriment of positive historical reconstructions) he reiterated its historicity:

> As one may imagine, given the lack of the indispensable documents, there must be gaps in the narration, and it is believed that some potentates have been omitted, perhaps because there are no notable events related to them that would cause them to be remembered in the popular memory. Even so, the elements collected do not cease to have their value as testimonies to inform scholars about the main stages in the existence of this important fraction of the great African family that I am concerned with. (ibid.: 523)

Lunda's turbulent political history is presented in an extraordinarily colorful and vivid way, with quotations in direct speech and with details that make it possible to imagine the dramaturgy behind the various accounts. (Some episodes, involving Carvalho, are developed in the travelogue, and he himself used footnotes to refer the reader to the volumes and pages of the travelogue in question on several occasions.)

As Carvalho's exposition of each reign is too long to be reproduced here, let us focus on contemporary events. At the end of 1884, around the time of Carvalho's crossing of the Kwango River, one of Samadiamb's younger brothers, known as Mudib,[61] appropriated the *rukan* and began a reign of terror. Some disgusted courtiers left the *Musumb*, taking refuge in the bush, but others clandestinely planned to replace Mudib with Samadiamb. Emissaries were sent on a mission to transmit an urgent appeal to the prince for putting an end to his long exile, in the hope that his preserved figure would restore the morality of the dynasty and the integrity of the empire, threatened by the intrusion of the Cokwe.

Another faction, however, was preparing an alternative succession to the throne that did not involve bringing Samadiamb back to the *Musumb*; instead, they planned to install a Lunda prince who had been entrusted as a boy to Cokwe potentates, friends of his father's, and who would therefore be in a good position to organize a "Cokwe war" against Mudib. What is certain is that he had no hand in these hosts who were allegedly under his command but who not only killed the *Mwant Yaav* in combat but also razed the *Musumb* and imprisoned thousands of Lunda, ultimately helping to aggravate rather than resolve the political crisis. Carvalho witnessed himself the "manifestations of joy" with which news of Mudib's death was received and how they gave way to a dreadful feeling as some survivors brought more details from the Nkalaany region about the destruction of the capital of the empire. In addition to the kidnapping of high nobility figures, important state insignia had fallen into the possession of the Cokwe—including Mudib's own *rukan*, taken from his corpse.

When Carvalho finally arrived at the *Musumb*—without Samadiamb, who had given up—Carvalho found a court deflated and discouraged, afraid, and even hungry. The Angolan colony suffered as well. The good news was that the *Musumb* was rebuilt in the main, although on smaller dimensions. Mukanza, brother of Samadiamb, was acting as interim *Mwant Yaav*, with a daughter of Samadiamb as *Rukonkish*.

A gilded rococo chair that Carvalho had brought as a gift to the *Mwant Yaav* was solemnly mounted. But the only man to occupy this "throne" was a *Mwant Yaav* who lacked the *rukan* and other state insignia that had been in the possession of the Cokwe since Mudib's death. When Mukanza sat, all nobles present prostrated themselves at his feet and rubbed their chest, arms, and face with earth. On 18 January 1887, Henrique de Carvalho succeeded in signing a treaty with the interim *Mwant Yaav* and the entire court, in which they committed themselves to "never acknowledge any other sovereignty than that of Portugal, under the protectorate of which their grandparents long ago placed all territories governed by them."[62] The Portuguese expedition had to withdraw as soon as possible, since its leader was worn out and disillusioned by the condition of the "once famous great empire" of the *Mwant Yaav*. He had indeed succeeded in renewing Portugal's political influence in Lunda, but in a very different way than he had imagined. In fact, the rococo object sent from Lisbon now represented the fall of two related myths: that of the mighty *Mwant Yaav* and that of the powerful *Mwene Puto*.

Once in Lisbon, Carvalho fought a relentless battle, nationally and internationally, to have Portugal's rights over the Lunda territories recognized.[63] Convinced that his ethnographic monograph satisfied "the most rigorous demands of works of this nature," he sent a letter to the minister of the navy and of overseas affairs in which he emphasized the "urgency" of its publication and its "great interest from a political point of view," in order to show Belgium, Britain, France, and Germany the historic role of Portugal in Central Africa.[64] The Portuguese eventually settled in several of the "civilizing stations" founded by Carvalho's expedition, which greatly expanded the borders of Angola, giving birth to the administrative province of Lunda, of which he, by then colonel, was the first governor.[65]

The Posthumous Destiny of an Excluded Ancestor

In the twentieth century, Belgian ethnographers collected other versions of the Lunda foundational mytho-history of Princess Ruwej and Cibind Yirung, as the Lunda region was eventually divided between Portuguese Angola and the Belgian Congo—into which its historical heartland was incorporated in 1891 (see Bustin 1975). In 1957 the Belgian Africanist and professor of ethnology at the Lovanium University of Leopoldville (Kinshasa), Daniel P. Biebuyck (1925–2019), conducted research at the *Musumb* (then a chieftaincy of the Belgian Congo with local dimensions) through interpreters with whom he spoke in Swahili. In an article in the magazine *Zaïre* in which he did not mention Carvalho's work, this former student of the London School of Economics wrote: "it is astonishing that the powerful group of Lunda still has to be classified among those cultures of which we know practically nothing positive" (Biebuyck 1957: 77). One year later, Belgian colonial administrator Léon Duysters (1900–1985), reacted to Biebuyck's all too brief footnote on previous authors: "Should we infer from this that D. Biebuyck is somewhat averse to using the work of non-experts in ethnological matters? That would be unfortunate" (Duysters 1958: 75). Among several contributions to (Northern) Lunda, Duysters made no reference to Carvalho's work, even if he highlighted an article published in 1937 by District Commissioner Van den Byvang who knew *Etnografia e História Tradicional dos Povos da Lunda* and drew much from it.[66]

The foundational love story of the Lunda empire is perhaps the only (relatively) famous passage of Carvalho's work. Excerpts of *Etnografia e História Tradicional dos Povos da Lunda* were translated by Victor Turner (1920–83) and published in 1955 in *The Rhodes-Livingstone Journal* under the title "A Lunda Love Story and Its Consequences: Selected Texts from Traditions Collected by Henrique Dias de Carvalho at the Court of the Mwantianvwa in 1887."[67] Along with Belgian colonial ethnographies and other sources—including new oral traditions— on Lunda and related contexts, this corpus nourished a scholarly debate of significant proportions, especially in the 1970s and 1980s.

Historians of Africa gathered around tutelary figures such as Jan Vansina (1929–2017) and Joseph C. Miller (1939–2019), who used these ethnographic materials to reconstruct the formation of Central African kingdoms, namely those of Lunda origin; while structural anthropologists led by Luc de Heusch (1927–2012) short-circuited the historical reading of what they considered to be a symbolical construct whose variants occurred within a geographically and ethnically broad mythological cycle: that of the foreign hunter who marries the autochthonous princess and establishes sacred kingship. Further divergences and rapprochements within and between the two camps have complicated the debate.[68] But Carvalho's monograph appears in this literature as a footnote reference (e.g., Vansina 1966: 60–75; Heusch 1972: 182). Besides, the version he documented, according to which Ruwej was the mother of the first *Mwant Yaav*,[69] is not really favored by Luc de Heusch and others who insist on the role of the alien hunter-king Cibind Yirung as a cultural hero and who suspect that Carvalho's sources for this origin myth were not Lunda (Palmeirim 2006: 26, 46). This contention, as we have seen, is not true.

The debate has had its successors to the present day, including the Portuguese anthropologist Manuela Palmeirim, who stresses the import of Carvalho's variant the most. From a structuralist—perhaps unavowedly feminist—perspective, she uses it to surpass a dichotomous reasoning and better appreciate the role of the feminine figure. Ruwej emerges as a contributor to the new sacred kingship on an equal footing with Cibind Yirung, not just as the bearer of previously existing, autochthonous royal insignia but also as the mother of the first emperor (Palmeirim 2006; see also 2016; Heintze 2012: 210). No wonder, then, that Palmeirim is also the one participant in the debate who most explicitly praises Carvalho's monograph as "a most precious ethnographic document" with "a very considerable amount of stimulating data" (Palmeirim 2006: 5–6).

Scholars from Angola and the Democratic Republic of Congo have also taken an interest in early Lunda history, sometimes following alternative epistemologies that stress the endurance of precolonial legacies while highlighting the historicity of the foundational characters and events of the Lunda empire. The lawyer, politician, and local historian Matadiwamba Kamba Mutu Tharcisse (2009), himself of Lunda/Ruwund descent, combines varied sources—including new oral traditions—in ways that challenge the debates of Western anthropologists and historians, at least implicitly. Carvalho's work, however, is not necessarily taken into account. In 2012 an international conference on Queen Ruwej took place at the university named after this mytho-historical character, Universidade Lueji A'Nkonde, which had been established three years earlier in the Angolan district of Northern Lunda. During the conference, Carvalho's work was mentioned by one participant in particular, the acclaimed Angolan writer Pepetela, author of *Lueji—O Nascimento de um Império* (2004), a novel whose heroes are Ruwej and Cibind Yirung: "In composing the book, I was helped by the writings of authors who researched Lunda and its history, among which I highlight Henrique de Carvalho, perhaps the first European to collect the data of oral tradition on the spot, but already in the late nineteenth century" (Pepetela 2013: 30).[70]

The radical decolonization of the discipline as practiced today in Portugal implies a disregard of Carvalho by the anthropological community, with a few exceptions, in particular Manuela Palmeirim. (Carvalho as a primary source for historians of Africa is another matter.) One has to take into account that the Portuguese colonial empire was the last to fall—only after the Carnation Revolution of 1974—and that the country endured the longest fascist-type dictatorship in Europe (1926–74). During Salazar's regime (called Estado Novo) Carvalho was included in the "pantheon" of "overseas heroes" of the late nineteenth and the early twentieth centuries, and a few hagiographic works about him were produced. Even before that, in 1923, his name had been attributed to the capital of the Lunda district. It is still possible today, however, within certain Portuguese scholarly institutions, to praise Carvalho in terms that contrast with the postcolonial critique of the anthropological and ethnographic production of his time. The Geographical Society of Lisbon plays a leading role in this regard. This institution's investment in its own historical legacy culminated in a state-funded project on Carvalho, resulting, among others, in an exhibition and a collective volume (Aires-Barros and Cantinho 2012). Without aiming at an assessment of Carvalho's import as an excluded ancestor on the international level, the following passage by the project's head, Manuela Cantinho, sounds more like an aspiration than a synthesis of his actual place in the history of anthropology in Portugal:

> The innovative character of the collecting carried out by the Portuguese expedition to Lunda allows us to consider it as a crucial moment in the history of Portuguese colonial anthropology, similar to what would happen a decade later with the Cambridge Anthropological Expedition to Torres Straits . . . which came to be identified as a milestone in the history of British anthropology. (Cantinho 2012: 130)[71]

As stated above, the dimensions and meticulousness of Carvalho's work contribute, in a way, to Carvalho's invisibility. Beatrix Heintze, a historian specializing in the region, goes even further and states that "in terms of the number and variety of details presented there, as well as its multiple dimensions, the monumental work of Henrique Dias de Carvalho has so far been not only insufficiently recognized, but completely ignored outside the Portuguese-speaking world" (2011: 97). Heintze has worked for many years to achieve recognition for the importance of Carvalho. As his staunchest defendant, she writes:

> Anyone who is not particularly interested in details will soon feel overwhelmed by Carvalho's accounts. And even scholars of late nineteenth-century eastern Angola and southern Congo, in spite of being eager for knowledge, seem to have capitulated at some point in the face of his writings. This hesitation is indicated by the fact that, whenever Carvalho is cited as a source at all, reference is basically made to his ethnographic-historical synthesis only. (Heintze 2011: 96–97)

She laments the fact that the all-too-brief references to his work disregard the four-volume travelogue—not to mention the eight handwritten volumes of the original journal, the systematic examination of which "has only just begun" (Heintze 2011: 95)—and only concern the single-volume *Etnografia e História Tradicional dos Povos da Lunda*. Moreover, as we have seen, only a small fraction of it is usually taken into account: the foundational myth of Ruwej and Cibind Ilunga translated by Victor Turner. Therefore, this book in itself represents a challenge to twenty-first-century readers, as the present chapter has tried to demonstrate.

Conclusion

There is no doubt that Carvalho went to the limits of human capabilities in his scientific and political efforts in the country of Lunda, driven by an exacerbated form of nationalism and imperialism. It is no wonder that he became so ill in late March and early April 1887 that his fevers caused a coma and brought him on the verge of death, yet with full awareness in brief glimpses of lucidity. His head throbbed, and his own voice sounded like that of a four-year-old child as he still managed to add a few words to his journal by dictating them to Manuel Correia da Rocha on 31 March: "Our Lady of the Martyrs and my Jesus, the Savior of the World, do not abandon me here after so many works and sacrifices. May they let me go to die in my country beside my own, and may I see all those I have left."[72] As stated at the beginning of the present chapter, this is when he decided to write *Etnografia e História Tradicional dos Povos da Lunda*. In the last chapter, titled "Concluding Remarks," Carvalho resumed several interconnected themes of the book, from the "good character" of the Lunda peoples to their "progressive capabilities" as measured by their "ease of adaptation to our ways and customs" (Carvalho 1890a: 667). But the final pages of the volume are dedicated to two orphan boys from Lunda who were among those who stayed by his side and most cared about him during his illness. Carvalho adopted them and took them with him to Lisbon. As they did not speak Portuguese and had "all the native habits" (ibid.: 730), their later transformation through education in Lisbon, even their portrait dressed up as little sailors, were the living proof, so Carvalho believed, of his own contention.

Carvalho unsettles the history of anthropology for many reasons, not in the least by his attention to historical events, which in practice meant giving anthropological primacy to the individual and resulted in complex descriptions of (and insightful observations into) Lunda politics, both in the contemporary present and in the recent past. The ethnographic epiphany Carvalho had while convalescing may be seen as a symbolical event, representing the emergence of the monograph from the travelogue. At the same time, it demonstrates that the two genres not only coexisted but had powerful communicating vessels between them. Furthermore, the tension between expeditionary and intensive fieldwork is clearly brought into question by this case study. The same applies to other alleged dichotomies, such as evolutionism versus particularism. The monograph's undeniably ethnocentric and imperialistic motives appear to be inseparable from its relativistic and antiracist dimensions. A man of his time, with paternalistic attitudes toward Africans, Carvalho did, however, anticipate certain aspects of the modern anthropological sensibility. If he didn't belong to a minor tradition of a peripheral country, he might have had a better chance of being recognized as one of the important forerunners of the ethnographic revolution.

In his monograph, Henrique de Carvalho never uses the word *taboo*, whose international repercussion is associated mostly with *The Golden Bough* (1890), the celebrated anthropological bestseller published in the same year as his own ethnographic historiography. In the following, expanded editions, James George Frazer (1854–1941), ever the polyglot, might have perused Carvalho's ethnography—if only he knew about it—for its abundant data on sacred kingship. A comparison between the two men and their respective works would be meaningful. Who does not know Frazer's *The Golden Bough*? But the invisibility of Carvalho's *Etnografia e História Tradicional dos Povos da Lunda* also stands for the oblivion of ethnographers before Malinowski whose place in the history of anthropology has been overshadowed by their contemporary armchair anthropologists.

Carvalho's monograph contrasts profoundly with Malinowski's *Argonauts of the Western Pacific* (published thirty-two years later) both in terms of structure and of style. It lacks explicit holistic connections. But we may say without a fear of presentism that its opening pages sound like a nineteenth-century version of Malinowski's charter myth. One of the local proverbs Carvalho collected encapsulates the greatest lesson he brought from Africa: "When among the Lunda, do as the Lunda do; when among the Cokwe, do as the Cokwe do" (Carvalho 1890b: 2:667). If Carvalho was a forerunner, though, this is not just because of his methodological reflections on the need for long stays, on the importance of learning the native languages, and on stripping oneself of prejudices. He actually pioneered and gave more depth of time to another, later theme of Malinowski's anthropology: culture contact in colonial Africa. To be sure, he did so in strident nationalistic terms, by claiming the centuries-old Portuguese influence. There is, however, a maxim of no other than Prince Samadiamb that reveals, again, a layer of local wisdom grafted into the anthropological thought of Carvalho: "Mwene Puto is white, he has his customs, and we blacks have ours."[73] Several passages of his diary confirm the Lunda perception of European (namely Portuguese) ways, but the following is particularly revealing of a mutual projection, a kind of chained understanding of each other's differences:

> They then manifested their joy, kneeling down and clapping their hands together and rubbing their arms with earth. All this time I was holding my hat in my hand. *They told the interpreter that because of this gesture they knew I understood that they were thanking me.*[74]

Frederico Delgado Rosa is a lecturer at NOVA University, Lisbon (Portugal) and a researcher in the history of anthropology at CRIA: Centre for Research in Anthropology (Lisbon) and HERITAGES (Paris). He is the author, among other works, of *L'Âge d'or du totémisme* (CNRS Éditions, 2003); *Exploradores portugueses e reis africanos* (Portuguese explorers and African kings, A Esfera dos Livros, 2013, with Filipe Verde); and *Elsdon Best, l'ethnographe immémorial* (Les Carnets de Bérose, 2018). He is currently co-director, with Christine Laurière, of *BEROSE International Encyclopedia of the Histories of Anthropology* and co-convenor, with Fabiana Dimpflmeier, of the "History of Anthropology Network" within the European Association of Social Anthropologists (EASA).

Notes

1. Carvalho's full name and rank was Henrique Augusto Dias de Carvalho, infantry major of the army of Portugal, later promoted colonel.
2. On Carvalho's political terminology as applied to the Lunda case, see below.
3. AHU-SEMU-DGU-ANG 1154, 02/04/1887.
4. AHU-SEMU-DGU-ANG 1092. A fifth notebook was the prototype for his monograph on the Lunda language (1890c). See below.
5. This word is spelled in various ways, such as *Mwant Yaav*, *Mwant Yav*, *Mwantayaav*, *Mwantianvwa*, *Muatianfu*, etc. This problem is alleviated but still unsolved today. From the beginning, Carvalho paid special attention to the etymology of the word. Relying on linguistic and historical arguments, in persistent dialog with his informants, he maintained that *Muatiânvua* was a compound word and should not be transliterated into two separate terms (see Carvalho 1890a: 74). Considering, however, that Carvalho's efforts to make Lunda words more readable to a Portuguese readership (except in his monograph on Lunda language, 1890c;

see below) are of no consequence here, I shall use the *Mwant Yaav* version prevailing among specialists (see Palmeirim 2006: xiii–xvi; 18n1), plus *Ant Yaav* for the plural. Carvalho's transliterations of this and other Lunda/Uruwund terms appear in endnotes between quotation marks.

6. Carvalho published other works, both political and scientific.
7. Instructions of the minister of the navy and of overseas affairs to Major Henrique de Carvalho (28/04/1884), as quoted in Carvalho (1890b: 1:35–42).
8. AHU-SEMU-DGU-ANG 1091. Letter of H. de Carvalho (9 June 1890) donating the tattered expedition flag to the Geographical Society of Lisbon, where it stands to this day.
9. For a critique of this perspective, see Clarence-Smith 1979.
10. See Manuscript Collections below. See Heintze (1990, 2011), Cantinho (2012: 148–55). The photographs were taken by Captain Sertório de Aguiar, but all captions were written by Carvalho. The European members of the expedition, apart from Carvalho, were the army pharmacist Agostinho Sizenando Marques (?–1923), deployed from the colony of São Tomé and Príncipe, and artillery captain (and photographer) Manuel Sertório de Aguiar (1851–?), head of the municipality of Massangano, Angola. The human resources and the logistics of the expedition are described in detail by Cantinho (2012: 29–43).
11. Carvalho tried, at some point, to follow the life cycle ethnographic template, but he did not persevere with this intention.
12. Carvalho opened the volume with a quote from the antiracist work of the Portuguese Africanist António Francisco Nogueira (1834–?), *A Raça Negra sob o Ponto de Vista da Civilização Africana*, published in Lisbon in 1880. This standpoint was not a matter of course in Portugal, where some scholars held racist views. In order to challenge those who asserted the mental or emotional inferiority of Africans and their inability to improve their conditions, Carvalho referred to examples of black individuals who had attained positions of social and intellectual prestige in both Portugal and Brazil.
13. AHU-SEMU-DGU-ANG 1152, 01/12/1885
14. The *Musumb* had no fixed location; it could be successively rebuilt in different places, but it had to be in the same region, around the Nkalaany River, which was held to be the historical core of the empire.
15. On his return to Portugal, Carvalho published *Método prático para falar a lingua da Lunda* (1890c).
16. AHU-SEMU-DGU-ANG 1092.
17. In Portuguese: *de me tornar gentio*.
18. In Portuguese, *sua cultura*.
19. "To be exact," Kroeber wrote, "he [Tylor] already had used the word 'culture' . . . six years earlier in his *Researches*, as if trying it out on the British public. He may have got it from the German ethnographer, Klemm, whom he read and cited. Klemm spells the word with a C—

Cultur—in his 1843 as well as his 1854 book. The word appears to have been in general German usage at that period with its modern meaning, and was in no sense handled then like a new coinage. I do not know precisely how far back the German word *Cultur* goes with its modern scientific meaning" (1949: 183).

20. Data from different ethnic groups are mixed up.

21. He explicitly avoided universal comparativism, namely between African and ancient customs, as this would deviate from his descriptive goal.

22. Not to be confused with Friedrich Max Müller.

23. Chapter 3, on "Ethnic Features," is dedicated to observable physical traits.

24. *Potentado* can also apply, more or less metaphorically, to an economic powerholder, a great enterprise, for example.

25. It is beyond the scope of the present chapter to examine later criticism, by professional anthropologists of the twentieth and twenty-first centuries, of terms such as *state* and *empire* as applied to African chiefdom (see Skalník 2009).

26. "Luéji" or "Luéji-ià-Cônti."

27. "Quingúri."

28. "Suana Murunda."

29. Cibind: hunter. "Cibinda/Chibinda Ilunga."

30. "Bângalas" and "Quiocos." Mention should also be made to the Ndembu, or Southern Lunda (see note 67) and to Kazemb, the eastern potentate of Lunda origin to which Carvalho dedicates some passages, mostly based on the testimony of a Portuguese officer, António Gamito (1806–66), who had lived at the Kazemb's *Musumb* in 1831–32.

31. Or Lourenço Bezerra Correia Pinto. Dates unknown. All other dates unknown if unmentioned.

32. On the Bezerra family, see Heintze (2004 [2002]: 98 et seq). According to Carvalho, António Bezerra had children everywhere, and this reinforced his importance as a cultural mediator. Let us also mention António Bezerra's brother, Agostinho Bezerra, and wife, Maria Bezerra, who was Lunda. "Maria de Bezerra helped us in our research," Carvalho wrote (1890a: 3:110; see also "Álbum da Expedição ao Muatiânvua," folio 29, verso, caption n. 3, National Library of Portugal; and B. Heintze, 2004 [2002]: 102). This African mediator checked and corrected her husband's propensity to mix different languages.

33. AHU-SEMU-DGU-ANG 1150, 24/08/1884; see Carvalho (1890a: 578).

34. "Muatiânvuas"; AHU-SEMU-DGU-ANG 1151, 16/04/1885.

35. The Cokwe had gradually encroached on Lunda territory during the nineteenth century. The Imbangala informants were caravan leaders associated with the *Kasanje*, the great potentate allegedly founded by Kinguri, Ruwej's brother. In spite of their formal allegiance to Angola, the Imbangala controlled the passage of the Kwango river and their hold on trade with the Lunda was a threat to the Portuguese.

36. "Lucuoquexe."

37. "Suana Murunda."
38. A third woman represented the role of the mother of the current *Mwant Yaav*, and although she could be his own mother, she was not necessarily maternally related.
39. This was also the case in the original notebook (AHU-SEMU-DGU-ANG 1092).
40. "Xa Madiamba."
41. AHU-SEMU-DGU-ANG 1157, folio 35.
42. Luso-African would be a more consensual term today.
43. The Imbangala invasion of Angola, according to Joseph Miller (1976): see below.
44. AHU-SEMU-DGU-ANG 1152, 23/12/1885; also 10/12/1885.
45. In this he was in contrast with other, more famous Portuguese figures who emulated the European model of the heroic white male explorer, most of all Alexandre de Serpa Pinto (1846–1900), whose *How I Crossed Africa* (1881) was first published in English in London.
46. The Jesuits were expulsed from Portugal by the Marquis of Pombal, prime minister of Portugal and "enlightened despot" in the name of King Joseph I.
47. Dates unknown.
48. Letter of H. de Carvalho to the Geographical Society of Lisbon, 9 June 1890 (AHU-SEMU-DGU-ANG 1091).
49. The original drawings are at the Overseas Historical Archive (Lisbon), AHU-ICONm-001-DD921. Carvalho dispatched many objects to Lisbon that were eventually incorporated into the Museum of the Geographical Society of Lisbon, where they remain to this day (Cantinho 2012: 155).
50. "Muatiânvuas."
51. Also from his official correspondence, namely to the Ministry of the Navy and Overseas Affairs. AHU-SEMU-DGU-ANG 1149, 1155, 1157.
52. "A-t-iânvua."
53. AHU-SEMU-DGU-ANG 1092.
54. This was possibly a sign of gratitude. Another way to compensate the most helpful was to grant them honorary patents of the Portuguese army.
55. AHU-SEMU-DGU-ANG 1152, 28/12/1885.
56. "Calau." Dates unknown.
57. "Mona Quiessa." Dates unknown.
58. "Noéji." Dates unknown.
59. While in Malanje, Carvalho had also had the occasion of conversing about dynastic history with Lunda envoys who happened to be there. But at that early point, he struggled with linguistic misunderstandings and the extreme complexity of the subject: "Wanting to inquire about the Ant Yaav succession . . . I found myself caught in a web that I may not unravel until later" (AHU-SEMU-DGU-ANG 1150, 10/07/1884).

60. "Ilunga."
61. "Muriba." Dates unknown.
62. AHU-SEMU-DGU-ANG 1157, folio 35v.
63. An event with great impact on Portugal's contemporary history was the British Ultimatum of January 1890, which put an end to the old Portuguese dream of uniting Angola and Mozambique. This basically concerned Rhodesia, not Lunda (claimed by Leopold II), but the climate of Carvalho's actions was one of injured national pride.
64. 14 June 1890, AHU-SEMU-DHU-ANG 1091.
65. Nevertheless, Carvalho served as such only between 1895 and 1896 because, following his opposition to a military campaign against the Kasanje potentate, he was unjustly accused of deviating state funds.
66. Duysters also added his own version of the Lunda charter myth, which he had collected in 1927. This also applies to the Belgian Jesuit missionary Yvon Struyf (1876–1950), who published a version (1948) corroborating Carvalho's. I omit other references for reasons of space (see Palmeirim 2006: 17; Nziem 1999: 643n2), but mention should be made of the German ethnologist Hermann Baumann (1902–72), who led an expedition to Lunda on behalf of the Ethnological Museum in Berlin and acknowledged that Carvalho was the best older connoisseur of Lunda, "der beste ältere Kenner Lundas" (1935: 224).
67. The Ndembu, made famous in anthropology by Turner, are southern Lunda and historically descendants of the northern Lunda/Aruwund. For this reason, Turner's monographs include occasional references to Carvalho.
68. Due to lack of space, an exhaustive version of the bibliography in question is not given. See Palmeirim (2006: 40–44).
69. As opposed to other versions stating that she was sterile and that it was her husband's second wife who gave birth to the first *Mwant Yaav*.
70. In websites and documentation associated with a political movement that claims autonomy for the "Lunda/Cokwe nation," it is possible to find references to the works and political treaties signed by Henrique de Carvalho, a matter that goes beyond the scope of this chapter.
71. It is paradoxical that the history of Portuguese anthropology during the age of empire was (or has been considered) a nation-building project, mostly focused on the metropole's peasantry, rather than an empire-building one (Leal 2008). However, Portuguese colonial anthropology and ethnology is getting increased attention. The actual presence of Carvalho in works by twentieth-century Portuguese anthropologists and ethnographers, both professional and amateur, has still to be meticulously studied.
72. AHU-SEMU-DGU-ANG 1157, 31/03/1887; see 1890a.
73. Samadiamb, as quoted by Carvalho, AHU-SEMU DGU-ANG 1152 (11/09/1885).
74. AHU-SEMU-DGU-ANG 1150, 13/07/1884 (my emphasis).

References

Manuscript Collections

Arquivo Histórico Ultramarino (Overseas Historical Archive), Lisbon.
Carvalho, Henrique de, 1884–87. Diário da "Expedição Portuguesa ao
Muatiânvua" (journal of the Portuguese expedition to the Mwant
Yaav), 8 vols.: AHU-SEMU-DGU-ANG 1150 (1884); 1151 (1885/I);
1152 (1885/II); 1145 (1886/I); 1146 (1886/II); 1156 (1886/III); 1153
(1886/IV); 1154 (1887)
Carvalho, Henrique de, 1886–87. Ethnographic manuscripts: AHU-
SEMU-DGU-ANG 1092
Correspondence and other documents related to the Portuguese expedi-
tion to the Mwant Yaav (1884–96): AHU-SEMU-DGU-ANG 1091
Official documents of the Portuguese expedition to the Mwant Yaav:
AHU-SEMU-DGU-ANG 1149 (1884–85); 1155 (1885–86); 1157
(1884–87)
Iconography, Portuguese Expedition to the Mwant Yaav: AHU-ICONm-
001-DD921
Sociedade de Geografia de Lisboa (Geographical Society of Lisbon, Portu-
gal); and Biblioteca Nacional de Portugal (National Library, Portugal).
Carvalho, Henrique de, and Manuel Sertório de Aguiar (phot.), 1890.
"Álbum da Expedição ao Muatiânvua," Sociedade de Geografia de
Lisboa; and Biblioteca Nacional de Portugal, E.A. 95 P.

Published Sources

Aires-Barros, Luís, and Manuela Cantinho, eds. 2012. *Memórias de um Ex-
plorador: A Colecção Henrique de Carvalho da Sociedade de Geografia
de Lisboa*. Lisboa: Sociedade de Geografia de Lisboa.
Baumann, Hermann. 1935. *Lunda: Bei Bauern und Jägern in Inner-Angola;
Ergebnisse der Angola-Expedition des Museums für Völkerkunde, Berlin*.
Berlin: Würfel Verlag.
Biebuyck, Daniel. 1957. "Fondements de l'organisation politique des Lunda
du Mwaantayaav dans le territoire de Kapanga." *Zaïre* 11(8): 787–817.
Buchner, Max. 1879–81. "Die Buchner'sche Expedition." *Mitteilungen der
Afrikanischen Gesellschaft in Deutschland* 1: 222–46; 2: 44–51, 129–30,
147–78; 3: 88–95.
———. 1882. "Über seine Reise in das Lunda-Reich, 1879–1882." *Verhand-
lungen der Geselschaft für Erdkunde zu Berlin* 9: 77–103.
———. 1883. "Das Reich des Mwata Yamvo und seine Nachbarländer."
Deutsche Geographische Blätter 7: 56–67.
Bunzl, Matti 1996 "Franz Boas and the Humboldtian Tradition: From
Volksgeist and *Nationalcharakter* to an Anthropological Concept of Culture." In *Volksgeist as Method and Ethic: Essays on Boasian Ethnography
and the German Anthropological Tradition*, edited by George W. Stock-

ing, Jr., 17–78. Madison, WI: University of Wisconsin Press (History of Anthropology 8).

Bustin, Édouard. 1975. *Lunda under Belgian Rule: The Politics of Ethnicity,* Cambridge, MA: Harvard University Press.

Byvang, M. Van den. 1937. "Notice historique sur les Baluunda." *Congo* 1(4): 426–38.

Cantinho, Manuela. 2012. "In Memoriam." In *Memórias de um Explorador: A Colecção Henrique de Carvalho da Sociedade de Geografia de Lisboa,* edited by L. Aires-Barros and M. Cantinho, 15–160. Lisbon: Sociedade de Geografia de Lisboa.

Carvalho, Henrique Augusto Dias de. 1890a. *Etnografia e história tradicional dos povos da Lunda.* Lisbon: Imprensa Nacional.

———. 1890b [1890–94]. *Descrição da viagem à mussumba do Muatiânvua.* 4 vols. Lisbon: Imprensa Nacional.

———. 1890c. *Método prático para falar a língua da Lunda contendo narrações históricas dos diversos povos.* Lisbon: Imprensa Nacional.

Clarence-Smith, W. G. 1979. "The Myth of Uneconomic Imperialism: The Portuguese in Angola, 1836–1926." *Journal of Southern African Studies* 5(2): 165–80.

Carvalho, João Augusto Dias de. 1975. *Henrique de Carvalho: Uma Vida ao serviço da pátria.* Lisbon: Liga dos Combatentes.

Cunnison, Ian (trans.), and António Gamito. 1960. *King Kazembe and the Marave, Cheva, Bisa, Bemba, Lunda and Other Peoples of Southern Africa.* Lisbon: Junta de Investigações do Ultramar.

Duysters, Léon. 1958. "Histoire des Aluunda." *Problèmes d'Afrique Centrale* 40: 79–98.

Gamito, António. 1854. *O Muata Cazembe e os Povos Maraves, Chévas, Muízas, Muembas, Lundas e Outros da África Austral: Diário da Expedição Portuguesa Comandada pelo Major Monteiro . . . Redigida pelo Major A. C. P. Gamito.* Lisbon: Imprensa Nacional.

Frazer, James George. 1890. *The Golden Bough: A Study in Comparative Religion.* London: Macmillan & Co.

Graça, Joaquim Rodrigues. 1890 [1867]. "Expedição ao Muatiânvua. Diário." *Boletim da Sociedade de Geografia de Lisboa* 8–9: 365–466. [Originally published as "Descrição da viagem feita de Luanda com destino às cabeceiras do Rio Sena," *Anais do Conselho Ultramarino* (1867): 101–45].

Gregorio, Mario A. di. 2002. "Reflections of a Nonpolitical Naturalist: Ernst Haeckel, Wilhelm Bleek, Friedrich Müller and the Meaning of Language." *Journal of the History of Biology* 35(1): 79–109.

Hammond, Richard J. 1966. *Portugal and Africa, 1815–1910: A Study in Uneconomic Imperialism.* Stanford, CA: Stanford University Press.

Heintze, Beatrix. 1990. "In Pursuit of a Chameleon: Early Ethnographic Photography from Angola in Context." *History in Africa* 17: 131–56.

———. 2004 [2002] *Pioneiros africanos: Caravanas de carregadores na África Centro-Ocidental (entre 1850 e 1890).* Lisbon: Caminho. [Portuguese ed.

of *Afrikanische Pioniere: Trägerkarawanen im westlichen Zentralafrika (ca. 1850–1890)*. Frankfurt am Main: Lembeck, 2002].

———. 2007. *Deutsche Forschungsreisenden in Angola: Ethnographische Aneignungen zwischen Sklavenhandel, Kolonialismus und Wissenschaft*. Frankfurt am Main: Verlag Otto Lembeck. [Exp. and rev. ed. of *Ethnographische Aneignungen: Deutsche Forschungsreisende in Angola*. Frankfurt am Main: Verlag Otto Lembeck, 1999].

———. 2011 "A Rare Insight into African Aspects of Angolan History: Henrique Dias de Carvalho's Records of his Lunda Expedition, 1880–1884." *Portuguese Studies Review* 19(1–2): 93–113.

———. 2012. "Casamentos Políticos na África Centro-Ocidental: As Averiguações de Henrique Dias de Carvalho (1884–1888)." In *Memórias de um Explorador: A Colecção Henrique de Carvalho da Sociedade de Geografia de Lisboa*, edited by L. Aires-Barros and M. Cantinho, 207–20. Lisbon: Sociedade de Geografia de Lisboa.

Heusch, Luc de. 1972. *Le Roi ivre ou l'origine de l'État*. Paris: Gallimard.

Hovelacque, Abel. 1877. *La Linguistique*. Paris: C. Reinwald.

Kalmar, Ivan. 1987. "The Völkerpsychologie of Lazarus and Steinthal and the Modern Concept of Culture." *Journal of the History of Ideas* 48: 671–90.

Kroeber, Alfred L. 1949. "The Concept of Culture in Science." *Journal of General Education* 3(3): 182–96.

Leal, João. 2008, "The Hidden Empire: Peasants, Nation Building and the Empire in Portuguese Anthropology." In *Recasting Culture and Space in Iberian Contexts*, edited by Shawn Parkhurst and Sharon Roseman, 35–53. New York: SUNY Press.

Martins, Joaquim de Oliveira. 1880. *Elementos de Antropologia*. Lisbon: Bertrand.

———. 1882. *Sistema dos Mitos Religiosos*. Lisbon: Bertrand.

Matadiamba, Kamba Mutu Tharcisse. 2009. *Espace lunda et identités en Afrique centrale: Lieux de mémoire*. Paris: L'Harmattan.

Miller, Joseph Calder. 1976. *Kings and Kingsmen: Early Mbundu States in Angola*. Oxford: Clarendon.

———. 1988. *Way of Death: Merchant Capitalism and the Angolan Slave Trade 1730–1830*. Madison: University of Wisconsin Press.

Nogueira, António Francisco. 1880. *A Raça Negra sob o Ponto de Vista da Civilização da África: Usos e Costumes de Alguns Povos Gentílicos do Interior de Mossâmedes e as Colónias Portuguesas*. Lisbon: Tipografia Nova Minerva.

Nziem, Nadaywel È. 1999. "Le Système politique luba et lunda: émergence et expansion." In *L'Afrique du XVIe au XVIIIe siècle (Histoire générale de l'Afrique*, vol. 5), edited by B. A. Ogot, 643–64. Paris: Éditions de l'UNESCO.

Palmeirim, Manuela. 2006. *Of Alien Kings and Perpetual Kin: Contradiction and Ambiguity in Ruwund (Lunda) Symbolic Thought*. Wantage (Oxon): Sean Kingston Publishing.

———. 2016. "Do 'Culture Heroes' Exist? A Dialogue with Luc de Heusch on the Limits of the Structuralist Approach to Myth." *SAGE Open* 6(2): 1–9.

Pepetela. 2004. *Lueji—O Nascimento de um império*. Luanda: Editorial Nzila.

———. 2013. "A Escrita de *Lueji—O Nascimento de um império*." In *A Rainha Lueji A'Nkonde e o Império Lunda. Actas da Conferência Internacional sobre a Rainha Lueji A'Nkonde (19 a 21 de Outubro de 2012)*, edited by S. C. Victorino et al., 28–33. Centro Urbano do Dundo: Lueji Editora, Universidade Lueji A'Nkonde, CEDES—Centro de Estudos de Desenvolvimento Social.

Pinto, Alexandre de Serpa. 1881. *How I Crossed Africa: From the Atlantic to the Indian Ocean*. Translated from the author's manuscript by A. Elwes. London: Sampson Low & Co.

Pogge, Paul. 1880. *Im Reich des Muata Jamwo: Tagebuch meiner im Auftrage der Deutschen Gesellschaft zur Erforschung Aequatorial-Afrika's in die Lunda-Staaten unternommenen Reise*. Berlin: Dietrich Reimer Verlag (Beiträge zur Entdeckungsgeschichte Afrikas 3).

Santos, Maria Emília Madeira. 1998. *Nos Caminhos de África: Serventia e Posse; Angola Século XIX*. Lisbon: Instituto de Investigação Científica Tropical.

Skalník, Peter. 2009. "Early State Concept in Anthropological Theory." *Social Evolution & History* 8(1): 5–24.

Stocking, George W., Jr. 1963. "Mathew Arnold, E. B. Tylor, and the Uses of Invention." *American Anthropologist* 65(3): 783–99.

———. 1966 "Franz Boas and the Culture Concept in Historical Perspective." *American Anthropologist* 68(4): 867–82.

Struyf, Yvon, 1948. "Kahemba: Envahisseurs Badjok et conquérants Balunda." *Zaïre* 2(4): 351–90.

Tylor, Edward B. 1871. *Primitive Culture: Researches into the Development of Mythology, Philosophy, Religion, Art, and Custom*. 2 vols. London: John Murray.

Turner, Victor (trans.), and Henrique de Carvalho. 1955. "A Lunda Love Story and Its Consequences: Selected Texts from Traditions Collected by Henrique Dias de Carvalho at the Court of the Mwantianvwa in 1887." *Rhodes-Livingstone Journal* 19: 1–26.

Urry, James. 1998. Comment on Susan Wright, "The Politicization of 'Culture'" [On Tylor's Definition of "Culture"]. *Anthropology Today* 14(2): 23.

Vansina, Jan. 1966. *Kingdoms of the Savanna (A History of Central African States until the European Occupation)*. Madison: University of Wisconsin Press.

Vellut, Jean-Luc. 1972. "Notes sur le Lunda et la frontière luso-africaine (1700–1900)." *Études d'histoire africaine* 3: 61–166.

Vermeulen, Han F. 2015. *Before Boas: The Genesis of Ethnography and Ethnology in the German Enlightenment*. Lincoln: University of Nebraska Press.

11

"Do in the Tundra as the Tundra-Dwellers Do"

Maria Czaplicka, Her Yenisei Expedition (1914–15), and *My Siberian Year* (1916)

Grażyna Kubica

The Polish-British scholar Maria Czaplicka (1884–1921) organized and led the Yenisei Expedition to north-central Siberia, starting in May 1914, just before the outbreak of World War I.[1] Being a trained geographer and anthropologist, Czaplicka was well prepared for this task. Moreover, before going to the field herself, she had studied the ethnographic work of Russian and Polish researchers in Siberia, mostly political exiles, and published *Aboriginal Siberia: A Study in Social Anthropology* in 1914. In the summer, the expedition stayed at the mouth of the Yenisei River, and during the winter it covered the vast territory between the Yenisei and Lena Rivers. Its aim was to collect ethnographic data, gather collections for museums, and make anthropometric measurements. On the one hand, its ethnographic results were modest, considering that only some academic articles were published and the field materials were never fully processed due to the early death of Czaplicka at the age of thirty-six. On the other hand, Czaplicka wrote a series of magazine articles, as well as her travelogue *My Siberian Year* (1916b), using ethnographic data collected during the research. This travelogue is a good example of literary ethnographic writing, which I understand to mean a form of literary work created on the basis of the field experience of researchers. Czaplicka's texts went beyond the framework of "science" and were written for a wider audience in addition to regular academic papers (and sometimes instead of them). The distinguishing feature was the interesting literary form of the work (drawing attention and providing aesthetic pleasure to readers) and the wide audience to whom the work was addressed (Kubica 2020b).

In her travelogue as a literary and reflexive ethnography, complemented by a few academic articles and examples of handwritten archival material, including her correspondence, we can depict anthropological issues that were rarely addressed by contemporary anthropological texts and monographs, such as the everyday experience of fieldwork, the role of local collaborators (Sibiriaks, Aboriginals, and political exiles), and the anthropologist's relations with Indigenous people. Czaplicka's legacy invites historiographical contextualization and inspires contemporary questions on the intersubjective experience of fieldwork as presented in her various ethnographic texts. Engaging and evocative, but also informative and sometimes educational, her writings reveal intensive tones in spite of the extensive nature of an expeditionary survey. The concept of multisited fieldwork might be appropriate here, as she was actually doing participant observation in different times and places in her expedition. The title of one of her articles, "On the Track of the Tungus"[2] (1917), encapsulates these intertwined dimensions of Czaplicka's ethnographic praxis, which may be reassessed today as sensitive if not visionary.

This chapter is one result of my long-time research on the biographies of several Poles who became British and American anthropologists: Bronisław Malinowski (e.g., Kubica 1988), his friend and colleague, Maria Czaplicka (Kubica 2020a), and his students Andrzej Waligórski (1908–74) and Feliks Gross (1906–2006), and also Alicja Iwańska (1918–96). In my attempts to trace their work I am following a critical feminist approach to the history of anthropology (Cole 2003), which enables "really challenging reflexivity" (Kuper 1991: 129), analyzes political dimensions of anthropology's history (Vincent 1991; Mills 2008), and rehabilitates "excluded ancestors" (Handler 2000).

From Warsaw to London and Oxford: A Glimpse into Czaplicka's Early Career

Before relating how an intrepid and knowledgeable woman, as Czaplicka was, went to Siberia, I have to sketch the historical and biographical context of her expedition.[3] During the long nineteenth century, Poland was deprived of statehood, and its territory partitioned among its neighboring empires, Russia, Prussia, and Austria. Warsaw was the capital of the Russian part of partitioned Poland, where the political situation was the most difficult: public education was only done in Russian, and national activities were persecuted. This led to several military uprisings, which were unsuccessful but caused thousands of Poles to be banned from the country or sent to Siberia in exile, and their estates confiscated. These political and economic factors caused the impoverishment of the important social class, *szlachta* (landed gentry), whose representatives had to move to towns and start professional careers benefitting from their main capital — education. This is how the class of intelligentsia originated, a typical and specific social formation in Eastern Europe.

Maria Antonina Czaplicka was born in Warsaw in 1884 into a family that proudly possessed their coat of arms but had long lost their family estates. Her father worked as a railway official. She attended one of Warsaw's private girls' schools (1894–1902) and later prepared herself for being a teacher. She had to pass a school leaving exam in a boys' grammar school (girls' schools did not give any qualifications) and a geography teachers' exam (both in 1906). Apart from her own education, she also ran a clandestine teaching group for working-class boys, which was a part of the system of underground Polish education. Czaplicka later described the work in her novel for young people (Czaplicka 1911). She also took part in another clandestine educational activity, this time as a student, called "Uniwersytet Latający" (Flying university), which featured high-level courses for women and lectures by eminent scholars. Later, after the "school strike," the institution was legalized by the Russian authorities as a Society of Academic Courses, where Czaplicka also worked as secretary of the scientific section. She started to work as a geography teacher in a girls' school (1906) and supplemented her modest earnings by tutoring landowners' children during the summer and functioning as a *dame de compagnie*, a lady's companion to rich women. She was also active in various civic institutions as Uniwersytet dla Wszystkich (University for everybody) and the Towarzystwo Kultury Polskiej (Society for Polish culture), which aimed at providing adult education to the working class. All such activity came out of the ethos of radical Warsaw intelligentsia, of which Czaplicka was part, which combined a socialist agenda with the idea of national independence. Her main mentor then was Wacław Nałkowski (1851–1911), an eminent geographer and a man of letters as well as a socialist. Czaplicka also befriended his daughter, Zofia Nałkowska (1884–1954), a future renowned novelist.

Due to overwork, the young geography teacher had to slow down, and in 1910 she went to Zakopane for several months, a famous resort in the Tatra Mountains (in the Austrian part of partitioned Poland), where she led an exuberant bohemian and sporting life. In her poems from the time, one can trace her struggle with the situation of being a woman scientist. That same year she obtained a prestigious scholarship to study abroad (the first woman to do so) from a Polish private institution, the Mianowski Fund, the only one at the time supporting research and publications. Czaplicka wanted to study anthropology to enrich her knowledge and specialize in ethnogeography.

By historical accident, Maria Czaplicka arrived in London several months after her acquaintance, Bronisław Malinowski had landed there. They knew each other from Warsaw and Zakopane. They were both twenty-six years old and quite experienced academically: she was a trained geographer, and he had his PhD from the Jagiellonian University in Kraków (in science and philosophy). They both started their English university studies at the London School of Economics under Charles Seligman (1873–1940), who lectured in ethnology (see Kuper 2017), and also attended Edward Westermarck's (1862–1939) sociological seminar (see Shankland 2014). Czaplicka and Malinowski were both members of the international circle of Westermarck's students.[4] The next year, Czaplicka moved to Oxford to continue her education at the School of Anthropology, residing at the women's Somerville College. Soon she became one of the favorite pupils of Robert Marett (1866–1943), the successor of Edward B. Tylor (1832–1917) to the chair of anthropology at Oxford University. It was Marett who suggested she digest major Russian and Polish ethnographic scholarship on Siberia, as this body of knowledge was completely unknown to British scholars. This is how her important first academic book originated.

It should be noted that *Aboriginal Siberia: A Study in Social Anthropology* (1914) consisted of chapters on ethnogeography of Siberian peoples, their sociology (social organization, marriage, birth, and death customs), religion (the longest part), and pathology ("Arctic hysteria"). For many years to come it became a major source of knowledge about Siberia and shamanism for the English-language public. In it Czaplicka also tackled other interesting topics, like gender transformation of shamans (obviously not using the term *gender*), what she saw in sociological terms as representing a third category of people besides men and women (see Balzer 1996); or "Arctic hysteria," which she in fact deconstructed, but she was later accused of grounding the psychopathologizing discourse on shamanism, particularly by Mircea Eliade (2004 [1951]: 24).

Czaplicka was an active participant in British academic life: she knew major British anthropologists (e.g., Alfred Haddon of Cambridge), and she took part in the International Congress of Americanists in 1912, where she became acquainted with Franz Boas

(1858–1942) as well as Russian ethnographers Lev Sternberg (1861–1927) and Waldemar Jochelson (1855–1937). She also attended several meetings of the British Association for the Advancement of Science, as well as the Royal Anthropological Institute, of which she became a member in 1914.

Czaplicka's mentor Marett was a transitional figure between evolutionism and functionalism. He himself remained an armchair anthropologist but was becoming aware of the importance of fieldwork and was helping his students organize their own expeditions (Rivière 2007). That was the case with his Polish protégé as well. Czaplicka's work on Siberian ethnographies made her an expert on the theme and raised her ambitions to carry out her own research there. She consulted on her ideas with Lev Sternberg in November 1913:

> I am particularly interested in the Tungus, I read and familiarize myself with works about them. . . . The aim of my expedition to Siberia is twofold: a) to bring back a museum collection, b) to study the social (cultural) sphere of the Tungus life. If possible, we will perform anthropometric measurements. . . . Without your advice, I cannot decide which Tungus exactly I would like to investigate. For I will have to learn one dialect better than the others.[5]

Other members of the Yenisei Expedition besides the leader — Czaplicka herself, who represented the Oxford University Anthropological Committee and was sponsored by Somerville College — were two British women, Maud Haviland (1889–1941), an ornithologist, and Dora Curtis (1875–1926), an artist, and an American anthropologist, Henry Usher Hall (1876–1944). Hall had studied at LSE and was to help Czaplicka in anthropometric measurements and collecting Siberian artefacts for the University of Pennsylvania Museum of Archeology and Anthropology, which sponsored his participation. Here again Czaplicka and Malinowski's lives ran in parallel: she left for her expedition to Siberia at the same time he headed for Australia and then to Melanesia for what became his famous fieldwork. Moreover, Marett revealed how Czaplicka supported him: "Thereupon that brilliant pupil of mine Miss A. Czaplicka (for whom, I hope, a special niche is reserved in the Polish Temple of Fame) besought me to assist her compatriot that he might see with his own eyes those peoples of the Antipodes about whom he had hitherto known from books alone" (Marett 1943: 7). Marett brought Malinowski as his assistant (thus for free) for a British Association for the Advancement of Science meeting that took place in Australia in 1914.

Outline of Czaplicka's Expedition (1914–15) and Later Accomplishments

Czaplicka left London in May 1914. She then stopped at St. Petersburg, where she met Russian scholars and collected letters of introduction and various permits necessary for traveling in the Russian Empire. In Moscow she was joined by the other members of the expedition. From there they traveled together via the Trans-Siberian Railway to Krasnoyarsk on the Yenisei. They boarded a steamer there and started their long journey down the river. On the way they encountered Aboriginal Siberians, the Ostiaks, about whom Czaplicka wrote to the principal of her college, Miss Emily Penrose (1858–1942):

> Nearly all the natives that we have seen before Golchikha were already drunk or hurrying to take advantage of the steamer's stopping to get alcohol enough to make them drunk as quickly as possible. We often had to hurry to reach their "chums" (tents) and occupy them with ourselves before they became incapable of occupying themselves with anything. I had to witness several pictures of merchants making the natives drunk before buying furs from them, in order to drive a harder bargain.[6]

Landing at the mouth of Yenisei at the end of June they raised their summer camp in a settlement called Golchikha. They all lived in two rooms of a small wooden hut that belonged to a local merchant. They benefitted from the occasion that the Samoyed and the Dolgan were fishing in the area nearby and coming to the trading post where they could be measured, photographed, and recorded. Czaplicka was the only person of the expedition able to communicate in Russian and later also in Samoyed and Tungus, languages she picked up while in Siberia.

The Yenisei Expedition learned about the outbreak of war only at the end of the summer.[7] The British women Maud Haviland and Dora Curtis decided to return to Europe, while the anthropologists Maria Czaplicka and Henry Hall would continue their expedition as planned and become apparently quite close emotionally (see figure 11.1). They traveled south to Turukhansk and waited for winter in order to be able to travel eastward toward the Lena River in long stretches, each time hiring a local guide with his reindeer train (see figure 11.2). On subsequent stops of their journey they rested in Tungus *chums* for several days. Reaching Lake Chirinda in February 1915, they stayed for three weeks and participated in a native court and other activities. They covered a distance of thirty-two hundred kilometers that winter. The temperature dropped to -60°C. They were accompanied by a Tungus woman, Michikha,[8] whom Czaplicka referred to as her *dame de compagnie*. They reached Lake Yessei, an area mostly inhabited by the Yakut, as the most eastern part of their journey. Later they headed back west and reached Turukhansk in mid-April and waited for the river to be navigable, arranging and sorting their ethnographic material, packing their collections, and developing photographs. As the war caused an increase in all prices, they ran out of money and had to ask their sponsors for help.

Figure 11.1. *Maria Czaplicka and Henry Hall in Tungus costumes (photograph from* My Siberian Year, *1916).*

They took a short trip south to Abakan Steppe and then started on their way back to Europe, again by the Trans-Siberian Railway. Czaplicka rushed to see her mother and Warsaw, deserted by the Russians.[9] Hall headed to St. Petersburg to secure permits for exporting their collections. Later they traveled together by train via Scandinavia because the Baltic Sea was controlled by German U-boats, and then by ship to Newcastle. They arrived in London on 4 September 1915.

Czaplicka's expedition received extensive media coverage, and she was invited by many English and Scottish institutions to deliver public lectures. She became a member of the Royal Geographical Society. Helped by Hall, she also soon wrote her travelogue *My Siberian Year* (Czaplicka 1916b), which is an interesting account of their adventures in the Arctic and the everyday life of their fieldwork, an engaging memoir of their encounters with many Aboriginal figures, and an interesting presentation of Siberia's major issues. It also strikes a nostalgic tone and features an undoubted literary quality as can be seen in the following fragment:

> I am just wondering if I shall ever see a warm hearth again and thaw out my numbed fingers and toes before a blazing Tungus and Yakut fire, when the barking of a dog breaks the silence, and as our sledge train clears the fringes of a belt of larch thicket, the sight of a column of sparks rising from the smoke-hole of a chum into the darkness sends a pleasant anticipatory thrill of warmth through me. (Czaplicka 1916b: 60)

She never returned to Siberia.

In October 1916 she was appointed a lecturer in ethnology by the Anthropological Committee at Oxford to replace a male colleague who had been called up to the army, becoming the first female lecturer of anthropology at Oxford. She then became a member of another women's college, Lady Margaret Hall. Continuing with her public lecture tour she added a new topic: Poland and its independence—an idea that was not very popular in Britain at the time. At the School of Oriental and African Studies (SOAS) of the University of London she gave a talk about the Turks of Central Asia (to discredit German efforts to extend their influence there), which was expanded into book form (Czaplicka 1919). That was also the time she started to write for newspapers on a regular basis: the "Russian Supplement" of *The Times*, *Land and Water*, and *New Europe*. In June 1919 she had to end her lectureship at Oxford University because the male colleague she was standing in for had returned from the war. She traveled to her homeland, which regained independence in November 1918, to write a series of reports on the new Poland but also hoping to get some academic position. Her efforts were in vain. At the end of 1919 she went to the United States, where she was to become an assistant to Franz Boas at the women's Barnard College.[10] This plan also did not work, and moreover Henry Hall, her expeditionary companion and intimate friend, got married. After coming back to England, she received an honorary Murchison Award from the Royal Geographical Society and finally landed a lectureship at Bristol University. This could have heralded a new chapter in her life, but she tragically decided to take her life on 27 May 1921. It is difficult to define the reasons for that decision: she suffered from financial and personal problems, which may have been compounded by the sense of instability of her career and lack of collegial support.[11] She was buried in Oxford as she wished.

The Polish Exiled Context to Czaplicka's Siberian Writing

Following the literary critic Mary Louise Pratt (1986), Kirsten Hastrup wrote that the imperial gaze first noticed Others and represented them in travel writing, only later identifying them in anthropological writing (Hastrup 1995: 2). This was possibly true in several Western colonial situations and also in the case of Siberia and in writing about Siberian Others. In the case of Polish writers, their travels to Siberia were not of a voluntary nature. The first descriptions of Siberian peoples came from Polish prisoners of war who were sent to Siberia by the tsar in the early seventeenth century and who, after returning home, published their diaries or wrote their memoirs. Later, when Poland lost its independence, Siberia hosted (though this is probably not a good expression) thousands of political exiles after each military uprising. They often published their accounts of exile and living among the Siberian Natives upon their return home (Kuczyński 1989). While in Siberia, some of these political prisoners became interested in the systematic ethnographic observation of Siberian Aboriginals. Often this had a salvatory effect on the ethnographers themselves, giving them a sense of life. There were several such figures. The most important and thorough were literary, although some, such as Wacław Sieroszewski (1858–1945), who lived among the Yakuts, and Bronisław Piłsudski (1866–1918), who resided with the Ainu and Giliaks, wrote scientific works. Czaplicka included short biographies of them at the end of her *Aboriginal Siberia* in order to show how they experienced Siberia during their stay (this concerned not only Polish exile-ethnographers but also Russian revolutionaries). At the beginning of the twentieth century, Russian authorities drained the Polish land of professionals who were needed for the development of Siberia, offering them very good economic conditions. These people—doctors, engineers, forestry specialists—went there voluntarily and also developed an interest in Aboriginal peoples.

This was the Polish background of Czaplicka's Siberian project. Thus it is not surprising that she started her travelogue as follows:

> When, as a child, I heard the word "Siberia" it meant but one thing for me: dire peril to the bodies, sore torture for the souls, of the bravest, cleverest, and most independently-minded of our people. . . . It was only as I grew older that I came to know of another aspect which more recently Siberia has assumed for the Poles, as a place in which to seek opportunities for the development of their abilities—opportunities denied them at home. . . . Finally . . . it was among the shady gardens of Oxford, in the midst of the splendid wealth of British libraries, and under the influence of British methods of research, that a new side of my interest in Siberia was awakened. (Czaplicka 1916b: 1, 2, 3)

Thus, from the very beginning of *My Siberian Year*, Czaplicka positions herself as a Pole, sketching the history of Polish presence in Siberia. This was to present her perspective, but one can also see this as showing nineteenth-century Siberia as a "contact zone." Hastrup wrote that anthropology grew in a contact zone and noticed that, "while the contact zone may form a space of coercive relationship between peoples that were previously apart, the fact of coercion and inequality itself should not blur our vision from the noticeable feature that 'contact' implies an interactive copresence of historical subjects, responding to and improvising the encounter" (Hastrup 1995: 4). The situation of the Polish accidental ethnographers in the Siberian contact zone was quite different. The political exiles, though white Europeans, spent prolonged periods of time living with Aboriginal Siberians and shared their position of subordination to the Russian Empire. And this had the potential for making a good platform for successful ethnography.

In the case of Czaplicka, something else played a role as well: she had read major ethnographic works on Siberia (and probably earlier also memoirs of exiles) before going there herself. She was not a political exile but a member of an *anglijska speditzia* (English expedition), as they were called in Siberia, not a member of a colonial power but still a white European.

Czaplicka's Siberian Ethnography:
Constructing the Field

How did Czaplicka perceive "the field" itself? At first sight, she thought of it in a rather traditional way, as being "out-there" and "waiting for being discovered" (Amit 2000: 6), not so much as the biographical and political process of building mutual relations, context, and places (Marcus 1995). By attentively reading her travelogue and other texts, however, one can trace a more nuanced picture, a processual image of the field. She unwittingly revealed what contemporary ethnographers often concealed and present-day researchers highlight and conceptualize. This can be found for instance in a prolonged description of a visit to a Tungus *chum* during the winter part of the expedition and the cultural norms that ruled such encounters:

> Among all these people there are certain conventions that have to be observed by visitors to their tents, and spending, as I did, most of my time in the tundra as a guest in native *chums*, it was necessary to conform to the rules of native etiquette. . . . At the entrance, somebody hands me a stick with which to beat the snow from my boots. The family sits round the fire, apparently quite unconcerned and uninterested, but really consumed with curiosity about the wandering strangers.
>
> Now it is *de rigueur* to make your way around the circle and offer your hand to every one—not to shake; if there is any shaking, you will have to do it; the small, shapely, listless hand lies in yours till you drop it. Then you will notice a white deerskin, unoccupied, in the centre of the circle on the far side of the fire, opposite the entrance. This is the seat of honour for a guest.
>
> On this you will squat with your legs doubled up under you tailor fashion, after first unwinding your muffler from your head, pulling off your second fur tunic, and hanging both over the pole that stretches from side to side of the *chum* above the fire, while every one gazes silently at the blazing hearth. (Czaplicka 1916b: 59–61)

Subsequently, the travelers were treated with the necessary amount of hot tea and food (while insisting on also using their own supplies) and helped by their hosts to get marrow out of a reindeer bone. Then *mahorka* (tobacco) was smoked in pipes.

> Now is the time for conversation, led by the host. He addresses himself to me through my Tungus woman, at any rate at first, even if he is aware that I speak his language [Tungus]. It is more in keeping with the importance of the occasion, perhaps, not to address me directly. Or perhaps it has something to do with their custom of avoidance, in accordance with

which, for example, one may not address one's daughter-in-law or sister-in-law directly. To be sure, I do not come within any of the degrees of affinity specifically tabooed, but my host does not know exactly how to classify me, and in any case it is better to be on the safe side. Usually it was only after we had been acquainted with each other for some little time that a man would address me directly. (ibid.)

A kind of examination followed when Czaplicka had to discuss her own "tundra" (country) and the people and animals living there. She found it difficult to "translate" Western life into aboriginal categories. This passage shows the biographical element and reflexivity of her encounters with the Others, the use of reciprocity and tactfulness as an ethnographic tool.

When I had satisfied their curiosity, their sense of the fitness of things led them to feel that it was only just they should satisfy mine, and it was but seldom that my most searching questions appeared to excite any suspicion of my motives. If they demurred at the proposal to measure their heads and stature, I would say that when I returned to my own people and they asked me, "What are the Tungus like?" and I said, "They are such and such," my people might want proof that I spoke the truth. "That," I said, "is why I want to write (measure) you, that I may show my people on paper who the Tungus are." The promise to make them known to distant lands seldom failed to break down their reticence. (ibid.: 66–67)

Figure 11.2. *Czaplicka's train in the tundra (photograph from* My Siberian Year, *1916).*

Another issue I would like to address here is connected with the very nature of Czaplicka's field. It was not as comprehensive and intensive as the Trobriand village of her colleague, Bronisław Malinowski,[12] which later became an ethnographic norm, but diffused and migratory: while in summer she stayed in one place, a small settlement called Golchikha at the mouth of the Yenisei to which the members of various Aboriginal tribes would come, during the winter she followed the tracks of the Tungus over a huge territory between the Yenisei and Lena Rivers. The Yenisei Expedition took summer residence in a building that was formerly a bath, where they "kept open house for the Samoyed, Yurak, and Dolgan" (ibid.: 22).

> This was their fishing season, when many of them come to the river to fish for themselves or for the Russian traders; but there were many days when the river was too rough for fishing, and their occasional excursions after geese did not occupy nearly the whole of their abundant leisure. So we were almost certain to find some one at home when we visited the chums, and we generally had our hut full of visitors when we were in. (Czaplicka 1916a: 31)

One of the reasons for these visits was the content of the Burroughs and Wellcome medicine chest, which Czaplicka possessed and often shared with the local inhabitants.

In both cases—summer residence and winter journey—the relations that Czaplicka nurtured with the people she met were of import. Vered Amit suggests "constructing" new fields out of diasporas and routs of transitions, and through aggregation of interactions (virtual or supra-local) (Amit 2000: 6). And this is what Czaplicka did: she constructed her field in this way; in summer, by waiting for people to come in for fishing and trading and by visiting their *chums* near Golchikha; in winter, by following their routes, staying in their *chums*, and taking part in their life as a strange guest, who came to "make the acquaintance of all the Tungus 'in this tundra'" (Czaplicka 1915a: 2). She also took advantage of the "supra-local aggregation of interaction" (Amit 2000), as the Tungus court can be called. Many Limpijsk Tungus came there; she participated in the hearings and became quite close with the former prince, Chunga, among others. One can call this type of research an early multisited ethnography because of a "complex object of study" (Marcus 1995) that was forced by real, not metaphorical nomadism of the people studied.

What were her methods of ethnographic enquiry? Maria Czaplicka did not write a comprehensive description of her methods or a methodological introduction. I had to compile information about it from clues scattered throughout her various texts. Generally speaking, she focused on the following areas of enquiry: physical anthropology, social anthropology, folklore, linguistics, archaeology, technology, and photography. Czaplicka wrote about her various research activities during the summer part of the expedition and the level of predicament connected with them:

> While we did not have much difficulty in securing measurements, conversation and the collection of tales, with the help of a native interpreter, was still easier; but they were less approachable when it was a question of actually observing customs or shamanist ceremonies. Most risky of all was our exploration of the tombs scattered about the hills near Golchikha. We had to be very careful not to be observed, lest we should be taken for cannibals, or, still worse, as offering a deliberate offence to the spirits of their ancestors.[13] ... As I have said, they are very communicative, and many hours passed in talk with old men about birth, death, marriage, the worship of good spirits, the struggle with bad ones—all this curiously schematized into a cycle of ceremonies, *rites de passage*, which mark the chief epochs of their simple lives. (Czaplicka 1916a: 30–31)

She was certainly interested in collecting folkloristic texts, or oral literature of all peoples she encountered in Siberia. One of her major informants in summer was Dens, a Samoyed prince, one of the heroes of her "mental portrait gallery of native friends" (ibid.: 70):

> He had an inexhaustible stock of Samoyed story, and loved, especially when his mood was mellowed by a glass or two of *spir't*, to recount with all the dramatic emphasis of an accomplished actor, the interminable adventures of some Samoyedic hero, while I, a willing victim of his tireless fantasy, wrote them down as they came from his lips, to be later turned into Russian with the aid of my interpreter Silkin. (Czaplicka 1916b: 71)

Silkin was an impoverished member of a Samoyedic Bai clan residing permanently in Golchikha who knew Russian and taught Czaplicka Samoyed and Yurak languages. She presented his literary portrait in *My Siberian Year*. It was full of sympathy but ended with a remark: "[I] was generally able to forestall his almost daily efforts to cheat me in some trifling way" (ibid.: 73).

She apparently also recorded voices on wax cylinders, but this was only mentioned once in a short account of her expedition:

> First I spoke into it myself and let them hear the machine repeat my words. Then everybody wanted to try the experiment. "Prince" Dens, incomparable teller of tales, drones a Samoyed love song into the recorder.

Next a notable smith, an ancient widower, repeated in a broken voice the dirge he had composed years ago by the graveside of his wife. Then a shaman sang an incantation. When I put on the reproducer, and they recognized the sound of their own voices, the enthusiasm and excitement were uproarious. The aged smith blubbered noisily, weeping large tears into his last cup of tea; the shaman yelled with delight at the revelation of a new magic; old Dens spoiled the show by shouting down the machine as he joined in the refrain of his own ditty. When I put on the record of a gay Polish folk-song the applause fairly raised the roof. Our fatigue forgotten, we kept up the fun until it was almost too late to go to bed at all. But it was worth while: I reaped a rich reward of folk-tales and accounts of native customs. (Czaplicka 1915b: 59)

The winter trip to the Tungus territory was quite successful as well. Czaplicka realized the significance of a good rapport with people, which enabled ethnographic enquiry. She wrote in one of her popular accounts of the Yenisei Expedition:

"And laugh much!" Indeed no work would have been possible without "laughing much" and making your interlocutors laugh. What appealed most strongly to their sense of humour was my "foreign accent" speaking in Tungus. They are a cheerful people, and though not apt to be communicative about the things I wanted to learn, a lively story or an opportune jest would usually put them in the right humour to relate a legend, tell a tribal custom, or submit to be measured—anthropologically. (Czaplicka 1915a: 3)

Thus it was not just a kind of exchange, as she suggested in a fragment of *My Siberian Year* cited earlier, but the establishment of democratic ground that made all participants of the interaction equal partners, and laughter strengthened that effect. Her mention of a comic dimension of her speaking Tungus adds a new and interesting point to a problem of good rapport.

She was learning the Tungus language intensively, first by studying its grammar—thanks to *Grammaire de la langue tongouse* (1874) by French linguist Lucien Adam (1833–1918)—and later through being tutored by Mikhail Suslov (1869–1929), a Sibiriak. She reported her achievements to Lev Sternberg in a letter from April 1915:

Before we travelled to the tundra, I took Tungus lessons with one gentleman, Suslov, who was a missionary among the Tungus, and has now become a trader. As a teacher he was not too good, because he wanted to teach everything using Russian grammar, which he did not really know. But he knows the spoken language well, and even compiled a dictionary, which he wants to offer to you. I have not seen this dictionary, because he wants 500 roubles for it, which I could not give him. . . . I would very much like to speak to your specialist in the Tungus language, whom I did not manage to meet previously. I have become slightly acquainted with this language, as well, to a certain extent, with Samoyed (Yurak). I recorded certain stories in these languages.[14]

She also had another teacher, cunning Michikha, whose capacity she put as follows:

> This lady, whom I called my *dame de compagnie*, called herself my teacher, in virtue of my efforts to derive from her a speaking acquaintance with the Tungus language to supplement what I had already gained from collected vocabularies and Adam's Grammar. The other Tungus called her my interpreter, which was indeed her chief function, though it was fortunate for me that I soon gained enough practical knowledge of her language to be able to guide and check her translations of my questions and of the answers that were returned to them. (Czaplicka 1916b: 74)

Her main Tungus informant, Hunta, also got his portrait in *My Siberian Year*: "Hunta, the peer among the Tungus of the Samoyed Dens as a story-teller—the Sterne of the Limpiisk tundra, but without Sterne's fondness for the sentimental *panache*. To Hunta life was a pageant of jest. No Tungus dignitary was sacrosanct to his satire, no tradition but he would allude to with his tongue in his cheek" (ibid.: 77).

In her 1917 paper "On the Track of the Tungus," Czaplicka summarized one important aspect of her dialogic enquiries, namely the collection of oral literature:

> Their tales and songs are, on the whole, much poorer in style and imagination than the flowery and heroic tales of the Yakut. Neither have they anything like the Samoyedic epos—realistic and naive, yet highly poetical in their directness and simplicity. The tales in which Tungus folklore is really rich are such as may best be described as "improper stories." And while in a Samoyed tent the point of highest tension comes at the description of some great deed of a shaman or a hero-child, during the recital of a Tungus tale emotion is expressed by a cynical laugh when the favourite hero, the malicious spirit Gamondo, has most cleverly cheated, murdered, and robbed some well-meaning member of the community. No god or goddess, no plant or animal, no shaman or warrior, is so often met with in their mythology as the wicked Gamondo. And only to see the indulgent smile with which the name of Gamondo is pronounced by Tungus lips! (Czaplicka 1917: 302)

Several other stories are also quoted in *My Siberian Year*: one recounting the struggle between shamans, one about bears (an Ostiak and a Tungus bear), a Yurak legend about hunting wild geese, a Tungus tale about clever Hulan, among others.[15]

The concept of the ethnographic fieldwork that Czaplicka implemented, with its focus on transcribed texts of various Siberian peoples in their languages, seems to have a clear Boasian provenance. Collecting texts was the primary research technique of Franz Boas himself, but other figures may be involved. Dmitry Arzyutov and Sergei Kan analyze the concept of the "field" of Russian ethnographers such as Sternberg, Vladimir Bogoras (1865–1936), and Jochelson (Czaplicka's mentors) and point out that they also followed that Boasian track. In the case of Boas, this predilection was connected to other aspects of his anthropology: for him, mythology, language, and physical traits of people were "means of identifying and studying the relationships between the tribes on the northwest coast of North America"; myths were for him very important in disclosing customs and the "character" of a people; transcribed texts were more resistant to distortion; to work on texts one or few informants sufficed (Arzyutov and Kan 2017: 38). Characterizing Boas's anthropology, Regna Darnell wrote that—according to him—historical accounts should be supplemented with "psychology": "This Native standpoint was accessible through linguistic texts obtained from the contemporary keepers of oral tradition" (Darnell 2008: 41; see Darnell 2001). Apart from that, Boas's fieldwork concentrated also on collecting material objects for museums as sponsors of his ethnographic enterprises and on physical anthropology that was always of interest to him (Arzyutov and Kan 2017: 38; Stocking 1982).

All these were also Czaplicka's concerns and preoccupations. She wanted to find cultural and "racial" characteristics of Siberian peoples, and she considered texts of folklore as important means for studying the languages; their deeper meaning was also to be investigated. She could work only with a limited number of informants. Thus Czaplicka fully realized the Boas format of fieldwork, as did her Russian mentors. There is no surprise that after familiarizing herself with the ethnographic scholarship on Siberia, to which the Jesup North Pacific Expedition (1897–1902), organized by Boas, contributed to a large extent, Czaplicka soaked up his ideas. She knew his works well and referred to them in her early work, *Aboriginal Siberia*. She knew him personally from 1912 on. Their earliest correspondence dates from 1914, when she informed Boas about her progress: "Following the natives we are now going south from the Samoyed country at the mouth of Yenisei by way of the Dolgan to the Tungus."[16] Another important factor was Boas's inclusion of environment into ethnographic enquiry, which appealed to Czaplicka. The geographical training of both was of import here, but also the very nature of the Arctic environment they encountered, which imposed such an approach.

But there is also another source of methodological-ethnographic knowledge that Czaplicka acquired, namely the well-known compendium *Notes and Queries on Anthropology*, then in its fourth edition (1912), edited by her Oxford friend, Barbara Freire-Marreco (1879–1967) and the archaeologist John Linton Myres (1869–1954). Czaplicka knew this manual very well, as she wrote a review of it for the Polish ethnographic journal *Lud* (People), suggesting that it be translated into Polish (which was never to happen). She briefly discussed the content: physical anthropology; technology; sociology; art, science, and religion; and language. *Notes and Queries* was intended to give guidance to amateur ethnographers in the field, but it was also very useful for Czaplicka and other academically trained anthropologists.[17] Her own mentor at Oxford, Robert Marett, as well as the representatives of the "Cambridge School," W. H. R. Rivers (1864–1922), Alfred C. Haddon (1855–1940), and her former teacher Charles Seligman were all involved in the updated edition of 1912 as members of the editorial committee and contributors, and *Notes and Queries* certainly matched Czaplicka's university studies in significant ways. "The description of the 'genealogical method' by its inventor himself, Dr. W.H.R. Rivers of Cambridge deserves special attention," she wrote (1914a: 231).

Thus Czaplicka's ethnography was rooted in these two anthropological traditions: Boasian and British. If Boasian anthropology together with its Siberian realizations gave her the actual format of her research, the British tradition, thanks both to her academic training in London and Oxford and to her thorough perusal of the latest edition of *Notes and Queries on Anthropology*, furnished her with a long and detailed list of topics for investigation, including sociology.

Czaplicka's Literary Ethnographic Writing as "Thick Description"

Apart from measuring and photographing the Natives, composing genealogies, and interrogating informants on social anthropology and folklore, Czaplicka also carried out participant observation. The results were narrated in Czaplicka's travelogue, which contains several prolonged, detailed, and engaging descriptions of various institutions or events that were based on thorough participant observation. Her report of *munyak*, a native court, is perhaps the best and can be called an early example of *thick description* (Geertz 1973). Czaplicka devoted a whole chapter of *My Siberian Year* to this institution. She began with general information, such as: "The native council appears to be a truly native institution common to all these tribes and dating back to very remote times" (Czaplicka 1916b: 160); "A prince is elected by the council for a term of three years, and may be re-elected any number of times" (ibid.: 161). The institutions had been recognized by Russian law because they were necessary to collect taxes. Then she reported her archival research in Russian official records, proving that originally there were much more democratic conditions and that later the role of prince had increased. The council met annually, and it was an important event, accompanied by more informal discussions and "a ceaseless stir of bustle and gaiety" (ibid.: 162).

She wrote further: "The longest and most interesting session of a *munyak* that I witnessed was that of the Limpiisk territorial group of Tungus held in February 1915. This was at Lake Chirinda . . . Here the prince had made his home for the winter" (ibid.: 163). They waited for several days until the representatives of all ten "families" arrived. Then the men gathered in a log hut.

> Inside, a populous gloom, thick with the stench of crowded fur-clad bodies, and pungent with the reek of half a hundred pipes. . . . The three of us, including my Tungus lady-companion—who was admitted only on the strength of being one of the *speditzia* [expedition] to an assembly from which women are usually excluded [footnote: They did not object to my being present, because I was not a Tungus woman]—reached our corner at last in a state of breathless exhaustion; . . . Prince Piroi sat behind a rickety table—he is a great admirer of Russian culture—and beside him on either hand a *starosta*. (ibid.: 165–66)

Elaborating on the system of taxes and *podvody* (free transport of Russian functionaries organized by princes), the problems of which were being discussed when she attended the court, she not only cited cases but also explained them, presenting the point of view of the actors.

There were also disputed individual cases, mostly concerning reindeer being taken over. "In pronouncing his decisions, as in his examination of the parties to the dispute, the prince adopted a hectoring and dictatorial tone, apparently designed to impress the assembly with a due sense of the importance of his office, or rather of himself as its incumbent" (ibid.: 170). The next case was of special interest to Czaplicka herself, prompting her to discuss the problem of political and criminal exiles and malicious Russian politics.

> A Yakut trader had a complaint to bring against a member of the important Hukachar clan. This man had outraged the feelings of the Yakut by calling him a *Palak*. This is the Russian pronunciation of *Polak* (Pole). The Hukachar, however, had used the word without any consciousness of its real meaning, but in the sense which it has acquired among the peasants on the Yenisei, for whom *palak* is an abbreviation of *paliticheski*, the cant term for political exiles ... a new and sinister meaning, viz. "bandits," "criminals." (ibid.: 171–72)

Czaplicka explained that double misunderstanding by alluding to the conscious policy of Russian authorities to add criminal exiles to the category of political, thus causing the change of attitude of Sibiriaks toward political exiles from sympathetic to negative. She reported details about the whole libel action from both sides. "The hearing of the case, what with the difficulties put in the way of progress by the interpreter, the voluble protests of the defendant, and the fondness these people have for argument at the best of times, continued for some two hours before the prince succeeded in bullying the Hukachar into consenting to pay the fine" (ibid.: 175). At that moment, the Yakut man said he did not want money but "the Hukachar's hand in token of renewed friendship and esteem" (ibid.: 175). The dispute started again. And then an interesting turning point took place:

> The defendant hereupon turned to me and asked me to say what I thought about the matter; for I, he said, was *gramotnyi* (able to read and write). I told him that a *palak* or *paliticheski* was most emphatically not considered by our people as a thief or a robber, and that many *paliticheski* were men whom we greatly admired and esteemed. But the prince cut me short; whatever, he said, we in our country thought about *palaks*, in the tundra to call a man by this name was considered a greater insult than to call him *ulak* (Tungus for "bad man," "cheat"). This, of course, settled the matter, and, indeed, I am quite sure that the prince spoke no more than the simple truth. (ibid.: 176)

This is really a remarkable lesson on her own ethnocentrism that Czaplicka got from the prince, and even more praiseworthy that she took it. This also shows how the participant observer was being received by the Tungus: at best as an advisor.

The *munyak* proceeded, and next cases were considered: the theft of foxes from a trap, the "borrowing" of tobacco from a store, and the escape of a woman from the *chum* of her deceased husband's brother, where she should live. That was a good occasion to discuss the issue of Tungus customary law and the agency of women (the law won, though the woman also had supporters). And finally, the last case was put at the end because it was very difficult, as it concerned a Russian individual: "It was curious to see how cautious they were in dealing with him," showing "their reluctance to take action at all against a Russian." He was a useless carpenter who was sent there by the authorities to finish a little church, which had to be maintained by local Tungus, but he also wanted a local bride with a dowry. That was too much for the council. The father of an intent bride, old Chunga Hiragir, "spoke up like a man: 'We do not want you here any longer. You know that you despise the Avankil [Evenki]. Do we not know also that you have said that the Tungus are quite savage and good-for-nothing? Shall I marry my daughter to a Russian who holds her people in contempt, and will not do the work he is paid for?' This patriotic note stiffened everybody up wonderfully" (ibid.: 184–85). The carpenter was summarily sent back to Turukhansk. The next day everybody had departed, and "only blackened circles on the snow showed where the chums had stood" (ibid.: 186). She finished the whole chapter on a posthumanist note: "Outside, the still air echoed only the grunts of the prince's reindeer, or the rattle of antlers which betokened a dispute over the turning-up of a succulent clump of moss" (ibid.).

The chapter on "Native Law: Crime and Punishment," which consists of the vivid report of the *munyak*, shows the high quality of Czaplicka as an ethnographic observer. It reveals both her literary skills to tell the story and her analytical capacity, as the chapter is an excellent example of anthropological situational analysis (Van Velsen 1978).

Her book also contains other important elements, like a chapter on religion, which is a discussion of religious syncretism (though she does not use the term) of Siberian "Christian shamanists." There is a thorough report of a shamanistic séance anthropologists ordered from "the great Samoyed shaman Bokkobushka." It was a very clever idea to ask him to shamanize for them, as they had problems observing any such procedure earlier. Czaplicka wrote about it: "Over three months of close intercourse and friendly relations with these people, and yet I had not hitherto been considered sufficiently initiated to be allowed to witness a shamanist ceremony" (Czaplicka 1916b:

197). She described the whole context of the event (Russian perse-
cutions of shamans until then), how she had managed to persuade
Bokkobushka to shamanize for them, and how the whole procedure
unfolded, step by step, explaining its meanings. She also reported instances of shamans' interventions and some ceremonies.

The whole chapter was devoted to "A Shaman's Curse" placed on
Chunga Hiragir and his fate-ridden family, who had experienced a
whole series of misfortunes and deaths. Reporting on all those ca-
lamities, she saw them as "partly a series of coincidences and partly
a matter of psycho-pathology" (ibid.: 213). To show how persuasive
fatalistic thinking is, she ended the chapter with the following remark: "But even now it makes me shudder to think—it is absurd, of
course—that perhaps I, too, was drawn into the meshes of the web
spun for Chunga's undoing, and made an unwitting instrument of the
dead shaman's vengeance" (ibid.: 224). Her suicide would certainly
be seen as such by her Siberian friends, if they knew about it.

Although her ethnography was not very theoretical, there were
theories she was preoccupied with and used her ethnographic material to support. Her main concern was the problem of the division of
Arctic peoples into two groups: Palaeo-Siberians, who were the oldest inhabitants of the area pushed there by newcomers from southern
Siberia, and Neo-Siberians, "the later comers . . . who, although they
have become adapted to the new environment, dropping in the process many of the characteristic features of their former culture, have
not had time to develop thoroughly distinctive Arctic industries or
art" (ibid.: 52). She had tackled the problem in her *Aboriginal Siberia* earlier and apparently wanted to confirm her ideas in the field.
Czaplicka used her ethnographic material as evidence to support her
theory (1914) that the Tungus were Neo-Siberians, even if they had
left the south a long time ago. The Tungusic tribes still lived then in
the Transbaikal and Amur regions, and she afforded evidence that the
Northern Tungus had come from there.

> Thus in mythology we have descriptions of plants and animals which my
> Northern Tungus could never have seen. On the ceremonial costume of
> the Tungus priest, or shaman, we find representations of many animals
> which they do not possess in the north, and in fact the forms of these
> are in some cases so much degenerated that I would scarcely dare to de-
> fine them without native help. I remember once examining the figures
> of animals carved in driftwood and placed at a deceased shaman's grave.
> . . . I asked a friendly Tungus who was explaining to me the meaning of
> the figures what two particularly shapeless forms represented. After some
> time I found that the pig-like form with enormous horns was *hali*, which

in the Tungus language means mammoth, whose remains are familiar to the Tungus, and whose teeth they imagine to be horns. About the other figure, I think I am right in supposing that it was a dromedary, like the one found in the Transbaikal region. My supposition was based on the information that the animal had by nature a saddle on its back, which was all my informant could tell me. I take this as a curious proof of the persistence of the old tradition, because this description of the ceremonial figure must have been repeated from mouth to mouth through at least twelve generations. A last, but not least important, proof of their southern origin is their custom of riding reindeer, just as they once rode horses in the south, a custom unknown to the truly northern peoples. (Czaplicka 1917: 293–95)

She was also very much preoccupied with the racial characteristics of various Siberian peoples, and she extensively measured their representatives. Moreover, she used Rivers's genealogical method to secure physical-anthropological results: "Thanks to our inquiry into the genealogical trees of the Tungus we measured, we have been able to distinguish four grades of Tungus metisation": the pure Tungus, the Tungus-Yakut, the Dolgan, and the Tungusizes Yakut (Czaplicka 1917: 299). Today, the use of genealogies to differentiate racial types may be seen as inappropriate from the genetic point of view. But it should be stressed that today's physical anthropology tries to answer questions about the migrations of Siberian populations, which preoccupied Czaplicka, by sequencing DNA.

Another important characteristic of the ethnography in her travelogue is that she included not only Aboriginal inhabitants of Siberia in the picture but also European settlers:

The Sibiriak—that is, broadly speaking, the colonial whose ancestors have been settling in Siberia, voluntarily or involuntarily, since, say, the end of the Middle Ages—is a man in whose veins there may run the blood of the Little Russian [Ukrainian], the Great Russian, the Pole, the German, the Jew, and the aborigine, who is himself the representative of much mixed Finno-Turko-Mongoloid and other strains. (Czaplicka 1916b: 243)

Claiming that "the growth of a new Russian nation in Siberia" is of interest to ethnographers and sociologists, she reported the aspirations of Sibiriaks, who "like to call themselves the Canada of Old World," and expressed her deep sympathy toward them. To finish the sociological picture of Siberia, she presented another important group of its inhabitants, namely the exiles.

She crowned her account with a chapter titled "Siberia as a Russian Colony," in which she drew an outline of the political and economic history of the region, mentioning also the destruction of Aboriginal peoples:

> These extensions of Russian rule were not unaccompanied by forcible, if unavailing, protests on the part of the native inhabitants. But, unfortunately no Sibiriak Longfellow or Cooper has arisen to record the heroism of the old possessors of the land, who were forced, like the "red" man in America, to retreat before the colonists. Some of the tribes have quite disappeared in the unequal struggle, other have remained, to sink into a condition of greater or less degeneracy, still others have withdrawn to wilder regions in Siberia or to lands beyond the southern border. (ibid. 293)

She finished with a strong accent of an engaged anthropologist:

> Perhaps Siberia may yet become what she is potentially already—the Canada of the East—the home of a great self-governing people, free to educate themselves, to direct in their own way and for their own benefit as well as that of the Russian Empire the development of the great resources of a country rich in minerals ... ; abounding in fine timber; spread with wide fields, growing wider every year, of grain and hemp; with vast grazing lands; with vaster tracts teeming with every kind of fur-bearing animal; and peopled by a hardy stock of democratically minded Europeans, trained to self-reliance and resourcefulness in no easy school. (ibid.: 306).

In her utopian vision of the future of the economically powerful and politically democratic Siberia as the Canada of the East, Czaplicka does not mention Aboriginal Siberians. It may be the case that in her admiration for these brave inhabitants of the inhospitable Arctic she believed they could thrive in the old ways instead of becoming full citizens of the modern world.

Maria Czaplicka's ethnography as presented in *My Siberian Year* and other texts was very thorough and insightful, but it represented only a fraction of her findings. In fact, the bulk of the expedition's field materials were to be worked out later by Czaplicka and Hall in a proper monograph the anthropologists planned to write together. The task was never completed, and only the table of contents and the introduction of it have survived. It was to be titled *The Natives of the Yenisei* and written in a standard way as the "Report of the Expedition to the Yenisei 1914–1915" (as in the subtitle). The preface would present the expedition itself. The chapter called "The Country" would elaborate on the environment, the population, and history of the region. Then the main section, "The Natives," would examine various subjects in reference to three peoples: "The Samoyed," "The Tungus," and "The Turks of S. Yenisei." The subjects would include mental characters (social customs, culture and technology, religion and mythology, language) and bodily characters (the results of measurements) (Kubica 2020a). It is probable that the innovation inherent in Czaplicka's ethnography would not have been found in this monograph. It can be best traced in *My Siberian Year*, which I maintain is not a mere travelogue but an ethnographic text with important rhizomes connecting it to her other anthropological writings.

The Reception of Czaplicka's Ethnography

Czaplicka is mostly remembered as the author of one book—*Aboriginal Siberia*—and almost all of the numerous references to her name relate to it. Cited mostly by anthropologists (e.g., Ruth Benedict 2005 [1934]; Lewis 1989) and researchers on shamanism (e.g., Eliade 2004 [1951]; Hultkrantz 1989), some mistook it for Czaplicka's own Siberian fieldwork ethnography (e.g., Wasilewski 1989; Rivière 2007: 53). In fact, it was only Nora Chadwick, a medievalist interested in oral literature, who referred to Czaplicka's ethnography in *My Siberian Year*, for instance the passages on the competition of the Samoyed and Yakut shamans, in which Chadwick saw an example of the literary tradition of battles between rival shamans (Chadwick 1936).

An attempt to find Czaplicka's field materials was undertaken in the 1930s by the Cambridge-based American sinologist and anthropologist Ethel Lindgren (1904–88). She studied the Southern Tungus (Lindgren 1938) and wanted to compare her own field material with that of the Yenisei Expedition. Lindgren learned that after Czaplicka's death her work had been sent to Henry Hall in Philadelphia. In the meantime, however, World War II had broken out, Hall died, and the materials vanished.[18]

In the 1990s, Curzon Press undertook a project to publish *The Collected Works of Maria A. Czaplicka*, a four-volume set that included her three books and a collection of papers and letters from the field, edited by a Slavist from Leeds University, David Norman Collins, who, together with James Urry, also wrote an article on Czaplicka (Urry and Collins 1997).

George W. Stocking, in *After Tylor*, made an all too brief reference to her as a member of the "pre-war cohort" (1995: 119, 406) of academically trained ethnographers aside from Malinowski. It is only quite recently that Maria Czaplicka has gained some attention as a fieldworker, but even so in footnote only—in a book on the history of Oxford anthropology: "She was also one of the first to publish a popular and personal account of fieldwork, *My Siberian Year* (1916), published by Mills and Boon" (Rivière 2007: 60). Czaplicka has been appreciated mostly as a museum collector (Skowron-Markowska 2012; Vider 2017).

What is really striking is the absence of any reference to Cza-plicka's ethnography in Russian-language scholarship on Siberia. Her *Aboriginal Siberia* is hardly cited, not to mention *My Siberian Year* or other texts. Even the recent book on Tungus peoples' folklore in Polish does not refer to any of Czaplicka's texts (Tulisow 2009). It is really a pity that Gamondo, a trickster-type personality, did not make it to a book on Evenki folklore.

What was the reason for this concealment or ignorance of Cza-plicka's ethnographic achievements? Primarily it was the positivist model of anthropology that dominated then and excluded popular works like *My Siberian Year* from the rubric of "science," and only with the literary turn in anthropology did such works come to be perceived as ethnographies.

Conclusion: A Presentist Assessment of Czaplicka's Ethnography

The ethnography that Maria Czaplicka presented in her travelogue can be assessed and analyzed using today's concepts and ideas. Because of its harsh character, the Arctic environment tends to be treated by contemporary researchers as a third party, as if endowed with agency. In Czaplicka's case, this was strengthened by her geographic education and her tendency toward environmental determinism. She saw anthropology very broadly as a discipline that deals with the human being in a biological sense as well as a cultural sense. With her geographical predilection for environmental explanations, she would certainly be an enthusiast of Tim Ingold's theory; and as a Siberian researcher she would especially appreciate his concept of the weather-world, which refers to the combination and continuities of weather phenomena and earthly landscape in both human and nonhuman existence (Ingold 2010). One can find such a perspective in a literary piece, in which she described her parting with Golchikha:

> The short, vivid summer passed only too quickly away, with its perpetual daylight, the short-lived splendor of purple, red and yellow wild flowers with which it carpeted the hills, the not less varied and picturesque

nomads appearing out of a misty nowhere, disappearing again into the vague limbo beyond the low horizon, like the migrant birds.[19]

These poetic phrases, however, only reveal the "weather-world" of those Aboriginal Siberians that she saw as a part of nature. These "picturesque nomads," whose lives she beautifully sketched, were for her part of an enchanted landscape, not of Siberia as a future political entity. In spite of her social and ethnographic sensitivity, Maria Czaplicka was a daughter of her time.

Another contemporary concept that applies to Czaplicka's literary ethnographic writing is intersubjectivity, conceived as a difficult but possible epistemological road. Michael Jackson described this concept as striving to experience one's own world, while remaining in relation to the life and world of other people—which is not only difficult but can also sometimes be impossible. Complicity and conflict are complementary poles of intersubjectivity (Jackson 1998: 4). Thus, acquired knowledge is not the result of some emphatic cognition but the effect of active, remembered "trading places." It is submerged in action and "thick participation." Ethnography is thus a record of embodied and intersubjective experience, present in a transformed world under study that is experienced by ethnographers in their "inner way" (Rakowski 2018). Johannes Fabian relates the concept of intersubjectivity to language and writes about "ethnography *as* communication," that language then is not a system of signs but of speaking: "interpersonal acts and modes of communication" (Fabian 2014: 202). Fabian concludes that, "like coevalness, intersubjectivity must be made or achieved, opening myself to misunderstandings or getting embroiled in contradiction" (Fabian 2014: 204, 207).

Certainly, Maria Czaplicka cannot be seen as a predecessor of any antipositivist anthropology; she was a devoted positivist scholar. But thanks to her literary ethnography in *My Siberian Year* we can find various elements and clues that would probably be absent in her (and Hall's) definite, "properly scientific" ethnographic monograph on *The Natives of the Yenisei*. Her travelogue provides the chance to look at fieldwork practice being told in a narrative way before it would be transformed into "proper" ethnographic discourse. In the Czaplicka travelogue it was the shared experience of braving the cold, traveling whole days on a sledge, inhaling the smell of reindeer, feeling hunger, and—also—telling stories. The title of her paper "On the Track of the Tungus" refers to her knowledge acquired through intersubjective experience, by doing what they were doing, following them, appreciating their ways of protecting against the cold, their sense of orientation in an indiscriminate terrain. All these were shared experiences. And even if interactions with Indigenous people were not very prolonged, these shared experiences enabled abductive knowledge on the part of the anthropologist (Hastrup 2018).

Present-day ethnographers endeavor at best to articulate embodied, sensed, motoric knowledge, which they possess in the course of an active, participatory cognitive process.

All this knowledge would hardly enter into Czaplicka's regular monograph. Her travelogue, as a piece of literary ethnographic writing, therefore represented the best opportunity for her embodied knowledge to be part of a text, as it manifests in the following fragment describing a Tungus woman's morning:

> The housewife requires no small effort of resolution to get herself out of the sleeping-bag before anyone else is up, in the bitter cold of winter, when the moisture of the breath freezes on the coverings that she has pulled up over her head, so that she has cautiously to pull away the hide or cloth that has stuck to her face, slip into her clothes, all of which she removed on retiring, and set to work in a temperature many degrees below zero to rekindle the fire on the hearth immediately below the smoke-hole in the middle of the tent, where the ashes have retained just enough heat to melt the snow that has fallen on the hearth, and make the place damp. (Czaplicka 1916b: 57–58)

Only actual cohabitation and shared experience enabled Czaplicka to describe in very sensual terms the difficult role every Tungus woman played: carer of the hearth in a literary meaning of the phrase.

Another good example of shared intersubjective experience is the shamanistic séance (mentioned earlier) that Czaplicka and Hall ordered, went through, and observed, and which she later described in *My Siberian Year*. This could also be seen as the situation Kirsten Hastrup wrote about, when an ethnographer is herself or himself an informant.

In the expeditionary report Czaplicka intended to write as an ethnographic monograph, we would probably have but a collection of Tungus stories, or some fixed versions of them, together with an overview of customs and *rites de passage*. But thanks to the open narrative of Czaplicka's travelogue, we can learn about the ethnographic situation and its context and imagine her intersubjective experience (see Kubica 2020b). By relying on memory and referring to imagination, her literary ethnography is not closed in stabilizing categories of ethnographic discourse and represents an alternative genre. *My Siberian Year* is no mere travelogue in the sense of continuing a nineteenth-century tradition but is instead a literary ethnographic text by a woman who had been trained in a male-dominated academic world to produce something quite different. It was mostly women who were authors of literary ethnographic writing, and that was mostly due to being outside academia or occupying some minor position. Proper academics (mostly male) rarely dared to publish literary texts, as these might threaten their academic position. When writing her travelogue, Czaplicka had not yet been a lecturer at Oxford (see Kubica 2013).

Tomasz Rakowski (2018) suggests "participation-understanding" — the phenomenological work resulting from the practices of comprehending and recalling the existing "facts" — as a separate work besides text, essay, novel, film, or performance. I can search for the reflections of this "participation-understanding" in Czaplicka's writings. Glimpses of this are scattered in her literary writing, such as the fragment cited above, or in such reports as their being lost in the *purga* and almost freezing to death: "Now I understood how the Tungus could drink with relish the blood of freshly slaughtered deer, and tear the smoking raw flesh with their teeth" (Czaplicka 1916b: 125). Only through the intersubjective experience did she conceive the "savage" way of life.

Tamara Kohn elaborated on "pre-verbal ethnographic skills and sensitivity of fieldworkers" that are crucial for the vocation (Kohn 1994). Czaplicka quickly acquired Siberian etiquette and knew how to behave by observing and adapting to the situation. But verbal skills were also important. She used her narrative skills (as a novelist she was a good narrator) in the field situation to create a good rapport and a democratically shared interpersonal space that prompted the Tungus to speak. Vladimir Bogoraz, who was also a talented author, used the same "trick" while in the field (Morgunova 2020).

Czaplicka called Michikha her *dame de compagnie*. She had to use the French phrase as there is no English equivalent of the Polish expression *dama do towarzystwa*. Czaplicka herself used to play that role: a lady companion to rich women who was paid but whose role was to assist, not to serve. The social status of a *dame de compagnie* was ambivalent: she was usually an impoverished member of the intelligentsia and thus economically unequal to the lady she assisted, but they both belonged to high society. Czaplicka found that the phrase was quite appropriate to define the role that Michikha performed in the winter part of the Yenisei Expedition. Michikha was paid, but she was not a servant. She came from a noble Tungus clan, and her connections were very useful to the anthropologists. But at the same time the expression *dame de compagnie*, applied to a Siberian Aboriginal woman, also had an ambivalent tone. And this symbolizes Czaplicka's attitude toward Siberian Aboriginals very well: respectful and, at the same time, ironic.

Grażyna Kubica is a professor in the Social Anthropology Section at the Institute of Sociology, Jagiellonian University, Krakow (Poland). She coedited the volume *Malinowski—Between Two Worlds* (Cambridge University Press, 1988) and authored the introduction and annotations of the complete version of Malinowski's diaries in their original language: *Dziennik w ścisłym znaczeniu tego wyrazu* (2002). Her last book is an anthropological biography of Maria Czaplicka, published by the University of Nebraska Press in the series Critical Studies in the History of Anthropology (2020). She was a member of the Executive Committee of the European Association of Social Anthropologists and vice-chairman of the Board of the Social Anthropology Section of the Polish Sociological Association.

Notes

1. This chapter was written as part of the National Science Center project "'Written with the Other Hand'—Literary Ethnographic Writing and its Polish Specificity" (2019/33 / B / HS3 / 00272).
2. The spelling of the names of Siberian tribes presents a problem. Currently, their representatives use their own names, but Czaplicka used contemporary names of colonial provenance. Samoyedic tribes do not currently have one collective name, but several: Nenets (formerly known as Samoyeds-Yuraks), Enets (Yenisei Samoyeds), Nganasan (Tawgi Samoyeds), and Selkups (Samoyeds-Ostiaks). Czaplicka also encountered Khanty (Ostiaks). In the case of the Tungus, it is quite simple, because those who Czaplicka dealt with are now called Evenki. As the present chapter deals with historical situations, I am using the historical names.
3. The biography of Czaplicka is extensively presented in my recent book (Kubica 2015b, 2020a) as well as in a shorter paper (Kubica 2015a).
4. They were also in quite close contact later. In the private archive of Malinowski's daughter, Helena Wayne, I found a note written in Polish by Czaplicka in which she gave her opinion on his outline of a future book, *The Family among Australian Aborigines*. There is also a letter written by her in 1919 reporting her situation; Malinowski Papers, Archive of the London School of Economics.

5. Letter in Russian of 12 November 1913, Archive of the Russian Academy of Sciences, St. Petersburg. Polish translation published in Kubica and Yakubova 2013: 326.
6. Letter of 3 July 1914, Archive of Somerville College, Oxford; Collins 1999: 67.
7. World War I began on 28 July 1914 and ended on 11 November 1918.
8. Dates unknown. All other dates unknown if unmentioned.
9. Warsaw, the capital of the Russian partition of Poland, hosted many Russian officials, soldiers, clerks, and businessmen. In 1915 the Russian-German front was approaching Warsaw from the West. The Russians deserted the city on 4 August 1915, blowing up bridges on the Vistula River and taking out the factory equipment. The city was managed by the Polish Central Citizens Committee. From 6 August 1915 until the end of the war, Warsaw was occupied by the Germans, who reactivated Polish education on all levels. Poland regained independence on 11 November 1918.
10. Correspondence between Czaplicka, Boas, and Dean Virginia Gildersleeve of Barnard College bears witness to those plans, which did not work probably due to lack of funding and Boas's own problems at Columbia University then. I write about it extensively in Kubica 2020a: 438–52. See BC 2.4, Archives of Barnard College, New York; Boas Papers, Archive of the Philosophical Society, Philadelphia.
11. I have written about likely reasons with the help of the theory of Émile Durkheim in Kubica 2020a: 471–72; 541. Malinowski considered applying for Czaplicka's position at Bristol, but his mentor, Seligman, dissuaded him from doing this (see Kubica 2020a: 470–71).
12. We have to remember, however, that Malinowski's ethnography concerned not just the Trobriands but also other islands in the Kula ring.
13. She does not seem too troubled by the moral aspect of that "overground archeology."
14. A letter in Russian of 3 April 1915 (old calendar), Archive of the Russian Academy of Sciences, St. Petersburg; Polish translation published in Kubica and Yakubova 2013: 329.
15. Henry Hall also reported a legend about shaman Langa (Hall 1919).
16. A letter of 6 September 1914; Boas Papers, B:B61, Archive of the Philosophical Society, Philadelphia.
17. Bronisław Malinowski was also studying the fourth edition of *Notes and Queries* while preparing for his fieldwork, to which the Polish (full and comprehensive) edition of his diaries bears witness (Malinowski 2002: 310).
18. I have documented the whole affair in my book on Czaplicka (Kubica 2020a).
19. This is a citation from Czaplicka's public lecture on her expedition. The manuscript is held at Lindgren Papers, Archive of Lucy Cavendish College, Cambridge.

References

Manuscript Collections

Archives of Barnard College, New York.
Archive of the London School of Economics, Malinowski Papers.
Archive of Somerville College, Oxford.
Archive of the Russian Academy of Sciences, St. Petersburg.
Archive of the Philosophical Society, Philadelphia: Boas Papers.
Archive of Lucy Cavendish College, Cambridge, Lindgren Papers.

Published Sources

Adam, Lucien. 1874. *Grammaire de la langue tongouse*. Paris: Maisonneuve et cie.
Amit, Vered. 2000. "Introduction: Constructing the Field." In *Constructing the Field: Ethnographic Fieldwork in the Contemporary World*, edited by Vered Amit, 2–18. London: Routledge.
Arzyutov, Dmitry, and Sergei A. Kan. 2017. "The Concept of the 'Field' in Early Soviet Ethnography: A Northern Perspective." *Sibirica* 16(1): 31–74.
Balzer, Marjorie Mandelstam. 1996. "Sacred Genders in Siberia: Shamans, Bear Festivals, and Androgyny." In *Gender Reversals and Gender Cultures: Anthropological and Historical Perspectives*, edited by Sabrina Petra Ramet, 164–82. London: Routledge.
Benedict, Ruth. 2005 [1934]. *Patterns of Culture*. New York: Houghton Mifflin.
Chadwick, Nora. 1936. "Shamanism among the Tartars of Central Asia." *Journal of the Royal Anthropological Institute* 66: 75–112.
Cole, Sally, 2003, *Ruth Landes: A Life in Anthropology*. Lincoln: University of Nebraska Press.
Collins, David N. 1999. "Letters from Siberia by M.A. Czaplicka." In *The Collected Works of M.A. Czaplicka*. Vol. 1. Richmond: Curzon Press.
Czaplicka, Maria Antonina. 1911. *Olek Niedziela: Powieść dla młodzieży* [Olek Niedziela: A novel for young people]. Warsaw: Księgarnia Sadowskiego.
———. 1914a. Review of *Notes and Queries on Anthropology*. *Lud* 12(1): 230–31.
———. 1914b. *Aboriginal Siberia: A Study in Social Anthropology*. Oxford: Clarendon Press.
———. 1915a. "Tribes of the Yenisei: The Oxford Expedition." *The Times Russian Supplement*, 13: 1–6.
———. 1915b. "A Year in Arctic Siberia." *Wide World Magazine* 37(217): 52–60.
———. 1916a. "Siberia and Some Siberians." *Journal of the Manchester Geographic Society* 32: 27–42.

—— [Czaplicka, Mary Antoinette]. 1916b. *My Siberian Year*. London: Mills & Boon.

——. 1917. "On the Track of the Tungus." *Scottish Geographical Magazine* 23: 289–303.

——. 1919. *The Turks of Central Asia in History and the Present Day*. Oxford: Clarendon Press.

——. 1999. *The Collected Works of M. A. Czaplicka*. Edited by David Norman Collins. 4 vols. Richmond: Curzon Press.

Darnell, Regna. 2001. *Invisible Genealogies: A History of Americanist Anthropology*. Lincoln: University of Nebraska Press.

——. 2008. "North American Tradition in Anthropology: The Historiographic Baseline." In *A New History of Anthropology*, edited by Henrika Kuklick, 35–51. Malden: Blackwell Publishing.

Eliade, Mircea. 2004 [1951]. *Shamanism: Archaic Techniques of Ecstasy*. Foreword by Wendy Doniger. Translated by Willard R. Trask. Princeton, NJ: Princeton University Press.

Fabian, Johannes. 2014. "Ethnography and Intersubjectivity: Loose Ends." *HAU: Journal of Ethnographic Theory* 4(1): 199–209.

Geertz, Clifford. 1973. *The Interpretation of Cultures*. New York: Basic Books.

Hall, Henry U. 1919. "Shamanist Bird Figures of the Yenisei Ostyak." *Museum Journal*, no. 10: 210–12.

Handler, Richard, ed. 2000. *Excluded Ancestors, Inventible Traditions: Essays Toward a More Inclusive History of Anthropology*. Madison: University of Wisconsin Press (History of Anthropology 9).

Hastrup, Kirsten. 1995. *A Passage to Anthropology: Between Experience and Theory*. London: Routledge.

——. 2018. "Muscular Consciousness: Knowledge-Making in an Arctic Environment." In *Pre-Textual Ethnographies: Challenging the Phenomenological Level of Anthropological Knowledge-Making*, edited by Tomasz Rakowski and Helena Patzer, 116–37. London: Sean Kingston Publishing.

Hultkrantz, Åke. 1989. "The Place of Shamanism in the History of Religions." In *Shamanism: Past and Present*, edited by Mihály Hoppál and Otto von Sadovszky, 43–52. Budapest: Hungarian Academy of Sciences.

Ingold, Tim. 2010. "Footprints through the Weather-World: Walking, Breathing, Knowing." *Journal of the Royal Anthropological Institute*: 121–39.

Jackson, Michael. 1998. *Minima Ethnographica: Intersubjectivity and the Anthropological Project*. Chicago: University of Chicago Press.

Kohn, Tamara. 1994. "Incomers and Fieldworkers: A Comparative Study of Social Experience." In *Social Experience & Anthropological Knowledge*, edited by Kirsten Hastrup and P. Hervik, 13–27. London: Routledge.

Kubica, Grażyna. 1988. "Malinowski's Years in Poland." In *Malinowski between Two Worlds: The Polish Roots of an Anthropological Tradition*, edited by Roy Ellen, Ernest Gellner, Grażyna Kubica, and Janusz Mucha, 88–104. Cambridge: Cambridge University Press.

———. 2013. "Wytyczanie granic między nauką a literaturą: Proza etnograficzna" [Making borders between science and literature: Ethnographic prose]. In *Granice i pogranicza: państw, grup, dyskursów . . . Perspektywa antropologiczna i socjologiczna* [Borders and borderlines of states, groups, discourses . . . Antropological and sociological perspectives], edited by Grażyna Kubica and Halina Rusek, 65–85. Katowice: Wydawnictwo Uniwersytetu Śląskiego.

———. 2015a. "Maria Czaplicka and Her Siberian Expedition, 1914–1915: A Centenary Tribute." *Arctic Anthropology* 25(1): 1–22.

———. 2015b. *Maria Czaplicka: Płeć, szamanizm, rasa; Biografia antropologiczna.* Kraków: Wydawnictwo Uniwersytetu Jagiellońskiego.

———. 2020a. *Maria Czaplicka: Gender, Shamanism, Race.* Critical Studies in the History of Anthropology. Translated by Ben Koschalka. Lincoln: University of Nebraska Press.

———. 2020b. "Emphatic Hegemony and Patriotic Gestures of the Literary Writing of Polish Women-Ethnographers." *East European Politics and Societies and Cultures* 34(3): 712–29. DOI: https://doi.org/10.1177/0888325419891226.

Kubica, Grażyna, and Natalia Yakubova. 2015. "Listy Marii Czaplickiej do Lwa Szternberga" [Letters of Maria Czaplicka to Lev Sternberg]. *Lud* 99: 321–36.

Kuczyński, Antoni. 1989. *Ludy dalekie a bliskie: Antologia polskich relacji o ludach Syberii.* [Peoples far away but close: An anthology of Polish accounts on Siberian peoples] Wrocław: Ossolineum.

Kuper, Adam. 1991. "Anthropologists and the History of Anthropology." *Critique of Anthropology* 11(2): 125–42.

———. 2017. "C. G. Seligman: 'Sligs.'" In *BEROSE International Encyclopaedia of the Histories of Anthropology*, Paris.

Lewis, Ian M. 1989. *Ecstatic Religion: A Study of Shamanism and Spirit Possession.* 2nd ed. London: Routledge.

Lindgren, Ethel John. 1938. "An Example of Culture Contact without Conflict: Reindeer Tungus and Cossacks of Northwestern Manchuria." *American Anthropologists* 40(4): 605–21.

Malinowski, Bronisław. 2002. *Dziennik w ścisłym tego słowa znaczeniu* [A diary in the strict sense of the term]. Annotation and introduction by Grażyna Kubica. Kraków: Wydawnictwo Literackie.

Marcus, George. 1995. "Ethnography in/of the World System: The Emergence of Multi-sited Ethnography." *Annual Review of Anthropology* 24: 95–117.

Marett, Robert R. 1921. "Obituary: Marie A. de Czaplicka: Died May 27th, 1921." *Man* 21(60): 105–6, Royal Anthropological Institute of Great Britain and Ireland.

———. 1943. "An Address." In *Professor Bronislaw Malinowski: An Account of the Memorial Meeting Held at the Royal Institution in London on July 13th 1942.* Oxford: Oxford University Press (Association of Polish University Professors and Lectures in Great Britain).

Mills, David. 2008. *Difficult Folk? A Political History of Social Anthropology*. New York: Berghahn Books.

Morgunova, Ekaterina. 2020. "'The Art of Diplomacy': Political Exiles, Imperial Authorities and Indigenous People in Northeast Siberian Ethnography." Paper presented at the conference "History of Arctic Anthropology," Royal Anthropological Institute, London, 27–28 February 2020.

Pratt, Mary Louise. 1986. "Fieldwork in Common Places." In *Writing Culture: The Poetics and Politics of Ethnography*, edited by James Clifford and George E. Marcus, 27–50. Berkeley: University of California Press.

Rakowski, Tomasz. 2018. "Introduction." In *Pre-Textual Ethnographies: Challenging the Phenomenological Level of Anthropological Knowledge-Making*, edited by Tomasz Rakowski and Helena Patzer, 1–22. London: Sean Kingston Publishing.

Rivière, Peter. 2007. "The Formative Years: The Committee for Anthropology 1905–1938." In *A History of Oxford Anthropology*, edited by Peter Rivière, 43–61. Oxford: Berghahn Books.

Shankland, David. 2014. "Westermarck, Anthropology and the Royal Anthropological Institute." In *Westermarck*, edited by David Shankland, 19–27. London: Sean Kingston Publishing.

Skowron-Markowska, Stefania. 2012. *Z Oksfordu na Syberię: Dziedzictwo naukowe Marii Antoniny Czaplickiej* [From Oxford to Siberia: Scientific heritage of Maria Antonina Czaplicka]. Wrocław: Polskie Towarzystwo Ludoznawcze.

Stocking, George W., Jr. 1982. "Franz Boas and the Culture Concept in Historical Perspective." In *Race, Culture, and Evolution: Essays in the History of Anthropology*, edited by George W. Stocking Jr., 195–233. Chicago: University of Chicago Press.

———. 1995. *After Tylor: British Social Anthropology 1888–1951*. Madison: University of Wisconsin Press.

Tulisow, Jerzy. 2009. *Folklor ludów tunguskich* [Folklore of Tungus people]. Warsaw: Wydawnicwo Akademickie Dialog.

Urry, James, and David N. Collins. 1997. "A Flame Too Intense for Mortal Body to Support." *Anthropology Today* 13(6): 18–20.

Van Velsen, Jan. 1978. "The Extended-Case Method and Situational Analysis." In *The Craft of Social Anthropology*, edited by A. L. Epstein and Max Gluckman, 129–49. London: Routledge.

Vider, Jaanika. 2017. "Marginal Anthropology? Rethinking Maria Czaplicka and the Development of British Anthropology from a Material History Perspective." PhD thesis, School of Anthropology and Museum Ethnography, University of Oxford.

Vincent, Joan. 1991. "Engaging Historicism." In *Recapturing Anthropology: Working in the Present*, edited by Richard G. Fox, 45–58. Santa Fe: School of American Research Press.

Wasilewski, Jerzy Sławomir. 1985. *Podróże do piekieł. Rzecz o szamańskich misteriach* [Travels to hell: On shamanistic mysteries]. Warsaw: Ludowa Spółdzielnia Wydawnicza.

12

Developing Fieldwork in the South American Lowlands

Debates and Practices in the Work of German Ethnographers (1884–1928)

Michael Kraus

On 25 July 1884 Karl von den Steinen (1855–1929) embarked with nineteen travel companions in eight canoes on the Rio Xingu to study the Indigenous groups living in its headwaters (Steinen 1886: 147).[1] The members of the expedition were two other German scholars, three Brazilian helpers—called *camaradas* (comrades) in Portuguese—the Bakairi Indian Antonio,[2] and an escort, mostly soldiers provided by the Baron of Batovy (1828–94), governor of the Brazilian state of Mato Grosso.[3] In his travelogue *Durch Central-Brasilien: Expedition zur Erforschung des Schingú im Jahre 1884* (Through Central Brazil: An expedition to explore the River Xingu in 1884) published in 1886, von den Steinen described the travel route and brief contacts with members of various ethnic groups they had met en route, among them the Bakairi, Kustenau, Trumai, Suya (Kisêdjê), Manitsaua, and Juruna (Yudjá). These encounters lasted from a few hours to a few days.

Three years after the first expedition, von den Steinen set off again for the upper Xingu. His goal was to continue the ethnographic studies begun during the first trip. This time his team consisted of thirteen people: three other scholars, three *camaradas*, a Brazilian lieutenant of German descent, a retired Brazilian lieutenant, four soldiers, and, once more, Bakairi Antonio.[4] On the way, von den Steinen forsook his team for several days in September 1887 and lived in a Bakairi village, where he was the only white man. In retrospect, he regarded "those idyllic days as the happiest" he had experienced. He described how the familiarity with his hosts increased due to his being alone in the village. The Amazon lowland inhabitants, often described as somber and taciturn in the literature, were, so von den Steinen stated, cheerful and talkative. On the Bakairi's openhearted behavior he wrote: "Much of it disappeared when the rest of the expedition arrived; the complete candor with which I was met when alone did not persist, and their behavior was more similar to the familiar pattern as recorded in the books" (Steinen 1894: 56).

Even if this episode does not meet later standards of ethnographic fieldwork, not least in terms of its duration, moments like these contributed significantly to the reflection on and improvement of ethnographic research methods.[5] Alone in the Bakairi village, von den Steinen experienced a qualitative change in his relationships with his hosts, which gave him new insights into their lives. Von den Steinen not only described these experiences but also reflected methodologically on the new quality of investigation that emerged from the changed situation. Both aspects led to a more accurate description of the people he visited and significantly influenced the work of the next generation of scholars.

A Discipline of Travelers:
The Beginnings of Professional Ethnology in Germany

In this chapter I address the debates and practices of Karl von den Steinen and other German ethnologists, above all Konrad Theodor Preuss (1869–1938), Theodor Koch-Grünberg (1872–1924), Max Schmidt (1874–1950), and Fritz Krause (1881–1963). Unlike the other chapters in this book, mine will not focus on a single ethnographer or a single text but will analyze the work of some of the most prominent representatives of two generations of German ethnologists who worked in South America around the turn of the twentieth century. My intention is to highlight some guiding research principles and the development of shared standards and variations upon these as well as open or sometimes also hidden discussions about methods, research topics, and questions of representation among these scholars. Subsequently, I compare the results with the classical paradigm of ethnographic methodology as presented in the introductory chapter of Bronisław Malinowski's *Argonauts of the Western Pacific* (1922).

While their experiences in the field transformed the thinking of these ethnologists, their texts contributed to a reconsideration of firmly anchored ideas in Germany about Indigenous peoples. They helped to correct the "familiar pattern as recorded in the books" about these Indians, as von den Steinen (1894: 56) put it in the passage cited above. I will conclude with some remarks on these new insights and demonstrate the value of these early studies.

As discussed in the introduction to the present volume, ethnographic fieldwork was not a novel scholarly practice at the turn of the century. As the volume clearly shows, this research tradition was not invented by a single person, by a single school, or by representatives of a particular nation. Many different events and encounters helped to develop this central method of ethnological data collection. Thus, my present discussion of German ethnographers in the Amazon Basin reflects a small but vital part of this far more extensive history.

In fact, since the beginning of its professional institutionalization,[6] and thus long before World War I, ethnology in Germany had been anything but an armchair science. Instead, it was often characterized by expeditions that aimed—mostly but not exclusively—to describe indigenous living conditions and to collect material culture (Penny 2002; 2019; Chevron 2006–7; Fischer, Bolz, and Kamel 2007). One important aspect differentiating the scholars discussed in this chapter from other German travelers who amassed collections in South America was that they practiced ethnology as a profession. Both Karl von den Steinen and the abovementioned representatives of the "second generation" (Petschelies 2019a: 297), on the one hand, conducted ethnographic field studies in South America; on the other, they were employed in one of the newly founded ethnological museums in Germany that emerged at the end of the nineteenth and the beginning of the twentieth centuries, sometimes after carrying out their fieldwork, in most cases, however, before that. In addition, all of the individuals mentioned gained their *Habilitation*—their *venia legendi* or teaching credential—with an ethnological treatise at a university. In this way, they contributed both to the development of research methods in the field and to the institutionalization of ethnology as an academic discipline in Germany.

What is remarkable about these scholars is that—almost without exception—they participated in several research expeditions. The later expeditions sometimes took them back to their previous areas of study or to new regions that were previously unknown to them. Von den Steinen traveled twice to the upper Xingu region of Central Brazil for research purposes. He also carried out research in the Marquesas Islands in the Pacific during 1897 and 1898. Theodor Koch-Grünberg traveled through Central Brazil in 1899 as a member of the large-scale but unsuccessful second Xingu expedition led by Herrmann Meyer (1871–1932). From 1903 to 1905 he studied nu-

merous Indigenous groups on the upper Rio Negro, primarily belonging to the Aruak and the Tucano language families. From 1911
to 1913, Koch-Grünberg traveled to northern Brazil and southern
Venezuela, mainly living with the Pemón, Wapichana, Macuxi and
Ye'kwana. Max Schmidt first studied various Indigenous groups
in the Brazilian Xingu region and subsequently the Guató on the
border with Bolivia in 1900–1901. Like von den Steinen, he also returned—sometimes several times—to the areas he had visited on his
first trip. In 1910 he visited the Guató again and also studied a group
of Paresí-Cabishí (Halíti). In 1914 he was in Paraguay among the
Toba and Kainguá. From 1926 to 1928 Schmidt worked again on the
Xingu and continued his studies in the area inhabited by the Guató.
He also visited the Umutina and came into contact with the Kaiabi,
Paresí, and Iranxe, albeit on a limited scale. In 1929 he quit his job
at the Ethnological Museum in Berlin and moved to Brazil for two
years, mostly living in his previous research region of Mato Grosso
before relocating to Paraguay in 1931, where he continued to work as
an ethnologist until his death in 1950. Konrad Theodor Preuss lived
in Cora, Huichol, and Mexicanero villages in Mexico from 1905 to
1907. In 1914–15, in addition to his archaeological activities, Preuss
conducted ethnographic research among the Uitoto and Kogi of Colombia. Fritz Krause undertook only one research trip, visiting the
Karajá and Kayapó along the Rio Araguaia in Brazil in 1908.[7]

The Ambivalence of Collecting
and the Emphasis on Language

Adolf Bastian (1826–1905), one of the founding fathers of an independent and professional ethnology in Germany, exerted a great deal
of influence on the ethnographers presented in this chapter. They
took up his ideas, though not without critical distance, and tried to
move beyond them or develop them further (Kraus 2007).[8] A former
ship's doctor who spent more than twenty years of his life traveling, Bastian was the first to earn a *venia legendi* in ethnography at
the Friedrich-Wilhelms-University (today Humboldt University) in
Berlin, doing so in December 1866.[9] Later, he became director of the
Royal Museum of Ethnology (today the Ethnological Museum of
Berlin), which was founded in 1873.

In the context of the present topic, I want to highlight a short text
from the vast number of his publications. In 1885, Bastian published
Ueber ethnologische Sammlungen (On ethnological collections), in

which he suggested assembling comprehensive collections of material culture. According to Bastian, collectors "should not let themselves be blinded by unusual and remarkable pieces, which in the earlier style of the cabinets of curiosities appear suitable to be hung as trophies" (Bastian 1885: 42). Such objects had been collected and displayed "for entertainment," to inspire "either horror or laughter, depending on the mood" (ibid.: 41). Instead, the aim of scientific collecting should be to "reveal the normal average character of ethnic life and thus to collect tools and devices with all the associated details (preliminary stages in the manufacturing process) down to the last variations" (ibid.: 42). To Bastian, the artifacts collected were extremely valuable for understanding other ways of life. He described them as "the only texts from which the intellectual life of tribes without writing can be read in the future" (ibid.: 40).[10]

In addition to such a collecting strategy, focused not on spectacular pieces but on holistic representations, Bastian's essay contains a number of ideas that go far beyond the collecting of material culture. Quite a few of these anticipate considerations that Malinowski addressed almost forty years later in *Argonauts of the Western Pacific.* As early as 1885, Bastian saw the need for scientific training of travelers, and he criticized the poor quality of data that resulted from "fleeting observations during brief sojourns" (ibid.: 38). He further emphasized the need for patient listening. In scientific research, there should be no question of "asking, or even questioning, but only of listening, of hearing during conversation [*vom Lauschen nur, im gesprächsweisen Heraushören*]" because with "incorrect questions, everything becomes an illusion, the information is falsified and much more spoiled. No instruction can help determine which question is the right one in a particular case if it does not emerge instinctively" (ibid.: 39–40). And, much in line with Malinowski's (1922: 25) famous formulation of the "native's point of view," for Bastian one of ethnology's central tasks was to "follow the native's train of thought [*den Gedankengang des Naturmenschen nachzudenken*]" (Bastian 1885: 38–39).

In contrast to the mere "observing and collecting," suggested by the various *Anleitungen* (manuals) published by the Ethnological Museum at the turn of the century, which were also directed to lay travelers (see, for example, Luschan 1904 and Ankermann 1914)—and to the alleged hostility to the spoken word and written texts in early German ethnology claimed by some modern historians of anthropology[11]—philological research methods were among the central tools applied by the ethnographers presented here (Kraus 2007: 145–

48). After his first expedition to the Xingu, von den Steinen already stressed that "linguistics ... was the key" in any attempt to classify the ethnic diversity of the Amazon Basin (Steinen 1886: 325). Years later, von den Steinen gave his subordinate at the Ethnological Museum, Koch-Grünberg, a paper with a "travel instruction" that was also given in similar form to other scientists who carried out research on behalf of the museum. In it, Koch-Grünberg was told to generate, "if at all possible among those [tribes] who live away from the usual traffic routes and who are still little known or not known at all—a systematic collection with the greatest possible consideration of series [of objects] and record them both ethnographically and linguistically." He should also "give preference under all circumstances to a longer stay with a single tribe over superficial visits with a number of them."[12]

In addition to mentioning the task of collecting material culture, precisely documenting it, and establishing contacts for the museum, the "travel instruction" states explicitly that the researcher would have to collect, "apart from useful word lists, above all original texts on tradition and mythology" of the Indian groups to be visited.[13]

Preuss, who among the ethnographers presented here committed himself most intensely to the study of indigenous language and thought during his researches in Mexico and Colombia, emphasized that in the field, the ethnographer should "feel fully like the learner and record as precisely as possible the worldview passed down in the indigenous language" (Preuss 1926a: 11).

As clear as the findings are regarding the importance of language for the ethnographers of the Amazon region, they are contradictory regarding the seemingly unambiguous aspect of collecting. Looking at the practice of his scientific research, we can see that even Bastian's handling of material culture was contradictory. One of the interesting peculiarities of his biography is that he himself, while publicly committed to expanding the ethnographic collections of the Ethnological Museum and repeatedly emphasizing their theoretical and methodological value, hardly ever conducted research on the basis of these objects, as his contemporaries von den Steinen (1905: 247) or Preuss observed (1926b: 6). A look at his diverse publications, where discussions on mythology, religious philosophy, psychology, linguistics, physical anthropology, or legal issues prevail, confirms this.[14]

As for the ethnologists examined here, collecting material culture was one of the common aspects of their ethnographic work.[15] They regularly and thoroughly described the objects they had acquired themselves or worked with objects from collections already held in the museum. However, despite their uniform research practice—the extensive acquisition of objects in the field and the detailed analysis of their use—they held quite ambivalent attitudes to their actual value. For example, von den Steinen, like Bastian, attached a good deal of scientific value to these objects but had little illusion about their effect when exhibited in a museum:

> The image of past times preserved in our ethnological museums is basically that of a poor assortment. The life of a people in a glass cabinet! But for the lack of anything better, these brightly colored rags and whimsical devices must serve future generations as testimonies of the development of humankind, and therefore what appears to be junk gradually acquires the value of priceless documents. (Steinen 1886: 328)

In his letters, Koch-Grünberg complained several times that he ultimately had little time for mythological studies during his trip to the upper Rio Negro, "because I had to collect for museums."[16] When he later became director of the museum in Stuttgart, he himself had to point out to Curt Nimuendajú (1882–1945), who had already emigrated to Brazil, that the museum he directed could unfortunately only finance the collection of objects, not the study of myths or the documenting of languages.[17] In a letter to Nimuendajú he wrote:

> To be honest, although I am a museum director, I do not put too much value on ethnographic collections. If one has lived among the natives in their freedom and seen them in their splendid jewelry, one feels repelled by the often battered objects in the glass cabinets. I think Bastian once said: "One cannot display the soul of a people in a glass cabinet!"[18]

It cannot be ruled out that Koch-Grünberg confused the "Bastian quote" in his letter with the above cited passage from von den Steinen. In any case, in his answer, Nimuendajú referred to this passage and commented that von den Steinen had seen "the Redskin too long in their natural setting to still be able to enjoy ethnographic cabinets."[19] These quotes demonstrate the ethnographers' skepticism about the value of the now lifeless-appearing objects in the museum—a result of their vivid experiences in the field.[20]

Preuss, who had carried out archaeological work in Colombia as well and who presented the results in a large, special exhibit after World War I (Reyes 2019: 309–24), brought back extensive ethnographic collections from his trips to Mexico and Colombia (Fischer, Haas, and Theis 2007; Reyes 2019). At least in Mexico he sometimes seemed to be pragmatic about his collecting: he let his local assistants manage the collection of the objects so that he could concentrate on his linguistic and religious studies, which interested him even more (Valdovinos 2012: 73). Krause pointed out that funding these research expeditions was often only possible through museums, which automatically entailed the obligation to collect objects of material culture.[21]

Consequently, even if the assembling of material culture collections was a central part of the scholarly work of these ethnographers, the huge number of objects they collected did not always reflect their real interests. What was often claimed as "collecting mania" (*Sammelwut*) was sometimes as much an obligation or an economic necessity as it was a personal interest.[22] Therefore, an examination of the collection process needs to consider both the theoretical debates about the significance of material culture and the specific acquisition processes in the field—including the behavior and interests of Indigenous partners. However, a distinction also needs to be made between the interests of individual scholars and the constraints put on them by institutional research funding structures (cf. Kraus 2014).

One more aspect of Bastian's 1885 text needs to be considered at this point. Prioritizing the growth of collections as the basis for future research in the museums, Bastian in the very same article took back one of his other central requirements of ethnographic research for practical reasons—the avoidance of "fleeting observations during brief sojourns." Because he feared the disappearance of what were then still called *Naturvölker* (natural peoples), he called for action: to record and collect as quickly as possible everything that was still possible to be recorded and collected. "These documents," he wrote, "are disappearing before our very eyes, every day all around us, because they are being torn away by the current of destructive time, washed away and waning; we are often left only to amass, to hoard them as quickly and as much as the circumstances allow (although 'the better, all the better,' of course)" (Bastian 1885: 40).

This section reveals the sometimes contradictory nature of the guidelines and methodological considerations of the time. Meeting the parallel requirements of collecting as comprehensively as possible and, at the same time, remaining in one place for as long as possible could pose difficulties in practice. Almost twenty years later this problem returned in von den Steinen's "travel instruction" to Koch-Grünberg. However, while Bastian prioritized the collection of what was to date unknown, reducing the longer stay to a desirable extra, von den Steinen prioritized the longer stay "under all circumstances." Visits to previously unknown villages and the collection of their material culture should only take place "if at all possible."[23]

Fatalistic Views of History, Violent Contexts, and the Reduction of Power Asymmetries

Beyond Bastian's interesting but somewhat contradictory method-ological suggestions and the shift in research priorities two decades later, the passage on the urgency of recording and collecting reflects another important aspect of this era. While the ethnographers appar-ently held themselves to be apolitical, in reality their journeys were shaped by political constellations. What Bastian paraphrased euphe-mistically as "the current of destructive time" was in reality a result of brutal human violence—a context that also influenced the encoun-ters that took place during the research expeditions. Bastian's fatalis-tic position can also be found in the writings of von den Steinen, who was convinced of the inevitability of such tragic developments, which called forth a good deal of sympathy for the Indians but did not lead to a fundamental criticism of the "expansion of the higher races" (Steinen 1886: 327). Von den Steinen identified the causes and real actors in these developments as an abstract collective. He remained vague, even if he was a little closer to the mark than Bastian: "Danger is imminent! A great flood could not wreak greater havoc, destroy less mercilessly the old conditions than the march of civilization . . . the flood kills and buries, civilization kills and destroys" (ibid.).

Therefore, before going into the individual research strategies in more detail, let us take a look at the reactions of the researchers to the political conditions in which they worked. In fact, there was an am-bivalent interplay between the realities on the ground, often charac-terized by violence, and the reactions to them in the research context and in fulfilling research interests.[24] The ethnologists found them-selves torn between the interests of different Indian groups, gov-ernments, and a large number of other actors, such as missionaries, traders, settlers, adventurers, and not least the rubber barons, who in many cases acted very brutally in their relations with the Indigenous populations. Previous experiences with non-Indigenous peoples in turn influenced the attitudes of the Indians toward the ethnogra-phers. How did the ethnologists deal with this initial condition of entangled but asymmetrical power relations?[25]

In a letter written in 1884, von den Steinen reflected the ambiva-lent and unpredictable situation his expedition faced when they left Cuiabá, the provincial capital. On the one hand, he wrote, the mil-itary escort provided by the governor could easily become "an un-fortunate factor in our calculations"; on the other, "febre, fome und frecha" (fever, hunger, and arrow, in Portuguese) were to be expected during the trip. "Regardless of all desires for friendship [*Freund-schaftsgelüste*] we have for the sons of the wilderness," he continued, a "good armament should be seriously considered."[26] The ethnographers were caught in a difficult and by no means easily navigable situation. Developments "in the field" were defined not only by their own actions vis-à-vis the Indians; instead, they were characterized and influenced by a large number of factors that are difficult to grasp or control. Depending on the situation, they responded quite differently to the conditions they found. While von den Steinen set out with a comparatively large team and Koch-Grünberg co-opted the greater political situation for his own purposes from time to time, claiming, for example, that the Brazilian government was interested in the results of his research (Kraus 2004: 311–12; 2018: 117), Max Schmidt chose the opposite path. He laid down his weapons and took off his clothes demonstratively to bathe in the river in front of the Indians so as to show his personal harmlessness and peaceful intentions (Schmidt 1905: 71).

Thus, the attitudes held and strategies applied by the ethnologists ranged from "desires for friendship" to the exchange of goods and to "good armament" (for more detail, see Kraus 2004: 144–247). The weapons carried on both sides symbolize the multifaceted nature of possible relations. They were used for demonstrations of power, but also for hunting and sharing food, or even for trading. Trading, intensified due to the ethnographers' obligation to collect material culture for museums in Germany, was also a central element of the relationships from an indigenous point of view. A recent analysis of the oral traditions of the Kuikuro gives an example of how von den Steinen's expeditions were interpreted by inhabitants of the upper Xingu. In contrast to violent earlier clashes, they are remembered as the arrival of "tame" whites with whom exchange relations could be consolidated. In addition to objects, private names were also exchanged with von den Steinen, a sign of friendship according to Indian understanding (Franchetto 1992: 347–48; see Steinen 1894: 125, 129).

Despite all potential conflicts and dangers, what seems to be of great importance in this context is that over time, the German ethnographers in South America made a notable shift toward ever smaller expedition teams and an increased reliance on indigenous support. On their early twentieth-century travels, Konrad Theodor Preuss, Max Schmidt, and Theodor Koch-Grünberg were accompanied for the most part by only one non-Indigenous assistant. For everything else, they relied on Indigenous companions, whom the researchers recruited on site both as informants and for logistical support. Only

Fritz Krause hired additional Brazilian *camaradas* for his trip on the Rio Araguaia; however, he declined the offer of a military escort with explicit reference to the negative experiences of Francis De Laporte de Castelnau (1810–80) and von den Steinen (Krause 1911: 28).

The overall political situation in which the expeditions took place did not change due to the reduced number of non-Indigenous expedition members; and yet, the decision as to how the concrete relations at the village level or during the journey were to be structured was now to a much greater extent in the hands of the Indians. There are many examples of how the latter were able to determine what happened during the visits of the ethnographers: a Tucano village chief, for example, prohibited Koch-Grünberg from taking pictures at a ceremony; Krause was asked by the Javaé to leave their village after a few days, and he complied—unlike von den Steinen, who in 1887 refused a similar request by the Nahukuá. Masks that Krause wanted to acquire were deemed too valuable to be sold to him. Particularly impressive was the conduct of the Uitoto Rïgasẹdyue, who was one of Preuss's most important informants. He demonstrated to the ethnographer the limits of his power and influence when he carved a figurine that Preuss would have liked to have acquired and then demonstratively destroyed it in front of his eyes. Schmidt, in turn, had to leave the Aweti village he was visiting during his first trip in some haste after the villagers had decided to simply take the trade goods he had brought along for themselves.[27]

That said, the encounters in the field were often characterized by "desires for friendship" on both sides. However, the events outlined illustrate how fragile social relations were during the research, how both sides were involved in shaping them, and how they were constantly being renegotiated.

Between Research Expeditions and Stationary Research

Apart from common characteristics and the initial conditions with which these ethnologists had to contend, their strategies to implement the guidelines of their sponsors and their personal interests present differences. This can be demonstrated by comparing the research done by Koch-Grünberg and Preuss.[28] The ambitious goal of breaking new geographic and ethnographic ground, admitted by von den Steinen to have been a motivating factor during his first expedition—"Why shouldn't one admit his weakness? I confess that when I considered the plan to explore the Xingu, I was not free from a certain joyful ambition: one wants to try something that no one has done before" (Steinen 1886: 8)—can be found in Koch-Grünberg as well.[29] On each of his expeditions, Koch-Grünberg crossed very large areas that had scarcely been documented by scientists before. However, he also lived for a few weeks at a time in individual villages[30] and developed a strong relationship with some of his hosts and companions. In between extensive and intensive modes of doing ethnography, this travel practice with repeated, longer stays in several villages along the route is reflected in the material results of Koch-Grünberg's research. In the case of his Rio Negro expedition, apart from the ethnographic observations, this included linguistic material in the form of long lists of words and sentences from more than forty ethnic groups, about one thousand photographs, a collection of more than eighteen hundred objects[31] from various groups, plant and rock samples, a butterfly collection, weather observations, and notes on the geography of the territory.

Konrad Theodor Preuss, on the other hand, spent almost nineteen months in Indian villages in northwestern Mexico between 1905 and 1907. He was a guest of the Cora for almost seven months, worked with the Huichol for nine months, and then spent another three with the Mexicaneros. In a letter from Mexico he described his approach: "I worked 10–12 hours a day; with my H[uichol] I always made strict 14-day contracts with promises of a high gratification at the end, if they would not miss a single day. And I got my will."[32] In 1914–15, following his archaeological work in San Agustin, Colombia, he was a guest for three months each with the Uitoto in the Amazon lowlands and with the Kogi in the Sierra Nevada. Here too the focus of his work was on the transcription of stories and myths. In his view, even a longer stay would be inadequate if the researcher concentrated on observation alone. Preuss's main intention was not to document the everyday cultural expressions of the people he visited. Instead, he wanted to understand their thinking and their worldview. To do so, the ethnographer had "to bring those persons knowledgeable of the old traditions, songs, prayers and magical formulæ to slowly dictate all their wisdom in their language, and to discuss every word with them, in order that he could bring home a kind of bible from each tribe" (Preuss 1926a: 10).

As his extensive and mostly bilingual transcriptions from the Cora, Uitoto, and Kogi show,[33] this was no lofty goal on Preuss's part, and he also realized this. In addition to the transcriptions he made and later published, he likewise brought extensive collections to Berlin: 2,300 objects from Mexico (Fischer, Haas, and Theis 2007:

96) and 791 (mainly archaeological) pieces from Colombia (Reyes 2019: 283).

For Preuss, the intensification of stationary research was a fundamental necessity. To him, Karl von den Steinen had initiated "the study of Brazilian Indians by using modern methods that consider nothing to be unworthy of consideration and understand the Indian psyche from the proper perspective."[34] However, he felt it necessary to add that

> research only progressed, following the master's example, . . . in its [geographical] scope; it was and is considered the greatest achievement to be the first to visit a tribe or even to find one that has never been seen by a white man. The size of Brazil and the small number of scholars . . . repeatedly obscure the fact that not a single Indian tribe has been thoroughly examined so far, with the documentation of their oral traditions and their observation over months or even years, which is what under all circumstances needs to be demanded of ethnology today. (Preuss 1914: 255, 257)

Already after his research in Mexico, Preuss had declared that in ethnology the "time of traveling around" was over. He pointed out that fieldwork should ideally take at least a year, as this would, for example, allow one "to observe the cycle of annual festivals" (Preuss 1912: iv; 1908: 149). After his fieldwork in Colombia, he again emphasized that "ethnographic travelers must have the courage to go where others have already been fleetingly, that is, to almost all tribes of South America, and [they must] renounce their ambition to find only previously unvisited Indians or even those who have never seen a white man. Because hardly any of them are left" (Preuss 1926c: 2–3). He criticized the tendency to "chase the phantom of so-called untouched children of nature, from whom one can acquire collections and theories but never precise knowledge, as supplies for a longer stay are unavailable and no Indian is fluent in a common language" (Preuss 1921: 24–25).

Thus, Preuss can be called a pioneer of stationary ethnographic fieldwork. However, the aspect of the "journey" must be examined more closely. While to Preuss an "ethnographic study essentially requires sitting still" (Preuss 1926c: 3) and travel was "unusual" and, indeed, "forced idleness" (ibid.: 8), on other expeditions the process of traveling with Indian companions constituted an essential part of the research. Shared activities such as hunting, paddling, and the preparation of food provided significant insights, as did their joint guest status in the villages of other ethnic groups and the resulting opportunity to get to know how relationships between members of different ethnic groups functioned. In addition, traveling together also offered the opportunity to improve one's language skills. While Karl von den Steinen spent only a few days in the Indian villages of the Rio Xingu's upper reaches, he spent a total of almost a year in the company of the Bakairi Antonio during his two expeditions. At the end of the first expedition in 1884 the latter even accompanied him to Rio de Janeiro. Antonio was von den Steinen's key informant on the culture of the Bakairi, and a photograph of him adorns the frontispiece of his 1892 book on their language. In addition, the learning process was mutual: "During our long time together, his broken Portuguese improved to such an extent that I was able to learn, my Bakairi progressing as well, everything that was essential from him" (Steinen 1892: v). For Koch-Grünberg, an extensive collection of myths was one of the results of the time spent traveling. These were told to him during "idle hours . . . around the campfire" and "during the journey in the rocking canoe" (Koch-Grünberg 1916–28: 2:v) by the Arekuna Möseuaípu and the Taurepan Mayuluaípu, who accompanied him in early 1912 on his expedition up the Rio Uraricuera from northern Brazil to southern Venezuela (see figure 12.1).

Thus, both "staying longer" and "moving on" could help realize another important aspect of the research methodology: the intensification of social relationships. In their reports, the ethnographers showed a willingness to take part in Indian life beyond observing, exchanging, collecting, and recording. Koch-Grünberg, for example, regularly took part in dances and feasts, in everyday activities such as eating or bathing together, hunting, fishing, or even playing with both adults and children. During his stay in Pari-Cachoeira he wrote, for example: "The children had the greatest pleasure when we let them pull us half across the village square [trapped] in the 'snake'" (Koch-Grünberg 1909–10: 1:274).[35] Similar to von den Steinen, cited in the introduction to this chapter, Koch-Grünberg occasionally separated from his Brazilian companion. A short passage about his stay in Urubú-Lago on the Rio Tiquié illustrates on the one hand the informal atmosphere that often prevailed; on the other, the exchange was by no means limited to material items but also comprised reciprocal information and stories:

> In the next two weeks I spent peaceful and enjoyable days here alone with the Indians. Soon I was as familiar with these magnificent and unspoiled people as if we had known each other for years. . . . Every evening we sat together and carried out scientific studies. I told them about the tribes on the distant Xingú and they provided me with ethnographic details about the inhabitants of the Caiarí and its tributaries. Later we

Figure 12.1. *The Taurepan Mayuluaípu and Theodor Koch-Grünberg recording myths. Photograph by Hermann Schmidt, 1911–12. © Nachlass Theodor Koch-Grünberg, Ethnographische Sammlung der Philipps-Universität Marburg (KG-H-III, 122).*

crouched in front of the Maloka, on the white sand of the village square, to enjoy the fresh night air, and then we turned [our attention] to astronomy. (Koch-Grünberg 1909–10: 1:244)

Attempts to participate also occur among ethnographers who did not travel for such long periods and were more distant in their social encounters. Walter Krickeberg (1885–1962), at the time a staff member at the Ethnological Museum in Berlin, reported on a lecture Fritz Krause had given there: "Krause had every technique shown to him and learned all the basic activities—pottery, mask making, net weaving."[36]

As outlined above, the early expeditions were by no means free from conflict. Diverging interests influenced the field of their encounters and their research. However, one characteristic feature of the expeditions was increased participation in the activities of the respective other and, closely and directly connected with it, an increase in the scope of exchange relationships. In addition to paying for objects, food, and services with goods brought along, the ethnographers tried to intensify their relations with the Indians they visited by participating in their day-to-day social lives, which by no means meant only observing events or adapting their own behavior to local customs; it also included showing photographs and picture books, telling stories about home or their experiences among other Indian groups, singing or playing songs on the phonograph, or explaining the technical equipment and other things they had brought with them (see figure 12.2). Even if the asymmetries caused by superordinate structures remained, reciprocity as a characteristic of the concrete relationships increased significantly.

Figure 12.2. *Demonstration of a bird whistle in the village of the Mehinakú during the second Xingu expedition of Karl von den Steinen. Photograph by Paul Ehrenreich, 1887. © Ethnologisches Museum Berlin (P 6110).*

Description with Public Appeal
versus Scientific Theory Building

Thus, apart from traveling and collecting, the following developed as methodological standards in their work: longer stays in the field, access through language, the intensification of social contacts by means of an increase in reciprocal relations, and an active participation in local life. However, these developments were not linear. Despite the establishment of standards and common features, a large range of approaches was possible. Focusing on the field studies undertaken by Preuss and Koch-Grünberg, taking place almost simultaneously, one more aspect in which both ethnographers differed should be addressed: How was the collected data to be analyzed? Who was being addressed, and what was the best form of presentation? A comparison of passages from their respective oeuvres—not always published and not always chronological—reveals what can almost be considered a hidden dialogue.

The central publication that emerged from Koch-Grünberg's expedition to the northwestern Amazon was his two-volume work *Zwei Jahre unter den Indianern: Reisen in Nordwest-Brasilien in 1903/1905* (Two years among the Indians: Travels through Northwestern Brazil in 1903–1905). This account addressed both colleagues in academia and lay readers. Originally published in 1909 and 1910, it was reissued twice in abridged "people's editions" or *Volksausgaben* during the 1920s. The lively narrative reflects the tension of the journey, its adventurous character, the regular changes in location, and the various encounters in villages. These accounts are combined with extensive ethnographic descriptions. The results of the subsequent voyage, which took the ethnographer "from Roraima to the Orinoco" between 1911 and 1913, was published in five volumes dealing with travel experiences, myths, ethnography, type photographs, and linguistics. Even if certain aspects were treated separately, Koch-Grünberg remained faithful to the large number of topics dealt with and to the requirements of a detailed and lively travelogue. The travel description formed the first volume and closely followed his handwritten notes made en route. In the introduction, Koch-Grünberg emphasized that the first volume was "a description of the journey, most of it diary pages in informal diction, with immediate impressions recorded on the spot" (Koch-Grünberg 1916–28: 1:v). A systematic presentation of the ethnographic data can be found in volume 3, but even here Koch-Grünberg refrained for the most part from theoretical excursions. His primary concern was to "publish the collected material," he wrote in a letter to the musicologist Erich M. von Hornbostel (1877–1935). "Any parallels only play a subordinate role. This is how I did it in the manuscript in which my material is in the main text, while all the parallels are in the footnotes."[37] What was important to Koch-Grünberg both in his writing and his many public lectures was to address not only his fellow scholars but also a broader audience (see Kraus 2004: 65–68, 455–57). In a letter to his Czech colleague Alberto Vojtěch Frič (1882–1944) he wrote that he wanted to "correct the preposterous misconceptions of the great mass about 'natural peoples' [*Naturvölker*]."[38]

In a diary entry during his Roraima-Orinoco expedition Koch-Grünberg criticized with explicit reference to the work of Preuss the use of too much interpretation in ethnographic descriptions, calling it "hypothetical."[39] In a letter to Walter Lehmann (1878–1939) he polemicized against Preuss's lunar interpretation of Uitoto mythology: "He seems to have become 'moonstruck'! Too bad about all his beautiful material! It will in future be difficult to separate the wheat from the chaff, and the Uitoto would be astonished to see what has become of their myths."[40]

Preuss, on the other hand, only briefly discussed the circumstances surrounding his research or the general situation in the villages he visited in his three large monographs on the Cora, Uitoto, and Kogi (Preuss 1912, 1921, 1926c). His focus was on the interpretation of the texts he recorded with reference to the festivals and rites he had observed as well as on an analysis of the respective religious systems. Nevertheless, the most extensive part of each volume was not the interpretation of the songs, stories, and myths he had recorded but their respective texts, printed verbatim in both the indigenous language and in German translation. His works on the Cora, Uitoto, and Kagaba also include extensive glossaries. In his foreword to *Die Nayarit-Expedition*, he emphasized the value of this approach by stating that, "in a publication, it is no longer enough to simply print the diary notes and a list of vocabularies." Instead, "an analysis of the textual material and a critical comparison of all information and observations" was needed (Preuss 1912: iv). In contrast to Koch-Grünberg, Preuss dealt extensively with contemporary theories and analytical models and tried to use his data for a general conceptualization of "religion"—which he defined as "life care by supernatural means [*Lebensfürsorge mit übernatürlichen Mitteln*]" (Preuss 1937: 98; 1926a). He explicitly defended this approach. For example, regarding his interpretation that the myths of the Uitoto were based on the phases of the moon, he stated that "it would have been more convenient to refrain from this chapter because a perfect result is impossible to reach. Nevertheless, a scholar has the duty to arrive at a conclusion as much as possible and then to express it, if only to further knowledge by encouraging criticism" (Preuss 1921: 115).

Argonauts of the Western Pacific: Nihil Novi sub Sole?

As mentioned at the beginning, ethnographic fieldwork was practiced and developed simultaneously by many people in many places. The scholars presented in this chapter are only a sample of a broader process. In the introductory chapter "The Subject, Method and Scope of This Inquiry" of *Argonauts of the Western Pacific*, Bronisław Malinowski also cited a short list of predecessors (Malinowski 1922: 9, 14). In the following I shall compare this text, which has become a *locus classicus* in anthropology, with the developments described above. It turns out that a significant number of the methodological principles discussed by Malinowski had already been debated and practiced by the ethnographers of the Amazon Basin and thus were far from being genuine innovations. Therefore, passages found at the beginning of the *Argonauts* appear to be a bundling of methodological approaches that had become fairly well known elsewhere in the meantime.

As described in my introduction above, von den Steinen had already emphasized the qualitative benefits of being alone in the field. In turn, Malinowski wrote: "Indeed, in my first piece of Ethnographic research on the South coast, it was not until I was alone in the district that I began to make some headway" (ibid.: 6). The value Malinowski attached to everyday life, but also to special events such as healing or funeral rites, "the capacity of enjoying their company and sharing some of their games and amusements" (ibid.: 8), as well as his general willingness "to put aside camera, note book and pencil, and to join in himself in what is going on" (ibid.: 21), are also reminiscent of the practices of the ethnographers discussed here, most certainly Koch-Grünberg's. In Krickeberg's description of Krause's practical approach, the latter not only observed but also practiced the first steps of craftsmanship, thus learning indigenous skills and technologies.

Malinowski's findings that the principles of religious beliefs were "mangled by being forced into pidgin English" (ibid.: 5), that no serious insights could be obtained even from those whites who had lived in the region for a long time (ibid.), and that "translation often robbed the text of all its significant characteristics" (ibid.: 23) correspond to Preuss's convictions, implemented during his fieldwork in the Americas. With his elaborated collections of texts in native languages, Preuss compiled a real *"corpus inscriptionum"* (ibid.: 24, italics in the original) of the societies visited. In turn, the view emphasized by Malinowski that scholarship had "the fundamental obligation of giving a complete survey of the phenomena, and not of picking out the sensational, the singular, still less the funny and quaint" (ibid.: 11) recalls Bastian's position on curiosity cabinets, even if Bastian focused his attention on the collection of material culture.

The *"imponderabilia of actual life"* (ibid.: 18, italics in the original), as Malinowski called the exact observation of everyday life that often deviated from normative, vernacular descriptions, was documented by the ethnographers of the Amazon Basin both during their research travels and during their stays in the villages. Malinowski wrote about the registration of imponderable facts that "so far, it has been done only by amateurs" (ibid.: 19), but as we have seen, this label does not apply to the German ethnographers under consideration. Moreover, diary writing was so much a part of their lives that Indigenous informants sometimes perceived their pen and paper as a typical characteristic of their behavior (see figure 12.3).[41]

Even Malinowski's insistence that the methodology applied be disclosed (ibid.: 2) can be seen in the work and writings of his German predecessors. In their travel descriptions or *Reiseschilderungen*, which usually precede or at times even intertwine directly with the ethnographic data as well as in their short essays or the "travel letters" (*Reisebriefe*) published from the field

Figure 12.3. *A native's point of view: Making a pencil sketch of Koch-Grünberg, the Siusí Tarú drew him with pen and paper as utensils. From Koch-Grünberg 1905.*

in academic journals, these early ethnographers usually gave very detailed insights into the specific course of their research. While these reports were often criticized in later discussions as a form of self-aggrandizement or the staging of ethnographic authority, they also had two more practical functions. On the one hand, they provided exact information on the travel routes and conditions, up to and including discussions about the quality of equipment taken along or health aspects, which in turn could be of great value for later travelers (Kraus 2004: 204–18). On the other hand, the sometimes diary-like descriptions of concrete experiences provide clues on the context and the conditions under which the data had been collected as well as on the personal attitude of the author in question. Fritz Krause was explicit in identifying this as a methodological necessity, since data collected during a research expedition could only "be appraised correctly when the manner of their attainment is known, that is, the conditions under which the studies took place" (Krause 1911: iii; see also Preuss 1912: v). Preuss, in turn, emphasized the need to publish glossaries so as to be able to verify the published texts and interpretations. Otherwise, the data would "assume the character of secret knowledge, guarded warily by the scholar" (Preuss 1912: v).

Malinowski's consideration "that only such ethnographic sources are of unquestionable scientific value, in which we can clearly draw the line between, on the one hand, the results of direct observation and of native statements and interpretations, and on the other, the inferences of the author" (Malinowski 1922: 3), was also anticipated by Krause when he wrote in the ethnographic part of his book on the 1908 expedition to Brazil:

> A strict distinction has been made between those events that have been observed once or several times and those about which information had been solely reported. In my view, this distinction cannot be made strict enough, if errors are to be avoided that afterwards are passed on and on. Some reports that seemed uncertain to me are dealt with in the footnotes, as a sign to later researchers that they should be checked. (Krause 1911: iv; see also Preuss 1912: v)

Nevertheless, a significant difference to Malinowski's aspiration can be found in Krause's next sentence:

> I believe to pay the best service to scholarship by publishing the material itself and only as such. In such a way it remains usable forever. While this method, which does not seek to solve problems or demonstrate far-reaching relations, is considered "out of date" by some people, I consider it the

> only correct way to maintain the scientific value of each notification and thus verify data that alone can advance us in our science. (Krause 1911: iv)

Similar to the dispute between Koch-Grünberg and Preuss, what distinguishes Malinowski from many of the ethnographers presented here is the degree to which he theoretically ordered and analyzed the data collected. What was new was not so much Malinowski's methodological considerations of fieldwork or his appeal for considering "the whole area of tribal culture *in all its aspects*" (Malinowski 1922: 11, italics in the original); rather, compared to the discussions between German ethnographers of the Amazon Basin, it was his call to analyze the interrelations and interactions between the individual aspects of culture: "The consistency, the law and order which obtain within each aspect make also for joining them into one coherent whole. An ethnographer who sets out to study only religion, or only technology, or only social organisation cuts out an artificial field for inquiry, and he will be seriously handicapped in his work" (ibid.).

German ethnographers of the Amazon region were influenced by contemporary theories and dealt with them directly or indirectly — the influence of evolutionism and how fieldwork softened these views, or the almost uniform rejection of diffusionism (Kraus 2019), for example, was typical. What remained an exception were attempts at developing new grand models or suggesting overarching interpretations. The rare attempts in this direction included approaches to structural-functional considerations on the part of Krause, or more detailed theoretical considerations by Schmidt on cultural change among the Aruak or Preuss's discussion of mythology and religion. Paul Ehrenreich's comparative mythology studies can also be mentioned in this context (Kraus 2004: chap. 4).

As for the majority of published studies, it needs to be noted that when the German ethnographers tried to discuss "the whole area of tribal culture *in all its aspects*" (to use Malinowski's phrasing), they did so on the basis of European categories, stringing together chapters like "technology," "economy," or "art." Dichotomies between "intellectual" and "material culture" marked these discussions much more than the idea of immanent, cultural consistency.[42] In those cases where they left the empirical for the sphere of "speculative and comparative theories" (as Malinowski 1922: 9n, stated it), they generally limited themselves to a particular aspect of culture, such as "cultural change" or "religion." A "new type of theory" (ibid.: 515) that focuses on the interactions between cultural institutions, considering "the influence on one another of the various aspects of an institution, the study of the social and psychological mechanism on which the institution is based" (ibid.: 516), was only rarely taken into account by this generation of pre–World War I ethnographers, although Schmidt and Preuss came quite close to fulfilling Malinowski's ideal.

A closer look at the views of individual ethnographers also shows how inappropriate it is to think in terms of one theory replacing another. Instead, parts of different approaches and theoretical conceptualizations shaped the thinking of particular epochs or of individual scholars. A 1926 text dealing with the restructuring of the Ethnological Museum in Berlin shows, on the one hand, that Preuss still adhered to evolutionist ideas and the division of peoples into stages of development. In his opinion, ethnology was primarily concerned with peoples who "provide the substrata for higher cultures" (Preuss 1926d: 67). In the very same text, however, he also argued in functionalist terms comparable to Malinowski's approach, emphasizing the semantic intertwining of the collections. A single object, Preuss argued, says little to the ethnologist: "It is always, rather, its relation to the entire culture of the people in question that gives it its value" (Preuss 1926d: 67; see also Reyes 2018: 12).[43] And this is why ethnological museums also show objects of art and technology, even if they are not—or even more than—museums of art and museums of technology.

Reducing the Distance

I want to close with one final point. Edward E. Evans-Pritchard (1902–73) once wrote about fieldwork that anyone "could produce a new fact"; however, "the thing is to produce a new idea" (Evans-Pritchard 1973: 3). Even if the ethnographers discussed above prioritized the ethnographic description of Indigenous groups over theory building,[44] it would be wrong to reduce them to mere collectors of data. The understanding that the collection of "raw data" or "facts" is a complex, creative process that in itself includes a great deal of interpretation (Sperber 1989; Dürr 2017) was still in its infancy—both among the ethnographers of the Amazon Basin and Malinowski. They were all convinced of the questionable and sometimes self-deceptive, positivist ideas of "common sense" or a "prejudice-free perspective" (Malinowski 1922: 3; Steinen 1897: vii; Koch-Grünberg 1909–10: 1:iv). It is precisely because each and every representation of a foreign culture is an interpretive process, in which anthropologists themselves are the central instrument for data collection (Dürr

2017: 90) and thus the reliability of the results presented is subject to narrow limits, that it is important to ask which ideas were conveyed to the writings of the scholars examined here.

For a time at least, the publication of Malinowski's diary resulted in a major scandal due to the derogatory statements it contains. The rather candid and personal ways of writing of the pre-Malinowskian German ethnographers also reveal manners of thought and categorizations we would reject today. This includes, for example, the description of old women as "witches" by von den Steinen (1886: 160, 179; 1894: 58, 123) or the disparaging depiction of the "Makú" by Koch-Grünberg (1906).[45] It is necessary to be aware of such passages in these early ethnographic texts and to reflect on their possible effects. However, one also has to ask which views dominated a scholar's overall work. In order to avoid a presentist or "chronocentric" interpretation (Streck 1997: 42, 51), that is, an assessment of the past based exclusively on the standards of the present, it is necessary to consider how the respective representations were assessed in the context of their time. From what contemporary ideas and ideologies did scholars of that time distance themselves? Which convictions shine through in their writings? In spite of later criticism of his often rather simplistic functionalism, Malinowski did manage to foreground the rationality, the "functionality," and the individuality of indigenous behavior in contrast to contemporary ideas of homogenous collective traditions or primitive superstition (Kohl 1990: 236). The Amazon scholars examined here were free from neither evolutionist assumptions nor paternalistic attitudes. However, their writings show how their fieldwork contributed to their questioning of existing assumptions and how the reduction of social distance as a result of longer stays in the Indian villages, characterized by increasing participation and language competence, led to representations that did not deny the people being described their history, their culture, their reason, or their humanity.

When Karl von den Steinen returned from the upper reaches of the Rio Xingu for the second time, he criticized the description of Indians living there as "stone age people," seeing it now as "a folly I realized because I had often committed it myself." He added, "As an impartial observer, I would never have had the idea that the Xingu Indians were living in the 'stone age'" (Steinen 1894: 203). Rejecting the equation of prehistory and stone age, and consistently putting the adjective "prehistoric" in quotation marks, he even wrote that he considered it "delusional . . . to call these 'hordes,' to which we have just brought metal goods, crude hunting peoples at the mercy of an unknown fate . . . We will have to get used to distinguishing in the ungainly masses that in our eyes epitomize the 'stone age' many regular, neatly ordered layers of culture" (ibid.: 212). In the abridged "popular edition" (*Volksausgabe*) of his publication, he emphasized in the preface "that there is no such thing as the 'savage,' because everywhere a social order is present as well as a linguistic and cultural bedrock that is already furnished with the most essential elements of higher development" (Steinen 1897: vii–viii.). A few sentences later he wrote: "Savagery, as it really is, still rests deep in our minds and hearts and often has the shine of a venerable, valuable possession; the culture of the savages is much higher on average, ours is much lower than commonly thought" (see also chapter 1 on Boas in the present volume). While thinking in evolutionary stages was still recognizable in von den Steinen's writings, the imagined distance between cultures was drastically reduced. As the passages cited above demonstrate, terms such as "savages" or "natural peoples," still used by him and his successors, cannot be equated with a conception of people without history or culture.

Likewise, Theodor Koch-Grünberg regularly tried to reduce the distance in his representation of different cultures by comparing behavior he had encountered among the Indians with customs in his homeland, the German state of Hesse. At the height of the Wilhelmine Empire, his writings about the inhabitants of the upper Rio Negro Basin led a staff member of the publishing house Strecker & Schröder to write: "I feel compelled, my dear doctor, to express my full sympathy for the philanthropic viewpoint you take toward the despised children of nature, that you see them as . . . fellow human beings and do not share the obnoxiously arrogant perspective that knows no bounds."[46] Concrete encounters in the field had made Koch-Grünberg increasingly cautious in his judgments. In contrast to the broad generalizations he made about "the South Americans" in his first texts, written before his first expedition into the field, he concluded the last book he published during his lifetime with the following words: "The more one absorbs oneself in the inner lives of the Indians, the more one realizes how little one knows about them. Perhaps I have succeeded after all in gaining some insight into the soul of these people" (Koch-Grünberg 1916–28: 3:389).

In his discussion of the worldviews of the Indians he visited, Konrad Theodor Preuss, in turn, emphasized both the "great intellectual achievements" and the aspiring ethics that these cultural systems embodied (Preuss 1920–21: 95; 1926c: 31; see also Jáuregui and Neurath 2003: 177).

In his introductory volume *Völkerkunde*, published a few years after World War I, Max Schmidt wrote:

> What makes Europeans so hated by most natives of foreign countries is the delusional grandeur they all too often display so openly. . . . This is not the place to list all atrocities the penetration of European culture has brought about among the natives of foreign countries, especially in the European colonies. The literature is full of them . . . Here only so much should be said that everyone who does not have at least a certain measure of respect for people outside the Eurasian cultural sphere, who does not have the virtue to respect the native in his family and economic life, will have more success with other fields of knowledge than with ethnology. Strict self-control in every sense and respect for the natives are the first prerequisites for every ethnological explorer. (Schmidt 1924: 48)

Schmidt's words are impressive, but once again we would not accept every single statement today. Even Bastian would have taken issue with his reducing the science of ethnology to the study of cultures outside the "Eurasian cultural sphere." Likewise, Schmidt's use of the German term *Eingeborene* (natives) is questionable, especially when the inhabitants of Europe are designated as *Einheimische* (which has the positive undertone of being a "local"). What is meant by "self-control" (*Selbstbeherrschung*) remains unclear and ultimately becomes a point of projection for the reader. And respect for the people one meets during fieldwork (or before or after) should surely be more than "a certain measure." Yet the passages sketched in this chapter show an essential tendency that was characteristic of the fieldwork of these first professional German ethnologists in the Amazon Basin and makes their texts worth reading to this day: they did not simply observe behavior or collect objects, impressions, images, and words; rather, they shared in everyday life in the villages they visited and recognized their inhabitants as fellow human beings. And they reflected on the experiences of their encounters during fieldwork in ways that contradicted contemporary beliefs on many levels. In this manner, they contributed not only to questioning the "familiar pattern as recorded in the books" (Steinen 1894: 56) but also to raising the very limited "measure of respect" (Schmidt 1924: 48) that Indigenous peoples enjoyed in Germany at the beginning of the twentieth century.

Michael Kraus is curator of the ethnographic collection at the University of Göttingen (Germany). He studied ethnology, sociology, and comparative religious studies in Tübingen, Guadalajara, and

Marburg. He was a research assistant in cultural anthropology at the Universities of Marburg and Bonn and worked at the Deutsches Historisches Museum, the Humboldt-Universität, and the Ethnological Museum in Berlin. His fields of interest are the history of anthropology, curatorial practices and museum studies, material culture, and visual anthropology. His main regional focus is on Indigenous societies of the South American lowlands.

Notes

1. This chapter was written at the invitation of the editors. I am grateful to Christiane Falck and Mark Münzel for critical comments and suggestions. The Ethnological Museum in Berlin, in the person of Manuela Fischer, and the Department of Social and Cultural Anthropology of the University of Marburg, in the person of Ernst Halbmayer, granted permission to reproduce the photographs. Andreas Hemming translated this chapter from the original German.
2. Dates unknown. All other dates unknown if unmentioned.
3. The expedition members included Karl von den Steinen, his cousin Wilhelm von den Steinen (1859–1934) and the German physicist Otto Clauss (1858–1921), the Brazilian *camaradas* Daniel and Pedro Alvarez, the Bakairi Antonio, Captain Francisco de Paula Castro, Castro's *camarada* Valentin, and twelve more people, mostly soldiers who had volunteered for this duty (Steinen 1886: 74, 76f., 83, 109, 145). Von den Steinen's travelogue opens with an illustration of the three German scientists; a photograph in the travel report also shows Antonio Bakairi (ibid.: 121), and another image shows Antonio, Valentin, Daniel, and Pedro with the caption "Our four comrades" (*Unsere vier Kameraden*) (ibid.: 129).
4. Not only did von den Steinen introduce the entire team of his second Xingu expedition to the reader (1894: v–vi, 12–13) but he also published two photographs that showed all its members (ibid.: tables 2 and 3). The first photograph had the caption "The gentlemen" (*Die Herren*) and showed Januario, a retired Brazilian lieutenant, who had accompanied von den Steinen during his first trip until the point of embarkation; Luiz Perrot, a lieutenant of German descent; Antonio Bakairi; and the four German scientists Karl von den Steinen, Wilhelm von den Steinen, Paul Ehrenreich (1855–1914), and Peter Vogel (1856–1915). The second photograph with the caption "The comrades" (*Die Kameraden*) shows Pedro and Carlos Dhein, sons of colonists from Rio Grande do Sul, who had previously accompanied the US-American natural scientist Herbert Smith (1851–1919); the four corporals João Pedro, Columna, Raymundo, and Satyro, who had been chosen by Perrot; and the young Manoel, who had insisted on accompanying the expedition and mostly

worked as a kitchen boy. It is interesting to note that on the first expedition the Bakairi Antonio was counted among the "comrades," but on the second he found himself among the "gentlemen" or leaders of the expedition.

5. Anita Hermannstädter already described von den Steinen's two Xingu expeditions as "a transition in the methodology of the discipline," which is why they have a "special place in the history of ethnology" (1996: 211).

6. The second half of the nineteenth century saw the institutionalization and professionalization of ethnology as a scientific discipline in Germany, reflected in the founding of new museums, the first ethnologists gaining their *venia legendi* (teaching credentials) in this discipline at the universities, and these scholars identifying themselves as ethnologists or *Völkerkundler*. This is also how the scholars examined here saw themselves (cf. Preuss 1926d: 67). The systematic scientific description of peoples was, by then, more than a century old—and should not be confused with the even older genre of travel writing. For the development of *Ethnographie*, *Völkerkunde*, and *Ethnologie* in the eighteenth century, the systematization of ethnographic description in the context of Russian expeditions to northeastern Asia, and the conceptualization of *Völkerkunde* by historians at the University of Göttingen, see Vermeulen 2015, 2019.

7. For a comprehensive overview of the work of these ethnographers, see Kraus 2004, and Petschelies 2019; another work that was still in preparation during the writing of this text appeared recently (Fernández 2020). There exist many other works on these scholars or the expeditions they headed; on von den Steinen, see, for example, Coelho 1993; Hermannstädter 1996, 2002a; Petschelies 2018; Viertler 2019. On Preuss in Mexico, see Jáuregui and Neurath 1998; Jáuregui and Neurath 2003; Valdovinos 2012; and the 85/2007 volume of the journal *Artes de México*. On Preuss in Colombia, see Reyes 2019. On Schmidt, see Bossert and Villar 2013, 2015; Kraus 2019. On Koch-Grünberg, see Ortiz 1995; Hempel 2009; Kraus 2018. Another important scholar of this generation was Paul Ehrenreich, who traveled several times to Brazil and visited various ethnic groups; he also acquired his *venia legendi* in ethnology in Germany. Due to his financial independence, however, he never sought employment in a museum. For Ehrenreich, who accompanied von den Steinen on his second Xingu expedition, see Hempel 2015.

8. Bastian's influence was not merely methodological or theoretical but, in many cases, more direct. This can be seen in the professional biographies of some of his younger colleagues. Von den Steinen (1905: 243) reports how a meeting with Bastian in Honolulu motivated him to take up ethnology. Bastian also paved the way for Koch-Grünberg's first job at the Ethnological Museum in Berlin (Kraus 2007: 141n4). Preuss (1926b: 7) praised his "expert eye" for winning outstanding specialists as museum employees.

9. When Bastian received his *venia legendi* in 1866, it was in *Ethnographie*; according to the university files on von den Steinen, the *venia legendi* he received in 1889 was in *Ethnologie* (HU ACTA 1207, 1216).
10. In the cited paper, Bastian writes of objects as "the only texts" (*die einzigen Texte*) from which the intellectual life of these groups can be read in the future. However, he also championed the recording of oral traditions like myths, tales, legends, etc.
11. See, for example, Zimmerman (2001: 49): "Anthropologists' faith in objects and mistrust of narrative and language determined nearly all the practices of anthropology, which centered almost exclusively on collecting, measuring, depicting, describing, and displaying objects."
12. Reise-Instruktion für Herrn Dr. Theodor Koch, EM Bln Acta Koch I [E 190/03] and VK Mr A.1. This "travel instruction" originally referred to the study of ethnic groups belonging to the Pano language family on the Rio Purus and Rio Ucayali. After his arrival in Brazil, however, much to the annoyance of his superior von den Steinen, Koch-Grünberg traveled first to the upper Rio Negro. As this trip took longer than planned, the following trip up the Purus and Ucayali Rivers could not take place (cf. Kraus 2018: 106f.). Preuss also extended his studies in Mexico beyond their planned duration and neglected the orders of his superior at the museum, Eduard Seler (1849–1922), in favor of his own research interests (Valdovinos 2012: 72; cf. also Jáuregui and Neurath 2003).
13. A similar document to von den Steinen's travel instruction to Koch-Grünberg, partly reiterating it word for word and also emphasizing the need to collect "word lists [and] original texts on tradition and mythology," was given to Richard Thurnwald (1869–1954) when he left for fieldwork on the island of New Britain in the West Pacific. It was signed by Thurnwald, by Felix von Luschan (1854–1929), then head of the department for Africa and Oceania at the Ethnological Museum in Berlin, and by Arthur Baessler (1857–1907), whose "Arthur Baessler Foundation" funded the trip. Marion Melk-Koch, who published the document in its original wording, described it as a "contract" (1989: 53–54). Thurnwald's expedition was explicitly to be a "collecting expedition." One of the differences with von den Steinen's "Reise-Instruktion" for Koch-Grünberg was that Thurnwald was not only committed to acquiring an ethnographic but also a physical anthropological collection.
14. A detailed description of Bastian's expeditions and a comprehensive list of his publications can be found in Fischer, Bolz, and Kamel 2007. On the value of collecting according to Bastian, see also Hermannstädter 1996: 217–18; Chevron 2006–7. Overall, Bastian's research and collection practices are as diverse as they are controversial. Kramer (1981: 74–81), for example, came to a critical assessment of his travels while Penny (2019) presented a more benevolent evaluation of the collections of the Ethnological Museum and the travels of its first director. Bastian's theoretical work has been the topic of several studies; apart from the edited volume of Fischer, Bolz, and Kamel, see for example, Koepping 1983.

15. Discussions about the practice of collecting and the social relationships during this exchange can be found, for example, in Kraus 2004: 334–56; Kraus 2014; Fernández 2018; and Petschelies 2019b.
16. Koch-Grünberg to Frič, 18 April 1916 (ES MR, A. 20); Koch-Grünberg to Schmidt, 10 May 1916. (ES Mr, A. 23).
17. Koch-Grünberg to Nimuendajú, 7 December 1915 (ES Mr, A. 19).
18. Koch-Grünberg to Nimuendajú, 12 March 1922 (ES Mr, A. 33).
19. Nimuendajú to Koch-Grünberg, 10 May 1922 (ES Mr, A. 33).
20. How closely mythology and material culture can be connected was little known to the scholars discussed here. The same applies to the fact that "objects" can be living actors from an Indigenous perspective. Compare, for example, specifically for the Amazon Basin, Panlõn Kumu and Kenhíri 1980; Münzel 1988; Santos-Granero 2009; Kraus, Kummels, Halbmayer 2018.
21. Krause to Koch-Grünberg, 16 June 1916 (ES Mr, A. 21).
22. At this point, I am less concerned with "defending" the behavior of the ethnographers than with pointing out various factors that had an effect within a particular system.
23. See note 12.
24. The political positions taken by the scholars mentioned in this chapter are ambivalent. At the Sixteenth International Congress of Americanists, held in Vienna in 1908, Czech ethnographer Alberto Vojtěch Frič condemned the brutal treatment of Indian groups in Brazil by German settlers and compared the conditions he encountered with those in the Belgian Congo. Instead of getting support from other scholars, Frič was marginalized: "Berlin ethnologists Karl von den Steinen and Eduard Seler, who had initially sent Frič to Brazil, denounced him for mixing politics and science" (Penny 2003: 250). The response was different when the actions of German settlers were not at stake. In his speech to the Geographical Society in Rio de Janeiro, von den Steinen explicitly defended not only the way of life of the Indians but also their violent forms of resistance as being a reaction to the abuse by the non-Indigenous society (Petschelies 2018: 561–62). In some of his texts, Koch-Grünberg defended the violent resistance of the Indians against the attacks of the "whites" and also condemned the crimes of the rubber barons. He even refused to lay the blame at the feet of a single nation, Britain, for example, pointing out that the capitalists responsible for these horrors might as well have been German. At the same time, however, he cooperated in the field with the local power brokers, like various rubber collectors, in order to facilitate the conduct of his own research (Kraus 2018).
25. For a detailed analysis of Koch-Grünberg's conduct during his fieldwork in the region of the upper Rio Negro and his description of various local actors during the rubber boom, see Kraus 2018. For a historical analysis of the conditions on the upper Rio Negro, see Meira 2017.
26. Steinen, Cuiaba, 2 May 1884 (EM Bln Acta Steinen/Ehrenreich).

27. Koch-Grünberg 1909–10: 1:350; Preuss 1921: 16; Krause 1911: 82, 142; Steinen 1894: 98; Schmidt 1905: 79–91. For further examples, see Kraus 2004: 313–34.

28. I first presented my thoughts about a comparison of the methodological practices of Preuss and Koch-Grünberg at the International Symposium "Siguiendo las huellas de Alexander von Humboldt: La antropología alemana, Walter Lehmann y las culturas indígenas de Centroamérica" in San José (Costa Rica) in October 2019. I thank the conveners, Werner Mackenbach and Martin Künne, for inviting me and for the inspiring discussions that took place during the conference.

29. There was also a discussion about the advantages of a longer stay in contrast with the search for "new ground" during Wilhelm Kissenberth's (1878–1944) expedition to the Rio Araguaia in 1908–9, financed by the Ethnological Museum in Berlin. This time it was Eduard Seler who, as representative of the museum's interests, urged that "new ground" should be broken, while Koch-Grünberg and Preuss argued for more in-depth studies among the Kayapó and Karajá (see Hermannstädter 2002b: 124–25; Kraus 2015: 253–54).

30. In 1903–4 this was the case among the Aruak-speaking Siusí in Cururú-Cuára, the Tucano in Pari-Cachoeira and the Cubeo (Pãmiwa) in Namocoliba (today's Puerto López) at the tributaries of the upper Rio Negro. Koch-Grünberg revisited some villages on this trip. In 1911 he spent several weeks in Koimélomeng, inhabited by Macuxi and Wapichana, and in 1912 he lived with the Ye'kwana in southern Venezuela, in the latter case at least partly involuntarily because he lacked options for moving on. The relationship with his hosts in this case was strained.

31. According to inventory lists, Koch-Grünberg presented the Ethnological Museum in Berlin with 1,298 objects from this expedition; 510 other objects are held by the Museu Paraense Emilio Goeldi in Belém, Brazil, to which Koch-Grünberg had already sold a first partial collection (López 2018). Smaller numbers of objects can be found in museums in Munich and Gießen, for example, while some remain privately owned.

32. Preuss to Koch-Grünberg, 11 February 1907 (ES Mr A. 3); see also Valdovinos (2012: 68).

33. Preuss initially only published his results on the Cora because he was preoccupied with his expedition to Colombia. The unpublished material on the Huichol was destroyed during World War II. An unpublished Nahua text was edited thirty years after Preuss's death by Elsa Ziehm (Fischer, Haas, and Theis 2007: 96).

34. Karl von den Steinen (1894: 397) himself described Carl Friedrich Philipp von Martius (1794–1868) as the "founder of Brazilian ethnography"; Koch-Grünberg (1903: 28) spoke of the Jesuits as "forerunners of modern South American ethnology."

35. The "snake" is a small woven hose, similar to a miniature manioc press. If a person sticks their finger in the weave and it is pulled tight, s/he has been "trapped."

36. Krickeberg to Koch-Grünberg, 26 April 1909 (ES Mr, A.6).
37. Koch-Grünberg to Hornbostel, 31 October 1922 (ES Mr, A. 32).
38. Koch-Grünberg to Frič, 2 May 1916 (ES Mr, A. 20).
39. Koch-Grünberg, Diary 1911–13, Notebook 3, 7 September 1911 (ES Mr, B.I.3).
40. Koch-Grünberg to Lehmann, 11 July 1921 (ES Mr, A.31).
41. Cf. Koch-Grünberg 1905: table 26; see also Hugh-Jones 2018: 209, 213.
42. Robert Lowie (1883–1957) and Herbert Baldus (1899–1970) had already criticized the lack of sociological analysis in the research done by these early ethnographers of the Amazon Basin (cf. Kraus 2004: 402n55).
43. When dealing with religion, Preuss called for the same holistic view: "The separation of particular beliefs from the whole, i.e., from religion in general, is a constant source of error for the scholar, since one needs to consider faith as a whole [*den Glauben als Ganzes*] in order to grasp the particular in a supernatural sense" (Preuss 1926a: 14). He later wrote: "To study the religion of Indigenous peoples [*Naturvölker*] is, as we have seen, not possible without constantly keeping developments as a whole in mind. Today, however, scholars who deal with the particulars of religious phenomena are often ignorant of the whole [*das Ganze*]" (Preuss 1937: 117).
44. On the assessment of the German scholars of the Amazon as "ethnographers," see also Petschelies 2019a: 19.
45. In the places mentioned, von den Steinen was not discussing the phenomenon of witchcraft as such; he used the term pejoratively for old or, from his point of view, ugly women. However, the derogatory description of the "Makú" by Koch-Grünberg appears not to have been his own but an adoption of the view of members of Tucano-speaking ethnic groups. Therefore, a critique of this representation should also include a critical analysis of intertribal relations.
46. Strecker and Schröder to Koch-Grünberg, 31 August 1908 (ES Mr, A. 4).

References

Manuscript Collections

Ethnologisches Museum Berlin (EM).
    Acta betreffend die Erwerbung der Sammlung 1. Karl von den Steinen 2. Paul Ehrenreich Pars I. B. Litt: K.
    Acta betreffend die Reise des Dr. Koch nach Amerika 1903/1905. Pars I B 44.
Philipps-Universität Marburg, Ethnographische Sammlung. Nachlass Theodor Koch-Grünberg (ES Mr).
    A.1–37 Korrespondenz
    B.I.3 Tagebuch-Hefte 1911–1913 ("Vom Roroima zum Orinoco")

Humboldt Universität Berlin, Universitätsarchiv (HU).
   ACTA der Königl. Friedrich Wilhelms Universität zu Berlin betreffend:
   Habilitation der Privatdozenten von März 1859 bis August 1867. Phil-
   osophische Facultät Littr. H. No. 1. Vol. X. 1207 (Blatt 257–262: Ha-
   bil. Bastian).
   ACTA der Königl. Friedrich Wilhelms Universität zu Berlin betreffend:
   Habilitationen der Privat-Docenten 1888/9. Philosophische Facultät.
   Littr. H. No. 1 Vol. XIX. 1216 (Blatt 107–117a: Habilitation des von
   den Steinen).

Published Sources

Ankermann, Bernhard. 1914. *Anleitung zum ethnologischen Beobachten
   und Sammeln*. Berlin: Reimer Verlag.
Bastian, Adolf. 1885. "Ueber ethnologische Sammlungen." *Zeitschrift für
   Ethnologie* 17: 38–42.
Bossert, Federico, and Diego Villar. 2013. *Hijos de la selva: La fotografía
   etnográfica de Max Schmidt. Sons of the Forest: The Ethnographic Photography of Max Schmidt*. Edited by Viggo Mortensen. Santa Monica:
   Perceval Press.
———. 2015. "Max Schmidt in Mato Grosso." In *Exploring the Archive: Historical Photography form Latin America—The Collection of the Ethnologisches Museum Berlin*, edited by Manuela Fischer and Michael Kraus,
   280–298. Köln/Weimar/Wien: Böhlau Verlag.
Chevron, Marie-France. 2006–7. "Reisen und Sammeln aus wissenschaftlicher Überzeugung heute und zur Zeit von Adolf Bastian (1826–1905)."
   Mitteilungen der Anthropologischen Gesellschaft in Wien 136/137:
   187–202.
Coelho, Vera Penteado, ed. 1993. *Karl von den Steinen: Um Século de Antropologia no Xingú*. São Paulo: Editora da Universidade de São Paulo.
Dürr, Eveline. 2017. "Feldforschung." In *Ethnologie. Einführung in die Erforschung kultureller Vielfalt*, edited by Bettina Beer, Hans Fischer, and
   Julia Pauli, 89–106. Berlin: Dietrich Reimer Verlag.
Evans-Pritchard, Edward Evan. 1973. "Some Reminiscences and Reflections
   on Fieldwork." *Journal of the Anthropological Society of Oxford* 4(1):
   1–12.
Fernández Castro, Johanna. 2018. "Translation, Austausch und Handel in
   der ethnographischen Forschung: Zugänge zu einer Kulturgeschichte
   der Begegnung zwischen Ethnologen und Indigenen in der Amazonas-
   region." In: Benjamin Brendel, Corinne Geering and Sebastian Zylinski
   (eds.) *Perspektiven der Kulturgeschichte. Gegenstände, Konzepte, Quel-
   len*. Trier: Wissenschaftlicher Verlag, 95–111.
———. 2020. *Kulturübersetzung als interaktive Praxis: Die frühe deutsche
   Ethnologie im Amazonasgebiet (1884–1914)*. Bielefeld: transcript Verlag.

Fischer, Manuela, Peter Bolz, and Susan Kamel, eds. 2007. *Adolf Bastian and His Universal Archive of Humanity: The Origins of German Anthropology.* Hildesheim: Georg Olms Verlag.

Fischer, Manuela, Richard Haas, and Edith Theis. 2007. "Eine Reise zu den lebenden Kulturen des Nayar." *Artes de México* (Arte Antiguo. Cora y Huichol) 85: 93–96.

Franchetto, Bruna. 1992. "'O aparecimento dos caraíba': Para uma história kuikuro e alto-xinguano." In *História dos Índios no Brasil,* edited by Manuela Carneiro da Cunha, 339–56. São Paulo: Companhia das Letras/ Secretaria Municipal de Cultura/FAPESP.

Hempel, Paul. 2009. "Theodor Koch-Grünberg and Visual Anthropology in Early Twentieth-Century German Anthropology." In *Photography, Anthropology and History: Expanding the Frame,* edited by Christopher Morton and Elizabeth Edwards, 193–219. Farnham: Ashgate.

——. 2015. "Paul Ehrenreich—The Photographer in the Shadows during the Second Xingu Expedition 1887–88." In *Exploring the Archive: Historical Photography from Latin America—The Collection of the Ethnologisches Museum Berlin,* edited by Manuela Fischer and Michael Kraus, 209–43. Köln/Weimar/Wien: Böhlau Verlag.

Hermannstädter, Anita. 1996. "Karl von den Steinen und die Xingú-Bevölkerung: Zur Wahrnehmung und Darstellung fremder Kulturen in der Ethnographie des 19. Jahrhunderts." *Baessler-Archiv* 44: 211–42.

——. 2002a. "Abenteuer Ethnologie: Karl von den Steinen und die Xingú-Expeditionen." In *Deutsche am Amazonas: Forscher oder Abenteurer? Expeditionen in Brasilien 1800 bis 1914,* edited by Ethnologisches Museum—SPK, 66–85. Berlin/Münster: LIT.

——. 2002b. "Eine vergessene Expedition: Wilhelm Kissenberth am Rio Araguaya 1908–1910." In *Deutsche am Amazonas: Forscher oder Abenteurer? Expeditionen in Brasilien 1800 bis 1914,* edited by Ethnologisches Museum—SPK, 106–31. Berlin/Münster: LIT.

Hugh-Jones, Stephen. 2018. "Su riqueza es nuestra riqueza: Perspectivas interculturales de objetos o *gaheuni.*" In *Objetos como testigos del contacto cultural: Perspectivas interculturales de la historia y del presente de las poblaciones indígenas del alto río Negro (Brasil/Colombia),* edited by Michael Kraus, Ernst Halbmayer, and Ingrid Kummels, 197–226. Berlin: Gebrüder Mann Verlag.

Jáuregui, Jesús, and Johannes Neurath, eds. 1998. *Fiesta, literatura y magia en el Nayarit: Ensayos sobre coras, huicholes y mexicaneros de Konrad Theodor Preuss.* México: Instituto Nacional Indigenista/Centro Francés de Estudios Mexicanos y Centroamericanos.

——. 2003. "El pasado prehispánico y el presente indígena: Seler, Preuss y las culturas del Gran Nayar." In *Eduard y Caecilie Seler: Sistematización de los estudios americanistas y sus repercusiones,* edited by Renata von Hanffstengel and Cecilia Tercero Vasconcelos, 175–195. México: UNAM/INAH.

Koch-Grünberg, Theodor. 1903. "Die Guaikurú-Gruppe." *Mittheilungen der Anthropologischen Gesellschaft Wien* 33: 1–128.

———. 1905. *Anfänge der Kunst im Urwald: Indianer-Handzeichnungen auf seinen Reisen in Brasilien gesammelt.* Berlin: Ernst Wasmuth A.G. Portuguese translation Manaus 2009.

———. 1906. "Die Makú." *Anthropos* 1: 877–906.

———. 1909–10. *Zwei Jahre unter den Indianern: Reisen in Nordwest-Brasilien 1903/1905.* 2 vols. Berlin: Ernst Wasmuth A.-G. Spanish translation Bogotá 1995; Portuguese translation Manaus 2005.

———. 1916–28. *Vom Roroima zum Orinoco: Ergebnisse einer Reise in Nordbrasilien und Venezuela in den Jahren 1911–1913.* Vols. 1–2: Berlin: Dietrich Reimer, Vols. 3–5: Stuttgart: Strecker & Schröder. Vol. 1, *Schilderung der Reise*, 1917. Vol. 2, *Mythen und Legenden der Taulipang- und Arekuna-Indianer*, 1916. Vol. 3, *Ethnographie*, 1923. Vol. 4, *Sprachen*, 1928. Vol. 5, *Typen-Atlas*, 1923. Spanish translation of vols. 1–3 Caracas 1981/82; Portuguese translation of vol. 1 São Paulo 2006.

———. 1921. *Zwei Jahre bei den Indianern Nordwest-Brasiliens.* Stuttgart: Strecker und Schröder. Abridged popular edition of Koch-Grünberg 1909/1910.

Koepping, Klaus-Peter. 1983. *Adolf Bastian and the Psychic Unity of Mankind: The Foundations of Anthropology in Nineteenth Century Germany.* St. Lucia: University of Queensland Press.

Kohl, Karl-Heinz. 1990. "Bronislaw Kaspar Malinowski (1884–1942)." In *Klassiker der Kulturanthropologie: Von Montaigne bis Margared Mead*, edited by Wolfgang Marschall, 227–47. München: Verlag C. H. Beck.

Kramer, Fritz. 1981. *Verkehrte Welten: Zur imaginären Ethnographie des 19. Jahrhunderts.* Frankfurt am Main: Syndikat.

Kraus, Michael. 2004. *Bildungsbürger im Urwald: Die deutsche ethnologische Amazonienforschung (1884–1929).* Marburg: Curupira.

———. 2007. "Philological Embedments — Ethnological Research in South America in the Ambience of Adolf Bastian." In *Adolf Bastian and His Universal Archive of Humanity. The Origins of German Anthropology*, edited by Manuela Fischer, Peter Bolz, and Susan Kamel, 140–52. Hildesheim: Georg Olms Verlag.

———. 2014. "Perspectivas multiples: El intercambio de objetos entre etnólogos e indígenas en las tierras bajas de América del Sur." *Nuevo Mundo Mundos Nuevos.* DOI: 10.4000/nuevomundo.67209.

———. 2015. "'More news will follow' — Wilhelm Kissenberth's Ethnographic Photographs from Northeast and Central Brazil." In *Exploring the Archive: Historical Photography from Latein America — The Collection of the Ethnologisches Museum Berlin*, edited by Manuela Fischer and Michael Kraus, 245–79. Köln/Weimar/Wien: Böhlau Verlag.

———. 2018. "Testigos de la época del caucho: experiencias de Theodor Koch-Grünberg y Hermann Schmidt en el alto río Negro." In *Objetos como testigos del contacto cultural: Perspectivas interculturales de la his-*

toria y del presente de las poblaciones indígenas del alto río Negro (Brasil/ Colombia), edited by Michael Kraus, Ernst Halbmayer, and Ingrid Kummels, 97–133. Berlin: Gebrüder Mann Verlag.

———. 2019. "Beyond the Mainstream: Max Schmidt's Research on 'The Arawak' in the Context of Contemporary German Ethnology." *Revista de Antropologia* 62(1): 162–91.

Kraus, Michael, Ernst Halbmayer, and Ingrid Kummels. 2018. "La perspectiva desde Alemania: Pasos hacia un diálogo en torno a los objetos." In *Objetos como testigos del contacto cultural: Perspectivas interculturales de la historia y del presente de las poblaciones indígenas del alto río Negro (Brasil/Colombia)*, edited by Michael Kraus, Ernst Halbmayer, and Ingrid Kummels, 9–47. Berlin: Gebrüder Mann Verlag.

Krause, Fritz. 1911. *In den Wildnissen Brasiliens: Bericht und Ergebnisse der Leipziger Araguaya-Expedition 1908*. Leipzig: Voigtländer.

López, Claudia. 2018. "Las colecciones etnográficas del alto río Negro en el *Museu Paraense Emílio Goeldi*: Notas históricas y diálogos contemporáneos." In *Objetos como testigos del contacto cultural: Perspectivas interculturales de la historia y del presente de las poblaciones indígenas del alto río Negro (Brasil/Colombia)*, edited by Michael Kraus, Ernst Halbmayer, and Ingrid Kummels, 155–70. Berlin: Gebrüder Mann Verlag.

Luschan, Felix von. 1904. *Anleitung für ethnographische Beobachtungen und Sammlungen in Afrika und Oceanien*. Berlin: Königliches Museum für Völkerkunde in Berlin/Gebrüder Unger.

Malinowski, Bronisław. 1922. *Argonauts of the Western Pacific: An Account of Native Enterprise and Adventure in the Archipelagoes of Melanesian New Guinea*. London/New York: Routledge/E.P. Dutton & Co.

———. 1967. *A Diary in the Strict Sense of the Term*. New York: Harcourt, Brace & World.

Meira, Márcio Augusto Freitas de. 2017. "A Persistência do aviamento: Colonialismo e história no Noroeste Amazônico." PhD thesis, Centro de Ciências Humanas e Sociais, Universidade Federal do Estado do Rio de Janeiro.

Melk-Koch, Marion. 1989. *Auf der Suche nach der menschlichen Gesellschaft: Richard Thurnwald*. Berlin: Staatliche Museen Preußischer Kulturbesitz.

Münzel, Mark, ed. 1988. *Die Mythen sehen: Bilder und Zeichen vom Amazonas*. 2 vols. Frankfurt am Main: Museum für Völkerkunde/Dezernat für Kultur und Freizeit.

Ortiz Rodriguez, María Mercedes. 1995. "Caminando selva: Vida y obra del etnógrafo alemán Theodor Koch-Grünberg." *Universitas Humanistica* 41: 74–86.

Panlõn Kumu, Umúsin, and Tolamãn Kenhíri. 1980. *Antes o mundo não existia: A mitologia heróica dos índios Desana*. Introduction by Berta G. Ribeiro. São Paulo: Livraria Cultura Editora.

Penny, H. Glenn. 2002. *Objects of Culture: Ethnology and Ethnographic Museums in Imperial Germany*. Chapel Hill/London: The University of North Carolina Press.

———. 2003. "The Politics of Anthropology in the Age of Empire: German Colonists, Brazilian Indians, and the Case of Alberto Vojtech Frič." *Comparative Studies in Society and History* 45(2): 249–80.

———. 2019. *Im Schatten Humboldts: Eine tragische Geschichte der deutschen Ethnologie.* München: Verlag C. H. Beck.

Petschelies, Erik. 2018. "Karl von den Steinen's Ethnography in the Context of the Brazilian Empire." *Sociologia e Antropologia* 8(2): 543–69.

———. 2019a. *As redes da etnografia alemã no Brasil (1884–1929).* PhD thesis, Universidade Estadual de Campinas, Instituto de Filosofia e Ciências Humanas.

———. 2019b. "From Berlin to Belém: Theodor Koch-Grünberg's Rio Negro collections." *Museum History Journal* 12(1): 29–51.

Preuss, Konrad Theodor. 1908. "Reise zu den Stämmen der westlichen Sierra Madre in Mexiko." *Zeitschrift der Gesellschaft für Erdkunde zu Berlin* 3: 147–67.

———. 1912. *Die Nayarit-Expedition: Textaufnahmen und Beobachtungen unter mexikanischen Indianern.* Erster Band. *Die Religion der Cora-Indianer.* Leipzig: B. G. Teubner.

———. 1914. "Die Indianer Brasiliens." *Illustrierte Zeitung* 3684: 255–58.

———. 1920/21. "Bericht über meine archäologischen und ethnologischen Forschungsreisen in Kolumbien." *Zeitschrift für Ethnologie* 52: 89–128.

———. 1921. *Religion und Mythologie der Uitoto: Textaufnahmen und Beobachtungen bei einem Indianerstamm in Kolumbien, Südamerika.* Erster Band. *Einführung und Texte.* Göttingen: Vandenhoeck & Ruprecht.

———. 1926a. *Glauben und Mystik im Schatten des höchsten Wesens.* Leipzig: C. L. Hirschfeld.

———. 1926b. "Adolf Bastian und die Völkerkunde: Zum Gedächtnis seines hundertjährigen Geburtstages am 26. Juni 1926." *Baessler-Archiv* 10: 2–15.

———. 1926c. *Forschungsreise zu den Kágaba: Beobachtungen, Textaufnahmen und sprachliche Studien bei einem Indianerstamme in Kolumbien, Südamerika.* St. Gabriel-Mödling: Administration des *Anthropos.*

———. 1926d. "Die Neuaufstellung des Museums für Völkerkunde." *Berliner Museen: Berichte aus den Preussischen Kunstsammlungen; Beiblatt zum Jahrbuch der Preussischen Kunstsammlungen* 47: 67–72.

———. 1937. "Die Religion." In *Lehrbuch der Völkerkunde,* edited by Konrad Theodor Preuss, 57–123. Stuttgart: Ferdinand Enke.

Reyes, Aura Lisette. 2018. "La materialidad amerindia, entre relatos míticos y colecciones: Una biografía de Konrad Theodor Preuss." BEROSE International Encyclopaedia of the Histories of Anthropology, Paris.

———. 2019. *Ensamble de una colección: Trayectos de Konrad Theodor Preuss durante su expedición en Colombia (1913–1919).* Barranquilla: Editorial Universidad del Norte.

Santos-Granero, Fernando, ed. 2009. *The Occult Life of Things: Native Amazonian Theories of Materiality and Personhood.* Tucson: University of Arizona Press.

Schmidt, Max 1905. *Indianerstudien in Zentralbrasilien: Erlebnisse und ethnologische Ergebnisse einer Reise in den Jahren 1900 bis 1901.* Berlin: Dietrich Reimer.

———. 1924. *Völkerkunde.* Berlin: Ullstein.

Sperber, Dan. 1989. *Das Wissen des Ethnologen.* Frankfurt am Main: Edition Qumran/Campus Verlag.

Steinen, Karl von den. 1886. *Durch Central-Brasilien: Expedition zur Erforschung des Schingú im Jahre 1884.* Leipzig: F. A. Brockhaus.

———. 1892. *Die Bakaïrí-Sprache: Wörterverzeichnis, Sätze, Sagen, Grammatik; Mit Beiträgen zu einer Lautlehre der karaïbischen Grundsprache.* Leipzig: Koehler"s Antiquarium.

———. 1894. *Unter den Naturvölkern Zentral-Brasiliens: Reiseschilderung und Ergebnisse der Zweiten Schingú-Expedition 1887–1888.* Berlin: Dietrich Reimer. Portuguese translation São Paulo 1940.

———. 1897. *Unter den Naturvölkern Zentral-Brasiliens: Reiseschilderung und Ergebnisse der Zweiten Schingú-Expedition 1887–1888; Zweite Auflage als Volksausgabe.* Berlin: Dietrich Reimer. Abridged popular edition of Steinen 1894.

———. 1905. "Gedächtnisrede auf Adolf Bastian." *Zeitschrift für Ethnologie* 37: 236–49.

Streck, Bernhard. 1997. *Fröhliche Wissenschaft Ethnologie: Eine Führung.* Wuppertal: Edition Trickster/Peter Hammer Verlag.

Valdovinos, Margarita. 2012. "La materialidad de la palabra: La labor etnolingüística de Konrad Theodor Preuss en torno a su expedición a México." *Baessler-Archiv* 60: 67–86.

Vermeulen, Han F. 2015. *Before Boas: The Genesis of Ethnography and Ethnology in the German Enlightenment.* Lincoln: University of Nebraska Press.

———. 2019. "Ethnographie, Ethnologie und Anthropologie im 18. und 19. Jahrhundert: Einheit, Vielfalt und Zusammenhang." *Mitteilungen der Berliner Gesellschaft für Anthropologie, Ethnologie und Urgeschichte* 40: 91–117.

Viertler, Renate. 2019. "Karl von den Steinen's Ethnographic Research among Indigenous Peoples in Brazil, 1884–1888." *Revista de Antropologia* 62(1): 97–133.

Zimmerman, Andrew. 2001. *Anthropology and Antihumanism in Imperial Germany.* Chicago: University of Chicago Press.

Conclusion

Founders of Anthropology
and Their Predecessors

Han F. Vermeulen and Frederico Delgado Rosa

In 1909 . . . a meeting of teachers from Oxford, Cambridge and London was held to discuss the terminology of our subject. We agreed to use "ethnography" as the term for descriptive accounts of non-literate peoples.
— Alfred Radcliffe-Brown, "Historical Note on British Social Anthropology," 1952[1]

New Zealand ethnographer Elsdon Best (1856–1931) persistently issued warnings about the variety, complexity, and depth of the "spiritual concepts of the Maori" (Best 1900–1901; also 1922)—each with multiple uses and meanings. "I prefer not to say," he wrote in *The Maori*, "how many years I sought to grasp the signification of the terms *mauri* and *hau*" (Best 1924: 1:311). If Best described his own writings "as the jottings of a bush collector" with "no pretense of presenting a scientific work" (Best 1924: 1:xi), this probably had something to do with him being humbled by the intricacies of his long-term ethnographic experience. Raymond Firth (1901–2002) paid tribute to "the unrivalled research of Mr. Elsdon Best" among other amateur ethnographers of the nineteenth and early twentieth centuries working on the Māori context. Despite "inevitable lacunae, especially in the sphere of social organization," that body of "fieldwork material" formed "a solid basis for theoretical treatment" (Firth 1959 [1929]: 17–18). Although Firth never mastered the language in any way comparable to Best, he tacitly took his place as a brighter authority on all subjects Māori.

Firth's exercise of subtly debunking his predecessors is similar to Malinowski's systematic perusal of a vast bibliography by amateur ethnographers and firsthand observers of Australian Aboriginal societies from 1793 to 1911. In his armchair monograph on *The Family among the Australian Aborigines* (1913), Malinowski was confronted with the following paradox: his purpose was to "collect sufficiently complete evidence" by using "some of the older sources whose trustworthiness might be disputed."[2] His answer was that "many of their observations are highly valuable if properly interpreted" (Malinowski 1913: ix). He considered that ethnographic records produced by amateurs should be subjected to "the rules of criticism of sources" just like in any historic science.[3] By focusing on the "modes in which evidence was obtained" and on the "kind of relation [that] existed between the respective author and the material of his observation," Malinowski's source criticism included an awareness of the various grades of colonial impact in Australia. Alfred William Howitt (1830–1908), for example, had never seen the Kurnai tribe "in its primitive state," so he had "probably" worked with Native individuals' "recollections of the bygone times" (ibid.: 21). Lamenting the fact that such contextual information was more easily found in "memoirs, diaries, descriptions of travels, expeditions, etc." than in properly ethnographic texts, Malinowski added: "In the case of ethnographers . . .—like Howitt, Spencer and Gillen, Roth,[4] and some others—we might expect to be informed minutely about the way in which they obtained their information. Unfortunately this is only partly the case" (ibid.: 22–23). Another reason for subjecting their writings to source criticism was their propensity toward theoretically biased speculations not sustained by descriptive material. "Many of the difficulties," Malinowski wrote, "may be solved by understanding some of the statements made as referring to hypothetical earlier stages." This is how he could eventually highlight the import of the individual family in Australian Aboriginal contexts to the detriment of so-called group marriage (ibid.: 4).

A similar attitude to that of Firth and Malinowski, a sort of academic haughtiness, is detectable in modern anthropologists whose writings replicate the theme of the professional who found himself or herself in worse historical conditions—that is, further transformed by colonialism—but did a better and quicker job than the amateurs working in a previous period, sometimes for decades. Notwithstanding the common mistake—or historiographical prejudice—that equates modern fieldwork with long-standing sojourns, the opposite is true: modern fieldwork often lasted for far less time than the lifetime sojourns of many amateur ethnographers. Behind this "inconvenient truth" we can see a historiographic challenge. The *idea* of a long sojourn, long enough to learn the native language and grasp "the native's point of view," is at the core of the Malinowskian charter myth. But were post-Malinowskian ethnographic experiences necessarily more Malinowskian than those taking place in a previous period? A preconceived notion about earlier accounts being theoretically irrelevant can lead to hasty conclusions about the types of ethnographic fieldwork—and ethnographic writing—taking place in the nineteenth and early twentieth centuries. This is because 1922 is usually considered the year when a fruitful combination of theory and firsthand ethnographic data finally happened in anthropology.

The *Annus Mirabilis* of British Social Anthropology

What we see here, *in nuce*, is a paradigm shift from ethnography as a broad descriptive and comparative research program welcoming rigorous accounts of all kinds to a theoretically infused fieldwork approach that became dominant thanks to Malinowski and A. R. Radcliffe-Brown (1881–1955) and their students and associates during the 1920s and 1930s. A stronger emphasis on the synchronic interdependence of social institutions was the hallmark of a new anthropology that rejected conjectural history by evolutionist and diffusionist scholars and championed professional fieldwork by academically trained anthropologists. "The 1920s saw the challenge to the . . . historical approach, and the acceptance of intensive fieldwork by participant observation as the basis for a career in anthropology" (Kuper 1996 [1973]: 63).

This development was enhanced in the 1930s and 1940s when E. E. Evans-Pritchard (1902–73), Meyer Fortes (1906–83), Raymond Firth, Isaac Schapera (1905–2003), Max Gluckman (1911–75), and others consistently promoted a specific combination of fieldwork and theory, namely, participant observation and structural functionalism. As Raymond Firth summarized the situation in 1951: "For well over a quarter of a century, *Problemstellung* has been a leading trait in British social anthropological thought—for which Malinowski deserves as much credit as anyone" (Firth 1951: 477). However, the reluctance of British social anthropologists to recognize the work of predecessors in the field and their emphasis on social anthropology as the only branch of anthropology worth developing led to the sidetracking and overshadowing of earlier ethnographic monographs that effectively disappeared behind the anthropological horizon. Comparing Malinowski to other famous anthropologists, Ivan Strenski stated: "Malinowski was neither the first nor even the best fieldworker of his day. Boas and Radcliffe-Brown were at least Malinowski's equals and earlier into the field. . . . What distinguished Malinowski was his skill at selling fieldwork" (1987: 45)—plus, we may add, his captivating style of writing.[5]

In 1922, the same year as Malinowski's *Argonauts of the Western Pacific*, Radcliffe-Brown published his monograph *The Andaman Islanders: A Study in Social Anthropology*. An extensive volume of 504 pages, published by Cambridge University Press, the book has received much less of the limelight than Malinowski's opus of about the same length (527 pages). Apart from a few articles dedicated to it (Tax 1955; Stocking 1984a; Hogbin 1988; Tomas 1991), and an important chapter in Kuper (1996 [1973]), the book was only reprinted in 1933, when Radcliffe-Brown was teaching in Chicago and expanding his theoretical views on social anthropology. While Malinowski is primarily seen as the inventor of "holistic fieldwork" (Kuper 1996 [1973]: 49), Radcliffe-Brown is regarded as the promotor of "comparative sociology" in the tradition of Durkheim (ibid.: 50, 63; see Hogbin 1988). Both Adam Kuper and Ian Hogbin (1904–1989) present Radcliffe-Brown as the founder of social anthropology, together with Malinowski, and their names appearing in combination as "founding fathers" had an enduring impact on the perception of disciplinary history beyond Britain. While it is impossible to overlook Boas, the leader of ethnographic studies in the United States (Zumwalt 2019), and his cohort of brilliant disciples,[6] other—if not older—developments in various other countries may be obscured by an obsessive focus on the rise of social anthropology in Great Britain.

Malinowski's and Radcliffe-Brown's fieldwork experiences, their methodological insights, and theoretical approaches had significant points of divergence. As is well known from the literature, Malinowski used the metaphor of the skeleton, the flesh and blood, and the spirit, to define the three avenues through which ethnographic fieldwork should be approached. The *skeleton* referred to the normative side of social life, to behavior as prescribed by custom and tradition, which in the absence of written law should be systematized by the ethnographer. The *flesh and blood* metaphor referred to actual behavior, to real-life episodes and incidents hardly predictable nor fully rendered by the study of rules alone—hence Malinowski's insistence on the import of this line of inquiry in terms of ethnographic writing. Finally, the *spirit* referred to the Natives' "commentary" about their own "cultural items," reflecting shared ideas and feelings, not individual opinions on the subject (Malinowski 1922: 22). Since these collective states of mind could be "too elusive and shapeless" to be formulated, the record of any explicit statement should be complemented by an indirect method: the *verbatim* transcription of a particular kind of cultural item, namely oral traditions, as these vernacular texts could be read "as documents of native mentality" (ibid.: 24). Malinowski resorted to a Latin formula, *corpus inscriptionum*, to designate this kind of compilation. Recording "the spirit" was particularly near to grasping "the native's point of view," even if all three avenues were related in their subordination to this "final goal" (ibid.: 25).

Under the rivaling influence of Radcliffe-Brown, ethnographies produced within British social anthropology did not necessarily follow Malinowski's program. As Phyllis Kaberry (1910–1977) pointed out (1957: 87), some structural functionalist monographs were like skeletons with hardly any flesh and blood, or they lacked spirit, one might add, having in view Radcliffe-Brown's canonical ideas on the uselessness of vernacular records—as those produced by Boasian anthropologists in the United States (Duvernay-Bolens 2001–2: 16). Malinowski's mistrust of "kinshipology," the Radcliffe-Brownian emphasis on almost-mathematical kinship rules to the detriment of *imponderabilia* in the real lives of real people, is another symptom of their clash of sensibilities. While Radcliffe-Brown lacked "Malinowski's interest in individual motivation and strategy," Kuper considers that his "detachment was a source of strength too, for it gave a controlled power to his analyses of social systems, which Malinowski never achieved" (1996 [1973]: 39; see Stocking 1984b; and Mancuso 2021). If they were influential in different ways, the fact remains that today, one hundred years after the so-called *annus mirabilis* of British social anthropology and the enduring recognition of intensive fieldwork as the central requirement for anthropological theory and praxis, we can conclude that there is a forgotten yet important point in common between these two founding figures. The complex, ambivalent developments associated with Malinowski's and Radcliffe-Brown's first major works published in 1922 have overshadowed previous ethnographies. Beyond the paradigmatic or simplified contrast between "functionalist" and "amateur" accounts is a richer history of anthropology and ethnography to be told.

Radcliffe-Brown, E. H. Man,
and *Notes and Queries on Anthropology*

Radcliffe-Brown, known as A. R. Brown until the early 1920s, had spent "about eighteen months" in the Andaman Islands south of Burma (now Myanmar) on behalf of an Anthony Wilkin Student-ship from Cambridge in 1906–8. The manuscript of the resulting monograph *The Andaman Islanders: A Study in Social Anthropol-ogy* (1922) was written in 1908–9—when Brown was a reader in eth-nology at the University of London (1908–10), taking over Alfred C. Haddon's lectures—and completed in 1914. Due to subsequent fieldwork in Western Australia,[7] and World War I, the book appeared only in 1922. In his preface to the second edition, written in Chicago in 1932, Radcliffe-Brown criticized the work of ethnologists "con-cerned . . . with attempts to provide hypothetical reconstructions of the details of culture history" and hailed that of French sociologists of the Durkheimian school such as Henri Hubert (1872–1927) that had given him "the method . . . to apply to the beliefs and customs of the Andaman Islanders," particularly in the fifth and sixth chap-ters of his book. These chapters formed a separate section, dealing with ceremonial, myths and legends (1922: 229–406; preface to the second edition, 1933: vii–viii). Earlier chapters dealt with social or-ganization, ceremonial customs, and religious and magical beliefs. The subjects "ceremonial" and "myths and legends" appear twice, as they were first described and then interpreted. His book ends with a long appendix on "the technical culture," while the second edition also includes an appendix on Andaman languages. Radcliffe-Brown considered that "the most urgent need of ethnology at the present time is a series of investigations of the kind here attempted, in which the observation and the analysis and interpretation . . . are carried on together by the ethnologist working in the field" (1922: 231–32) and added that "we must be careful not to fall into the error of attrib-uting to him [the Andaman Islander] the conceptions by which we make clear to ourselves his indefinite sentiments and notions and the ceremonies in which they are expressed" (ibid.: 324). He later wrote: "Ethnology is faced with the dilemma that it must either give up for ever all hope of understanding such things as myth or ritual, or it must develop proper methods for determining as accurately as can be what meaning they have for the people to whose culture they be-long" (preface to the second edition, 1933: vii–viii).

After serving as foundation professor of anthropology at the Uni-versity of Cape Town, South Africa (1921–25) and at Sydney, Australia (1926–31), Radcliffe-Brown began teaching a fresh cohort of students in the United States before accepting the first chair in social anthropology at Oxford (1937–46). An influential professor, already giving a series of lectures on "Comparative Sociology" at the University of Cambridge in 1910 (Stocking 1984a; Tomas 1991: 98), he published theoretical statements on the "Concept of Function in Social Science" (1935) and "On Social Structure" (1940), as well as analyses of kinship and social organization, myth and ceremony, and religion and totemism, along with essays on method and theory. Nevertheless, apart from his study of social organization in Australia, Radcliffe-Brown never published another ethnographic monograph, and he is described by Ian Hogbin (1988) as a "theoretician rather than a field worker." Meyer Fortes (1953: 16–17) credited Radcliffe-Brown for having made the "first serious attempt" to carry out an "intensive study of limited areas."

In reality, Radcliffe-Brown had limited access to the vernacular language and was working with people close to a penal colony of the British Empire.[8] David Tomas (1991: 101) surmises that his fieldwork actually lasted "little more than a year." Focusing on the historical background of Radcliffe-Brown's Andamanese ethnography, Tomas considers that it illustrates the ideology of professional authority: "In the emergent disciplinary market of modern anthropology, . . . the currency of time could be converted into that of academic training at rates very favorable to the latter" (Tomas 1991: 101). According to Tomas, Brown's claim to methodological authority had to do less with his actual fieldwork than with his academic status, as a new type of ethnographer:

> In the end, when the Andamanese in the vicinity of the colonial settlement had been almost wiped out or assimilated into the everyday life of a penal colony, the meaning of Andamanese cultural practices and beliefs within a now increasingly inaccessible Andamanese culture could be authoritatively reconstituted, even in the aftermath of a relatively unsuccessful fieldwork sojourn, by a university-trained anthropologist attuned to the latest developments in French social theory. (Tomas 1991: 76)

Thus, *The Andaman Islanders* resulted from a peculiar, not particularly "Malinowskian" ethnographic experience. Acknowledging the limitations of his research, including the fact that he had to rely on interpreters speaking Pidgin English or Hindustani, Radcliffe-Brown developed a theoretical orientation that "made it possible for him to salvage his fieldwork experience in the name of modern ethnography's first encounter with the Andamanese" (Tomas 1991: 97).

As a "fusion of the 'armchair worker' and the 'labourer in the field,'" Radcliffe-Brown's *Andaman Islanders* contrasted sharply, Tomas suggests, with the earlier epistemological model epitomized by the *Notes and Queries on Anthropology, for the Use of Travellers and Residents in Uncivilized Lands*. Originally published in 1874,[9] this is probably the best known if not "the most important" (Urry 1984: 38) of several guidelines produced by armchair anthropologists that were addressed to amateur ethnographers. These men and women "on the spot" had a subordinate place and attitude toward the "proper" scholars in the metropoles, who were perceived as having better capacities to handle data, namely from a theoretical and comparatist perspective. Perhaps due to the modesty codes of his own time, James George Frazer (1854–1941) proclaimed that only the compilation of ethnographies would survive, and not the thesis binding them together in *The Golden Bough*.[10] Yet that compilation was certainly his. In spite of all the praise anthropologists might give to certain observers, the pre-Malinowskian hero was the scholar who knew *all* travel literature, in the wide sense of the term, and who could afford *not* to be there, as epitomized by Frazer's anecdotal answer when asked about his direct acquaintance with the natives: "But Heaven forbid!" (Evans-Pritchard 1951: 72)

The "men on the spot" were supposed to stick to the "facts" and avoid combining observation and theory, so their respectability as ethnographers was very different from Radcliffe-Brown's. One case in point is that of his predecessor in the Andaman Islands, Edward Horace Man (1846–1929), who had resorted to *Notes and Queries* in order to produce his ethnographic monograph *On the Aboriginal Inhabitants of the Andaman Islands* (1932 [1885]).[11] According to Man, the "unavoidable" contact between the native people and the convict population from British India represented an "evil influence" amounting to a "deterioration" (Man 1932 [1885]: xxiii). Man himself was in charge of the so-called "Andaman Homes," encampments erected by the British to supply "civilized" goods and services to the "savages." This had undesired side effects, from loss of hunting skills to gain of weight, from indolence to excessive tobacco smoking, and so on. Thus, when Man affirmed that his position as an administrator gave him "exceptional advantages" as an ethnographer, he had in mind not the coastal habitués[12] but the far-off "junglees" who approached the "Andaman Homes" sporadically and could be "fairly considered as representatives of the race," if not living "in their primitive state" (Man 1932 [1885]: ix).

Unlike Radcliffe-Brown's, Man's ethnographic authority resulted from a long stay in the islands (almost thirty years), and from learning the native language(s). Considering "ignorance of the language" as "the most important obstacle to be surmounted," he distanced himself from prior observers who could not communicate fluently with the Andaman natives and were therefore "betrayed into the repetition of many erroneous assertions" that could be traced back to the hearsay and "hasty observations of earlier travellers" (Man 1932 [1885]: 1).[13] From the first edition of *Notes and Queries*, learning the native language was considered of maximum import. Obtaining independence from interpreters and Pidgin English, along with the gradual production of texts fully in the vernacular, particularly from the dictation of traditional formulas, was recommended in all editions of *Notes and Queries*, whether in methodological chapters or as a dispersed theme in various sections.[14]

The continued existence of the *Notes and Queries* well after the consolidation of modern field-centered anthropology may be seen as a manifestation of conservative forces in British society that somehow prevented the suppression of scientific instructions for untrained men and women "on the spot." The twentieth-century editions of 1912, 1929, and 1951 reflect paradigmatic shifts of the discipline: an overall movement from fragmented to holistic perspectives, from "savage" to "nonliterate," from ethnography as an inclusive research program to fieldwork as the hallmark of academic anthropology. James Urry stated that the 1912 edition, including Rivers's "General Account of Method" (the opening section of part 3, on "Sociology"), marks "a radical change" and "hints of the functionalism to come," thanks to a new perception of the "interrelationship of the different aspects of social life" (Urry 1993: 29–31). Several principles usually associated with Malinowski were put forward by W. H. R. Rivers (1864–1922), who further developed them one year later in a "Report on Anthropological Research outside America" (1913; see Stocking 1995: 122–23; Eriksen in this volume). However, the abovementioned dichotomies were never absolute or abrupt. To the contrary, the surviving and the transformational dimensions of *Notes and Queries* were connected.

Some of the preoccupations that were supposed to be modern innovations had been there long before the work of Malinowski, Radcliffe-Brown, or, for that matter, Rivers. Prejudice avoidance was an important recommendation in *Notes and Queries* from the first edition on, and it kept being recycled all the way through (see

Tylor 1892 [1874]b: 146–47). Other Malinowskian themes, such as "friendly intercourse" (BAAS 1874: iv, v), appear from the earliest editions of *Notes and Queries*. The discredit of long residence as sufficient credentials (RAI 1951: 30, 31; Rivers 1912: 110) is detectable in the Victorian versions, where it was stated that even "a long-continued residence" could end in "superficial answers" to the suggested queries (Read 1892: 87). In his "Prefatory Note" to the second edition, Charles H. Read (1857–1929) wrote that direct questions on religious doctrine and morals should be avoided (1892: 88). Instead, native religion would be "more easily learnt" through the observation of "religious ceremonies, such as prayer, sacrifice, festivals, &c.," which could raise more spontaneous explanations of those acts (Tylor 1892: 130). This dialogues with Malinowski's (and Rivers's) method of "concrete instances," according to which social regulations could and should be identified through real-life cases, to the detriment of abstract questions. It was always better to obtain information "on the spot to which the questions relate" (Read 1892: 88)—and this sounds like an *avant la lettre* warning against verandah ethnography.

If several pre-Malinowskian ethnographers knew and followed the available queries, many others did not. As the case studies in the present volume exemplify, the nineteenth-century label of data collectors was a conceptual construct that hid a myriad of different occurrences. Moreover, *Notes and Queries* might be helpful to professionally trained ethnographers, including Malinowski. The case of *Notes and Queries* is paradigmatic in that it reveals significant overlaps and rhizomes, not a clear-cut dichotomy, between professional and amateur ethnographies in the late nineteenth and the early twentieth centuries.[15]

Malinowski's Departure from "Amateur Productions"

Radcliffe-Brown was three years Malinowski's senior, and during the meeting of the British Association for the Advancement of Science in Melbourne (1914), where Malinowski acted as secretary to Robert R. Marett (1866–1943), Radcliffe-Brown had given him advice on the research Malinowski was planning to carry out on the islands off the coast of southern New Guinea. Malinowski later spoke of this advice as "valuable hints about field-work" (Firth 1951: 3), and Radcliffe-Brown (1946: 38) recalled: "We had many lengthy discussions on anthropology and the aims and methods of field research, and we reached fairly complete agreement." That same year (1914),

Radcliffe-Brown reviewed Malinowski's first book, *The Family among the Australian Aborigines* (1913). These events took place after Radcliffe-Brown had concluded his research in Western Australia.

In his first fieldwork report, "The Natives of Mailu" (1915), Malinowski "had relied heavily on *Notes and Queries* for the categories which structured his text," as Michael Young found out. Young describes "The Natives of Mailu" as "a window on the past" in contrast to *Argonauts of the Western Pacific* (1922), which he characterizes as "a window on the future" (Young 1988: 27, 24). Malinowski conducted fieldwork at Mailu Island (south of Papua New Guinea) for four weeks in October–November 1914, and for another month in December 1914–January 1915. He finished his report on Mailu in June 1915.

Malinowski then spent ten months in Kiriwina on the Trobriand Islands, from June 1915 to February 1916, "doing fieldwork ... in the only way it is possible" (letter to Seligman, 30 July 1915, cited in Alvarez Roldán 1995: 144). In September–October 1915, he wrote to Seligman that he was "beginning to talk Kiriwinian quite sufficiently," to Rivers that he was "doing 'intensive work' in the Trobriands," and to Haddon that he was "living right among the natives in a village" (cited in Alvarez Roldán 1995: 147–48, 153n3). After recuperating in Sydney and writing a long essay titled "Baloma: The Spirits of the Dead in the Trobriand Islands" (published in 1916), Malinowski carried out a third expedition and his final fieldwork among the Trobrianders from October 1917 to October 1918, concluding about two years of fieldwork. While his Mailu ethnography "had been done from ... [a] historicist point of view, he looked at native society [in Kiriwina] from a synchronic, functionalist point of view," and this change in perspective had "persuaded Malinowski to learn the vernacular language and to observe natives' behaviour" (Alvarez Roldán 1995: 147). By collating "The Natives of Mailu" (1915) and "Baloma" (1916), Arturo Alvarez Roldán highlighted the pioneering aspect of this second ethnographic account by Malinowski—his first Trobriand monograph, which was actually a seventy-seven-page article published in the *Journal of the Royal Anthropological Institute*: "This essay contains the basic lines of the new model of ethnography that he later improved in writing *Argonauts*" (Alvarez Roldán 1995: 151). Regarding the debate on whether and when ethnographic fieldwork had been revolutionized by introducing participant observation, Alvarez Roldán opined: "It is of no interest to continue arguing about who was the inventor of this research method, or where the invention first took place" (1995: 143). This is because he had no doubt that it was indeed Malinowski who had "discovered" it while carrying out research in Kiriwina.

The magnitude and diversity of the ethnographic archive world-wide may, however, force a suspension of judgment regarding the pioneering nature of Malinowski's fieldwork and its results, whether *Argonauts of the Western Pacific* or "Baloma."[16] The way Malinowski explicitly obfuscated previous ethnographic accounts is also part of the equation. In the introduction to *Argonauts of the Western Pacific*, he compared "scientific" and "amateur" ethnography, resorting to the metaphor of the skeleton, flesh and blood, and the spirit summarized above. A closer look at the passages in question reveals that Malinowski had his own views on the shortcomings and achievements of previous ethnographers with and without scientific training. In everything having to do with "the skeleton," he had no doubt that "scientific" fieldwork was "far above even the best amateur productions" (Malinowski 1922: 22–23). No systematic outline of the normative side of social life, he believed, was "found or at least practised in Ethnography till field work was taken up by men of science" (ibid.: 12). Questionable as this harsh judgment may sound today, it was counterbalanced by a startling comment in relation to the flesh-and-blood avenue of ethnographic fieldwork:

> There is, however, one point in which the latter [amateur productions] often excel. This is in the presentation of intimate touches of native life, in bringing home to us these aspects of it which one is made familiar [with] only through being in close contact with the natives, one way or the other, for a long period of time. In certain results of the scientific work ... we are given an excellent skeleton, so to speak, of the tribal constitution, but it lacks flesh and blood. ... And that is the reason why certain works of amateur residents of long standing ... surpass in plasticity and vividness most of the purely scientific accounts. (Malinowski 1922: 17–18)

Knowing that the white residents had other priorities than carrying out ethnography and, most of all, that "none of them lives right in a native village," this positive side of their writings had, in turn, to be put into perspective. When done by untrained observers, the description of the *imponderabilia* of social life usually amounted to "a superficial registration of details." In short, amateur accounts were like flesh and blood with no skeleton, whereas scientific accounts were like skeletons with no flesh and blood: "Neither aspect, the intimate, as little as the legal, ought to be glossed over. Yet as a rule in ethnographic accounts we have not both but either the one or the other—and, so far, the intimate has hardly ever been properly treated" (ibid.: 19).

But what about "the third and last aim of scientific field-work," grasping "the spirit"? In the two and a half pages dedicated to the all-important matter of producing a *corpus inscriptionum* of the societies visited in the native language, Malinowski no longer compared scientific accounts with amateur ones. He wrote: "The best ethnographical writers—here again the Cambridge school with Haddon, Rivers, and Seligman rank first among English-language ethnographers—have always tried to quote *verbatim* statements of crucial importance." This may be read as an ambiguous statement (note his choice of verb: "have tried to . . ."), as if Malinowski had in mind his mentors resorting to Pidgin English on the colonial verandas of Torres Straits.[17] Then he added: "One step further in this line can be made by the Ethnographer who acquires a knowledge of the native language and can use it as an instrument of inquiry" (1922: 22–23). No need to say that the goal of obtaining independence from interpreters and from "Pidgin English," along with the gradual production of texts fully in the vernacular, particularly by dictating traditional formulas, was not a twentieth-century invention. To the contrary, numerous *corpora inscriptionum* had been produced in the nineteenth century, even if Malinowski abstained from giving examples.

Conclusion: Opening the Field, Delimiting Ethnography

To this day no one has questioned the fact that Malinowski's introduction to *Argonauts of the Western Pacific* (1922), however "self-mythicizing," comprises "arguably the most influential twenty-five pages in the history of the discipline" (Young 2018: 11). "The possibilities of the systematic field investigation of one culture were first demonstrated by Malinowski in his work on the Trobriand Islands . . . , and his constant emphasis on methodological problems has deeply influenced the development of field technique," his disciple Audrey Richards (1899–1984) wrote in "The Development of Field Work Methods in Social Anthropology" (1939: 285). "There can be no question of Malinowski's radical influence on fieldwork methods," Phyllis Kaberry opined in a chapter dedicated to her master's way of doing and writing ethnography (1957: 86). The vividness of Malinowski's ethnographic accounts, allowing the reader "to know the inhabitants, not as paid and perhaps bored informants, but as actors in a changing scene" (ibid.: 71), resulted from and was inseparable from his innovative fieldwork experience. Malinowski was more than "a participant observer," Kaberry added: "He actively sought his information by employing a range of techniques" (ibid.: 78). Following the publication of Malinowski's diary, reassessments were less benevolent, in any case less unanimous about the methodological candor with which he described his praxis in the Trobriand Islands. Noting that Malinowski's field diaries, published in 1967, "reveal that he did not achieve that separation from European contacts which he advocated,"[18] Adam Kuper insists that Malinowski "really did invent modern fieldwork methods in the two years he spent on the Trobriand islands" (1996 [1973]: 12–13).

By contrast, Ian Jarvie did not defend the "Malinowskian revolution" in *The Revolution in Anthropology* (1964). He criticized the scientism underlying the call to do fieldwork for being "a false religion," comparable to cargo cults (the subject of three chapters in his book). According to Jarvie, the hegemonic understanding of fieldwork as anthropology's alpha and omega precluded other ways of being an anthropologist, such as an armchair anthropologist resorting to ethnographic accounts for comparative and theoretical purposes. Defending the figure he considered to have played the role of scapegoat, the revolution's slain king, Frazer, he admitted:

> I must say I find Frazer [*The Golden Bough*] glorious and thrilling reading; there is an excitement to be found there which is sadly lacking in the work of the later generations and I am ashamed to have to report that he is not properly appreciated. ... Minds must be made up. Do we want comparative sociology, and are we going to excuse its practitioners from the ritual of fieldwork or not? And if we do want this and we will let them off, let us be more careful how we treat those who we can count as precursors, especially when their problems were different from those we are now interested in. (Jarvie 1967 [1964]: 33)

Considering that Frazer perused the vast ethnographic literature of his era like no other, Jarvie's "plea for a 'Back to Frazer' movement" (ibid.: 175) can be rephrased today as a back-to-reading movement—not necessarily Frazer, but the numerous ethnographic accounts that he mastered. It is not just Frazer's problems that were different from ours. Today, generations of students in anthropology are pushed to pursue new ethnographies in contemporary settings at home to the detriment of the ethnographic archive and its potentialities. Under the pretext that studying non-Western societies is unethical, this trend affects the ways in which anthropologists (do not) relate to the ethnographic archive, particularly to salvage ethnography conducted in the nineteenth and twentieth centuries—except as colonial violence.

Notwithstanding the alleged "historic turn" in anthropology, the discipline risks becoming more and more estranged from the past— that is, from disciplinary history and from the *longue durée* of other societies and cultures. The hegemony of present- and future-oriented anthropology significantly reduces the possibility of it also being a past-oriented discipline.

If we today are less confident about the "Revolution in Anthropology," this is not because we question Malinowski's undeniable merits and the innovations he brought to the monographic genre. It is because "the age of armchair anthropologists" was also the era of ethnographers, producing a vast literature, sufficiently varied, rich, and complex to deserve a case-by-case analysis of form and content. As to the fieldwork experiences at the basis of earlier ethnographic accounts, 365 of which are listed in the appendix to the present volume, produced by at least 220 ethnographers between ca. 1870 and ca. 1922, it is clear that intensive, long-term fieldwork had been practiced by many late nineteenth- and early twentieth-century ethnographers—though not necessarily "by tenting in the [proverbial] village."

One of the best-known examples of intensive research conducted in the nineteenth century is that of Frank Hamilton Cushing (1857–1900), who lived at a Zuni pueblo from 1879 to 1884, learned the local language, and engaged "with the people and culture as deeply as possible, providing an early example of a participant-observer" (Lewis 2014: 77). Adopting a Zuni name, Cushing started a Zuni family (Pandey 1972) and became a Zuni priest and chief. Within the entangled realities of colonial settings, other intensive approaches were possible, whether in past-, present-, or future-oriented projects. A lesser-known case is that of the Dutch Orientalist Christiaan Snouck Hurgonje (1857–1936), who became a Muslim in Jeddah and carried out research among Acehnese Muslims in both Mecca (1884–85) and Aceh, Sumatra (1891–92). Working as an ethnographer and Islam scholar (*mufti*), Snouck Hurgonje produced monographs on Mecca and Aceh, married twice a Sundanese woman on Java, and was a political advisor to the Dutch East Indies government before accepting a chair in Arabic and Islam studies at Leiden University, the Netherlands, in 1906 (Koningsveld 2015).

Malinowski was not the inventor of intensive fieldwork—scores of other ethnographers, including Franz Boas, Frank Hamilton Cushing, James Mooney, Katie Langloh Parker, Henrique de Carvalho, Alice C. Fletcher, Francis La Flesche, Maria Czaplicka, Elsdon Best,

Theodor Koch-Grünberg, Robert S. Rattray, Edward Westermarck, etc., practiced that long before him, as the case studies in the present collection demonstrate. But Malinowski brought its merits into the open and instructed his students to put the method into practice. Later followers routinized the charismatic authority of Malinowski as the prophet of modern anthropology, and many of them found positions in social anthropology departments as universities expanded after World War II (see Shankland 2019 and Shankland, this volume).

One fundamental side effect of ignoring older texts and early ethnographers has been the neglect of women ethnographers doing fieldwork before Malinowski. Fortunately, the present book includes solid analyses of the ethnographic work carried out by three such women: Katie Langloh Parker, Alice C. Fletcher, and Maria Czaplicka (see Dawson, Scherer, and Kubica, this volume).[19] Likewise, Indigenous individuals engaged in ethnographic projects in the period ca. 1870–ca. 1922, whether as interlocutors, collaborators, or ethnographers in their own right, deserve their place in the history of anthropology in order to be acknowledged in more consequential ways. The chapters in part 2 of this volume highlight the cases of Mpengula Mbande, Tutakangahau, and Francis La Flesche (see Chidester, Paparoa Holman, and Scherer, this volume).

Moreover, Malinowski's predecessors in Germany, the land where he had studied for three semesters in Leipzig (1908–10), were no amateurs. Karl von den Steinen, Theodor Koch-Grünberg, Konrad Theodor Preuss, Max Schmidt, Paul Ehrenreich, and Fritz Krause were among the first professional ethnographers in the Amazon Basin. They prioritized the description of Indigenous groups over theory building, but it would be wrong to regard them as mere collectors of data (see Kraus, this volume).

Most pre-Malinowskian ethnographers, women or men of European or Indigenous descent, are excluded ancestors, absent from disciplinary memory. This happened not only because Malinowski contributed to setting the canon but also because successive generations of practicing anthropologists and lecturers repeated—and continue to repeat—the idea that he did so. Within such a complex "pre-Malinowskian" world, we suggest surpassing preconceived ideas on the irrelevance of nineteenth- and early twentieth-century ethnographers and focus on their texts, which bring out the plurality in anthropological writing. Before reproducing the hasty judgment that such ethnographic accounts were mostly miscellaneous, dry compilations of odds and ends, we should get back to reading them with an open mind.

Han F. Vermeulen is research associate at the Max Planck Institute for Social Anthropology in Halle (Saale), Germany, specializing in the history and theory of anthropology. He is editor or co-editor of a dozen books, including *Fieldwork and Footnotes: Studies in the History of European Anthropology* (1995); *Treasure Hunting? Collectors and Collections of Indonesian Artefacts* (2002); and *Tales from Academia: History of Anthropology in the Netherlands* (2002). His latest book, *Before Boas: The Genesis of Ethnography and Ethnology in the German Enlightenment* (University of Nebraska Press, 2015), was listed by the *Süddeutsche Zeitung* as one of the most important books of 2016, awarded the ICAS Book Prize 2017 by the International Convention of Asia Scholars, and published in a paperback edition in 2018. He is a founding member of the the "History of Anthropology Network" (HOAN) within the European Association of Social Anthropologists (EASA).

Frederico Delgado Rosa is lecturer at NOVA University, Lisbon (Portugal) and a researcher in the history of anthropology at CRIA: Centre for Research in Anthropology (Lisbon) and HERITAGES (Paris). He is the author, among other works, of *L'Âge d'or du totémisme* (CNRS Éditions, 2003); *Exploradores portugueses e reis africanos* (Portuguese explorers and African kings, A Esfera dos Livros, 2013, with Filipe Verde); and *Elsdon Best, l'ethnographe immémorial* (Les Carnets de Bérose, 2018). He is currently co-director, with Christine Laurière, of *BEROSE International Encyclopedia of the Histories of Anthropology* and co-convenor, with Fabiana Dimpflmeier, of the "History of Anthropology Network" within the European Association of Social Anthropologists (EASA).

Notes

1. In that meeting, it was also agreed that the "comparative study of the institutions of primitive societies was accepted as the task of social anthropology, and this name was preferred to 'sociology.'" Radcliffe-Brown added that Frazer had defined social anthropology in 1906 "as the branch of sociology that deals with primitive peoples" and that Westermarck held the position of "Professor of Sociology, though his work was really in the field of social anthropology" (1952: 276).
2. Malinowski's "List of Books Used as Ethnographic Sources, Referring to the Australian Aborigines" comprised forty-seven books, thirty-five articles (with many more referred to through journal titles), twelve book chapters, and over twenty regional and museum bulletins. Vari-

ous genres were considered. Many texts were not produced under the label of ethnography, but Malinowski's list also contained ethnographic accounts properly speaking, including several monographs dedicated to specific tribes and certain areas or to Australia in general but with chapters on specific tribes or areas.

3. In this regard, Malinowski acknowledged his debt to the French historians Charles-Victor Langlois (1863–1928) and Charles Seignobos (1854–1942), authors of the canonical textbook *Introduction aux études historiques (1898)*.

4. Walter Edmund Roth (1861–1933) was a physician and an ethnographer who served as chief protector of Aborigines in Queensland.

5. Malinowski dictated the *Argonauts* to his wife, Elsie Rosaline Masson (1890–1935), "an accomplished writer, who edited it before it was again revised by Malinowski" (Skalník 1995: 138). Between 1922 and 1935 Malinowski published five detailed monographs on Trobriand culture and society.

6. Including such prominent women anthropologists as Ruth Fulton Benedict (1887–1948), Ella Cara Deloria (1889–1971), Zora Neale Hurston (1891–1960), and Margaret Mead (1901–78) (King 2019).

7. His reserch on kinship and marriage among Australian aborigines, conducted in 1910–12, was basically "survey work of the kind practised by Rivers or Seligman." It provided the basis for his article on "Three Tribes of Western Australia" (1913) and his later work on the "Social Organization of Australian Tribes" (1930–31). Although his Australian work was primarily "survey and salvage" ethnography, his studies "stand as a remarkable synthesis" and "a significant advance" (Kuper 1996 [1973]: 40–43).

8. Radcliffe-Brown presented his book as that of an apprentice. He dedicated it to "Dr. A. C. Haddon, F.R.S. and Dr. W. H. R. Rivers, F.R.S. to whose instruction and kind encouragement is due whatever value it may possess, this work of apprenticeship is dedicated."

9. Under the auspices of the British Association for the Advancement of Science, in liaison with the Anthropological Institute of Great Britain and Ireland, established in 1871.

10. After having been awarded the Praemium Erasmianum in Amsterdam, Claude Lévi-Strauss said the same thing. During a May 1973 lecture at the Institute of Cultural Anthropology in Leiden he gave the following answer to a graduate student who asked what the most important problem was in current anthropology: "To do fieldwork." This was quite unexpected, as Lévi-Strauss was known as an eminent structural anthropologist and a major theoretician. Apparently, his intensive studies of ethnographic accounts by Boas and other representatives of the "Americanist tradition" for his comparative works on kinship and mythology, plus the idea of a disappearing world, had prompted Lévi-Strauss to give priority to ethnographic fieldwork as a basic requirement of anthropology.

11. Originally published in the *Journal of the Anthropological Institute of Great Britain and Ireland* between 1882 and 1885.

12. Some of whom might actually be "prisoners," or at least "hostages" (see Tomas 1991: 77–83).

13. A sign of Man's new rigor was the assertion that there were at least nine tribes in the islands, with different dialects and the possibility of further divisions in the lesser-known Little Andaman, whose inhabitants remained aloof to the British. Man's linguistic authority was to be challenged at the turn of the century by his successor in the field, Maurice Vidal Portman (1860–1935), who implied that Man spoke a mixture of various dialects (see Tomas 1991: 90–91).

14. Here is one example by none less than Edward B. Tylor, regarding the "collection of mythic stories": "It is desirable to take them down verbatim from the lips of a skilled storyteller, as they thus form specimens of the language in its best form, exhibiting native metaphor, wit, and picturesque diction. They should be copied out with an exact translation between the lines or on the same page" (Tylor 1892 [1874]a: 140).

15. The fact that the nineteenth-century editions of *Notes and Queries* created a fragmented model of more than seventy sections, with no particular emphasis on interdependence, does not mean that there were no suggested connections between them. In fact, systemic views connecting different dimensions of social life, particularly of "primitive" social life, are detectable in anthropological literature from Auguste Comte (1798–1857) and Herbert Spencer (1820–1903) on, if not from, Joseph-François Lafitau (1681–1746); see Tax 1955. At the turn of the twentieth century, the comparison between social institutions and the organs of a living body could even be found in literature directed at a popular audience (for example, Jenks 1909 [1900]). The comparison between the precepts of modern, particularly functionalist anthropology and *Notes and Queries on Anthropology* might be further illuminated by other contemporary manuals, such as *Führer durch die ethnographische Abteilung* (1877) by Adolf Bastian (1826–1905); *Questionnaire* (1903) by Paul Sébillot (1843–1918); *Queries in Ethnography* (1903) by Albert Galloway Keller (1874–1956); *Anleitung für ethnographische Beobachtungen und Sammlungen in Afrika und Oceanien* (1899) by Felix von Luschan (1854–1924); and *The Handbook of Folklore* (1890) by George Laurence Gomme (1853–1916), among many others.

16. Here is one exemplary comparison. Malinowski's anti-amateur bias can be detected in the 1916 article, in which he disparaged the German missionary and ethnographer Carl Strehlow for denying the Arunta nescience of physiological paternity: "Here the explanation lies in the insufficient mental training of the observer (Strehlow). You can no more expect good all round ethnographical work from an untrained observer than you can expect a good geological statement from a miner, or hydrodynamic theory from a diver. It is not enough to have the facts right in front of one, the faculty to deal with them must be there" (1916: 415).

Today, Malinowski's contention reads problematic because (a) the alleged Trobriand ignorance of physiological paternity is among his most disputed "findings" and (b) Strehlow's work, with its "innovative" linear translations of myth, has recently been considered "the first" vernacular record of Australian oral literature, providing "some of the earliest insight into the true sophistication of Aboriginal cultures" (Kenny 2013: 7, 10). Ironically, it was Malinowski, not the amateur ethnographer, who was championing supernatural birth, a category strongly connoted with nineteenth-century armchair anthropology.

17. Malinowski's reserved attitude toward amateur ethnographers was anticipated by Rivers (1912, 1913), who acknowledged, however, that "the total mass of the contribution of missionaries to ethnology is so great that it is difficult to imagine what would have been the position of the science today without it." This paradox was solved by saying that "only exceptional men"—such as Robert Henry Codrington, Henri-Alexandre Junod (1863–1934), John Roscoe (1861–1932), and Carl Strehlow—had overcome these obstacles (Rivers 1913: 8–10).

18. One year earlier, Murray L. Wax had noted: "The unhappy truth in Malinowski's diaries is that he neither participated in the ordinary run of the native life nor was able to reciprocate native trust and honor" (Wax 1972: 10). Although Malinowski pitched his tent "in the heart of the native habitat" (ibid.: 11), he lived like a European sahib (lord), did not participate (ibid.: 10) nor "establish parity with native people" (ibid.), and was more an interrogator and observer than a participant (ibid.: 12). Therefore, "it is hard to classify his work as participant observation, although he did move the next generation of anthropologists toward that style of fieldwork" (ibid.: 7).

19. Thanks to the development of gender studies, a focus on women anthropologists has resulted in the biographical dictionary of Ute Gacs et al. (1998) and the handbook of Bettina Beer (2007), presenting no less than seventy German-speaking women anthropologists, many of whom conducted fieldwork (see also Kuper 1999; Bank 2016; Larson 2021).

References

Alvarez Roldán, Arturo. 1995. "Malinowski and the Origins of the Ethnographic Method." In *Fieldwork and Footnotes: Studies in the History of European Anthropology*, edited by Han F. Vermeulen and A. Alvarez Roldán, 143–55. EASA Series. New York: Routledge.

BAAS [British Association for the Advancement of Science]. 1874. *Notes and Queries on Anthropology, for the Use of Travellers and Residents in Uncivilized Lands*. London: Edward Stanford.

———. 1929. *Notes and Queries on Anthropology*. 5th ed. London: The Royal Anthropological Institute.

Bank, Andrew. 2016. *Pioneers of the Field: South Africa's Women Anthropologists*. Cambridge: Cambridge University Press.

Bastian, Adolf. 1877. *Führer durch die ethnographische Abteilung*. Berlin: Königliche Museen zu Berlin.

Beer, Bettina. 2007. *Frauen in der deutschsprachigen Ethnologie: Ein Handbuch*. Köln/Weimar/Wien: Böhlau Verlag.

Best, Elsdon. 1900–1. "Spiritual Concepts of the Maori." *Journal of the Polynesian Society* 9: 173–99; 10: 107–65.

———. 1922. *Spiritual and Mental Concepts of the Maori*. Wellington: Dominion Museum, the Government Printer.

———. 1924. *The Maori*. 2 vols. Wellington: H. Tombs.

Duvernay-Bolens, Jacqueline. 2001–2. "L'oral et l'écrit: De Franz Boas à Lévi-Strauss." *Gradhiva* 30–31: 15–30.

Evans-Pritchard, Edward Evan. 1951. *Social Anthropology*. London: Cohen & West.

Fortes, Meyer. 1953. *Social Anthropology at Cambridge since 1900*, 1–30. Inaugural Lecture. Cambridge: Cambridge University Press. Repr. in Regna Darnell, ed. 1974. *Readings in the History of Anthropology*, 426–39. New York: Harper and Row.

Firth, Raymond. 1951. "Contemporary British Social Anthropology." *American Anthropologist* 53(4): 474–89.

———. 1959 [1929]. *Economics of the New Zealand Maori*. Wellington: R. E. Owen.

———. 1957. "Introduction: Malinowski as Scientist and as Man." In *Man and Culture: An Evaluation of the Work of Bronislaw Malinowski*, edited by Raymond Firth, 1–14. London: Routledge & Kegan Paul.

Frazer, James George. 1890. *The Golden Bough: A Study in Comparative Religion*. London: Macmillan and Co.

Freire-Marreco, Barbara, and John Lynton Myres, eds. 1912. *Notes and Queries on Anthropology*. 4th ed. London: The Royal Anthropological Institute.

Gacs, Ute, Aisha Khan, Jerrie McIntyre, and Ruth Weinberg, eds. 1998. *Women Anthropologists: A Biographical Dictionary*. New York: Greenwood Press.

Garson, John George, and Charles Hercules Read, eds. 1892. *Notes and Queries on Anthropology; or, A Guide to Anthropological Research for the Use of Travellers and Others: Edited for the Council of the Anthropological Institute*. 2nd ed. London: The Anthropological Institute.

———. 1899. *Notes and Queries on Anthropology: Edited for the British Association for the Advancement of Science*. 3rd ed. London: The Anthropological Institute.

Gomme, George Laurence, ed. 1890. *The Handbook of Folklore*. London: David Nutt.

Hogbin, Ian. 1988. "Radcliffe-Brown, Alfred Reginald (1881–1955)." *Australian Dictionary of Biography*. Vol. 11. Online at https://adb.anu.edu.au/biography

Jarvie, Ian C. 1967 [1964]. *The Revolution in Anthropology*. Foreword by Ernest Gellner. London: Routledge & Kegan Paul.

Jenks, Edward. 1909 [1900]. *A History of Politics*. New York: The Macmillan Co.

Kaberry, Phyllis M. 1957. "Malinowski's Contribution to Field-Work Methods and the Writing of Ethnography." In *Man and Culture: An Evaluation of the Work of Bronislaw Malinowski*, edited by Raymond Firth, 71–91. London: Routledge & Kegan Paul.

Keller, Albert Galloway. 1903. *Queries in Ethnography*. New York: Longmans and Co.

Kenny, Anna. 2013. *The Aranda's Pepa: An Introduction to Carl Strehlow's Masterpiece* Die Aranda- und Loritja-Stämme in Zentral-Australien *(1907–1920)*. Acton [Canberra]: ANU Press.

King, Charles. 2019. *Gods of the Upper Air: How a Circle of Renegade Anthropologists Reinvented Race, Sex, and Gender in the Twentieth Century*. Garden City, NY: Doubleday. UK ed.: *The Reinvention of Humanity: A Story of Race, Sex, Gender and the Discovery of Culture*. London: The Bodley Head (Vintage).

Koningsveld, Pieter Sjoerd van. 2015. "Conversion of European Intellectuals to Islam: The Case of Christiaan Snouck Hurgronje alias Abd al-Ghaffar." In *Muslims in Interwar Europe: A Transcultural Historical Perspective*, edited by Bekim Agai, Umar Ryad, and Mehdi Sajid, 88–104. Leiden: Brill.

Kuper, Adam, ed. 1977. *The Social Anthropology of Radcliffe-Brown*. London: Routledge and Kegan Paul.

———. 1996 [1973]. *Anthropology and Anthropologists: The Modern British School*. 3rd rev. and enlarged ed. New York: Routledge.

———. 1999. "Audrey Richards: A Career in Anthropology." In *Among the Anthropologists: History and Contexts in Anthropology*, edited by Adam Kuper, 115–37. London: Athlone Press. French version in *BEROSE International Encyclopedia of the Histories of Anthropology* 2017.

Langlois, Charles-Victor, and Charles Seignobos. 1898. *Introduction aux études historiques*. Paris: Hachette.

Larson, Frances. 2021. *Undreamed Shores: The Hidden Heroines of British Anthropology*. London: Granta Book.

Lewis, Herbert S. 2014. *In Defense of Anthropology: An Investigation of the Critique of Anthropology*. New Brunswick, NJ: Transaction Publishers.

Luschan, Felix von. 1899. *Anleitung für ethnographische Beobachtungen und Sammlungen in Afrika und Oceanien*. Berlin: Königliches Museum in Berlin.

Mancuso, Alessandro. 2021. "Before and After Science: Radcliffe-Brown, British Social Anthropology, and the Relationship Between Field Research, Ethnography, and Theory." In *Ethnography: A Theoretically Oriented Practice*, edited by Vincenzo Matera and Angela Biscaldi, 51–80. Basingstoke: Palgrave Macmillan, an imprint of Springer Nature.

Malinowski, Bronisław. 1913. *The Family among the Australian Aborigines: A Sociological Study*. London: University of London Press.

——. 1915. "The Natives of Mailu: Preliminary Results of the Robert Mond Research Work in British New Guinea." *Transactions and Proceedings of the Royal Society of South Australia* 39: 494–706.

——. 1916. "Baloma: The Spirits of the Dead in the Trobriand Islands." *Journal of the Royal Anthropological Institute* 46: 353–430.

——. 1922. *Argonauts of the Western Pacific: An Account of Native Enterprise and Adventure in the Archipelagoes of Melanesian New Guinea*. Preface by Sir James George Frazer. London: George Routledge & Sons.

——. 1967. *A Diary in the Strict Sense of the Term*. Preface by Valetta Malinowska. Introduction by Raymond Firth (editor). Translated [from the Polish] by Norbert Guterman. London: Athlone Press/London: Routledge & Kegan Paul.

Man, Edward Horace. 1932 [1885]. *On the Aboriginal Inhabitants of the Andaman Islands* (With *Report of the Researches into the Language of the South Andaman Island*, by Alexander J. Ellis). London: Royal Anthropological Institute of Great Britain and Ireland. Repr. from the *Journal of the Royal Anthropological Institute of Great Britain and Ireland* 1882–83 and 1885.

Pandey, Triloki Nath. 1972. "Anthropologists at Zuni." *Proceedings of the American Philosophical Society* 116(4): 321–37.

Radcliffe-Brown, Alfred Reginald [Brown, A. R.]. 1913. "Three Tribes of Western Australia." *Journal of the Royal Anthropological Institute of Great Britain and Ireland* 43: 143–94.

——. 1922. *The Andaman Islanders: A Study in Social Anthropology*. Cambridge: The University Press.

——. 1933. *The Andaman Islanders*. 2nd ed. with a new preface. Cambridge: The University Press.

——. 1946. "A Note on Functional Anthropology." *Man* 46: 38–41.

——. 1952. "Historical Note on British Social Anthropology." *American Anthropologist* 54(2): 275–77.

RAI [Royal Anthropological Institute of Great Britain and Ireland]. 1951. *Notes and Queries on Anthropology*. 6th ed. London: Routledge and Kegan Paul.

Read, Charles Hercules. 1892. "Prefatory Note" (to Part II, "Ethnography"). In *Notes and Queries on Anthropology; or, A Guide to Anthropological Research for the Use of Travellers and Others; Edited for the Council of the Anthropological Institute*, 2nd ed., edited by J. G. Garson and C. H. Read, 87–88. London: The Anthropological Institute.

Richards, Audrey I. 1939. "The Development of Field Work Methods in Social Anthropology." In *The Study of Society: Methods and Problems*, edited by F. C. Bartlett, M. Ginsberg, E. J. Lindgren, and R. H. Thouless, 272–316. London: Kegan Paul, Trench, Trubner & Co.

Rivers, William Halse Rivers. 1912. "A General Account of Method." In *Notes and Queries on Anthropology*, 4th ed., edited by B. Freire-Marreco and J. Linton Myres, 108–27. London: The Royal Anthropological Institute.

———. 1913. "Report on Anthropological Research outside America." In W. H. R. Rivers, A. E. Jenks, and S. G. Morley, *Reports upon the Present Condition and Future Needs of the Science of Anthropology*, 5–28. Washington, DC: The Carnegie Institution of Washington.

Sébillot, Paul. 1903. *Questionnaire*. Paris: E. Malbet.

Shankland, David. 2019. "Social Anthropology and Its History." *Zeitschrift für Ethnologie* 144: 51–76.

Skalník, Peter. 1995. "Bronislaw Kasper Malinowski and Stanislaw Ignacy Witkiewicz: Science versus Art in the Conceptualization of Culture." In *Fieldwork and Footnotes: Studies in the History of European Anthropology*, edited by Han F. Vermeulen and A. Alvarez Roldán, 129–142. EASA Series. London/New York: Routledge.

Stocking, George W., Jr. 1984a. "Dr. Durkheim and Mr. Brown: Comparative Sociology at Cambridge in 1910." In *Functionalism Historicized: Essays on British Social Anthropology*, edited by G. W. Stocking Jr., 106–30. Madison: University of Wisconsin Press (History of Anthropology 2).

———. 1984b. "Radcliffe-Brown and British Social Anthropology." In *Functionalism Historicized: Essays on British Social Anthropology*, edited by G. W. Stocking Jr., 131–91. Madison: University of Wisconsin Press (History of Anthropology 2).

———. 1995. *After Tylor: British Social Anthropology, 1888–1951*. Madison: University of Wisconsin Press.

Strenski, Ivan. 1987. *Four Theories of Myth in Twentieth-Century History: Cassirer, Eliade, Lévi-Strauss, and Malinowski*. Iowa City: University of Iowa Press.

Tax, Sol. 1955. "From Lafitau to Radcliffe-Brown: A Short History of the Study of Social Organization." In *Social Anthropology of North American Tribes*, 2nd enlarged ed., edited by Fred Eggan, 445–81. Chicago: University of Chicago Press.

Tomas, David. 1991. "Tools of the Trade: The Production of Ethnographic Observations on the Andaman Islands, 1858–1922." In *Colonial Situations: Essays on the Contextualization of Ethnographic Knowledge*, History of Anthropology 7, edited by G. W. Stocking Jr., 75–108. Madison: University of Wisconsin Press.

Tylor, Edward B. 1892 [1874]a. "Mythology." In *Notes and Queries on Anthropology; or, A Guide to Anthropological Research for the Use of Travellers and Others: Edited for the Council of the Anthropological Institute*, 2nd ed., edited by J. G. Garson and C. H. Read, 140–42. London: The Anthropological Institute.

———. 1892 [1874]b. "Morals." *Notes and Queries on Anthropology; or, A Guide to Anthropological Research for the Use of Travellers and Others: Edited for the Council of the Anthropological Institute*, 2nd ed., edited by J. G. Garson and C. H. Read, 146–49. London: The Anthropological Institute.

———. 1892 [1874]c. "Religion, Fetishes, &c." *Notes and Queries on Anthropology; or, A Guide to Anthropological Research for the Use of Travellers and Others: Edited for the Council of the Anthropological Institute*, 2nd ed., edited by J. G. Garson and C. H. Read, 130–40. London: The Anthropological Institute.

Urry, James. 1984. "A History of Field Methods." In *Ethnographic Research: A Guide to General Conduct*, edited by Roy F. Ellen, 35–61. Foreword by Sir Raymond Firth. London: Academic Press.

———. 1993. *Before Social Anthropology: Essays on the History of British Anthropology*. Chur: Harwood Academic Publishers.

Vermeulen, Han F. 2015. *Before Boas: The Genesis of Ethnography and Ethnology in the German Enlightenment*. Lincoln: University of Nebraska Press (Critical Studies in the History of Anthropology).

Young, Michael W. 1988. "Malinowski among the Magi: Editor's Introduction." In Bronislaw Malinowski, *Malinowski Among the Magi: "The Natives of Mailu,"* 1–76. Edited with an Introduction by M. W. Young. New York: Routledge.

Wax, Murray L. 1972. "Tenting with Malinowski." *American Sociological Review* 37: 1–13.

Zumwalt, Rosemary Lévy. 2019. *Franz Boas: The Emergence of the Anthropologist*. Critical Studies in the History of Anthropology. Lincoln: University of Nebraska Press.

Appendix

Selected Bibliography of Ethnographic Accounts, ca. 1870–1922

In the first edition of his *History of Anthropology* (1910),[1] Alfred Cort Haddon paid tribute to missionaries of the nineteenth century for their contributions to the growth of ethnology (Haddon 1910: 103). He mentioned eight cases of missionary ethnographers, namely Jean-Antoine Dubois (1765–1848), William Ellis (1794–1872), John Williams (1796–1839), David Livingstone (1813–73), Évariste-Régis Huc (1813–60), George Turner (1818–91), William Wyatt Gill (1828–96), and Henry Callaway (1817–90). In the second edition of 1934, reprinted in 1949, Haddon added a paragraph saying that the "increasingly valuable" contributions of missionaries responded to "the modern requirements of ethnology" (Haddon 1934: 102–3). As an illustration, he selected "but a very few" representatives of this trend: Henri-Alexandre Junod (1863–1934), John Roscoe (1861–1932), and Carl Strehlow (1871–1922). No names were evoked of other colonial agents, and thus Haddon kept the following words unchanged: "Besides the missionaries, we owe a deep debt of gratitude to the early explorers and civil servants in all parts of the world, who have provided, consciously or unconsciously, a vast amount of information about the peoples among whom they travelled or over whom they ruled" (Haddon 1910: 1034; 1934: 103). Not counting the "further material" acquired by scientific expeditions, "even before these were undertaken in the interests of anthropology," he acknowledged the historical importance of nonprofessional ethnographers in the following manner: "Such varied data, often of unequal value, have formed the foundation on which the science of ethnology has been *and is being* laboriously built" (Haddon 1934, 1949: 103; our emphasis).

As interesting as such lists are, they always exclude work by other ethnographers. For instance, Haddon did not mention the following eight monographs on Africa authored by three colonial administrators and army officers: *The Tshi-Speaking Peoples of the Gold Coast of West Africa* (1887), *The Ewe-Speaking Peoples of the Slave Coast* (1890), and *The Yoruba-Speaking Peoples of the Slave Coast of West Africa* (1894) by Alfred Burdon Ellis (1852–94); *The Masai* (1905) and *The Nandi* (1909) by Alfred Claud Hollis (1874–1961); and *The Tailed Head-Hunters of Nigeria* (1912), *Hausa Superstitions and Customs* (1913), and *The Ban of the Bori* (1914) by Arthur John Newman Tremearne (1877–1915).

Prepared during the professionalization of ethnography in the United Kingdom, Haddon's short list can be taken as a sample of what the present volume aims at. Both intersecting with and complementing his selection, other short lists exist. In *The Rise of Anthropological Theory* (1968), for example, Marvin Harris made a "brief analysis" of the sources in Edward Tylor's *Researches into the Early History of Mankind* (1865). Along with the "poorly qualified travelers or missionaries," there were "trained and skilled observers" such as William Mariner (1791–1853), Thomas Williams (1815–91), and Eugène Casalis (1812–91).[2] From the late 1920s, Margaret Mead's pile of "famous monographs of the period" included *The Baganda* (1911) by John Roscoe and *The Cheyenne Indians* (1923) by George Bird Grinnell (1849–1938)—alongside *The Argonauts of the Western Pacific* (1922) by Bronisław Malinowski and *The Todas* (1906) by W. H. R. Rivers.[3] In *After Tylor* (1995), George W. Stocking Jr. enumerated eight anthropologists who were trained in British academia to undertake "the intensive study of a limited area before the Great War" (1995: 117–19, see introduction above). He also made reference to colonial officers with no academic training in anthropology who collected ethnographic materials in the same period or after World War I, but he paid more attention to those who received diplomas or took courses in anthropology, such as Hubert Murray (1861–1940), Charles Kingsley Meek (1885–1965), or Robert S. Rattray (1881–1938). Focusing on monographs written by English-speaking authors, such lists do not necessarily consider authors from other language areas.

The following bibliography of 365 ethnographic accounts by 220 ethnographers tries to correct the one-sidedness of the all-too-short lists from the Anglo-Saxon part of the ethnographic archive. Far from being exhaustive, it is a selection from the period ca. 1870–ca. 1922 based on our own perusal of the discipline's archive, with a focus on texts published in book form or at book length. We were assisted by colleagues from Brazil, Portugal, Italy, Sweden, Russia, Lithuania, India, Japan, and China specializing in the history of area studies. It would be possible to expand this sample by exploring the vast literature of specific ethnographic traditions, for example the collection of Russian oral literature following the pioneer work of Alexander Afanasyev (1826–71); by giving the full series of monographs sponsored by a single institution, for example the Field Columbian Museum; by listing all monographs produced by a single author, for example the twenty-five volumes of Italian folklorist Giuseppe Pitrè's (1841–1916) "Biblioteca delle tradizioni popolari siciliane" (1870–1913); or by adding shorter ethnographic articles, not to mention unpublished manuscripts.

Expanding its time frame would increase the size of our selection. Moreover, the history of the very notion of ethnography from the earliest records in the eighteenth century[4] reveals that conflating ethnography with fieldwork leaves aside other kinds of *Völker-Beschreibung* (description of peoples and nations), from statistical questionnaires to armchair compilations of firsthand sources, an abundant nineteenth-century literature that is routinely left out of consideration. Therefore, the list presented below focuses on texts resulting from their authors' own ethnographic fieldwork (albeit including, in some cases, complementary materials produced by others), with a monographic focus on a single group or various groups within a relatively circumscribed cultural region. Compilations of oral texts, or *corpora inscriptionum*, have also been selected. With a few exceptions, only first editions are considered. Articles shorter than one hundred pages were not included.

As with the case studies presented in the preceding chapters, the chosen monographs and other ethnographic accounts, whether by professional or amateur ethnographers, are not necessarily the most important from the period under consideration—*after Tylor* and *before Malinowski*—nor are they inescapable references, for the simple reason that, as the present volume argues, there are many angles from which to reassess them. Pre-Malinowskian ethnographies are a fundamental part of the history of ethnography and anthropology, each account containing several layers of meaning, style, and content that inspire open-ended readings and are projectable into the future. Considering the vast scope of the archive, a selection of ethnographic texts from the period can never be final, let alone complete, thus only a tentative experiment in a process that will be resumed, transformed, and criticized by future researchers.

Ajisafe, Ajayi Kolawole. 1924. *Laws and Customs of the Yoruba People*. London: G. Routledge & Sons.

Arsen'ev, Vladimir K. 1921. *Po Ussuriiskomu kraiu (Dersu Uzala): Puteshestvie v gornoi oblasti Sikhote-Alin'* [Through the Ussuri Krai (Dersu Uzala): A journey in the mountainous region of Sikhote-Alin]. Vladivostok: Ekho.

——. 1923. *Dersu Uzala: Iz vospominanii o puteshestvii po Ussuriiskomu kraiu v 1907 g.* [Dersu Uzala: From memories after the journey through the Ussuri Krai in 1907]. Vladivostok: Svobodnaia Rossiia.

Bastian, Adolf. 1866–71. *Die Völker des östlichen Asien* [The peoples of East Asia]. 6 vols. Leipzig: Otto Wigand/Jena: Hermann Costenoble.

——. 1874–75. *Die deutsche Expedition an der Loango-Küste, nebst älteren Nachrichten über die zu erforschenden Länder* [The German expedition to the Loango Coast, with earlier reports about the countries to be explored]. 2 vols. Jena: Costenoble.

——. 1878–89. *Die Culturländer des Alten Amerika* [The cultural centers of ancient America]. 3 vols. Berlin: Weidmannsche Buchhandlung.

——. 1881. *Die heilige Sage der Polynesier. Kosmogonie und Theogonie* [The sacred saga of the Polynesians: Cosmogony and theogony]. Leipzig: F. A. Brockhaus.

Beckwith, Martha Warren. 1919. "The Hawaiian Romance of Laieikawai" [with ethnological notes collected in the field]. In *Thirty-Third Annual Report of the Bureau of American Ethnology Presented to the Secretary of the Smithsonian Institution 1911–12*, 285–666. Washington, DC: Government Printing Office.

Bell, Gertrude L. 1907. *The Desert and the Sown*. London: William Heinemann.

Bérenger-Féraud, Laurent-Jean-Baptiste de. 1879. *Les Peuplades de la Sénégambie: Histoire, ethnographie, mœurs et coutumes, etc.* [The peoples of Senegambia: History, ethnography, customs and manners, etc.] Paris: Ernest Leroux.

——. 1883a. *La Race provençale: Caractères anthropologiques, mœurs, coutumes, aptitudes, etc., etc., de ses peuplades d'origine* [The race of the Provence: Anthropological characteristics, manners, customs, aptitudes, etc., of its native peoples]. Paris: O. Doin.

——. 1883b. *Réminiscences populaires de la Provence* [Folk reminiscences of the Provence]. Paris: Ernest Leroux.

——. 1885. *Recueil de contes populaires de la Sénégambie* [Collection of folk tales from Senegambia]. Paris: Ernest Leroux.

Best, Elsdon. 1897. *Waikare-moana: The Sea of the Rippling Waters*. Wellington: Government Printer. [See chapter 5 in this volume.]

——. 1924a. *The Maori*. 2 vols. Wellington: Harry H. Tombs.

——. 1924b. *Maori Religion and Mythology*. Wellington: Dominion Museum, the Government Printer.

——. 1924c. *The Maori as He Was*. Wellington: Government Printer.

——. 1925. *Tuhoe: The Children of the Mist*. 2 vols. New Plymouth, New Zealand: Thomas Avery & Sons.

Bleek, Wilhelm. 1870. *Reineke Fuchs in Afrika: Fabeln und Märchen der Eingeborenen* [Reynard the Fox in Africa: Native fables and fairy tales]. Weimar: Hermann Böhlau.

——. 1875. *A Brief Account of Bushman Folk-Lore, and Other Texts*. Cape Town/London/Leipzig: J. C. Juta/Trübner & Co./F. A. Brockhaus.

Bleek, Wilhelm, and Lucy Lloyd. 1911. *Specimens of Bushman Folklore*. Introduction by George McCall Theal. London: George Allen and Co.

Boas, Franz. 1888. "The Central Eskimo." In *Sixth Annual Report of the Bureau of Ethnology to the Secretary of the Smithsonian Institution 1884–'85*, 399–669. Washington, DC: Government Printing Office. [See chapter 1 in this volume.]

——. 1894. *Chinook Texts*. Washington, DC: Government Printing Office (Bureau of American Ethnology Bulletin 20).

——. 1895. *Indianische Sagen von der Nord-Pacifischen Küste Amerikas* [Indian legends from the North Pacific Coast of America] (offprint from *Verhandlungen der Berliner Gesellschaft für Anthropologie, Ethnologie und Urgeschichte* 23[8] [1891–1895]: vi + 363 pp.). Berlin: Verlag von A. Asher & Co.

——. 1897. *The Social Organization and the Secret Societies of the Kwakiutl Indians*. Based on Personal Observations and on Notes made by Mr. George Hunt. Report of the U.S. National Museum for 1895, 311–738, 215 ills.

——. 1898. *The Mythology of the Bella Coola Indians*. New York: Published by Order of the Trustees [AMNH] (Memoirs of the American Museum of Natural History, 2/1, Publications of the Jesup North Pacific Expedition 1: 25–127).

——. 1901a. *Kathlamet Texts*. Washington, DC: Government Printing Office (Bureau of American Ethnology Bulletin 26).

——. 1901b. *The Eskimo of Baffin Land and Hudson Bay: From Notes Collected by Capt. George Comer, Capt. James S. Mutch, and Rev. E. J. Peck*. New York: Published by Order of the Trustees [AMNH] (Bulletin of the American Museum of Natural History 15/1: 1–370).

——. 1902. *Tsimshian Texts*. Washington, DC: Government Printing Office. (Bureau of American Ethnology, Bulletin 27: 1–244.)

——. 1907. *Second Report on the Eskimo of Baffin Land and Hudson Bay*. New York: Published by Order of the Trustees [AMNH]. (Bulletin of the American Museum of Natural History 15/2, 371–570.)

——. 1909. *The Kwakiutl of Vancouver Island*. Leiden: E. J. Brill/New York: G. E. Stechert & Co. (Memoirs of the American Museum of Natural History, 8/2; Publications of the Jesup North Pacific Expedition 5/2, 301–522.)

———. 1910–35. *Kwakiutl Tales*. 2 vols. New York: Columbia University Press/Leiden: E. J. Brill. (Columbia University Contributions to Anthropology 2 and 26.)

———. 1912. *Tsimshian Texts. New Series*. Leiden: E. J. Brill. (Publications of the American Ethnological Society).

Boas, Franz, and Alexander Chamberlain. 1918. *Kutenai Tales*. Washington, DC: Government Printing Office. (Bureau of American Ethnology, Bulletin 59, xii + 387 pp.)

Boas, Franz, and Henry Wellington Tate. 1916. "Tsimshian Mythology: Based on Texts Recorded by Henry W. Tate." In *Thirty-First Annual Report of the Bureau of American Ethnology Presented to the Secretary of the Smithsonian Institution 1909–1910*, 27–1036. Washington, DC: Government Printing Office.

Boas, Franz, and George Hunt. 1905. *Kwakiutl Texts*. Leiden: E. J. Brill/New York: G. E. Stechert (Memoirs of the American Museum of Natural History, 5; Publications of the Jesup North Pacific Expedition, 3, vii + 532 pp.)

———. 1906. *Kwakiutl Texts, Second Series*. Leiden: E. J. Brill/New York: G. E. Stechert. (Memoirs of the American Museum of Natural History, 14/1; Publications of the Jesup North Pacific Expedition 10/1: vi + 269 pp.)

———. 1921. "Ethnology of the Kwakiutl. Based on Data Collected by George Hunt." In *Thirty-Fifth Annual Report of the Bureau of American Ethnology Presented to the Secretary of the Smithsonian Institution*, parts 1 and 2, 42–794, i–xi [index]. Washington, DC: Government Printing Office.

Bogoraz, Vladimir Germanovich [Bogoras, Waldemar]. 1900. *Materialy po izucheniiu chukotskogo iazyka i fol'klora, sobrannye v Kolymskom okruge V.G. Bogorazom* [Materials for the study of the Chukchee language and folklore, collected in the Kolyma District by V.G. Bogoraz]. Part 1. St. Petersburg: Imperatorskaia akademiia nauk.

———. 1904–9. *The Chukchee*. Leiden: E. J. Brill/New York: G. E. Stechert & Co. (Memoirs of the American Museum of Natural History 11; Publications of the Jesup North Pacific Expedition, 7/1–3; part 1: *Material Culture*, part 2: *Religion*, part 3: *Social Organization*).

———. 1910. *Chukchee Mythology*. Leiden: E. J. Brill/New York: G. E. Stechert & Co. (Memoirs of the American Museum of Natural History 12/1; Publications of the Jesup North Pacific Expedition 8/1).

———. 1913. *The Eskimo of Siberia*. Leiden: E. J. Brill/New York: G. E. Stechert & Co. (Memoirs of the American Museum of Natural History 12/3; Publications of the Jesup North Pacific Expedition 8/3).

———. 1917. *Koryak Texts*. Leiden: E. J. Brill/New York: G. E. Stechert & Co. (Publications of the American Ethnological Society, 5).

———. 1918. *Tales of Yukaghir, Lamut, and Russionized Natives of Eastern Siberia*. New York: Published by Order of the Trustees [AMNH] (Anthropological Papers of the American Museum of Natural History 20/1).

Bonwick, James. 1870. *The Last of the Tasmanians; or, the Black War of Van Diemen's Land*. London: Sampson Low & Co.

———. 1870. *The Daily Life and Origin of the Tasmanians*. London: Sampson Low and Marston.

Borie, Pierre-Henri Dumoulin. 1886. *La presqu'île de Malacca, les Malais et les sauvages*. Tulle: Imprimerie de J. Mazeyrie.

Bourke, John Gregory. 1884. *The Snake-Dance of the Moquis of Arizona*. London: Sampson Low, Marston, Searle & Rivington. [See chapter 7 in this volume.]

Breeks, James Wilkinson. 1873. *An Account of the Primitive Tribes and Monuments of the Nilagiris*. Edited with a preface by S. M. Breeks. London, India Museum: W. H. Allen and Co.

Busk, Rachel Harriette. 1870. *Patrañas or Spanish Stories, Legendary and Traditional*. London: Gilbert and Rivington.

———. 1871. *Household Stories from the Land of Hofer; or, Popular Myths of Tirol*. London: Griffith and Farran.

———. 1874a. *Valleys of Tirol: Their Traditions and Customs and How to Visit Them*. London: Longmans, Green and Co.

———. 1874b. *The Folk-Lore of Rome, Collected by Word of Mouth from the People*. London: Longmans, Green and Co.

———. 1887. *The Folk-Songs of Italy: Specimens with Translations and Notes, from Each Province*. London: Swan Sonnenschein & Co.

Calder, James Erskine. 1875. *Some Account of the Wars, Extirpation, Habits, etc., of the Native Tribes of Tasmania*. Hobart: Fullers Bookshop.

Callaway, Henry. 1868. *Nursery Tales, Traditions, and Histories of the Zulus in Their Own Words*. Springvale, Natal: J. A. Blair/London: Trübner.

———. 1868–70 *The Religious System of the Amazulu*. 3 vols. Springvale, Natal: John A. Blair/Cape Town: J. C. Juta/London: Trübner.

Carvalho, Henrique Augusto Dias de. 1890a. *Etnografia e história tradicional dos povos da Lunda* [Ethnography and traditional history of the Lunda peoples]. Lisbon: Imprensa Nacional. [See chapter 10 in this volume.]

———. 1890b [1890–94]. *Descrição da viagem à mussumba do Muatiânvua* [Description of the voyage to the Mwant Yaav's mussumba]. 4 vols. Lisbon: Imprensa Nacional.

———. 1890c. *Método prático para falar a língua da Lunda contendo narrações históricas dos diversos povos* [A practical method for speaking the Lunda language, with historical accounts of the various peoples]. Lisbon: Imprensa Nacional.

———. 1898. *O Jagado de Cassange na província de Angola* [The Kasanje Jaga kingdom in the Province of Angola]. Lisboa: Tipografia de Cristóvão Augusto Rodrigues.

Chatelain, Héli. 1894. *Folk-Tales of Angola. Fifty Tales, with Ki-Mbundu Text, Literal English Translation, Introduction, and Notes*. Boston, New York: G. E. Stechert & Co.

Chubinskii, Pavel Platonovich. 1872–78. *Trudy Etnografichesko-statisticheskoi ekspeditsii v Zapadno-russkii krai, snariazhennoi Russkim geogra-*

ficheskim obshchestvom [Works of the ethnographic and statistical expedition to the Western-Russian krai, organized by the Russian Geographical Society]. 7 vols. St. Petersburg: Russkoe Geograficheskoe obshchestvo.

Clifford, Hugh C. 1897. *In Court and Kampong; Being Tales & Sketches of Native Life in the Malay Peninsula.* London: Grant Richards.

Codrington, Robert Henry. 1891. *The Melanesians: Studies in Their Anthropology and Folk-Lore.* Oxford: Clarendon Press.

Cole, Fay-Cooper. 1913. *The Wild Tribes of Davao District, Mindanao.* Chicago: Field Museum of Natural History (Anthropological Series 12/2).

Corso, Raffaele. 1920. *L'arte dei pastori* [The art of shepherds]. Roma: Edizioni La Fionda.

Crooke, William. 1890. *An Ethnographical Hand-Book for the North-Western Provinces and Oudh.* Allahabad: Government Press.

———. 1896. *The Tribes and Castes of the North-Western Provinces and Oudh.* 4 vols. Calcutta: Government Printing.

———. 1897. *The North-Western Provinces of India: Their History, Ethnology and Administration.* London: Methuen.

Curtin, Jeremiah, and John Napoleon Brinton Hewitt. 1918. "Seneca Fiction, Legends, and Myths." In *Thirty-Second Annual Report of the Bureau of American Ethnology Presented to the Secretary of the Smithsonian Institution*, 37–814. Washington, DC: Government Printing Office.

Cushing, Frank Hamilton. 1883. *Zuñi Fetishes* (extract from the *Second Annual Report of the Bureau of Ethnology*). Washington, DC: Government Printing Office.

———. 1896. "Outlines of Zuñi Creation Myths." In *Thirteenth Annual Report of the Bureau of Ethnology to the Secretary of the Smithsonian Institution 1891–'92*, 321–447. Washington, DC: Government Printing Office.

———. 1901. *Zuñi Folk Tales.* Introduction by John Wesley Powell. New York/London: G. P. Putnam's Sons.

Czaplicka, Maria. 1916. *My Siberian Year.* London: Mills and Boon. [See chapter 11 in this volume.]

Dannert, Eduard. 1906. *Zum Rechte der Herero, insbesondere über ihr Familien- und Erbrecht* [On Herero law, especially their family and inheritance law]. Berlin: Dietrich Reimer.

Davis, Charles Oliver. 1876. *The Life and Times of Patuone, the Celebrated Ngapuhi Chief.* Auckland: J. H. Field.

Delhaise, Charles. 1909. *Les Warega (Congo Belge).* With a preface by C. Van Overbergh. Brussels: Albert Dewit.

Dennett, Richard Edward. 1898. *Notes on the Folklore of the Fjort (French Congo).* Introduction by Mary H. Kingsley. London: David Nutt.

Dorsey, George Amos. 1903. *The Arapaho Sun Dance: The Ceremony of the Offerings Lodge.* Chicago: Field Columbian Museum (Field Columbian Museum Publication 75, Anthropological Series 4).

———. 1903. *The Cheyenne.* Vol. 1: *Ceremonial Organization.* Chicago: Field Columbian Museum (Field Columbian Museum Publication 99, IX[1]).

――――. 1905. *The Cheyenne.* Vol. 2: *The Sun Dance.* Chicago: Field Columbian Museum (Field Columbian Museum Publication 103, IX[2]).

Dorsey, George Amos, and Alfred L. Kroeber. 1903. *Traditions of the Arapaho.* Chicago: Field Columbian Museum (Field Columbian Museum
Publications 81/5).

Dorsey, George Amos, and Heinrich (Henry) Richard Voth. 1902. *The Mis-
hongnovi Ceremonies of the Snake and Antelope Fraternities (The Stanley
McCormick Hopi Expedition).* Chicago: Field Columbian Museum (Field
Columbian Museum Publication 66, Anthropological Series III/3).

Dorsey, James Owen. 1884. "Omaha Sociology." *Third Annual Report of
the Bureau of Ethnology Presented to the Secretary of the Smithsonian
Institution,* 205–370. Washington, DC: Government Printing Office.

――――. 1897. "A Study of Siouan Cults." In *Eleventh Report of the Bureau
of Ethnology to the Secretary of the Smithsonian Institution 1889–'90 by
J. W. Powell, Director,* 361–544. Washington, DC: Government Printing
Office.

Doutté, Edmond. 1914. *Missions au Maroc: En tribu* [Missions in Morocco:
Within the tribe]. Paris: Paul Geuthner.

Durham, Mary Edith. 1909. *High Albania.* London: Edward Arnold.

Efimenko, Petr Savvich. 1877–78. *Materialy po etnografii russkogo nasele-
niia Arkhangel'skoi gubernii, sobrannye P.S. Efimenkom* [Materials on
ethnography of the Russian population of the Arkhangelsk region collected by P. S. Efimenko]. 2 parts. Moscow: Tipografiia F. B. Millera.

Ehrenreich, Paul. 1891. *Beiträge zur Völkerkunde Brasiliens* [Contributi-
ons to the ethnology of Brazil]. Berlin: Spemann (Veröffentlichungen aus
dem Königlichen Museum für Völkerkunde 2, 1/2).

――――. 1905. *Die Mythen und Legenden der südamerikanischen Urvölker
und ihre Beziehungen zu denen Nordamerikas und der alten Welt* [Myths
and legends of the Indigenous peoples of South America and their relations with those of North America and the Old World]. Berlin: Asher
(*Zeitschrift für Ethnologie,* Band 37, Supplement).

Ellis, Alfred Burdon, 1887. *The Tshi-Speaking Peoples of the Gold Coast
of West Africa: Their Religion, Manners, Customs, Laws, Languages, etc.*
London: Chapman and Hall.

――――. 1890. *The Ewe-Speaking Peoples of the Slave Coast: Their Religion,
Manners, Customs, Laws, Languages, etc.* London: Chapman and Hall

――――. 1894. *The Yoruba-Speaking Peoples of the Slave Coast of West Af-
rica: Their Religion, Manners, Customs, Laws, Languages, etc., with an
Appendix Containing a Comparison of the Tshi, Ga, Ewe, and Yoruba
Languages.* London: Chapman and Hall.

Endle, Sidney. 1911. *The Kachâris.* Introduction by J. D. Anderson. London: Macmillan & Co.

Erdland, August. 1914. *Die Marshall-Insulaner: Leben und Sitte, Sinn und
Religion eines Südsee-Volkes* [The Marshall Islanders: Life and customs,
manners and religion of a South Sea people]. Münster: Aschendorff
(Anthropos-Bibliothek 2/1).

Evans, Ivor Hugh Norman. 1923. *Studies in Religion, Folk-lore, & Custom in British North Borneo and the Malay Peninsula*. Cambridge: Cambridge University Press.

Fewkes, Jesse Walter. 1903. "Hopi Katcinas Drawn by Native Artists." In *Twenty-First Report of the Bureau of American Ethnology to the Secretary of the Smithsonian Institution 1899–1900*, 13–126. Washington, DC: Government Printing Office.

———. 1986 [1894–98]. *Hopi Snake Ceremonies*. Albuquerque, NM: Avanyu.

Finnamore, Gennaro. 1890. *Credenze, usi e costumi abruzzesi* [Abruzzo beliefs, customs, and traditions]. Palermo: Libreria Internazionale L. Pedone Lauriel di Carlo Clausen.

Finsch, Otto. 1865. *Neu-Guinea und seine Bewohner* [New Guinea and its inhabitants]. Bremen: C. Ed. Müller.

———. 1914. *Südseearbeiten: Gewerbe- und Kunstfleiß, Tauschmittel und "Geld" der Eingeborenen auf Grundlage der Rohstoffe und der geographischen Verbreitung* [South Sea trades: Indigenous trade and artistry, means of exchange, and "money" based on raw materials and geographical distribution]. Hamburg: L. Friedrichsen & Co.

Fison, Lorimer. 1904. *Tales from Old Fiji*. London: Alexander Moring, the De La More Press.

Fison, Lorimer, and Alfred William Howitt. 1880. *Kamilaroi and Kurnai: Group-Marriage and Relationship, and Marriage by Elopement, Drawn Chiefly from the Usage of the Australian Aborigines; Also the Kurnai Tribe, Their Customs in Peace and War*. Melbourne/Sydney/Adelaide/Brisbane: George Robinson.

Fletcher, Alice Cunningham, and Francis La Flesche. 1911. "The Omaha Tribe." In *Twenty-Seventh Annual Report of the Bureau of American Ethnology 1905–'06*, 17–672. Washington, DC: Smithsonian Institution; U.S. Government Printing Office. [See chapter 6 in this volume.]

Fletcher, Alice C., and James R. Murie. 1904. "The Hako: A Pawnee Ceremony." In *Twenty-Second Annual Report of the Bureau of American Ethnology to the Secretary of the Smithsonian Institution 1900–'01*, 1–368. Washington, DC: Smithsonian Institution; U.S. Government Printing Office.

Fornander, Abraham. 1878–86. *An Account of the Polynesian Race: Its Origin and Migrations, and the Ancient History of the Hawaiian People to the Times of Kamehameha I*. 3 vols. London: Trübner and Co.

Freeman, Richard Austin. 1898. *Travels and Life in Ashanti and Jaman*. Westminster: Archibald Constable and Co.

Gatschet, Albert Samuel. 1884. *A Migration Legend of the Creek Indians, with a Linguistic, Historic and Ethnographic Introduction*. Philadelphia: D. G. Brinton (Brinton's Library of Aboriginal American Literature 1).

———. 1888. "Tchikilli's Kasi'hta Legend in the Creek and Hitchiti Languages." *Transactions of the Saint Louis Academy of Sciences* 5: 33–239.

Gaud, Fernand. 1911. *Les Mandja (Congo Français)*. With the collaboration of C. Van Overbergh. Brussels: Albert Dewit.

Gill, William Wyatt. 1876. *Myths and Songs from the South Pacific*. London: Henry S. King & Co.

Grinnell, George Bird. 1889. *Pawnee Hero Stories and Folk-Tales, with Notes on the Origin, Customs and Character of the Pawnee People*. New York: Forest & Stream Publishing Co.

——. 1893. *Blackfoot Lodge Tales: The Story of a Prairie People*. London/Boston: D. Nutt.

——. 1915. *The Fighting Cheyennes*. New York: C. Scribner's Sons.

——. 1923. *The Cheyenne Indians: Their History and Ways of Life*. 2 vols. New Haven, CT: Yale University Press.

Grube, Wilhelm. 1901. *Zur Pekinger Volkskunde* [On Beijing folklore]. Berlin: W. Spemann.

Guppy, Henry Brougham. 1887. *The Solomon Islands and Their Natives*. London: Swan Sonnenschein, Lowrey & Co.

Gurdon, Philip R. T. 1907. *The Khasis*. Introduction by Charles Lyall. London: Nutt.

Haddon, Alfred Cort. 1894. *Decorative Art of British New Guinea: A Study in Papuan Ethnography*. Dublin: The Academy House.

Hahn, Theophilus. 1881. *Tsuni-Goam: The Supreme Being of the Khoi-Khoi*. London: Trübner and Co.

Hale, Horatio, ed. 1883. *The Iroquois Book of Rites*. Philadelphia: D. G. Brinton (Brinton's Library of Aboriginal American Literature 2).

Halkin, Joseph. 1910. *Les Ababua*. With the collaboration of Ernest Viaene. Brussels: Albert Dewit.

Hall, H. Fielding. 1898. *The Soul of a People*. London: MacMillan and Co.

Hatt, Emilie Demant. 1913. *Med lapperne i højfeldet [With the Lapps in the High Mountains]*. Stockholm: A.-B. Nordiska Bokhandeln.

——. 2013. *With the Lapps in the High Mountains: A Woman Among the Sami 1907–8*. Translated from the Danish with an introduction by Barbara Sjoholm. Madison: University of Wisconsin Press.

Henry, Joseph. 1910. *L'Ame d'un peuple africain: Les Bambara, leur vie psychique, éthique, sociale, religieuse*. Münster: Aschendorff.

Hewitt, John Napoleon Brinton. 1903. "Iroquoian Cosmology: First Part." In *Twenty-First Report of the Bureau of American Ethnology to the Secretary of the Smithsonian Institution 1899–1900*, 127–339. Washington, DC: Government Printing Office.

——. 1928. "Iroquoian Cosmology: Second Part, with Introduction and Notes." In *Forty-Third Annual Report of the Bureau of American Ethnology to the Secretary of the Smithsonian Institution 1925–1926*, 449–819. Washington, DC: Government Printing Office.

Hewitt, John Napoleon Brinton, and Jeremiah Curtin. 1918. "Seneca Fiction, Legends, and Myths." In *Thirty-Second Annual Report of the Bureau of American Ethnology to the Secretary of the Smithsonian Institution 1910–1911*, 37–813. Washington, DC: Government Printing Office.

Hinde, Sidney Langford, and Hildegarde Hinde. 1901. *The Last of the Masai*. London: William Heinemann.

Hodson, Thomas Callan. 1908. *The Meitheis*. Introduction by Charles Lyall. London: David Nutt.

———. 1911. *The Naga Tribes of Manipur*. London: Macmillan.

Hoffman, Walter James, 1891. "The Mide'wiwin or 'Grand Medicine Society' of the Ojibwa." In *Seventh Annual Report of the Bureau of Ethnology to the Secretary of the Smithsonian Institution 1885–86*, 143–300. Washington, DC: Government Printing Office.

———. 1896. "The Menomini Indians." In *Fourteenth Annual Report of the Bureau of American Ethnology 1892–'93: Part 1*, 3–328. Washington, DC: Government Printing Office.

Hollis, Alfred Claud. 1905. *The Masai: Their Language and Folk-lore*. Introduction by Sir Charles Eliot. Oxford: Clarendon Press.

———. 1909. *The Nandi: Their Language and Folk-lore*. Introduction by Sir Charles Eliot. Oxford: Clarendon Press.

Holm, Gustav F. 1914. "Ethnological Sketch of the Angmagsalik Eskimo." In *The Ammassalik Eskimo: Contributions to the Ethnology of the East Greenland Natives*, edited by William Thalbitzer, part 1. Copenhagen: C. A. Reitzels Forlag (Meddelelser om Grønland, Vol. 39, Part 1). [Containing the ethnological and anthropological results of G. Holm's expedition in 1883–85 and G. Amdrup's expedition in 1898–1900. Originally published in Danish in *Meddelelser om Grønland*, vol. 10 (1896, 1898).]

Hose, Charles, and William Macdougall. 1912. *The Pagan Tribes of Borneo: A Description of Their Physical, Moral and Intellectual Condition with Some Discussion of Their Ethnic Relations* (with an Appendix on the Physical Characters of the Races of Borneo by A. C. Haddon). 2 vols. London: Macmillan and Co.

Howitt, Alfred William. 1904. *The Native Tribes of South-East Australia*. London/New York: Macmillan and Co./The Macmillan Company.

Hutton, John Henry. 1921. *The Angami Nagas: With Some Notes on Neighbouring Tribes*. London: Macmillan and Co.

———. 1921. *The Sema Nagas*. Foreword by Henry Balfour. London: Macmillan and Co.

Hyltén-Cavallius, Gunnar Olof. 1863–68. *Wärend och Wirdarne: Ett Försök I Svensk Ethnologi* [Wärend and Wirdarne: An experiment in Swedish ethnology]. 2 vols. Stockholm: P. A. Norstedt & Söner.

Im Thurn, Everhard Ferdinand. 1883. *Among the Indians of Guiana: Being Sketches, Chiefly Anthropological, from the Interior of British Guiana, etc.* London: Kegan Paul & Co.

Iokhel'son, Vladimir Il'ich [Jochelson, Waldemar]. 1895. *Zametki o naselenii Iakutskoi oblasti v istoriko-etnograficheskom otnoshenii* [Historical and ethnographic notes on the population of the Yakut region]. St. Petersburg: Tipografiia S.N. Khudekova.

———. 1900. *Materialy po izucheniiu iukagirskogo iazyka i fol'klora*. Vol. 1: *Obraztsy narodnoi slovesnosti iukagirov* [Material on the study of the Yukagir language and folklore. Vol. 1: Samples of the folklore of the Yukagirs]. St. Petersburg: Imperatorskoi akademiia nauk.

———. 1905–8. *The Koryak*. Leiden: E. J. Brill/New York: G. E. Stechert (Memoirs of the American Museum of Natural History 10/1–2; The Jesup North Pacific Expedition 6/1–2; Part 1: *Religion and Myths*; Part 2: *Material Culture and Social Organization*).

———. 1910–26. *The Yukaghir and the Yukaghirized Tungus*. Leiden: E. J. Brill/New York: G. E. Stechert (Memoirs of the American Museum of Natural History 13; The Jesup North Pacific Expedition, 9/1–3).

Irle, Johann Jakob. 1906. *Die Herero: Ein Beitrag zur Landes-, Volks- & Missionskunde* [The Herero: A contribution to the study of the country, the people, and the missions]. Gütersloh: Druck und Verlag von C. Bertelsman.

Iyer, L. K. Anantha Krishna. 1909–12. *The Cochin Tribes and Castes*. 2 vols. Preface by John Beddoe, Introduction by A. H. Keane. Madras: Higginbotham & Co./Cochin Government Press.

Jackson, Henry Cecil. 1923. *The Nuer of the Upper Nile Province*. Karthoum: El Hadara Printing Press. First published in *Sudan Notes and Records*.

Jenks, Albert Ernest. 1905. *The Bontoc Igorot*. Manila: Bureau of Public Printing.

Jenness, Diamond. 1922. *The Life of the Copper Eskimos*. Ottawa: F. A. Acland (Report of the Canadian Arctic Expedition 1913–18, vol. 12).

Jenness, Diamond, and Andrew Ballantyne. 1920. *The Northern D'Entrecasteaux*. Preface by Robert R. Marett. Oxford: Clarendon Press.

Johnson, James. 1899. *Yoruba Heathenism*. Exeter: James Townsend and Sons.

———. 1921. *The History of the Yorubas: From the Earliest Times to the Beginning of the British Protectorate*. Lagos: C. M. S. (Nigeria) Bookshops.

Junod, Henri-Alexandre. 1897. *Les Chants et les contes des Ba-Ronga de la baie de Delagoa* [Songs and folktales of the Delagoa Bay Ba-Ronga]. Lausanne: Georges Bridel & Cie. Éditeurs.

———. 1898. *Les BaRonga: Étude ethnographique sur les indigènes de la baie de Delagoa* [The Baronga: Ethnographic study of the Delagoa Bay natives]. Neuchâtel: Attinger Frères (Bulletin de la Société de Géographie de Neuchâtel 10).

———. 1911. *Zidji: Étude de mœurs sud-africaines* [Zidji: A study of South-African customs]. Saint-Blaise: Foyer Solidariste.

———. 1912–13. *The Life of a South-African Tribe*. 2 vols. Neuchâtel: Attinger Frères.

Kaggwa, Apollo. 1907. *Empisa za Baganda* [Customs of the Baganda]. Kampala: Uganda Bookshop.

Kalakaua, David. 1888. *Legends and Myths of Hawaii: The Fables and Folklore of a Strange People*. Edited with an introduction by Rollin Mallory Daggett. New York: Charles L. Webster & Company.

Karsten, Rafael. 1920a. "Studies in South American Anthropology." *Finska Vetenskaps-Societetens Förhandlingar* 62(2): 1–232.

———. 1920–21. *Bland indianer i Ekvadors urskogar* [Among Indians in the primeval forests of Ecuador]. 2 vols. Helsinki: Söderström & Co förlagsaktiebolag.

——. 1920c. *Blodshämnd, krig och segerfester bland Jibaroindianerna i östra Ecuador.* Helsinki: Holger Schildts förlagsaktiebolag. English edition 1923.

——. 1923. *Blood Revenge, War and Victory Feast among the Jibaro Indians of Eastern Ecuador.* Washington, DC: Smithsonian Institution, U.S. Government Printing Office (Bureau of American Ethnology Bulletin 79).

Kharuzin, Aleksei Nikolaevich. 1889–91. *Kirgizy Bukeevskoi ordy: Antropologo-etnologicheskii ocherk* [The Kirgiz of the Bukeevsraia horde: Anthropological and ethnological outline]. 2 vols. Moscow: Tipografiia A. Levenson i K°.

Kharuzin, Nikolai Nikolaevich. 1890. *Russkie lopari: Ocherki proshlogo i sovremennogo byta* [Russian Sami: An outline of past and present everyday life]. Moscow: T-vo skoropech. A. A. Levenson.

Kingsley, Mary H. 1897. *Travels in West Africa: Congo Français, Corisco and Cameroons.* London: MacMillan and Co./New York: The MacMillan Company.

——. 1899. *West African Studies.* London: MacMillan and Co./New York: The MacMillan Company.

Koch-Grünberg, Theodor. 1903. "Die Guaikurú-Gruppe" [The Guaikurú family]. *Mittheilungen der Anthropologischen Gesellschaft Wien* 33: 1–128.

——. 1905. *Anfänge der Kunst im Urwald: Indianer-Handzeichnungen auf seinen Reisen in Brasilien gesammelt* [Beginnings of art in the jungle: Indian drawings collected on his travels in Brazil]. Berlin: Ernst Wasmuth A. G. Portuguese translation Belém 2010.

——. 1906. *Indianertypen aus dem Amazonasgebiet nach eigenen Aufnahmen während seiner Reise in Brasilien* [Indian types from the Amazon region after photographs taken during his journey in Brazil]. Berlin: Ernst Wasmuth A. G.

——. 1909–10. *Zwei Jahre unter den Indianern: Reisen in Nordwest-Brasilien, 1903–1905* [Two years among the Indians: Travels in Northwest Brazil, 1903–1905]. Berlin: Ernst Wasmuth A. G. 2nd abridged ed. published as *Volksausgabe*, 1921. Portuguese translation Manaus 2005.

——. 1916–28. *Vom Roroima zum Orinoco: Ergebnisse einer Reise in Nordbrasilien und Venezuela in den Jahren 1911–1913* [From the Roroima to the Orinoco: Results of a journey in Northern Brazil and Venezuela during the years 1911–1913]. 5 vols. Berlin: Dietrich Reimer (Ernst Vohsen) (Vols. 1–2)/Stuttgart: Strecker & Schröder (Vols. 3–5). Vol. 1: *Schilderung der Reise* [Description of the voyage], 1917; Vol. 2: *Mythen und Legenden der Taulipang- und Arekuna-Indianer* [Myths and legends of the Taulipang and Arekuna Indians], 1916; Vol. 3: *Ethnographie* [Ethnography], 1923; Vol. 4: *Sprachen* [Languages], 1928; Vol. 5: *Typen-Atlas* [Atlas of types], 1923. 2nd abridged ed. of vol. 1 published as *Volksausgabe*, 1934. Portuguese translation of vol. 1, São Paulo 2006. [See chapter 12 in this volume.]

———. 1920. *Indianermärchen aus Südamerika* [Indian tales from South America]. Jena: Diedrichs.

Kovalevskii, Maksim Maksimovich. 1890. *Zakon i obychai na Kavkaze* [Law and custom in the Caucasus]. 2 vols. Moscow: Tipografiia A. I. Mamontova i K°.

Krämer, Augustin. 1902–3. *Die Samoa-Inseln: Entwurf einer Monographie mit besonderer Berücksichtigung Deutsch-Samoas* [The Samoa Islands: Draft of a monograph with special reference to German Samoa]. 2 vols. Stuttgart: E. Schweizerbartsche Verlagsbuchhandlung (E. Nägele). Vol. 1: *Verfassung, Stammbäume und Überlieferungen* [Constitution, genealogies, and folklore]; Vol. 2: *Ethnographie.*

Krause, Fritz. 1911. *In den Wildnissen Brasiliens: Bericht und Ergebnisse der Leipziger Araguaya-Expedition 1908* [In the wildernesses of Brazil: Report and results of the Leipzig Araguaya Expedition 1908]. Leipzig: R. Voigtländer Verlag. [See chapter 12 in this volume.]

———. 1921. *Die Kultur der kalifornischen Indianer in ihrer Bedeutung für die Ethnologie und die nordamerikanische Völkerkunde* [The culture of Californian Indians and its significance for ethnology and the ehnology of North America]. Leipzig: Verlag von Otto Spamer.

Kroeber, Alfred L. 1902–7. *The Arapaho.* New York: Published by Order of the Trustees [AMNH] (Bulletin of the American Museum of Natural History 18/1–4; Publication of the Mrs. Jesup Arapaho Expedition 1899–1901).

———. 1908. *Ethnology of the Gros Ventre.* New York: Published by Order of the Trustees [AMNH] (Anthropological Papers of the American Museum of Natural History 1/4; Publication of the Mrs. Jesup Arapaho Expedition 1899–1901).

Kubary, Johann Stanislaus [Jan Stanisław]. 1889–95. *Ethnographische Beiträge zur Kenntnis des Karolinen Archipels* [Ethnographic contributions to the study of the Caroline Islands]. Veröffentlicht im Auftrag der Direktion des Kgl. Museums für Völkerkunde zu Berlin. Unter Mitwirkung von J. D. E. Schmeltz. Leiden: P. W. M. Trap (Commission: C. F. Winter'sche Verlagshandlung in Leipzig).

La Flesche, Francis. 1921. "The Osage Tribe: Rite of the Chiefs; Sayings of the Ancient Men." In *Thirty-Sixth Annual Report of the Bureau of American Ethnology to the Secretary of the Smithsonian Institution 1914–1915*, 37–640. Washington, DC: Smithsonian Institution; U.S. Government Printing Office.

———. 1925. "The Osage Tribe: Rite of Vigil." In *Thirty-Nineth Annual Report of the Bureau of American Ethnology to the Secretary of the Smithsonian Institution 1917–1918*, 31–630. Washington, DC: Smithsonian Institution; U.S. Government Printing Office.

———. 1928. "The Osage Tribe: Two Versions of the Child-Naming Rite." In *Forty-Third Annual Report of the Bureau of American Ethnology to the Secretary of the Smithsonian Institution 1925–1926*, 23–164. Washington, DC: Smithsonian Institution; U.S. Government Printing Office.

———. 1930. "The Osage Tribe: Rite of the Wa-xo'-be." In *Forty-Fifth Annual Report of the Bureau of Ethnology to the Secretary of the Smithsonian Institution 1927–1928*, 523–833. Washington, DC: Government Printing Office.

Lagden, Godfrey. 1909. *The Basutos; The Mountaineers & Their Country; Being a Narrative of Events Relating to the Tribe from Its Formation Early in the Nineteenth Century to the Present Day*. 2 vols. London: Hutchinson & Co.

Landtman, Gunnar. 1917. *Ur sagans barndom berättelser av vildfolket i Nya Guinea* [Folktales and legends from the natives of New Guinea]. Helsinki: Holger Schildts Förlag.

———. 1927. *The Kiwai Papuans of British New Guinea: A Nature-Born Instance of Rousseau's Ideal Community*. Introduction by Alfred C. Haddon. London: Macmillan & Co.

Langloh Parker, Katie. 1896. *Australian Legendary Tales: Folk-lore of the Noongahburrahs as told to the Piccaninnies*. London: David Nutt/Melbourne: Melville, Mullen and Slade.

———. 1905. *The Euahlayi Tribe: A Study of Aboriginal Life in Australia*. Introduction by Andrew Lang. London: Archibald Constable. [See chapter 2 in this volume.]

Machado y Álvarez, Antonio. 1881. *Colección de Cantes Flamencos Recogidos y Anotados* [Collection of flamenco songs collected and annotated]. Seville: Imp. El Porvenir.

———. 1887. *Cantes Flamencos y Cantares* [Flamenco songs and chants]. Madrid: Bibliotecea de El Motín, Imprenta Popular a cargo de Tomás Rey.

McNair, John Frederick Adolphus. 1878. *Perak and the Malays: "Sarong" and "Kris."* London: Tinsley Brothers.

Maksimov, Sergei Vasil'evich. 1871. *Lesnaia glush': Kartiny narodnogo byta iz vospominanii i putevykh zametok* [Forest wilderness: Pictures of a people's life from memories and fieldnotes]. 2 vols. St. Petersburg: K. N. Plotnikov.

Malinowski, Bronislaw. 1915. "The Natives of Mailu: Preliminary Results of the Robert Mond Research Work in British New Guinea." *Transactions and Proceedings of the Royal Society of South Australia* 39: 494–706.

———. 1916. "Baloma: The Spirits of the Dead in the Trobriand Islands." *Journal of the Royal Anthropological Institute* 46: 353–430.

———. 1922. *Argonauts of the Western Pacific: An Account of Native Enterprise and Adventure in the Archipelagoes of Melanesian New Guinea*. Preface by Sir James George Frazer. London: George Routledge & Sons.

Man, Edward Horace, and A. J. Ellis. 1885. *On the Aboriginal Inhabitants of the Andaman Islands* [by E. H. Man]; *With Report of Research into the Languages of the South Andaman Island* [by A. J. Ellis]. London: Royal Anthropological Institute of Great Britain and Ireland.

Martin, Minnie. 1903. *Basutoland: Its Legends and Customs*. London: Nichols and Co.

Matsumura, Akira. 1918. "Contributions to the Ethnography of Micronesia." *Journal of the College of Science, Imperial University of Tokyo* 40.

McGee, William J. [and J. N. B. Hewitt]. 1898. "The Seri Indians." In *Seventeenth Annual Report of the Bureau of American Ethnology Presented to the Secretary of the Smithsonian Institution: Part 1, 1895–96*, 1–344. Washington, DC: Government Printing Office.

Merker, Moritz. 1904. *Die Masai: Ethnographische Monographie eines ostafrikanischen Semitenvolkes* [The Masai: Ethnographic monograph of an Eastern African Semitic people]. Berlin: Dietrich Reimer.

Meyer, Hans [1858–1929]. 1916. *Die Barundi: Eine völkerkundliche Studie aus Deutsch-Ostafrika* [The Barundi: An ethnological study from German East Africa]. Leipzig: Otto Spamer (Veröffentlichungen des Staatlich-Sächsischen Forschungsinstitutes für Völkerkunde in Leipzig, Reihe 1).

Miklukho-Maklai, Nikolai Nikolaevich. 1885. *Soobshchenie o puteshestviiakh N.N. Miklukho-Maklaia ob issledovanii ostrovov Tikhogo okeana* [Report on the travels of N. N. Miklukho-Maklai, with a study of the islands of the Pacific Ocean]. St. Petersburg: Tipografiia V. Bezobrazova i K°.

———. 1982. *Travels to New Guinea: Diaries, Letters, Documents.* Moscow: Progress Publishers.

———. 1990–96. *Sobranie sochineniy v shesti tomakh* [Collected works in six volumes]. Moscow: Nauka.

Mills, James Philip. 1922. *The Lhota Nagas.* Introduction and notes by John Henry Hutton. London: Macmillan.

Mooney, James. 1891. "The Sacred Formulas of the Cherokees." In *Seventh Annual Report of the Bureau of Ethnology to the Secretary of the Smithsonian Institution 1885–86*, 307–97. Washington, DC: Government Printing Office.

———. 1896. "The Ghost-Dance Religion and the Sioux Outbreak of 1890." In *Fourteenth Annual Report of the Bureau of American Ethnology 1892–'93: Part 2*, 641–1110. Washington, DC: Government Printing Office.

———. 1898. "Calendar History of the Kiowa Indians." In *Seventeenth Annual Report of the Bureau of Ethnology Presented to the Secretary of the Smithsonian Institution: Part 1*, 129–445. Washington, DC: Government Printing Office.

———. 1900. "Myths of the Cherokee." In *Nineteenth Annual Report of the Bureau of Ethnology to the Secretary of the Smithsonian Institution 1897–98: Part 1*, 3–548. Washington, DC: Government Printing Office.

Murray, John Hubert Plunkett. 1912. *Papua or British New Guinea.* Introduction by William McGregor. London: T. Fischer Unwin.

Nelson, Edward William. 1899. "The Eskimo About Bering Strait." In *Eighteenth Annual Report of the Bureau of Ethnology to the Secretary of the Smithsonian Institution 1896–97*, 3–518. Washington, DC: Government Printing Office.

Newton, Henry. 1914. *In Far New Guinea: A Stirring Record of Work and Observation amongst the People of New Guinea, with a Description of Their Manners, Customs, & Religions, &c.* Philadelphia: J. B. Lippincott Company; London: Seeley, Service & Co.

Nigmann, Ernest. 1908. *Die Wahehe. Ihre Geschichte, Kult-, Rechts-, Kriegs- und Jagd-Gebräuche* [The Wahehe: Their history, religious, legal, war and hunting customs]. Berlin: Mittler.

Nigra, Costantino. 1888. *Canti popolari del Piemonte* [Folk songs of Piemonte]. Torino: Loescher.

Nimuendajú, Curt [Curt Unckel]. 1914. "Die Sagen von der Erschaffung und Vernichtung der Welt als Grundlagen der Religion der Apapocúva-Guaraní" [Legends of the creation and destruction of the world as foundations of the Apapocúva-Guaraní religion]. *Zeitschrift für Ethnologie* 46: 284–403.

Nordenskiöld, Erland. 1910. *Indianlif i El Gran Chaco (Sydamerika)* [Indian life in the Grand Chaco (South America)]. Stockholm: Albert Bonniers Förlag.

———. 1911. *Indianer och Hvita i nordöstra Bolivia* [Indians and Whites in Northeastern Bolivia]. Stockholm: Albert Bonniers Förlag.

———. 1915. *Forskningar och äventyr i Sydamerika 1913–1914* [Research and adventure in South America 1913–1914]. Stockholm: Albert Bonniers Förlag.

Ostermann, Valentino. 1894. *La vita in Friuli; usi, costumi, credenze, pregiudizi e superstizioni popolari* [Life in Friuli: Folk customs, manners, beliefs, prejudices, and superstitions]. Udine: Domenico del Bianco.

Partridge, Charles. 1905. *Cross River Natives; Being Some Notes on the Primitive Pagans of Obubura Hill District, Southern Nigeria, Including a Description of Upright Sculptured Stones on the Left Bank of the Aweyong River*. London: Hutchinson & Co.

Paulitschke, Philipp Viktor. 1893–96. *Ethnographie Nordost-Afrikas* [Ethnography of North-East Africa]. 2 vols. Vol. 1: *Die materielle Cultur der Danakil, Galla und Somâl* [The material culture of the Danakil, Galla, and Somali]; Vol. 2: *Die geistige Cultur der Danakil, Galla und Somâl* [The spiritual culture of the Danakil, Galla, and Somali]. Berlin: Geographische Verlagshandlung Dietrich Reimer.

Pedroso, Zófimo Consiglieri. 1882. *Portuguese Folk-Tales*. Translated by Henriqueta Monteiro. Introduction by William R. S. Ralston. London: The Folklore Society, Elliot Stock.

Pevtsov, Mikhail Vasil'evich. 1883. *Ocherk puteshestviia po Mongolii i severnym provintsiiam Vnutrennego Kitaia* [Outline of a travel to Mongolia and the northern regions of inner China]. Omsk: Zapadno-Sibirskoe otdelenie Russkogo geograficheskogo obshchestva.

Pigorini Beri, Caterina. 1889. *Costu mi e superstizioni dell'Appenino Marchigiano* [Costumes and superstitions of the Marche Apennines]. Città di Castello: S. Lapi Tip. Editore.

Piłsudski, Bronisław. 1912. *Materials for the Study of the Ainu Language and Folklore*. Edited by Jan Michał Rozwadowski. Cracow: Imperial Academy of Sciences.

Pitrè, Giuseppe. 1875. *Fiabe, novelle e racconti popolari siciliani* [Sicilian folk tales]. 4 vols. Palermo: Luigi Pedone Lauriel.

———. 1913. *La Famiglia, la casa, la vita del popolo siciliano* [The family, the house and the life of the Sicilian people]. Palermo: Libreria Internazionale A. Reber (Biblioteca delle tradizioni popolari siciliane).

Plas, Joseph Van den. 1910. *Les Kuku (possessions anglo-égyptiennes)*. With a preface and an introduction by C. Van Overbergh. Brussels: Albert Dewitt (Collection de monographies ethnographiques).

Playfair, Alan. 1909. *The Garos*. Introduction by J. Bampfylde Fuller. London: David Nutt.

Potanin, Grigorii Nikolaevich. 1893. *Tangutsko-Tibetskaia okraina Kitaia i Tsentral'naia Mongoliia: Puteshestvie G.N. Potanina: 1884–1886* [The Tangut-Tibetan fringe of China and Central Mongolia: Travels by G. N. Potanina, 1884–1886]. 2 vols. St. Petersburg: Imperatorskoe Russkoe geograficheskoe obshchestvo.

Preuss, Konrad Theodor. 1912. *Die Nayarit-Expedition. Textaufnahmen und Beobachtungen unter mexikanischen Indianern* [The Nayarit Expedition: Textual recordings and observations among Mexican Indians]. Vol. 1: *Die Religion der Cora-Indianer*. Leipzig: B.G. Teubner. [See chapter 12 in this volume.]

———. 1921. *Religion und Mythologie der Uitoto: Textaufnahmen und Beobachtungen bei einem Indianerstamm in Kolumbien, Südamerika* [Religion and mythology of the Uitoto: Textual recordings and observations among an Indian tribe in Colombia, South America]. Vol. 1: *Einführung und Texte*. Göttingen: Vandenhoeck & Ruprecht.

Pryzhov, Ivan Gavrilovich. 1913. *Nishchie na sviatoi Rusi: Materialy dlia istorii obshchestvennogo i narodnogo byta v Rossii* [Beggars in Holy Rus': Materials for a history of the social and folk life in Russia]. Kazan: Molodye sily.

Radcliffe-Brown, Alfred Reginald [Brown, A. R.]. 1913. "Three Tribes of Western Australia." *Journal of the Royal Anthropological Institute of Great Britain and Ireland* 43: 143–94.

———. 1922. *The Andaman Islanders: A Study in Social Anthropology*. Cambridge: The University Press. 2nd ed. with a new preface, 1933.

Rattray, Robert Sutherland. 1907. *Some Folk-Lore Stories and Songs in Chinyanja, with English Translation and Notes*. London: Christian Knowledge Society.

———. 1913. *Hausa Folk-Lore*. Oxford: Clarendon Press.

———. 1916. *Ashanti Proverbs: Primitive Ethics of a Savage People*. Oxford: Clarendon Press.

———. 1923. *Ashanti*. Oxford: Clarendon Press. [See chapter 9 in this volume.]

Reed, William Allan. 1904. *Negritos of Zambales*. Manila: Bureau of Public Printing.

Rémy, Jules. 1868. *Contributions of a Venerable Savage to the Ancient History of the Hawaiian Islands*. Translated from the French by William Tufts Brigham. Boston: A. A. Kingman, Museum of the Boston Society of Natural History.

Reyes y Florentino, Isabelo de los. 1889–90. *El Folk-Lore Filipino* [Philippine folk-lore]. 2 vols. Manila: TipoLitografía de Chofré y Cía, Imprenta de Santa Cruz.

Riggs, Stephen Return. 1893. *Dakota Grammar, Texts and Ethnography.* Edited by James Owen Dorsey. Washington, DC: Government Printing Office.

Rink, Henry [Hinrich Johannes]. 1875. *Tales and Traditions of the Eskimo — with a Sketch of Their Habits, Religion, Language, and Other Peculiarities.* London: William Blackwood & Sons.

——. 1887–91. *The Eskimo Tribes: Their Distribution and Characteristics, Especially in Regard to Language; With a Comparative Vocabulary and a Sketch-Map.* 2 vols. London: Williams and Norgate/Copenhagen: C. A. Reitzel.

Risley, Herbert H. 1891. *The Tribes and Castes of Bengal: Ethnographic Glossary.* 2 vols. Calcutta: Bengal Secretariat Press

——. 1915 [1908]. *The People of India.* Revised edition, W. Crooke. Calcutta: Thacker, Spink.

Rivers, William Halse Rivers. 1906. *The Todas.* London: Macmillan and Co.

——. 1914. *The History of Melanesian Society.* Percy Sladen Trust Expedition to Melanesia. 2 vols. Cambridge: Cambridge University Press.

Rodrigues, Raimundo Nina. 1900 [1896–97]. *L'Animisme fétichiste des nègres de Bahia* [Fetishist animism of the Black people of Bahia]. Salvador: Reis & Companhia.

Roquette-Pinto, Edgard. 1912. *Nota sobre os índios nambiquaras do Brasil Central* [Notes on the Nambikwara Indians of Central Brazil]. Rio de Janeiro: Museu Nacional do Rio de Janeiro.

——. 1917. *Rondonia: Anthropologia, Ethnographia.* Rio de Janeiro: Imprensa Nacional.

Roscoe, John. 1911. *The Baganda: An Account of Their Native Customs and Beliefs.* London: Macmillan and Co.

Roth, Henry Ling. 1878. *A Sketch of the Agriculture and Peasantry of Eastern Russia.* London: Ballière, Tindale & Cox.

——. 1896. *The Natives of Sarawak and British North Borneo: Based Chiefly on the Mss. of the Late Hugh Brooke Low, Sarawak Government Service.* Preface by Andrew Lang. 2 vols. London: Truslove & Hanson.

——. 1903. *Great Benin: Its Customs, Art and Horrors.* Halifax: F. King & Sons.

Roth, Walter Edmund. 1897. *Ethnological Studies among the North-West-Central Queensland Aborigines.* Brisbane/London: Edmund Gregory, Queensland Agent-General's Office.

——. 1908–10. "North Queensland Ethnography." Bulletin no. 10–17. Miscellaneous Papers. *Records of the Australian Museum* 7 and 8.

——. 1915. "An Inquiry into the Animism and Folk-lore of the Guiana Indians." In *Thirtieth Annual Report of the Bureau of Ethnology to the Secretary of the Smithsonian Institution 1909–1910,* 103–386. Washington, DC: Government Printing Office.

——. 1924. "An Introductory Study of the Arts, Crafts, and Customs of the Guiana Indians." In *Thirty-Eight Annual Report of the Bureau of Ethnology to the Secretary of the Smithsonian Institution 1916–1917*, 25–720. Washington, DC: Government Printing Office.

Roy, Sarat Chandra. 1912. *The Mundas and Their Country*. Introduction by E. A. Gait. Calcutta: The Kuntaline Press/The City Book Society.

Russell, Frank. 1908. "The Pima Indians." In *Twenty-Sixth Annual Report of the Bureau of Ethnology to the Secretary of the Smithsonian Institution 1904–1905*, 3–389. Washington, DC: Government Printing Office.

Salomone Marini, Salvatore. 1880. *Leggende popolari siciliane in poesie* [Sicilian folk legends in poetry]. Palermo: Luigi Pedone Lauriel Editore.

Sapir, Edward, and Jeremiah Curtin. 1909. *Wishram Texts (Together with Wasco Tales and Myths, Collected by Jeremiah Curtin and Edited by Edward Sapir)*. Leiden: E. J. Brill (Publications of the American Ethnological Society 2).

Schmidt, Max. 1905. *Indianerstudien in Zentralbrasilien: Erlebnisse und ethnologische Ergebnisse einer Reise in den Jahren 1900 bis 1901* [Indian studies in Central Brazil: Encounters and ethnological results of a journey in the years 1900 to 1901]. Berlin: Dietrich Reimer (Ernst Vohsen). [See chapter 12 in this volume.]

——. 1917. *Die Aruaken: Ein Beitrag zum Problem der Kulturverbreitung* [The Arawak: A contribution to the problem of culture diffusion]. Leipzig: Veit und Comp. Portuguese translation São Paulo 2021.

Sébillot, Paul. 1880. *Contes populaires de la Haute-Bretagne* [Folk tales of Upper Brittany]. Paris: Charpentier.

——. 1881. *Littérature orale de la Haute-Bretagne* [Oral literature of Upper Brittany]. Paris: Maisonneuve.

——. 1882. *Traditions, et superstitions de la Haute-Bretagne* [Traditions and superstitions of Upper Brittany]. 2 vols. Paris: Maisonneuve.

Seligmann, Charles Gabriel. 1910. *The Melanesians of British New Guinea*. With a chapter by F. R. Barton and an appendix by E. L. Giblin. Cambridge: Cambridge University Press.

Seligman, Charles G., and Brenda Z. Seligman. 1911. *The Veddas*. Cambridge: Cambridge University Press.

Seroshevskii, Vatslav Leopol'dovich. 1896. *Iakuty: Opyt etnograficheskogo* [The Jakuts: Outline of an ethnographic study]. Vol. 1. St. Petersburg: Russkoe geograficheskoe obshchestvo.

Shakespear, John. 1912. *The Lushei Kuki Clans*. London: Macmillan & Co.

Shirokogorov, Sergei Mikhailovich [Shirokogoroff, S. M.] 1919. *Opyt issledovaniya osnov shamansta u tungusov* [Effort to study the basics of shamanism of the Tungus]. Vladivostok: Tipografiia Oblastnoi Zemskoi Upravi.

Shortland, Edward. 1882. *Maori Religion and Mythology: Illustrated by Translations of Traditions, Karakia, &c., to Which are Added Notes on Maori Tenure of Land*. London, Longmans, Green, and Co.

Shternberg, Lev Iakovlevich. 1904. "Gilyaki" [The Gilyak]. *Etnograficheskoe Obozrenie* [Ethnographic Review] 60: 1–42; 61: 19–55; 63: 66–119.

———. 1908. *Materialy po izucheniiu giliatskogo iazyka i fol'klora, sobran-nye i obrabotannye L.Ia. Shternbergom* [Materials for the study of the Gilyak language and folklore, collected and adapted by L. I. Shternberg]. Vol. 1. St. Petersburg: Tipografiia Imperatorskaia akademiia nauk.

———. 1999. *The Social Organization of the Gilyak.* Edited by Bruce Grant. New York: American Museum of Natural History.

Skeat, Walter William. 1900. *Malay Magic, Being an Introduction to the Folklore and Popular Religion of the Malay Peninsula.* Preface by Charles Otto Blagden. London: MacMillan and Co./New York: The MacMillan Company.

Skeat, Walter William, and Charles Otto Blagden. 1906. *Pagan Races of the Malay Peninsula.* 2 vols. London: Macmillan & Co.

Smith, Edwin William, and Andre Murray Dale. 1920. *The Ila-Speaking Peoples of Northern Rhodesia.* 2 vols. London: Macmillan and Co.

Smith, Stephenson Percy. 1904 [1898]. *Hawaiki: The Original Home of the Maori, with a Sketch of Polynesian History, Being an Introduction to the Native History of Rarotonga.* Christchurch: Whitcombe & Tombs.

———. 1910 [1904]. *Maori Wars of the Nineteenth Century: The Struggle of the Northern against the Southern Maori Tribes prior to the Colonisation of New Zealand in 1840.* Christchurch: Whitcombe & Tombs.

———. 1910. *History and Traditions of the Maoris of the West Coast, North Island of New Zealand prior to 1840.* Wellington: The Polynesian Society.

Snouck Hurgronje, Christiaan. 1888–89. *Mekka.* 2 vols. The Hague: Martinus Nijhoff. Separate vol. *Bilder-Atlas.* The Hague: Nijhoff. English translation of vol. 2: *Mekka in the Latter Part of the Nineteenth Century: Daily Life, Customs and Learning, the Moslims of the East-Indian Archipelago.* Leiden: E. J. Brill/London: Luzac & Co. 1931.

———. 1893–94. *De Atjèhers* [The Achenese]. 2 vols. Batavia: Landsdrukkerij/ Leiden: E. J. Brill. English translation of vol. 1, Leiden 1906. Indonesian translation, 1985.

———. 1903. *Het Gajoland en zijne bewoners* [The land of the Gajonese and its inhabitants]. Batavia: Landsdrukkerij.

Soppitt, C. A. 1887. *A Short Account of the Kuki-Lushai Tribes on the North-East Frontier, with an Outline Grammar of the Ranghol-Lushai Language and Comparison of Lushai with Other Dialects.* Shillong: Assam Secretariat Press.

Spencer, Baldwin, and Francis James Gillen. 1899. *The Native Tribes of Central Australia.* London: Macmillan and Co.

———. 1904. *The Northern Tribes of Central Australia.* London: Macmillan and Co.

Spieth, Jakob. 1906. *Die Ewe-Stämme: Material zur Kunde des Ewe-Volkes in Deutsch-Togo* [The Ewe tribes: Materials on the Ewe people in German Togo]. Berlin: Dietrich Reimer.

———. 1906. *Die Eweer: Schilderung von Land und Leuten in Deutsch-Togo* [The Ewe: Description of country and people in German Togo]. Bremen: In Kommission bei der Norddeutschen Missions-Gesellschaft. English translation 2011.

——. 2011. *The Ewe People: A Study of the Ewe People in German Togo.* Edited by Komla Amoaku. Translated by Marcellinus Edroh et al. Accra: Sub-Saharan Publishers.

Stack, Edward. 1908. *The Mikirs.* Edited by Charles Lyall. London: David Nutt.

Stack, James West. 1898. *South Island Maoris: A Sketch of Their History and Legendary Lore.* Christchurch: Whitcomb & Tombs.

Steinen, Karl von den. 1886. *Durch Central-Brasilien: Expedition zur Erforschung des Schingú im Jahre 1884* [Through Central Brazil: Expedition to explore the Xingu in 1884]. Leipzig: F. A. Brockhaus. Portuguese translation São Paulo 1942.

——. 1892. *Die Bakaïri-Sprache: Wörterverzeichniss, Sätze, Sagen, Grammatik; mit Beiträgen zu einer Lautlehre der Karaïbischen Grundsprache* [The Bakairi language: Vocabulary, proverbs, legends, grammar; with contributions to a phonetics of the basic Carib language]. Leipzig: Koehler.

——. 1894. *Unter den Naturvölkern Zentral-Brasiliens: Reiseschilderung und Ergebnisse der zweiten Schingú-Expedition 1887–1888* [Among the natural peoples of Central Brazil: Travel account and results of the Second Xingu Expedition 1887–1888]. Berlin: Dietrich Reimer. 2nd abridged ed. published as *Volksausgabe*, 1897. Portuguese translation São Paulo 1940. [See chapter 12 in this volume.]

Stevenson, Matilda Coxe. 1894. "The Sia." In *Eleventh Report of the Bureau of Ethnology to the Secretary of the Smithsonian Institution 1889–'90,* 5–157. Washington, DC: Government Printing Office.

——. 1904. "The Zuñi Indians: Their Mythology, Esoteric Societies, and Ceremonies." In *Twenty-Third Annual Report of the Bureau of Ethnology to the Secretary of the Smithsonian Institution 1901–1902,* 1–608. Washington, DC: Government Printing Office.

Strehlow, Carl Friedrich Theodor. 1907–20. *Die Aranda- und Loritja-Stämme in Zentral-Australien* [The Arunta and Luritcha tribes of Central Australia]. 5 vols. in 7 parts. Frankfurt am Main: Joseph Baer & Co.

Stuebel, Oskar. 1896. *Samoanische Texte, unter Beihülfe von Eingeborenen Gesammelt und Übersetzt* [Samoan texts, collected and translated with the help of Indigenous people]. Berlin: Königlichen Museum für Volkerkunde.

Swanton, John Reed. 1905a. *Contributions to the Ethnology of the Haida.* Leiden: E. J. Brill/New York: G. E. Stechert (Memoirs of the American Museum of Natural History 8/1; Publications of the Jesup North Pacific Expedition 5/1).

——. 1905b. *Haida Texts and Myths: Skidegate Dialect.* Washington, DC: Government Printing Office (Bureau of American Ethnology Bulletin, no. 29).

——. 1908. "Social Condition, Beliefs, and Linguistic Relationship of the Tlingit Indians." In *Twenty-Sixth Annual Report of the Bureau of Ethnology to the Secretary of the Smithsonian Institution 1904–1905,* 391–485. Washington, DC: Government Printing Office.

——. 1909. *Tlingit Myths and Texts*. Washington, DC: Government Printing Office (Bureau of American Ethnology Bulletin, no. 39).

——. 1911. *Indian Tribes of the Lower Mississippi Valley and Adjacent Coast of the Gulf of Mexico*. Washington, DC: Government Printing Office (Bureau of American Ethnology Bulletin, no. 43).

——. 1922. *Early History of the Creek Indians and Their Neighbors*. Washington, DC: Government Printing Office. (Bureau of American Ethnology Bulletin, no. 73.)

Talbot, Dorothy Amaury. 1915. *Woman's Mysteries of a Primitive People: The Ibibios of Southern Nigeria*. London/New York/Toronto/Melbourne: Cassell and Co.

Talbot, Percy Amaury. 1912. *In the Shadow of the Bush*. New York: George H. Doran/London: William Heinemann.

——. 1926. *The Peoples of Southern Nigeria: A Sketch of Their History, Ethnology and Languages, with an Abstract of the 1921 Census*. 4 vols. London: Humphrey Milford.

Teit, James. 1900. *The Thompson Indians of British Columbia*. Edited with a chapter on art and the conclusions of the volume by Franz Boas. New York: Published by Order of the Trustees [AMNH] (Memoirs of the American Museum of Natural History 2/4; Publications of the Jesup North Pacific Expedition 1/4).

——. 1906. *The Lillooet Indians*. Leiden: E. J. Brill/New York: G. E. Stechert (Memoirs of the American Museum of Natural History 4/5; Publications of the Jesup North Pacific Expedition 2/5).

——. 1909. *The Shuswap*. Leiden, E. J. Brill/New York: G. E. Stechert (Memoirs of the American Museum of Natural History 4/7; Publications of the Jesup North Pacific Expedition 2/7).

——. 1912. *Mythology of the Thompson Indians*. Leiden: E. J. Brill/New York: G. E. Stechert (Memoirs of the American Museum of Natural History 12/2; Publications of the Jesup North Pacific Expedition 8/2).

Te Matohoranga and Nepia Pohuhu. 1913–15. *The Lore of the Wharewānanga, or Teachings of the Maori College on Religion, Cosmogony, and History*. Written down by Hoani Te Whatahoro Jury. Translated with an introduction by Stephenson Percy Smith. New Plymouth: Thomas Avery, The Polynesian Society.

Temple, Richard Carnac. 1884. *Legends of the Panjâb*. 2 vols. London: Trübner & Co.; Bombay: Education Society's Press.

Tessmann, Günther, 1913. *Die Pangwe: Völkerkundliche Monographie eines westafrikanischen Negerstammes* [The Fang: Ethnographic monograph of a West African Black tribe]. Ergebnisse der Lübecker Pangwe-Expedition 1907–1909 und früherer Forschungen 1904–1907. 2 vols. Berlin: Ernst Wasmuth.

Thomas, Northcote W. 1910. *Anthropological Report on the Edo-Speaking Peoples of Nigeria*. 2 vols. London: Harrison & Sons.

——. 1913–14. *Anthropological Report on the Ibo-Speaking Peoples of Nigeria*. 6 vols. London: Harrison & Sons.

——. 1916. *Anthropological Report on Sierra Leone.* 3 vols. London: Harrison & Sons.

Thomson, Basil. 1908. *The Fijians: A Study of the Decay of Custom.* London: William Heynemann.

Thrum, Thomas G. 1907. *Hawaiian Folk Tales: A Collection of Native Legends.* Chicago: A. C. McLurg & Co.

Thurnwald, Richard. 1916. *Banaro Society: Social Organization and Kinship System of a Tribe in the Interior of New Guinea.* New York: American Anthropological Association (Memoirs of the American Anthropological Association 8).

——. 1921. *Die Gemeinde der Bánaro: Ehe, Verwandtschaft und Gesellschaftsbau eines Stammes im Innern von Neu-Guinea (aus den Ergebnissen einer Forschungsreise 1913–25); Ein Beitrag zur Entstehungsgeschichte von Familie und Staat* [The Banaro community: Marriage, kinship, and social system of a tribe in the interior of New Guinea (from the results of a research journey 1913–25); A contribution to the genesis of family and state]. Stuttgart: Verlag von Ferdinand Enke.

Torii, Ryūzō. 1902. *Kōtōsho Dozoku chōsa hōkoku* [Research report on the customs of Botel Tobago Aborigines]. Tōkyō Teikoku Daigaku, Jinruigaku Kyōshitsu [Tokyo Imperial University, Institute of Anthropology].

——. 1907. *Byōzoku chōsa hōkoku* [Research report on the Miao]. Tōkyō Teikoku Daigaku, Jinruigaku Kyōshitsu [Tokyo Imperial University, Institute of Anthropology].

——. 1919. "Etudes archéologiques et ethnologiques: Les Aïnou des Iles Kouriles." *Journal of the College of Science, Imperial University of Tokyo* 42.

Tremearne, Arthur John Newman. 1912. *The Tailed Head-Hunters of Nigeria: An Account of an Official's Seven Years' Experiences in the Northern Nigerian Pagan Belt, and a Description of the Manners, Habits, and Customs of Some of Its Native Tribes.* London: Seeley, Service & Co.

——. 1913. *Hausa Superstitions and Customs: An Introduction to the Folk-Lore and the Folk.* London: John Bale, Sons & Danielsson.

——. 1914. *The Ban of the Bori: Demons and Demon-Dancing in West and North Africa.* London: Heath, Cranton & Ouseley.

Trilles, Henri. 1912a. *Le totémisme chez les Fân* [Totemism among the Fang]. Preface by Monseigneur Alexandre Le Roy. Münster: Bibliothek Anthropos.

——. 1912b. *Chez les Fang, ou Quinze années de séjour au Congo français* [Among the Fang, or fifteen years in the French Congo]. Lilles/Paris/Bruges: Société Saint-Augustin, Desclée, De Brouwer et Cie. [See chapter 8 in this volume.]

Tsybikov, Gombozhab Tsebekovich. 1919. *Buddist palomnik u sviatyn' Tibeta: Po dnevnikam, vedennym v 1899–1902 gg.* [A Buddhist pilgrim to the holy sites of Tibet: According to fieldnotes from 1899–1902]. Petrograd: Rusckoe geograficheskoe obshchestvo.

Turi, Johan. 1910. *Muitalus sámiid birra: En bog om lappernes liv* [An Account of the Sámi: A book about the life of the Lapps]. Translated and edited with an introduction by Emilie Demant Hatt. Stockholm: A.-B. Nordiska Bokhandeln.

———. 1931 [1910]. *Turi's Book of Lappland.* Translated by E. G. Nash. London: Jonathan Cape.

———. 2012 [1910]. *An Account of the Sámi: A Translation of* Muitalus sámiid birra, *Based on the Sámi Original.* Translated by Mikael Svonni and Thomas A. DuBois. Karasjok: ČálliidLágádus.

Turner, George. 1884. *Samoa: A Hundred Years Ago and Long Before, Together with Notes on the Cults and Customs of Twenty-Three Other Islands in the Pacific.* Preface by Edward B. Tylor. London: MacMillan and Co.

Van Gennep, Arnold. 1914. *En Algérie* [In Algeria]. Paris: Mercure de France.

Volkov, Fedor Kondrat'evich. 1916. "Ėtnograficheskie osobennosti ukrainskogo naroda" [Ethnographic characteristics of the Ukrainian people]. In *Ukrainskiĭ narod v ego proshlom i nastoĭashchem* [The Ukrainian people in its past and present], edited by F. K. Volkov, M. S. Grushevskiĭ, M. M. Kovalevskiĭ, F. E. Korsh, A. E. Krymskiĭ, M. I. Tugan'-Baranovskiĭ, and A. A. Shakhmatov, 455–647. Petrograd: Tipografiia tov-va "Obshchestvennaia pol'za."

Volters, Eduards [Voliteri E. A.] 1887. *Ob etnograficheskoi poezdke po Litve i Zmydi letom 1887 goda* [About an ethnographic trip to Lithuanians and Zhmud' in the summer of 1887]. St. Petersburg: Imperatorskaia akademiia nauk.

———. 1901. *Spiski naselennykh mest Suvalkskoi gubernii, kak materialy dlia istoriko-etnograficheskoi geografii kraia* [Lists of inhabited settlements of the Suvalki Guberniia as material for a historical and ethnographic geography of the region]. St. Petersburg: Imperatorskaia akademiia nauk.

Voth, Heinrich (Henry) Richard. 1901. *The Oraibi Powamu Ceremony.* Field Columbian Museum Publication, 61; Anthropological Series, 3/2. Chicago: Field Columbian Museum.

Walker, James R. 1917. *The Sun Dance and Other Ceremonies of the Oglala Division of the Teton Dakota.* New York: American Museum of Natural History.

Wehrli, Hans Jacob. 1904. *Beitrag zur Ethnologie der Chingpaw (Kachin) von Ober-Burma.* Leiden: E. J. Brill.

Wessmann, Richard. 1908. *The Bawenda of the Spelonken (Transvaal): A Contribution towards the Psychology and Folk-lore of African Peoples.* Translated from the German by Leo Weinthal. London: The African World Ltd.

Westermarck, Edward. 1914. *Marriage Ceremonies in Morocco.* London: Macmillan.

———. 1926. *Ritual and Belief in Morocco.* 2 vols. London: Macmillan. [See chapter 3 in this volume.]

Weule, Karl. 1908. *Wissenschaftliche Ergebnisse meiner ethnographischen Forschungsreise in den Südosten Deutsch-Ostafrikas* [Scholarly results from my ethnographic expedition to the southeastern parts of German East Africa]. Berlin: Mittler (Mitteilungen aus den deutschen Schutzgebieten, Ergänzungshefte, 1).

White, John. 1879–90. *The Ancient History of the Maori, His Mythology and Traditions: Horo-Uta or Taki-Tumu Migration.* Wellington: George Didsbury, Government Printer.

White, Walter Grainge. 1922. *The Sea Gipsies of Malaya: An Account of the Nomadic Mawken People of the Mergui Archipelago with a Description of Their Ways of Living, Customs, Habits, Boats, Occupations, etc. etc.* London: Seeley, Service & Co.

Wilken, George Alexander. 1884–85. *Het animisme bij de volken van den Indischen archipel* [Animism among the peoples of the East Indian archipelago]. Amsterdam: J. H. de Bussy/Leiden: E. J. Brill.

———. 1921. *The Sociology of Malayan Peoples: Being Three Essays on Kinship, Marriage, and Inheritance in Indonesia.* Translated by G. Hunt. Introduction by C. O. Blagden. Kuala Lumpur: Committee for Malay Studies (Papers on Malay Subjects, 2nd series, Malayan Sociology, 5).

Wilkin, Anthony. 1900. *Among the Berbers of Algeria.* London: T. Fisher Unwin Ltd.

Wilkinson, Richard James. 1906. *Malay Beliefs.* London: Luzac & Co./Leiden: E. J. Brill.

Williamson, Robert Wood. 1912. *The Mafulu Mountain People of British New Guinea.* Introduction by A. C. Haddon. London: Macmillan & Co.

———. 1914. *The Ways of the South Sea Savage: A Record of Travel & Observation Amongst the Savages of the Solomon Islands & Primitive Coast & Mountain Peoples of New Guinea.* London: Seeley, Service & Co.

Wissler, Clark, and D. C. Duvall. 1908. *Mythology of the Blackfoot Indians.* New York: Published by Order of the Trustees [AMNH] (Anthropological Papers of the American Museum of Natural History 2/1).

Witort, Jan. 1898. *Zarysy prawa zwyczajowego ludu litewskiego* [Patterns of Lithuanian customary law]. Lwów: Nakładem Towarzystwa Ludoznawczego [Polish Folklore Society].

Wollaston, Alexander Frederick Richmond. 1912. *Pygmies & Papuans: The Stone Age To-day in Dutch New Guinea.* With appendices by William Robert Ogilvie-Grant, Alfred C. Haddon, Sidney Herbert Ray. New York: Sturgis & Walton Company.

Young, Ernest. 1898. *The Kingdom of the Yellow Robe, Being Sketches of the Domestic and Religious Rites and Ceremonies of the Siamese.* London: Archibald Constable & Co.

Number of ethnographers in this Appendix: 220
Number of ethnographic accounts: 365
Halle (Saale) and Lisbon, January 2022

Notes

1. Alfred C. Haddon (with the help of A. Hingston Quiggin), *History of Anthropology* (London: Watts & Co., 1910); also published in New York and London by G. P. Putnam's Sons, 1910 (A History of the Sciences series); 2nd rev. ed. London: Watts & Co. (The Thinker's Library 42), 1934; 3rd impression 1949.
2. Marvin Harris, *The Rise of Anthropological Theory* (London: Routledge & Kegan Paul, 1968).
3. Margaret Mead as quoted in Roger Sanjek, *Ethnography in Today's World: Color Full before Color Blind* (Philadelphia: University of Pennsylvania Press, 2014), 40.
4. Han F. Vermeulen, *Before Boas: The Genesis of Ethnography and Ethnology in the German Enlightenment* (Lincoln: University of Nebraska Press, 2015).

Index